Traditional Housing in African Cities

Traditional Housing in African Cities

A COMPARATIVE STUDY OF HOUSES IN ZARIA, IBADAN, AND MARRAKECH

Friedrich W. Schwerdtfeger Ph.D.
Ahmadu Bello University
Zaria, Nigeria

John Wiley & Sons
Chichester • New York • Brisbane • Toronto • Singapore

British Library Cataloguing in Publication Data:

Schwerdtfeger, Friedrich W.
Traditional housing in African cities.
1. Architecture and society – Morocco
2. Architecture and society – Nigeria
I. Title
301.5′4′0964 NA1590 80-41693

ISBN 0 471 27953 6

Typeset by Pintail Studios Ltd, Ringwood, Hampshire.
Printed at the Pitman Press Ltd, Bath, Avon.

The history of utopias has shown that model settlements have never made model societies; but there is at least a sporting chance that model societies might generate model settlements.

Duccio A. Turin

Contents

Acknowledgements

I wish to dedicate this book to my teacher Professor Duccio A. Turin whose tragic and untimely death in 1976 was a great loss for all who worked with him and benefited from his advice and friendship.

I owe appreciation and thanks to Professor O. H. Koenigsberger, who in the course of many years has kindly helped me to clarify my thoughts on buildings in the tropics, and who has given me help and valuable advice for my work. I am especially indebted to Professor M. G. Smith, who introduced me to Social Anthropology, and who has given so freely of his time, guidance, and encouragement for this research project.

During the course of my fieldwork in Nigeria I was generously helped by Professor A. L. Mabogunje of the Department of Geography at the University of Ibadan, and Professor W. J. Kidd, at the time Head of Department of Architecture at Ahmadu Bello University in Zaria. I owe a very considerable debt to Alhaji Muhammadu Aminu, the late Emir of Zaria, as well as to his then Private Secretary Alhaji Shehu Idris, the present Emir of Zaria, and to many officials in their administrations for their kindness which was always combined with a genuine desire to help wherever possible.

In Marrakech, I received assistance from Monsieur A. Masson, Chef de la Division Technique, Ministère de'Intérieur, Rabat, and from Monsieur Michel de Leenheer, head of the ministry's local architects' and town-planning office, who provided me with plans, maps, and aerial photographs, and whose kind help and friendship made my stay in Marrakech very pleasant indeed. I would also like to thank Monsieur Papini, Ministère de l'Intérieur, who, after I lost my camera on my journey across the Sahara, came all the way from Rabat to take some pictures in Marrakech, six of which are given on pages 218, 219, 259, and 260.

I am further indebted to D. M. Steward whose assistance never failed throughout my survey in Africa, and to my interpreters Yahaya Ahmed Jere in Zaria, Sylvanus Nzesi in Ibadan, and Aitm Hammed Mohammed Miki in Marrakech.

My greatest debt, of course, is to the many citizens of Zaria, Ibadan, and Marrakech who welcomed us into their homes and devoted much valuable time to answering my questions with courtesy and good humour. I hope I have not betrayed their trust.

I wish to acknowledge the help received from the library staff of the School of Oriental and African Studies and the Institute of Commonwealth Studies of the University of London; the Commonwealth Society; and the British Library of Political and Economic Science at the London School of Economics and Political Science.

This research was generously financed by the German Academic Exchange Service in Bonn. Mr George Martin kindly read the whole manuscript, and for help in typing the text, I am grateful to Miss J. Browne.

Foreword

As the author of this pioneer study rightly observes, 'Traditional urban houses have hitherto received very little attention, yet they provide shelter for the overwhelming majority of the urban population in Africa and Asia'. Archaeologists, of course, give special attention in their excavations to the sites, layouts, and sizes of settlements, ground plans of their monumental buildings, and particularly to the forms and details of human dwellings in cities, towns and lesser population centres which provide the most abundant and revealing stores of evidence for many earlier civilizations. To archaeologists, such information as they can glean on and from the scale, layout, orientation, modes, and materials of construction, patterns and durations of occupancy and patterns of daily use in the homesteads of earlier populations, often provides the most decisive clues to interpretations of data drawn from other sectors of cultural activity such as tombs and monuments, temples, city walls, moats, palaces, town plans and irrigation works. Despite their relatively humble character, data drawn from human habitations normally provide more reliable guidance to the interests, orientations, social organization, economic activities, aesthetic standards, technical capacities, and religious concepts of a people than more elaborate monuments that glorify their rulers and noble dead. Nor should this evoke surprise, since habitations are among the first truly human creations, and embody the resources, technical knowledge, and skills, the central ideas and values that organize the domestic and family life of the people who build and inhabit them. They are accordingly very close to the hearts of their makers and occupants, and so exercise a strong claim on the first fruits of any new acquisitions or developments of taste, technique, material resources, labour organization, or design that indicate cultural progress. In this way the habitations of men richly embody and illustrate their cultural aptitudes, preferences, and development.

What is true of housing in dead cultures holds equally for living ones. Given its cultural centrality and social significance, the form of housing that a people has developed and uses offers a direct and strategic entrance to the study of their culture and society. Accordingly, we might expect that social and cultural anthropologists would have devoted special attention to the systematic study of housing patterns and practices in pre-industrial societies. However, despite L. H. Morgan's early impressive demonstration of the potential value of such studies,[1] anthropologists have usually been content to dismiss the topic with perfunctory photographs and ground plans of typical dwellings, and perhaps a brief account of prevailing patterns of construction and use. More systematic study of the domestic architecture of simpler societies is a rather recent development which so far owes more to the efforts of architects, town planners, and others with specialist training and interest in human settlements and construction than to social and cultural anthropologists. The various volumes edited by Paul Oliver illustrate this nicely.[2]

Most contemporary anthropological accounts of housing and house styles in exotic pre-industrial cultures illustrate the predominantly semiotic interests and goals of their authors. Under such influences, social and cultural anthropologists seem to regard dwellings and other types of construction as primarily of interest because of their symbolic character and significance. From such perspectives, a house is readily perceived as a code to be cracked by a semiotic analysis which will no doubt display a deep structure that integrates and coordinates the redundant symbolic contrast sets which together order and constitute the house.[3] Now clearly, all human dwellings must embody and reflect the symbolism that pervades the culture of those who constructed and occupy them; but such expression occurs within limits set by the materials and techniques of construction, the affluence, number, and rank of the occupants, the location, layout, and size of the building, and similar mundane but relevant factors. These material constraints are normally sufficient to ensure that dwellings, though laden with symbolic purposes and meanings, must first fulfil certain practical requirements as suitable homes, before serving as vehicles for symbolism. These limiting conditions and functions should therefore be particularly important objects of ethnographic documentation and analysis in order properly to contextualize and illuminate the symbolic motivations and patterns that inform and overlay the house itself. Unfortunately it is precisely in this respect that anthropological studies of housing in pre-industrial societies have been most systematically incomplete, perhaps because ethnographers have generally assumed that the additional knowledge and insights into a people's society and culture to be gleaned from comprehensive studies of a systematic sample of their traditional dwellings would not adequately repay the considerable efforts such studies require.

The present volume neatly demonstrates the error of such an assumption, and advances our knowledge of the cultures and domestic organization of the three populations with which it deals, namely, the Hausa-Fulani of Zaria, the Yoruba of Ibadan, and the Berber of Marrakech, separately and together, by the careful comparison which identifies their differences and what they have in common. At the same time, and perhaps most importantly, Friedrich Schwerdtfeger, in this long overdue and path-breaking work, demonstrates and applies a fully developed methodology for detailed study of relationships between the forms of housing and the forms of domestic organization in urban centres of pre-industrial cultures of widely differing history, economy, ecology, and demographic structure. To complete his investigation of these relationships, Dr Schwerdtfeger examines systematically the relationships between the occupations and incomes of household and family heads and their expenditures on house repair and construction, together with the occasions, purposes and frequencies of such outlays. Systematic study of the distribution and use of living space within dwellings is complemented by detailed attention to the technology, raw materials, finance, and organization of the local construction industry in each of the cities studied. In these and other respects, Dr Schwerdtfeger's monograph brilliantly realizes the aims and standards set for all students of urban housing and settlement by the remarkable scholar whose teaching inspired much of the present work, the late Professor Duccio Turin.[4]

Traditional houses must either illustrate the conscious cultural preferences of those who construct and inhabit them, or the responses to formally open situations of choice of those people who rightly or wrongly feel that alternative forms of accommodation, including imported Western models, are beyond their economic reach, or otherwise inappropriate and unsuitable for them. Such freedom of individual choice between traditional and other kinds of dwelling presupposes relatively free access to land required for building sites and to the skills and resources required for construction of traditional homes. To an extraordinary degree, these requisites were normatively and operationally fulfilled in traditional Hausa society, illustrated in this volume by the city of Zaria in northern Nigeria. At the other extreme, in the following comparison, lies the southern Moroccan city of Marrakech, whose population, at least in the old city, the *medina*, occupies 'permanent' buildings in the densely congested medieval quarter. Predictably, newcomers to Marrakech, young adults from the country or from other towns seeking work and fortune, sometimes singly, sometimes in couples, are obliged to rent accommodation, often at rates they can ill afford and in overcrowded buildings. Among contemporary Hausa, parallel patterns occur in Kano, the much larger metropolitan city situated a hundred miles north of Zaria, which was formerly the major terminus in the central Sudan for the Saharan caravan trade. Zaria, however, with lower levels of congestion, rental, tenancy, and overcrowding, was a decade or so ago still sufficiently spacious to sustain traditional Hausa patterns of settlement, land tenure, and domestic architecture.

At Ibadan, the largest Yoruba city and the most populous black African township, both the style of housing and the pattern of domestic organization differ radically from those at Marrakech and Zaria. There, compounds are normally the typical and most inclusive homesteads. They are relatively permanent structures with little interior open space. Each compound accommodates several agnatically linked family units, and is normally administered by its oldest resident male member in the agnatic line, who as compound head is responsible to the town authorities, ancestors, and future generations for the welfare of all within it. In short, Yoruba compounds house patrilineages or patrilineal segments of wider units. In consequence, each Yoruba compound accommodates a plurality of families which are often polygynous, linked to one another by the agnatic relations of their senior male members. Ideally these families are aligned serially in an order of seniority which corresponds to the birth order of their male heads. Being exogamous, Yoruba patrilineages recruit wives for their members from other descent groups. Thereby they engage in an unavoidable complex of relations with one another through which women are exchanged and move to live with their husbands in the latter's patrilineal compounds. Thus, unlike those at Zaria and Marrakech, all adult women in Yoruba compounds are necessarily descended from males with whom their husbands have no agnatic ties. The Yoruba compound accordingly houses an exogamous corporate group, and its sections are occupied by domestic units whose status and rights of occupancy derive from their leading male members, themselves members of one or other of the senior generations of the agnatic group.

At Marrakech and Zaria, by contrast, though patriliny predominates as a principle for the affiliation of successive generations, exogamous corporate lineages are absent. Instead, at Marrakech, where polygyny, though legitimate, is relatively infrequent, individual elementary families prevail and often, as is normally the case in tenant households, these have no kinship ties to other units in the building or compound. At Zaria city, by contrast, in 1968 rental of domestic accommodation was still very rare; and there most compounds contained the families of two or more agnatically linked adult males. However, following Islamic norms and Arabic models, the Hausa of Zaria had long ago rejected exogamy and corporate lineages as basic conditions of their social organization. Indeed, without exception, by 1960 Hausa descent lines and groups were, while patrilineal, not exogamous, and few operated as corporate groups. Instead, as the author demonstrates, the composition of Hausa households typically reflected various stages in the developmental cycle of the agnatic extended families which formed, established and occupied them.[5]

Thus, while modally Muslim like the citizens of Zaria and Marrakech, the Yoruba of Ibadan differed radically in their domestic organization as a function of their organization in corporate exogamous virilocal patrilineages which formed the framework of their domestic life. These lineages were also the basic units of the Yoruba city-states, since each participated in the administration of its chiefdom through its lineage hierarchy and its compound heads, having one or more titles with executive positions and advisory duties appropriated to it in the rank order of state officials. Accordingly the Yoruba compound was both an externally indivisible and presumptively indissoluble corporate unit, and an essential element in the patrilineally based constitution of these Yoruba chiefdoms. In consequence, Yoruba compounds tended to show an identical basic form and framework, being based on sets of adult males whose common agnatic descent furnished their inner organization and moral unity. One consequence of this which has often puzzled students of Islam is the apparent indifference of Yoruba household arrangements to the usual Muslim concern for privacy that prescribes differing degrees of seclusion or purdah for wives, as illustrated at Zaria and Marrakech. Evidently, these Middle Eastern or Arabic rules of wife seclusion are irrelevant in the context of exogamous corporate patrilineal households like those of the Yoruba. For, unless specifically authorized by kinship norms, under such circumstances the most heinous possible crime is adultery with the wife of a patrikinsman, and above all, one living in the same compound. This being so, there is no reason for women to be secluded within the compound, since they are guaranteed protection by the basic kinship rules that constitute Yoruba patrilineages. Moreover, such freedom as Yoruba women enjoy within their homes is an essential condition for the freedom which they exercise outside them, in their varied roles in the economic, religious, and other spheres of public social life.

As this brief comparison indicates, this richly documented study enables us to raise and consider many stimulating questions concerning domiciles and household arrangements which have hitherto received little attention, due primarily to lack of detailed studies of indigenous systems of traditional housing in exotic cultures. In this regard the present monograph is primarily an exploration into important but neglected territory; and in this respect, as also in the thoroughness of its design and execution, this investigation of housing patterns and practice in southern Morocco, Yorubaland, and Hausaland, follows worthily in the tradition of the author's predecessors and compatriots, Heinrich Barth and Gustav Nachtigal, who so fully and vividly recorded the cultures and histories of the then little-known peoples of the Sahara and Sudan.

M. G. SMITH

Notes and references

1 Lewis H. Morgan, 1881, *Houses and House-life of the American Aborigines.* Contributions to North American Ethnology Vol. IV. Washington D.C., Government Printing Office. (Reprinted 1965, University of Chicago Press.)

2 Paul Oliver (ed.), 1969, *Shelter and Society*, New York, Praeger.
Paul Oliver (ed.), 1971, *Shelter in Africa*, London, Barrie & Jenkins.
Paul Oliver (ed.), 1975, *Shelter, Sign and Symbol*, London, Barrie & Jenkins.

3 For examples, see: James Littlejohn, 1960, 'The Temne House', *Sierra Leone Studies*, no. 14, pp. 63–79; Pierre Bourdieu, 1973, 'The Berber House', in Mary Douglas (ed.), *Rules and Meanings*, Penguin Books, Harmondsworth; Mary Douglas, 'Symbolic Orders in the Use of Domestic Space', in Peter J. Ucko, Ruth Tringham, and G. W. Dimbleby (eds), 1972, *Man, Settlement and Urbanism*, London, Duckworth; or Adam Kuper, 1980, 'Symbolic Dimensions of the Southern Bantu Homestead', *Africa*, vol. 50, no. 1, pp. 8–23.

4 For tributes to Duccio Turin, a moving personal memoir, and four brief examples of his thought, see Otto Koenigsberger and Steven Groak (eds), *Habitat International: Duccio Turin Memorial Issue*, 1978, vol. 3, nos 1 and 2.

5 v. Joseph Greenberg, 1947. 'Islam and Clan Organisation among the Hausa', *Southwestern Journal of Anthropology*, vol. 3, pp. 193–211.

Preface

The material for this book was collected from 1967 to 1969, when I investigated 215 houses or compounds which held a total of 676 households containing 3,248 persons in Zaria and Ibadan, two Nigerian cities, and Marrakech in Morocco.* Since then rapid economic development in Nigeria, and to a lesser degree in Morocco, has strengthened the building industry in both countries and increased the production of modern houses but has neglected the traditional housing sector. After reviewing my own material, which covers a period of approximately ten years from 1960 to 1970, I decided to include most of the data, even though some seem dated – particularly those which relate to Nigeria and Morocco as a whole – since they are all clearly needed for a full understanding of the urban housing situation in the three towns studied. Furthermore, official policies and public attitudes towards the traditional housing sector have not substantially changed since my investigation was completed.

The subject discussed here overlaps several disciplines, for example, architecture, social anthropology, history, and economics to name only the most important. The multi-disciplinary approach followed here was necessary – indeed unavoidable – to describe and analyse the complex relationships that hold between traditional urban houses and their inhabitants. These relationships were investigated in detail and no doubt form the most

*This book is a revised version of my Ph.D. thesis at University College, London, in 1975.

important part of this book. In fact, the construction and layout of traditional urban houses – and for that matter of all houses built by their inhabitants – are incomprehensible without an understanding of the structure and development of co-residential kinship groups that have built, enlarged, and maintained these houses in order to meet their housing needs. In other words, housing should never be examined as an isolated phenomenon but only as an integral part of culture. Not only can traditional architecture best be understood by studying society but conversely a better understanding of society can be obtained by examining the houses to which they gave rise. Even among architects, the once accepted notion that one could simply study architecture as a spatial–structural entity without examining the society and the socio-economic structure of the people concerned is no longer tenable.

As little work has been done in the field of traditional architecture and society, this study must remain essentially exploratory, and some of my interpretations and conclusions will no doubt have to be elaborated in future.

It is hoped that this study will provide some information which architects, town planners, and sociologists concerned with the urban housing situation in the Third World may find of relevance and interest as they seek better housing solutions, particularly in African cities.

Zaria, August 1980 FRIEDRICH W. SCHWERDTFEGER

List of tables, plans, and diagrams

Each chapter includes some tables and diagrams, but the main bulk of the tables and diagrams can be found in the appendixes. The tables and diagrams in the main text bear the number of the chapter and of the table itself, i.e. Table 3.1 means table number 1 in Chapter 3. Tables and diagrams in the appendixes are numbered from 1 to 20 according to the chapter numbers, and are signified with a letter A, i.e. Table A.3.1 means table number 1, Chapter 3.

Part I Zaria

Tables

Diagrams

Graphs

Plans

Pictures

Part II Ibadan

Tables

Diagrams

Graphs

Plans

Pictures

Part III Marrakech

Tables

Diagrams

Graphs

Plans

Pictures

Part IV Comparison and Conclusion

Tables

Plans

Appendixes Part I Zaria

Tables

Diagrams

Graphs

Plans and Maps

Appendixes Part II Ibadan

Tables

Diagrams

Graphs

Plans and Maps

Picture

Appendixes Part III Marrakech

Tables

Diagrams

Graphs

Plans and Maps

Introduction

Traditional urban houses have hitherto received very little attention, yet they provide shelter for the overwhelming majority of the urban population in Africa, Asia, and Latin America. Most countries in Africa have made genuine efforts to increase the production of modern houses constructed with permanent building materials, but this effort, though often and widely publicized, has benefited only a relatively small section of the community, whereas the rest of the population still have to rely for their housing needs almost entirely on traditional building materials and techniques, on traditional craftsmen, and on their own meagre financial resources. It is the houses and people of this latter group that will be described and analysed in this book.

The towns chosen for this research were Zaria, a Hausa city in Northern Nigeria, the Yoruba metropolis of Ibadan in Western Nigeria, and Marrakech, the ancient capital of Morocco. These three precolonial cities have undergone broadly similar changes, linked first with colonization at the start of this century and then with the emergence of independent states in Morocco and Nigeria in 1956 and 1960 respectively. The predominantly Muslim population of all three towns has grown rapidly during the last 50 years,[1] but the physical expansion associated with this growth has taken place outside the traditional cities, leaving their central areas virtually untouched.

Aims and objectives

The primary aims of this study are, first, to provide some information on the housing conditions of the indigenous population of three selected African towns; second, to investigate the relations between traditional forms of housing and the organization of domestic groups, and finally to find out how these groups build, finance, and maintain their houses.

As most houses or compounds included in my survey were constructed in several stages according to the needs of their inhabitants, I have devoted special attention to domestic groups and their kinship organization in order to determine what relationship exists between the development of co-residential kinship groups and the layout and size of their compounds or houses. This is an essential part of my study and stems from the belief that we cannot understand the construction, use, abandonment, and decay of traditional urban compounds, let alone plan new houses to supplement or replace them, unless we have a sound understanding of the structure and development of the co-residential kinship groups that have built and developed these compounds in order to meet their housing needs.

It is hoped that this study will provide useful information on the social and economic aspects of domestic groups as well as on the physical and financial aspects of housing. Such information may be of some relevance when we seek to identify areas which are in need of improvement, and to analyse past failures in the modern housing sector. Furthermore, this research project was undertaken to develop a method and to collect the data which are essential to study the various aspects of the relationship between co-residential kinship groups and their houses.

However, it should be noted that this study cannot provide solutions for housing problems encountered in the three towns under investigation, nor does it seek to supply ready-made solutions for these problems. Instead I merely try to provide a more comprehensive view of the urban housing situation by including the often neglected development of co-residential kinship groups which, as we shall see in this book, play a decisive part in determining the layout and size of these compounds.

Problem and method of study

Selection of towns

Selection of the towns to be studied was guided by three broad principles. First, to ensure that they represented distinct cultures, it was necessary that the towns should have been firmly established long before colonial rule. Second, each town had to have a largely undisturbed central area in which the pattern of domestic groups and their building activities could be studied; and finally, to exclude problems that might arise due to differences of religion, I decided to restrict the study to towns having a predominantly Muslim population. Furthermore, each of the three towns chosen should be situated in one of Africa's main climatic regions, i.e. the warm/humid, the monsoon, and the hot/dry climate. Beyond these criteria, the choice of towns was arbitrary and depended largely on the existence of supporting facilities such as universities, and on the willingness of the municipal authority to permit the survey.

Main characteristics of the towns

The city of Zaria was founded as the capital of a Hausa state with that name in the fifteenth century and has been the seat of an emir or chief for the last four centuries. The city is the cultural, economic, and political centre of the contemporary emirate. Its inhabitants are mainly engaged in subsistence farming, handicrafts, and trade. In the early 1970s the population of the city and its suburbs was estimated at between 160,000 and 180,000.[2]

Ibadan was established as a Yoruba army camp early in the nineteenth century. From this unusual beginning, the city has grown rapidly due mainly to large-scale immigration from the northern parts of Yorubaland. By 1900, Ibadan was the largest native city in sub-Saharan Africa, and after the First World War Ibadan became the commercial centre for the cocoa-growing region of Western Nigeria. Its inhabitants derive their wealth and livelihood mainly from cash-crop cultivation, craft production, and trading. It has been estimated that the population of the city reached a million in the early 1970s.[3]

Marrakech was founded by Berber tribesmen in the late eleventh century, and served as the capital of the Moroccan empire for over three centuries. During the Middle Ages the city was one of the most important northern entrepôts for the long-distance caravan trade across the Sahara. As the regional capital of southern Morocco, contemporary Marrakech retains some of its former economic importance, and its inhabitants are mainly engaged in trade, craft activities, and local administration. According to the 1971 census report the city then had a population of 333,000.[4]

The only modern industries at the time of my survey

consisted of a few food-producing factories in the three towns.

Sample procedure

Nonexistence or incompleteness of housing lists in all three towns chosen for study meant that the selection of houses had to be based on areal samples. A standard procedure was adopted for all three towns. The first step was to define the central area of the town, i.e. the area surrounded by the old city wall.[5] It was then decided to exclude all modern residential areas, any fallow land, parks, and land used for agriculture, as well as markets and other nonresidential areas. The territory defined by this procedure was then divided into contiguous plots which varied in size depending on the town and on the density of housing in each area. Once these plots were transposed on an aerial photograph of the city, they were carefully examined and one house, typical of houses in each plot, was selected and marked on the photograph. Specific care was taken in each city to select a cross-section of large, medium, and small houses, although the very largest compounds had to be left out because of difficulties in dealing with them adequately due to shortage of time. Nevertheless, some very large compounds – mostly houses of chiefs – were studied separately though they were not included in the survey.[6]

From this description of my selection procedure it is quite clear that the houses chosen in the three cities do not represent a random sample. Hence, my survey data cannot be regarded as statistically representative of the towns studied, even though some comparison with other relevant data has occasionally been made.

The houses selected on the aerial photographs were then listed and identified with the help of the ward head in the area. When this had been done for all areas in a town, each ward head was asked to approach the heads of all houses in his area and to obtain their permission to survey the houses and their occupants. This procedure provided me with sponsorship and an official introduction; and although some compound heads did have misgivings about the investigation, they seldom refused the ward head's request that I should be allowed to survey their homes.

Demographic factors

The three samples chosen in this way varied in absolute size and in the proportions of the universes which they represent. Thus, the sample taken in Zaria included 77 compounds with 1,067 inhabitants, and represented about 2.6 per cent of the total population living in the walled city. In Ibadan the sample consisted of only 63 houses with 1,285 persons or about 0.2 per cent of the city's total population; while at Marrakech the sample included 75 houses with 896 inhabitants or about 0.5 per cent of the population in the *medina* or old walled city. In spite of their differing ratios the three samples have equivalent status because they were chosen, studied and analysed by a uniform method.

Unit of analysis

The unit of analysis throughout this study consisted of a house or compound and its inhabitants, who may be divided into two or more households or economic units. However, as data on current household composition are insufficient by themselves to document and explain the various changes which frequently occur in domestic groups, additional kinship data based on a common reference point – in our case relation to the compound head – were collected and analysed for all households and compounds in these samples.

Method of survey

The survey of compounds and houses followed a systematic pattern throughout my investigation. After the compound head[7] had agreed to permit a survey of his house, I visited the house at a prearranged time, often accompanied by the ward head. Following a detailed explanation of the aim and purpose of my survey, I encouraged the compound head to ask questions in order to clear up any possible misunderstandings. This informal discussion before each investigation proved invaluable on both sides as it put the compound head at ease and acquainted us with one another.

In each compound I began my survey by measuring the house and all its rooms and interior spaces, the sizes of all doors and windows within it, the height of rooms and the thickness of walls. The contents of all rooms were then recorded on a specially prepared list. Inquiries were then made about the use of each room and the number of its occupants. In the course of this inventory, new constructions, improvements, and recent repairs carried out by the compound head or any other household head were easily detected and marked on the plan. Depending on the size of the house, the first part of the inquiry lasted on average between one and three hours.

This first part of the compound survey supplied a wealth of useful information by direct observation which proved invaluable during the following interviews. For example, the distribution of radios, sewing machines, record players, bicycles, and occasionally television sets found in the houses surveyed, gave a fair indication of the economic positions of their occupants. The state of repair of the house and the use of traditional or expensive modern building materials supplied another set of useful information, which served as a check on some of the compound head's answers and as reminder when inquiries into the cost of new construction, improvements, and repairs were carried out.

The first part of a personally administered questionnaire was designed to obtain basic information on the number of people living in the house, their relationships to the compound head, their age, birthplace, ethnic identity, length of residence in the town and the house, then educational standards and occupations as well as the history of the family. The second part of the questionnaire began with more detailed questions on the occupations of all adult males and females in the compound's households. This was followed by questions about household consumption of food, hygiene, children, extended kinship links, and expenditures on food, clothing, other consumer goods, and outlays for festivals. With this information I could then start to estimate annual, monthly, weekly and/or daily incomes which were always checked with the informant. The third part of the questionnaire dealt in detail with the house, its construction, improvements, and maintenance, seeking information on actual expenditures over the past five years. Costs of these building activities were calculated with the help of the compound head, who was also questioned on the method and sources of finance.

As only a few informants could speak either English or French as fluently as needed for the interview, I used interpreters who were trained for about three weeks preceding the date of the first interview in each town.

Fieldwork, general notes

On my arrival in Nigeria in November 1967, the civil war with Biafra in the former Eastern Region of the country was at its height. Although not directly involved in the war, the people of Ibadan, and to a lesser degree those of

Zaria, were understandably suspicious of strangers at the time and particularly of those who came to probe into their personal affairs. In spite of repeated official explanations of the nature of my inquiry and repeated efforts at personal persuasion, some compound heads were not convinced of the good faith of the inquiry and refused to cooperate. One compound head, a soldier, actually went so far as to report us to his superior officer, declaring that we were spies engaged in collecting information which could be used by enemy aircraft for air raids against the town. While such wild accusations could be dealt with relatively easily, there were other obstacles which were less immediately evident but more persistent and severe. Having agreed to let me survey their houses, some compound heads tried with considerable skill to lead me systematically astray by giving deliberately false information about their incomes. To overcome these difficulties I decided to base my financial inquiry on reports of the regular daily, weekly, and monthly expenditures of household heads, then infrequent annual outlays – subjects about which most informants were quite willing to speak freely. Some additional information was also obtained from urban consumer surveys. Only after all major regular and irregular items of expenditure were listed was household income investigated. Income and expenditure were then compared and only when they balanced within about 10 per cent was the budget accepted as sufficiently accurate for inclusion in the analysis.

The plans of compounds and houses reproduced in this book were drawn during the survey. As it has not been my aim to enumerate every detail here, it has not been necessary to provide keys for all the reference numbers and letters appearing on them.

Diagrammatic representation of kinship organization throughout the book takes the following form:

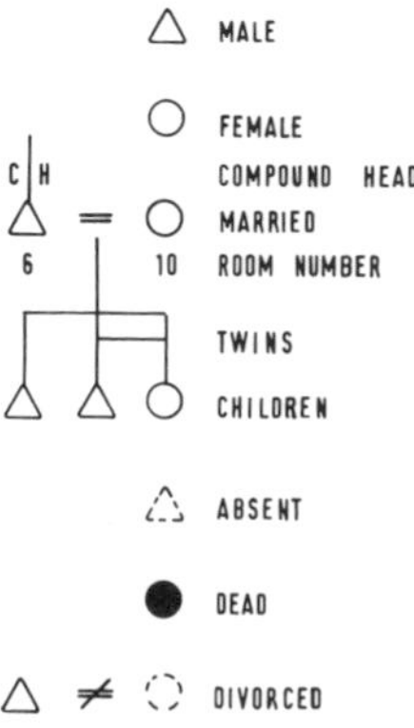

Notes and references

1 In the 1960s over 90 per cent of the population in the walled cities of Zaria and Marrakech, and nearly 60 per cent of Ibadan's population, were Muslims. (For Ibadan see A. L. Mabogunje, *Urbanization in Nigeria*, London, 1968, pp. 219–220.)
2 H. Bedawi, *Housing in Zaria: Present Condition and Future Needs*, ABU, Department of Urban and Regional Planning, Zaria, 1977, p. 51.
3 Mabogunje, op. cit., p. 236.
4 Service Central des Statistiques, Royaume du Maroc, *Population légale du Maroc 1971*, Rabat, 1971, p. 6.
5 In 1967/1968 all three towns still had parts of old city walls.
6 See pp. 125–126.
7 A distinction has been made between the compound head, who is in control of the house and its inhabitants, and the head of a household or economic unit of which more than one may be found in any given house or compound. For more detailed discussion, see p. 34.

Part I

ZARIA

Chapter 1

Context

Environmental setting

Geography and climate

Nigeria is the largest country on the west coast of Africa. It is sited entirely within the tropical zone between latitudes 4° 20′ and 13° 53′ north and between longitudes 2° 40′ and 14° 40′ east, and covers an area of 923,737 sq. km (356,669 sq. miles). The main features of the country's topography are the valleys and flood plains of the Niger and Benue rivers, which, together with the coastal region and the Chad Basin in the north-east of the country, are less than 300 m above sea-level. The greater part of Northern Nigeria lies between 300 and 1,200 m above sea-level, but the Jos plateau situated approximately in the centre of the country and the Cameroon highlands on the south-east border rise up to 1,780 m and 2,020 m respectively.

The vegetation of the country may be roughly divided into three zones.[1] First, the swamp and tropical rainforest of the coastal belt; second, the high forest of the humid south; and third, the Guinea and Sudan savannah of the north. The forest and the southern part of the savannah are suitable for growing cocoa, kola, rubber plants, palm trees, yam, and cassava, while in the northern part of the savannah there is herding of cattle and sheep with cultivation of cotton, groundnuts, millet, and guinea corn.

The climate of Nigeria is conditioned by the seasonal

shifting of pressure belts, the continental air masses blowing from the north-east from November to March, which is the dry or harmattan season, while the equatorial maritime air masses blow from the south-west from May to September to create the rainy season.

In Zaria the temperatures vary from an average maximum of 35.8 °C in April to an average minimum of 14.0 °C in January. The mean annual rainfall (1928–1967) is 1,110 mm and most of it falls between May and September.[2] (See also Diagram A.1.1 on p. 317.) However, the local people in Hausaland distinguish four seasons as follows. First, *bazara* from mid-February to mid-May, the hot dry season of the harmattan; second, *damina* from mid-May to the end of August, the rainy season; third, *kaka* from the beginning of September to the end of November, the harvest season; and fourth, *rani* from the end of November to mid-February, the cold dry season of the harmattan which is also the building season.

Human pattern

Over 90 per cent of the various linguistic and cultural groups found in Nigeria belong to the Sudanic language family.[3] According to Buchanan and Pugh, three divisions of the Sudanic language family are recognized today.[4] There are, first, the Negro languages; second, the Semi-Bantu languages; and third, the Inner Sudanic languages. The Kwa language group, a subdivision of the Negro languages, is further divided into a northern section including Nupe, Jukun, and Gwari and a southern section including Yoruba, Ibo, Ijaw, and Edo.* The Semi-Bantu language group stretches in a broken semi-circle to the north of the Yoruba–Ibo speaking area and includes the Ibibio, Tiv, and Fulani.[5] The Inner Sudanic languages, which are subdivided into the Hausa–Kotoko and Kanuri groups, are spoken in all northern states of Nigeria.

The people who live and work in the walled city of Zaria speak Hausa, but the pastoral Fulani (*filanih daji*), who come to the city from the surrounding countryside to sell milk products, speak Fulfulde. These pasturalists are distinguished from the settled Fulani (*filanih gida*) who speak Hausa and have provided the ruling families (*dangin sarauta*) in most Hausa states since the beginning of the nineteenth century.

*See Ethnic Composition on p. 19.

Historical background

The recorded history of Hausaland can be divided into four periods: the Habe kingdoms, which lasted from the fifteenth to the end of the eighteenth century, the Fulani empire, 1804–1900; the colonial period, 1900–1960; followed by independence. The origin and early history of the Hausa people are obscure, but it seems probable that during the ninth and tenth centuries AD several waves of immigrants from the east came into the area which is now part of north-western Nigeria including the former provinces of Sokoto, Katsina, Kano, and Zaria.[6] *Daura makas sarki*,[7] a legend probably written only in the eighteenth or early nineteenth century AD, speaks of a Hausa kingdom in Daura (80 km north of Kano) which was ruled by a queen. The legend tells that a traveller named Ba'ijidda, son of Abdullah, Sultan of Baghdad, came to Daura and killed the snake which was living in the town's main well, preventing people from drawing water. For this he was chosen by the queen as her husband and their descendants became the first kings and queens of seven Hausa kingdoms (*Hausa bakwai*). One of these kingdoms was Zazzau or Zaria. In their early history the seven Hausa kingdoms formed a loose collection of culturally related units and it is reported that Zaria, due to her position to the south, had the task of capturing and supplying slaves to her northern neighbours. The chronicle of the Hausa kingdom of Zaria mentions queen Bakwa who ruled Zaria from 1492 to 1522. It is further reported that Bakwa was the last queen who ruled in Turunku, a place 25 km south of Zaria, and that her second daughter Zaria built the last of the five capitals of Zaria in its present position and gave it her name. According to Arnett, Islam was introduced to Kano in the first half of the fourteenth century AD by Arab traders, and may have reached Zaria in the middle of the fifteenth century.[8] The new religion seems to have spread rapidly among the nobility in the capital, but until the early eighteenth century the occasional pagan ruler appears on the list of local chiefs.

The Fulani cattle nomads, first mentioned as *peul* (sing. *pullo*) in the eleventh century AD, were a small group living in what is now known as Senegal. Over the years they wandered eastwards, and they crossed the border of Hausaland in the early sixteenth century. There they were generally welcomed by the Hausa kings and either continued as nomads or settled in towns as *filanih gida*. By the middle of the eighteenth century wars and corruption had weakened the political and administrative organization of the Hausa kingdoms. But it was the impurity of Islam as practised by the Hausa elite which compelled Uthman dan Fodio, a Fulani religious leader and clan head, to preach his holy war (*jihad*) against the Hausa king of Gobir during the last years of the eighteenth century, thus initiating developments which led to a holy war in 1804–1810 which caused the downfall of the Hausa dynasties.

After the victory over Makau, the last Hausa king of Zaria in about 1807 Malam Musa was appointed by Uthman dan Fodio to rule Zaria. The new Fulani rulers of Hausaland, who enjoyed a great measure of autonomy, recognized the Sultan of Sokoto as their spiritual and political head and paid him an annual tribute. Emirates in difficulties could appeal to the sultan for help, who, in case peace was threatened, did intervene in the political administration of the state concerned. The emirate of Zaria, which extended southwards to the bank of the river Benue in the middle of the nineteenth century, was divided into a number of areas and vassal states controlled by the emir who either appointed Fulani noblemen as fiefs or installed locally chosen heads after they had sworn allegiance to him.[9]

In the second half of the nineteenth century the Royal Niger Company, which traded along the Niger and Benue, entered into a number of commercial treaties with the emirs of the Fulani empire in order to protect their trade and trading establishments. These agreements, it was later argued, gave the company and its successor, the British Government, the right over large areas of land, particularly alongside the two rivers, and some undefined political power over the emirates. How wrong this assumption was, was shown by the tough resistance of most emirs to the British occupation which started under the command of Frederick Lugard (later Lord Lugard) at the beginning of 1900, from Lokoya and was only firmly established after the battle of Burmi in July 1903 where Attahiru, the last independent Fulani sultan, died with over 700 of his followers.

With the advance of British forces Zaria came under British rule in 1902. The colonial administration deposed Kwassau, Emir of Zaria and replaced him with Aliyu, a grandson of Malam Musa, the Galadima Suleimanu acting as regent for a six months' period. (See Table A.1.1, p. 318.) After the battle of Burmi, the Zaria emirate was reduced in size and its former vassal states of Keffi, Nassarawa, and Jema'a were made independent chiefdoms. Slavery was gradually abolished and in the following years the foundations of a modern economy with its infrastructure, new laws, an educational system, and a health service were gradually laid down, leading to independence in September 1960.

Economic development

The overall performance of the Nigerian economy between 1960 and 1970, as reflected in the changes in Gross Domestic Product (GDP), was one of unsteady expansion. For example, in 1962 the GDP at 1962/1963 factor cost was 1,299 million Nigerian pounds (£N)[10] and rose to £N1,522 million in 1966,[11] giving per capita income of approximately £N28 and £N31 respectively.[12] (See Table A.1.2 on p. 319.) While the average annual rate of growth of GDP was about 5 per cent between 1962 and 1966, that of per capita GDP was 2.5 per cent. However, after the outbreak of the civil war in mid-1967, GDP fell to £N1,286 million.[13] After the decline in 1967 and stagnation in 1968, the economy adjusted to the civil war in the country and started to pick up again in 1969, a trend which was even more pronounced after the fighting had stopped in January 1970.

Nigeria has a wealth of natural resources which include *inter alia* crude petroleum, coal, natural gas, tin, columbite, limestone, and a wide variety of timber. Nevertheless, agriculture occupied a dominant position in the country's economic development and accounted for about £N764 million or 47.7 per cent of GDP, and about 43 per cent of total overseas export earnings in 1969. About three quarters of the population of Nigeria then worked on the land. However, since the early 1960s the relative position of agriculture as a major foreign exchange earner has declined from £N123 million or 75 per cent of the total domestic export in 1962 to £N121 million or 19 per cent in 1971,[14] while income from petroleum export has risen sharply and so increased the nation's GDP. (See Tables A.1.4 and A.1.5 on p. 320.)

Until quite recently, Nigeria's manufacturing industry consisted overwhelmingly of small processing plants that were mainly engaged in producing consumer goods such as textiles, canned food, paints, beer and soft drinks, flour, car tyres, and cement. In 1960 the contribution of manufacturing industry (including crafts) to the GDP amounted to £N60 million or 4.8 per cent. By 1969 its value had risen to £N132 million or 8.2 per cent of GDP. During this period the average growth rate of manufactured goods was roughly 10 per cent per annum. Approximately one quarter of the contribution of these industries to GDP came from the semi-processing of primary raw materials for export, such as palm oil processing and sawmilling, while industrial production accounted for the rest. In addition there are a great number of indigenous small-scale enterprises run by local craftsmen and artisans, e.g. weaving, traditional building construction, smithing, and leather working, the contribution of which are not included in GDP.

In 1969, other important sectors of the national economy were distribution with £N206 million or 12.8 per cent of GDP; government, other services and education, health, electricity, and water supply together with £N240.7 million or 15.0 per cent; crude oil and mining with £N127 million or 7.9 per cent; building construction with £N70 million or 4.4 per cent, and transport and communication with £N64 million or 4.0 per cent.* (See Tables A.1.2 and A.1.3 on p. 319.)

From 1960 to 1965 Nigeria had a trade deficit which led in 1964/1965 to legislation to restrain consumer demand by imposing higher taxes and higher customs duties on a wide range of imported consumer goods. As a result of these measures and, later, the increasing revenue from crude petroleum export, the balance of trade showed a surplus of £N27 million in 1966, which increased to £N107 million in 1971.[15] (See Table A.1.6 on p. 320.)

As indicated above, the production of crude petroleum has come to play a vital role in the country's economic development. The export of crude petroleum rose from £N4.4 million or 2.7 per cent of total domestic export in 1960 to £N92 million or 33.0 per cent in 1966. During the civil war, exports fell to £N72 million in 1967 and still further to £N37 million or 18 per cent of total export value in 1968. In 1969 export of crude petroleum increased again, reaching £N477 million or 74.4 per cent of total domestic export in 1971. The share of crude petroleum and mining in GDP at 1962/1963 factor cost rose from 1.2 per cent in 1960 to 6.9 per cent in 1966, and fell to 3.3 per cent in 1968, only to rise again to 14.9 per cent in 1971. Known reserves of crude petroleum are estimated at about 200 million tons which, at the present rate of exploitation, would last until the early 1990s. However, probable aggregate estimation ranges between 600 and 1,200 million tons.

Nigeria's Gross Fixed Capital Formation (GFCF) at 1962/1963 prices rose from £N176 million or 13.6 per cent of GDP in 1962, to £N275 million or 17.7 per cent of GDP in 1966. After the outbreak of the civil war in 1967, capital formation fell to £N236 million or 18 per cent of GDP in 1967 and further to £N221.6 million in 1969.[16] Closer

*Agriculture and manufacturing industry mentioned earlier accounted together for 55.9 per cent of GDP.

examination of total capital formation by type of asset shows that the value of investment in building increased from £N64.9 million in 1960 to £N94.3 million in 1965, and decreased to £N65.3 million in 1969. The percentage distribution in building works fell from 40.4 per cent in 1960 to 29.5 per cent in 1969, while civil engineering works increased from 16.9 per cent to 29.0 per cent over the same time. (See Tables A.1.7 and A.1.8 on p. 321.) As already mentioned, total building investment averaged about 33.0 per cent from 1960 to 1969, of which privately financed dwellings accounted for up to 10 per cent of GFCF in both cases. Most of these privately financed dwellings are located in urban centres, while the overwhelming majority of dwellings in rural and semi-urban areas, where about 80 per cent of the total population live, are all within the traditional sector of the economy which never enters into any national accounts.

Notes and references

1 R. W. J. Keay, *An Outline of Nigerian Vegetation*, Lagos, 1949, pp. 33–36. Keay distinguishes between Forest Region and Savannah Region which are divided into three subgroups each.
2 M. W. Walter, 'Observation on rainfall at the Institute for Agricultural Research', Samaru Miscellaneous Paper No. 15, Ahmadu Bello University, Zaria, 1967, pp. 3–5.
3 H. Baumann and D. Westermann, *Les Peuples et les civilisations de l'Afrique*, Paris, 1948, pp. 449–468.
4 K. M. Buchanan and J. C. Pugh, *Land and People in Nigeria*, London, 1955, p. 82.
5 Baumann and Westermann, op. cit., p. 457. Baumann includes the Fulani in the Semi-Bantu language group, although this has been disputed by other scholars.
6 M. G. Smith, 'The beginning of Hausa society AD 1000 to 1500', in *The Historian in Tropical Africa*, by J. Vansina *et al.*, London, 1964, pp. 339–354.
7 E. J. Arnett, 'A Hausa chronicle', *Journal of the Royal African Society*, (London), **IX**, 1909–1910, pp. 161–167.
8 Arnett, op. cit., p. 163.
9 M. G. Smith, *Government in Zazzau 1800–1950*, Oxford, 1960.
10 The naira was introduced in January 1973. As this was about three years after my investigation was completed, all currency for Nigeria is given in Nigerian pounds.
11 Federal Office of Statistics, Nigeria, *Annual Abstract of Statistics 1971*, Lagos, 1972, p. 141.
12 The estimated population of Nigeria was about 47 million in 1962 and 52 million in 1966.
13 From 1967 to 1970 Biafra was excluded from GDP calculations.
14 Federal Office of Statistics, Nigeria, op. cit., pp. 84–86.
15 Federal Office of Statistics, Nigeria, op. cit., p. 68.
16 Ibid., p. 142.

Chapter 2

Land tenure and land use in Zaria walled city

Historical notes on land tenure

The present Land Tenure Law, passed by the legislature of Northern Nigeria in 1962, contains three diverse and often contradictory elements; first, the customary law (*al'ada*); second, the Muslim land law (*shari'a*) based on the Maliki school or rite which was introduced after the Fulani *jihad** from 1804 to 1810; and third, colonial land legislation following the establishment of the protectorate of Northern Nigeria in 1900.

It is difficult to give a definite account of the customary land law in the pre-Fulani state of Zaria. According to C. K. Meek,[1] most of the land was communally owned. The ultimate authority on land matters was the local chief. He was the trustee of the group and distributed land among his people who enjoyed usufructuary rights during occupancy against any other member of the community. Fallow land remained with its occupant until no longer needed when it reverted to the general pool for reallocation. The formal sale of land was unknown though long- and short-term loans of land were practised.

After the Fulani conquest of Zaria in 1807 the new rulers recognized most of the customs relating to land.[2] The land was divided into two broad categories following the customary division: first, dead land, i.e. land which has not been brought under cultivation; and second, living

*See pp. 5–6.

land which has either been cleared, cultivated, or inhabited.[3] Living land was further subdivided into tithe land and *kharaj* land. Tithe land was farmed by Muslims on which the statutory tithe (*zakka*) was payable, while *kharaj* land was cultivated by heathens who paid the *kharaj*, a tribute levied on the vanquished in return for the privilege of being allowed to remain in possession of their land. After the Fulani had conquered the former Hausa kingdoms, they divided the territory and allotted land to Fulani noblemen as fiefs in return for their active support during the *jihad*.[4] The Muslim land law, which is based on the Maliki law,[5] was gradually introduced by the Fulani rulers into the Hausa courts. However, the new law was seldom applied in practice because the majority of people settled their land transactions and inheritance disputes informally amongst themselves, but land disputes brought before the courts would be settled according to the rule of Maliki law.[6] Nevertheless, 'Hausa courts', as M. G. Smith observed in Zaria, 'administer a variable mixture of Maliki law and Hausa custom', which coexisted and functioned side by side during nearly one hundred years of independent Fulani rule in Zaria.[7]

The protectorate of Northern Nigeria was created on 1 January 1900, but it was not until the fall of Kano and Sokoto in the first half of 1903 that colonial rule was finally established over the whole territory.[8] The most important land legislation introduced by the British Government included *inter alia*, first, the Land Proclamation No. 8 of 1900 which enacted that the title to land, which was formerly vested in the emirs, henceforth passed to the colonial government, and that a non-Nigerian could not acquire land without written consent from the High Commissioner; second, the Crown Land Proclamation No. 16 of 1902 which dealt with land acquired from the Royal Niger Company, while the Public Land Proclamation No. 13 of the same year dealt with the land which was the property of conquered or deposed rulers or land not actually occupied. In 1908 the government appointed a committee to advise on land policy for the protectorate. The report of the committee, which was later approved and embodied in the Land and Native Rights Proclamation No. 9 of 1910, and 1 of 1916, recommended that all land should be declared 'Native Land' and that the earlier distinction between Public Land (Government administered) and Crown Land (Government owned) should be abandoned.[9] In analysing land legislation in the first decade of colonial rule, two important factors emerge: first the government's determination to preserve local forms of land tenure and second its ban on land alienation have helped to preserve precolonial patterns of landholding to an astonishing degree.[10] It should be remembered that in practice the Governor's power regarding land legislation has for the most part been delegated to the Native Authorities or emirs who have thus continued to exercise their executive control of land disposal and revocation. Thus despite or because of colonial land legislation, it can be said that the majority of people living in the walled city of Zaria continue to hold and use land in much the same way as their forefathers. However, exceptions are the British colonial settlements which were established and built in the first half of this century on the outskirts of all major cities in Northern Nigeria. These settlements were administered by British civil servants whose outlook and philosophy they portrayed, and housed the colonial administration, trading establishments and the labour force which came mostly from the southern parts of the country.[11]

Land tenure and transfer today

The main features of land tenure in Zaria Province were studied by C. W. Cole in 1948, and the situation has not changed substantially since then.[12] However, Cole concentrated on rural land tenure and gives only a brief description of the situation within the walled city of Zaria.[13] Further research on land tenure was carried out by the Institute of Administration, Ahmadu Bello University, Zaria, in 1963.[14] The investigation of ownership and acquisition of land described below is based on my 1968 survey of 77 compounds situated in the walled city. The following three types of landholdings were found: first, community holdings, i.e. land belonging to the Native Authority and includes sites for its offices and departments of the administration, the main city market, all roads, rivers, public footpaths, as well as rock outcrops and borrow-pits;* second, family holdings, i.e. land owned by a family or lineage; and third, individual holdings, i.e. privately owned land which has usually been acquired by the present owner, and which becomes family land when inherited.

Permanent transfers of land

Inheritance of land (*gado*) accounted for 65.0 per cent of compounds surveyed. Inheritance is by far the most

*See p. 15.

important mode of land transfer and the 'normal' means of acquisition. On the death of its compound head, the family compound is not normally subdivided among the inheritors, but passes undivided into the care of the senior resident male agnate. However, if the heirs cannot agree upon the division of the agricultural land and other items among themselves, which is extremely rare, the *alkali* or judge, if called on, will subdivide the land as required by Maliki law. Farmland is generally divided equally among the resident male heirs. Any surplus of unapportioned land is usually worked as a *gandu* or joint farm by all the adult males and their families in the compound.*

Purchase of land (*saye*) accounted for 24.6 per cent of compounds surveyed. The sale of suitable building sites in Zaria walled city is now common practice and plays an important role particularly in the densely populated areas. By contrast, farmland is normally not sold, though it may be transferred on a temporary basis. The price of a plot of land varies enormously, between £N2 and £N80, and depends not only on the size and location, but also on the relationship between the parties involved.

Allocation of land is made by the Native Authority normally to employees of the emir's administration but also to other families in need. This category accounted for 6.5 per cent of the compounds surveyed. These building sites, which often include small adjacent farm plots, are usually located near the emir's palace. Land allocated by the emir is held on usufructuary rather than proprietary bases though it is heritable and, if the grant is not revoked progressively, acquires the status of family land.

Gift of land (*kyauta*) between private individuals accounts for 2.6 per cent of compounds surveyed. Land may be given, for example, by a compound head to his adult son, to a cognatic kinsman, a client or a good friend of the family.

Reclaiming of land occurred in 1.3 per cent of compounds surveyed. Such reclaiming of land for building purposes is done by filling in disused borrow-pits. This was undertaken by several compounds surveyed, but only in one case of the sample was a new compound built entirely on such reclaimed land. (See Table A.2.1 on p. 322.)

*See discussion on p. 34.

Temporary transfers of land

The temporary transfer of land is restricted to farm land but outright sales are more frequently conducted today. Two types of temporary land transfer are recognized today:

Pledge of land (jingina or *dangana)* Pledging is a customary transaction by which one person or group obtains temporary rights to farm a plot of land as security for a loan made to its proprietor. Pledged land remains perpetually redeemable by the pledgor on repayment of the loan. However, adequate notice must be given and the pledgee must be allowed to harvest his crops. While the loan made to the owner of the land varies and does not necessarily bear any relationship to the value of the land, it is normally free of interest (*ushra*) as required by Muslim law. Pledging is an increasingly important feature of the local economy used for short- and long-term land conveyance, and for raising money to finance trading activities, marriage payments and building construction or improvements.

Loan of land (*aro*) Renting of farm land is widely practised in the walled city and usually takes place when the holder is unable to work all his fields. The rent for the land consists either of *galla*,* a token payment from the crop, e.g. one or two bundles of guinea corn or millet, or an annual cash payment (*suhuri*). The latter form of payment was unknown in precolonial times and developed only after the introduction of the money economy.[15]

Land use in Zaria walled city

The study of land use given below is based partly on an air survey carried out in December 1963 and partly on a large-scale map at 1:2,400 published by Northern Nigerian Survey, Kaduna, in 1964. The walled city has a total area of 16,577,670 sq. m or 1,658 hectares (4,097 acres). The circumference of its wall is 14.9 km long. The diameter of the walled city varies between 4,080 m in the north–south direction and 5,000 m in the east–west direction. The total area has been divided into six categories:

*This term was also used in precolonial times to denote the slave or serf's payment to the landowner, his owner. This was at least one third, often one half, of the crop.

1 Cultivated land is 66.2 per cent of the total area within the city walls. Cultivated land is by far the most important category and comprises upland farms on light sandy soil farmed in the wet season, and lowland farms (*fadama*) characterized by heavier soil worked mainly during the dry season. (See Map A.2.1, p. 323.) Upland farms, 93.3 per cent of the total cultivated land, are planted in rotation with millet, sorghum, guinea corn and groundnuts, while on irrigated lowland farms, 6.7 per cent of the total cultivated land, which are situated alongside river banks and in well-watered depressions, cash-crops such as sugar-cane, tobacco, rice, and vegetables are produced.

2 Building sites account for 18.6 per cent of the total area within the city walls if we include the narrow footpaths between compounds in the densely built-up areas. Land use within compounds is separately discussed on pp. 30 and 32.

3 Waste land represents 9.1 per cent of the enclosed area. Most of this land is uncultivable and consists of stony plots, land liable to irregular flooding, gullies and stretches of erosive slopes bordering the dilapidated town wall.

4 Roads, if we define this to include all roads and tracks wide enough to carry motor vehicles, are then 2.1 per cent of the enclosed area is appropriated to these ends.

5 Rock surfaces are 2.1 per cent of the total area inside the walls. This includes patches of flat solid rock surface as well as two major areas of granite outcrops in the north-east area of the walled city.

6 Borrow-pits and brooks account for 1.9 per cent of the total area. However, this proportion represents the area under water in December 1963 and changes with the seasons. The many borrow-pits, created by the excavation of building material (mud), that contain stagnant water are typical of all Hausa towns and still constitute a large public health problem. (See Table A.2.2 on p. 322.)

Notes and references

1 C. K. Meek, *Land Tenure and Land Administration in Nigeria and the Cameroons*, London, 1957, pp. 113–117.

2 M. G. Smith, 'Hausa inheritance and succession', in *Studies in the Laws of Succession in Nigeria*, by J. D. M. Derrett *et al.*, Oxford, 1965, p. 245.

3 Meek, op. cit., p. 164. Meek, discussing the different land types, mentioned *wakf* land as a third category, but according to F. H. Ruxton, *Maliki Law*, London, 1916, p. 216, *wakf*

land as a separate subcategory did not exist in Northern Nigeria. However, the term 'territorial *wakf*' was used by the Fulani rulers to describe conquered land in general.

4 M. G. Smith, *The Economy of Hausa Communities of Zaria*, London, 1955, p. 105.

5 Ruxton, op. cit.

6 C. W. Michie, 'Notes on land tenure in the northern districts of Zaria emirate', in *Report on Land Tenure, Zaria Province*, by C. W. Cole, Kaduna, 1952, p. 72. 'The case of Ibrahim versus Musa (before the native court in Zaria walled City on the 23rd Dec. 1937) is a case in point. Two brothers and two sisters failed to live amicably and the *alkali* gave each brother one-third of the compound and the two sisters the remaining third.'

7 M. G. Smith, 'Hausa inheritance and succession', p. 246.

8 Colonial Office, *Annual Report, Northern Nigeria*, London, 1902–1903.

9 Colonial Office, C.D. 5102, *Report of the Northern Nigeria Land Committee*, London, 1910, p. 23.

10 Colonial Office, *Land and Native Rights Ordinance No. 1 of 1916*, Preamble: 'And whereas it is expedient that existing native customs with regard to the use and occupation of land should, as far as possible, be preserved.'

11 For a description of this development see A. W. Urquhart, *Planned Urban Landscapes of Northern Nigeria*, Zaria, 1977.

12 Cole, op. cit.

13 Ibid., pp. 46–47.

14 J. R. N. Marshall, *Traditional Land Tenure Survey 1963*, 'Report on parts of Zaria province' by I. A. Bijimi, pp. 43–143. Institute of Administration, ABU, Zaria, 1965, mimeo.

15 C. W. Rowling, *Report on Land Tenure, Kano Province*, Kaduna, 1949, p. 51.

Chapter 3

Demography

General characteristics

Nigeria: the demographic situation

According to the Nigerian census of 1973, the detailed figures of which were never released, the country then had a total population of 77.8 million.[1] However, the United Nations statistical yearbook estimated the population of Nigeria at 59.6 million in the same year.[2] In 1963, an attempt was made by the United Nations Statistical Office to project the population of Nigeria on the basis of an annual increase of 2.4 per cent, estimating a population of 91.2 million in 1980.[3] Although all these figures have been disputed for one reason or another, Nigeria is by far the most populous country in tropical Africa and holds about one fifth of the total population on that continent.

Crude population estimates with very limited statistical value were made by the British colonial administration in 1911, 1921, and 1931 yielding totals of 16.0 million, 18.7 million, and 20.0 million respectively.[4] The first and still the most reliable and detailed census was taken in 1952/1953, giving a total population of 31.1 million for Nigeria plus that part of the Cameroons then under UK trusteeship.[5] During the 1952/1953 census the following age groups were counted: 0–1, 2–6, 7–14, 15–50, and over 50. Data were also collected on ethnic groupings, occupation, literacy, and religious affiliation. A national census was taken in 1962 but never officially published. However, unofficial sources estimated the country's total population at between 42 and 52 million that time.[6] Another census taken in 1963 yielded a population of 55.6 million.[7] This result was regarded by leading demographers as at least 10 per cent too high when compared with the 1952/1953 census.[8]

In spite of four national censuses taken in Nigeria over a period of 20 years (1952/1953, 1962, 1963, and 1973), it is still impossible to give a reasonably accurate estimate of the size of the total population in the country. This is mainly due to the confusion of political with statistical issues, particularly in the national censuses taken after 1960. Hence, until there is a new and reliable census, the published demographic material on Nigeria must be considered with the utmost caution. However, in the absence of other data I will make use of some of the 1952/1953 and 1963 census results for Zaria and Ibadan keeping their limitations in mind.

Regional distribution and density

Until the creation of the twelve new states in May 1967,[9] which were increased to 19 states in 1976, Nigeria was divided into three major regions: first, the Northern Region with a population of 29.8 million or 53.6 per cent of the total in 1963; second, the Western Region including the Colony with Lagos as well as the Mid-Western Region created in 1963, with 13.4 million or 24.1 per cent; and third, the Eastern Region with 12.3 million or 21.3 per cent.

The density of population per square mile in the 26 provinces, as found in 1963, is summarized in Map A.3.1 on p. 324. The map clearly shows three densely populated provinces which coincide with 'key areas' in the country's cultural and economic geography. First, Kano Province in the former Northern Region, with a density of 350 persons per square mile, is the centre of Nigeria's groundnut, cotton, and hide and skin processing industries. Second, the Western Region, reaching 740 persons per square mile in Ibadan Province, is regarded as the central area of the cocoa-producing belt. Third, Owerri Province in the Eastern Region, with a density of about 850 persons per square mile, is situated in the heart of the palm tree belt. Central Nigeria, including the former provinces of Adamawa, Benue, Ilorin, Kaba, Niger, Plateau, and Sardauna, shows a remarkably low overall density of about 80 persons per square mile which still reflects tribal wars and slave-raiding activities by the Fulani emirates and the Yoruba kingdoms in the last century.

Ethnic composition

Nigeria is composed of a heterogeneous population of more than 35 major ethnic groups recorded in the 1963 census, of which 13 accounted for over 84 per cent of the country's total population. They are: Hausa 20.9 per cent, Yoruba 20.3 per cent, Ibo 16.7 per cent, Fulani 8.6 per cent, Kanuri 4.0 per cent, Ibibio 3.6 per cent, Tiv 2.5 per cent, Ijaw 1.9 per cent, Edo 1.7 per cent, Annang 1.2 per cent, Nupe 1.2 per cent, Urhobo 1.1 per cent, and Igala with 1.0 per cent. The non-African population represented only 0.08 per cent of the total in Nigeria at that time.[10]

A survey of the population in the three former regions gives a much clearer picture of the distribution of the major ethnic groups. According to the 1952/1953 census report, no detailed data are available for 1963; the Hausa–Fulani group in the Northern Region was represented with 51.0 per cent, the Yoruba in the Western Region with 71.0 per cent, and the Ibos in the Eastern Region with 68.0 per cent of the total regional population.

Age and sex distribution

In the 1963 census the distribution of age was recorded in five-year intervals and showed as many as 43.0 per cent of the total population to be under the age of 15. (See Table A.3.1 on p. 326.) This large proportion of young people is a salient feature of all rapidly developing countries in Africa and indicates a decreasing infant mortality rate combined with a high fertility rate in the recent past. The Gross Reproduction Rate (total number of live female births per woman) was estimated at 3.2 for Nigeria.[11]

The sex distribution taken from the 1952/1953 census was 957 males to 1,000 females or 49.0 per cent to 51.0 per cent, and in 1963 1,020 males to 1,000 females or 50.6 per cent to 49.4 per cent respectively.

Level of urbanization

According to the 1963 census report (no detailed data are available for the 1973 census), nearly 11.0 million people or 19.2 per cent were living in urban centres of 20,000 or more inhabitants. The level of urbanization varies considerably from region to region. The census figures for 1963 show the ratio of urbanization as high as 45.8 per cent in the former Western Region, increasing to 53.9 per cent in Yorubaland which includes the former provinces of Oyo, Ibadan, Abeokuta, Ijebu, Ondo, and the Colony, 11.4 per cent in the former Eastern Region, and 10.5 per cent in the former Northern Region.[12]

Zaria

The growth and development of Zaria

As already mentioned in Chapter 1, the city of Zaria, or Zazzau, was founded in the fifteenth century as the capital of a Hausa state with that name. Unfortunately, little is known of the city's early history. The construction of a city wall, known as the Madarkaci wall, is believed to date back to the foundation of the city. (See Plan 3.1.) There are at least three other still recognizable walls within the neighbourhood of the city, known respectively as the Kona, Amina, and Tukur-Tukur walls, but their origins and dates of construction are unknown. A second and larger wall encircling the old city, known as the Fulani or Main wall, may date back to the eighteenth century, but unless new archaeological excavations have taken place the dates of all these walls must remain tentative.[13]

After the British occupation of Zaria in 1902, a Government Station was built about 3 km to the north of the old city. This was followed by the establishment of a commercial centre, a new town or Sabon Gari, and the settlement of Tudun Wada in 1912 and 1914 respectively.[14] Due to the colonial policy of strict racial segregation, these last two settlements were built for and occupied by African labourers, artisans, and clerks from Southern and Northern Nigeria, while the Government Station with its Residential Area (GRA) was inhabited by Europeans. In 1925 an Agricultural Station was established at Samaru village about 12 km north-west of the old city, which later expanded rapidly following the foundation of the Nigerian College of Arts, Science, and Technology that was subsequently transformed into Ahmadu Bello University in 1962.

The diverse settlements created in the first three decades of colonial rule together with the old city constitute what is known today as Zaria Urban Area, which according to recent estimates holds about 200,000 people.[15]

Population growth

Zaria Urban Area is divided into Zaria City District and Sabon Gari District and coincides roughly with the built-

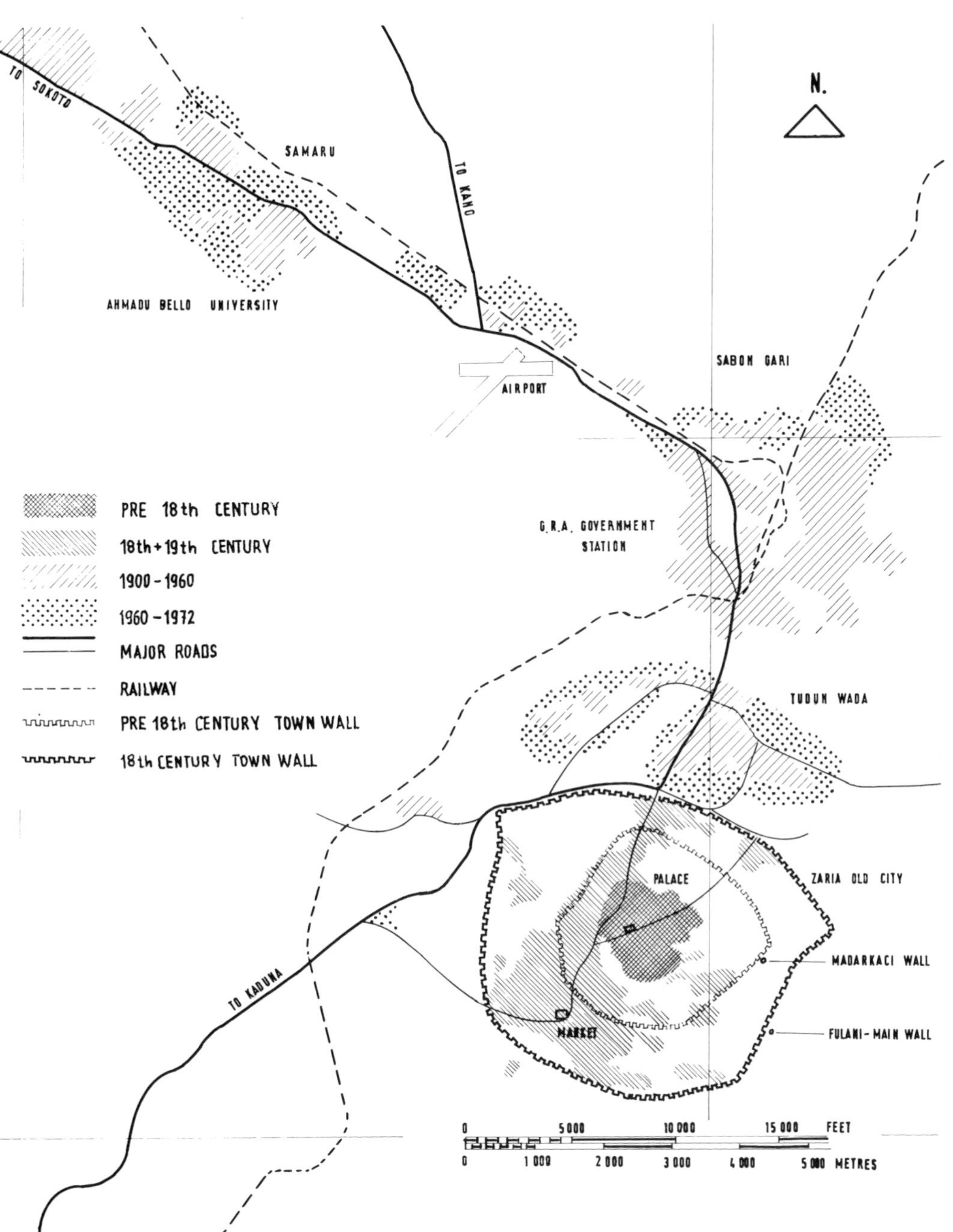

Plan 3.1
Zaria: stages of growth fifteenth century to 1970

up area of the town. Census data for 1952 and 1963 indicate an increase for both districts together from about 92,000 to 166,000, or 5.5 per cent per annum over the 11-year period. The large increase in recent years is due to a combination of natural growth and migration, the latter being mainly responsible for the rapid growth of Zaria as a whole. But there are marked differences in the pattern of growth between the walled city and the new urban areas which were established after the British occupation at the beginning of this century.

Both Sabon Gari and Tudun Wada are typical immigrant communities, which have grown from a few hundred families in 1915 to about 20,000 inhabitants in 1952/1953, and an estimated 40,000 to 50,000 inhabitants in 1963. This represents a growth rate of over 6.0 per cent per annum. This development was briefly interrupted when, after the disturbances in May and September 1966, nearly all Ibos left Sabon Gari for the former Eastern Region whence most returned after the end of the civil war in 1970.

After a decrease of its population in the early days of colonial rule, the walled city increased rather slowly, mainly through natural growth, reaching totals of 32,600 in 1952/1953, 34,900 in 1963, and about 40,600 in 1968 when my survey was made. The last figure was obtained from the population files of the four ward heads in the walled city and is therefore most likely an underestimate. However, this also applies to the 1952/1953 census which, when compared with the latest figures, showed an average growth rate of approximately 1.5 per cent per annum. This relatively modest increase is due to the role of infant mortality, the absence of any sizeable immigration, and the emigration of young persons to new urban centres such as Kaduna, Jos, and Kano which offer better employment opportunities. Assuming that this very modest growth rate has continued over the past ten years, the population of the walled city will have reached between 50,000 and 55,000 in 1980. (See Graph A.3.1 on p. 327.)

A comparison of the census results of 1952/1953 and 1963 for different parts of Zaria illustrates the various patterns of growth experienced by the new and old towns. (See Table 3.1.) The populations of the Township Area (GRA) and particularly of Tudun Wada show increases which are probably too high while, for different reasons, in Sabon Gari and the walled city the growth rate seems to be very small. The uneven growth rates of these different urban areas may be due partly to the confusion of places and names in the two census reports, and partly to inaccuracy during the counting.

Table 3.1 Population increase in different parts of Zaria city

	1952/1953 census[a]	1963 census[b]	Annual growth in percentages
Walled city	32,560	34,870	0.62
Sabon Gari	10,720	15,870	3.61
Tudun Wada	8,420	37,360	14.55
Township Area	2,280	5,970	9.15
Total	53,980	94,070	

[a]Department of Statistics, Nigeria, *Population Census of Nigeria 1952/53*, Lagos, 1956.
[b]Federal Office of Statistics, Nigeria, 'Population census, Northern Region 1963' (mimeo), vol. 1, Lagos, 1968, p. 235.

Ethnic composition

The ethnic composition of the Zaria City District, which includes Tudun Wada and other nearby hamlets but not Sabon Gari and the former European township area, is given in the 1952/1953 census as follows: Hausa 74.5 per cent, Fulani 18.9 per cent, other northern Nigerian tribes 3.8 per cent, other Nigerian tribes 2.7 per cent, and non-Nigerians 0.02 per cent.[16]

The ethnic composition of the Sabon Gari District was as follows: Hausa 48.7 per cent, Ibo 20.6 per cent, Yoruba 12.1 per cent, Fulani 8.9 per cent, other northern Nigerian tribes 4.1 per cent, other Nigerian tribes 4.9 per cent, and non-Nigerians 0.7 per cent.[17]

Administrative division

Until 1976 Zaria was divided into two administrative units, namely the new Township Area which could best be described as a municipal enclave within the Native Authority, and that territory to which all other parts of the town belonged.

The new Township Area was established under the enlarged and amended Township Ordinance of 1963, and came under the control of a governing body known as the Local Authority.[18] The Township Area was run by an advisory board with its members drawn from a cross-section of the local community under the chairmanship of an administrative officer appointed by the Central Government.

The walled city, on the other hand, was governed by the Native Authority, that is the emir and his Native

Administration established by F. D. Lugard in the first decade of the twentieth century. The Zaria Native Authority consisted of a Chief-in-Council, namely the emir, who presided over all meetings of the council which was composed of appointed senior members of the local community.

However, since the introduction of the Local Government Reform throughout Nigeria in 1976, Zaria Urban Area and its immediate environs have been governed by a Local Authority Council whose members are elected by general suffrage.

The walled city of Zaria is further divided into four main administrative units or wards, namely Juma, Iya, Kaura and Kwarbai.[19] (See Map A.3.3 on p. 228.) In 1971/1972, these wards were slightly reorganized and placed under officials known as *wakili*; they were renamed Arewa, Yamma, Kudu, and Gabas, with a total of 43 subdivisions headed by 14 *masu angowoyi*.

Sample survey

The results of the sample survey regarding age and sex distribution, ethnic composition, and migration are discussed below. The number of people included in my survey was 1,067 or about 2.6 per cent of the total population in the walled city in 1968. However, a number of problems encountered during the collection of the demographic data must be briefly mentioned first.

Age and sex distribution

All African demographic surveys share the problem of trying to record the ages of people who do not know their exact ages and are not fundamentally interested in knowing them.'[20] In order to overcome this problem, the so-called Historical Calendar Method was used. In this method, the age of people is linked to well-known historical events; thus older persons were asked to give their ages according to the reigns of local emirs, or other widely known events such as the British occupation in 1902 and the outbreak of the Second World War. The age of a woman could be further clarified by investigating the number and duration of her marriages as well as the ages of her first and last-born child. However, it must be stressed that the ages of people obtained in this way can never be accurate, but they are probably more exact than could be achieved by any other known method.

Table 3.2 Population distribution by age groups in percentages

	Zaria Div. 1952/1953 Tot. pop. 795,900	Zaria Div. 1963 Tot. pop. 1,183,100	Sample survey, 1968 Tot. pop. 1,067
0–14	44.6	45.9	46.7
15–49	45.7	47.7	44.3
50+	9.7	6.4	9.0
Male	48.6	49.6	45.2
Female	51.4	50.4	54.8
Total	100.0	100.0	100.0

In Table 3.2 the age distribution of the sample population is compared with the divisional census returns for Zaria Division in 1952/1953 and 1963. The divisional census data as well as my own survey data show the typical high proportion of young people. There was also an excess of females over males, particularly in my survey data.

The amount of distortion which frequently occurs in African demographic data – including my own – can be linked to specific cultural conditions. For example, there is a tendency to under-report females in the age group 10 to 14, whereas the age group 15 to 29 is correspondingly inflated. An explanation for this bias has been given in a number of census reports, all of which agree that in countries where girls marry at an early age, usually between the ages of 10 and 14,* married girls under the age of 15 are unconsciously graded upwards, thus causing a serious imbalance in the sex ratio of the affected age groups.[21]

The sex and age distribution of the sample population is shown in Diagram A.3.1 on p. 329. As indicated on the bar-chart, the distorted sex ratio of the sample population is due to three main reasons. First, in spite of careful age recording there is a certain amount of differential age misreporting in both sexes, but more noticeably in the female age groups 10 to 29 already discussed above. Second, the excess of females over males in the age group 20 to 29 may partly reflect the large number of polygamous marriages recorded in the sample.† A third part of the imbalance may reflect the emigration of males in the age group 20 to 24 to new urban centres such as Kaduna and Jos which offer better employment opportunities.

*In the sample population all females over the age of 15 were married.
†See page 38.

Ethnic composition

The ethnic composition of the survey population showed the expected close resemblance to the figures given for Zaria City District on p. 23 and were as follows: 79.3 per cent Hausa, 16.8 per cent Fulani, 1.4 per cent other northern Nigerian tribes, and 2.5 per cent other Nigerian tribes.

Migration

Immigration has been of limited importance in the sample population. Only 125 persons – 55 males and 70 females, or 11.7 per cent of the sample – were born outside the walled city. Most of these came as children or in their early teens. By far the most important group of immigrants were wives. Altogether 46 females were counted of whom the majority came from Zaria and other northern provinces, but several came from farther afield including six from Ibadan and one from Fort-Lamy in the republic of Chad. A second group consisted of 22 male and female children who had been adopted by their relatives in the walled city. A total of 13 compound heads born outside the city are of interest: six came from Zaria Province, three from Kano Province, two from Plateau province, and one each from Katsina and Ibadan. Their average age was 39.7 years, while the average number of years spent in the walled city was 26.8.

Only seven adult males including four Koranic teachers (*malamai*), two traders, and one embroiderer had immigrated in the last 10 years. The motivation given for coming to Zaria was, in the case of the *malamai*, better teaching opportunities; the rest gave economic reasons.

In conclusion, contemporary Zaria contains two contrasting types of urban settlements: first, the traditional pre-industrial walled city, from which all the houses included in my survey were chosen; and second, a new, technologically advanced urban area. The new town has grown rapidly mainly due to large-scale immigration from the southern part of Nigeria, whereas the population of the walled city has increased rather slowly. The age distribution of the sample population showed, with 46.7 per cent, a high proportion of young people under the age of 15. The absence of any sizeable male immigration, combined with the slow integration of newcomers into the community, has preserved the traditional urban community in the walled city more or less intact.

Notes and references

1 Africa Research Ltd, *African Research Bulletin* (Exeter), **11** (7), 1974, p. 3298.
2 United Nations, *Demographic Year Book 1973*, New York, 1974, p. 82.
3 United Nations, *World Population Prospects as Assessed in 1963*, New York, 1965, ST/SOA/Series A/41, p. 142.
4 *Daily Times, Nigeria Year Book 1971*, Lagos, 1971, p. 21; S. M. Jacob, *Census of Nigeria 1931*, London, 1933, p. 95.
5 Department of Statistics, Nigeria, *Population Census of Nigeria 1952/53*, Lagos, 1956. Subsequently this section of the Cameroons was incorporated into Nigeria.
6 S. A. Aluko, 'How many Nigerians? An analysis of Nigeria's census problems 1901–63', *Journal of Modern African Studies* (Cambridge), **III** (3), 1965, pp. 371–392.
7 Federal Office of Statistics, Nigeria, *Population Census of Nigeria 1963* (mimeo), vol. 3, Lagos, 1968, p. 7.
8 W. Brass *et al.*, *The Demography of Tropical Africa*, Princeton, NJ, 1968, pp. 6 and 515.
9 In 1976/1977 more states were created, bringing the total to 19.
10 Federal Office of Statistics, Nigeria, op. cit., p. 10.
11 E. Wallé, van de, 'Fertility in Nigeria', in Brass *et al.*, op. cit., p. 527.
12 Federal Office of Statistics, Nigeria, *Annual Abstract of Statistics 1971*, Lagos, 1972, pp. 10 and 12–14.
13 A. Smith, 'Some notes on the history of Zazzau under the Hausa kings', in *Zaria and its Region*, ABU, Department of Geography, Occasional Paper No. 4, pp. 82–101.
14 A. W. Urquhart, *Planned Urban Landscapes of Northern Nigeria*, ABU, Zaria, 1977.
15 H. Bedawi, *Housing in Zaria, Present Condition and Future Needs*, ABU, Department of Urban and Regional Planning, Zaria, 1977, p. 51.
16 Department of Statistics, Nigeria, *Population Census of Northern Nigeria 1952*, Bulletin No. 4, Zaria Province, Kaduna, 1956, p. 12.
17 Ibid.
18 Northern States of Nigeria, *Local Government Year Book 1968*, Kaduna, 1968, p. 33.
19 In 1968 the population of the walled city was, according to the tax and population files, as follows: Kwarbai 14,670 or 36.1 per cent of the total population in the walled city; Kaura 13,860 or 34.2 per cent; Iya 6,170 or 15.2 per cent; and Juma 5,900 or 14.5 per cent.
20 Brass *et al.*, op. cit., p. 13.
21 Department of Statistics, Nigeria, *Population Census of the Northern Region of Nigeria 1952*, pp. 8–9. Zanzibar Protectorate, *Report on the [1958] Census of the Population of Zanzibar Protectorate*, Zanzibar, 1960, p. 27. Service de Statistique Haute-Volta, *La Situation démographique en Haute-Volta, Resultats partiels de l'enquête démographique 1960–61*, Paris, 1962, p. 29. J. L. Boutillier, *et al.*, *La Moyenne Vallée du Sénégal*, Paris, 1962, p. 26.

Chapter 4

Domestic groupings and the house

The compound

Layout and organization

The following description of the layout and organization of compounds in Zaria walled city is a necessary introduction to the discussion on domestic groupings.

Islam had no doubt some influence on the layout of compounds, particularly in the urban areas of Hausaland.* Polygamy and the different modes of religious marriages, of which *auren kulle* and *auren tsare* lay great emphasis on complete or partial seclusion of women respectively, require a high degree of privacy which, combined with the genuine desire for security in precolonial times as well as building materials, techniques, and skill available to the community, has produced the present-day compound with several courtyards surrounded by high mud walls.

A compound (*gida,* pl. *gidaje*) is usually divided into a forecourt (*kofar gida*) and the central courtyard (*cikin gida*) which contains several huts inhabited by a family or group of families which are descended from common ancestors. The only access into the compound is through an entrance hut (*zaure*) which is the domain of the compound head (*maigida*). Here he entertains his visitors and friends, takes his meals and, if possible, pursues his occupation such as weaving, tailoring, embroidery, or

*See discussion on p. 299.

teaching the Koran. The entrance hut may also be used as a sleeping room for students and other overnight guests. The door leading from here into the interior is always covered with a straw mat (*tufaniya kofar*) to prevent male visitors from looking into the forecourt. No male stranger is normally allowed further into the compound, but all females, and boys under the age of puberty, are free to enter the house.

The forecourt functions as an intermediate zone between the outside world and the centre of the compound. The huts found here house the compound's adolescent, unmarried sons. If the compound head possesses a horse it is usually tethered in the forecourt. The second entrance hut (*shigifa*), which gives access to the centre courtyard of the compound, is sometimes divided into a larger room which is often used as an additional sitting room, and a smaller interior one which is always used as a storeroom for mortars, large pots, and other heavy kitchen equipment.

The centre courtyard of the compound contains the compound head's hut (*turaka*), the rooms of his wife or wives grouped around an open area with a wet season kitchen (*dakin girki*), one or two general store rooms, and the huts of any other related family group or groups. Poultry pens and granaries (if any) are always located in the central courtyard. (See Plan 4.1.) Since most women in the walled city live under the arrangement of *purdah* nearly every compound in Zaria walled city has at least one pit-latrine, a washing place, and a well.

This is the usual layout of a compound but there are great variations in size, number of rooms, and type of construction depending on the wealth and status of its inhabitants. A poor man's compound may not have a second entrance hut, a wet season kitchen or a separate room for the compound head, while a well-to-do man may have a compound with several entrance huts, a two-storey building (*bene* – the upper storey) covered with a corrugated iron roof and richly decorated outside walls. In areas where building space is limited the forecourt may be replaced by a succession of small rooms which give access to the central courtyard, while in some compounds the wives' rooms are built around a central hall which serves as a common working, sitting, and storage place. (See Plan 4.2.)

Most rooms are sparsely furnished. People are accustomed to sit and work on grass mats or goatskins which cover part of the floor, and the only built-in equipment is a raised earthen bed (*gadan kasa*). Better-off people may have an additional wooden or iron bed. A

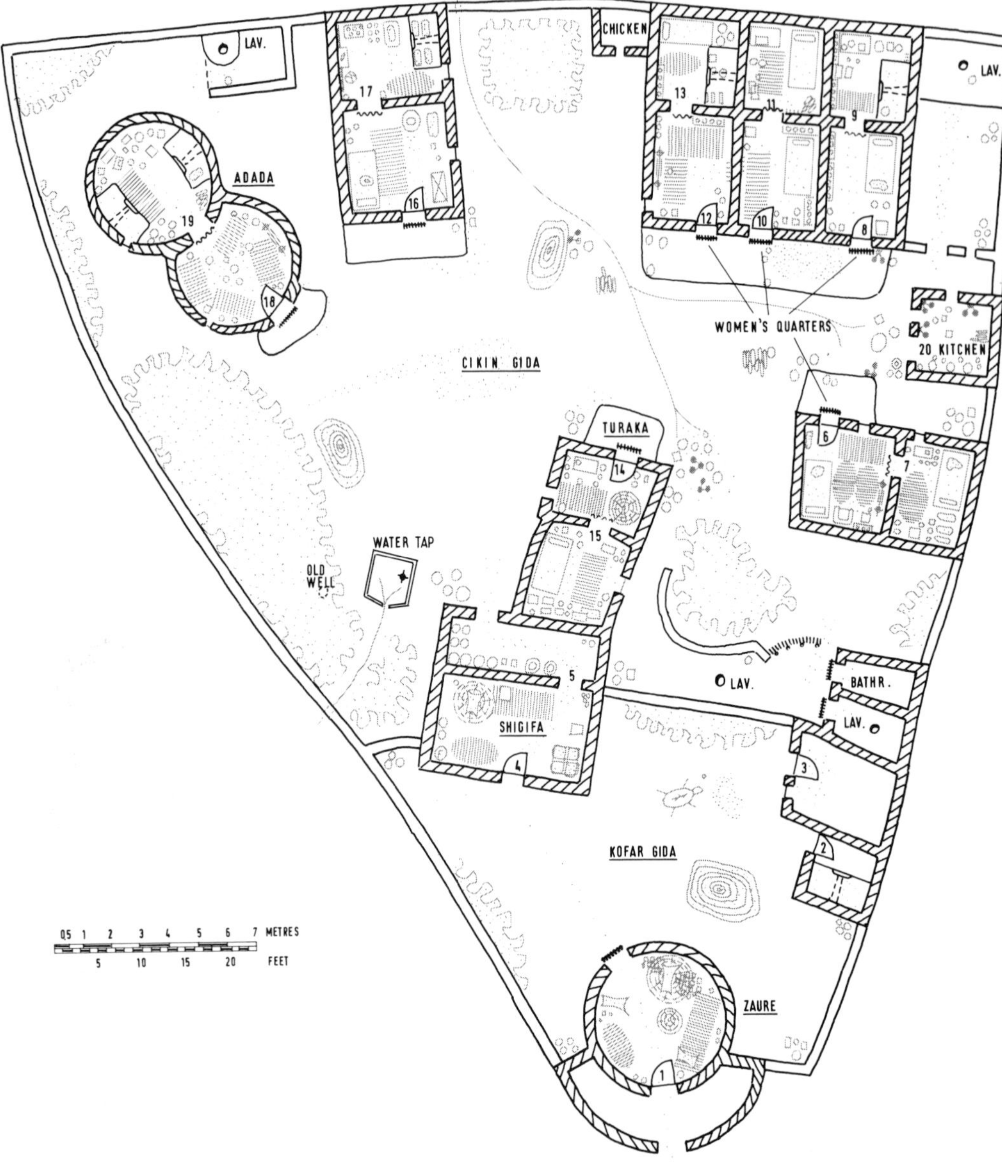

Plan 4.1
House 39

typical woman's room may also contain an upright loom, a low, round, wooden stool, a small table and a collection of various pots, baskets, and calabashes. A cement platform in front of the room is used as an outside working place for food preparation, cooking, and handicrafts, as well as to dry rice and/or pepper.

Land use inside the compound

The data on land use given below derives from measurements taken in 77 compounds surveyed in the walled city.

Plan 4.2
House 78

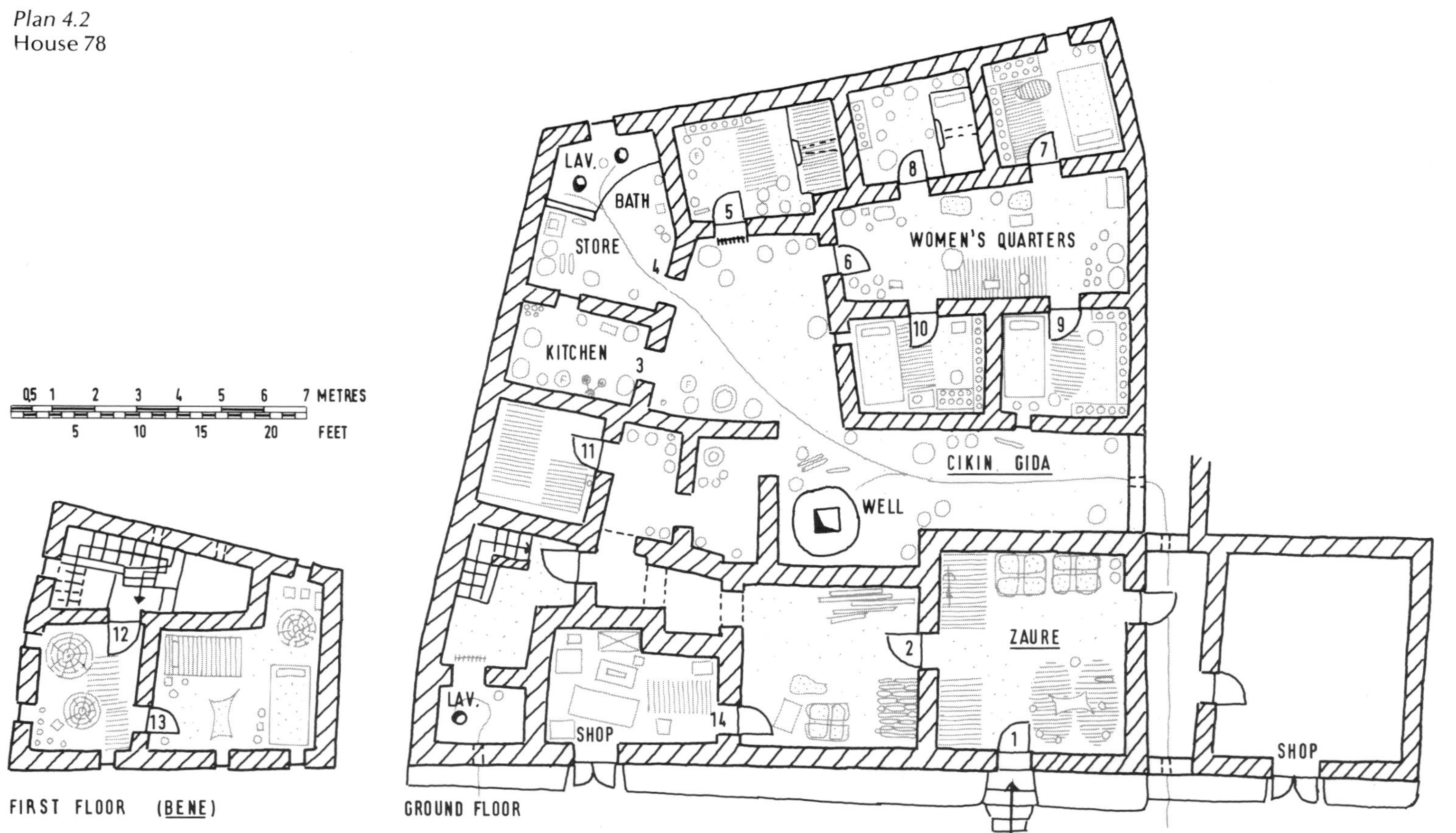

These compounds had a total area of 47,552 sq. m which was divided into the open area of 31,284 sq. m or 65.8 per cent, and the built-up area of 16,268 sq. m or 34.2 per cent. The average size of these compounds was about 620 sq. m or 6,670 sq. ft.

The open area of 31,284 sq. m was subdivided into five categories. First, the general courtyard area accounted for 76.4 per cent of the total open area. This included all unpaved areas not used for any particular purpose. In 65 compounds about one quarter of this area had been set aside for further construction should the need arise, whereas in 12 compounds, with an average open area of only about 9 sq. m per person, no expansion was possible without demolishing an old building.

Second, cultivated land accounted for 13.1 per cent of the total open area. Cultivated land found in 44 compounds was used as vegetable gardens. The average area per compound was 93 sq. m, but in six compounds over 300 sq. m were found to be under cultivation.

Third, cement platforms accounted for 6.8 per cent of the open area. The use of cement platforms, particularly in front of rooms, has already been mentioned. In 63 compounds at least one cement platform was found, the average area being 34 sq. m.

Fourth, pit-latrines and personal washing places covered 3.2 per cent of the total open area. Pit-latrines and personal washing places were usually located behind sleeping rooms. These areas, which were specially screened off with mud walls or a fence made of grass mats (*zanaku*), accounted for an average of 14 sq. m per compound; the average number of pit-latrines was 2.5 per compound.

Fifth, storage space accounted for only 0.5 per cent of the total open area. The most frequently stored items were building materials, firewood, and old clay pots; the average area per compound was 4.3 sq. m. (See Table A.4.1 on p. 331.) The area used for grain storage (granaries) was small as only eight compounds had one or more granaries.

Type and size of rooms

The built-up area in 77 compounds contained 1,284 rooms or 16.8 per compound. The total floor area of 10,473 sq. m was divided into four categories.

First, the *living area* which accounted for 67.6 per cent of the total floor area. This category includes all sleeping and sitting rooms, as well as store rooms used for personal articles. With a total of 883 rooms, this was by far the most important group.

Second, commonly used rooms accounted for 16.1 per cent of the total floor area. This category includes 71 main entrance huts,* 91 second entrance huts, and all staircases and passages.

Third, basic ancillary facilities covered 12.5 per cent of the total floor area. This included 97 kitchens, 64 kitchen stores as well as general store rooms and 29 toilets and/or bathrooms.

Fourth, commercially used rooms accounted for 3.8 per cent of the total floor area. This included 12 shops or workshops, 9 storage rooms used for trading commodities, 3 garages, and 25 permanent stables for horses, donkeys, goats, and sheep. (See Table A.4.2 on p. 332.)

Social structure and kinship organization

In the following pages the social structure of the sample population will be analysed in order to show the principles which govern the development of co-residential kinship groups in Zaria walled city. The main features of Hausa kinship organization and marriage were investigated by M. G. Smith in various rural and urban communities in the emirate of Zaria in 1949–1950, and provided the basis for my own investigation as well as an excellent opportunity for cross-checking.[1]

In this book the unit of analysis is the population of a compound divided into households or economic units. However, as household data alone are insufficient to explain the changes which frequently occur in co-residential groups, additional kinship data, based on a common reference point – in our case relations with the compound head – are essential. This will enable me later to illustrate the cyclic tendency which regulates the development of co-residential kinship groups.

The first essential step in the study of kinship organizations is the identification of the compound head by uniform criteria. In the Hausa–Fulani community at Zaria, the status and role of the compound head is clearly defined and receives clear socio-political recognition and support. In the absence of house numbers, a compound in the walled city of Zaria is generally known by the name of its present head who is usually the senior resident male in age and status. He is responsible for the payment of

* Seven entrance huts were used for sleeping, and one compound had two entrance huts.

tax due from all male residents and is consulted by the authority in all matters concerning the compound and its inhabitants. To identify the head of a chosen compound these external criteria were used even though they did not always reflect the internal distribution of authority which, in a few cases, lay with younger brothers of the head, or was divided between full or half brothers living in the same compound. Changes in headship which always occur after the death of the compound head, and are accompanied by a re-definition of the relations between members of a kinship group, may thus lead to a split of the old group and the establishment of a new one elsewhere by the secession of some households.

Before going into these matters it is necessary to define the terms 'individual family' and 'household' as used in this analysis. The term individual family (*iyali*) denotes both monogamous and polygamous families consisting of a man, his wife or wives, and their own or adopted children; but in 19 cases of the sample the man's widowed mother was also included. A household, on the other hand, is a separate unit of domestic economy consisting of all persons who eat together from the same pot (*tukunya*), dwell together in one part of the compound known as *sassa*, and who contribute most of the time in kind, labour, service, and/or money to the household budget. A further distinction should be made between the compound head and his immediate household, and the heads of all other dependent or semi-dependent households living in the compound. The compound head is clearly distinguished by his capacity to take independent action, which may include the building of new rooms or the accommodation of other family members, whereas dependent or semi-dependent household heads cannot make these decisions independently without infringing the compound head's authority.

If the inhabitants of a compound depend largely on agriculture as a means of livelihood, they may form a single work unit known as *gandu* which then consists of all the adult males and their families. During the rainy season from May to September, individual families within a *gandu* farm a common field and cook together, their common meals being prepared by each of the members' wives in turn until the harvest is over. In the dry season each household head may pursue his own occupation such as weaving, embroidery, trading, or teaching the Koran, and at this time each household operates a separate domestic economy. However, in Zaria walled city only four compounds with one *gandu* each were found, although the survey was carried out during the rainy season. In all other compounds surveyed, the various household heads farmed their plots independently either with the help of an unmarried son or with paid labour (*kodago*). In the majority of cases the commercial or subsistence crops are essential income which is supplemented by non-agricultural activities that are also pursued during the rains at reduced rates, and often exclusively after the harvest. It is evident that the *gandu* as a work unit for the common production and consumption of food, plays a far less important role in the walled city than in the rural areas, but the basic idea remains. For example, in some compounds token exchanges of cooked food amongst the different branches of the family are practised, and all will cooperate in repairing the compound wall, and in rebuilding commonly used rooms. Before the first marriage of a young male compound member, all resident household heads are expected to contribute towards the bride-price and later towards the construction of the new hut for the young couple.

Population and household data

The population distribution of 77 compounds surveyed in Zaria is given in Diagram 4.1. The majority of the sample compounds (83.0 per cent) have populations that range between 5 and 19 persons, the average being 13.8 per compound. However, there were three compounds which had 34, 38, and 39 persons respectively, the largest containing the family of a former District Head.

Diagram 4.2 compares the size of compound heads' households with those of all other dependent or semi-dependent households found in the compounds surveyed. The remarkable differences in household size are important, particularly the high 57.2 per cent of compound heads' households with more than 6 persons.

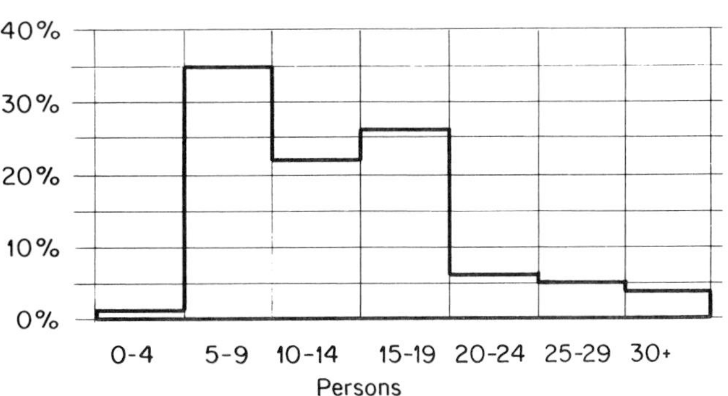

Diagram 4.1
Number of persons per compound in percentages

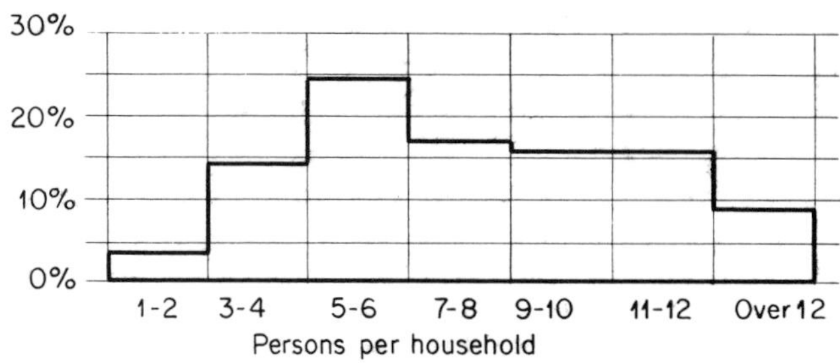

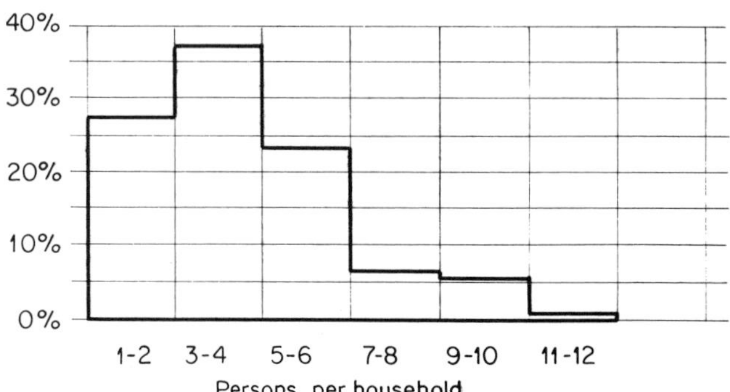

Diagram 4.2
Number of persons per household in percentages.[a] This includes eleven strangers' or clients' families who lived in the 77 surveyed compounds. (See also p. 44)

Dependent or semi-dependent households of the same size are represented only by 12.4 per cent. The average size of compound heads' households was found to be 7.8 persons, whereas dependent or semi-dependent households had on average only 4.1 persons. (See Table A.4.5 on p. 338.) These differences in household size are partly due to the fact that the latter type consists mainly of 'young households'. For example, only 5.1 per cent of all wives of dependent household heads have passed childbearing age (40 plus), as against 24.3 per cent of all compound heads' wives. (For the age distribution of compound and dependent household heads see Table A.4.6 on p. 339.) Furthermore, the generally lower income of dependent household heads, a topic which will be discussed in the next chapter, tends to limit, at least temporarily, the number of children in these households.

The age and sex distribution as well as the marital status of the sample population are given in Diagram 4.3 and Table 4.1. The bar-chart indicates that females marry early. About 36.0 per cent of all females between the ages of 10 and 14 were already married, and there were no unmarried females over the age of 15. Males, on the other hand, on average marry later, normally between the ages of 20 and 29.

The number of 51 resident divorced and/or widowed

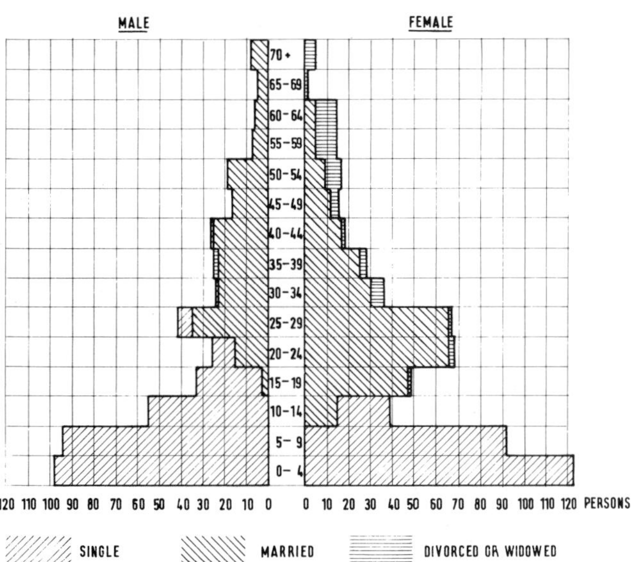

Diagram 4.3
Survey sample population by sex, age, and marital status

females is noteworthy. Further study shows that of these females, 19 were the widowed mothers of compound heads, while four were widowed mothers of compound heads' half brothers, and one was the compound head's grandmother. The majority of these females will probably stay with their next of kin, whereas a large proportion of the remaining 27 females will marry again and leave the compound. (For more detailed information see Table A.4.4 on p. 336.)

Table 4.2 gives the number of wives per compound head and all other dependent or semi-dependent household heads (*masu-iyali*). The difference between the number of wives married by compound heads and by all other dependent household heads is noteworthy and shows the dominant economic position of compound heads as well as the prestige of polygamous marriage. The five dependent household heads with three wives each directed economically independent households whose cash income exceeded that of their compound heads.

As shown in Tables A.4.3 and A.4.4 on pp. 234–237, adoption (*tallafi*) is widely practised in Zaria, but generally restricted to children of members of the kinship group including the kinship group of wives. Women usually adopt girls and men boys. Of the 88 adopted children (44 boys and 44 girls) in 77 compounds surveyed, 75 children were adopted by the compound head and his wife or wives. The male children most commonly adopted were sons of the compound heads' brothers (20), and the sons of compound heads' sisters (5). The most commonly

Table 4.1 Survey sample population by sex, age, and marital status

Age	Male					Female					Grand
	Sing.	Mar.	Div.	Wid.	Total	Sing.	Mar.	Div.	Wid.	Total	total
0–4	98				98	122				122	220
5–9	94				94	91				91	185
10–14	55				55	25	14			39	94
15–19	30	3			33		48	1		49	82
20–24	11	15			26		66	2		68	94
25–29	6	35			41		66	1		67	108
30–34	1	23			24		30	3	3	36	60
35–39		23	2		25		25	1	2	28	53
40–44	1	25			26		17	1		18	44
45–49		16			16		11	2	3	16	32
50–54		18			18		9		8	17	35
55–59		7			7		5		9	14	21
60–64		6			6		5		9	14	20
65–69		5			5				1	1	6
70+		8			8				5	5	13
Total	296	184	2	—	482	238	296	11	40	585	1,067

Table 4.2 Distribution of wives per married man

Column	1		2		3	
Type of household	Compound head (CH)		Dependent household head[a] (DHH)		Total household heads (HHs)	
	No.	%	No.	%	No.	%
Male with 1 wife	25	32.9	90	78.9	115	60.5
Male with 2 wives	32	42.1	19	16.7	51	26.9
Male with 3 wives	12	15.8	5	4.4	17	8.9
with 4 wives	7	9.2			7	3.7
Total	76[b]	100.0	114	100.0	190	100.0
No. of wives	153		143		296[c]	
% of males in polygamous fam.		67.1		21.1		39.5
% of females in polygamous fam.		83.7		37.1		61.1
Av. no. of wives per married man	2.0		1.3		1.6	

[a] Includes 11 strangers' households.
[b] One compound head was a widowed female.
[c] Eight wives were temporarily absent.

adopted female children were the daughters of compound heads' wives' brothers (15), followed by the daughters of the compound heads' brothers (5), and the daughters of compound heads' sons (5).

Family groupings

In the following pages I will analyse the structure, size, and development of co-residential kinship groups. I will also show how certain changes in the structure and size of kinship groups affect the layout and occupational patterns of compounds in the walled city of Zaria. The kinship groups surveyed are based on agnatic descent and virilocal marriage. The development of these kinship groups can best be illustrated by using an ideal growth model that describes successive stages in the development of co-residential agnatic groups among the Hausa. The differing kinds of domestic groups found in the compounds surveyed may then be placed into the relevant categories or stages. To avoid misplacements the preceding stage(s) of each domestic group was investigated. For exposition, the kinship diagrams are given in their simplest essentials, though in real life we may find many more related persons belonging to any one given kinship group. The compound head (CH) has two wives and two or three children, while other married relatives have only one wife and one or two children apiece. The aims of these diagrams are to illustrate the cyclic tendency which regulates the development of these domestic groups, and to expose the factors that limit their expansion.

Kinship groups of the type shown in Diagram 4.4 were found in 31 compounds containing 31 households or 17.2 per cent of all related households included in the sample. However, strangers' and clients' households which do not influence or contribute to the development of co-residential kinship groups are omitted here but will be analysed separately later.

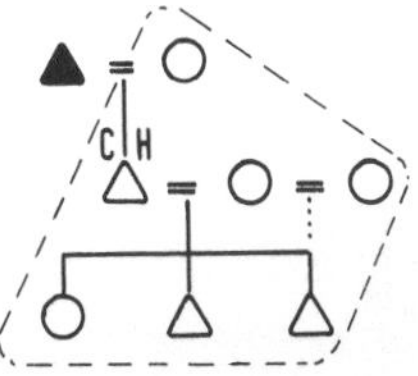

Diagram 4.4
Kinship development: stage 1. (See also Diagram A.4.1 on p. 330)

The second stage of kinship development is reached when one or more sons of the compound head have married and form, as shown in Diagram 4.5, two or more semi-dependent households under the leadership of their father. The compound head's daughter will have left the house on her marriage. In rural areas this type of family grouping provides the natural basis for a *gandu* under the guidance of the compound head who normally will pay

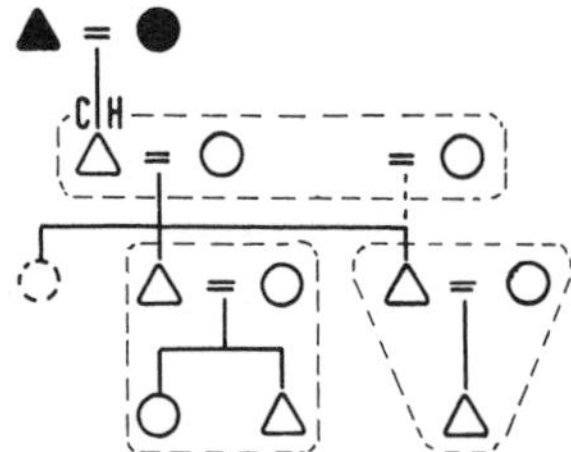

Diagram 4.5
Kinship development: stage 2

the tax for his sons. Kinship groups of this type were found in nine compounds containing 27 households or 15.0 per cent of all related households.

The death of the compound head gives rise to the third stage in the development of co-residential units (Diagram 4.6) by converting it into a grouping of collateral agnates and their families, with the older brother usually succeeding as compound head. After the mourning period is over, barren and junior widows of the dead compound head will normally leave the house for re-marriage. This type of kinship group was found in 17 compounds with 41 households or 22.8 per cent of all related households.

The fourth stage in the development of co-residential kinship groups (Diagram 4.7) is reached when the new compound head's son and/or one of the full or half brothers' sons has married. As always, since women move to their husbands' homes, the marriage of girls reared in the compound does not affect the structure of agnatic kinship groups. As shown in the diagram, the two daughters have left their father's house on marriage. 'Stage 4 groups' are usually large co-residential groups with complex kinship networks and average a population of 24.2 persons per compound. These extended collateral families are of particular interest because their internal structure normally generates a split of the old kinship group and the establishment of a new residential unit, which then begins the cycle at stage 1 as shown above. Co-residential kinship groups of this type were found in eleven compounds containing 57 households or 31.6 per cent of all related households.

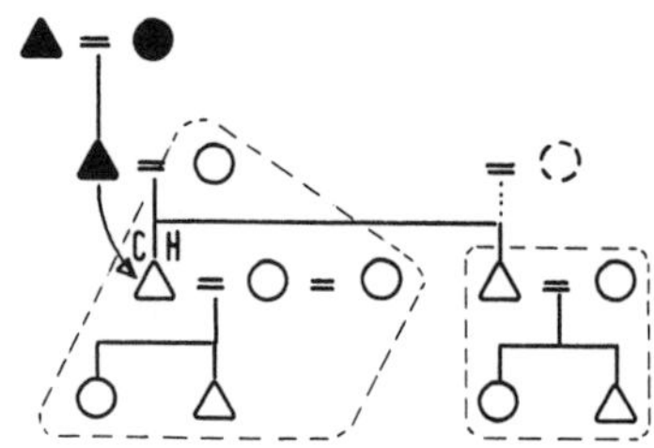

Diagram 4.6
Kinship development: stage 3

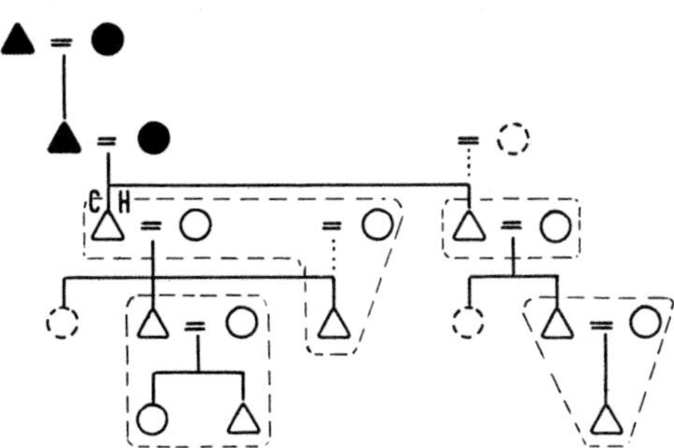

Diagram 4.7
Kinship development: stage 4

After the death of the compound head his senior surviving brother takes over the responsibility for the co-residential kinship group. At this stage, (Diagram 4.8), divergence of interest and ensuing friction amongst the various household heads may result in the split of the kinship group. Groups of this type were found in one compound with five households or 2.8 per cent of all related households included in the sample. However, it must be stressed here that a division of a co-residential kinship group can occur at earlier stages when, for example, the compound head has built a new compound for his eldest son, or if one of the dependent household heads has become economically independent and wishes to build a compound of his own.

Stage 6 (Diagram 4.9) shows a relatively rare combination of parallel agnatic cousins and their families and

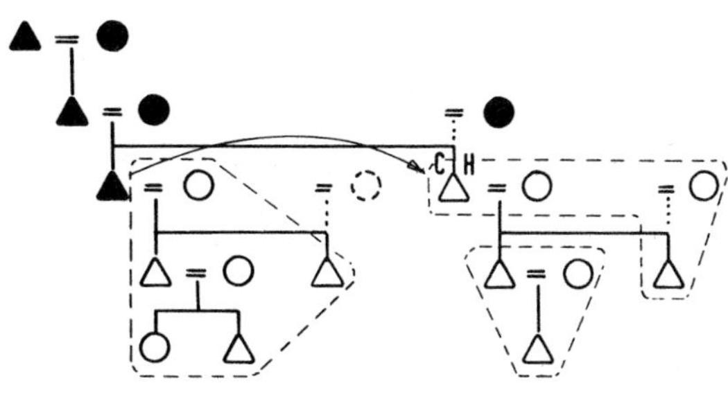

Diagram 4.8
Kinship development: stage 5

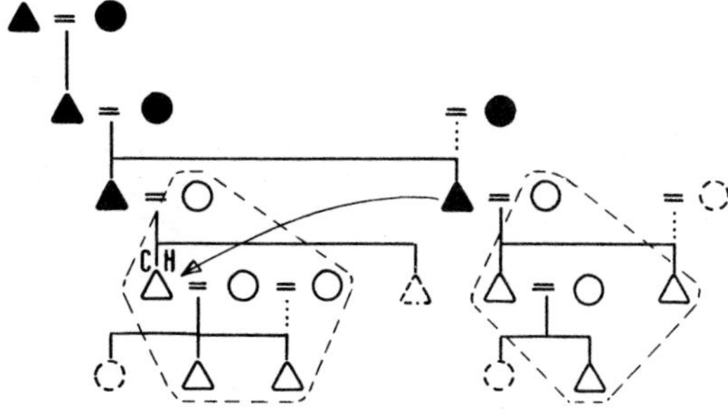

Diagram 4.9
Kinship development: stage 6

possibly their married sons living together in one compound. The two household heads are related through agnates in the second degree of kinship, and this was the widest span of kinship that formed a basis for a co-residential group observed in the survey. Groups of this type were found in one compound with three households or 1.7 per cent of all related households included in my survey.

To summarize, a total of 31 households or 17.2 per cent of all related households included in the survey lived in kinship groups at stage 1, i.e. the compound head, his wife or wives, and their own unmarried children, whereas 133 households or 73.9 per cent lived in composite co-residential kinship groups which had developed under the rules of patrilineal descent; but there were seven compounds with 16 households or 8.9 per cent which did not. The seven compounds contained nine households which had joined these compounds and increased their populations by immigration and not by natural growth.

Except for the last category, the individual family as a separate residential unit represents the first and simplest stage in the developmental cycle that gives rise to composite co-residential kinship groups often containing three or more generations of males linked in direct line of descent. In the second stage these kinship groups consist of the families of the compound head and his son or sons. As time passes and the compound head dies, this reconstitutes the residential unit as a kinship group composed of siblings, whose deaths in due course redefine the unit as one of paternal cousins. This development has been further illustrated in Table 4.3 by tabulating the ages of compound heads at each stage of development.

As expected, heads of compounds in stages 1, 3, and 6 tend to be younger than their counterparts in stages 2, and 4 + 5. In the lower part of the table the average number of households per compound increases from 1 household in stage 1 to 5.2 households in stages 4 + 5. The same upward tendency can be observed in the average number of persons per compound which rises from 7.7 persons in stage 1 to 24.2 persons in stages 4 + 5. The average number of persons per household, on the other hand, shows the reverse tendency by falling from 7.7 persons in stage 1 to 4.7 persons in stages 4 + 5. This fall in the number of persons per household is clearly due to the emigration of larger dependent households. The number of households in stage 6 is too small for generalization although the 3 households found in this category do not basically depart from the earlier observed patterns.

As has been shown above, the death of the compound

Table 4.3 Age of compound heads by stages of kinship development

Column	1	2	3	4	5	6	7
Stage	1	2	3	4 + 5	6	Joint hhs	Total
Age of CH							
20–24	1						1
25–29	2		3			1	6
30–34	3		3		1	2	9
35–39	4		1				5
40–44	8	1	3	1			13
45–49	5	1	3	1		2	12
50–54	2	1	2	3		1	9
55–59	2	2	1	2			7
60–64	3	1		1		1	6
65–69	1		1	1			3
70+		3		3			6
No. of CHs	31	9	17	12	1	7	77
No. of HHs	31	27	41	62	3	16	180
No. of persons	240	141	244	290	28	85	1,028
Av. households hhs per compound	1.0	3.0	2.4	5.2	3.0	2.3	2.3
Av. persons per compound	7.7	15.7	14.4	24.2	28.0	12.1	13.4
Av. persons per hh	7.7	5.2	5.9	4.7	9.3	5.3	5.7
Kinship diagrams	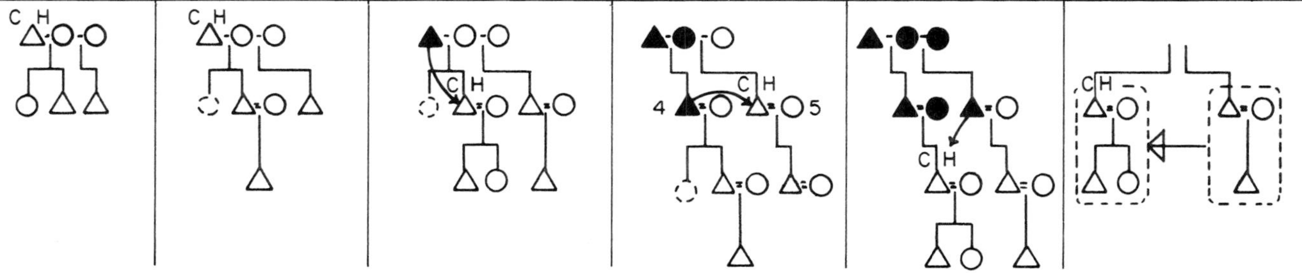 C H	C H	C H	C H 4 5	C H	C H	

head, lack of space for new construction, internal tension between group members, and differential economic success achieved by junior heads of dependent or semi-dependent households are the major reasons for emigration of dependent households. This can occur at any stage of the kinship development, but particularly at stage 4. However, such centrifugal tendencies are counterbalanced to some degree by adoption of children, the mode of land tenure (commonly owned land), and, especially in poorer lineages, by the need to live and work together to ensure at least some degree of economic security.

Thus far we have discussed those co-residential kinship groups which contained the compound head and other related dependent or semi-dependent households, but we must now briefly consider the eleven client* and strangers' households which were found in eight out of 77 compounds surveyed. All of these household heads had immigrated to Zaria. In Table 4.4 these eleven households have been divided into four main categories based on kinship organization. The first category (columns 1–3) has heads who were either single, divorced, or widowed; the second category (column 4) contains female heads whose husbands had been absent for more than one month preceding the time of the interview; the third category (column 5) consists of couples without children including those whose children were away; while the fourth category (column 6) contains individual families. As can be seen, there were one divorced household head, one wife whose husband was temporarily absent, and one childless couple. The remaining eight households consisted of individual families.

Compound and kinship organization

In the following pages I will relate some of the facts which emerged from the discussion on household pattern and kinship organization to a number of compounds surveyed in Zaria. Three case studies have been chosen from the sample to illustrate various stages in the development of co-residential agnatic kinship groups and the repercussions of these developments on the layout and size of compounds.

The first example is a compound situated in the southern part of the walled city which has belonged to a family of weavers for several generations. With the help of

* The head of a client household is an unrelated servant who joined the compound in his early teens and for whom the compound head has provided a wife and free shelter.

Table 4.4 Structure of strangers' families

Column	1	2	3	4	5	6	7	8	9
Type of HH	Single	Div.	Wid.	Female with temp. absent hus.	Childless couples	Individual families	Female HH	Male HH	Grand total HH
Age of Stranger HHs									
15–19				1			1		1
20–24						1		1	1
25–29						1		1	1
30–34						1		1	1
35–39		1			1			2	2
40–44						3		3	3
45–49						1		1	1
50–54						1		1	1
55–59									
60–64									
65–69									
70+									
Total M + F							1	10	
No. of households (hhs)	–	1	–	1	1	8			11
No. of persons	–	2	–	2	2	33			39
Av. no. of persons per hh	–	2.0	–	2.0	2.0	4.1			3.5
Kinship diagrams	H H	 H H	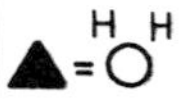 H H	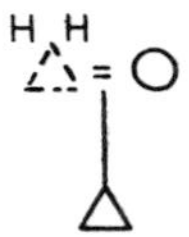 H H	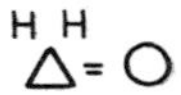 H H	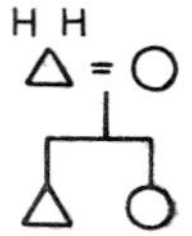 H H			

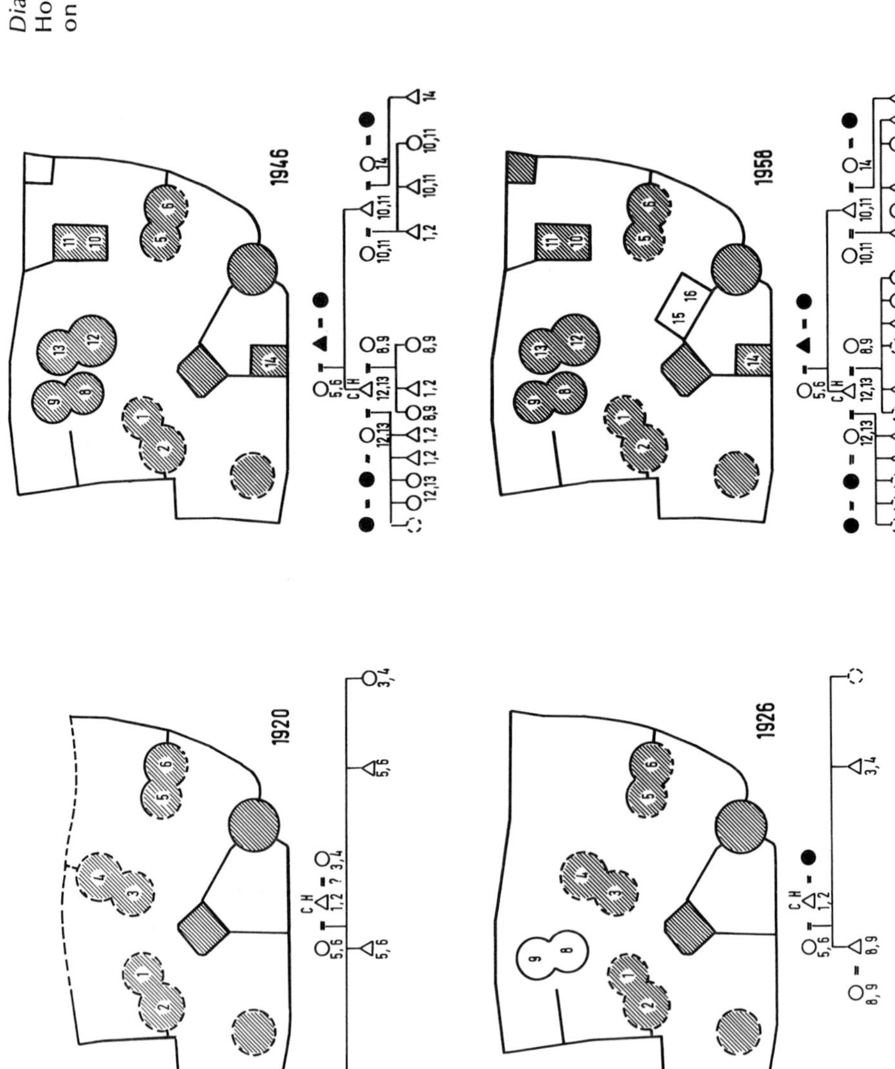

Diagram 4.10
House 68. (See also Plan A.4.1 on p. 343)

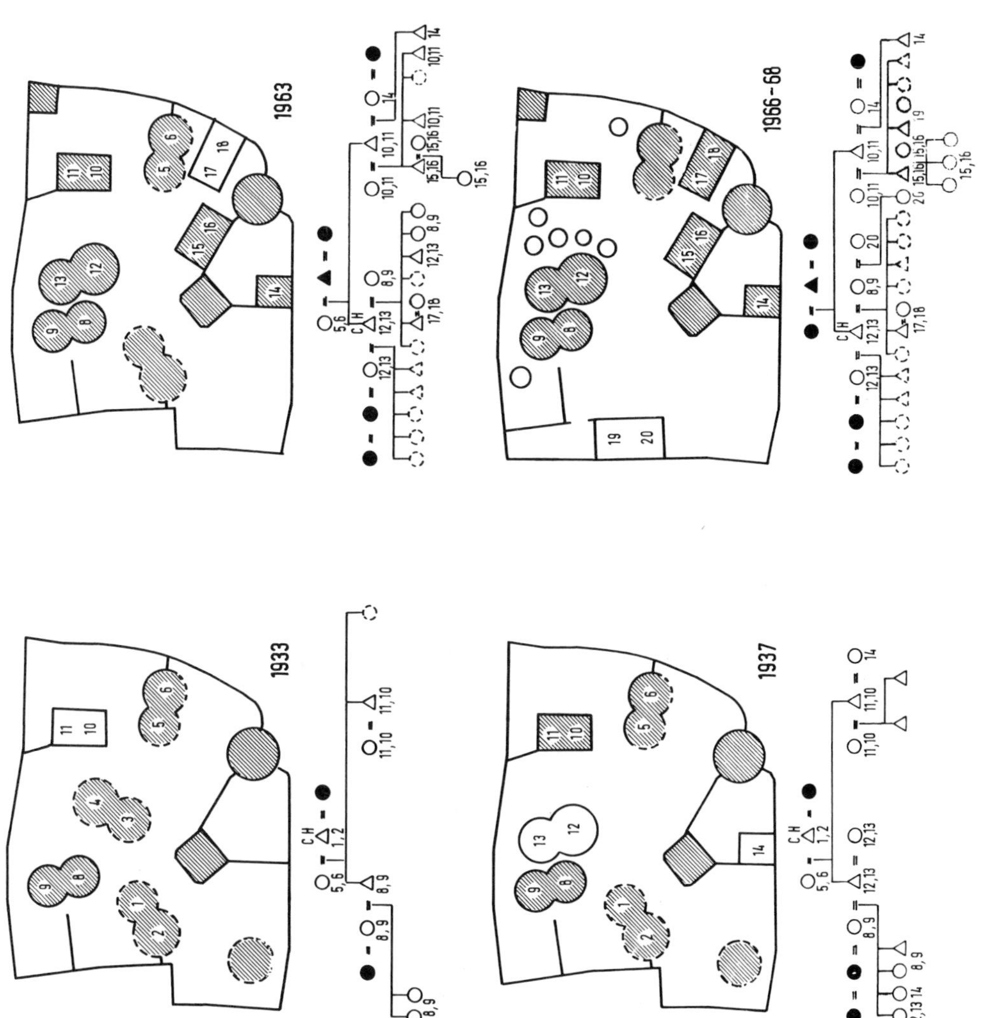
1933
1937
1963
1966–68

the compound head and the older kinsmen, the history of this compound and its inhabitants was traced backwards to the turn of this century when the present compound head was born. The kinship pattern and the architectural development of the compound were compiled independently for the given time span and then compared, all apparent inconsistencies being discussed with the compound head to make whatever corrections were necessary.

According to the compound head, his father had rebuilt the compound around 1900 shortly before the British occupation. There the old man lived with his wives and children in three double-roomed round huts (*adadai*), which are indicated in Diagram 4.10 by dotted lines. There was some uncertainty about the father's second wife and the number of children by this marriage. The plans and the kinship diagrams are therefore incomplete for the early stages of the compound's history. Nevertheless, from the data collected it was possible to produce a series of plans showing the development of this compound from about 1920 to 1968.

After the First World War the compound was occupied by one individual family; it illustrated stage 1 in the kinship development discussed above. In 1926, when the first-born son of the compound head married, the co-residential kinship group reached stage 2. Following an extension of the compound area, a hut with two rooms was built for the young couple. The marriage of the compound head's second son in 1933 led to the construction of a new hut. Between 1935 and 1937 three more rooms were built to house the compound head's sons' newly married additional wives. After the death of that compound head in 1946, the oldest son assumed responsibility for the compound and its inhabitants. As a result of this move the co-residential kinship group had reached stage 3 in the kinship development. With the marriage of the compound head's brother's oldest son in 1958 the group changed to stage 4. In the same year a new hut was built for the young couple. Further rooms were built in 1963 and 1965–1966 to house the then rapidly expanding family.

However, as already mentioned above, composite kinship groups are liable to changes at any stage of kinship development which may not proceed progressively from stage 1 to stage 6 but is frequently interrupted. This is shown in the second example. (See Diagram 4.11.)

This compound is situated near the market in the walled city and has belonged to a family of butchers for at least three generations. In the late 1920s when the compound was occupied by the families of the compound head and

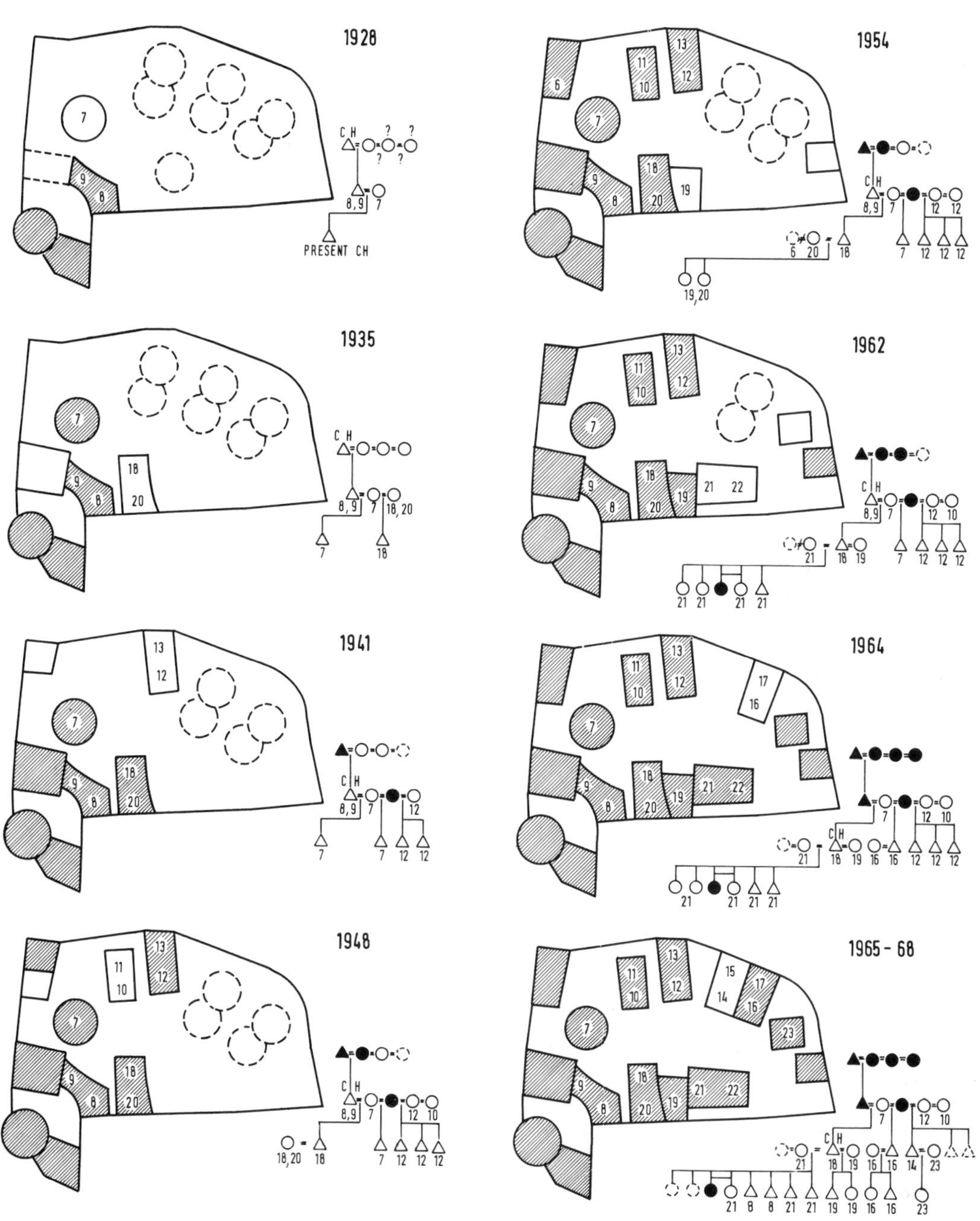

Diagram 4.11
House 71. (See also Plan A.4.2 on p. 344)

his son, it illustrated stage 2 in the kinship development. However, after the compound head's death in 1939, the compound was occupied by only one individual family, thus representing a reversal to stage 1. With the marriage of the new compound head's son in 1948, stage 2 was reached again. The death of that compound head in 1963 again reduced the residential kinship group to stage 1; but with the marriage of the new compound head's half brother in 1964 the group reached stage 3 in the development cycle. In 1965, when the compound head's second half brother married his first wife, a hut with two rooms was built to accommodate the young couple. As the group could not expand further due to the lack of adequate building sites within the compound, the two remaining half brothers moved out. One half brother married in 1966 and has since built a compound of his own elsewhere.

The third compound was investigated in 1968 and revisited in 1979 in order to record changes which had taken place in the co-residential kinship group and consequently in the layout of the compound over the last decade. This compound is situated about ten minutes' walk from the main market to the north. The present compound head is a *mai tsire* who grills meat for sale in the main street and the market.

In the early 1930s, the compound was occupied by two full brothers, their wives and unmarried children. This combination represents stage 3 in the development cycle of co-residential kinship groups. In the late 1930s, the younger brother of the compound head left the compound for Jos, taking his wife and children with him, and the remaining kinship group reverted to stage 1 which represents a nucleus or elementary family with unmarried children.

In 1946, when the oldest son of the compound head married, two new rooms (11 and 12) were built for him and his young wife. This was repeated when the second son married a few years later (rooms 5 and 6). With the marriage of the oldest son the co-residential kinship group had reached stage 2 in the developmental cycle, which consists of the compound head and his married son(s). Throughout the 1940s the layout and structural features of the compound represented the classical example of a traditional Hausa compound, consisting of several free-standing, two-roomed, round, thatched huts surrounded by a high mud wall. (See Plan 4.3.)

The compound head's death in 1951 resulted in his oldest son taking over the headship of the compound, following which, the kinship group entered stage 3, i.e. brothers, their wives, and unmarried children. In 1955, the third brother of the new compound head married and moved with his young wife temporarily into the two rooms (3 and 4) vacated by his dead father's younger brother, who had left the compound in the late 1930s.

Following the unexpected death of the relatively young compound head in 1960, the third brother, though

Plan 4.3
House 77, survey sample population by sex, age, and marital status

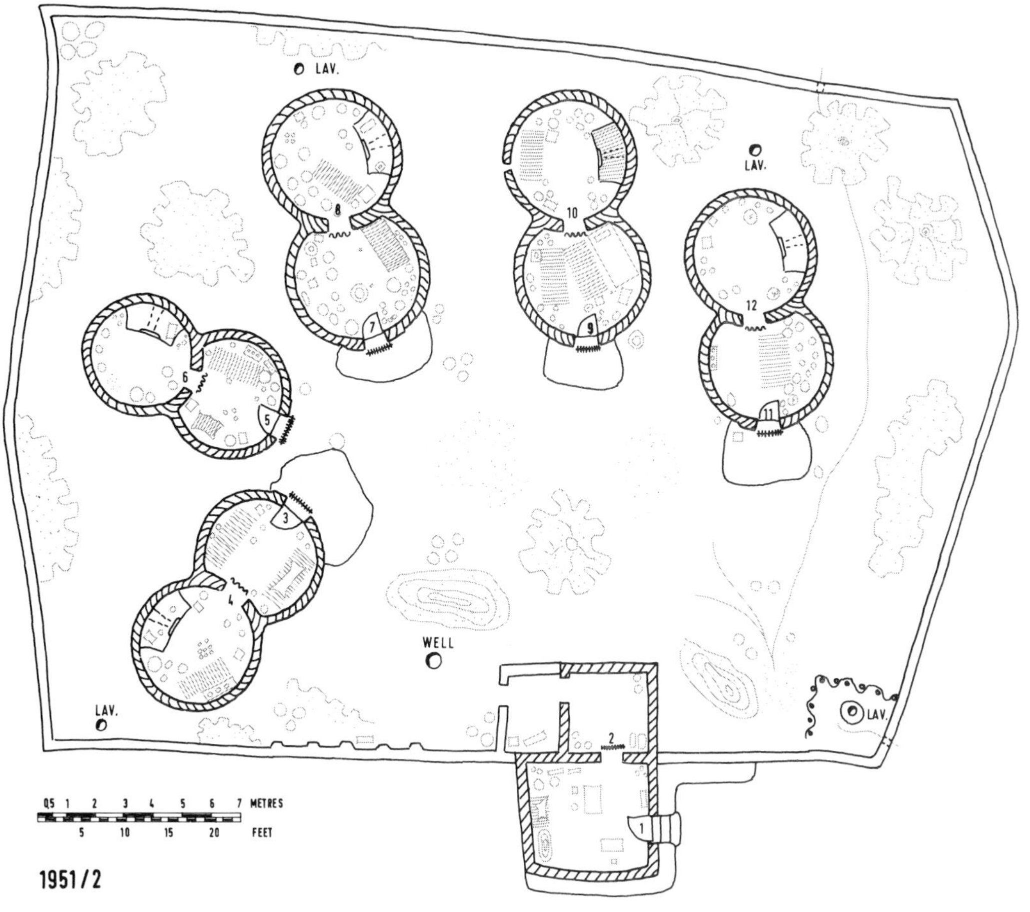

LAV.
LAV.
LAV.
LAV.
WELL
1
2
3
4
5
6
7
8
9
10
11
12
0.5 1 2 3 4 5 6 7 METRES
5 10 15 20 FEET
1951/2

C H
7/8
9/10
(3)
(4)
(3/4)
C H.
11
12
5
6
3/4
3/4
11/12
?

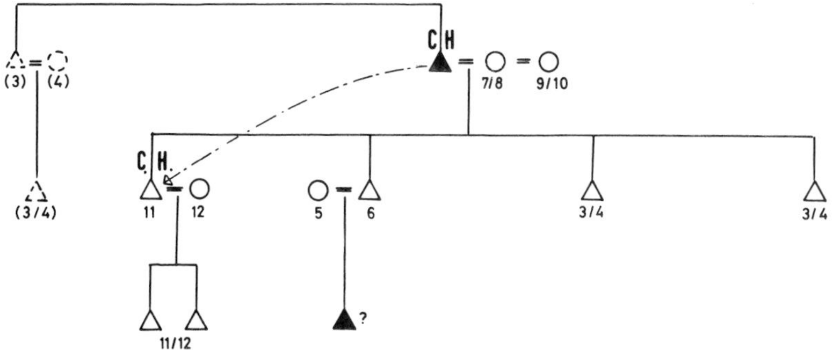

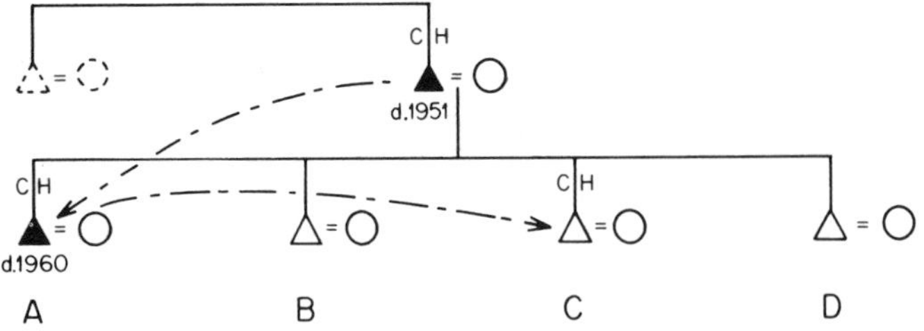

Diagram 4.12
Sequence of headship

junior, took over the headship and the responsibility for the inhabitants of the compound, bypassing his older brother C who then had no children.[2] (See Diagram 4.12.) Moreover, though senior in age, brother B was economically rather inactive and largely dependent for his livelihood on brother C, the new compound head. Owing to the unexpected death of the older brother A, the co-residential kinship group moved to stage 5 in the development cycle although none of the children of the remaining three brothers had by then married. In 1961 the youngest brother D married and moved temporarily into the two rooms (11 and 12) left empty by the death of his senior brother. He also shared responsibility with the new compound head for their dead brother's children. As can be seen on Plan 4.4, the position of rooms within the compound and, more important, who occupied them are decisive factors in the physical development of the compound. The territorial division of the house between the compound head and his younger but very ambitious brother (D) is noteworthy. The building activities listed below, which at times assumed a competitive character,[3] were made possible by the economic success of brother D who had already initiated his own independent meat-frying business.

The first two rooms having rectangular floor plans (nos 13 and 14) were built by brother D for himself and his wife in 1962. In 1964 he constructed the first shop (no. 15), followed by a kitchen (no. 16). The compound head, after moving temporarily into rooms (nos 11 and 12) vacated by brother D, demolished his old quarters and built in its place three rectangular rooms (nos 17–19) for himself and his wife in 1964/1965. Three years later brother D added two more rooms (nos 20 and 21) next to his own quarters for his dead brother's eldest son who helped him with his business. This was the situation I found when visiting the compound in 1968 (see Plan 4.5).[4] In 1971/1972 another two rooms (nos 22 and 23) plus a shop (no. 24) were added by brother D.

In 1972, when the compound head married his second wife, one room (no. 25) was built for her next to his own

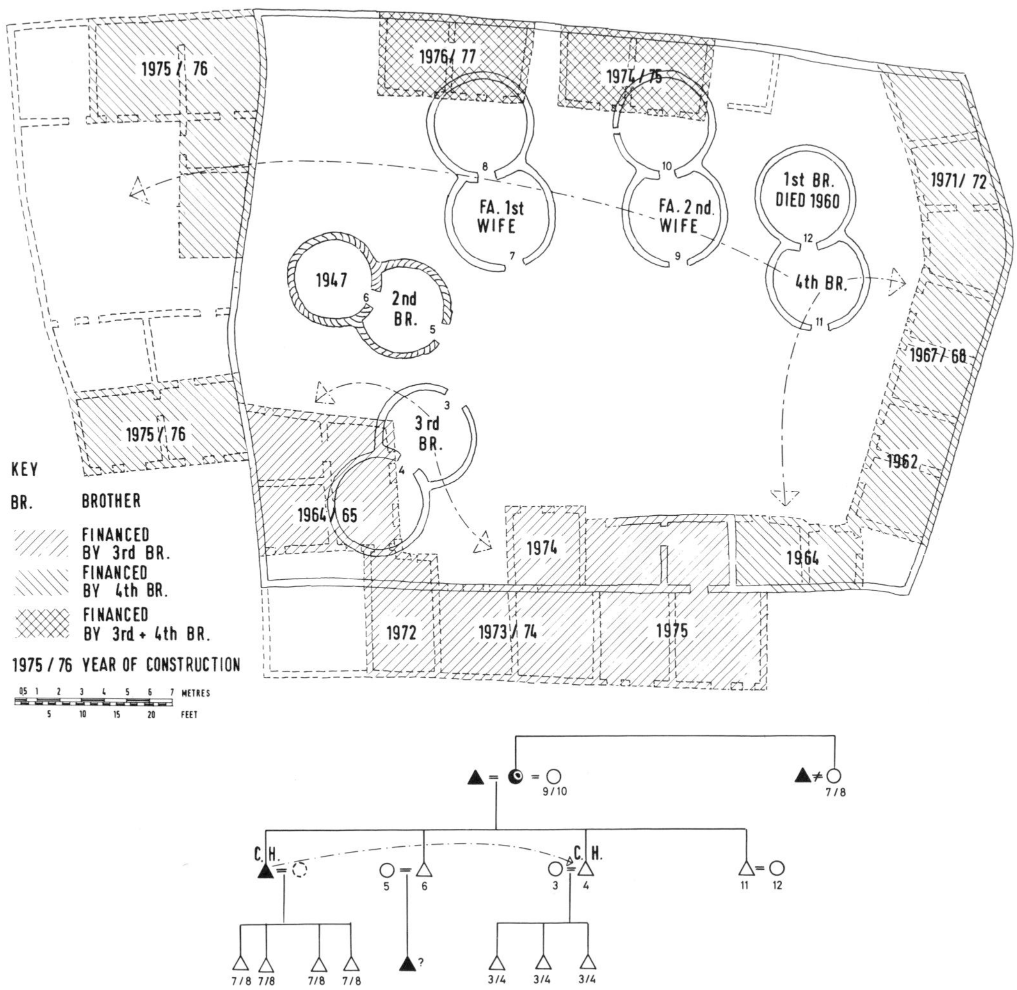

Plan 4.4
House 77, development 1961–1979

room. This sparked of a major redevelopment of the front portion of the compound, including six new rooms. On the marriages of the compound head's first and second sons in 1973 and 1974 respectively, three more rooms (nos 26–28) were added, and one year later a second shop (no. 31) and a new entrance hut (*zaure*) were constructed and paid for by the compound head. The two rooms immediately behind the *zaure* (nos 2 and 32) were then upgraded by converting their roof structure from thatch to mud (*soro*).

In late 1974, brother D decided after all to build his own compound next to the old one. An entrance hut (no. 33), a shop (no. 34), one kitchen (no. 38) and three rooms (nos 35–37) were constructed in 1975/1976 and ready for occupation at the beginning of 1977. An interior door set in the old compound wall to connect both houses was

Plan 4.5
House 77, 1968

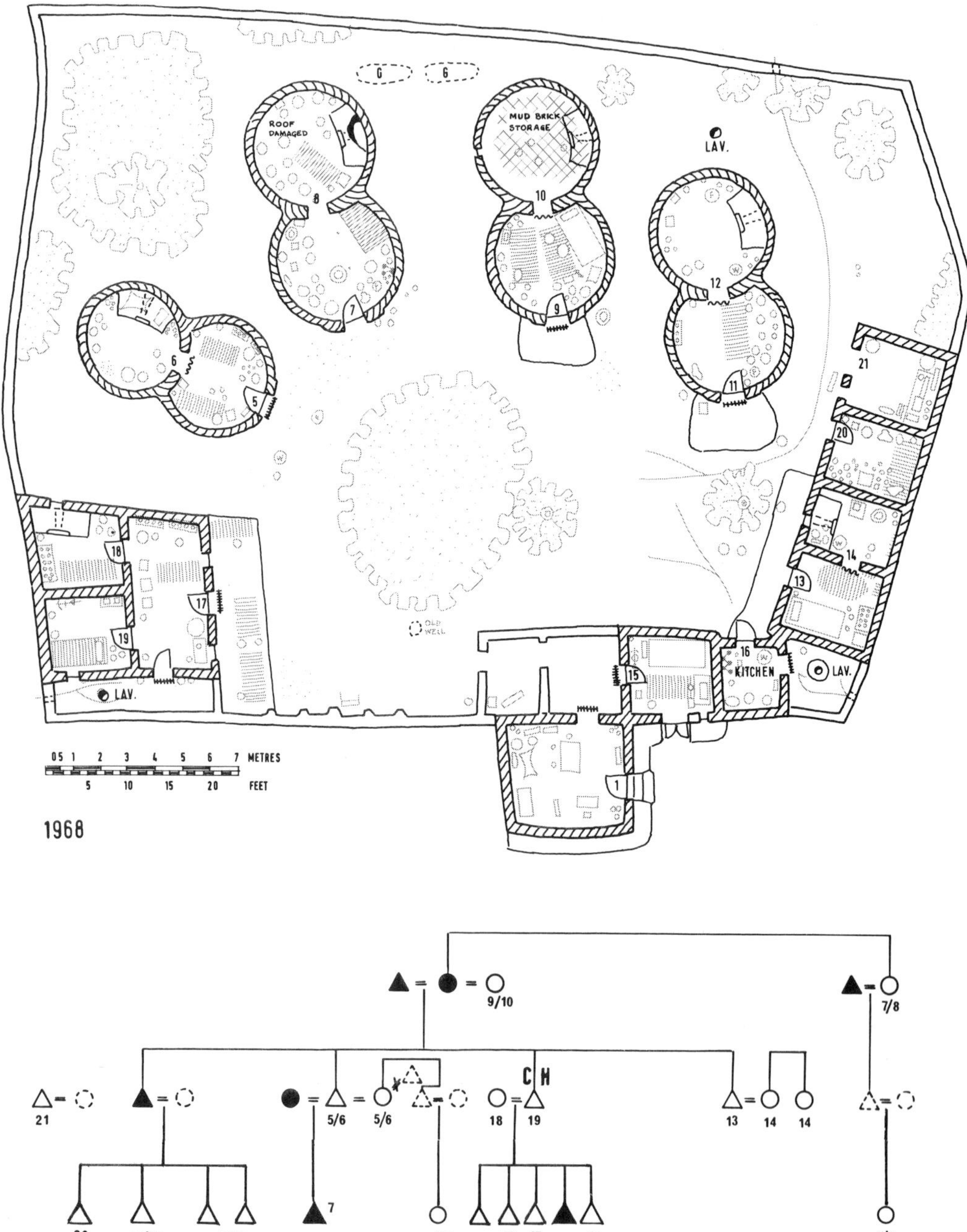

closed in 1978 after brother C – the compound head next door – had complained that his and his sons' wives, instead of working in the compound, were found far too often chatting with his younger brother's second wife in the new compound.

Only in the mid-1970s did the compound head (C) and his younger brother (D) combine their financial resources in order to build two double-roomed huts, one for the second son of their dead senior brother (nos 39 and 40), the other for their mother's junior brother's son (nos 29 and 30), on their respective marriages. It may be mentioned here that none of the three brothers had made the pilgrimage to Mecca (*hajji*), hence a substantial proportion of their incomes were available for investment in both compounds.

Table 4.5 compares the contributions that each of the brothers made to the compound's construction.

The type of construction carried out during the last two decades is also worth noting. When the present compound head took over the headship in 1960, the compound consisted of five two-roomed round huts plus two entrance rooms, all of which were covered with thatched roofs. Twenty years later, the only two circular thatched rooms that remained belonged to the oldest of the three brothers (B) who had contributed nothing to the compound's construction. All other 29 rooms, excluding one kitchen shed, had rectangular floor plans,[5] and mud roofs (*soraye*), and some walls had also been rendered with cement plaster. During my visit to the compound in 1979 (see Plan 4.6), I observed a pile of cement blocks next to the compound head's hut, a clear sign of future structural changes when cement blocks will be used for walls instead of mud bricks (*tubala*), and corrugated iron roofs may be used to cover the new as well as the remaining mud-walled rooms.

Table 4.5 Contributions to construction of compound

Family members	Sq. m	%
Father of compound head (died in 1951)	17.90	6.3
Brother B. No contribution; lives in hut provided by his father on marriage	0.00	0.0
Brother C (compound head)	108.10	37.8
Brother D. Including his own compound	126.00	44.1
Brothers C and D together built and financed	33.60	11.8
Total compound	285.60	100.0

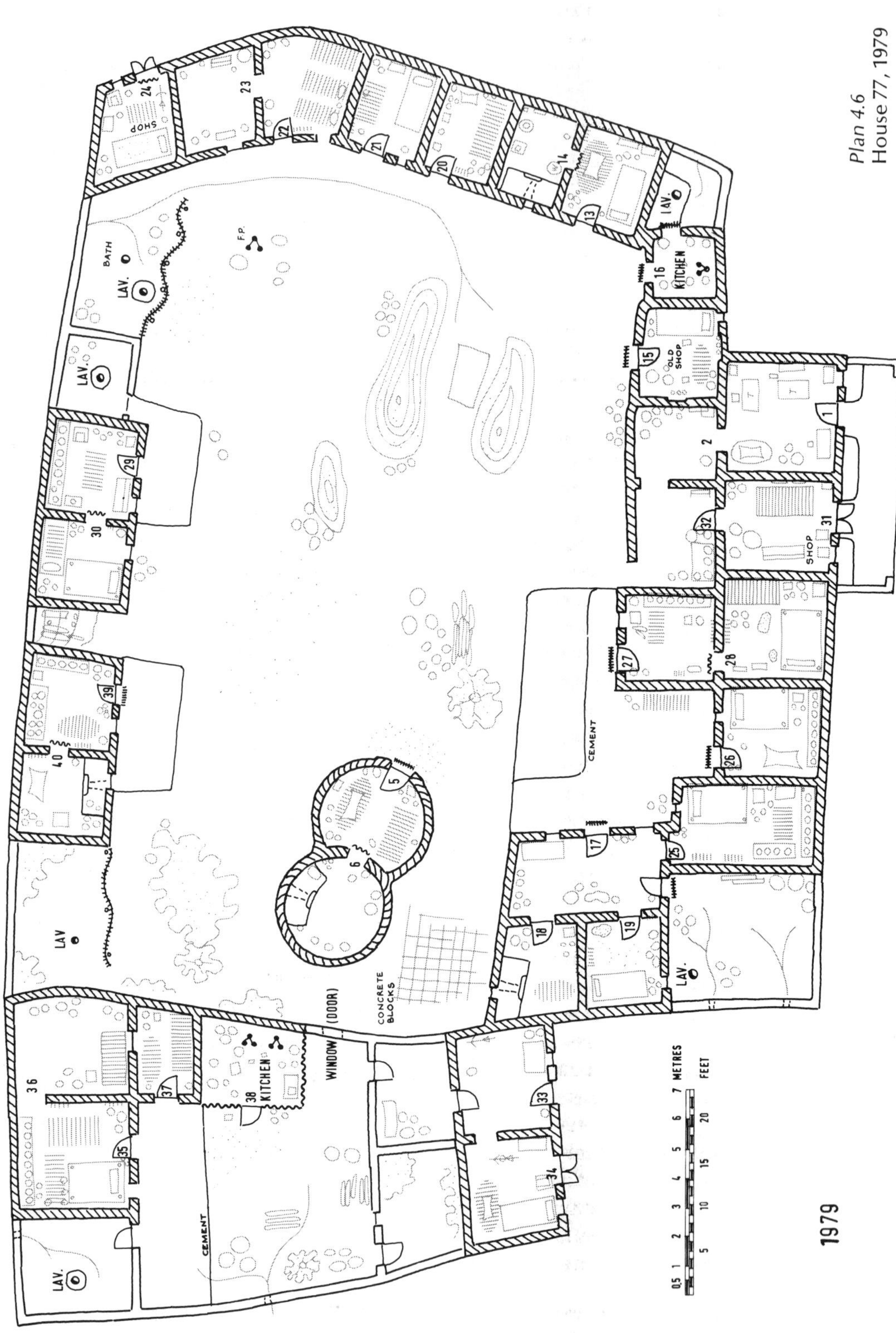

Plan 4.6
House 77, 1979

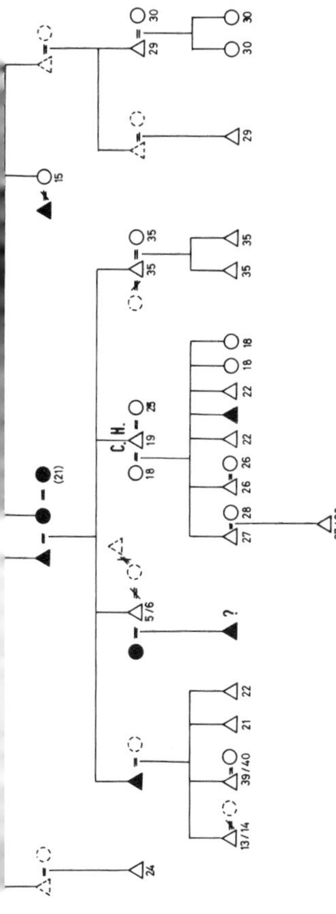

The co-residential kinship group and the building activities described above can only be fully understood if the socio-economic conflicts between the two brothers B and D on the one hand and the compound head (C) on the other are briefly discussed, because they have influenced the physical development of the compound.

The conflict between the compound head (C) and his older brother (B) centres around the headship and the authority and prestige associated with that status. Although not directly connected with the physical development of the compound, it is of importance for an understanding of the kinship group and their attitude towards building construction. After the first brother's death the oldest surviving brother (B) did not succeed as compound head because he had no children, and above all because his poverty and lack of enterprise counted heavily against him. Furthermore, he is regarded by the adult members of the kinship group as being rather unlucky; hence the headship passed to his younger brother on whom he is financially dependent. Although it seemed that the older brother resigned himself to his fate, he still resented the fact of being passed over. This became quite obvious during several conversations with both men. The present compound head (C) naturally insisted that all decisions regarding the compound and its inhabitants are taken together, which is probably true, and politely insisted that his older brother is the 'real compound head', a statement which was dismissed by most adult members of the kinship group as a polite gesture, but no more. In addition, representatives of the municipal administration always contact brother C in any matters concerning the compound and its inhabitants and the compound is now known by his name. Up to 1979, B had no income of his own but got his share of receipts from the meat-frying business run by his younger brother, the compound head, with whom he works.

The conflict and rivalry between the compound head (C) and his younger brother (D) clearly have an economic character and had a decisive impact on the physical development of the compound. There is little doubt that D is the more successful business man and that this has at times led to tension between the two men. To some degree this was expressed in the form of their competitive building activities, until finally the younger man decided to build his own compound and move out of his father's house, although there was not an acute shortage of space in the compound for future extension.

However, it must be stressed here that rivalries of the kind described are seldom discussed in public, however clearly expressed in the various actions. Conflicts of this nature have always played an important part in distributing influence and authority in the socio-economic sphere of Hausa extended family life.

This brief account identified four differing kinds of events that alter the kinship composition of co-residential kinship groups. These are, first, the death of the compound head or other adult married male; second, the marriages and divorces of males in each agnatic kinship category and generation; third, withdrawal by senior kinsmen for the lack of space; and, fourth, economic rivalries or disagreements between adult compound members.

Before the architectural development of these compounds can be related fully to the growth of the co-residential kinship groups, an old Hausa custom, which influenced building development in many compounds, should be noted. This custom, which is no longer universal and probably harks back to pre-Muslim times, enjoins the burial of a dead person in or next to his or her hut which is then abandoned and left to collapse.[6] After its roof and part of the walls have disintegrated, the roofing poles of deleb palm stems or bamboo are removed for use in new construction or as firewood. The remaining walls will then disintegrate quickly to form a small mound of earth which is left to mark the site of the former hut for several years. However, when new rooms are needed, this earth will be used to make bricks for the new building, thus recycling the basic raw materials needed for the construction of houses. As can be seen from Diagrams 4.10 and 4.11 this practice was followed in the first two compounds I used as illustrations.

In Diagram 4.10 a total floor area of 105.5 sq. m was constructed between 1926 and 1966. Of this, an area of 100.3 sq. m or 95.1 per cent was built as a direct response to a need for living and sleeping rooms for newly wedded couples or for additional wives, whereas only 5.2 sq. m or 4.9 per cent of the total area was built as a wet-season kitchen. Over the same period three double-round huts and one store room used by the compound head's later father disappeared.

Diagram 4.11 shows a slightly different distribution. Of the total floor area of 127.8 sq. m built between 1928 and 1967, 88.6 sq. m or 69.3 per cent was constructed to provide living and sleeping rooms for newly married couples, or for the rapidly growing family of the present compound head, while 22.8 sq. m or 17.9 per cent was built to provide such ancillary facilities as kitchens and kitchen stores. Only one commonly used room of 16.4

sq. m or 12.8 per cent of the total floor area was built between 1928 and 1967.

In the last example, on pp. 50–58, a total of 267.7 sq. m or 29 rooms were built between 1962 and 1976. Of the total floor area, 185.3 sq. m or 69.2 per cent were constructed as 20 living and sleeping rooms to house the rapidly growing family. In addition, four shops or commercially used rooms with, altogether, 35.7 sq. m or 13.4 per cent were built, one of which has since been converted into a sleeping room for the compound head's mother's widowed sister. Another three entrances/passages used by the whole family with 32.5 sq. m or 12.1 per cent and two kitchens with 14.2 sq. m or 5.3 per cent were built and financed by the compound head and his younger brother. Over the same period, a total of four double-roomed round huts and the old *zaure* or entrance hut had disappeared.

Distribution of floor area

The distribution of the floor area among the sample population may be studied from two points of view; first, the average floor area per household and per person classified by their relationship to the compound head, and, second, the average floor area per household and per person according to the number of persons per household. The first approach may tell us something about differential treatment of related and strangers' households regarding the allocation of space, whereas the second approach will indicate the compound head's ability to provide shelter for the growing family.

Floor area and household

The survey in Zaria walled city covered 191 households containing 1,067 persons in 77 compounds. Table 4.6 compares the total average floor area and the average sleeping area available to each household and its members, these households being classified by the relationship of their heads to the compound head. The substantial difference between the total average area occupied by compound heads' households (100.6 sq. m) and the total average area of all other dependent or semi-dependent households (24.9 sq. m) is noteworthy. These differences are due to the greater size of compound heads' households which contain an average of 7.8 persons as against 4.1 persons in all other households. Moreover, the total average area of

Table 4.6 Average floor area per household and person in square metres

Column	1		2		3	
	No. of hhs	No. of persons	Total av. area per hh	Total av. area per person	Av. sleep. area per hh	Av. sleep. area per person
CH's household	77	603	100.6	12.8	37.7	4.8
CH's full & half brs' hhs	39	172	31.0	7.0	18.1	4.1
CH's sons' households	29	106	20.1	5.5	14.3	3.9
CH's full & half brs' sons' hhs	25	118	21.4	4.5	16.0	3.4
Other related households	10	29	23.8	8.2	12.1	4.2
Subtotal dep. households	103	425	24.9	6.0	16.0	3.9
Strangers' households	11	39	15.1	4.3	13.5	3.8
Total hhs and persons	191	1,067				
Av. all hhs and persons			54.8	9.8	24.5	4.4

100.6 sq. m occupied by compound heads' households includes all rooms which are directly under the control of the compound head, including the various entrance huts, workshops, and corridors in the compound, even though these are available for general use by other residents. Dependent or semi-dependent household heads, on the other hand, are normally only responsible for their immediate sleeping and living rooms, plus the occasional kitchen and store room. Thus, the average floor areas cited above illustrate the differential distribution of responsibilities among households' heads within these compounds rather more precisely than the allocation of floor area between the households themselves. Furthermore, the differences in the average sleeping area available to individuals only fluctuate between 4.8 sq. m for the members of the compound head's household and 3.9 sq. m for persons belonging to all other dependent or semi-dependent households. However, it must be noted that the average sleeping area per person for households of compound heads is slightly inflated by the fact that 50 compound heads have their own private quarters.

Graphs 4.1 and 4.2 are based on Table A.4.8 on p. 342. Graph 4.1 shows the average floor area and the average sleeping area per household according to the number of persons per household. As can be seen, the average floor area per household increases from 17.2 sq. m in households with 1 or 2 persons to 118.4 sq. m in

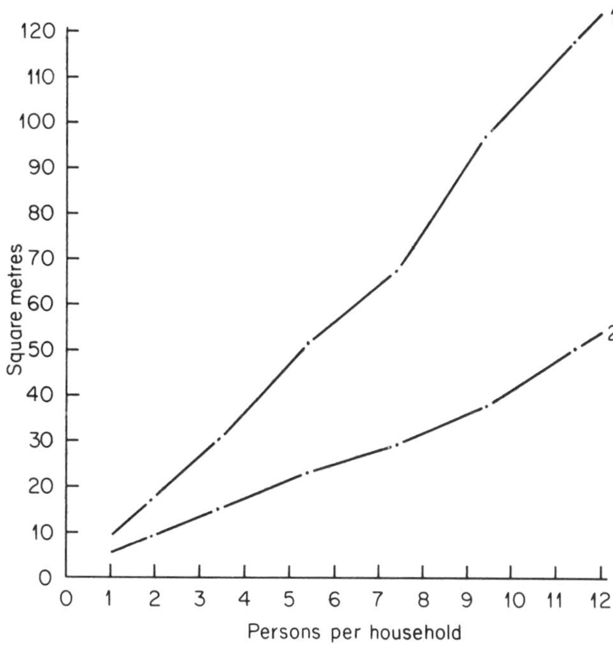

Graph 4.1
Average floor and sleeping area per household in square metres

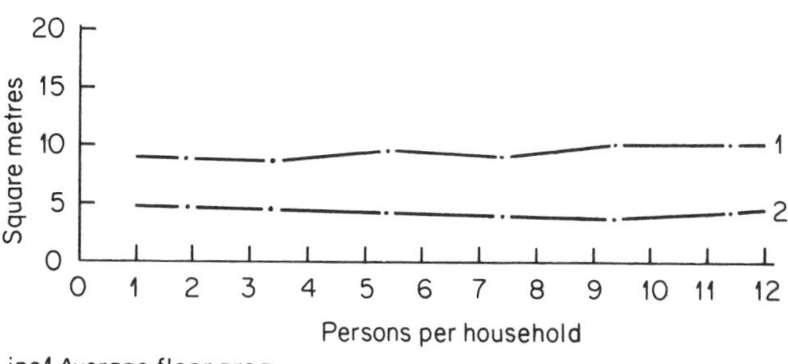

Graph 4.2
Average floor and sleeping area per person in square metres. (See Table A.4.8 on p. 342)

households having 11 or 12 persons. At the same time the average sleeping area per household also increases from 9.2 sq. m for households with 1 or 2 persons to 50.9 sq. m for 11 or 12 person households.

Graph 4.2 shows the average floor area per person and the average sleeping area per person according to the number of persons per household. The average floor area increases only marginally from 9.0 sq. m for households with 1 or 2 persons to 10.4 sq. m for households having 11 or 12 persons, while the average sleeping area per person remains almost stable between 4.8 sq. m per person for households with 1 or 2 persons and 4.5 sq. m for households having 11 or 12 persons. This finding confirms a preceding observation that new huts are built for nearly all women who enter the compound on marriage, and that further rooms are constructed to house the expanding family. It is evident that the lack of suitable building sites within compounds rather than overcrowding of existing rooms precipitates decisions of dependent household heads to leave the house and to establish independent new compounds elsewhere.

Notes and references

1 M. G. Smith, *The Economy of the Hausa Communities of Zaria*, London, 1955, pp. 4–48.
2 All adult compound members interviewed were unanimous in their statements that he had had no children at all, but he insisted on having had a son who died soon after birth.
3 This can be clearly shown in the construction of prestigious but unused shops of which three were built by brother D.
4 F. W. Schwerdtfeger, 'Housing in Zaria', in *Shelter in Africa*, ed. P. Oliver, London, 1971, p. 75.
5 Here are some reasons for the rapid change from round to rectangular rooms in Hausaland. First, historical: the preference of early Arabic settlers in Kano and other towns in Northern Nigeria to construct rectangular houses no doubt impressed wealthy Hausa traders who copied it later. See H. Barth, *Travel in North and Central Africa*, London, 1890, vol. I, pp. 286–310. Second, pragmatic: in constructing square rooms, the boundary wall of a compound can often be used as one wall of the proposed room and only three walls have to be built. Third, practical: furniture of Western design such as iron bed-steads, cupboards, tables, and shelves do not fit easily into round rooms.
6 See compound shown in Plan 4.5 where, between rooms 7/8 and 9/10, there are two graves marked G.

Chapter 5

Occupation and income

Nigeria and Zaria

Occupational pattern

The most significant feature of the occupational pattern in Nigeria is the predominance of agriculture. However, detailed data on the percentage distribution of the main occupational groups are confusing. According to the 1952/1953 census report, about 78 per cent of the country's total labour force was engaged in agriculture, 13 per cent in trade, clerical work, and services, 3 per cent in crafts, 2 per cent in administrative, professional and technical work, and 4 per cent in miscellaneous occupations.[1] The 1963 census report, on the other hand, gave about 57 per cent of the country's total labour force as being engaged in agriculture, 21 per cent in trade, 14 per cent in crafts, 3 per cent in administration, and 5 per cent in other occupations.[2] Unfortunately, no detailed data for the 1973 census are yet available.

According to the 1963 census report, the urban labour force in Zaria Province was in the region of 58,000 persons.* Agriculture, crafts, and trade each accounted for about 30 per cent of the urban working population, whereas persons engaged in administrative, professional, and technical work accounted for about 6 per cent and other occupations for 3 per cent.[3]

* Includes towns with 20,000 or more inhabitants.

In 1968 the largest single employer in Zaria Province was the Native Authority with about 2,350 employees.[4] The eleven industrial establishments in Zaria which participated in the 1967 Industrial Survey had a total of 1,500 Nigerian employees.[5] Local factories then included *inter alia* a cotton mill, a cigarette factory, a printing press, an oil-seed processing plant, and the Nigerian Railway engineering works.

Income

In 1970 the average per capita income for Nigeria was estimated at over £N30 per annum, and was expected to increase by about 3 to 4 per cent during the period of the Second National Development Plan from 1970 to 1974.[6] According to the Industrial Surveys of 1963 and 1967, the average annual wages for Nigerian employees increased by over 30 per cent from £N151 in 1963 to £N201 in 1967.[7] A substantial increase of over 12 per cent was awarded after the Morgan Commission on wages and salaries had published its findings early in 1964.[8] In its report the commission recomended a new wage structure, and a minimum wage rate that ranged from £N6 10 s. to £N12 per month according to location.[9] In a White Paper the Government adopted some of these recommendations and raised the minimum wages accordingly.[10]

In 1967 the average income by occupational groups in Nigerian industrial establishments of ten or more employees was £N124 per annum for unskilled labourers, £N191 per annum for semi-skilled and skilled workers, £N300 per annum for clerical workers, and £N1,073 per annum for professional and managerial staff. In this context it should be mentioned that non-Nigerian employees with an average income of £N2,660 per annum accounted for only 2.6 per cent of the industrial labour force but consumed 34.4 per cent of the total labour cost.[11] In Northern Nigeria the average income of employees in industry was for unskilled labourers £N104 per annum, for semi-skilled and skilled workers £N170 per annum, for clerical workers £N250 per annum, and for professional and managerial staff £N740 per annum.

Cost of living

Nigeria has experienced inflation since 1961, and as the cost of living has risen so have wages and salaries. The general cost of living indices for Ibadan and Kaduna are given in Tables A.5.1 and A.5.2 on pp. 345, 346. Over the ten year period from 1961 to 1971, the average annual increase in the general consumer price index for Ibadan and Kaduna was 3.1 and 3.8 per cent respectively, whereas between 1960 and 1965 the increase at Zaria was only 1.4 per cent per annum.[12] By contrast, the sharp rise in the cost of living from 1968 to 1971 indicates the inflationary pressures that developed towards the end of the civil war as the result of increasing expenditure on arms and some import restrictions on civilian consumer goods.

Sample survey

Occupational pattern

Occupational patterns and the division of labour within the sample population are discussed below. Broadly speaking, men work in trade, crafts, agriculture, and various other wage-earning occupations, and contribute mainly such goods as food, clothing, and shelter to the household economy, while women contribute services and pursue low-paid crafts or petty trade on their own account. The main occupations of the 191 household heads included in my sample are given in Table 5.1.

About 33.7 per cent of the 77 compound heads interviewed were engaged in trade, textiles and food produce being among the most frequently traded commodities. Services including persons employed by the local and regional government as well as by the army accounted for 28.6 per cent. Such arts and crafts as weaving, tailoring, building, and teaching the Koran together accounted for 27.3 per cent of the sample, and full-time agriculture for only 2.6 per cent. Six compound heads or 7.8 per cent had retired and received some

Table 5.1 Occupational pattern of 191 household heads

	Compound head		Dependent HHs		Total HHs	
	No.	%	No.	%	No.	%
Crafts	21	27.3	49	43.0	70	36.7
Trade	26	33.7	32	28.1	58	30.4
Service	22	28.6	18	15.8	40	20.9
Agriculture	2	2.6	8	7.0	10	5.2
Misc.	6	7.8	7	6.1	13	6.8
Total	77	100.0	114	100.0	191	100.0

financial support from their next of kin. (For more detailed information see Table A.5.3 on p. 348.)

The occupational distribution of the 114 dependent or semi-dependent household heads revealed a slightly different pattern. Here craftwork with 43.0 per cent was the most important occupation, followed by trade with 28.1 per cent, services with 15.8 per cent, farming with 7.0 per cent, and miscellaneous occupations with 6.1 per cent.

A total of 104 household heads or 54.5 per cent derived some additional income in cash from agricultural activities, while another five compound heads received rent in kind from their farmland. Nearly half of the 51 compound heads directly engaged in farming employed paid labour on their farms, whereas the majority of dependent household heads farmed themselves or with the help of their unmarried sons. (See Table A.5.3.)

As shown in Table 5.2, nearly 60.0 per cent of the compound heads were self-employed, 24.7 per cent were employed in the public sector, and only 5.2 per cent worked in private firms. About 40.0 per cent of all dependent household heads were self-employed, 34.2 per cent helped a senior family member, 14.9 per cent were employed by the public sector, and 6.1 per cent in private firms.

As most married women among the Muslim Hausa are largely confined to the compound, only older women and those who live in *auren jahilai* (marriage of the ignorant) are seen trading in the market. Out of 347 married, widowed, and divorced females living in the compounds surveyed, nearly 60.0 per cent were engaged in spinning, weaving country cloths known as *gwadanne* on the vertical

Table 5.2 How household heads are employed

	Compound head		Dependent HHs		Total HHs	
	No.	%	No.	%	No.	%
Self-empl.	46	59.7	44	38.6	90	47.1
Empl. publ. sector	19	24.7	17	14.9	36	18.8
Empl. priv. sector	4	5.2	7	6.1	11	5.8
Helps fam. member	2	2.6	39	34.2	41	21.5
Retired	6	7.8	1	0.9	7	3.7
Misc.	–	–	6	5.3	6	3.1
Total	77	100.0	114	100.0	191	100.0

loom, or embroidering caps and pillow cases for sale by the household head or through commission agents in the city market. Another 15.0 per cent of these housewives prepared food which was hawked by young girls through the city market and streets, and about 13.0 per cent were primarily engaged in petty trading. Of the remaining 41 women, 23 or 6.6 per cent of the sample had no gainful occupation, and for 18 women or 5.2 per cent I obtained no information. As women always pursue their crafts or trading activities independently of their husbands, their profits are their own. While no systematic attempt was made to collect information on women's incomes during the survey, the incomplete data available suggest profit margins that varied from 1 to 6 shillings per week.

Household budget

Any useful analysis of family budgets must be prefaced by a brief description of the method used in collecting the relevant economic information as well as a critical discussion on the reliability and shortcomings of the data. The aim of my budgetary inquiries was to establish the annual cash income of the compound head and that of all other dependent or semi-dependent household heads who lived in the compound surveyed.

During a pilot survey of five compounds, which are not included in the sample, useful information on the current and fluctuating market prices for food, clothing, other consumer goods, and building materials was collected, together with wage levels, turnover, and profit margins for the most important trading commodities. Data available from the socio-economic survey of the Hausa communities in Zaria by M. G. Smith, the Urban Consumer Survey for Zaria and Kaduna, the Industrial Surveys, and the Zaria market retail prices which the Federal Office of Statistics collected regularly proved most helpful.[13] Seasonal variations in economic activities, food prices, and supplies were noted in order to evaluate price movements linked with these fluctuations. Such seasonal variations were always discussed separately during interviews since information obtained from only one month or season could not serve as a sound basis for an annual expenditure/income calculation.

The financial inquiry started with an investigation of the household heads' regular daily, weekly, and monthly expenditure on food and drinks, firewood, transport, and accommodation where outlays for rent, new construction, improvements, and maintenance were clearly distinguished. This was followed by irregular expenditure on clothing, cash gifts or loans to family members and friends as well as outlays for religious and public festivals, childbirth, marriages, and/or funerals. After all major items of expenditure were listed income was investigated. To reduce cumulative errors, the daily, weekly, monthly, or seasonal incomes from agriculture, art and crafts, trade, services, and other professions were calculated. Further inquiries were made about income from cash gifts, loans, and other financial transactions. Income and expenditure were then compared and only when they balanced by about 10 per cent was the budget accepted as valid for inclusion in the analysis. Major mistakes caused by forgetfulness or deliberate misinformation were in most cases found out and could be corrected by discussing the discrepancy with the household heads concerned. Inaccuracies were further reduced by comparing the statements of cost and profit margins with those made independently at previous interviews by men practising the same trade or craft, and in the case of wage-earners by checking with the employers. Nevertheless, it is highly unlikely that the data collected are free of inaccuracies and omissions, though they are sufficiently detailed and close to the truth to illustrate the patterns of domestic economy in 1967/1968 and provided a valuable guide to the levels of cash income and expenditure at that time. The records of three representative budgets are given in Tables A.5.7, A.5.8, and A.5.9 on pp. 352–354. The household heads chosen to illustrate prevailing budgetary variations include a farmer who was also a farm labourer, a barber–doctor (*wanzami*), and a trader.

Before proceeding with the analysis some additional remarks on the limitations of the collected budgetary data are necessary. The first and obvious one is the size of the sample which included only 147 successfully interviewed household heads. Another problem arises from the relatively large number of dependent household heads who did not respond (38.6 per cent), of whom about half were absent at the time of interview, while the rest either refused to cooperate or deliberately gave misleading information and so had to be omitted from the sample. Fortunately, all compound heads participated fully in the budgetary inquiry and none had to be omitted. The last point to make is that no attempt was made to check information on income in kind, which derived mainly from farming activities and other non-monetary transactions such as rent in kind, or from barter, the informants' statements on this subject being normally accepted. For most households the additional income from agricultural produce was important, though variably so. The proportion of kind income as a percentage of gross income can vary from as much as 70 per cent in the case of a subsistence farmer to zero for a full-time trader, craftsman, or wage earner with no farmland.[14]

Income groups

The first consumer surveys conducted in Nigeria between 1953 and 1955 were limited to wage-earning households with an income not exceeding £N350 per annum. This limit was later raised to £N400 per annum in the Zaria–Kaduna survey of 1955/1956. In the early 1960s a new division into lower income households not exceeding £N450 per annum and middle income households between £N450 and £N1,200 per annum was adopted. For my own survey these income categories proved unsuitable due to the large proportion of non-wage earning households in the sample with very low incomes, particularly among the dependent or semi-dependent households. The income distribution given in Table 5.3 represents a more realistic classification and permits useful comparisons with other studies.[15]

The low-income households include some retired household heads who are supported by their next of kin, unskilled manual labourers engaged in agriculture, manufacturing industry, and local government, small-scale craftsmen and petty-traders, as well as some semi-skilled labourers.

Table 5.3 Income distribution

	Income per month in shillings	Income per annum in £N
Low-income households		
A.	Under 100s.	Under £N 60
B.	100s. to 199s. 11d.	£N 60 to £N 120
C.	200s. to 299s. 11d.	£N 120 to £N 180
Middle income households		
D.	300s. to 399s. 11d.	£N 180 to £N 240
E.	400s. to 599s. 11d.	£N 240 to £N 360
F.	600s. to 999s. 11d.	£N 360 to £N 600
High-income households		
G.	1,000s. to 1,999s. 11d.	£N 600 to £N 1,200
H.	2,000s. to 2,999s. 11d.	£N 1,200 to £N 1,800
I.	3,000s. and over	£N 1,800 and over

The middle income households include skilled workers and artisans, proprietors of medium-sized trading enterprises and craftsmen, clerical, supervisory, and semi-professional staff.

The high-income households contain a few large-scale kolanut and cloth traders, besides professional, executive, and managerial staff employed by local or regional governments and state-owned industries.

Income distribution

Of the 191 household heads interviewed, 44 or 23.0 per cent either refused to cooperate or gave such grossly misleading information about their incomes and expenditures that they had to be excluded from the following analysis. Of the remaining 147 valid household budgets, 101 or 68.7 per cent were in the low-income group (up to £N180 per annum), 42 or 28.6 per cent were in the middle income group (£N180 to £N600 per annum), and only 4 or 2.7 per cent were in the high-income group (above £N600 per annum). The income distribution for compound heads and all other dependent or semi-dependent household heads is given separately in Table A.5.5 on p. 347. As can be seen, compound heads have on average the highest income, with 53.2 per cent of them in the low-income group, 41.6 per cent in the middle, and 5.2 per cent in the high-income group. Dependent household heads, on the other hand, have 85.8 per cent in the low, 14.2 per cent in the middle, and none in the high-income group.

The income distribution by household size for all households is set out in Table A.5.6.A on p. 350. This table shows the predominance of small households with one to six persons in the low income group. However, as the number of persons per household increases, income tends to increase as well. This is clearly shown by the diagonal pattern of concentration which holds for households with up to eleven or twelve persons and with incomes of between 300 and 999 shillings per month. From there onwards, the few remaining households are scattered so widely that their distribution has uncertain statistical value.

While the average monthly income per household increased from about 157 shillings in households with one or two persons to 402 shillings in households with nine or ten persons, the per capita income decreased from about 80 shillings per month in households with one or two persons to about 42 shillings in households with nine or ten persons.

On Graph A.5.1, p. 355, the cumulative income distribution of 147 household heads is plotted on logarithmic probability paper in order to show the relationship between the income of the compound head and those of all dependent or semi-dependent household heads as well as their median income. The slightly curved line of the cumulative income distribution for all households indicates a log-normal distribution. The two types of households are distinguished by separate curves. Except for the dependent household heads in the middle income group, these curves show an approximately equal percentage change but differing incomes. As a result the curve representing the income distribution of dependent household heads, who have generally lower incomes, shifts leftwards. The median income of compound and dependent household heads is 290 and 150 shillings per month respectively. However, part of the higher income of compound heads which derives from farm produce and other financial benefits which are associated with the headship, is spent on new construction, improvements, and repair of the compound as well as on help given to other family members in need.

From the budgetary data collected a Lorenz Curve was constructed. Graph A.5.2 on p. 355 revealed the inequality in the distribution of income with about 50 per cent of the 147 household heads earning about 25 per cent of the total recorded annual income.

In conclusion, this study has shown that nearly 70 per cent of all household heads included in this analysis had a cash income of less than 300 shillings per month or £N180 per annum. The median cash income of all compound heads was, at 290 shillings per month, nearly double the income of dependent household heads which reached only 150 shillings per month. In the following chapter I intend to show how domestic groups with such limited financial resources can successfully build, improve, and maintain their compounds.

Notes and references

1 Department of Statistics, Nigeria, *Population Census of Nigeria 1952/53*, Lagos, 1956, p. 1.
2 Federal Office of Statistics, Nigeria, *Population Census of Nigeria 1963*, Combined National Figures, vol. III, Lagos, 1968, p. 39.
3 Federal Census Office, *Population Census of Nigeria, Northern Region* (Mimeo), vol. II, Lagos, 1968, p. 391.
4 Ahmadu Bello University, Zaria, Institute of Administration, *Northern States of Nigeria Local Government Year Book 1968*, Zaria, 1968, p. 87.

5 Federal Office of Statistics, Nigeria, *Industrial Survey of Nigeria 1967*, Lagos, 1968, p. 40.
6 Federal Ministry of Information, Nigeria, *Second National Development Plan 1970/4*, Lagos, 1970, p. 40.
7 Federal Office of Statistics, Nigeria, *Industrial Survey of Nigeria 1963* and *1967*, Lagos, 1965 and 1968.
8 Federal Ministry of Information, Nigeria, *Report of the Commission on the Review of Wages, Salaries and Conditions of Service of the Junior Employees of the Government of the Federation and in Private Establishments 1963 to 1964*, Lagos, 1964.
9 Ibid., pp. 20–21.
10 Federal Ministry of Information, Nigeria, *Conclusion of the Federal Government on the Report of the Morgan Commission on the Review of Wages, Salaries and Conditions of Service of the Junior Employees of the Government in the Federation and Private Establishments 1963–64*, Sessional Paper No. 5, Lagos, 1964.
11 Federal Office of Statistics, Nigeria, *Industrial Survey of Nigeria, 1967*, pp. 62–97.
12 Department of Statistics, Northern Nigeria, *Statistical Yearbook 1966*, Kaduna, 1967, p. 212.
13 M. G. Smith, *The Economy of Hausa Communities of Zaria*, London, 1955, reprint 1971. Federal Department of Statistics, Nigeria, *Urban Consumer Surveys in Nigeria Report on Enquiries into the Income and Expenditure Patterns of Wage-Earner Households in Kaduna and Zaria 1955/6*, Lagos, 1959. Federal Office of Statistics, Nigeria, *Industrial Surveys of Nigeria 1963* to *1968*. Department of Statistics, Northern Nigeria, op. cit., p. 209.
14 M. G. Smith, op. cit., p. 139.
15 A. Lubega, 'Financing and production of private houses in urban districts of Kampala (Uganda)', London, 1970, p. 60. Unpublished Ph.D. thesis.

Chapter 6

Production, cost, and financing of houses in Zaria walled city

Building materials and the construction of houses

The production and cost of residential buildings in Nigeria vary enormously as functions of the building materials, technology and techniques of construction used, the site's location, the complexity of the design, and the political as well as the socio-economic status of the client. In this chapter I will describe the construction, cost, and financing of traditional houses built with those indigenous materials and techniques which are still used by the overwhelming majority of the inhabitants in the walled city of Zaria. However, such modern building materials as cement, corrugated iron roofing sheets, and sawn wood, which are mainly used to modify and improve traditional buildings, will also be briefly discussed.

The construction of houses in Zaria walled city rests almost entirely with their occupants. Public initiative is unknown except for the delegation of building sites by the emir's administration discussed in Chapter 2, and for the occasional building loans allotted to better-paid local government employees. As shown in Chapter 4, the construction of residential buildings in the walled city of Zaria is a continuous process. Hence the availability of cheap building materials and labour is essential if co-residential kinship groups are to meet their demand for housing which is governed by changes in their size and composition. However, the increasing use of expensive modern building materials such as sawn wood, cement, and corrugated iron sheets indicates the rising standard of living which accompanies the changes from a subsistence economy to a monetary system.

Information on the production and consumption of building materials in Nigeria is haphazard and incomplete. However, some indication of the general trend can be obtained from data published by the Federal Office of Statistics and from various other studies carried out by universities and by commercial firms.

The demand for and the supply of traditional and modern building materials vary within Nigeria, since they depend on the type of construction and the level of building technology used in different parts of the country. Nigeria has an adequate supply of all the major raw materials required for the rapid development of industries to produce building materials both traditional and modern.

Earth and clay

Earth and clay have been used since time immemorial for the construction of walls and, in some areas, to cover the wooden structure of roofs. Today, the majority of houses in Nigeria still have mud walls built by locally trained craftsmen. Hence the demand for burned clay products is very small indeed. In 1969, the Industrial Survey of Nigeria listed only nine establishments with a total of 702 employees that specialized in this work.[1] Over half of the industry's gross output* of £N354,000 consisted of tiles, while bricks and pipes accounted for the rest. Other ceramic products such as sanitary porcelain ware and glazed tiles are imported.

Timber and wood products

Nigeria's wealth in timber is well known. Of the country's total land area of 923,740 sq. km, about one third is good forest land, but only about 10 per cent or 87,550 sq. km is classified as forest reserves. These forest reserves are subdivided into Savannah Forest with 68,760 sq. km or 79 per cent, and High or Equatorial Forest with 18,790 sq. km or 21 per cent.[2] It has been estimated that the volume of Nigeria's commercial timber totals about 70 million cu. m,

* Gross output is the sum of the values of products plus receipts for resale of goods, value of contract work, value of assets produced for own use, and work in process.

while the current removal of industrial wood stands at about 1.4 million cu. m per annum.[3]

In 1969 there were 65 sawmills with a total of 7,684 employees operating in the country.[4] The total production of lumber by the industry was estimated at 226,560 cu. m in 1967, of which 52,520 cu. m or 23 per cent were exported. Other exports that year included 331,570 cu. m of logs and 14,810 cu. m of plywood and veneers. (See Table A.6.1 on p. 356.) In 1967 the total export value of Nigerian timber was in the order of £N4.3 million.[5] Between 1963 and 1967 the average annual consumption of lumber within Nigeria was 176,000 cu. m of which about 140,000 cu. m or 80 per cent was used by the construction industry. (See Table A.6.2 on p. 356.) However, the quantity of *azara* beams cut from the stem of the deleb palm and used for the construction of traditional roof structures is unknown and therefore not included in Table A.6.2.

Cement and cement products

Effectively the Nigerian cement industry began in December 1957.[6] Between 1960 and 1966 the annual production of cement increased more than six-fold from 164,000 tons to 986,000 tons, while at the same time imports fell from 626,000 tons to 151,000 tons. Following the outbreak of the civil war in mid-1967, cement production fell to 565,000 tons in 1968; but with the restoration of peace early in 1970 demand for cement increased so sharply that 459,000 tons were imported that year. (See Table A.6.3 on p. 356.) According to the Industrial Survey of 1969 there were then three major cement plants in operation which together employed a total of 1,300 persons. Their total gross output was around £N6.1 million in 1969. Such associated industries as cement products were served by nine factories which produced mainly blocks and asbestos roofing sheets. This industry employed about 1,140 persons, paid £N307,000 in wages and salaries, and had a gross output of £N2.0 million in 1969.[7]

Iron and steel products

A detailed analysis of the consumption of iron and steel products in Nigeria was carried out by the British Steel Corporation in 1970.[8] Data cited here were extracted from this study. In 1970 Nigeria imported about 490,000 tons of steel, an amount which was nearly double its steel imports of 1965. (See Table A.6.4 on p. 357.) Throughout the 1970s no steel was produced in the country, but there was some re-rolling and steel processing which accounted for about 30 per cent of total steel imports. For example, in 1970 the two galvanizing plants at Ikeja in Lagos state had a combined output of approximately 40,000 tons of corrugated iron roofing sheets which represented nearly the total local supply, and about 75,000 tons of steel was re-rolled in various small plants as reinforcement bars and light gauge steel sections for the building industry. (See Table A.6.5 on p. 357.) It has been estimated that the Nigerian construction industry consumed about 214,000 tons or 44 per cent of the steel imports in 1970 followed by the oil industry (36 per cent), enamelware industry (7 per cent), and commercial vehicle and other industries which together accounted for about 13 per cent. Altogether iron and steel products formed the largest single item of imported building materials.

Zaria: type of construction

The construction of residential buildings in Zaria walled city is carried out by locally trained craftsmen who mainly use indigenous materials and traditional building techniques. Such modern building materials as corrugated iron roofing sheets and cement are largely employed for the protection and improvement of existing buildings rather than for the production of new and more permanent types of buildings. (See Picture 6.1.)

Mud walls

The building season, which starts when the rains have ceased in October, lasts until the beginning of March when water needed for house construction becomes increasingly scarce. Construction of a house will begin with the excavation of a sufficient quantity of earth from the nearest borrow-pit, unless this can be obtained from a collapsed hut within the compound to save the labour and transport costs. Near the building site the earth is stacked in heaps about one metre high, cut grass and water is added, and the earth is trampled several times until it has the consistency of mortar. This material is then moulded into bricks having the shape and size of half a rugby football; they are left to dry in the sun for at least two weeks. (See Picture 6.2.) Meanwhile the foundations of the building are dug to about half a metre in depth to penetrate below the loose top soil. The dried bricks are then laid in courses, each of which is covered with a layer of specially prepared mud mortar, until the walls reach the required height. (See Picture 6.3.) At ground-floor level the thickness of walls varies between 0.5 and 0.7 m for one-storey buildings, and 1 m or more for two-storey buildings.

Picture 6.1
New corrugated iron roof on top of existing building

Picture 6.2
Brick manufacturing

Picture 6.3
Construction of mud walls

Roof construction

There are basically two types of roof construction used in the walled city today: a thatched roof, and a mud roof which may be either flat or dome-shaped. Households in the upper income groups may also cover their mud roofs with corrugated iron sheets to protect the mud roof and walls from damage by rain. I shall denote structures of this latter type as corrugated iron roofs.

The rafters of a thatched roof consist either of bamboo or raphia palm stems in situ or, if the roof is small, of guinea corn stalks tied together on the ground with bands of straw and locally woven rope (*igiya*) before being lifted and placed in position. The thatch is bought in bundles approximately 1 m wide, but when unrolled they are at least 7 to 8 m long. These grass mats are wrapped around the frame of the roof, each layer being set 0.10 to 0.15 m above the previous one and bound to the rafters with a rope. The roof is then completed by tying a network of rope over the thatch to secure it from high winds. (See Picture 6.4.)

The beams needed for the construction of flat or vaulted mud roofs are cut by local craftsmen from the stem of the deleb palm (*Borassus aethiopum*; Hausa, *giginya*) which is selected because of its resistance to ter-

Picture 6.4
Underside of a conical thatched roof construction

mites and white ants. The average size of these beams is 0.05 × 0.10 × 2.40 m. Flat mud roofs are constructed mainly for rectangular rooms not larger than 3 × 4 m. To this end the roof beams of deleb palm are set side by side diagonally across the corners of the wall, and extended progressively inward until the roof is closed. (See Picture 6.5; also Diagram A.6.1 on p. 362.) A grass mat is spread over the beams and covered first with a layer of mud mortar approximately 0.05 m thick, and then by another layer of earth about 0.10 to 0.15 m deep. The external surfaces of the roof and walls are finished with a thin layer of waterproofing plaster made of mud mortar mixed with *katsi* which is a binding substance produced by the dyeing trade, or with *makuba* made from the fruit pod of the locust bean tree (*Parkia filicoidea*; Hausa, *dorawa*). Either plaster will keep the roof and walls reasonably waterproof for at least one year.[9]

Larger rooms are covered with mud domes supported by wooden arches sprung from opposing walls. After the arches have been erected, the open bays are laid out with beams and covered with mud as described above. (See Picture 6.6.) All mud roofs are drained by spouts made from old petrol tins which project down and outwards sufficiently to throw the rainwater well away from the base of the walls. One type of roof which has not been mentioned so far is the thin shell roof structure covered with thatch. The method of construction is similar to that used for granaries, but is no longer practised in the walled city of Zaria.

Picture 6.5
Underside of a flat mud roof construction

Picture 6.6
Underside of vaulted mud roof construction showing ribs

The internal walls of rooms are finished with an additional layer of smooth mud plaster overlaid with a layer of red mud mixed with fine sand which provides a good base for whitewash. The floor of a room is levelled, and compacted. In about half of the rooms surveyed the floor was finished with a layer of cement screed or soil-cement between 0.03 and 0.05 m thick.[10] Window openings average 0.40 × 0.40 m, and are covered with wooden shutters fixed with leather strips to the frame, while doors usually consist of planks or wooden frames covered with a sheet of corrugated iron. Doors are usually fixed to the frame with hinges.

The building trade

The building trade in the walled city of Zaria has an established tradition and status. Legend has it that Baban Gwani, Malam Mikaila a local craftsman who built the mosque in Zaria in the reign of Abdulkarim sometime between 1834 and 1846, was subsequently invited to build a mosque in Birnin Gwari about 100 km west of Zaria, on completion of which the local emir had him seized and executed so that no other mosque would ever be built to equal the one in Birnin Gwari.[11] To this day the descendants of Baban Gwani are the leading family of builders in the walled city and the chief builder *sarkin magina* is chosen by the adult male members of the family from the wider kinship group.

According to the 1968 local tax file there were 140 builders living in the walled city of Zaria. The majority of them still see the construction of houses as an inherited craft and instruct only their own children.

The most common way of building a house is to employ one of these builders, who will recruit several assistants and labourers from the walled city or nearby villages according to the size of the contract. Self-help in house building is rarely practised in the city, although family members frequently assist with the transport of building materials and the finishing of interior walls and floors.

The construction of a building with one or two rooms is normally completed within one building season. For example, out of 227 rooms built between 1963 and 1968 in the compounds surveyed, 174 rooms or 77 per cent were completed within one building season, and 53 rooms or 23 per cent, all of which had a mud roof, took a second year to complete. Such improvements as an additional corrugated iron roof or the rendering of mud walls with cement plaster were carried out after the household head had saved or borrowed some money to buy the required building materials. Table A.6.6 on p. 358 shows that of 109 corrugated iron roofs built between 1963 and 1968, 75 or 69 per cent were constructed on mud-roofed rooms which had been completed at least two building seasons earlier. The survey included six compounds built entirely between 1963 and 1968. In all these compounds the stages of construction were carried out according to a similar pattern. It took on average one building season to build the compound wall, the *zaure* or entrance hut and at least two rooms for the owner to live in. Other rooms were later added as the need arose.

Sample survey

The type of construction discussed in the first part of this chapter and the quantitative use of modern building material such as corrugated iron roofing sheets and cement in 77 surveyed compounds will be analysed below. Furthermore, I want to illustrate some structural changes which occurred in these compounds between December 1963 and November 1968. This discussion will combine data from the aerial survey of the walled city carried out on 17 December 1963 and from my own survey of May to November 1968. Each individual compound selected for study was examined carefully on the aerial photographs before a skeleton ground-plan 1:100 was drawn with the help of an epidiascope. These plans provided the base for measurements that were subsequently made within the compounds. Any changes which had occurred in these compounds were thus immediately noticed and discussed with the compound head. This procedure enabled me to obtain a complete picture of structural changes in these compounds over a period of five years.

Structural changes of compounds

The 77 compounds selected for study contained 1,227 rooms with a total area of 10,164 sq. m.* All 1,227 rooms had mud walls. Between 17 December 1963 and 1 November 1968, which marks the end of the survey in Zaria, a total of 227 new rooms were built in these compounds, while at the same time 144 rooms in use in 1963 had disappeared or were abandoned and decaying at the time

* This does not include 28 animal pens with a total area of 157.1 sq. m and 29 lavatories and/or bathrooms with 152.3 sq. m.

of the interviews. Thus the total net increase of rooms over nearly five years was 83 or 7.3 per cent which represents an overall growth rate of 1.5 per cent per annum. This figure corresponds very closely with the estimated overall annual increase of the population in the walled city which was shown to be in the region of 1.5 per cent per annum (see p. 22). Thus the increase of the population corresponds with the increase of rooms/houses in the area under investigation and could be regarded as a typical feature of traditional societies.

I divided the walled city into two districts: first, the area surrounding the palace and, second, the area around the market. Both areas together contained between 80 and 90 per cent of all compounds in the walled city. As shown in Table A.6.6 on p. 358, the difference between the palace area and the market area is striking. It appears that in the former area the annual growth rate of rooms was 3.2 per cent between December 1963 and November 1968, while in the latter area there was hardly any change at all, with 69 rooms decaying and 74 new ones, the annual growth rate being merely 0.2 per cent. Perhaps the simplest explanation is the lack of suitable land for further development in the densely populated market area, while the palace area contains ample land for further building.

The roof is an important structural part of any building. The local use of thatch, mud, or corrugated iron sheets reflects to some extent the economic position of its owner. Some 698 rooms or 57.0 per cent of the total rooms surveyed were covered with mud roofs, by far the most common type. In the five years preceding my survey, 133 new rooms with mud roofs had been built, while another 40 rooms had their roof structure converted from thatch to mud. A further 75 mud-roofed rooms were covered with corrugated iron roofing sheets, and seven mud roofs were converted to ceilings on the construction of upstairs rooms. Only 13 rooms with mud roofs had disappeared or were decaying at the time of my study. Thus the total net increase of mud-roofed rooms over the five-year period was 78 or 12.6 per cent which represents an annual growth rate of 2.6 per cent.

The total number of rooms with thatched roofs was 361 or 29.4 per cent in 1968. From 1963 to 1968, 60 new rooms with thatch were built, while at the same time 131 rooms with such roofs had disappeared and 40 rooms already mentioned earlier were converted from thatch into mud roofs. This gives a net decline of 111 thatch-roofed rooms or 23.5 per cent over these years, averaging a decrease of 4.8 per cent per annum.

The number of corrugated iron roofs increased nearly

four-fold from 39 rooms in 1963 to 148 rooms in 1968, giving an average annual growth rate of 57.3 per cent, which is remarkably clear evidence of changing local building standards and techniques. Although the corrugated iron roof was by far the most rapidly increasing type of roof within the walled city, it is still restricted to the middle and high income groups. (For more detailed information see Table A.6.6 on p. 358.)

There are other indications that the use of the corrugated iron roof, which is still regarded by the community as a status symbol, will continue to increase in the near future. When asked 'What improvement do you think the compound most needs?', 31 out of 77 compound heads or 40 per cent answered spontaneously 'A corrugated iron roof', followed by 15 compound heads or 19 per cent who cited more sleeping rooms, nine or 12 per cent who favoured the rendering of mud walls with cement plaster, and seven or 9 per cent who wanted to change thatched into mud roofs. Another twelve compound heads gave various other answers, while two did not respond, and one was satisfied. (See Table A.6.7 on p. 359.) A more detailed study of the 31 compound heads who wanted corrugated iron roofs revealed that the majority belonged to the middle income group with incomes of 300 to 999 shillings per month, and lived in compounds with predominantly mud-roofed rooms.

The use of cement for interior floors and for outside working platforms had also increased. Between 1963 and 1968 the area of cement floors nearly doubled from 2,852 sq. m to 5,477 sq. m. At the same time outdoor working platforms in these compounds increased by 58.5 per cent from a total of 1,339 sq. m to 2,122 sq. m, while the number of rooms rendered with cement plaster on at least one outside wall rose from 117 to 297. This substantial increase in the use of cement screed and plaster was unevenly distributed. To show the distribution and use of cement, I have classified these compounds into four groups according to type of roofs. It was clear that compound heads who could afford to build mud or corrugated iron roofed rooms would also be the most likely to spend more money on cement for floors and outside working platforms. Table 6.1 shows that the floor area covered with cement screed increased proportionately to the total floor area from 87.1 sq. m or 16.6 per cent in compounds with thatched roofs only to 2,083.4 sq. m or 68.7 per cent in compounds with predominantly mud and corrugated iron roofs. Likewise, the total area covered with cement screed (floor area and outside working platforms) increased from 178.0 sq. m, or 2.6 sq. m per person, in compounds with

Table 6.1 Distribution of cement area in four groups of compounds

Column	1	2	3	4	5	6	7	8	9
	No. of compounds	No. of rooms	Total floor area in sq. m	Cement floor in sq. m	Cement floor as % of total floor area	Cement platforms in sq. m	Total cement area in sq. m	No. of persons	Cement area per person in sq. m
1 Compounds with thatched roof only	6	67	523.1	87.1	16.6	90.9	178.0	69	2.6
2 Compounds with thatched and mud roofs	34	601	4,809.3	2,140.5	44.5	781.2	2,921.7	568	5.1
3 Compounds with mud roof only	15	216	1,797.0	1,166.4	64.9	402.4	1,568.8	166	9.5
4 Compounds with thatched, mud, and corrugated iron roofs	22	343	3,034.6	2,083.4	68.7	847.1	2,930.5	264	11.1
Total	77	1,227	10,164.0	5,477.4	53.9	2,121.6	7,599.0	1,067	7.1

thatched roofs to 2,930.5 sq. m, or 11.1 sq. m per person, in 'group 4' compounds. From the above discussion it becomes obvious that the use of modern building materials such as sawn wood, cement, and corrugated iron or asbestos cement roofing sheets will play an increasing role in the production and improvement of traditional and semi-traditional housing in the country.

Age and duration of houses

During the survey of compounds, information on the ages of 967 rooms were collected, whereas the ages of 299 rooms or 23.6 per cent of the total were uncertain or unknown and had to be omitted. As far as possible the data collected for these rooms were checked against information obtained on the development and change of co-residential kinship groups discussed in Chapter 4. Rooms built before 1940 were grouped together because it proved too difficult to collect sufficient additional information to check their precise age. Unfortunately the ages of most of the 144 rooms which had disappeared or been abandoned over the last five years were unknown, but this was so because most of these rooms had been built before the present generation of compound heads were born. In view of these difficulties it was not possible to construct life tables for buildings, since the data needed for such life tables include not only a census of the age distribution of occupied rooms but also records of the ages and numbers of rooms which have disappeared over a given period of time. Lack of the latter information is regrettable because life tables of various types of buildings could supply much-needed data on the life expectancy of a given house occupied for a known number of years. It is hoped that in future the collection of more detailed information may provide the data necessary for the construction of such life tables.

Graph 6.1 presents the age distribution of 967 rooms plotted against their cumulative percentage. It shows that about one fifth of the occupied rooms are older than 30 years and that the median age of these rooms is 11.8 years. The curve indicates that during the first years after completion, the change of a room being abandoned or even demolished is relatively small. However, in later years the risk naturally increases as more sleeping rooms are abandoned and collapse following their owner's death, until only those remain such as entrance huts (*zauruka* and/or *shigifu*) or other commonly used rooms which serve the whole compound population. These latter

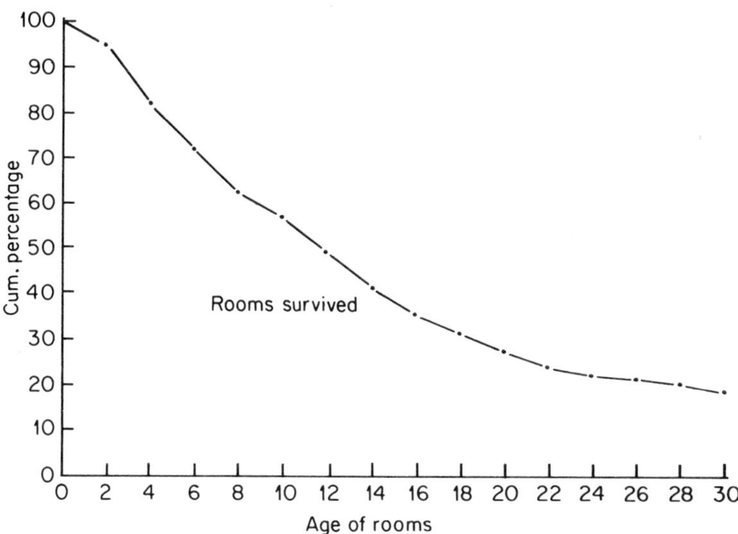

Graph 6.1
Age distribution of rooms

rooms, being repaired frequently, have much longer life spans and accordingly account for the majority of rooms at the tail end of the curve. (See also Table A.6.8 on p. 359.)

Thus far we have confined our attention almost exclusively to the age distribution of rooms and little has been said about the various environmental and social factors which influence the lifetime of rooms. The impermanence of earth used for the construction of walls and roofs and the tropical climate are the most important environmental factors which determine the lifetime of rooms. Averages for the durability of various roof types given below are tentative figures, based on information obtained from several local building contractors and my own observations in the surveyed compounds. The lifetime of a thatched roof is between 8 and 10 years (and 15-year-old thatched roofs are not unknown) unless it is eaten by termites or white ants. Regular annual maintenance may prolong its useful life by a few years. A mud roof, on the other hand, may last for 20 or even 30 years, depending in the first place on the soundness of its construction, and on the care taken regularly to replace the plaster that waterproofs it. A corrugated iron roof set on top of a mud roof will prolong the lifetime of the latter type even further. However, it must be stressed again that because of the very nature of the building materials and the tropical climate regular annual maintenance is decisive in determining the lifetime of any part of a building.

Among the social factors which influence the lifetime of buildings, the most important is no doubt the custom that obliges Hausa families to abandon a room after the owner's death. The dead man's hut, no longer maintained, collapses within two or three years, thereby providing space and raw material (earth) for new development. However, the age of abandoned huts is not a decisive factor here, as one example shows. After the death of one compound head's mother, her hut, which was then only three years old, was abandoned and left to collapse. But there were also a number of cases where the lifetime of a deceased person's hut had been prolonged by adapting it to new uses such as kitchen, general store room, or animal pen. It was also observed that in these compounds 96 rooms or 7.2 per cent of the total were empty at the time of my survey. Most of these rooms had formerly been occupied by the divorced wives of the compound heads, all of whom left their compounds on divorce. Thus although in 1968 the majority of these rooms were in good repair and suitable for new wives, failing remarriage many compound heads would probably allow these rooms to decay or replace them with new huts for other family members.

Cost of building

In the final part of this chapter I will first discuss the level of construction cost followed by the method of financing these building activities, both based on the data obtained from my survey of 77 compounds in the walled city of Zaria.

The cost of building covers a whole range of different activities which may be divided into five major categories as follows:

1 cost of construction (completed 1963–1968),
2 cost of buildings under construction,
3 cost of improvement,
4 cost of maintenance and repair, and
5 cost of such miscellaneous constructions as granaries and wells.

As mentioned elsewhere, the construction of new huts inside compounds is a continuous process which reflects the growth or decline of co-residential kinship groups. This pattern of development made it necessary for me to restrict my investigation on building cost within the compounds surveyed to a five-year period from December 1963 to November 1968. During this period a total of 227 new rooms were constructed within these compounds while 115 rooms were entirely re-roofed with different materials, a change I have classified as improvement.

Table 6.2 shows that of the total adjusted building

Table 6.2 Costs of construction in 77 surveyed compounds, 1963–1968

Column	1	2	3	4	5	Pilot Scheme[b] 6	7
	No. of rooms	Sq. m	Cost in shillings	Shillings per sq. m floor area	% of cost adjusted	Material cost only, sq. m	Material and labour cost, sq. m
New construction (completed)							
Thatch-roofed rooms	60	426.0	10,175	23.9		17.7	38.2
Mud-roofed rooms	133	990.0	40,244	40.6		30.2	54.0
C. iron roofed rooms	34	356.5	27,930	78.3		56.7	89.7
Compound walls			1,565				
Subtotal	227	1,772.5	79,914		44.4		
Improvement on existing buildings							
Change thatch to mud roof	40	309.8	5,893	19.0		16.0	24.9
C. iron roof on top of mud roof	75	663.9	22,441	33.8		26.5	35.7
Cement floor & platforms			13,602				
Electricity installed (16)			5,163				
Pipe-borne water installed (8)			2,845				
Subtotal	115	973.7	49,944		27.7		
Maintenance and repair							
Includes *inter alia* roofs, walls, doors, windows, cement plaster, painting, etc.			For details see Table 6.4.				
Subtotal (1966–1968, actual)			25,493				
Adjusted sub-total, 1963–1968[a]			42,488		23.6		
Buildings under construction							
Rooms: walls completed	17	129.5	707				
Rooms: mud roof completed	13	106.7	2,697				
Rooms: c. iron roof completed	9	72.4	929				
Subtotal	39	308.6	4,333		2.4		
Miscellaneous construction							
Includes *inter alia* wells, pit-latrines, bathrooms, stables, & granaries							
Subtotal			3,392		1.9		
Total expenditure, actual			163,076				
Total expenditure, adjusted			180,071		100.0		

[a] $\frac{25{,}493}{3} \times 5 = 42{,}488$ shillings. [b] See Table A.6.9 on p. 360.

expenditure of about 180,000 shillings or £N9,000, 44.4 per cent was spent on new construction, 27.7 per cent on improvements of existing buildings, 23.6 per cent on repair, 2.4 per cent on buildings under construction, and 1.9 per cent on miscellaneous construction.

Cost of new construction

During the five-year period from 1963 to 1968, 277 rooms with a total floor area of 1,772 sq. m were built in 52 out of 77 compounds surveyed. The recorded cost of construction for these rooms was 79,914 shillings (£N3,995) or 44.4 per cent of the total expenditure on buildings. As shown in column 4 in Table 6.2, the average cost per square metre for a room with a thatched roof was 23.9 shillings, for one with a mud roof 40.6 shillings, and for a room with a corrugated iron roof set on top of a domed mud roof 78.3 shillings.

Detailed studies of construction costs for a typical two-roomed house (16.0 sq. m floor area) with mud walls and three different roof types – i.e. thatch, mud, and corrugated iron sheets set on top of a domed or flat mud roof – were made with the help of two local builders. (See Table A.6.9 on p. 360.) Two sets of figures were collected, first, for the cost of materials only, expressed in shillings per square metre, the minimum cost (see column 6, Table 6.2); and second, for the total cost for materials and labour per square metre, which represents the maximum cost (see column 7, Table 6.2). Comparison of the data obtained from the survey and from this independent case study revealed that the survey data tabulated in column 4 (Table 6.2) are lower than the maximum cost per square metre in column 7 established by the case study. This confirms a well-known fact that most compound heads assist the builder throughout the construction period in order to keep the labour costs down.

A breakdown of cost by element of building for the typical two-roomed house discussed above is given in Table 6.3. That table presents costs for three different types of roof, the doors, windows, and finishings being of the same standard.

The considerable differences in the proportionate costs of building elements for these rooms reflect the differing expenditures for building materials on each. Expressed as percentages of total cost, building materials for a room roofed with thatch accounted for 46 per cent of the total cost, for a room roofed with mud 56 per cent, and for a room roofed with corrugated iron sheets on top of a mud roof 63 per cent (see Table A.6.9 on p. 360).

Table 6.3 Breakdown of cost by element of building in percentages[a]

Element of building	Thatch-roofed rooms	Mud-roofed rooms	C. iron roofed rooms
Sub & super structure	69.8	78.6	87.1
Doors and windows	7.3	5.2	3.1
Finishes	22.9	16.2	9.8
Total	100.0	100.0	100.0

[a]See Table A.6.9 on p. 360.

Altogether 39 rooms with a total floor area of 309 sq. m were under construction at the time of interview. The eleven compound heads who had undertaken these constructions paid 4,330 shillings or £N217 which represents about 2.4 per cent of the total expenditure on buildings.

Cost of improvements

The cost of improvements – which includes *inter alia* the change of roof structures from thatch to mud or the fixing of a corrugated iron roof on top of a mud roof, as well as new cement floors and the installation of piped water and/or an electricity supply – amounted to 49,940 shillings (£N2,497) or 27.7 per cent of the total expenditure on buildings. More detailed data on these improvement expenditures revealed that 22,440 shillings (£N1,122) or 45.0 per cent was spent on corrugated iron roofs, followed by cement screed and plaster with 27.2 per cent, changes from thatched to mud roofs 11.8 per cent, and the installation of piped water and an electricity supply 10.3 and 5.7 per cent respectively.

Cost of maintenance and repair

The adjusted cost of maintenance and repair accounted for 42,490 shillings (£N2,215) or 23.6 per cent of the total building expenditure. In spite of repeated efforts, it proved impossible to collect enough reliable data on maintenance and repair costs for the years 1964 and 1965, simply because most household heads could not remember the details. In contrast, such expenditures for the three years from 1966 to 1968 were recalled with confidence. The detailed data collected on this item show clearly the recurrent tendency of this kind of expenditure. Thus, after checking all available information I have assumed that repair and maintenance costs for the two incompletely documented years, 1964 and 1965 were not substantially different from the three later years and have made the necessary adjustments to cover the whole period from 1963 to 1968.

Because of their importance, the total actual maintenance and repair costs of 25,500 shillings or £N1,275 merit further attention. (See Table 6.4.) It is noteworthy that slightly under one third of the total maintenance cost was absorbed by repair work on compound walls. Repair cost for mud roofs, which represent over half of all roof types in the compounds surveyed, was 22.6 per cent of the total maintenance cost, while repairs to thatched roofs account for 21.5 per cent. The relatively high maintenance cost of thatched roofs is of interest since in contrast to mud roofs, the number of thatched roofs has steadily declined from 472 rooms or 41.3 per cent of total roof types in December 1963 to 361 rooms or 29.4 per cent in November 1968. Thus these data suggest that, while the thatched roof is relatively cheap to build, it is also rather expensive to maintain.

Table 6.4 Actual maintenance cost by element of building, 1966–1968

Element of building	Shillings	%
Compound walls	8,243	32.4
Mud roofs	5,766	22.6
Thatched roofs	5,486	21.5
Mud plaster on housewalls	3,979	15.6
Cement platforms and plaster	943	3.7
Painting and whitewash	554	2.2
Doors and shutters	411	1.6
Other repairs	111	0.4
Total	25,493	100.0

Financing of private houses

The following analysis is intended to show how houses included in the sample survey were financed. The investigation is again limited to the five-year period from December 1963 to November 1968. The two main sources of housing finance are personal sources and institutional sources.

Personal sources

Personal sources can be divided into three interrelated groups:

1 self-financing from income and savings,
2 contributions from family members and friends, and
3 funds from social security, gratuities or pensions.

Out of the 227 rooms built during the period under study, 182 or 80.2 per cent were either partly or wholly financed by 50 compound heads in whose compounds they were built, while the remaining 45 rooms or 19.8 per cent were financed by 23 dependent or semi-dependent household heads.

Self-financing from income and savings played an important part in house building at Zaria. As shown in Table A.6.11 on p. 364, about 84.0 per cent of the total expenditure on building between 1963 and 1968 came from personal income and savings of household heads. Altogether 45 compound heads, or 58.4 per cent of the total, had at one time or another saved amounts that ranged from £N15 to £N95 to finance building, while 29 compound heads or 37.7 per cent had never saved to this end, and three or 3.9 per cent did not respond.

Contributions from family members and friends have been subdivided into gifts and loans. During the five-year period from 1963 to 1968, eleven loans totalling 8,170 shillings or £N409 were made by private persons or private saving societies to eleven compound heads who used the money mainly for new construction. In Table 6.5 the creditors of these loans are arranged in order of importance.

Gifts received to finance either new construction, improvements, or repairs amounted to 17,820 shillings or £N891, and came mainly from close relatives and friends of the compound head. All 25 contributors lived outside the compound concerned. However, it is highly unlikely

Table 6.5 Types of creditors of private building loans

	No. of loans	Shillings	%
Personal friends of compound head	5	4,850	59.4
Private saving societies	4	2,200	26.9
Close relatives of compound head	2	1,120	13.7
Total	11	8,170	100.0

that this represents all instances of such help, as several compound heads were rather reluctant to speak freely on this topic and only when pressed hard admitted having received some aid. The sum received from family members and friends, including gifts and loans, amounted to 25,990 shillings (£N1,300) or 14.4 per cent of the total building expenditure from 1963 to 1968.

Contributions from employers encountered in my survey were relatively small and involved only three compound heads, all of whom were former employees of the local government. These three compound heads received gratuities totalling £N335 which were partly used for the construction of new buildings or to improve old ones.

The private saving societies (*adashi*) are worth citing because they are of general interest. The modern form of these saving societies probably originated among Ibo and Yoruba immigrants employed in Northern Nigeria by government, industry, and commerce. Most of these private saving societies have only a few members who, in return for a regular weekly or monthly subscription, receive in turn the total contributions, and often use this to buy household goods, to meet emergencies, to pay debts, or, as here, to finance new buildings as well as improvements on old buildings.

Institutional sources

Institutional sources of funds for housing include all building loans and grants made by the local government, housing corporations, and banks. From 1963 to 1968 only two compound heads received building loans and they totalled £N136. The two loans in question were made by the Zaria Native Authority to members of its staff at the generous interest rate of 2½ per cent. These are obviously special loans which are not available to the general public but are closely tied to the position and influence of the beneficiary. One additional grant of £N14 was given to one employee of the local police force who used the money to start the construction of a hut for himself. The two loans and one grant covered about 1.7 per cent of the total building expenditure between 1963 and 1968.

It is not surprising that loans from financial institutions such as housing corporations, building and/or cooperative housing societies, commerical banks, and insurance companies are conspicuously absent in the walled city of Zaria. This is due to three reasons. The first is the insistence of all Nigerian finance institutions, modelled on Western prototypes, that the borrower should have a clear title to the land intended for development. Land owned by lineages or sections of lineages is, in the case of mortgage default, regarded as a security risk.[12] (Most land in Zaria walled city is in the hands of lineages.) The second reason is the demand of such agencies that the mortgagee should use only such permanent building materials as concrete blocks and corrugated iron or asbestos cement roofing sheets for any construction financed by a mortgage loan[13]; and the third reason is the low average income of household heads in Zaria walled city. For example, as about 69 per cent of the sample households earned less than £N180 per annum, they were automatically excluded from funds distributed by the Northern Nigeria Housing Corporation. Hence housing loans from institutional sources are generally not available to the inhabitants of the walled city, who are thus left entirely to their own meagre financial resources as far as housing is concerned.

In short, between 1963 and 1968, a total sum of about £N9,000 was spent by 77 compound heads and various other dependent or semi-dependent household heads on new construction, improvement, and maintenance of their compounds. About 84 per cent of this money came from the personal savings and income of household heads, over 14 per cent came from loans and gifts made by family members and friends, while the rest – about 2 per cent – came from official loans and/or grants.

Internal subsidy

Thus far we have confined our attention almost exclusively to private and institutional resources for housing finance which may be available to compound heads for building purposes, and little has been said about internal subsidy. By internal subsidy I mean the provision of money, building materials, or new rooms for close relatives living inside the compound concerned. This may include rooms built by a compound head for his newly married son or for any other dependent individual or semi-dependent family in need, as well as the opposite – for example, the construction of a room by a well-to-do son of his ageing father. In these terms, of the 182 rooms* built between December 1963 and November 1968, 42 rooms or 18.5 per cent were fully or partly subsidized by the compound head and given to dependent families

* Forty-five rooms were built and paid for by dependent or semi-dependent household heads and were not subsidized by the compound head. See Table A.6.12 on p. 365.

living in the compound concerned, while another six rooms were fully or partly subsidized by five dependent or semi-dependent household heads and given to three compound heads and two dependent families. (See Table A.6.12 on p. 365.)

Diagram 6.1 illustrates the main characteristics of internal subsidies towards new construction made by various household heads during the five-year period from December 1963 to November 1968.

It will be noted that twelve rooms costing a total of 3,920 shillings were built and paid for by compound heads for their newly married sons. In addition, two compound heads also built three rooms for the families of full brothers' sons. Of the remaining six fully subsidized rooms four went to various other relatives, while two rooms were paid for by the son and the full brother's son of two compound heads.

It is interesting to observe that out of 27 partly financed rooms 17 belong to families of the compound heads' full and half brothers, while three rooms each were occupied by one compound head's mother's brother's family and the families of two compound head's full sisters' sons. A further three rooms were partly financed by the sons of two compound heads, and one by the compound head's full brother who shared the cost with his son.

In closing I should stress that the information collected covers only a relatively short period (1963–1968) and thus represents only a small proportion of the total internal subsidy that any compound head might give or receive during his lifetime.

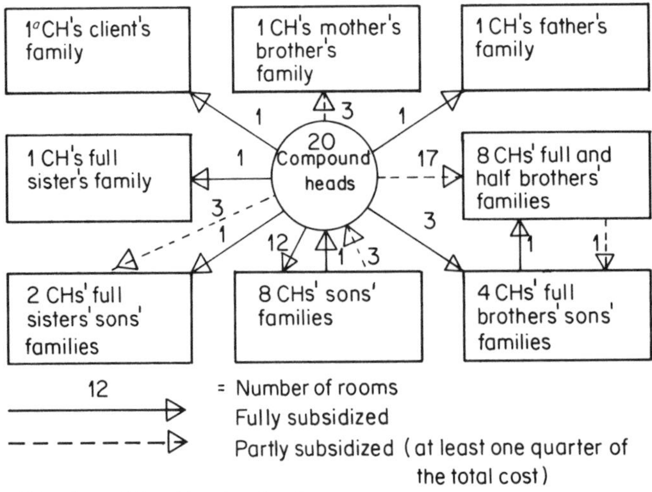

Diagram 6.1
Distribution of internal subsidy

Notes and references

1 Federal Office of Statistics, Nigeria, *Annual Abstract of Statistics 1971*, Lagos, 1972, p. 41. Only establishments with ten or more employees.

2 L. Okigbo, *Sawmill Industry in Nigeria*, Ibadan, 1964, p. 13.

3 Federal Ministry of Information, Nigeria, *Second National Development Plan 1970/4*, Lagos, 1970, p. 61.

4 Federal Office of Statistics, Nigeria, op. cit., p. 41. Only establishments with ten or more employees.

5 Organization for Economic Co-operation and Development (OECD), *Tropical Timber*, Paris, 1969, p. 152.

6 S. U. Ugoh, 'The Nigerian cement industry', *Journal of Economic and Social Studies* (Ibadan), **8** (1), 1966, pp. 97–111.

7 Federal Office of Statistics, Nigeria, op. cit., p. 48.

8 British Steel Corporation, 'Nigeria: Economic prospects and steel import potentials 1975' London, 1970. Unpublished report compiled by Ffowcs Williams, I. A. Market Research Officer, BSC.

9 F. A. Daldy, 'Temporary buildings in Northern Nigeria', Technical Paper No. 10, Public Works Department, Lagos, 1945, pp. 20–22.

10 Department of Economic and Social Affairs, United Nations, *Soil-Cement, its Use in Building*, New York, 1964, pp. 43–49.

11 J. C. Moughtin, 'The Friday Mosque, Zaria City' *Savanna, A Journal of the Environmental and Social Sciences* (Ahmadu Bello University, Zaria), **1** (2), December 1972.

12 Native Authority Housing Corporation, Northern Region of Nigeria, *First Annual Report . . . 1961*, Kaduna, 1962. Housing Loan Rules, No. 38 of 1960 §7 Section a., p. 12.

13 Native Authority Housing Corporation, Northern Region of Nigeria, *Second Annual Report 1962/63*, Kaduna, 1963, p. 13.

Part II

IBADAN

Chapter 7

Context

Environmental setting

Geography and climate

Ibadan, latitude 7° 26′ north, longitude 3° 54′ east, and about 200 m above sea-level, lies within the humid high forest zone of Nigeria. Owing to the prevalent system of shifting cultivation, in which bush is cleared by fire, virtually no virgin forest remains around Ibadan. The crops grown by farmers in the region include *inter alia* cocoa and oil-palm produce for export, kola, yams, maize, cassava, rice, oranges, bananas, pepper, and various vegetables for the home market.[1]

Temperatures in Ibadan vary from an average daily maximum of 33.9 °C in February and March to an average daily minimum of 20.6 °C in August and December. Relative humidity is high throughout the year, ranging from an average daily maximum of 98 per cent at 6.30 a.m. GMT in October, to an average daily minimum of 49 per cent in February at 12.30 p.m. GMT.[2] The mean annual rainfall over the period 1905 to 1952 was 1.230 mm and most rain falls between March and October. However, there is a slight break in rainfall at mid-summer which is called the 'little dry season', and in August rainfall averages 74 mm, as against 132 mm for July and 170 mm for September.[3] (See Diagram A.7.1 on p. 367.)

For most of the year, the prevailing winds blow from the

south-west, but in the harmattan season, December to February, as the tropical continental air mass moves south, they blow from the north and create a dry season.

Topographical features*

Ibadan is dominated by a range of hills that runs from north to south. The highest point on this range, the Eleiyele Hill, stands over 270 m above sea-level and about 60 m above the surrounding countryside. The contemporary city of Ibadan is built around the southern slope of the Aremo ridge and stretches down to the flood plains of the Ogunpa and Kudeti streams, a position which no doubt had strategic advantages that attracted the early settlers. (See Map A.7.1 on p. 369.)

Historical background

Unlike Zaria, Ibadan is a city of comparatively recent origin, and began as a war encampment for the Yoruba military forces in the early nineteenth century.

According to legend, the first known inhabitants in the area were refugees from neighbouring communities, and only after Lagelu, a chief and warrior from Ile-Ife, joined them was the first settlement called Eba-Odan (near the grassland) founded.[4] This settlement was soon destroyed;[5] but Lagelu, who survived the event, built a new village on a site near the central city market at Oja Iba.

By the beginning of the nineteenth century, the Oyo Empire, which covered an area reaching from Katunga (old Oyo) in the north to the Bight of Benin in the south, and which had enjoyed peace and stability for about 200 years, was tottering to its end. (See Map A.7.3 on p. 371.) Its subsequent collapse was due to internal rebellion, inter-tribal wars, and invasions of Fulani horsemen from the north who finally captured Ilorin in the early 1820s and then used it as their headquarters for attacks on other Yoruba settlements.[6]

Many Yoruba towns in the northern part of the Oyo Empire were destroyed by the Fulani forces, for example old Oyo in 1837, and an increasing flood of refugees fled south, with the result that the remaining part of the empire was soon plunged into civil war. Slave raiding between the various independent Yoruba kingdoms in

* The main topographical features of Nigeria have been sketched in Chapter 1 on p. 3.

the south, encouraged by Ijebu, sparked off the Owu war c. 1813.[7] The combined forces of the Ife and Ijebu, joined by Yoruba refugees from Oyo to the north, completely destroyed the town of Owu c. 1823.[8] After its victory the army routed many Egba towns which gave active support to Owu. It was during this campaign that the allied army chose Ibadan, an Egba village, as their camp.[9] What began as a war encampment in the mid-1820s soon became a permanent settlement, and so the present city of Ibadan came into existence.

Precolonial Ibadan, 1829–1893

The allied army that settled at Ibadan comprised the Yoruba from Ife and Oyo who occupied the area around Oja Iba central market and Oke Mapo, the Ijebu who built their houses in an area known today as Isale Ijebu, and the remaining Egba who resided at Iye Osa.[10]

This heterogeneous population was soon at loggerheads. Open hostilities broke out among the chiefs of these segments and resulted in the expulsion of Maye, the Ife army commander who had so far dominated the town, by the numerically stronger Oyo under Oluyole who thenceforward ruled the city, thus identifying Ibadan as a predominantly Oyo–Yoruba town which recognized the Alafin of Oyo as their overlord.[11] With Oluyole in power, an even greater number of Oyo refugees flocked to the city. By 1840 the Ibadan army under Balogun* Oderinlo was strong enough to inflict a decisive defeat on the Fulani forces at Oshogbo, which effectively checked their advances into Yorubaland.[12] The rapidly growing military power of Ibadan during the following two decades promoted an expansionist policy under Balogun Ibikunle who duly brought the Ekiti country, south of the city, under the control of Ibadan. (See Map A.7.3 on p. 371.)

Much of the evidence of Ibadan's history at this period is based on journals and letters written by the Reverend David Hinderer of the Church Missionary Society (CMS) who arrived in the city in 1851 (see Picture A.7.1 on page 368).[13] By 1858 Ibadan had so expanded that it was necessary to build a new town wall, and this extension is known today as Ibikunle's wall.[14] The new wall, which had four main gates, measured about 17.6 km in circumference and enclosed an area of approximately 2,240 hectares.

* Title of the commander-in-chief of the Ibadan army.

With the Ekiti and their country under Ibadan's control its only remaining challenger for effective leadership of the Oyo Yoruba was Ijaye, a town which had so far shared with Ibadan the burden of defending the southern Oyo territories. But with the destruction of Ijaye by a Yoruba army in 1862, Ibadan emerged as the leading military power in Yorubaland.[15] Other independent Yoruba kingdoms, particularly the Ijebu and Egba of Abeokuta due south of Ibadan, were alarmed by these developments which upset the balance of power in Ibadan's favour. Fear of Ibadan's growing military and economic power prompted the Egba and Ijebu kingdoms, which were ideally situated between Ibadan and the coast, to cut Ibadan's trade routes and block its supply of arms from Porto Novo and Lagos, thus initiating a war which lasted more than 16 years and which was only resolved by the intervention of the British colonial government at Lagos, when a peace treaty was signed in August 1893.

Before discussing the city under British rule it is necessary to outline briefly the political system of pre-colonial Ibadan, as this is relevant to the city's later development.[16]

Following the fierce power struggle in its early days, Oluyole, who ruled Ibadan for about twenty years until his death in 1847, established a system of government which persisted until the British occupation in 1893 and beyond. (See Table A.7.1 on p. 369.) At the head of the government was the *Bale** (literally, father of the town) and the *Balogun* (commander-in-chief of the army). The former was responsible for the civil administration of the town, while the latter was in charge of all major military operations. Both men had equal status and each was assisted by an *Otun Bale* or *Otun Balogun*, that is, his right-hand man, and an *Osi* or left-hand man, who was followed by the third, fourth and fifth in command. Ranked below the *Balogun* was the *Seriki*, a junior military leader, who was likewise assisted by an *Otun* and *Osi*. Women's interests were represented by the *Iyalode* who is described by Anna Hinderer in 1854 as 'a sort of queen, a person of much influence and looked upon with much respect'.[17] It is especially noteworthy that none of these chieftainship titles was hereditary. In fact any free-born male citizen could become a *mogaji* or head of his patrilineage and most junior title-holders were chosen from these lineage-heads. Chiefs of either division, the military or civil, moved up the social ladder to more prestigious and influential senior titles on the death of a

* A *Bale* ranks generally under an Oba or king.

senior title holder. Every patrilineage in town was attached to one important chief who directed the public affairs of the group concerned, but each *mogaji* could select the chief he preferred and was free to change his allegiance at will. It is clear that the political system of nineteenth century Ibadan was characterized by intense competition for power and influence both among the various lineage groups and among the leading warriors and title-holders.

Ibadan under British rule, 1893–1960

The agreement which the chiefs of Ibadan and G. C. Denton, the Acting Governor of the Colony of Lagos, signed in 1893 restored peace and stability to Yorubaland, but it also incorporated Ibadan and its vassal towns into the British Empire. In the same year Captain Bower became the first Resident in the city.

The British colonial administration established its base on the north-eastern outskirts of the town, and the railway which reached Ibadan in 1901 had its headquarters and repair shops at the west of the town, thus setting the pattern for Ibadan's future development. With the railway came a modern business community, with the result that the area around the station soon developed into the new commercial centre of Ibadan with warehouses and wholesale and retail shops mainly for goods imported from Europe.[18] These three institutions – i.e. the colonial administration, the railway and the modern business community – were the new elements which had the most decisive effects on the growth of the city. The rapid expansion of trade and the sharp increase in the number of immigrants to the city were among the first signs of change.

Among the earliest immigrants under colonial rule were the Hausa who already had traditional trading links with the Yoruba, and gradually settled in an area known today as Sabon Gari, or new town, on the northern outskirts of the city.[19] They were closely followed by the Ijebu, Egba, and Ijesha who settled in wards known as Agbeni, Amunigun, Idikan, Oke Foko, and Oke Padre. (For the location of these areas, see Map A.7.2 on p. 370.)

The increasing influx of non-Yoruba traders from Lagos, Benin, and Eastern Nigeria after 1920 duly led to the establishment of the suburb of Ekotedo just north of the railway station; but it was not until the early 1930s that the influx of educated young Nigerians to Ibadan to work as clerical staff in administration and commerce began. Most of these immigrants settled along the newly constructed Lagos bypass in the south-western part of the city.

In 1946 Ibadan became the headquarters of the Western Region of Nigeria and six years later the capital of a semi-autonomous region. Both events brought new waves of Nigerian and European administrators, businessmen, and technicians into the city, and most of these newcomers settled in the rapidly growing western and northern suburbs. After Nigeria became independent in 1960, Ibadan continued to attract a large number of people of all walks of life, until its population exceeded a million in the early 1970s.

Islam in Ibadan

According to Johnson[20] and Parrinder,[21] Islam was introduced into Yorubaland in the latter half of the eighteenth century, mainly by traders from the north. It is most likely that a group of Yoruba converts under the first Imam of Ibadan, Abdullahi (Gunnugun) (d. 1839), were among the founders of the city. The small Muslim community in Ibadan was strengthened when in the 1830s a number of learned Muslim teachers, mainly from Hausaland, settled in the city. Among them were Ahmad Qifu, and particularly Uthman b. Abu Bakr who served as the second Imam of Ibadan from 1839 to 1871.[22] During his period as Imam, some members of the ruling class, and in particular the war chiefs, if not formally converted, became so sympathetic towards Islam that a large number of their people accepted Islamic customs and rites.

By the mid-nineteenth century, Ilorin had become the centre for Islamic learning in Yorubaland. It was thence that Abu Bakr b. al Qasim came to Ibadan and established a school which contributed to the city's image as a place of learning, so that it attracted scholars from Sokoto and even further afield.

Although Muslims were not allowed to build mosques in the city until the end of the nineteenth century,[23] Ibadan had by then become a very important centre for Muslim learning in the heart of Yorubaland.[24] In 1908 Ibadan had three times as many mosques as Christian churches.[25] There is little doubt that the British occupation provided the peace and stability under which Islam could expand rapidly, although Christianity was actively encouraged by the colonial power. In 1913, it was estimated that about one third of the population of Ibadan were Muslims. Forty years later, the 1952 census report showed that the Muslim population had increased to nearly 60 per cent while Christians accounted for 32 per cent and Animists for 8 per cent.[26] Unfortunately, no data on religious beliefs are available from the 1963 census, and the 1973 census only gives an overall figure for Nigeria's population.

By the mid-1960s there were as many as 15 mosques for Friday prayers and about 500 smaller ones found in the city.[27] We need not speculate here why Christianity, in spite of official support, has advanced so slowly in Ibadan over the last 100 years. This subject has been dealt with by others.[28] However, there is little doubt that Islam has suited the people of Ibadan better, though they have remoulded it to some degree by inserting elements of traditional Yoruba beliefs and customs according to their own needs.

Notes and references

1 B. W. Hodder, 'The markets of Ibadan', in *The City of Ibadan*, ed. P. C. Lloyd *et al.*, Cambridge, 1967, pp. 173–190.
2 Meteorological Office, *Tables of Temperature, Relative Humidity and Precipitation for the World*, part IV, London, 1964, p. 121.
3 British West African Meteorological Services, Nigeria, *Preliminary Notes on Rainfall of Nigeria*, Meteorological Notes No. 2, Lagos, 1955. K. M. Buchanan and J. C. Pugh, *Land and People in Nigeria*, London, 1966, p. 28.
4 I. B. Akinyele, *The Outlines of Ibadan History*, Lagos, 1946, pp. 28–40.
5 Ibid. According to legend the first settlement situated near the campus of the University of Ife at Ibadan was destroyed because the inhabitants of Ibadan violated Yoruba customs by accidentally allowing women to see exposed Egungun masqueraders during annual ceremonies, who were regarded as representatives of ancestors on earth.
6 S. Johnson, *The History of the Yorubas*, Lagos, 1960, pp. 197–202.
7 R. S. Smith, *Kingdoms of the Yoruba*, London, 1969, p. 151.
8 A. L. Mabogunje and J. D. Omer-Cooper, *Owu in Yoruba History*, Ibadan, 1971, pp. 63–69 and 77.
9 Johnson, op. cit., pp. 223–225.
10 B. A. Awe, 'Ibadan, its early beginnings', in Lloyd *et al.*, op. cit., p. 14.
11 Johnson, op. cit., pp. 238–242. Johnson gives a detailed account of these events.
12 Johnson, op. cit., pp. 285–289.
13 The reports and letter of David Hinderer can be found in the Church Missionary Archives at 4 Salisbury Square, London EC4, under the serial number CA2/20. A. Hinderer, *Seventeen Years in the Yoruba Country*, London, 1873.
14 Johnson, op. cit., p. 327.
15 Ibid., pp. 336–345.
16 B. A. Awe, The Rise of Ibadan as a Yoruba Power in the 19th Century, unpublished Ph.D. Thesis, Oxford University, 1964.

17 A. Hinderer, op. cit., p. 110.
18 A. L. Mabogunje, *Urbanization in Nigeria*, London, 1968, pp. 209–213. R. A. Akinola, 'Ibadan: A study in urban geography', London, 1963. Unpublished Ph.D. thesis, pp. 139–157.
19 A. Cohen, 'The Hausa', in Lloyd *et al.*, op. cit., pp. 117–127. A. Cohen, *Custom and Politics in Ibadan*, London, 1969, p. 31.
20 Johnson, op. cit., p. 26.
21 G. Parrinder, *The Story of Ketu, an Ancient Yoruba Kingdom*, Lagos, 1956, p. 33.
22 F. H. El-Masri, 'Religion in Ibadan, B. Islam', in Lloyd *et al.*, op. cit., pp. 249–257.
23 S. J. Trimingham, *A History of Islam in West Africa*, Oxford, 1978, p. 231. Trimingham rightly points out that there were in fact mosques, 'since a market-out square or a room in a compound is all that is necessary'.
24 G. Parrinder, *Religion in an African City*, London, 1953, pp. 63–85.
25 Church Missionary Society (CMS), *Review*, 1908, p. 648.
26 Department of Statistics, Nigeria, *Population Census of the Western Region of Nigeria 1952*, Lagos, 1956.
27 El-Masri, op. cit., p. 256.
28 E. B. Idowu, 'Religion in Ibadan, A. Traditional religion and Christianity', in Lloyd *et al.*, op. cit. J. D. Y. Peel, *Aladura: A Religious Movement among the Yoruba, London, 1968.*

Chapter 8

Land tenure and land use in the older parts of Ibadan

Historical notes on land tenure

In the previous chapter we saw how Ibadan developed from an encampment of several groups of marauding soldiers in the early 1820s, into a Yoruba metropolis of about 100,000 inhabitants by 1893.[1] The various war chiefs who settled in Ibadan took whatever land they needed for their compounds which were closely surrounded by the houses of their followers. Land granted by these chiefs to their followers or to refugees was generally not recoverable by them and thus belonged to the head of the family and his heirs in perpetuity. However, serious crimes or rebellion against the chiefs were often punished by wholesale expulsion of the offending lineage, the destruction of their compounds, and the reallocation of their land to newcomers.

With the rapid increase of Ibadan's population the shortage of farmland around the city was soon apparent, and this situation forced people to move further away in order to find enough virgin bushland for cultivation. Land already cultivated or cleared was later seldom allocated to strangers, but newcomers were able to rent farms and grow food crops. However, such economic trees as oil palms, and later cocoa trees, belonged to the owner of the land unless covered by special arrangements. It must be stressed that before the British occupation, land in towns had no market value, and therefore was not sold or bought.[2]

During the first twenty years of colonial rule in Southern Nigeria, three important laws relating to land were introduced by the British Government. They were, first, the Native Lands Acquisition Proclamation No. 1 of 1900 which was designed to control the purchase of land by non-Nigerians; second, the Land Registration Ordinance No. 15 of 1907 which instituted compulsory registration of all sales of land with the colonial government; and third, the Crown Lands Ordinance No. 13 of 1908 which regulated the management, control, and disposal of Crown Land.[3] However, it is true to say that none of these laws affected the majority of the Yoruba who continued to hold, transfer, and use their land in much the same way as their ancestors did. With the development of an economy based on money, transfers of farms and building land for cash instead of for the customary gifts which consisted mainly of palm wine, gin, and kola nuts, increased steadily and in spite of the opposition of the traditional and colonial authorities alike.[4] As one consequence of this development, outright sale of land has now become the most frequent mode of acquisition for building in the cities of Yorubaland.

Land tenure and transfer today

The main features of Yoruba land tenure were investigated by H. L. Ward Price in 1933 and by P. C. Lloyd between 1956 and 1959.[5] The three basic categories of land tenure already identified in Chapter 2 apply fully to Ibadan. They are, first, community or public land; second, family land; and third, individually owned land. Community or public land includes *inter alia* land occupied by administrative buildings, most tarred roads, public markets, forest reserves, and reservoirs. Family land (*ilẹ ẹbi*) is inherited land which is owned corporately by a lineage and cannot be alienated outside the descent group without the consent of all adult male members of the lineage or section concerned; while individually owned land is usually acquired by purchase and the owner is free to sell or bequeath the land without the restrictions imposed on family land.[6]

Let us now consider in more detail the various types of land tenure which can be found in Ibadan city and the rights held in land by an individual or descent group. This analysis is based on interviews with 63 compound heads in the older parts of the city and is restricted to land on which the interviewee's compound was built.

Permanent transfers of land

Inheritance of compounds and compound sites accounted for 57.1 per cent of the compounds surveyed, and is by far the most important type of land transfer. (See Table A.8.1 on p. 372.) However, we should distinguish here between the inheritance of the houses (50.8 per cent) and inheritance of land (6.3 per cent) on which the new owner has since built a house. The first category consists mainly of 'family compounds' to which all the restrictions discussed earlier under family land apply. The second category is more difficult to define because it includes two different types of land first, corporately owned family land, for example, the sites of ancestral compounds; and second, land bought by the owner's father and inherited from him. Land of the first category cannot be sold without the consent of the grantor, though all improvements on it, such as a house built by the present occupant, may in theory be sold by him provided he has notified the lineage head of his intention well in advance. In the second case the land and any house on it can be freely sold by the heir without any restrictions. Thus, inherited land includes some in which the present occupier has only usufructuary rights, and freehold land which can be alienated by the heir without any obstruction.

As regards inheritance, after a man's death his rights in such property as land or a house usually remain with his own *omo iya*,* a group comprising his immediate family together with his remaining full siblings and their children.[7]

Purchase of house sites accounted for 22.2 per cent of the compounds surveyed. Purchase of land to build on is a relatively recent phenomenon in Ibadan and only developed during the last 50 years. Purchase, as contrasted with the customary modes of land transfer in precolonial Ibadan, requires that a relatively large cash payment should be made to the vendor, substantially above the value of the customary gifts. There seems to be no simple correlation between the size of a building plot and the price paid for it. For example, five compound heads paid so little for their land that these sums probably represented money substitutes for the traditional gifts presented in return for a customary grant,[8] while one compound head paid £N250 in 1965 for a plot measuring about 20 × 30 m.

*For definition of this term see Chapter 10, p. 133.

Allocation of family land is usually made by a landholding descent group to its members in need. This may consist of farmland or land for building, which accounted for 17.5 per cent of the sites surveyed. Land granted for house building is heritable, but cannot be sold by its present owner without the grantor's consent. However, any improvement made by the grantee on the land may be sold by him without the interference of his lineage group.

Temporary transfers of land

Temporary transfers of land are mainly restricted to farmland and areas of fruit-bearing trees, and may take two forms; first, the pledging or pawning of land in order to obtain a loan; and second, the renting of land for a fixed monthly or annual rent in kind or cash (*ishakọlẹ*). These alternatives have already been discussed in Chapter 2 on p. 14. However, the sample included two cases in which houses were rented as units by their present occupiers. In both cases, long-term arrangements had been made between the owner and tenant, which gave the tenant the right to sublet rooms.

In conclusion, some facts which have changed the traditional mode of land tenure on Ibadan over the last 50 years should be considered. There is little doubt that the concept introduced by the British colonial administration of land as a saleable commodity has substantially changed the attitudes of people towards their land. Historically, sale of land for money was regarded by the Yoruba as immoral and repugnant, and it was even declared illegal in some areas.[9] However, over the past 50 years sales of building land on the perimeters of larger cities have steadily increased. Many a household head seized this opportunity to free himself from the dependence on his descent group entailed by the traditional mode of land tenure, and built his house on purchased land well away from his ancestral compound in the old city.

In contrast, transfers of corporately owned land by succession or allocation are still in most cases conducted in accordance with the customary law which has changed little over the last 50 years. Hence a great number of families in the older parts of the city only hold usufructuary rights to the land they occupy.

Land use in Ibadan city

The following summary of data on land use in Ibadan is based on the researches of J. O. Oyelese at the University of Ibadan.[10] Using a set of aerial photographs from 1965, Oyelese measured and described twelve different categories of land use in the city area.* For convenience these categories have been reduced to five groups. They are:

1 Cultivated land which accounts for 39.0 per cent of the total city area. Cultivated land includes field-crop farms (35.2 per cent), private or government-owned experimental farms (3.2 per cent), and tree-crop farms (0.6 per cent). (See Table A.8.2 on p. 372.)
2 The built-up area which represents 33.4 per cent of the city area and includes roads as well as open spaces between houses. This category has been further subdivided into the traditional housing area (14.3 per cent) with an average density of about 23 compounds per hectare in the core of the city,[11] and the modern low and high density housing area (9.4 per cent) which, except for five former European housing reservations and some houses along the Lagos bypass, were built after the Second World War mainly in the western and northern suburbs of the city. The density of these areas is between four and twelve houses per hectare. A third subgroup comprises all public, educational, industrial, and commercial buildings including markets, and accounts for 9.7 per cent of the total city area.
3 Fallow and woodland areas which account for 18.8 per cent of the city area and include flood plains alongside the Ogunpa and Kudeti streams. According to Oyelese, this area has been reduced from 4,219 hectares in 1961 to 1,954 hectares in 1965. The reclaimed land is now partially used for food growing and new housing developments.
4 Forest reservations or fuel plantations in the immediate neighbourhood of the town which cover about 780 hectares or 7.5 per cent of the city area.
5 Lakes and reservoirs which cover about 125 hectares, or 1.2 per cent of the total area.

Notes and References

1 A. Millson, 'The Yoruba Country, West Africa', *Proceedings of the Royal Geographical Society*, **13**, October 1891, p. 583. Millson, who visited Ibadan in 1891, estimated its population at 120,000. Sir G. Carter, *Report of the Lagos Interior Expedition 1893*, Lagos, 1893, p. 47, c 7 227. Carter estimated the

*The total city area given as 10,379 hectares (25,646.5 acres) was slightly larger than the area of the 40 city wards, 9,763 hectares being controlled by the Town-planning Authority.

number of houses in Ibadan at 15,000 and its population at about 150,000. It is believed that this estimate was probably too high but it was accepted at the time as the official figure.

2 H. L. Ward Price, *Land Tenure in the Yoruba Provinces*, Lagos, 1939, p. 42.

3 C. K. Meek, *Land Tenure and Land, Administration in Nigeria and the Cameroons*, London, 1957, pp. 323–25. Crown Land consisted of land acquired from the Royal Niger Company in 1900 and land bought by the government from individuals, chiefs, and obas. Crown Land was sometimes leased to European commercial firms.

4 Ward Price, op. cit., p. 61. In 1903 a Public Note was issued in Ibadan bringing the sale of land under the supervision of the *bale*. See also Native Court Rule 1918.

5 Ward Price, op. cit. P. C. Lloyd, *Yoruba Land Law*, Oxford, 1962. (I did not carry out an investigation of Yoruba land law apart from interviewing the 63 household heads. This paragraph owes much to P. C. Lloyd's outstanding research on the subject.) C. W. Rowling, *Land Tenure in Ijebu Province*, Ibadan, 1956: J. O. Coker, *Family Property among the Yoruba*, London, 1958, pp. 16–57.

For a purely legal view of land tenure see T. O. Elias, *Nigerian Land Law and Custom*, London, 1951, pp. 88–164.

6 Lloyd, op. cit., pp. 76–86.

7 Ibid., pp. 296–298.

8 Ibid., p. 327. Lloyd lists three points in which sale differs from customary grant:

I. The land cannot be recovered by the vendor group.
II. The land does not revert to the group if it is merely abandoned by the purchaser or his heir.
III. The purchaser gains by the sale not only a usufructuary right in perpetuity but also a right to alienate the land.

9 Ibid., p. 328. According to Lloyd the sale of land in Ondo rural area was illegal. See also pp. 97–135.

10 J. O. Oyelese, 'The growth of Ibadan city and its impact on land-use patterns, 1961–1965', *Journal of Tropical Geography*, Singapore, **32**, June 1971, pp. 49–55.

11 Ibid., p. 49.

Chapter 9

Demography

Ibadan

The demographic situation of Nigeria has already been sketched in Chapter 3 and here I wish to concentrate on the population growth and accompanying developments in Ibadan. This will be followed by some data obtained from my survey in the city which include *inter alia* age and sex distribution, ethnic composition and rural–urban migration.

The growth of Ibadan's population

From its beginning, Ibadan's population increased rapidly, mainly due to the influx of refugees and free-lance soldiers from northern Yorubaland. Thus within the first three decades of its existence Ibadan grew remarkably, and by the second half of the nineteenth century it had already become a large city by any standards. According to David Hinderer, who was the first missionary to arrive in the city, in 1851 Ibadan had an estimated population of about 60,000 inhabitants.[1] Other missionaries who visited Ibadan in the early 1850s made similar estimates.[2]

About forty years later, on the eve of colonial rule, British Government officials estimated the population of Ibadan at between 120,000 and 150,000 inhabitants.[3] Official estimates of Ibadan's population gave totals in 1911 of 175,000, in 1921 of 238,000, and in 1931 of 387,000 inhabitants.[4] No population estimate was made in 1941. (See Table A.9.1 on p. 373.)

The first census with a house-to-house count was conducted in 1952 and gave a total of 459,000.[5] A second census in 1962 was never published, but another attempt one year later showed that the urban population of Ibadan had risen to about 627,000, yielding a growth rate of 2.9 per cent per annum over the preceding eleven years.[6] Tentative projections indicate that the population of Ibadan reached the 1 million mark by the early 1970s.[7]

However, all these estimates and census returns, which suggest an impressive and uninterrupted population growth, are somewhat misleading. One reason for this ambiguity lies in the perpetual movement of people which takes place between Ibadan and its rural hinterland. It is well known that a large proportion of families who have houses in the older parts of the city spend most of their time working on their farms, some of them up to 40 km away. While some of these people visit Ibadan quite regularly, normally once a week, others may only return for the big festivals such as Oke Badan in March and the Egungun festival in June, and important family occasions.[8] It has been estimated that at times when agricultural activities are reduced, and during the above mentioned festivals, the population of Ibadan may increase by as much as 30 to 40 per cent.[9] That such a substantial population fluctuation should occur frequently in the city raises an important question, namely: what population was counted in the censuses of 1952 and 1963 – the city's permanent residents, those who return regularly to the city, or those who live in surrounding villages and hamlets but none the less regard Ibadan as their home, and would probably come to the city in an event such as elections or censuses? Obviously, a clear definition of its various categories of residents is urgently needed for Ibadan, and until this has been achieved, any census of Ibadan's population will be highly ambiguous.

The growth of Ibadan city

Ibadan's growth and the development of its residential districts have been described in detail by A. L. Mabogunje.[10] As the result of the population growth sketched above, the development of Ibadan can be broadly divided into three periods: the precolonial period, 1820–1893; the colonial period, 1893–1952;* and the period after independence.

Each of these periods has left its mark on the city by creating an area with distinguished patterns of population density, house types, and socio-economic and cultural characteristics.

Developments during the precolonial period from the early 1820s to 1893 established two similar areas: first, the 'core region', an area which S. Johnson described as 'about half a mile around Oja Iba market',[11] and second a surrounding built-up area which stretched in 1893 as far as Agbeni and Foko in the west, Kudeti in the south, Elekuro and Aremo in the east, and Agodi in the north-east. (See Plan 9.1.) In the late 1960s these areas housed about half of Ibadan's population and are by far the most densely populated parts of the city. Levels of population density are attributed by A. L. Mabogunje to 'growth by fission', that is, 'the replacement of simple large structures; i.e. the traditional Yoruba compound built around one or more spacious courtyards; by more complex and more numerous smaller units'.[12] (See Table A.9.2, groups I and II, column 4, on p. 374.) Nearly all houses built in this central area have mud walls covered with corrugated iron roofs.

The colonial period from about 1893 to 1952 was marked by a rapid expansion of the city. Most immigrants to Ibadan during this period settled to the west and north of the old city. Some of the houses built in these areas have mud walls rendered with cement plaster and are covered with corrugated iron roofs, while others are constructed with modern building materials and include such amenities as piped water and electricity. The steady increase of European administrators, technicians, and businessmen from 58 in 1921 to over 2,000 in 1952 led to the construction of five residential reservations in the city. Until 1952 these reservations were exclusively occupied by Europeans, but since the transfer of political power that year, the Europeans have gradually been replaced by Nigerians of similar rank and income.

Since 1952, Ibadan's development has largely been initiated by a new class of Nigerian professionals who have taken over the administration of the region. Their demand for modern and more spacious houses equipped with all sanitary and household amenities sparked off new

*In 1952 Ibadan became the capital of a semi-autonomous Western Region with the transfer of political power from the British colonial government to the nationals of the region. The political independence of Nigeria came in October 1960.

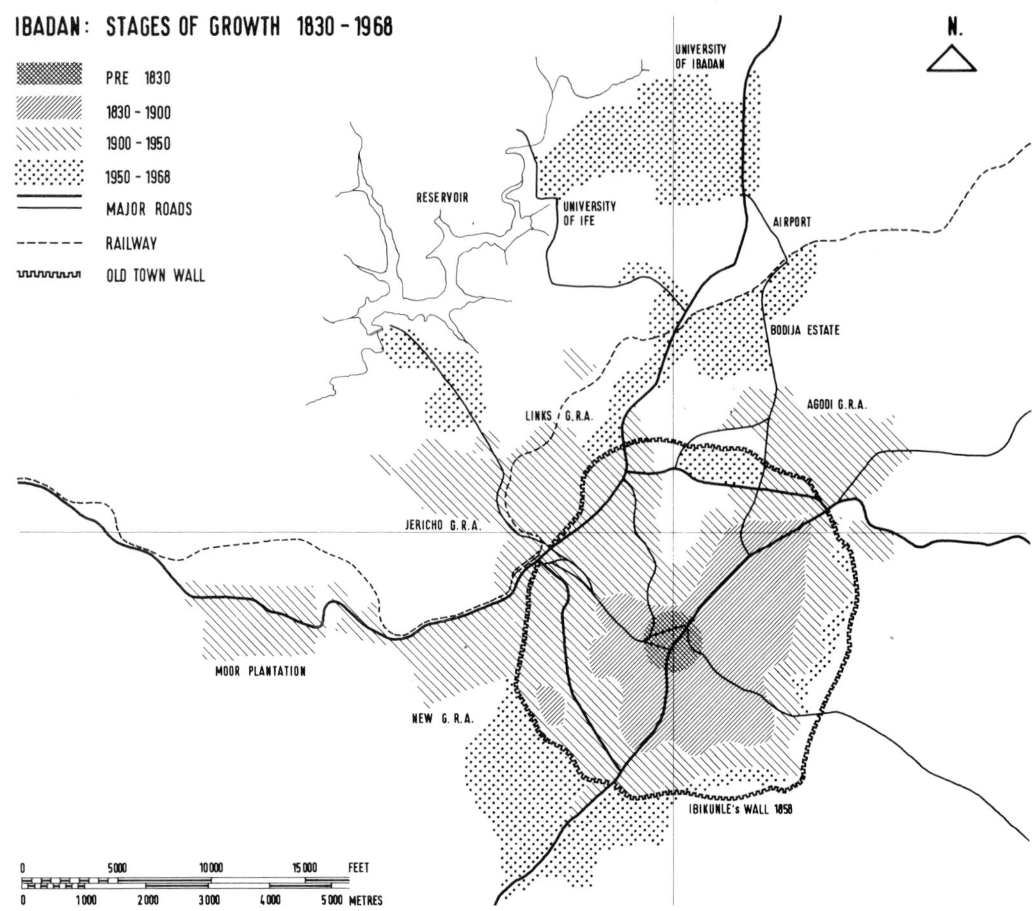

Plan 9.1
Ibadan, stages of growth, 1830–1968

developments in the south-western suburbs beyond the nineteenth-century town wall and to a lesser extent in the northern parts of the city including the Bodija Housing Estate. In the early 1960s the spatial expansion of the city was indeed impressive. For example, in 1961 Ibadan's total built-up area was about 2,630 hectares, but by 1965 this had increased to about 3,470 hectares, that is, by about 30 per cent in only four years. Of this expansion, traditional and modern housing areas accounted for about 530 hectares, while public, industrial, commercial, and educational building areas increased by about 310 hectares.[13] (For population density according to city wards, see Maps A.9.1 and A.9.2 on pp. 375 and 376.)

Ethnic composition

The ethnic composition of Ibadan Division as shown in Table 9.1 is derived from the 1952/1953 and 1963 census reports.

Table 9.1 Ethnic composition of Ibadan Division, censuses 1952–1953 and 1963, in percentages

	1952[a]	1963[b]
Yoruba	96.2	95.0
Other Southern Nigerian tribes	1.7	3.7
Northern Nigerian tribes	1.6	0.9
Non-Nigerians	0.1	0.2
Unspecified	0.4	0.2
Total	100.0	100.0

[a]Department of Statistics, Nigeria, *Population Census of the Western Region of Nigeria 1952*, Lagos, 1956, p. 18.
[b]Federal Office of Statistics, Nigeria, 'Population census of Nigeria 1963' (mimeo), Lagos, 1968, vol. 2, p. 70.

According to the 1963 census only about 5 per cent of the total divisional population were non-Yoruba. The largest group of these non-Yoruba immigrants were Ibo from Eastern Nigeria, who increased from 7,800 in 1952 to about 26,000 in 1963. Unfortunately none of these censuses provides us with a breakdown of the various Yoruba subgroups such as the Egba, Ijebu, and Oyo, to name only the most important groups, who together form the largest immigrant group in Ibadan. Data cited in Table A.9.3 on p. 378 give some indication of the proportion of non-indigenous Yoruba within my sample population.

Sample survey

Data from the sample survey regarding the age and sex distribution, ethnic composition, and some aspects of the rural–urban immigration are given below.

The sample population covered 1,285 persons representing about 0.2 per cent of the total population of Ibadan.

Age and sex distribution

The age composition of the sample population was collected with the help of the so-called 'historical calendar method' by which individual ages are estimated by reference to past events. However, it must be stressed again that while this method generally restricts errors within somewhat narrower limits, it does not entirely exclude misinformation.

Table 9.2 Population distribution by sex and age groups in Ibadan, in percentages

	Ibadan Div., 1952 Total pop. 796,900	Ibadan Div., 1963 Total pop. 1,258,600	Sample survey, 1968 Total pop. 1,285
0–14	50.9	31.9	41.3
15–49	41.0	62.3	49.6
50+	8.1	5.8	9.1
Male	51.4	53.9	48.1
Female	48.6	46.1	51.9
Total	100.0	100.0	100.0

Table 9.2 gives the age and sex ratios of the sample population for comparison with the census returns for Ibadan Division in 1952 and 1963.

A more detailed bar-chart, Diagram A.9.1 on p. 377, shows comparative percentage distribution for male and female at five-year intervals for Ibadan Division in 1963 and for the sample survey population. As can be seen, the sex and age distribution in 1963 was seriously affected by age-selective immigration which resulted in a substantial excess of males and females in the age groups 20–29. This pattern of age distribution, which has been widely accepted as 'normal' for rapidly growing urban centres in Africa, is far less pronounced in the survey sample population, as shown in Diagram A.9.2 on p. 377. Two likely explanations for this difference in age distribution are the smallness of the sample coupled with the fact that only 26 compounds, or 40 per cent of the sample, were situated in predominantly immigrant areas of the formally walled city. Furthermore, houses outside the old city wall where most of the immigrants settled are excluded from the survey.

The sex ratio given in Table 9.2 shows an excess of males over females in both the 1952 and 1963 census, while there are slightly more females than males in the sample population. However, it is interesting to note that for tenant households in the sample, most of whom are immigrants, the sex ratio is reversed with 53.2 per cent male and 46.8 per cent female. There is also a notable increase of males and females in the age groups between 25 and 34. (See Table A.10.3 on p. 381.)

Ethnic composition

The ethnic composition of the sample population closely resembles the figures given in Table 9.1 and is as follows: Yoruba 94.0 per cent; other Southern Nigerian tribes 3.7 per cent; Northern Nigerian tribes 2.3 per cent.

Migration

As we have seen, migration has always played an important part in Ibadan's population growth. It was the large number of immigrants who came to the city in the late 1830s and early 1840s who helped to establish Ibadan as the leading military power in Yorubaland; and, after the first years of British rule, it was again a never-ending stream of immigrants from all over Nigeria which contributed to the economic growth and wealth of the city.

It is thus not surprising that in all 330 persons, 164 males and 166 females, or together 25.7 per cent of the sample population, were born outside Ibadan. Most male immigrants in this group came to Ibadan in search of work or better trading opportunities, while nearly two thirds of the females came as wives.

Some distinction must be made here between the long-range migration of people coming from other parts of the country, and the short-distance population movements mentioned above that take place between Ibadan and its surrounding countryside. In this section we are concerned only with people of the first category.

As already shown in Table 9.1, only about 5 per cent of the population in Ibadan Division are not Yoruba. This relatively small proportion, which roughly corresponds with my own findings, about 6 per cent, indicates that the majority of immigrants must have come from Yoruba subgroups and for this reason were not separately counted among the immigrants in the censuses of 1952 and 1963. Table A.9.3 on p. 378 tries to answer this question for the household heads in the sample. Of the 295 household heads who replied, 135 or 45.8 per cent were born outside Ibadan. Of these latter, 115 or 39.0 per cent belonged to one of several Yoruba subgroups, 14 or 4.8 per cent were members of various other Southern Nigerian tribes such as Ibo and Edo, and 6 or 2.0 per cent came from Northern Nigeria. The largest tribal subgroup among the 115 Yoruba household heads was the Egba of Abeokuta, with 29 or 9.8 per cent, followed by Ijebu with 15 or 5.1 per cent, and Oyo with 11 or 3.7 per cent.

Since over 45 per cent of all household heads are

immigrants, what, one may ask, happens to newcomers when they move to Ibadan? Do they still group themselves according to their ethnic origin? In the past, immigrants of the same tribal group tended to congregate in certain areas. Thus when the first Ijebu and Egba arrived at the beginning of this century they settled at the western outskirts of the built-up area in districts now known as Agbeni, Idikan, Amunigun, and Oke Foko. (See Map A.7.2 on p. 370.) Hausa and Nupe from the north built their houses in the Sabon Gari or new town, and at Mokola on the northern fringe of the city, while Ibo, Edo, Ibibio, and the people from Lagos are mainly found in Ekotedo and the neighbouring Inalende. This general pattern has not substantially changed.

Informants among the sample of household heads who immigrated to Ibadan agreed on the central role played by kinsfolk, town or village unions, and associations in assisting newcomers in their search for employment in town; and immediate kin, or in their absence people from the same village, town, or ethnic group, provided the necessary shelter. Such close contact with his own group provided the newcomer with a sense of belonging and security which greatly helped him to adapt to the new urban environment. However, there are indications that after this initial stage of adaptation, well-to-do household heads often prefer to settle among people of their own status and income group, rather than in areas dominated by their own ethnic group.[14]

Notes and references

1 D. Hinderer, *Journals*, Church Missionary Society (CMS) Archives, CA2/049, London, September 1851.

2 A. W. Tucker, *Abeokuta or Sunrise within the Tropics*, London, 1853, pp. 231–234. Miss Tucker estimated the population of Ibadan at 60,000. It is not clear if this is an estimate arrived at independently or simply a repetition of Hinderer's earlier figure. T. J. Bowen, *Central Africa: Adventures and Missionary Labors in Several Countries in the Interior of Africa, from 1849–1856*. Charleston, South Carolina, 1857, p. 218. Bowen estimated the population of Ibadan at 70,000.

3 A. Moloney, 'Notes of Yoruba land and the colony and protectorate of Lagos', *Proceedings of the Royal Geographical Society* (London), new series, **12** (10), 1890, p. 596. Moloney estimated the population of Ibadan at 150,000. A. Millson, 'The Yoruba Country, West Africa', *Proceedings of the Royal Geographical society* (London), **13** (10), 1891, p. 583. Millson estimated the population of Ibadan at 120,000. G. Carter, 'Dispatch from Sir Gilbert Carter furnishing a general report of the Lagos Interior Expedition', C. 7227, London, 1893, p. 47. Carter estimated the population of Ibadan at 150,000.

4 Colonial Office, *Official Report on the Southern Nigeria Census 1911*, Southern Nigeria Annual Report, Lagos, 1912, pp. 629–656. H. B. Cox, *Census of the Southern Provinces*, vol. 3 of the Census of Nigeria, 1931; London, 1932.

5 Department of Statistics, Nigeria, *Population Census of the Western Region of Nigeria 1952*, Lagos, 1956, p. 23.

6 Federal Office of Statistics, Nigeria, *Population Census of Nigeria 1963*, Western Region, vol. 2, Lagos, 1968, p. 26.

7 A. L. Mabogunje, *Urbanization in Nigeria*, London, 1968, p. 236.

8 N. C. Mitchell, 'Some comments on the growth and character of Ibadan's population', Research Notes No. 4, Dept of Geography, University College, Ibadan, 1953, pp. 9–10. Mitchell reports that farmers who live in the immediate surrounding rural area spend on average four nights on their farms and three in Ibadan during any one week. Morgan, W. B. 'The change from shifting to fixed settlements in Southern Nigeria', Research Notes No. 7, Dept of Geography, University College, Ibadan, 1955, pp. 14–25. Morgan found that in spite of permanent residence in the villages, farmers return to Ibadan for the big festivals.

9 Millson, op. cit., p. 583. Millson mentioned that 'Ibadan counts over 200,000 souls while within the wall of the city itself at least 120,000 people are gathered'. The remaining people live in villages and work on their farms. P. C. Lloyd, *Yoruba Land Law*, Oxford, 1962, p. 55. Based on the 1952 census, Lloyd estimated that the 'sociological population' of Ibadan was about 700,000 of which approximately 459,000 or 66 per cent were living in Ibadan city.

10 A. L. Mabogunje, 'The growth of residential districts in Ibadan', *Geographical Review*, **52**, pp. 56–57. A. L. Mabogunje, 'The morphology of Ibadan', in *The City of Ibadan*, ed. P. C. Lloyd *et al.*, Cambridge, 1967, pp. 35–56. A. L. Mabogunje, *Urbanization in Nigeria*, pp. 205–237.

11 S. Johnson, *The History of the Yorubas*, Lagos, 1960, p. 244.

12 Mabogunje, 'The growth of residential districts in Ibadan', p. 60.

13 J. O. Oyelese, 'The growth of Ibadan city and its impact on land-use patterns, 1961–1965', *Journal of Tropical Geography* (Singapore) **32**, June 1971, pp. 49–55.

14 E. P. Skinner, 'Strangers in West African societies', *Africa*, **XXXIII**, 1963, pp. 307–320.

Chapter 10

Domestic groupings and the house

The compound

Layout and organization

Most compounds found in the older districts of the city can be grouped into two major categories first, the traditional Yoruba compound built around one or more spacious courtyards; and second, a much smaller house with fewer rooms grouped around a central hall or corridor.

The traditional Yoruba compound (*agbo-ile*) is inhabited by a lineage or section of a lineage consisting of a group of patrilineally related families (*ara-ile*, literally, residents of the house) descended through males from a common ancestor. The compound head (*bale*) usually has rooms opposite the main entrance where he receives visitors and entertains his friends. Strangers, clients, and more distant relatives usually have their rooms near the entrance gate.[1] Nearly all rooms in the compound face the courtyard(s), and each has a covered veranda or portico in front where most of the daily housework, including cooking, is done. Today, only a few such compounds have survived in Ibadan, and I only studied one of them, though it was not included in the survey. (See Plans 10.1 and 10.2.)

The second house-type mentioned above consists of a double row of rooms which open onto a common hall or

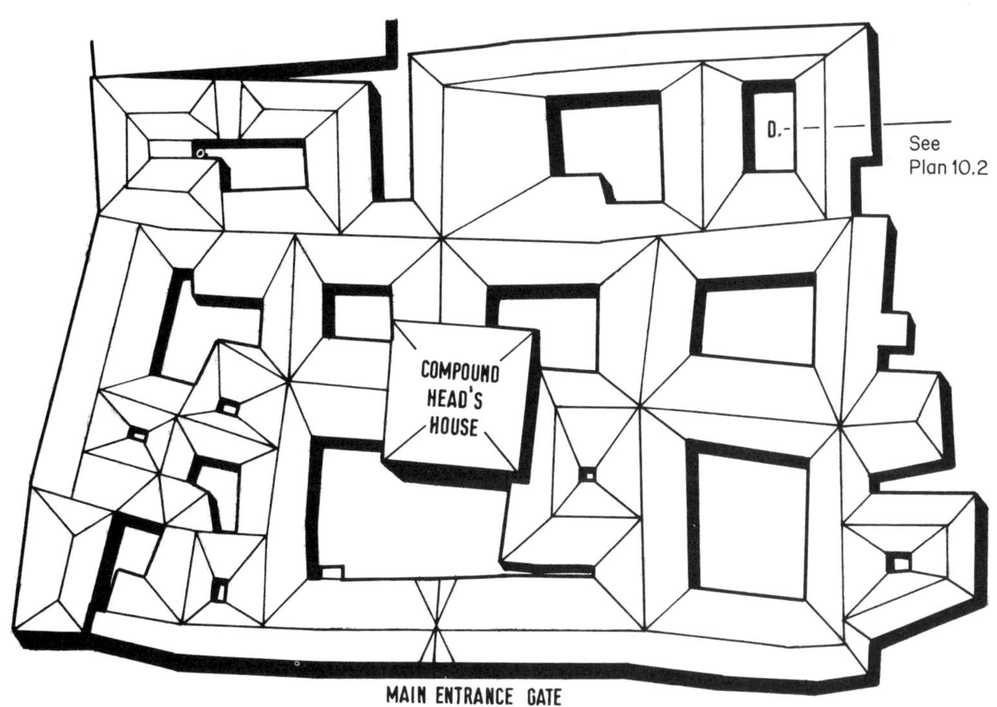

Plan 10.1
Traditional compound in Ibadan

passage. The central hall is of great importance for the running of the house and serves not only as a common place for working, sitting, and storage, but also as an additional sleeping area for overnight guests from the village. (See Plan 10.3.) In more recently built houses, the spacious central hall has been replaced by a central corridor or passage which leads onto a backyard which usually contains a common kitchen, bathroom, pit-latrine, and one or two storage rooms. (See Plan 10.4.) This latter type, which has on average between six and eight rooms, is by far the most frequently built house-type in the city today. In predominantly immigrant areas such as Ekotedo, Inalende, Mokola, and Molete, this type of house may have many more rooms, and even a second floor which is sometimes occupied by the owner and his family, while all other rooms are rented out to immigrant families. (See Plan 10.5.)

Another clearly recognizable house-type is the modern, self-contained dwelling built with permanent building materials and including all the necessary sanitary and other installations such as water and electricity. These houses are normally designed by architects for the government, housing corporations, housing societies, and wealthy individuals; they are described in various publications and have not been included in my survey.[2]

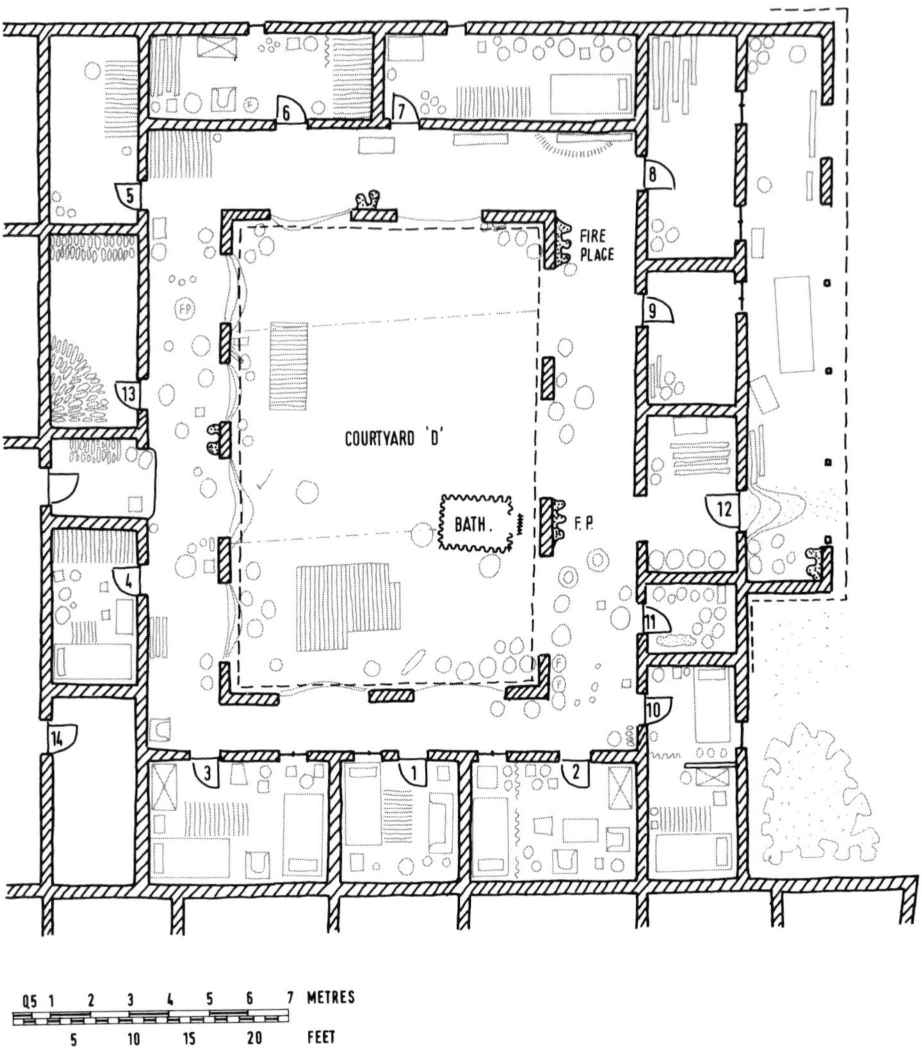

COURTYARD 'D'

FIRE PLACE

BATH.

F.P.

0.5 1 2 3 4 5 6 7 METRES

5 10 15 20 FEET

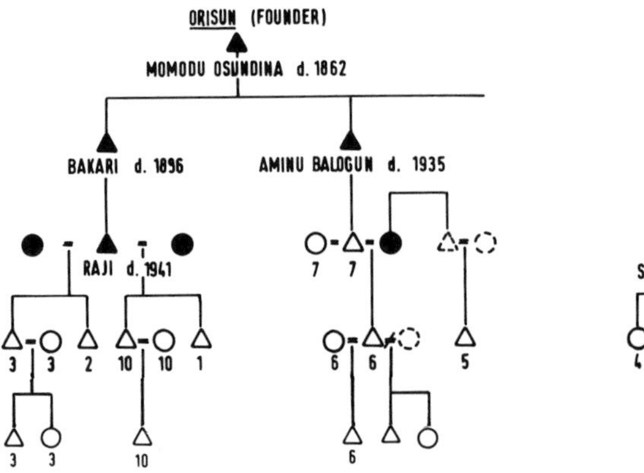

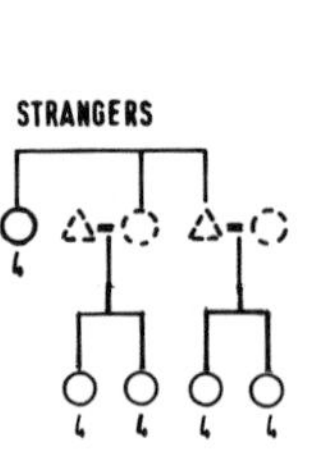

Plan 10.2
A courtyard in a traditional compound in Ibadan

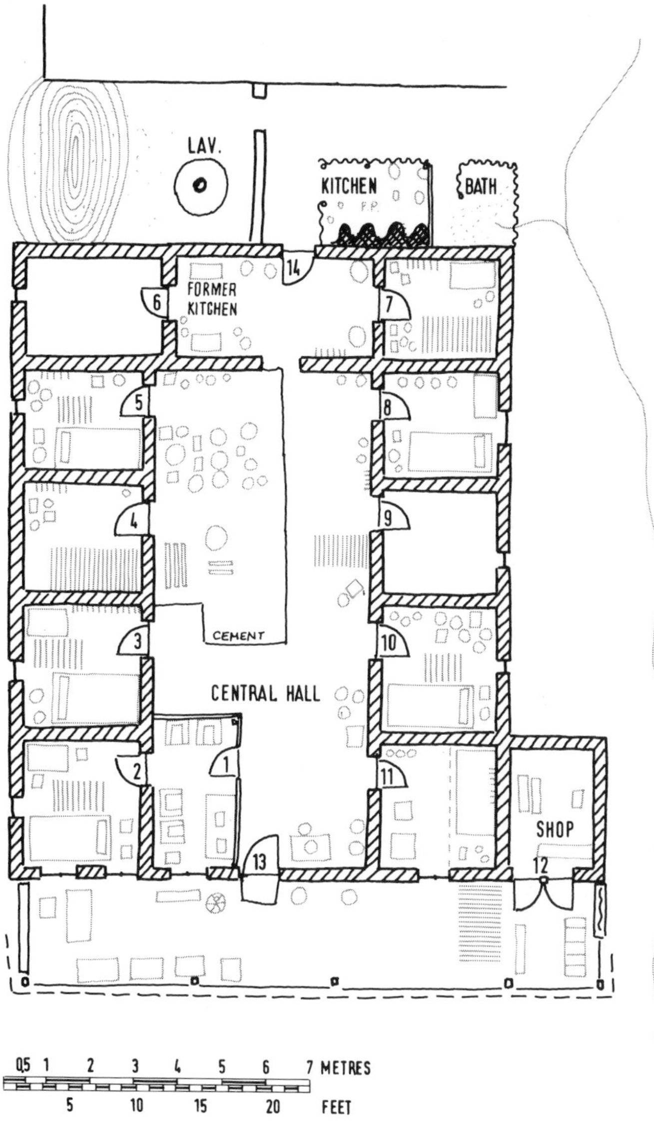

Plan 10.3
House 9

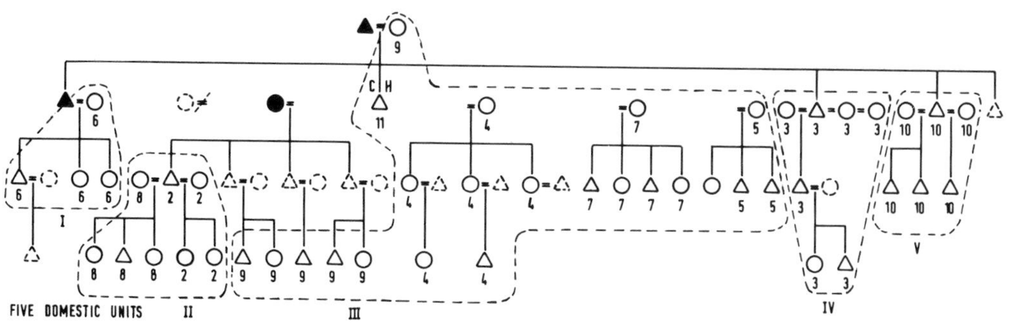

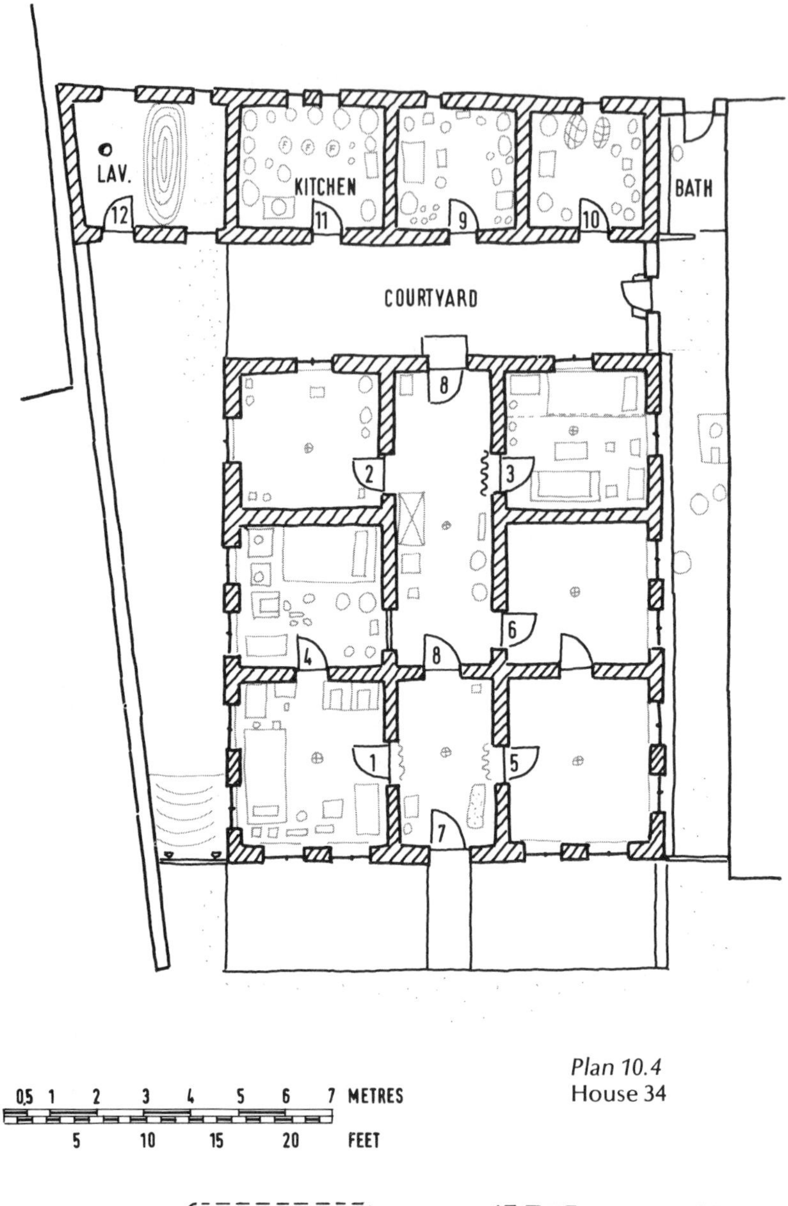

LAV.
KITCHEN
BATH
COURTYARD

0.5 1 2 3 4 5 6 7 METRES
5 10 15 20 FEET

Plan 10.4
House 34

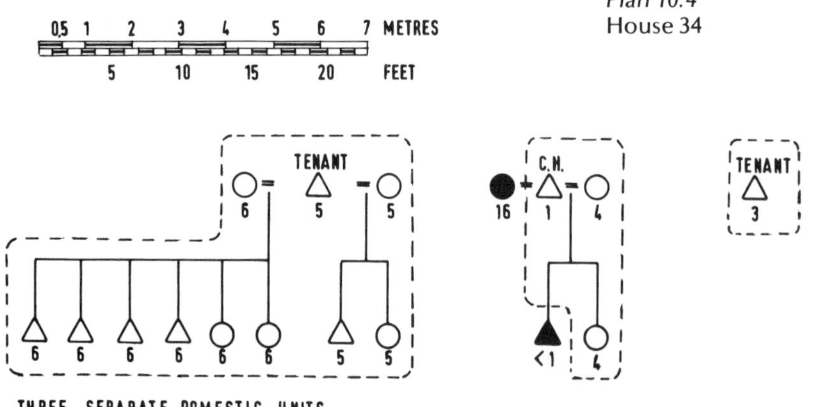

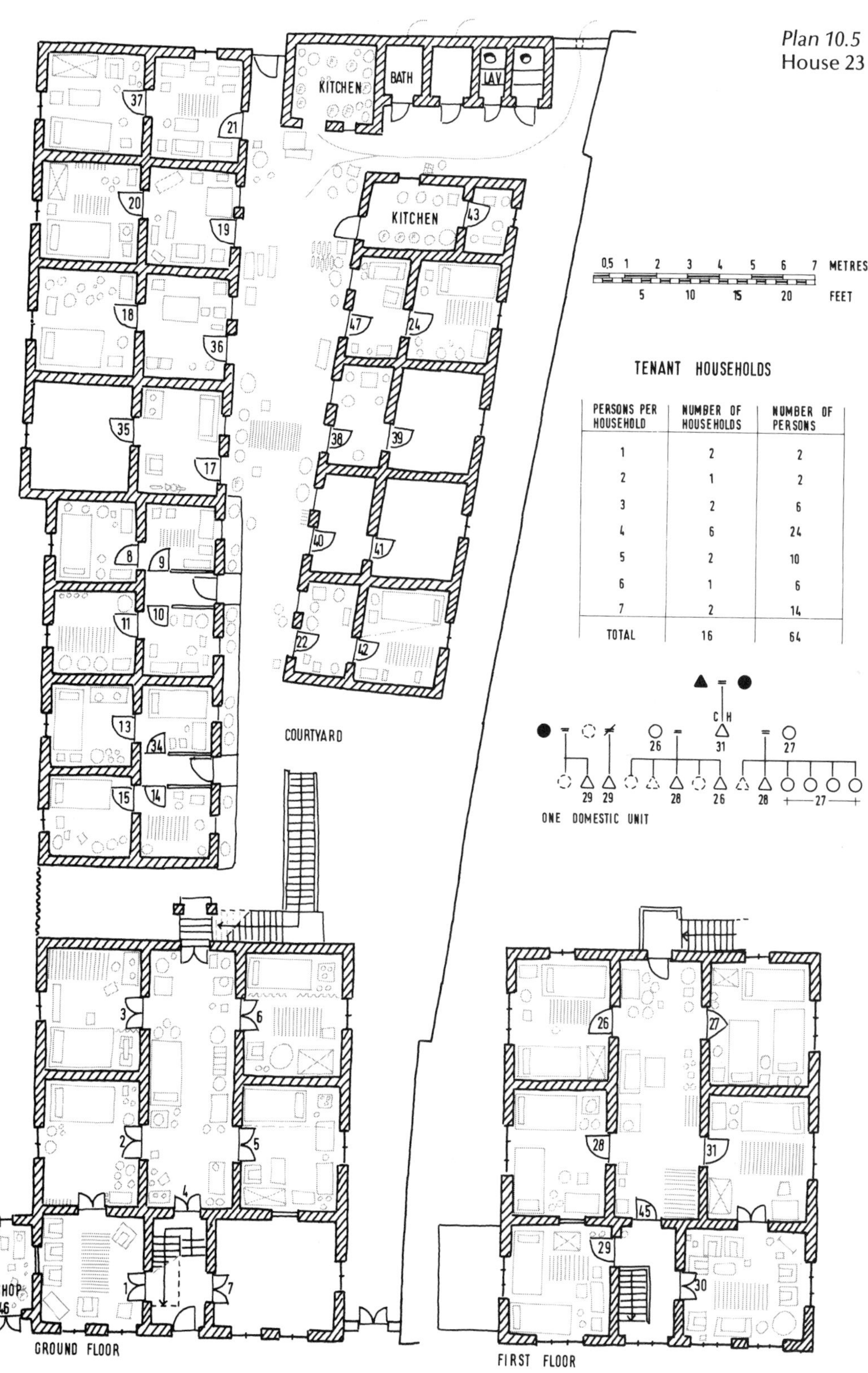

TENANT HOUSEHOLDS

PERSONS PER HOUSEHOLD	NUMBER OF HOUSEHOLDS	NUMBER OF PERSONS
1	2	2
2	1	2
3	2	6
4	6	24
5	2	10
6	1	6
7	2	14
TOTAL	16	64

Plan 10.5
House 23

Finally, the so-called 'Brazilian Houses' must be mentioned. Originally reserved for houses built in the second half of the nineteenth century in Lagos and other West African coastal towns by former slaves returning from South America, the term is now very loosely used to denote any two-storey house with a central corridor, a decorated street elevation, and brightly coloured balustrades. To the best of my knowledge there is no original 'Brazilian House' in Ibadan, but a few have survived in Lagos.

Land use

Data on land use given below derives from measurements taken in 63 compounds in Ibadan. The compounds surveyed cover a total area of 18,152 sq. m* divided between the built-up area of 12,379 sq. m or 68.2 per cent and the open area of 5,773 sq. m or 31.8 per cent, the average size per compound being 288.0 sq. m or 3,100.0 sq. ft. The open area can be subdivided into four categories:

1 Unpaved areas in courtyards and around compounds. These covered 3,878 sq. m or 67.2 per cent of the total open area.
2 Cement platforms which covered 1,549 sq. m or 26.8 per cent of the open area. Cement platforms found in courtyards are used as outdoor working areas, while those in front of compounds are occasionally occupied by traders to display their goods.
3 Pit-latrines and washing places covered 162 sq. m or 2.8 per cent of the open area.
4 Storage space occupied 184 sq. m or 3.2 per cent of the total open area. The items most frequently stored there included such building materials as sun-dried bricks and cement blocks as well as firewood and old clay pots. No cultivated land was found in any compound. (See Table A.10.1 on p. 379.)

Type and size of rooms

The built-up area in all the 63 compounds surveyed contained a total of 1,099 rooms, averaging 17.4 per com-

*The total area includes the built-up area, 47 courtyards (average size 62.5 sq. m), and other open areas surrounding the compound which are exclusively used by the inhabitants of the house. Public or semi-public footpaths and other open areas alongside the house are excluded. The area given above does not necessarily correspond with the total area owned by the family concerned.

pound. The total floor area of 9,522 sq. m is divided into four categories:

1 Living areas accounted for 7,958.6 sq. m or 83.6 per cent of the total floor area. This category includes 578 rooms with an average size of 8.0 sq. m which are used for sleeping; 50 sitting rooms or parlours with an average size of 10.9 sq. m; 86 central halls with an average size of 24.7 sq. m; 49 storage rooms for personal belongings with an average size of 6.3 sq. m; and 51 temporarily empty living and/or sleeping rooms. With a total of 814 rooms this is by far the most important group.
2 Common rooms accounted for 544.9 sq. m or 5.7 per cent of the total floor area. This category includes 66 entrance lobbies with an average size of 5.8 sq. m and 19 passages and staircases.
3 Basic ancillary facilities accounted for 728.3 sq. m or 7.6 per cent of the total floor area. This includes 57 kitchens with an average size of 7.1 sq. m, 35 store rooms with an average size of 4.6 sq. m, and 69 toilets and bathrooms.
4 Commercially used rooms accounted for 290.5 sq. m or 3.1 per cent of the total floor area. This category comprised 35 shops and/or workshops with an average size of 7.4 sq. m, 2 storage rooms for trade goods, and 2 permanent stables. (See Table A.10.7 on p. 390.)

Social structure and kinship organization

In the following pages I will first summarize some categories of Yoruba social structure and kinship organization, and then relate them to the compounds surveyed and their inhabitants. Among many distinguished scholars who have studied the Yoruba of south-western Nigeria, the works of W. R. Bascom, W. B. Schwab, and P. C. Lloyd were of particular interest for my study.

As already mentioned, the Yoruba of Nigeria* are an urban people who have lived in large urban communities for several centuries.[3] Today, over half of the total Yoruba population in Nigeria live in urban settlements having 20,000 and more inhabitants.

The kinship organization of the northern Yoruba, which includes the people of Ibadan, is based on agnatic kinship groups.[4] The Yoruba patrilineage (*idi'le*) is defined by reference to the lineage founder (*orisun*) and consists of all recognized agnatic descendants of that ancestor. The known history of a patrilineal descent group may be several generations in depth, and is often preserved in

*There are small groups of Yoruba living in Togo and Benin.

ritual chants (*rara*) and praise songs (*oriki*). In Ibadan the lineage founder is usually three to five generations remote from the oldest living member of the group. According to B. Lloyd, some large lineage groups contain more than one thousand living members who occupy several adjoining compounds.[5]

Within each lineage there are divisions into segments known as *igun* or *origun*. Each segment may occupy the rooms around one courtyard, or it may occupy a separate compound which is the base of a co-residential kinship group and the unit of analysis in this study. The population of a compound may be further divided into various related individual families. The individual family – which consists of the male head, his wife or wives, and his own children – is known among the Yoruba as *oba kan*.* As Yoruba are polygamous, an *oba kan* may be subdivided into the children of each of the head's wives. These groups are known as *omo iya* (literally, children of the same mother). Hence an *oba kan* group contains as many *omo iya* as the male head has wives with children. This pattern is illustrated in Diagram 10.1.

However, like the Yoruba, we have to extend an *omo iya* group beyond the limit of the individual family. Unless all his full siblings are dead, the family head, who is normally male, is a member of the *omo iya* group into which he was born; and he with his own children will be regarded as part of a wider close-knit kinship group, which may form the base of a co-residential kinship group.

So far we have briefly discussed the various kinds of kinship groups recognized by the Yoruba and we must now turn to the division of the compound population into economic units or households. As already pointed out in Chapter 4 on p. 34, the compound population is not necessarily divided into economic units along kinship lines, and a household may include several other related or unrelated persons.

The 63 compounds surveyed in Ibadan contained a total of 295 households which fall into three categories. First, there is the compound head's household; second, there are all other related households which are dependent or semi-dependent; and third, there are tenant households which pay a weekly or monthly rent for their rooms. I intend to examine these three different categories of households before discussing the various forms of family groupings and the cyclic tendency which regulates their growth, decline, and size.

**Oba kan* and *omo iya* are terms which describe the relationship between children and their parents. I will follow here P. C. Lloyd in extending both terms to denote a group of people so related.

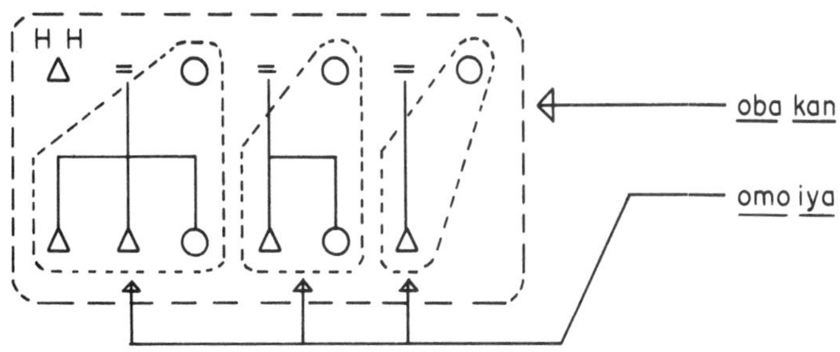

Diagram 10.1
Yoruba kinship and descent

Population and household data

The population distribution of these 63 compounds is given in Diagram 10.2. Over two thirds or 69.8 per cent of the sample compounds have populations that range between 5 and 24 persons, the average being 20.4 persons per compound. However, eleven or 17.4 per cent of these compounds contained between 30 and 49 persons, while two or 3.2 per cent had 52 and 76 persons respectively. The two largest compounds are 'tenement houses' situated in predominantly immigrant areas west of the old city. (See Table A.10.2 on page 380.)

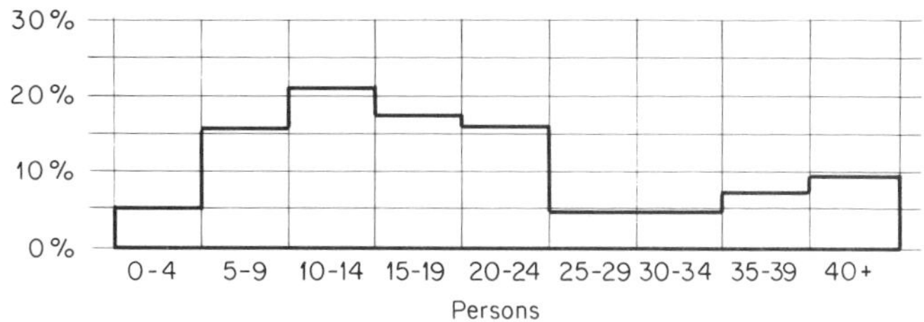

Diagram 10.2
Number of persons per compund in percentages

Variations in the size of the three types of households distinguished above are compared in Diagram 10.3. The three diagrams reveal some interesting features. Nearly three quarters of all compound heads' households have populations that range from 3 to 10 persons, whereas nearly half of all dependent households have populations of 3 to 4, and over 50 per cent of tenant households only 1 or 2 persons. The average size of households decreases from 7.2 persons per household in the first category to 4.2 persons in dependent households and 3.0 persons in tenant households. These differences in household size are partly due to the fact that the two latter types of households consist mainly of 'young households'.* For

*For the age of household heads see Tables A.10.3 and A.10.4 on pp. 381 and 382.

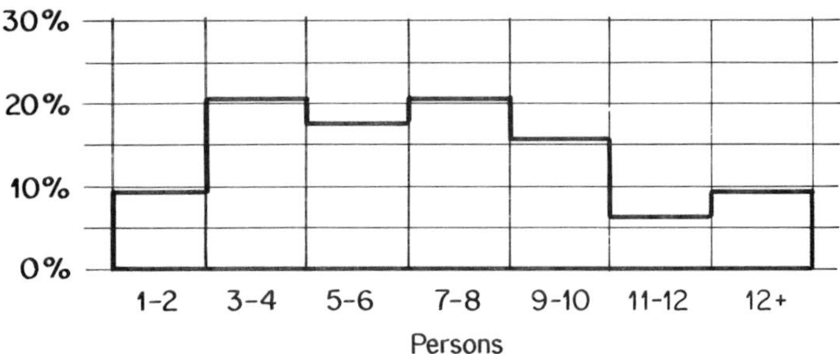

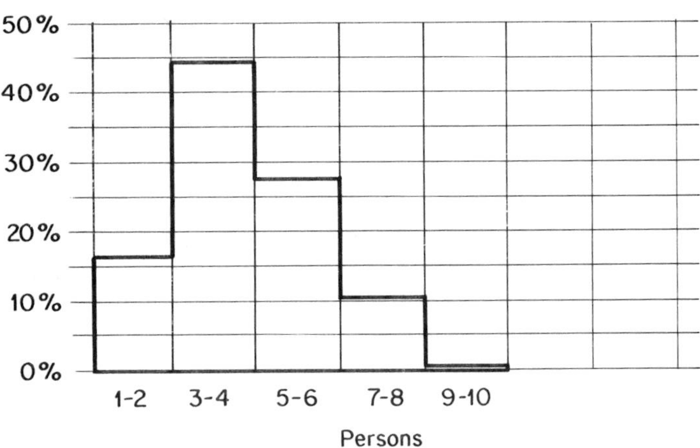

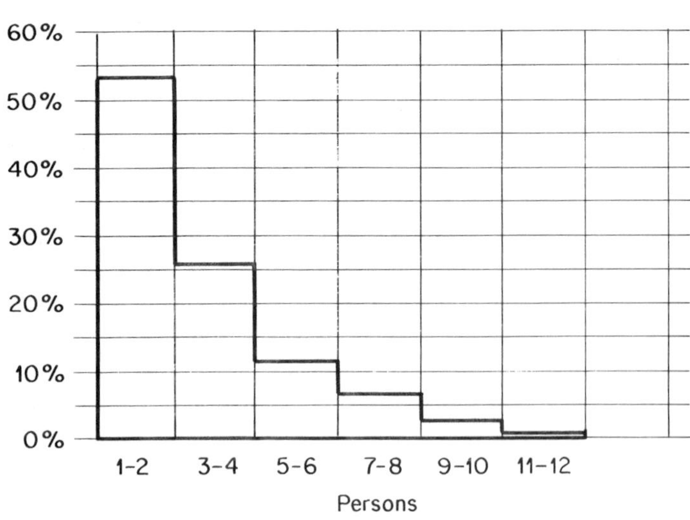

Diagram 10.3
Number of persons per household in percentages

Table 10.1 Distribution of wives per married man

Column	1		2		3		4	
	CH		DHH		THH		Total	
Type of household	No.	%	No.	%	No.	%	No.	%
Male with 1 wife	28	46.7	70	70.7	85	89.5	183	72.0
Male with 2 wives	19	31.6	23	23.2	10	10.5	52	20.5
Male with 3 wives	10	16.7	6	6.1	–	–	16	6.3
Male with 4 wives	3	5.0	–	–	–	–	3	1.2
Total	60	100.0	99	100.0	95	100.0	254[a]	100.0
No. of wives	108		134		105		347	
% of males in polygamous families		53.3		29.3		10.5		27.9
% of females in polygamous families		74.1		47.8		19.0		47.3
Av. no. of wives per married man	1.8		1.3		1.1		1.4	

[a]There were 41 households whose head was either single, divorced, or widowed.

example, only 14.9 per cent of wives of dependent household heads and 4.3 per cent of wives of tenant household heads have passed childbearing age (40 plus), as against 41.8 per cent of all compound heads' wives. Furthermore, the lack of cheap and suitable accommodation as well as the generally lower income of the heads of these dependent and tenant households – a topic discussed in the next chapter – tend to limit, at least temporarily, the number of children in these families.

In Table 10.1 a preliminary discrimination is made among men in each of these three households according to the number of their wives. The table shows clearly the dominant economic position of the compound head and the prestige generally associated with polygamous marriages among both the Christian* and Muslim communities in Ibadan.

The age and sex distribution as well as the marital status of the sample population is given in Diagram 10.4. and Table 10.2. The bar-chart indicates that young persons of both sexes, but particularly females, marry on average at a later age than their counterparts in Zaria. About half of the 49 widowed females who lived in the compounds surveyed are former wives of deceased compound heads. Some widows, who are no longer able to work, were supported by their next of kin, while the younger widows

*The 'African Churches', made up of splinter groups from Methodist and/or Anglican christians, leave the decision to establish monogamous or polygamous families entirely to their individual members.

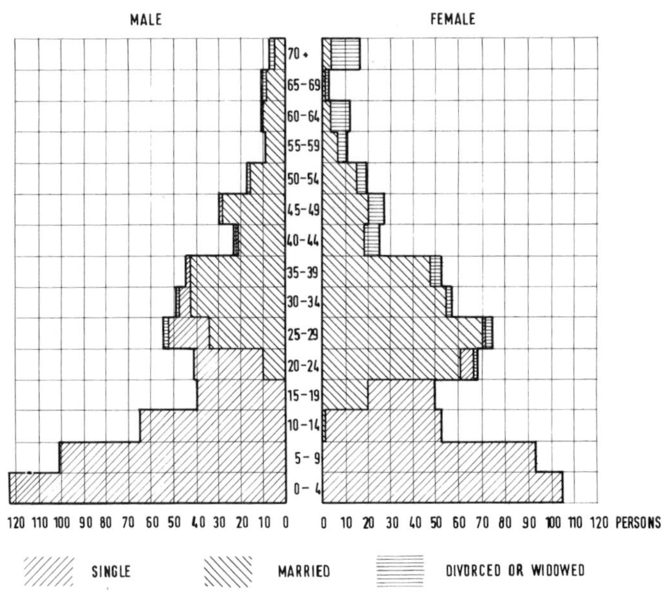

Diagram 10.4
Survey sample population by sex, age, and marital status

will leave the compound on remarriage. (For more detailed information see Table A.10.5 on p. 384.)

Family grouping

The following discussion on family groupings is partly based on household data; but as we cannot fully understand the principles that govern the constitution

Table 10.2 Survey sample population by sex, age, and marital status

Age	Male					Female					Grand
	Sing.	Mar.	Div.	Wid.	Total	Sing.	Mar.	Div.	Wid.	Total	total
0–4	123				123	105				105	228
5–9	91				91	93				93	184
10–14	65				65	52	1			53	118
15–19	40				40	30	20			50	90
20–24	32	10			42	6	61	1		68	110
25–29	19	34	2		55	1	70	3		74	129
30–34	5	43	1		49		55	1	1	57	106
35–39	2	43			45		48	1	4	53	98
40–44	1	21	1		23		18	1	6	25	48
45–49	1	29			30		20		7	27	57
50–54		16	1		17		15		4	19	36
55–59		9			9		7	1	3	11	20
60–64		10		1	11		4		8	12	23
65–69		9		2	11		1		2	3	14
70+		5		2	7		3		14	17	24
Total	379	229	5	5	618	287	323	8	49	667	1,285

Table 10.3 Age of compound heads by stages of kinship development

Column	1	2	3	4	5	6	7
Stage	1	2	3	4 + 5	6	Joint hhs	Total
Age of CH							
25–29			1		1		2
30–34	2		1		1	2	6
35–39	1		4			3	8
40–44			1		1		2
45–49	7		2		2	1	12
50–54			3	2		1	6
55–59	1		2	3	1	1	8
60–64	5						5
65–69	1	2	2	2		1	8
70+	2	3		1			6
No. of CHs	19	5	16	8	6	9	63
No. of HHs	19	12	44	38	36	22	171
No. of persons	130	66	228	199	166	118	907
Av. households (hh) per compound	1.0	2.4	2.7	4.7	6.0	2.4	2.7
Av. persons per compound	6.8	13.2	14.3	24.9	27.7	13.1	14.4
Av. persons per hh	6.8	5.5	5.2	5.2	4.6	5.4	5.3
Kinship diagrams	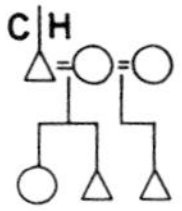	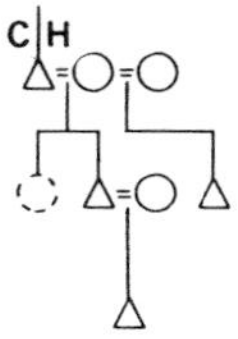	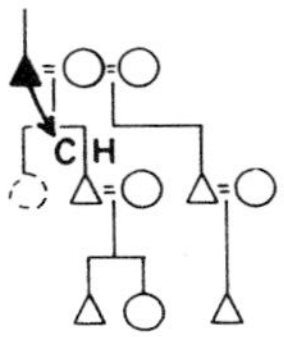	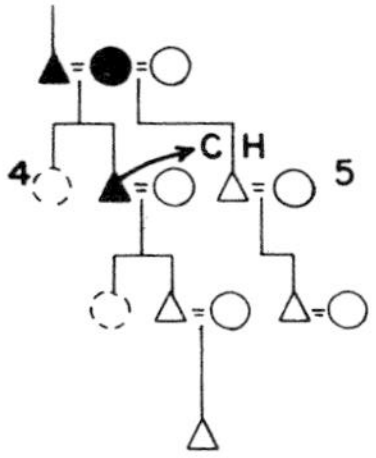	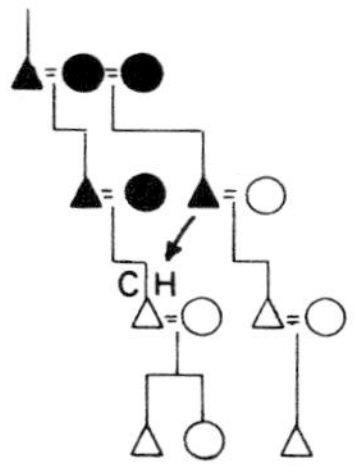	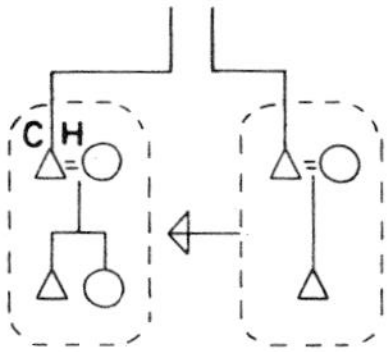	

and changes of family grouping by reference to household data alone, some additional kinship data having a common reference point are necessary. For this purpose, compound headship provides the natural focus, since by systematically classifying the sample population in terms of their individual relationship to the compound head, we are able to expose the internal fabric of kinship structure. (See Tables A.10.4 and A.10.5 on pp. 382, 384–386.) As already shown elsewhere, kinship groups are liable to constant change due to marriage, migration, and death of their male members. How such changes affect co-residential kinship groups and so modify the layout and size of compounds in Ibadan will be the subject of the following analysis.

We may begin by recalling some earlier findings on the development of co-residential kinship groups at Zaria. There, most co-residential kinship groups are based on agnatic descent. We also found that the individual family was the first and simplest stage in a development cycle that gave rise to composite co-residential kinship groups. Of the six such stages we identified, the last was that of a compound which housed paternal cousins and their descendants.

The majority of compounds surveyed in Ibadan also contained family groups based on agnatic kinship. We may therefore apply a similar mode of analysis to the kinship data collected there. However, one important difference must be briefly discussed first. Unlike our sample in Zaria, at Ibadan our sample included a total of 124 households containing 378 unrelated persons who lived as tenants in about half of the compounds surveyed. These tenant households, which neither contribute to nor influence the development of complex co-residential kinship groups, are omitted from the Table 10.3 and are analysed separately later.

The top part of Table 10.3 gives the age distribution of the 63 compound heads, according to the composition of the co-residential kinship groups. These age distributions, when compared with the simplified kinship diagrams in the lower part of the table, clearly show that compound heads in stages 1, 3, and 6, which result either from migration or the death of a former compound head, are on average younger than their counterparts in stages 2 and 4 + 5. A similar observation has already been made for the sample studied at Zaria. Column 6 lists nine compounds the populations of which increased by the immigration of 13 related families rather than by natural growth.

The centre of the table deserves special attention. It can be seen that the average number of households per compound increases from one household with an average of

6.8 persons in stage 1 to six households having an average total of 27.7 persons in stage 6. The average number of persons per household on the other hand decreases from 6.8 persons in stage 1 to 4.6 persons in stage 6. This decrease in the number of persons per household is partly due to the emigration of larger dependent family units in search of more spacious accommodation, while other dependent household heads, responsible for large units, may become compound heads. It is also of interest to note that none of the 63 compounds surveyed contained co-residential kinship groups which developed beyond stage 6, that is, to include paternal parallel cousins and their unmarried children. It is obvious that at this stage lack of space, the limited lifespan of these houses built of mud, tensions between group members, the differential economic success of junior household heads, and the death of the compound head combine to split the lineage segment into smaller units. (See Table A.10.6 on p. 388.)

So far we have discussed those co-residential kinship groups which contained the compound head and other related dependent or semi-dependent households, but we must now consider the 124 tenant households who live in rented accommodation in 32 out of 63 compounds surveyed. Only six of these tenant household heads were born in Ibadan,* while the rest are of a group of first-generation immigrants. In Table 10.4 these 124 tenant households have been divided into four main categories based on kinship organization to reveal the structure of this group. The first category (columns 1–3) has heads who are either single, divorced, or widowed, while the second category contains 18 female heads whose husbands had been absent for more than one month preceding the time of the interview (column 4). However, in ten cases there was considerable doubt if the women in question were still married. The third category consists of couples without children including those whose children were away (column 5), while the fourth category contains individual families (column 6). Among the couples without resident children (column 5) twelve women were temporarily absent. Three women were away during childbirth, while the rest were living with their parents until their husbands could secure suitable jobs. Thus 19 or 15.3 per cent of all tenant households consisted of single persons, 26 or 21.0 per cent contained widowed, divorced, and married persons who lived alone (excluding those households with wives away during childbirth), and 79 or 63.7 per cent contained couples without resident children and individual families.

*Four household heads were born in Ibadan but brought up by their mothers on the family farm, while two household heads had quit their fathers' compounds after a family dispute.

Table 10.4 Structure of tenant households

Column	1	2	3	4	5	6	7	8	9
Type of HH	Sing.	Div.	Wid.	Female with temp. absent husband	Childless couple	Individual family	Fem. HH	Male HH	Grand total
Age of THH									
15–19	2						1	1	2
20–24	7	1		2		1	3	8	11
25–29	8	2		3	6	7	5	21	26
30–34	1	2		2	5	14	3	21	24
35–39	1			8	4	14	8	19	27
40–44					5	5		10	10
45–49				1	5	5	1	10	11
50–54				1	2	4	1	6	7
55–59		1				1	1	1	2
60–64				1		1	1	1	2
65–69			1					1	1
70+			1				1		1
M + F hh							25	99	
No. of households	19	6	2	18	27	52			124
No. of persons	20	10	2	39	46	261			378
Av. no. of persons per hh	1.0	1.7	1.0	2.2	1.7	5.0			3.0
Kinship diagrams									

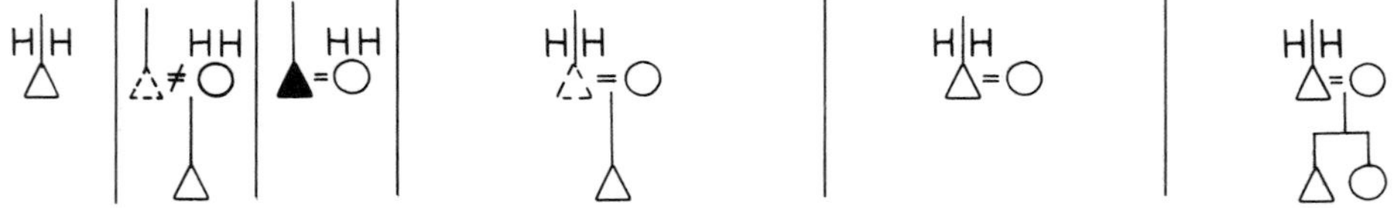

Another comment on this table is appropriate. In the 124 tenant households with 378 members, 25 or 6.6 per cent were dependent single relatives belonging either to the husband's or to the wives' kin group. For comparison, the households of compound heads contained 124 such persons or 27.3 per cent of their total population.

Finally, comparison of the age distribution of tenant household heads and compound heads provides some indication of the age distribution of first-generation immigrants within the sample population. Table 10.5 shows that nearly three quarters of the tenant household heads are under the age of 40 as against only one quarter of the compound heads.

In conclusion, the main differences between the households of compound heads and those of their tenants may be outlined briefly. The most obvious difference is the higher average population, 7.2 in the households of compound heads compared with 3.0 for their tenants. The number of dependants from their wider kinship groups in compound heads' households was 124 persons* or 27.3 per cent, and greatly exceeds that in tenant households with 25 persons or 6.6 per cent. Budgets taken from both types of households indicate that one factor associated with the smaller number of dependent persons in tenant households may be economic.

The different structures of the two types of households are perhaps even more important. A compound head's household is usually part of a co-residential kinship group which may include his married son or sons and their dependants, and his collateral agnates and their issue. This kinship group for which the compound head is partly responsible provides a certain amount of social stability as well as economic security for all its members. Tenant households, on the other hand, seem to be less stable groups, and 45 or 36.3 per cent of their heads are single or either divorced, widowed, or separated. As recent immigrants into the city, most tenants had suffered economic hardship until they established themselves.

Table 10.5 Age distribution of tenant household heads and compound heads, in percentages

Age group	15–24	25–39	40–54	55–69	70+	Total	No. of HHs
Tenant HHs	10.5	62.1	22.6	4.0	0.8	100.0	124
Compound heads	—	25.4	31.8	33.3	9.5	100.0	63

*This does not include seven married daughters and one married son of compound heads who live in their fathers' compounds but do not form separate households.

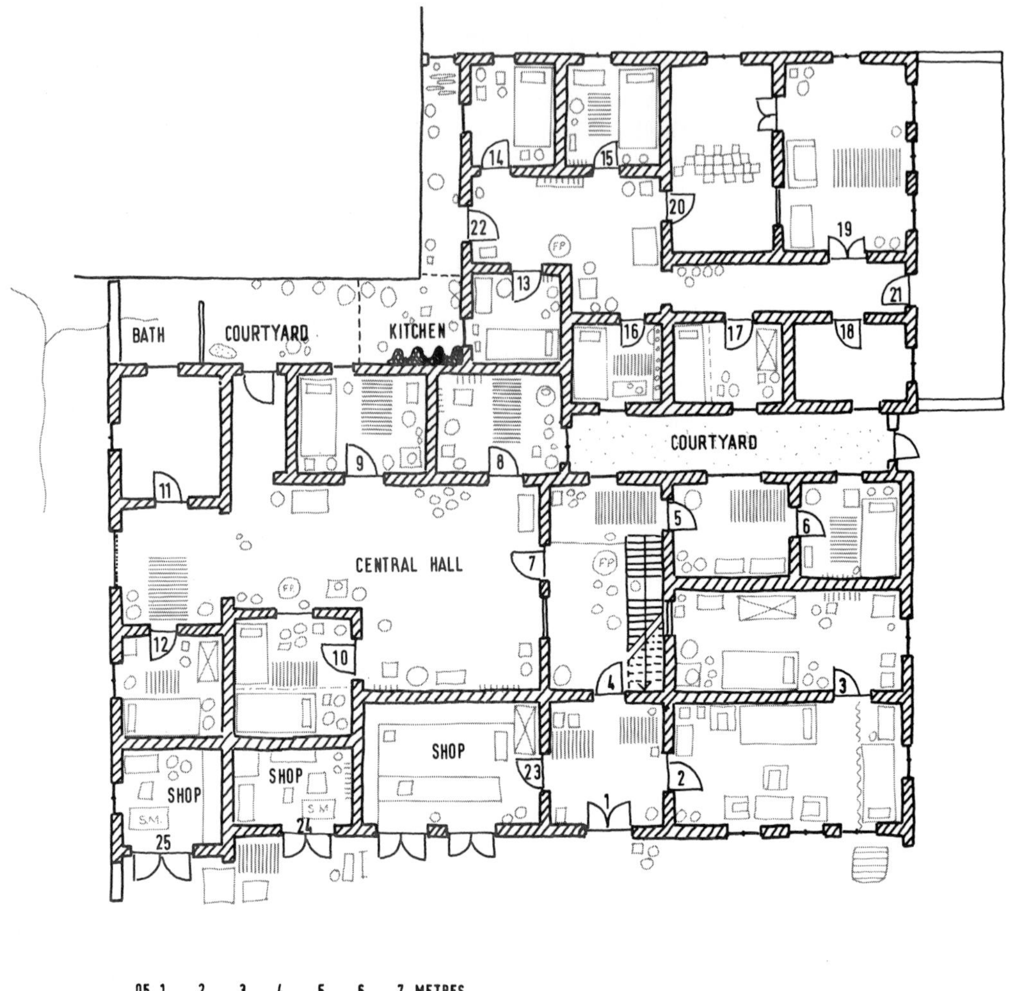

Plan 10.6
House 5

This brief comparison clearly shows the considerable variety in the structure and size of these three household types. It has also indicated the danger of using data on households indiscriminately without taking into account their respective backgrounds and positions within co-residential groups.

Compound and kinship organization

In the following pages I will relate some of the facts which emerged from the discussion on household and kinship organization to a number of compounds surveyed in Ibadan. Two case studies have been chosen from the sample to illustrate various stages in the development of co-residential agnatic kinship groups and the repercussions of these developments on the compounds.

The first example is a compound situated on the north-eastern outskirts of the city (see Plan 10.6). The land on which the house stands was given to the present compound head's late father by his mother's family shortly after the First World War. The core of the house was built between 1920 and 1922. In 1923 or 1924 the compound head's first child was born. The family who then occupied the house illustrated stage 1 in the kinship diagram discussed earlier. (See p. 39, and Plan 10.7A.) In 1930, the compound head's mother and younger full brother came to live in the house and, anticipating his marriage to a second wife, the compound head built two additional rooms plus a small shop to accommodate the newcomers (Plan 10.7B). Following the marriage of the compound head's full brother in 1935, a new house with four rooms was added. The enlarged compound then contained a 'stage 3 type' kinship group of two full brothers and their families (Plan 10.7C). The next two additions to the compound were constructed between 1947 and 1954 to house the rapidly growing group (Plans 10.7D and 10.7E). In 1949 the eldest son of the compound head married his first wife, thus moving the co-residential kinship group into stage 4. The premature death of the compound head's younger brother in 1964 gave rise to a 'stage 5 type' kinship group without affecting the headship (Plan 10.7F). With the death of the compound head two years later, his oldest son assumed responsibility for the late father's and father's brothers' wives and their unmarried children. As a result of this latest death, the co-residential kinship group moved to stage 6, which consists of several paternal parallel cousins and their unmarried children. At the time of my visit in 1968, the inhabitants of the compound discussed among themselves the possibility of constructing an upper floor. They told me that unless something was done some family members would be forced to look for alternative accommodation elsewhere, a step of which the compound head did not approve.

The second example shows a compound occupied by a co-residential kinship group which changed over a ten-year period (1958–1968) from stage 3, when it contained full or half brothers' families with unmarried children, into stage 4 containing full or half brothers' families with married children and their descendants. As a result of these changes, including the death of the compound head in 1961, several rooms changed hands, following certain principles generally observed by the Yoruba.

According to its compound head, the house was built on family land in the first decade of this century. A family dispute in the late 1940s led to the division of the com-

KINSHIP ORGANIZATION AND THE DEVELOPMENT OF THE COMPOUND

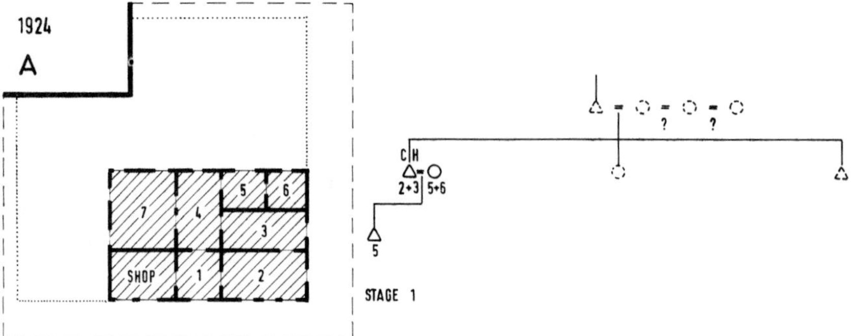

Plan 10.7A

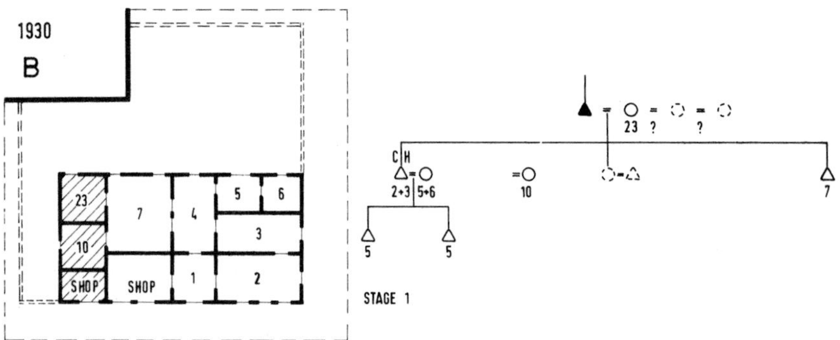

Plan 10.7B

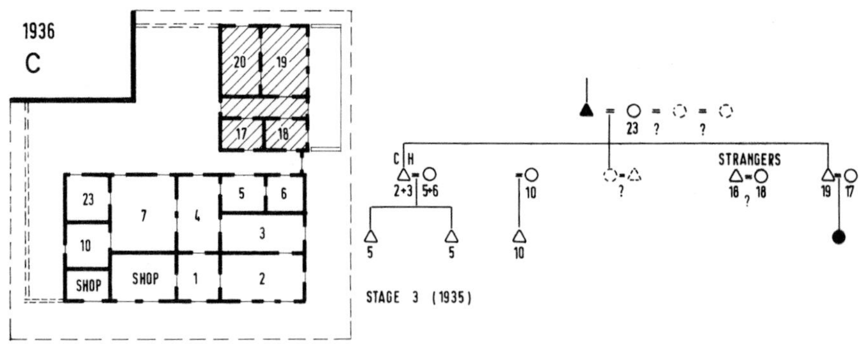

Plan 10.7C

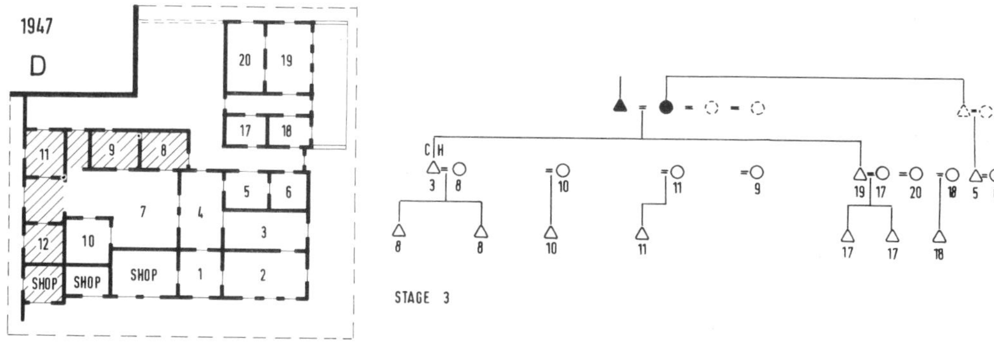

Plan 10.7D

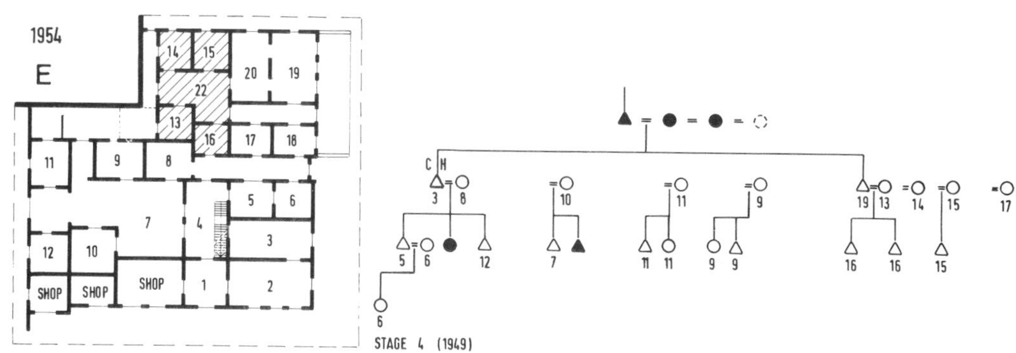

Plan 10.7E

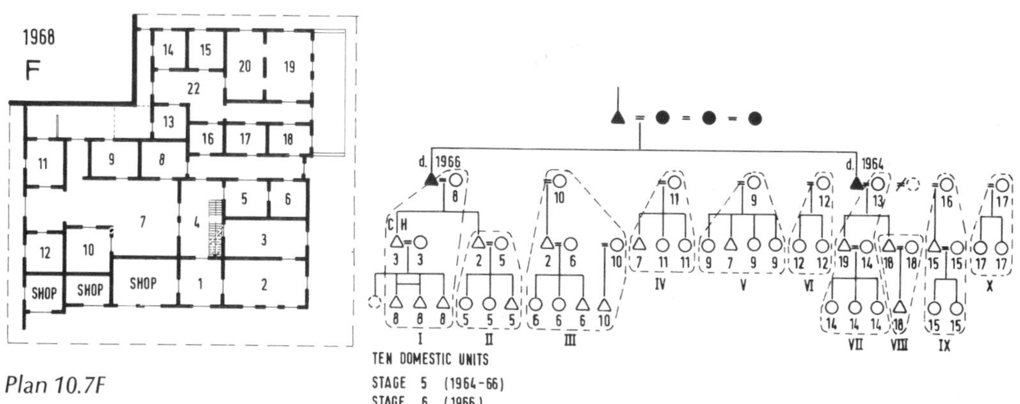

Plan 10.7F

Plan 10.7
Development of House 5

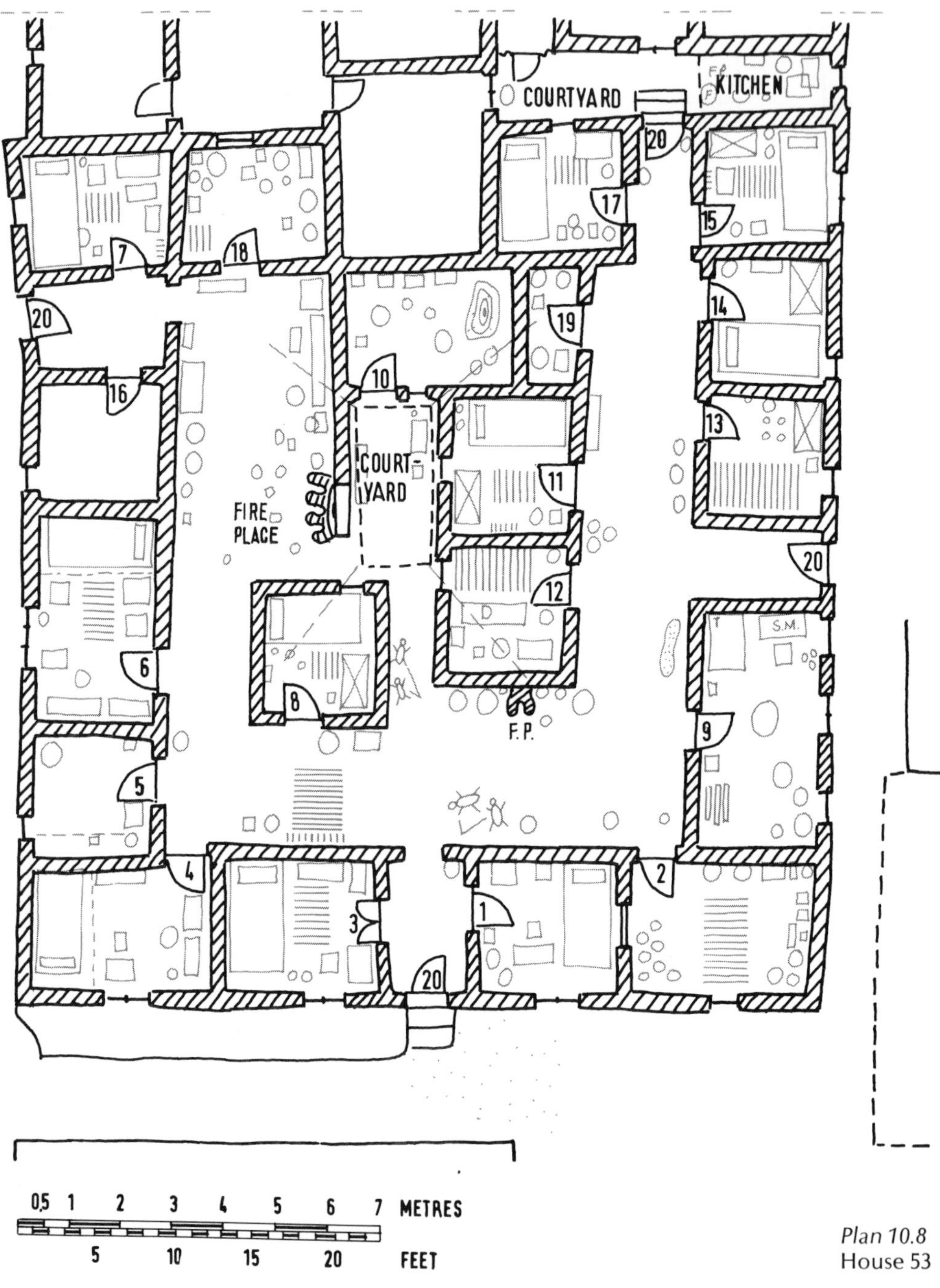

Plan 10.8
House 53

pound into two separate units, marked by the closing of its only internal passage. (See Plan 10.8 above.) In 1958 the rooms were distributed among the three half brothers and their families who lived in the house as follows: the compound head and his family occupied the front rooms numbered 1–4, while each of his two half brothers and their families occupied the rooms to the left and right of the courtyard respectively. (See Plan 10.9.) In the late 1950s, two marriages, the youngest brother's third and the compound head's oldest son's first, sparked off the construction of two new rooms which were completed in 1960. (See Plan 10.9B.) Following the death of the compound head in 1961, and the succession of the senior surviving half brother to the headship, several rooms changed hands. The new compound head moved into rooms 1 and 2, while the late compound head's oldest son occupied room 3. This move was made in recognition of the young man's increasing wealth as a successful craftsman and a future contender for the headship. In 1964 he built a room for his wife. (See Plan 10.9C.) The distribution of rooms in 1968 still reflected the pattern of occupancy laid down in 1960, with the oldest son of the new compound head remaining in the room formerly occupied by his father. (See Plan 10.9D.)

It was observed throughout my survey in Ibadan that at least one front room in each compound was always occupied by the compound head, and that any other room facing the main street or footpath was given to some important member of the house.

It is probably true to say that in the past a sizeable proportion of Ibadan's population lived in large compounds. These compounds were divided into segments known among the Oyo-Yoruba as *igun* or *origun*, i.e. people who live in the same courtyard. My investigation has shown that today kinship groups of this type live in smaller, self-contained houses which are often built on corporately owned family land. Apart from the large number of immigrant households and some well-educated household heads with above average income, there is little evidence to support the view that the Yoruba co-residential kinship group is breaking up into still smaller units. On the contrary, it seems that the social and economic strains associated with the rapid urban growth of towns such as Ibadan may serve to bind kinship groups even closer together.

Distribution of floor area

The distribution of the floor area among the population of compounds may be studied in two ways. First, we can examine the average floor area per household and per person classified by their relationship to the compound head; and second, we may study the average floor area per household and per person according to the number

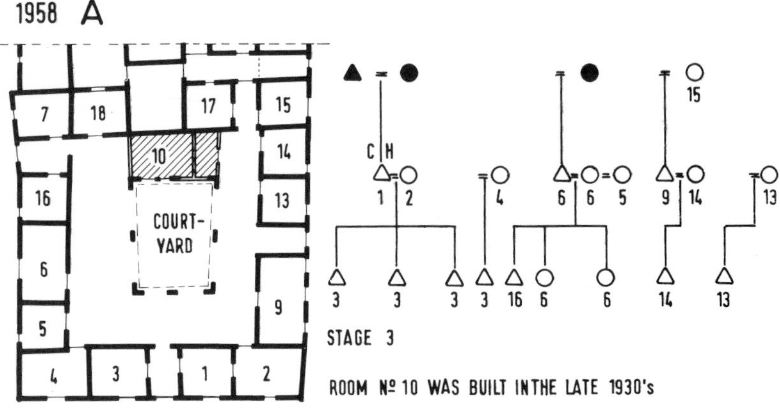

Plan 10.9A

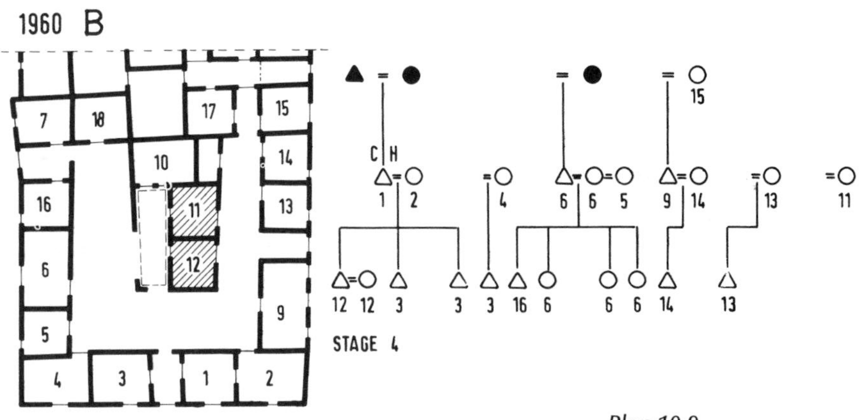

Plan 10.9B

Plan 10.9
Development of House 53

of persons per household. The first approach may tell us something about preferential treatment by certain household heads regarding the allocation of rooms, while the second will indicate the steps taken by compound heads to build new rooms, or to adapt available space for the growing number of people in compounds.

The survey in Ibadan included 295 households with 1,285 persons in 63 compounds. Table 10.6 compares the total average floor area (column 2) and the average sleeping area (column 3) available to each household and its members, classifying these households by the relationship of their head to the compound head. As can be seen in the table, the substantial difference between the total average floor area occupied by the compound head's own household (91.8 sq. m) on the one hand, and the total

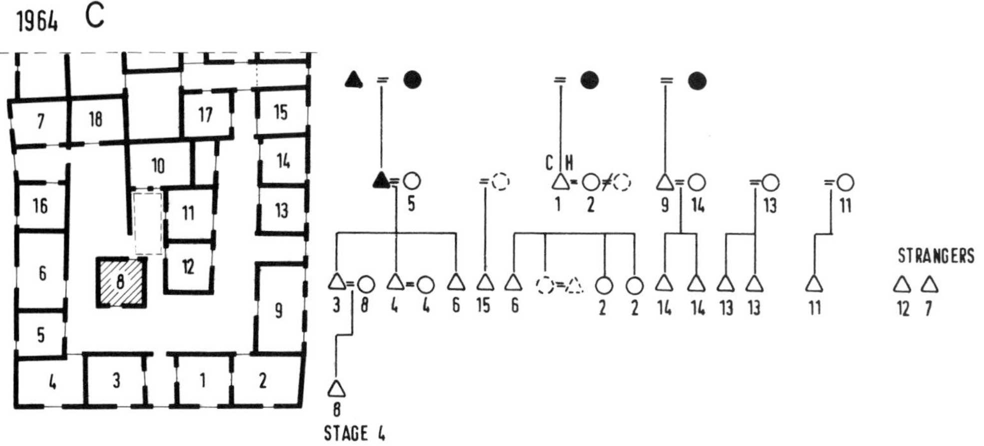

Plan 10.9C

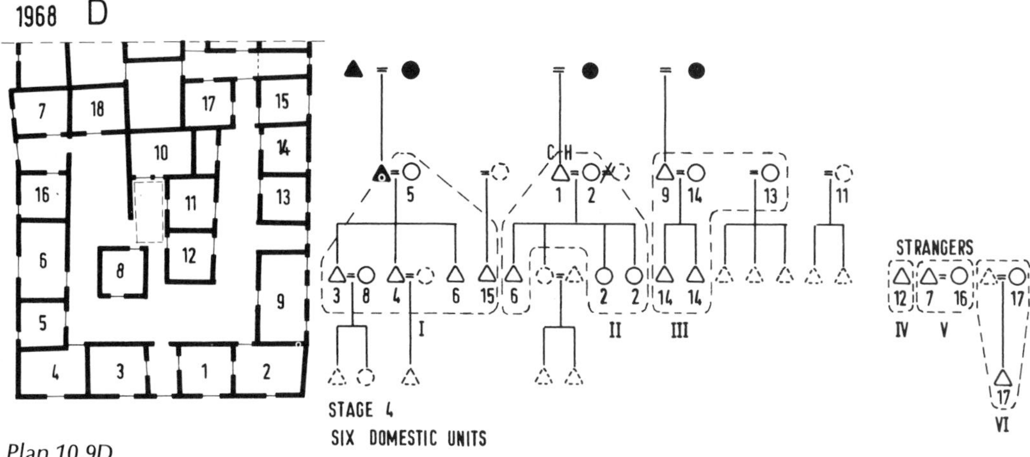

Plan 10.9D

average floor area of other related dependent or semi-dependent households (17.8 sq. m) and tenant households (14.6 sq. m) on the other, is noteworthy.

These differences are partly due to the larger average size of the compound head's household, 7.2 persons, as against 4.2 and 3.0 persons for all other dependent and tenant households respectively. Furthermore, the area occupied by the compound head's own household includes all rooms such as central halls, entrance lobbies, common kitchens, and stores for which he is directly responsible, although these rooms are normally available for general use by all other resident households. Therefore, the average floor area illustrates the differential distribution of responsibilities among household heads within the compound rather more precisely than

Table 10.6 Average floor area per household and person in square metres

Column	1		2		3	
	No. of hhs	No. of persons	Total av. area per hh	Total av. area per person	Av. sleep. area per hh	Av. sleep. area per person
CH's household	63	454	91.8	12.7	33.8	4.7
CH's full & half brs' hhs	42	195	19.0	4.1	14.7	3.2
CH's sons' hhs	11	54	24.9	5.1	12.9	2.6
CH's full & half brs' sons' hhs	14	48	18.0	4.9	12.6	3.4
CH's father's brs' sons' hhs	17	69	16.3	4.0	13.4	3.3
Other related hhs	24	87	14.0	3.9	11.4	2.4
Subtotal dep. hhs	108	453	17.8	4.2	12.6	3.0
Tenant hhs	124	378	14.6	4.8	11.0	3.6
Total hhs and persons	295	1,285				
Av. all hhs and persons			32.3	7.4	16.7	3.8

the allocation of living space between the households themselves.

The average sleeping area per person fluctuates between 4.7 sq. m for members of the compound head's household and 2.4 sq. m for other related households, the total average being 3.8 sq. m or 41.0 sq. ft. However, the average sleeping area per person in the compound heads' households is slightly inflated by the fact that some compound heads have their own sleeping rooms, a luxury not enjoyed by most other household heads.

Graphs 10.1 and 10.2 derive from Table A.10.8 on p. 392. Graph 10.1 shows the average floor area (line 1) and the average sleeping area (line 2) in households of differing size. As may be seen, the average floor area per household increases from 13.6 sq. m in households with 1 or 2 persons to 106.4 sq. m in households having 11 or 12 persons. At the same time the average sleeping area per household also increases from 8.4 sq. m for households with 1 or 2 persons to 46.8 sq. m for 11- or 12-person households.

Graph 10.2 shows the average floor area per person (line 1) and the average sleeping area per person (line 2) in households of differing size. As can be seen, the average floor area per person decreases from 8.8 sq. m for households with 1 or 2 persons to 6.1 sq. m for households with 3 or 4 persons, but increases steadily to 9.9 sq. m for

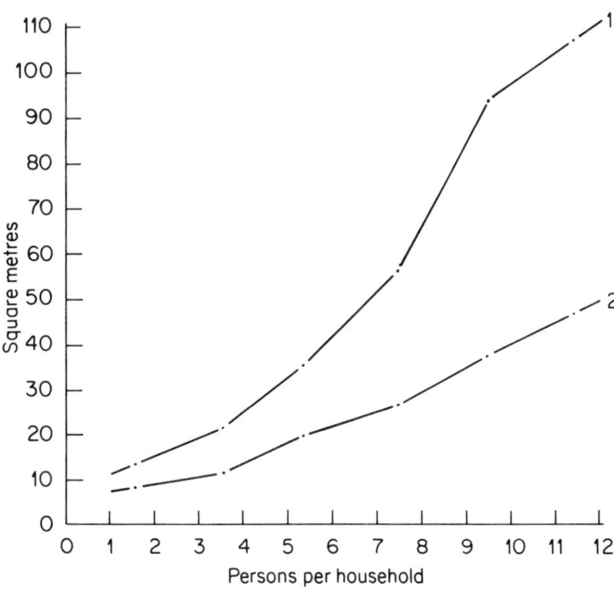

Graph 10.1
Average floor and sleeping area per household in square metres

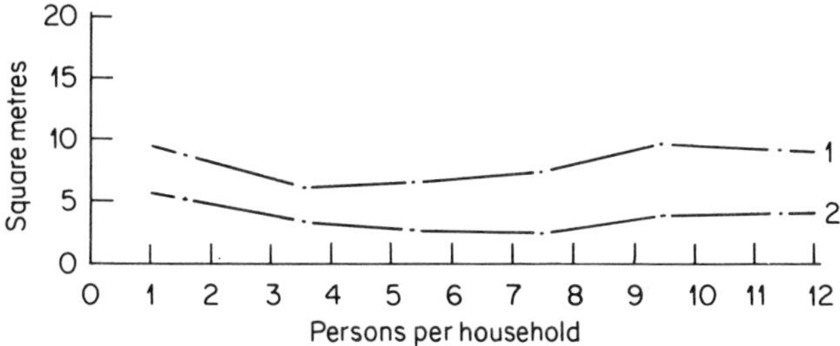

Graph 10.2
Average floor and sleeping area per person in square metres. (See Table A.10.8 on p. 392)

households having 9 or 10 persons. The same trend can be observed for the average sleeping area per person which decreases from 5.4 sq. m per person in households with 1 or 2 persons to 3.4 sq. m per person in households with 3 or 4 persons but remains fairly stable between 3.7 sq. m and 4.1 sq. m per person for all larger households. The total average floor area of 7.4 sq. m (80.0 sq. ft), and the average sleeping area of 3.8 sq. m (41.0 sq. ft), available per person in households surveyed in Ibadan, indicate no serious problem of overcrowding.[6] It is obvious that most compound heads were able to build new rooms or make old rooms available for the growing kinship groups, while some of the larger dependent households left their father's or brother's houses and established their own independent households elsewhere.

Notes and references

1 P. C. Lloyd, 'The Yoruba lineage', *Africa*, **XXV** (3), 1955, p. 238.

2 United Nations, *Housing in Africa*, E/CH/14/HOU/7/Rev., New York, 1965. Office of International Housing, *Housing in Nigeria*, Washington, DC, 1964, HHFA, Country Report Series.

3 W. R. Bascom, 'Urbanization among the Yoruba', *American Journal of Sociology*, **LX** (5), 1955, pp. 446–454.

4 P. C. Lloyd, 'Agnatic and cognatic descent among the Yoruba', *Man, The Journal of the Royal Anthropological Institute*, **I** (4), 1966, pp. 484–500. P. C. Lloyd, *Yoruba Land Law*, Oxford, 1962, p. 56. W. B. Schwab, 'Kinship and lineage among the Yoruba', *Africa*, **XXV** (4), 1955, pp. 352–374.

5 B. Lloyd, 'Indigenous Ibadan', in *The City of Ibadan*, ed. P. C. Lloyd *et al.*, Cambridge, 1967, pp. 59–83.

6 A. Lubega, 'Financing and production of private houses in urban districts of Kampala (Uganda), London, 1970. Unpublished Ph.D. thesis, pp. 152–156. The extent of overcrowding is usually measured by the ratio of persons per habitable room. It has been fairly widely accepted that an occupancy rate of more than two persons per habitable room can be regarded as overcrowded. In the 63 compounds the occupancy rate of the 814 habitable rooms was 1.6 persons per room. See also Table A.11.7 on p. 390.

Chapter 11

Occupation and income

Ibadan

Occupational patterns and income distribution for Nigeria have already been dealt with in Chapter 5. In this chapter I shall discuss the information available on occupational patterns and income distribution in Ibadan, before proceeding to the analysis of the data obtained from my survey of 63 compounds containing 295 households in that city.

Until the late 1960s, only a few scholars worked on the occupational pattern in Nigeria. One of the first systematic investigations into the craft activities of Ibadan's population was carried out by K. M. Buchanan in 1949–1950. According to Buchanan, there were then 2,700 small-scale industrial enterprises in the city. The most important of these industries was tailoring with 34.0 per cent of the total, followed by carpentry with 17.7 per cent, dyeing with 13.5 per cent, and mechanical work – i.e. cycle repairing and motor mechanics – with 12.8 per cent.[1] The numbers of persons employed by these enterprises are not given. Further investigations into craft activities in Ibadan city were conducted by A. Callaway in 1961 and 1963[2] and M. Koll in 1967.[3]

Despite its many shortcomings, the 1952 census provided the first comprehensive set of detailed data on the occupational structure of Ibadan's population.[4] The occupational distribution of the city's male population was then as follows: agriculture, 21.6 per cent; crafts, 13.4

per cent; trade, 12.0 per cent; administrative and professional workers, 5.3 per cent; miscellaneous occupations, 9.6 per cent; and unspecified, 38.1 per cent. An analysis of the occupational pattern in 39 city wards based on the 1952 census returns was carried out by A. L. Mabogunje.[5] Mabogunje shows that agriculture is especially important in the eastern parts of the city, while craft activities are more frequently found in immigrant areas to the west and north of the old city, with marked concentrations around Bere Square (N.1) and Ogunpa (S.W.6). (See Map A.7.2 on p. 370 and Map A.9.1 on p. 375.) On the other hand, trade is more evenly distributed throughout the city with concentrations between the Gebai business district, the Oja Iba market, and Mokola.[6]

The 1963 census return on occupational groups in Ibadan Province makes a distinction between urban and rural areas. These figures are less detailed, and as far as the city is concerned they are probably less accurate than those for 1952 and so do not permit a direct comparison with the earlier census.[7]

Income distribution in Ibadan

Before discussing the findings of my survey, the income distribution of Ibadan's working population should be briefly considered. Unfortunately, no reliable data are as yet available. However, the *Statistical Abstract* of 1971, published by the Western State of Nigeria, attempts some rough estimates of income for self-employed and wage-earning household heads, on the basis of taxation. These data are most likely grossly inaccurate and of little scientific value. Nevertheless, it may be worthwhile to give at least the income distribution of the 73,809 wage earners in Ibadan Division who were included in the PAYE scheme in 1970. According to the *Statistical Abstract* the low-income group with earnings of up to £N200 per annum accounted for 67.8 per cent of the total, the middle income group with earnings of £N200–600 per annum accounted for 24.4 per cent, and the group with incomes above £N600 per annum for 7.8 per cent.[8]

Sample survey

Occupational pattern

The main occupations of the 295 household heads in my sample are given in Table 11.1 column 4. It can be seen

Table 11.1 Occupational pattern of 295 household heads in Ibadan

Column	1		2		3		4	
	Compound heads		Dep. HHs		Tenant HHs		Total HHs	
	No.	%	No.	%	No.	%	No.	%
Services	17	27.0	37	34.3	50	40.4	104	35.3
Crafts	20	31.7	33	30.6	36	29.0	89	30.2
Trade	12	19.1	33	30.6	33	26.6	78	26.4
Agriculture	9	14.3	4	3.7	2	1.6	15	5.1
Miscellaneous	5	7.9	1	0.8	3	2.4	9	3.0
Total	63	100.0	108	100.0	124	100.0	295	100.0

that services, which include *inter alia* clerks, teachers, and police officers, is the most important occupational group among these household heads. Then follow traditional and modern crafts, trade, and agriculture. This order applies for the 108 dependent as well as the 124 tenant household heads. However, the occupations of the 63 compound heads differ slightly from these patterns. Here, the crafts are the most important occupation followed by services, trade, and agriculture.

The involvement in agriculture of the 63 compound heads must be further discussed. Apart from the 9 full-time farmers already listed in Table A.11.1, column 1, on p. 394, another 8 compound heads gave farming as their second occupation. A further 21 compound heads had some share in the proceeds from the family farm, but did not farm themselves. Among the 18 compound heads born outside Ibadan Province, 10 maintained an active interest in the family farm at their home town. Thus 48 compound heads or 76.2 per cent were either actively working on or had some vital interest in farm land, while the rest did not.

The 89 household heads employed in traditional or modern crafts deserve some notice. Table A.11.1 shows that among the most numerous in this category are 19 tailors, 12 mechanics, and 11 carpenters. This distribution corresponds with those reported by the earlier surveys of crafts in Ibadan which featured these three occupations at the top of the list. Table A.11.1 also shows that only 39 household heads or 13.2 per cent of the total had more than one occupation, which no doubt reflects the increasing specialization of work in Ibadan.

Table 11.2 shows how household heads in the sample are employed. Over 50 per cent of all compound heads and dependent household heads were self-employed,

Table 11.2 How household heads are employed

Column	1		2		3		4	
	Compound heads		Dep. HHs		Tenant HHs		Total HHs	
	No.	%	No.	%	No.	%	No.	%
Self-employed	37	58.7	58	53.7	56	45.2	151	51.2
Empl. priv. sector	10	15.9	35	32.5	38	30.6	83	28.1
Empl. public sector	11	17.5	13	12.0	26	21.0	50	17.0
Helps family member	—	—	1	0.9	—	—	1	0.3
Retired	5	7.9	—	—	—	—	5	1.7
Miscellaneous	—	—	1	0.9	4	3.2	5	1.7
Total	63	100.0	108	100.0	124	100.0	295	100.0

while 45 per cent of the tenant household heads had their own businesses. This reflects the substantial number of tenant household heads who were employed in government and in private firms.

The unique role played by Yoruba women in retail trade throughout the country is widely recognized, and the findings of my survey support this observation. In fact, 78.0 per cent of the 381 married, divorced, or widowed women in my sample, including one single female household head, are so employed. The kind of goods in which these women trade varies widely, and include provisions, cigarettes, and kola nuts, sold by 233 women or 61.2 per cent of the total; textiles were traded by 36 women or 9.4 per cent; firewood, crockery, mats, native medicine, shoes, and livestock were handled by 28 women or 7.4 per cent. Such crafts as the design and dyeing of cloth, weaving, and embroidery were practised by 18 women or 4.7 per cent of the sample. Another 14 women or 3.7 per cent who engaged in services included two primary school teachers, three hairplaiters, and four prostitutes. Of the remaining 52 women, 37 or 9.7 per cent were housewives with no gainful occupation,* 13 or 3.4 per cent had retired and were supported by their next of kin, and for 2 women or 0.5 per cent I lack information.

Except for 3 female compound heads and 25 female tenant household heads no systematic attempt was made to collect data on the monthly cash income of married

*Most of these women had only recently been married and most will start trading once they have settled down and their husbands have given them the capital they need to buy their initial stock.

women. However, the 18 completed budgets of female household heads show cash incomes that range from about 10 shillings per week to as much as £N50 per month for one well-to-do cloth trader who has recently made the pilgrimage to Mecca. It must be emphasized here that profit made from their trading and crafts belongs to the women who earn it, and that they are generally not obliged to contribute to the housekeeping costs. However, during my interviews it became quite obvious that many a household head would find himself in financial difficulties without the help of his wife or wives. Most women will also try to set aside at least some money for their families and/or their daughters' doweries; but except for wealthy female traders, this amount is probably small.[9]

Income distribution

The aim of my budgetary inquiries was to establish the annual cash incomes of the compound heads and those of dependent and tenant household heads who lived in the compound surveyed. In spite of painstaking inquiries, the data on household cash income and expenditure presented below must be treated with caution. The reasons for this caution may be mentioned briefly. During my investigation at Ibadan from January to May 1968, the civil war in Eastern Nigeria, then approaching its climax, had created a general slump in the country's economy. An almost stagnant industry and increasing unemployment, some of which was absorbed by the army, forced many local families to live, at least temporarily, on reduced incomes, which had in some cases to be subsidized by the household head's wife or wives or from savings. Other household heads relied on financial help from more fortunate family members. The various import restrictions imposed by the military government had also stimulated sharp increases in the prices for foreign goods and substantial profit margins for some traders, who were understandably unwilling to disclose their incomes.

In these circumstances it may be seen why my questions regarding income and, to a lesser extent, expenditure were met with suspicion, and in spite of repeated personal and official assurances, as well as exhaustive explanations about the nature and aims of my survey, 68 household heads or 23.1 per cent of the total sample remained evasive or gave grossly misleading answers and their budgets had to be omitted from the final analysis. (See Table A.11.2 on p. 393.) Hence of the total of 295 households covered by the survey only 227 are included in the following analysis. Of these, 122 households or 53.8 per cent were in the low-income group (up to £N180 per annum), 93 or 40.9 per cent in the middle income group (£N180 to £N600 per annum), and only 12 or 5.3 per cent in the high-income group (above £N600 per annum). (See Table A.11.3 on p. 393.) Table A.11.4B–D on pp. 396–397 gives the income distribution for compound heads, dependent or semi-dependent household heads, and tenant household heads separately. It shows that compound heads have the highest average income, with 32.8 per cent of them in the low-income group, 50.0 per cent in the middle, and 17.2 per cent in the high-income group. This is followed by tenant household heads with 58.7 per cent in the lowest bracket, 39.1 per cent in the middle, and only 2.2 per cent in the high-income group. Dependent or semi-dependent household heads have still lower average incomes, but similar distributions, though none of these household heads is in the high income group.

The combined distribution of incomes by household size is given in Table A.11.4A on p. 396 and shows the predominance of small-size households (1–4 persons) in the low-income group. As the number of persons per household increases income tends to increase as well. This is illustrated by the diagonal pattern of concentration up to households with 9–10 persons and income of 1,000 to 1,999 shillings per month. From there onwards the small number of households involved scatter so widely that the distribution has little statistical value.

The per capita income of households with 1–2 persons was found to be 130 shillings per month. This sum decreases to 81, 76, and 55 shillings per month for households with 3–4, 5–6 and 7–8 persons respectively. However, the per capita income of households with more than 9 persons increases to 75 shillings per month. This upward movement reflects the high proportion of large households of compound heads with general higher income.

On Graph A.11.1 on p. 398 the cumulative income distribution of the 227 households is plotted on logarithmic probability paper in order to show the relationship between the median income and the type of household. The nearly straight line of the cumulative income distribution curve for all 227 households indicates a lognormal distribution. All three types of households distinguished by separate curves show an approximately equal percentage change, which in the case of the dependent and tenant households is based on lower incomes. As a result, the curves of these two latter types of household shift leftwards but do not substantially alter their shape. The median incomes as shown on the graph are 460 shillings per month for the households of the compound heads, 265 shillings per month for tenant household heads, and 235 shillings per month for dependent or semi-dependent household heads. However, part of the higher incomes of the compound heads derives from rent and other financial benefits which are associated with the headship; and some of this is spent on improvements and repair to the family compound, and on financial help given to other family members in need, neither of which are generally expected from other compound members.

A Lorenz Curve was constructed from the collected data (Graph A.11.2 on p. 398) and illustrates clearly the inequality in distribution of income among the 227 household heads included in this analysis. The 'area of inequality' is 41.7 per cent and shows that about 50 per cent of all households earn about 25 per cent of the total recorded average monthly income.

The above analysis has shown that over 50 per cent of the household heads interviewed have cash incomes of less than £N180 per annum. To what extent these income levels and distributions were influenced by the civil war is difficult to say, but the general slump in the country's economy during the period of field study no doubt had some dampening effect on the retail trade and on other economic activities which were felt by nearly all household heads interviewed.

I have dealt with the annual income of the sample population at some length because it is often used as a measure to determine the creditworthiness and above all the size of loans given by various credit institutions for building activities. Furthermore, in planning to design and build for the poor, we should recognize that between two and four times the amount of their annual income is probably all that they can afford to invest in their houses, given their lack of easy credit. In the next chapter I will show how household heads with very low incomes actually build, improve, and maintain their houses.

Notes and references

1 K. M. Buchanan and J. C. Pugh, *Land and People in Nigeria*, 6th edition, London, 1966, p. 200.
2 A. Callaway, 'From traditional crafts to modern industry', in *The City of Ibadan*, ed. P. C. Lloyd *et al.*, Cambridge, 1967, pp. 153–171. Callaway carried out a complete survey of all

crafts and small industries with permanent premises in Ibadan in 1963. In all 5,135 establishments were counted and divided into 15 categories, the most important being tailors with 26.3 per cent, carpenters with 12.5 per cent, mechanics with 10.1 per cent, and photographers with 7.7 per cent. The total number of persons employed by these establishments were 14,500 persons or 2.9 per unit including apprentices, journeymen, and proprietors.

3 M. Koll, *Crafts and Cooperation in Western Nigeria*, Freiburg i.B., 1969, pp. 20 and 124. Koll took an area sample which covered approximately 10 per cent of all small industrial establishments in the city. After calculating the standard error, the probable minimum number of units was estimated to be 12,200, the probable maximum 16,400. The total number of persons employed in the craft sector was estimated to be approximately 42,000 or 5 per cent of the total population in the city. The most important units were tailors with 29.2 per cent, carpenters with 12.6 per cent, and mechanics with 8.0 per cent.

4 Department of Statistics, Nigeria, *Population Census of the Western Region of Nigeria 1952*, Lagos, 1956, pp. 16–17.

5 A. L. Mabogunje, *Urbanization in Nigeria*, London, 1968, pp. 221–223.

6 Ibid., p. 211.

7 Federal Office of Statistics, Nigeria, 'Population Census Western Region of Nigeria 1963' (mimeo), Lagos, 1968, vol. 2, p. 160. The occupational structure of the male population in the urban areas of Ibadan Province was as follows: agriculture 31.5 per cent, crafts 27.9 per cent, trade 14.7 per cent, administrative and professionals 9.9 per cent, other occupations 11.4 per cent, and unemployed 4.6 per cent.

8 Ministry of Economic Planning and Reconstruction, Western State of Nigeria, *Statistical Abstract*, nos 1–2, vol. XII, 1970, Ibadan, 1971, pp. 37 and 60.

9 P. Marris, *Family and Social Change in an African City*, London, 1961, pp. 78–81.

Chapter 12

Production, cost, and financing of houses in the older parts of Ibadan

Building materials and the construction of houses

During the 1950s and 1960s private houses built in Ibadan ranged in type from the semi-traditional one-storey mud house covered with corrugated iron sheets in the older parts of the city, to multi-storey dwellings of reinforced concrete which are equipped with all modern amenities such as piped water and electricity. In the following pages I will be concerned mainly with houses of the semi-traditional type which are still being built in large numbers in the older parts of the city. This type of house is characterized by varying mixtures of traditional and modern building materials and techniques. Unfortunately, no quantitative assessment of the construction of houses during the 1950s and 1960s is available, but since 1950 the major expansion of Ibadan has taken place in areas beyond the nineteenth-century city wall, leaving the centre almost untouched. (See Plan 9.1 on p. 118.)

Building materials

Most houses built in the older parts of the city today require a limited number of basic building materials. These include earth for walling, forest timber for the roof frame, corrugated iron roofing sheets, sawn wood for doors and windows, cement for rendering the walls and floors, and asbestos-cement or fibreboard sheets for ceilings. (See Picture 12.1.) A prosperous man may also use stone for the foundations, cement blocks for walling, glazed windows, and paint for walls, ceilings, and joinery. He may also build a two-storey house with or without a reinforced concrete balcony and richly decorated balustrade. (See Picture 12.2.)

The increasing use of modern building materials entails a corresponding increase in the capital cost of housing, which, should the owner overrate his financial resources, may result in prolonging the period of construction for several years. For example, of 25 houses surveyed which were built by their present owners, two required about 6 years to construct, while one was finished within 4 months, and the average building time for all 25 houses was 3.2 years. The variable length of the construction period partly reflects differences in the incomes of these compound heads, but it also depends on their individual abilities to raise money from family members and friends, or by loan, for completion of the house. In most cases ceilings are fixed and floors and walls are cemented several years after the owner has moved into the house.

Picture 12.1
One-storey house in Ibadan city

Picture 12.2
Two-storey house with reinforced concrete balcony

The construction of walls

In 1962 an estimated 22,000 houses or 90 per cent of the city's total housing stock had mud walls.[1] These walls were either made of several layers of mud work or with square mud bricks often manufactured on the building site. The preparation of earth for wall building has already been described in some detail in Chapter 6 on p. 76. However, the Yoruba method of construction differs somewhat from the technique used at Zaria, and may take one of two forms. First, the house walls may be raised by several layers of mud work, usually 0.30 to 0.50 m high, depending largely on the clay content of the earth. In this process, each new layer can only be added after the one below is sufficiently hard to bear its weight. (See Picture 12.3.) This method of construction is slow and can only be carried out during the relatively short dry season which lasts from the beginning of November to the middle of March. (See Graph A.7.1 on p. 367.) The alternative method consists of manufacturing mud bricks with the help of a rectangular wooden mould. The moulded blocks of earth are then dried in the air for several days before being piled to form a simple kiln. The kiln is then lit and kept burning for one or two days after which it is broken down, and the walls of

Picture 12.3
Construction of mud walls

the house are built with the help of specially prepared mud or cement mortar.[2] (See Pictures 12.4 and 12.5.) However, brick firing is not regarded as absolutely essential, and many houses are built with sun-baked bricks.

The roof

The roof frame of a house is usually constructed from round, uncut forest timber or bamboo and covered with corrugated iron sheets. (See Picture 12.6.) The use of sawn wood for a roof frame is still rather rare, and is normally restricted to modern houses built by well-to-do compound heads. Ceilings fixed to the underside of the roof frame consist either of hand-woven straw mats or of asbestos-cement or fibreboard sheets.

The use of corrugated iron sheets as a roofing material is no new thing in Nigeria; it was introduced by European merchants at the beginning of the twentieth century.[3] Although not recommended by the colonial administration as ideal roofing material,* the change from thatch to corrugated iron roofs, known locally as 'pan', was almost complete in Ibadan by the late 1920s.[4] This rapid change

*Early colonial houses in Ibadan used tiles made of burnt clay as roofing material.

Picture 12.4
A kiln ready for firing

Picture 12.5
One-storey house built with sun-baked bricks

was made possible by the increasing demand for cocoa on the world market.[5] In the absence of alternative imported building materials, the relatively high prices received by cocoa farmers at this date prompted many to change the roofing material of their town houses from thatch to corrugated iron sheets. Moreover, although this change did substantially worsen the living conditions inside the house due to the intense heat radiation from the roof, it was regarded as a status symbol, and did after all reduce the risk of fire which in the last century periodically devastated large parts of the city.[6]

The kinds of construction described above are usually carried out by a wall builder or bricklayer who recruits several helpers to prepare the earth and to assist him in building the walls. After the walls are completed, a carpenter is asked to construct the roof frame and affix the corrugated iron sheets. He usually makes the window shutters and doors as well. In recent years increasing numbers of houses have been built by indigenous contractors who undertake all construction work and charge a lump sum for the whole house.

The local building industry

Very little is known about the size, performance, and output of the local building industry. Among the various

Picture 12.6
Roof construction

independent crafts which enter into this industry, only carpenters are included in all three crafts censuses carried out by various scholars in Ibadan between 1950 and 1970. (See Chapter 11, pp. 153–154.) The investigation conducted by M. Koll in 1967 revealed that an estimated 2,000 carpenters worked in the city. Other craftsmen engaged in construction, such as wall builders, bricklayers, plasterers, glass cutters, plumbers, painters, and electrical wiremen, were excluded from Koll's study, since they had no 'visible workshop'.[7]

It is interesting to note that in the grouping of Yoruba craftsmen into 'guilds' builders are not included as a separate occupation, and so there is no builders' cult.[8] This may be largely due to the fact that in the past the construction of houses was traditionally carried out on a communal basis known as *owe*. Under this arrangement a man wishing to build a house would call on all his relatives, friends, and/or neighbours for manual help, while he provided the necessary building materials, refreshments, and food for all who helped. With the emergence of an urban society in Yorubaland and, later, the introduction of an economy based on money in the early twentieth century, this practice of communal help was gradually abandoned in large towns like Ibadan, and building then became a paid and specialized occupation.

In the mid-1950s the emerging modern building industry enjoyed a major boom due mainly to an extensive school-building programme in Ibadan.[9] The number of contractors registered by the government of the former Western Region accordingly increased sharply. Table A.12.1 on p. 399 reveals that of the 357 contractors then registered in Ibadan, 271 were building contractors, 49 were civil engineers, and 37 were electrical contractors. However, of these groups 73.8, 28.6, and 81.1 per cent respectively belonged to the category of small operators for which the contract value of work undertaken usually does not exceed £N10,000. The majority of these small firms also carry out the construction of houses covered by the survey in Ibadan. Most of the small contractors, who are still in business, have no office or work-yard beside their living quarters.[10] They are notoriously undercapitalized, have no access to even short-term credit, and seldom have enough work to keep them busy throughout the year.

Sample survey

I will now discuss some changes in structure and in building materials observed in the 63 compounds surveyed. My investigation of their histories was limited to a five-year period from May 1963 to April 1968, because it proved impossible to collect reasonably accurate information beyond this period. Two sets of aerial photographs of the city taken in 1961 and 1965 were used to select the compounds for study and to identify the structural changes which had taken place in the compounds surveyed.

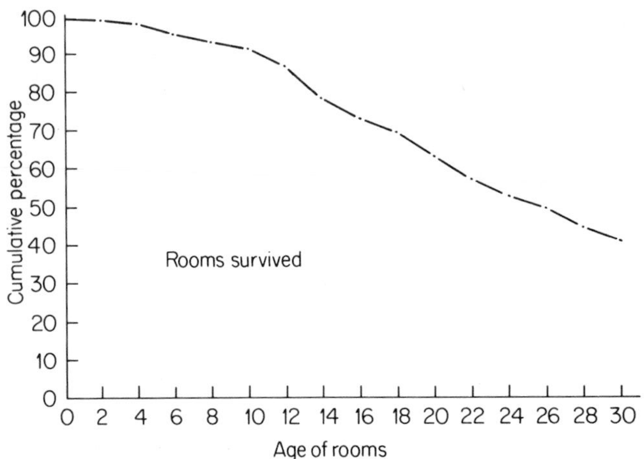

Graph 12.1
Age distribution of rooms

Age composition of rooms

I shall first examine the age composition of the rooms surveyed. This deserves special attention not only because it indicates the need to replace old and obsolete structures, but also because it reveals the type and quantity of new constructions, improvements, and maintenance which are necessary to the survival of any compound.

Graph 12.1 shows the age distribution of 1,093* rooms found in 63 compounds surveyed. The median age of these rooms is 25.6 years, which is appreciably older than the rooms surveyed at Zaria where the median age was only 11.8 years. (See Chapter 6, p. 86.) About 20 per cent of these rooms which are over 50 years old have so far accommodated at least two generations of compound heads. The two oldest compounds in the sample were built between 1890 and 1892 while the most recent was only 3 years old. There is little doubt that the corrugated iron roof has substantially contributed to the increased life span of these mud-walled buildings.

* The ages of six rooms were not known. See also Table A.12.2 on p. 400.

Structural changes of compounds

The 63 compounds surveyed in Ibadan contained 1,099 rooms with a total area of 9,522 sq. m. Between 1 May 1963 and 30 April 1968, when my survey in Ibadan concluded, only 69 new rooms were built in these compounds, while 12 rooms had disappeared or were decaying at the time of interview. Thus the total net increase over the five-year period was 57 rooms or 5.2 per cent which yields an average growth rate of about 1.0 per cent per annum. This very modest growth rate reflects the fact that all major housing developments over the previous two decades (1950–1970) had taken place in areas beyond the nineteenth-century city wall, whereas the older parts of the city, to which this survey was confined, were little affected by this expansion because of lack of suitable building space.*

Although about 80 per cent of the 69 rooms built between 1963 and 1968 had mud walls, there is some evidence that the use of cement blocks is increasing. A further indication of changes in local building practice and standards is the increased use of cement for rendering walls and internal floors. For example, on my data the total area of cement floor in these compounds increased from about 5,600 sq. m in 1963 to 6,260 sq. m in 1968, that is, by 11.8 per cent (see Table A.12.3 on page 401). Furthermore the use of cement for outdoor working platforms and terraces increased from 1,200 sq. m to 1,550 sq. m, that is, by 29.2 per cent, over the same period.

Amenities

I shall now examine the availability of such basic amenities as kitchens, bathrooms, toilets, electricity, and piped water in the 63 compounds surveyed accommodating 295 households.

Kitchens were found in 43 compounds which together accommodated 218 households. Of these only 7 households had their own private kitchens while the remaining 211 households shared 50 kitchens, giving an average of one kitchen per 4.2 households. The remaining 77 households (26.1 per cent) living in 20 compounds had no kitchen at all but cooked their meals either in the central halls or on verandas of their compounds.

* The only exception was the encroachment of some houses on the flood plains of the Ogunpa and Kudeti streams where there was a disastrous flood in 1963, and the loss of many lives and much property.

A total of 42 covered bathrooms were counted in 24 compounds and shared by 135 households. In 20 compounds having 91 households, sheltered cement platforms were available, whereas in 19 compounds with 69 households various unpaved areas inside and outside the house were used for personal washing.

The 27 covered toilets found in 20 compounds were shared by 114 households. Another 19 compounds with 76 households had at least one pit-latrine in or near the house, while 24 compounds with 105 households, or 35.6 per cent of the sample, had no toilets at all. The inhabitants of these compounds either used a public lavatory or the lavatory of a neighbour or friend.

An electricity supply had been installed in 30 compounds, but of the 174 households living in these compounds, only 126 had an electric bulb in their rooms, while 169 households or 57.3 per cent of the total had no electricity supply at all.

Finally, 13 compounds with 86 households had water taps in their courtyards, whereas 209 households or 70.8 per cent used a public stand-pipe in one of the streets nearby.

In short, 26.1 per cent of all households surveyed had no kitchen, 35.6 per cent had no toilet, 54.2 per cent had no bathroom, 57.3 per cent had no electric light, and 70.8 per cent had to fetch their water from a public stand-pipe.[11]

In spite of the appalling shortage of basic amenities, compound heads were not unduly disturbed about this situation. When asked what improvement they thought their compounds needed most, 19 or 30.2 per cent answered spontaneously 'an upstairs', 11 or 17.5 per cent wanted to paint or repaint the house, and another 5 or 7.9 per cent were keen on having ceilings in their rooms. Only 4 or 6.3 per cent felt the need for a lavatory or bathroom, while another 4 were generally dissatisfied and said they would prefer to demolish and rebuild the house. Three compound heads opted for piped water, more bedrooms, electricity supply, and roof repair, 5 had various other needs, 2 did not respond, and 1 was undecided. (See Table A.12.4 on p. 402.) It is interesting to note that nearly half of the compound heads interviewed wanted to build 'an upstairs' and paint the house, whereas such improvements as a new lavatory, bathroom, piped water, and electricity only ranked fourth and fifth in their collective list of needs.

Cost of building

Next I will examine the costs of house construction,

improvements, and maintenance as well as the method of financing these activities in Ibadan. The discussion is based on results obtained from my survey of 63 compounds. The period for which the costs of construction and improvements was studied was five years, from the beginning of May 1963 to the end of April 1968, whereas the study on maintenance costs was further limited to the three years immediately preceding the date of the interview. These time limits were necessary as most compound heads could not remember all expenditure on building activities accurately. As far as expenditure on maintenance is concerned, the very detailed annual data obtained for this period of three years enable me to adjust the spending on this item to cover the five-year period under study.

Cost of building materials and labour

During the first half of 1968 prices for imported building materials rose sharply, due mainly to import restrictions imposed by the military government during the civil war. As one result of these measures, building activities slowed down and almost came to a standstill in Ibadan. The prices quoted below for a number of basic building materials are average prices charged by building material merchants in late 1967 before the price increases took effect. In 1967, cement prices ranged from 14 to 15 shillings per 50 kg bag; sheets of corrugated iron for roofing were usually sold in bundles of 20 at between £N4.75 and £N5.00; and asbestos-cement sheets, 1.20 m × 1.20 m, for ceilings cost 6 or 7 shillings.

Daily wages paid to building workers then ranged from 3s. 6d. for unskilled labourers to 10 shillings or more for skilled assistants, while payments made by the household head to skilled craftsmen were normally on a job basis. For example, a common unit of charge is for the construction of the mud walls for a single room, of 9 to 12 sq. m in area. Job prices quoted to me for this work ranged from £N7 to £N10. If the building material has to be transported, an additional charge is made. Carpenters normally use the bundle of corrugated iron sheets as the unit-basis of their charge. Work done by carpenters includes construction of the roof frame, the timber necessary being supplied by the household head, and the fixing of the corrugated iron sheets. For a single-storey house their charge varies between £N1.50 and £N2.00 per bundle,* while for two-

* The roof of a six-roomed house requires on average eleven bundles.

storey houses the charge rises to about £N3.00 due to the greater risks involved. Doors and windows were quoted to me as costing between £N1.50 for a very simple internal door to over £N5.00 for a good quality external door. Windows and window-shutters fluctuated on a similar scale. All materials required are supplied by the household head but ready-made doors and windows are also available. Other prices charged by tradesmen include £N1.00 to £N1.50 for laying the cement floor for an average sized room and £N3.00 for fixing a ceiling of asbestos-cement sheets. All prices quoted here are average prices charged for 'one-off' work.

Cost of construction

Expenditure on building covers a range of different activities and may be divided into five major groups, as follows:

1 cost of construction completed between 1963 and 1968;
2 cost of buildings still under construction at 30 April 1968,
3 cost of improvements, 1963–1968,
4 cost of maintenance and repair, and
5 cost of such miscellaneous constructions as wells, pit-latrines, or stables.

Table 12.1 reveals that of the total adjusted building expenditure of about 104,000 shillings or £N5,200, 48.5 per cent was spent on new construction, 26.3 per cent on maintenance and repair, 22.1 per cent on improvements, and 3.1 per cent on miscellaneous constructions. There was no expenditure for buildings still under construction at 30 April 1968, although five compound heads had already bought some building materials such as bricks, cement blocks, cement, and sawn wood for future use at a total cost of about 4,500 shillings.

In the five-year period under study, 1963–1968, 67 rooms* with an area of 559.3 sq. m were built in 15 of the compounds surveyed. (See Table 12.1 and Table A.12.5 on page 403.) The total recorded cost for building these rooms was 50,410 shillings or £N2,520. The average cost per square metre is 98.2 shillings for 49 comparable living and sleeping rooms with a total area of 473.1 sq. m. Only three houses were entirely constructed within this period,

* This excludes two permanent stables which are grouped in Table 12.1 on p. 173 under miscellaneous construction.

Table 12.1 Cost of construction in 63 surveyed compounds, 1963–1968

Column	1	2	3	4	5
	No. of rooms	Sq. m	Cost in shillings	Cost per sq. m	%
New construction (completed)					
Corrugated iron roofed rooms, living area, common and commercial rooms	49	473.1	46,460	98.2	
Basic ancillary facilities	18	86.2	3,950		
Subtotal	67	559.3	50,410		48.5
Improvements on existing buildings					
Cement floors and plaster			11,966		
Electricity installed			2,920		
Piped water installed			975		
Ceilings			5,628		
Other improvements			1,506		
Subtotal	–		22,995		22.1
Maintenance and repair					
Mud walls					
Painting and/or whitewash					
Corrugated iron roof			For details see Table 12.2.		
Cement plaster and screed					
Subtotal (1966–1968, actual)	–		16,389		
Subtotal adjusted 1963–1968[a]			27,315		26.3
Buildings under construction					
Walls completed					
Roof completed					
Subtotal	–	–	–		–
Miscellaneous construction					
Includes wells, pit-latrines, bathrooms, and stables (2)	2		3,260		
Subtotal	–		3,260		3.1
Total actual expenditure			93,054		
Total adjusted expenditure			103,980		100.0

[a] $\frac{16,389}{3} \times 5 = 27,315$ shillings.

and details for two of these are given in Tables A.12.6 and A.12.7 on pp. 404–407. Another three compounds had major extensions including one upper storey. In the remaining nine compounds, only a few rooms and such basic ancillary facilities as kitchens, stores, bathrooms, and toilets were added. (For information on who built the core of houses, see Table A.12.9 on page 411.)

A break-down of *cost by element of building* has been attempted for the two newly constructed compounds and is given in Tables A.12.6 and A.12.7 on pp. 404–407. The first house (see Plan A.12.1 on p. 408 was built in 1963–1965 at a total cost of about 9,930 shillings or £N497. The superstructure, which includes the mud walls and roof, accounted for 61.2 per cent of the total cost, whereas finishes, i.e. all doors and windows, ceilings, cementing of floors and walls as well as painting, together accounted for 38.8 per cent. The *cost by element of cost* was divided between materials, 64.3 per cent, and labour, 35.7 per cent. The builder's overall profit margin, which is believed to be in the region of about 10–15 per cent,[12] is hidden in the cost of materials and labour, and could not be calculated separately for this house.

The second new house (see Plan A.12.2 on p. 409) was built by two brothers, one of whom was a bricklayer and the other a trained carpenter, at a total cost of about 6,310 shillings or £N316 in 1964/1965. The percentage distribution of the superstructure and finishes in this case was 59.9 per cent and 40.1 per cent respectively, which is very similar to the first example, whereas the cost by element of cost differed sharply, being 93.5 per cent for materials and only 6.5 per cent for labour as the two brothers built the house themselves.

The only data on Yoruba house construction costs available for comparison are for houses built in rural areas of Western Nigeria. These were collected by R. Galletti and P. Crooke in 1951 and 1965 respectively. Using these data, Table A.12.8 on p. 410 shows that the construction cost for an average room of 10 to 12 sq. m had risen from £N12.2 in 1920–1924 to £N32.50 in 1951 and £N37.30 in 1965. Galletti interprets the temporary fall in construction costs which occurred in the early 1930s and again during the Second World War by correlations with the exceptionally low cocoa prices and correspondingly low incomes for cocoa farmers who could not afford to build expensive houses. The rapid recovery of the cocoa market after 1945 yielded record incomes and is clearly reflected in the rising costs of construction of houses.[13] These increases were partly due to a gradual replacement of the traditional type of rural house with its long front room leading on to a row of smaller rooms at the rear, by an essentially urban house having a central corridor with rows of rooms on either side; but these changes of design were accompanied by increased use of expensive modern building materials such as corrugated iron roofing sheets, cement, and better finishes.[14] Nevertheless, comparison of these data with those I gathered in 1968 suggests that houses built in Ibadan city were on average twice as expensive as their counterparts built in the rural areas of Western Nigeria. The higher cost of house building in urban areas was mainly due to the increased use of modern building materials and appreciably higher labour costs.

Cost of maintenance and repair

The adjusted cost of maintenance and repair was the second largest item of expenditure on building in the compounds surveyed, namely 27,315 shillings or 26.3 per cent of the total. This relatively high maintenance cost to some extent reflects the median age of 25.6 years for 1,093 rooms in the sample. (See Graph 12.1 on p. 168.) However, it must be stressed that, unlike those for new construction and major improvements, maintenance and repair costs are very difficult to check, and in consequence I normally accepted each compound head's statements of these outlays after comparing his annual expenditures for each item with those of others. Given its importance, I have broken down the total actual maintenance cost of 16,389 shillings into six categories for presentation in Table 2.2.

It is interesting to note that mud walls absorbed over one third of the total maintenance cost, followed by painting and/or whitewash with 21.9 per cent, and corrugated iron roofs 19.4 per cent, cement plaster and

Table 12.2 Maintenance cost by element of building, 1966–1968

Element of building	Shillings	%
Mud walls	5,884	35.9
Painting and/or whitewash	3,589	21.9
Corrugated iron roof	3,179	19.4
Cement plaster and screed	2,147	13.1
Doors and windows	639	3.9
Other repairs	951	5.8
Total actual maintenance cost	16,389	100.0

screed 13.1 per cent, while outlays for doors and windows and for miscellaneous repairs were only 3.9 and 5.8 per cent respectively. Maintenance costs for mud walls and roofs deserve additional comment. During the heavy downpours which sometimes occur in June and September, unprotected house corners tend to collapse and the necessary repair work is generally expensive. Damage to the roof is normally caused by high winds which may blow away parts or even the whole roof including its frame.

Cost of improvements

By improvements I mean all building activities other than maintenance which are carried out after an owner has moved into a new house. A total of 22,995 shillings was spent on improvements in the compounds under study between 1963 and 1968. In order of importance, cementing of walls and floors accounted for 52.0 per cent of this total, the fixing of ceilings for 24.5 per cent, installation of electricity and piped water for 12.7 and 4.2 per cent respectively, and miscellaneous improvements such as insertion of bigger windows for 6.6 per cent.

The financing of private houses

In the previous pages I have examined the types and costs of various building activities carried out in the compounds surveyed. Now I wish to show how these building activities were financed by the various household heads. As has already been discussed in Chapter 6, the two main sources of funds for housing are personal and institutional.

Personal sources

Personal sources of building funds include self-finance from personal income and savings, contributions from family members and friends, and such social security funds as pensions or gratuity. Contributions from family members and friends were further subdivided into gifts and loans.

While 25 compound heads in the sample had built their own houses, only three had done so between 1963 and 1968. Another three compound heads had added major extensions to their compounds during the period under study. These six compound heads had together built a total of 56 rooms with an area of 507.0 sq. m, while the remaining 13 rooms, covering 68.1 sq. m and including 2 permanent stables, were built by seven compound heads and two heads of dependent households. As noted above, major improvements such as the cementing of walls and floors, the fixing of asbestos-cement ceilings, and the installation of electricity and piped water supplies had also been carried out by 37 compound heads at a total cost of about 23,000 shillings or £N1,150.

During the five-year period from 1963 to 1968 loans totalling 4,460 shillings (£N223) were made by private persons to four compound heads who used the money as follows: two loans having a total of 3,560 shillings for new construction, and two loans totalling 900 shillings for various improvements. The creditors of these loans were in order of importance as shown in Table 12.3.

There were three recorded gifts having a total of 1,995 shillings (£N100). These gifts were made by close relatives of the compound heads who used the money partly to pay for new construction and partly for improvements to their houses.

The four loans listed in Table 12.3 as well as the three cash gifts covered about 10.6 per cent of the total costs of new construction and 4.8 per cent of the expenditure on improvements.

In short, between 1963 and 1968 a total of 103,980 shillings (£N5,200) was spent by 63 compound heads on new construction, and on the improvement to and maintenance of their houses. Slightly less than 94 per cent of this money came from the personal savings and income of compound heads, while about 6 per cent came from loans and gifts made by family members and friends. (See Table A.12.10 on p. 412.) None of the interviewed compound heads received a loan or grant from such official institutions as building societies, housing corporations, banks, or other government sponsored agencies.

Table 12.3 Types of creditors of private building loans

	No. of loans	Shillings	%
Close relatives of compound head	1	3,000	67.3
Esusu[a]	2	900	20.2
Personal friend of compound head	1	560	12.5
Total	4	4,460	100.0

[a]Private saving society.

Given the lack of commercial and government aided loans or subsidies for housing for the lower-income groups of the population in Ibadan, independent savings are extremely important for the building activities of the urban Yoruba. In my sample 41 compound heads or 65.1 per cent had at one time or another saved amounts that ranged from £N25 to over £N300 to finance building, while 17 or 27.0 per cent had never saved for this end, and 5 or 7.9 per cent did not respond. Savings were carried out either with the help of commercial banks, or more often through the traditional saving societies called *esusu.*[15] These saving societies or clubs are believed to be of Yoruba origin and date back at least to the first half of the nineteenth century. The *esusu* is described by Shirley Ardener as: 'An association formed upon a core of participants who agree to make regular contributions to a fund which is given, in whole or part, to each contributor in rotation.'[16]

Private money-lenders are very much in evidence all over Yorubaland. However, in interviews it became obvious that most compound heads were rather reluctant to use their services, one reason being their exorbitant rates of interest which may range from 30 to 50 per cent per annum and over, a rate that makes such loans impracticable for private house building except perhaps as finance for tenant accommodation with relatively quick returns.

Internal subsidy and mutual help

By internal subsidy, I mean the financing of new rooms for close relatives living in the same compound. This includes help given by a compound head to his newly married son or any other dependent family member in need of shelter. In these terms, of 69 rooms built between May 1963 and April 1968, 10 or 14.5 per cent were either fully or partly subsidized by three compound heads. Another three compound heads invested some money in tenant accommodation (see page 179). Diagram 12.1 illustrates the main characteristics of internal subsidy and investment made by these six compound heads from 1963 to 1968.

As shown in the diagram, a total of eight rooms were partly subsidized by these compound heads and allocated to the families of two full brothers' sons. Of the other two fully subsidized rooms, one went to the compound head's father's brother's son's family, the other to an unmarried son of the compound head.

Although mutual help in the form of labour is no longer

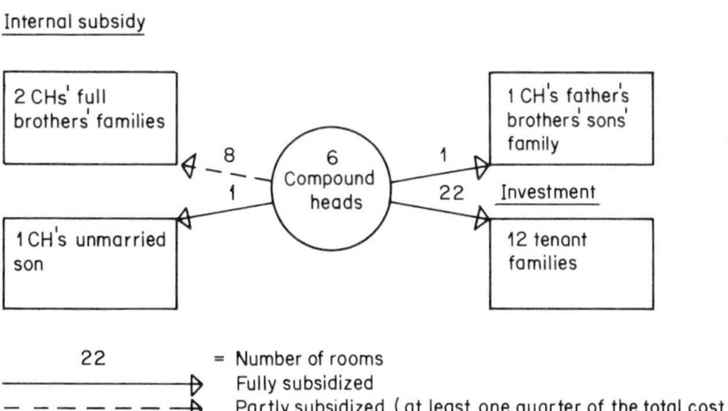

Diagram 12.1
Distribution of internal subsidy and investment

practised in such towns as Ibadan, many a compound head finds it difficult to build a new house independently because of the rapidly rising costs of building materials and labour. Hence, in all three new houses built between 1963 and 1968, two full brothers had pooled their financial resources to construct the building.* While this coincidence does not have statistical significance, it indicates a general trend among the lower-income groups to share the burden and costs of house building with one or more close relatives.

Inquiries into the financing of house maintenance showed that about half of the dependent or semi-dependent household heads were themselves responsible for any improvements and/or repairs they undertook in their rooms, while maintenance costs for the roof and outside walls were usually met from a general fund collected annually by the compound head from lineage kin in Ibadan and the surrounding villages. Such funds to cover the external maintenance costs applied only to family compounds, i.e. compounds which belonged to a lineage or section of a lineage, and were found in 18 cases.

Investment in building

Investment to provide accommodation for rental is fairly widespread in Ibadan, and particularly in areas to the north and south-west of the old city. Several compound heads in the sample had built houses in different parts of the city and rented them out either to one trustworthy tenant or more often to a number of people, most of whom occupied one or two rooms. Alternatively, some

* Two of these compounds are given in Tables A.12.6 and A.12.7 on pp. 404–406.

compound heads had simply built a few rooms for rental in their backyard. As mentioned on page 179, three compound heads had built 22 rooms for rental. The rent paid for an average room at Ibadan in 1968 ranged from £N1.50 to £N2.50 per week. Such relatively high rents guarantee owners quick returns for their investments, especially when the average building cost of about £N5 per square metre is considered.

To conclude, although only a small number of rooms were built in the sample compounds between 1963 and 1968, it can be shown that the average cost of these rooms was then around £N5 per square metre, which is considerably cheaper, in fact between four and five times less, than the cost of houses built by the Western State Housing Corporation at Ibadan. This substantial difference is partly due to the exclusive use of modern building materials, the installation of piped water and an electricity supply, and the higher labour cost in houses constructed by the corporation. It could also be shown that the financing of private houses built during the period under investigation was left entirely to the household heads concerned. Of the 50 compound heads who undertook new construction and/or major improvements between 1963 and 1968, not one received financial help of any kind from the banks, insurance companies, building societies, and housing corporations. Some reasons for this lack of commercial and official support already identified for Zaria apply equally to Ibadan. (See Chapter 6 on pp. 94–95.) These include the low average income of household heads, their use of traditional building materials and techniques, and the mode of urban land tenure, under which large areas of land belong to extended family groups which may only transfer usufructuary rights of occupancy to their members. As such conditions are generally regarded by modern financial institutions as high credit risks, the lack of commercial funds for the poorer section of the population most in need of help is easy to understand.

Notes and references

1 These data were supplied to me by the Ibadan City Council in 1968.

Federal Office of Statistics, Nigeria, 'Ibadan housing enquiry', unpublished MS, Lagos, 1963, p. 6. The survey was carried out in October 1962. A total of 350 houses containing 800 households were investigated. It was found that about 10 per cent of these houses had cement block or brick walls, the majority being situated in the south-western part of the city.

2 Author not given 'Yoruba brickmaking', *Nigeria Journal* (Ibadan), no. 25, 1946, pp. 297–298.

3 A. Hinderer, *Seventeen Years in the Yoruba Country*, London, 1872, pp. 99–100 and 188. The first corrugated iron roof was introduced by missionaries to Ibadan in 1854. In a letter dated 14 May 1854, Anna Hinderer wrote: 'Our new house, after all the toil in building it promises to possess all the comfort we could expect or desire in this country, it is water-tight! has a good sized sitting and bedroom, white washed walls and a good iron roof . . .' But in a letter dated 28 December 1858 she wrote: 'Our house is very comfortable now, a light grass roof over the iron makes it cooler . . .'

4 Colonial Office, Great Britain, *Blue Book, Colony and Protectorate of Nigeria*, Lagos 1914, 1915, 1920, 1925, 1930, 1935, and 1938. Importation of flat and corrugated iron sheets into Nigeria. Between 1914 and 1938 a total of 200,763 tons of corrugated iron sheets were imported into Nigeria. The pattern of the imports was as follows: in 1914 a total of 7,378 tons were imported; this amount dropped to a mere 447 tons in 1917, but rose again with some fluctuation to 16,971 tons in 1928. Imports then declined to 6,912 tons in 1934 and rose sharply to a new level of 19,283 tons in 1937. In 1938 the imports again fell to 3,741 tons. Of the total of 200,763 tons imported, over 60 per cent was imported between 1914 and 1930.

5 R. Galletti, *Nigerian Cocoa Farmers*, Oxford, 1956, pp. 1 and 253–256. Production of cocoa in Nigeria expanded twelvefold from a mere 4,100 tons in 1914 to 28,200 tons in 1930. By then the country produced about 10 per cent of the world supply. Galletti found a direct correlation between the price of cocoa paid to farmers and the amount of money spent by farmers on housing.

6 J. Barber, *Journals*, Church Mission Society, London, CA2/021, 1857. In January 1857 no fewer than four fires destroyed large parts of the city.

7 M. Koll, *Crafts and Cooperation in Western Nigeria*, Freiburg i.B., 1969, pp. 118–124.

8 P. Crooke, 'Rural settlement and housing trends in a developing country: an example in Nigeria', *International Labour Review* (Geneva), **96** (3), 1967, pp. 280–291.

9 Western State of Nigeria, Ministry of Economic Planning and Reconstruction, *Statistical Abstract* (Ibadan, **XII** (1–2), 1970, p. 34. The capital expenditure of the former Western Region, now Western State, of Nigeria between 1960 and 1970 was £N92.8 million. Of this £N12.3 million or 13.3 per cent was spent on buildings which include, *inter alia*, schools, offices, and residential buildings for civil servants, while another £N16.8 million or 18.1 per cent was spent on roads and bridges. Over 70 per cent of these projects were carried out by private builders and civil engineers by contract.

10 G. A. Ogunpola, 'The pattern of organization in the building industry – A Western Nigerian case study', *Nigerian Journal of Economic and Social Studies* (Ibadan), **10** (3), 1968, pp. 339–360.

11 Federal Office of Statistics, Nigeria, op. cit., p. 10. Out of 800 households surveyed 96 or 12.0 per cent had no kitchen, 71 or 8.9 per cent had no bathroom, 116 or 14.5 per cent had no

toilet, 508 or 63.5 per cent had no electricity supply, 625 or 78.1 per cent had no private water supply.

12 United Nations, *Housing in Africa*, E/CN/14/HOU/7/Rev., New York, 1965, p. 104.

13 Galletti, op. cit., pp. 252–259.

14 P. Crooke, 'Sample survey of Yoruba rural building' *Odu, University of Ife Journal of African Studies* (Ibadan), **2** (2), 1966, pp. 41–71.

15 W. R. Bascom, 'The Esusu: A credit institution among the Yoruba', *Journal of the Royal Anthropological Institute of Great Britain and Ireland* (London), **LXXII**, 1952, pp. 53–70.

16 S. Ardener, 'The comparative study of rotating credit associations', *Journal of the Royal Anthropological Institute* (London), **XCIV** (2) 1964, pp. 201–229.

Part III

MARRAKECH

Chapter 13

Context

Environmental setting

Geography and climate

Morocco, or al-Mamlaka al-Maghrebia (the kingdom of the west), as it is known among the Arabic-speaking people, is located at the north-western corner of Africa between latitudes 27° 40′ and 35° 55′ north and between longitudes 1° 00′ and 13° 10′ west. The country is over 1,200 km (750 miles) long and about 500 km (310 miles) wide at its greatest inland depth, and has an area of approximately 445,500 sq. km or 174,000 sq. miles.

The main features of the country's topography are the Rif and Atlas mountains. These mountains, which rise to a height of over 4,100 m (13,300 feet), are roughly aligned in a chain from north-east to south-west and are divided into four distinctive massifs: the Rif, and the Middle, the High, and the Anti Atlas.

The contrast between the fertile Atlantic lowlands situated to the west of the mountain range and the barren desert plains of Saharan Morocco to the east is very striking. The western slopes are covered by forests which consist mainly of cedars, cork, and evergreen oak, aleppo pine, and various kinds of cypresses, whereas the eastern slopes consist of bare sun-baked rocks giving way to almost waterless stony plateaux trenched by valleys from which cultivated palm groves extend like green fingers into the desert.

The vegetation found in the Atlantic coastal plains (0–200 m above sea-level) includes fruit-bearing trees and crops, asphodels, fennel, and dwarf palms, while on the Meseta Plateau further east (200–1,000 m above sea-level) shrubs and alfalfa grass dominate the landscape. The main crops grown by farmers in the Atlantic lowlands and on irrigated plots elsewhere include *inter alia* such cereals as wheat, barley, and corn as well as pulses, citrus fruits, vegetables, sugar-beet, cotton, oil-producing plants, potatoes, and rice.

Morocco's climate is determined by the Atlas Mountains which act as a barrier and watershed between the western and eastern parts of the country. North and central Morocco enjoy a Mediterranean type of climate with hot, dry summers, which are largely the result of anticyclones centred near the Azores, and warm, wet winters. Further south, as the rainfall gradually decreases, this climate gives way to semi-arid and eventually to desert conditions. For example, Tangier with 897 mm (35.3 in.) average annual rainfall is one of Morocco's wettest towns, followed by Fez with 536 mm (21.1 in.), Marrakech with 239 mm (9.4 in.), Quarzazate with 107 mm (4.2 in.), while Tabelbala just inside Algerian territory has a mere 20 mm or 0.8 in.[1] The only exceptions to this gradient are found in the high ridges of the Rif and Atlas mountains where the rainfall averages over 800 mm per annum.[2]

The city of Marrakech, at 30° 37′ latitude north, 8° 00′ longitude east, stands about 460 m above sea-level in the western foot-hills of the High Atlas Mountains. Temperatures in the city vary from an average daily maximum of 38.4 °C in July to an average daily minimum of 4.4 °C in January. The mean annual rainfall (1923–1958) is only 239 mm, mostly coming between November and April.[3] (See Diagram A.13.1 on p. 413.)

Human pattern

Since late Palaeolithic times North Africa has been inhabited by people of Caucasoid race. When the Phoenicians, Greeks, and later the Romans colonized the coast from the first millennium BC until the fourth century AD, they found the region occupied by people known collectively as Berbers (Latin, *barbarus*). After the conquest of Morocco by an Arab army at the beginning of the eighth century, Arabs and Berbers mixed freely and are today no longer distinguishable, particularly in towns and the Atlantic lowlands.

According to Greenberg, the languages of Morocco belong to the Afro-Asiatic group, also known as Hamito-Semitic, which includes *inter alia* both Berber and Arabic.[4] The spread of the Arabic language in Morocco since the eighth century, and especially after large-scale Bedouin/Arab immigration in the eleventh and fifteenth centuries, has resulted in the survival of Berber languages only in mountainous regions inaccessible to Arab power. Today, an estimated 60 per cent of the total population, most of whom live in urban areas, the Atlantic lowlands, and the Taza Corridor, speak Arabic, whereas the rest of the population, particularly those in the mountainous regions, speak one of several Berber languages.[5]

Historical background*

While many outstanding medieval and modern scholars have contributed to our knowledge of Morocco's history, the following summary is mainly based on the researches carried out by Henri Térrasse, Charles-André Julien, and Gaston Deverdun whose works enable us to follow the turbulent history of Marrakech from its foundation in the late eleventh century to the present day.[6]

The conquest of North Africa by an Arab army began in the middle of the seventh century and was almost completed when Musa b. Nusair conquered the western parts of the Maghrib between 704 and 711. Spain, except the far north, was in the hands of an Arab–Berber army by 713. The history of the western Maghrib after the successful Arab invasion until the middle of the eleventh century is one of confusion. The beginning of this period was characterized by tough Berber resistance to the Arab invaders. This was followed by the rise and fall of successive Arab and Berber states such as the Kharidjite, Idrisid, Aghladbid, and Fatimid dynasties, and massive invasions by two waves of nomads, the Banu Hilal who were Arab and the Sanhadja Berbers, who invaded Morocco in the early eleventh century. It is the invasion of the latter group which merits further attention.

Both the Almoravid and Almohad dynasties, which lasted for over 200 years from the middle of the eleventh century to the middle of the thirteenth, started as reformist religious movements. The Almoravid dynasty was founded by Sanhadja Berbers, a nomadic people, who roamed the western Sahara, trading mainly salt for gold in

* Spelling of Arabic names is based on the *Encyclopaedia of Islam*, ed. M. J. Houtsma *et al.*, vols 1–4, Leyden and London, 1913–1934.

the Sudan belt of West Africa. Islam had spread among the Sanhadja since about the ninth century, but it is alleged that their knowledge of the new religion remained rather rudimentary.[7] Around 1035 Abd Allah b. Yasin, a religious scholar from the Sous, appeared among the Sanhadja to preach the tenets of Islam. However, his mission was not successful and he left with a few followers and built a fortified monastery (*ribat*), the inhabitants of which were called *al-murabitun*, hence the name Almoravids.[8] In the early 1040s, having assembled a sizeable army of warrior-monks, Abd Allah b. Yasin launched a successful *jihad* or holy war against the surrounding tribes. By 1060 large parts of southern and central Morocco as well as the western trading routes to the Sudan belt were in the hands of the Sanhadja Berbers.[9] Yusuf b. Tashfin, a military leader, who gained control of the Sanhadja army in 1061, became the first Almoravid sultan. He founded the city of Marrakech in about 1070,[10] and made it the capital of a new empire.[11] Under Ibn Tashfin's son 'Ali b. Yusuf (1107–1143) the Almoravid empire was at its height. Territorially, it then included Muslim Spain, the Balearic Isles, the Mediterranean coast as far east as Algiers, and the western trading routes to the Sudan belt of West Africa.

Marrakech, which was first established by Yusuf b. Tashfin as an army camp for the Sanhadja Berbers, soon became a permanent settlement. But it was not until 1126–1127, when the city was seriously threatened by an army under Ibn Tumart, the religious leader and founder of the Almohad movement,[12] that Marrakech was surrounded by a defensive wall.[13] (See Plan 15.1 on p. 207.) However, 'Ali b. Yusuf's successors, Tashfin b. 'Ali and Ishak b. 'Ali b. Yusuf, could not prevent the already crumbling empire from falling into the hands of the Almohads. The city of Marrakech was taken after an eleven months' siege in the spring of 1147 by an army under 'Abd al-Mu'min (1133–1163), the first Almohad sultan, and then became again the capital of Morocco where the sultan and his successors resided when they were in the country. 'Abd al-Mu'min vigorously pursued further conquests along the Mediterranean coast of Morocco and beyond, and when he died at Ribat al-Fath (Rabat) in 1163 he left his son Abu Ya'kub Yusuf (1163–1184) an empire which comprised the whole of the Maghrib from the Atlantic coast to Tripoli and the greater part of Muslim Spain.

Under the Almohads Marrakech grew rapidly and became one of the most prosperous cities in the Maghrib. Ya'kub al-Mansur (1184–1199), the third Almohad sultan and the most renowned builder of the dynasty,[14] ordered the construction of the Casba, an extension of the city to the south. (See Plan 15.1 on p. 207.) Many important public buildings such as the Mosquee al Mansour situated in the Casba, a hospital, several schools (*médersas*), aqueducts, and magnificent gardens were laid out and constructed during his reign. However, his successors Muhammed al-Nasir (1199–1213) and Yusuf al-Mustansir (1214–1224) rapidly lost most of their influence in Muslim Spain. Eastern and central Maghrib, governed by the Hafsids and Zayamids, slipped out of Almohad control, and the last four decades of the dynasty (1224–1269) were disturbed by rivalries between the descendants of 'Abd al-Mu'min and those of Ibn Tumart which made it relatively easy for the Merinids to seize control of the country.

The occupation of Marrakech by an Merinid army in September 1269 not only brought the Almohad dynasty to an end but also the political unity of the Maghrib. The three Muslim states which succeeded the Almohads – the Merinids centred in Fez, the Zayanids in Tlemsen, and the Hafsids in Tunis – were, unlike their predecessors, politically oriented states rather than religiously inspired empires.[15] The first Merinid sultan, Abu Yusuf Ya'kub (1258–1286), ordered the construction of his new capital overlooking the old town of Fez which was founded by the Idrisids in the early ninth century; and during the two and a half centuries of Merinid rule Fez remained the capital of the dynasty, while Marrakech was administered by governors appointed by the reigning sultan. Abu' l-Hasan 'Ali (1286–1307) was the only Merinid sultan to build a mosque and a school there, but by the 1430s the city seems to have become *de facto* an independent kingdom ruled by Hintata emirs from the south of Morocco.

By the end of the fifteenth century the Moroccan system of government based on exclusive domination by one or two tribal groups was declining. Two new types of grouping were emerging: first, a powerful urban class of merchants and artisans who were passionately interested in stability and order and, second, a popular religious Sufi movement. These groupings, and a professional army founded by Ahmad al-Mansur in the late sixteenth century, played increasingly important parts in the political affairs of the Sa'dian and later the Alawite dynasties.

Ahmad al-A'radj, the first Sa'dian sultan (1517–1541), established himself peacefully in Marrakech, and made it the capital of the new dynasty. Abd al-Ghalib (1557–1574) and his brother Ahmad al-Mansur (1578–1603)[16] restored the city to its former splendour. Several mosques, schools, and a new palace (al-Badi) were built by them. The Jewish population of the city were rehoused in the Mellah, an area they still occupy today. (For names of localities see Plan A.15.3 on p. 423.) However, after al-Mansur's death in 1603, anarchy spread throughout the country. The struggle for power between his sons split Morocco into the kingdom of Marrakech under Abu Faris Abdallah and the kingdom of Fez under Zidan. This division hastened the decline of the Sa'dian dynasty which came to an end when Mawlay al-Rashid (1659–1671), the first Alawid sultan, occupied Marrakech in 1668.[17]

During the long reign of Mawlay Isma'il (1672–1727) peace and order were restored. The sultan made Meknès the capital of the Alawid dynasty and improved it by building a palace and several mosques there. He took little interest in Marrakech and destroyed most of its famous palaces in his search for valuable building materials to speed up his building at Meknès. However, Muhammad b. 'Abd Allah (1757–1790) restored Marrakech and some of its palaces and made it his residence. His successors, Abd al-Rahman (1822–1859) and Muhammad b. Abd al-Rahman (1859–1873) continued to take an active interest in the city by repairing some of its religious buildings, aqueducts, and water storage basins, although both sultans seldom stayed in Marrakech.

It is interesting to note that none of the Sa'dian and Alawid sultans was able to rule the whole country, which was then effectively divided into the *bled al-makhzan*, the areas in which the sultan exercised his supreme religious and secular authority, and the *bled es-siba* (land of the dissidents) whose inhabitants were hostile to the secular authority of the central government, though they usually recognized the sultan's authority as *imam* or religious leader.[18] The size of the area under the control of the sultan's central government varied from sultan to sultan and depended not only on his military strength but also on his ability and standing as a national leader.

The European struggle for influence in the Maghrib started with the occupation of Algeria by the French in 1830. This invasion forced the country out of her chosen isolation. It soon became clear that Morocco's independence could only be preserved as long as the European powers were prepared to check each other's colonial ambitions in this region. However, after protracted bargaining, which involved the colonial interests of France, Great Britain, Spain, Germany, and Italy, Morocco became a Franco-Spanish protectorate early in 1912.

After the defeat of Al-Hiba's army at Sidi bu-Uthman,* French forces under Colonel Mangin occupied Marrakech on 7 September 1912. Louis Lyautey, the first French Governor General (1912–1925), restored El Hadj Thamis, one of the influential Kaids† in southern Morocco, to his old post as Pasha of Marrakech‡ which he held until 1955. General de Lamothe, who assumed control over the region, built a fort and several barracks at the foot of Jbel Gueliz about 3 km south of the walled city. A modern European township, situated between the fort and the walled city, was laid out and developed rapidly after the First World War. In 1928 the railway reached Marrakech and linked the town with Casablanca.

In the French zone of Morocco, the colonial government embarked on a programme of introducing a modern economic infrastructure. Between 1912 and 1956 a total of 1,600 km of railway[19] and over 49,000 km of highways, 15,000 km of which were all-weather roads, were constructed by the French.[20] Special efforts were made to exploit the country's mineral wealth and to introduce modern agricultural methods. The French educational system as well as medical facilities were introduced and gradually extended to the Moroccan population. After the Second World War mounting resistance to the colonical regime spread throughout the country; and after skirmishes between the Moroccan National Movement and the colonial forces, which reached their height in mid-1955, the French Government granted Morocco its independence in March 1956.

Economic development

Between 1960 and 1970, the performance of the Moroccan economy, expressed in the changes in Gross Domestic Product (GDP) at current factor cost, was one of steady expansion. For example, the GDP rose from DH (dirham)§ 9,090 million in 1960 to DH16,960 million in 1970 at current factor cost, or DH13,540 million at 1960 prices,[21] yielding per capita incomes of approximately DH780 and DH940 respectively. During this period the estimated average annual growth rate of GDP was in the region of 3.9 per

* Al-Hiba was a marabout or holy man from Mauritania who had himself proclaimed sultan and established his headquarters at Marrakech in 1912.

† Tribal chiefs.

‡ Mayor of Marrakech.

§ The dirham (DH) is the unit of currency in Morocco and it was introduced in October 1959. The exchange rate was 100 Moroccan francs for 1 dirham.

cent, while per capita incomes rose by slightly over 1.0 per cent per annum.[22] (See Table A.13.1 on p. 414.)

Although Morocco is rich in mineral resources, notably phosphates, agriculture provides the basis of the country's economy, contributing 27.7 per cent of GDP and about 50 per cent of the total export earnings in 1970. Over half of the population of Morocco are engaged in agriculture and livestock raising. The mining industry contributes only 4.4 per cent to GDP, though minerals, mainly phospates, accounted for over 30 per cent of total export earnings in 1971. (See Table A.13.2 on p. 415.)

The manufacturing industry in Morocco consists mainly of small and medium sized processing plants producing such consumer goods as textiles, canned food, soft drinks, flour, sugar, motor car tyres, and cement. The contribution of the manufacturing industry, including crafts, to the GDP was 12.5 per cent in 1971. Export of manufactured goods rose substantially from DH132 million or 6.1 per cent of total export value in 1965 to DH395 million or 15.6 per cent in 1971. (See Tables A.13.3 and A.13.4 on pp. 416–417.)

Tourism has become Morocco's fastest growing industry in recent years. The number of tourists increased from about half a million in 1965 to an estimated 1 million in 1972. Revenue derived from tourism increased from DH406 million in 1968 to DH555 million in 1972.

Other important sectors of the national economy are commerce which in 1971 accounted for DH2,840 million or 20 per cent of GDP, transport and non-governmental services which totalled DH2,300 million or 16.2 per cent, government services with DH1,630 million or 11.5 per cent, construction with DH730 million or 5.1 per cent, and energy with DH370 million or 2.6 per cent.

Morocco's major trading partners are the EEC countries which took about 57.0 per cent of the country's exports and supplied approximately 50 per cent of its imports in 1971. Between 1965 and 1971 imports rose at an average annual rate of 7.4 per cent from DH2,295 million to DH3,533 million, while exports over the same period increased by only 2.5 per cent annually from DH2,176 million to DH2,525 million, leaving a trade deficit of over DH1,000 million in 1970 and 1971.[23]

Morocco's Gross Fixed Capital Formation (GFCF) at current prices rose from DH1,370 million or 12.3 per cent of GDP in 1964 to DH2,620 million or 15.5 per cent in 1971. More detailed examinations of Fixed Capital Formation by type of asset show that the share of investments in residential and non-residential buildings remained fairly stable at around 20 per cent over the last eight years

(1964–1971). Such public works as dams, roads, and bridge construction accounted for about 37.0 per cent over the same period, while the rest was invested in equipment and machinery. (See Tables A.13.5 and A.13.6 on p. 417.) As already mentioned, total investment in building represents about 20 per cent while residential buildings may account for an estimated 6 to 8 per cent of GFCF. As observed in Chapter 6, most private and government financed dwellings are located in cities and in the few selected rural development areas, while the majority of houses built in the rural and suburban areas where an estimated 70 per cent of the country's total population live are constructed outside the monetary sector and never appear in any national accounts.

Notes and references

1 Meteorological Office, *Tables of Temperature, Relative Humidity and Precipitation for the World*, part IV, Africa, etc., London, 1964, pp. 10, 106–109, 165.
2 W. Hance, *The Geography of Modern Africa*, New York, 1964, p. 78.
3 Meteorological Office, op. cit., p. 108.
4 J. H. Greenberg, *Languages in Africa*, The Hague, 1966, pp. 42–65.
5 R. Montagne, *La Vie sociale et la vie politique des Berbèrs*, Paris, 1931. Trans. by D. Seddon *The Berbers: Their Social and Political Organization*, London, 1973, p. 4.
6 C.-A. Julien, *Histoire de l'Afrique du Nord*, Paris, 1956, 2 vols. Trans. by J. Petrie as *History of North Africa*, London, 1970. H. Térrasse, *Histoire du Maroc des origines à l'establissement du protectorat français*, Casablanca, 1949–1950, 2 vols. G. Deverdun, *Marrakech des origines à 1912*, Rabat, 1959 and 1966, 2 vols.
7 Julien, op. cit., p. 77.
8 J. M. Abun-Nasr, *A History of the Maghrib*, Cambridge, 1971, p. 93.
9 Abou-Obeid-el-Bekri, *Kitab al-Masalik*, Trans. by Mac Guckin de Slane as *Description de l'Afrique septentrionale*, Paris, 1965, pp. 309–318.
10 Deverdun, op. cit., pp. 59–64.
11 Térrasse, op. cit., pp. 222–223.
12 I. Goldziher, *Mohammed Ibn Toumert et la théologie de l'Islam dans le Nord de l'Afrique au XIe siècle*, Algiers, 1903, pp. 54–71.
13 Deverdun, op. cit., pp. 109–110.
14 M. R. Mouline, *The Era of al-Mansur the Almohad, or the Political, Intellectual and Religious Life of the Maghrib from the Year 580 to the Year 595 (1185–1199)*, Rabat, 1946.
15 Abun-Nasr, op. cit., pp. 119–120.
16 E. W. Bovill, 'The Moorish invasion of the Sudan', *Journal de la Société des Africanistes* (Paris), **XXVI**, 1927, pp. 245–293, and **XXVII**, pp. 47–56. H. de Castries, 'La Conquête du Soudan', *Hesperis*, **3**, 1923, pp. 433–488.

17 R. le Tourneau, 'La Décadence sa'dienne et l'anarchie marocaine au XIIe siècle', *Annales de la Faculté des Lettres d'Aix*, **XXXII**, 1960, pp. 187–225.
18 Montagne, op. cit., pp. 12–17. D. M. Hart, 'The tribe in modern Morocco: Two case studies', in *Arabs and Berbers*, ed. E. Gellner *et al.*, London, 1973, pp. 27–28.
19 Gouvernement Chérifien Service Central des Statistiques, *Annuaire statistique de la zone française du Maroc*, Rabat, 1952, p. 282.
20 Encyclopedia Mensuelle d'Outre-mer, *Morocco 54*, Special Issue, Paris, 1954, p. 189.
21 Ministère du développement, Royaume du Maroc, *Annuaire statistique du Maroc 1964–1965* and *1971*, Rabat, 1966 and 1972, pp. 198, 250.
22 United Nations, *Yearbook of National Accounts Statistics 1971*, New York, 1973, vol. 2, p. 90.
23 United Nations, Economic Commission for Africa (ECA), 'Summaries of Economic Data, Morocco 1971', Addis Ababa, 1972, pp. 16–17.

Chapter 14

Land tenure and land use in the *medina* of Marrakech

Historical notes on land tenure

Before we turn our attention to the various types of land tenure which can be found in Marrakech today, a few introductory words should be said about the system of land ownership that existed in Morocco before 1912.

Broadly speaking, land ownership was divided into four major categories. First, there was *makhzen* land, or land which belonged to the state, i.e. the sultan, who had the right to retain these lands or grant their use to important individuals – in which case it was known as *azib* land – or to tribal communities who were usually of Arab origin, in return for military service. Under the latter type of arrangement, often referred to as *guich*, the land was granted in perpetuity and consisted mainly of agricultural and pasture land situated in the vicinity of large cities or near important strategic points.[1] A second category of tenure was represented by *habous* land.* This consisted mainly of urban and agricultural land left by pious people for the benefit of religious and/or charitable organizations. These lands were held and used by mosques, *médersas* (Muslim schools), or *zaouia* (religious

* There were two kinds of *habous* land: family *habous* and public *habous*. The characteristic feature of the first category was that before passing to the society or the establishment stipulated, the land was enjoyed by a series of intermediate beneficiaries, in the order prescribed by the donor, while the second category was constituted for the direct and immediate benefit of the charitable or social association.

brotherhoods), and administered by *nadirs** who were officials appointed by the reigning sultan.[2] *Habous* land was considered inalienable but could be rented or exchanged for parcels of equal value. The third category of tenure was *melk* or freehold land. *Melk* land was either inherited, bequeathed, or purchased and was owned by an individual, or more often by groups of related persons. The bulk of *melk* land was located in and around towns. Finally, there were collective tribal lands known as *arch* which belonged by traditions of continuous occupancy to a tribe as a whole. Most of this land, which consisted mainly of pasture grounds, was situated in the mountainous regions of the country and lay outside the sultan's authority.

After the Treaty of Fez, which marks the beginning of the French protectorate in Morocco, was signed in March 1912, it took the occupying forces over twenty years to pacify the territory. In the meantime, Louis H. G. Lyautey, the first French Governor General, introduced a number of important pieces of land legislation which were designed to give some land to the newly arrived French immigrants (*colons*) while protecting the indigenous Moroccan farmers.[3] The first step was a Circular issued by the Grand Vizir on 1 November 1912. In it were listed all property which could not be alienated such as roads, rivers, beaches, forest, as well as *arch*, *habous*, and *makhzen* land.

In early 1913 Lyautey appointed a Commission d'Études to advise him on land policy in the protectorate. The commission's report, which was based on the Australian Torrens Act of 1858,† recommended the voluntary registration of land ownership and laid down procedures thereto. Most of the commission's recommendations were approved by Lyautey and embodied in the *dahir* of 12 August 1913.‡ The new law decreed that registration of land was optional, except in the case of exchange, purchase, or alienation of *makhzen*, *habous*, and *arch*. All land registered was placed under the jurisdiction of French courts, although these courts, either the Tribunaux

* Traditionally there was one *nadir* in each mosque or *zaouir* chosen by notables of the quarter, town, or district. However, towards the middle of the nineteenth century, Abd al-Rahman (1822–1859) abolished private *nadirs* and replaced them with officially appointed civil servants.

† The Real Property Act No. 15 of 1857–1958 was first introduced on the recommendation of Sir Robert Torrens in South Australia in 1857. This act with its simplified procedure of registration became Australia's most important contribution in land legislation to the world as a whole.

‡ A *dahir* or statutory decree was drawn up by the French administration and approved by the resident Governor General before it was submitted to the Sultan for his seal. The *dahir* of 12 August 1913 was modified by others of October 1916, 2 May 1917, 24 September 1917, 10 June 1918, 10 March 1921, and 23 February 1924.

de Première Instance or the Cour d'Appel, could request Muslim legal consultants to give evidence should the need arise. As expected, the registration of land proved extremely slow and hazardous and René Besuard remarked somewhat bitterly: 'Depuis le grand Vizir jusqu'au plus petit Caid, on se disputa l'honneur de les tromper.'[4] In spite of these difficulties a total of over 116,000 registrations of land ownership (32,000 by Europeans and 84,000 by Moroccans) were requested, checked, and completed by the administration between 1914 and 1956.[5]

During his first year in office, Lyautey ordered a survey of all *habous* and *makhzen* or government land and, after having successfully completed this, he recovered some of these lands from persons who had obtained them irregularly shortly before 1912. In a *dahir* of 1 August 1914, *makhzen* land was divided into the Domaine Public de l'État which was controlled by the Administration des Travaux Publics, and the Domaine Privé which was run by the Service des Domaine. Land controlled by the Administration des Travaux Publics was inalienable, while land administered by the Service des Domaines was available to those *colons* who wished to purchase it and settle in Morocco. In 1913 approximately 73,000 hectares (180,000 acres) were under cultivation by Europeans, and this steadily increased to over 1,000,000 hectares (2,500,000 acres) or about 10 per cent of Morocco's total cropland in 1953.[6] This total was farmed by about 5,900 Europeans, with an average of about 170 hectares or 420 acres per farm.

In 1915 Lyautey placed the administration of *habous* land under Muslim authority by creating a Conseil Supérieur des Habous which was assisted by a French councillor. As already mentioned, *habous* land was inalienable, but a *dahir* of 21 July 1913 allowed such land to be let to *colons.*[7]

Arch was protected against alienation by a *dahir* of 15 July 1914, but this decree law was partly revised by a *dahir* of 27 April 1919, which placed collective tribal land under the control of the Conseil de Tutelle. The newly appointed council used its power freely to confiscate large parts of this land, often against the wishes of its lawful owners, and sold it to French settlers.[8]

Melk or freehold land, apart from the *dahir* which permitted its registration, was not affected by the land policy of the protectorate. Hence transactions in urban land and houses among the indigenous population were conducted in much the same way as before the French occupation in 1912.

In conclusion, all land in pre-protectorate Morocco

belonged at least in theory to the reigning sultan. In practice, however, there were four clearly distinguishable types of landholding, namely, *makhzen*, *habous*, *melk*, and *arch*. The bulk of the latter was situated in inaccessible mountainous regions and was therefore outside the sultan's authority. After the French occupation, the colonial government, unlike its British counterpart in Nigeria, was keen to provide some land for French settlers. This policy was regarded by the French Government in Paris as an important prerequisite for the successful pacification of the country.[9] Lyautey realized that the question of land was the most important and delicate he had to solve in order to establish a successful and lasting French presence in Morocco. There is little doubt that during his 13 years as Governor General (1912–1925), Lyautey tried to protect the Moroccan interest. That his policy failed in the long run was largely due to the open hostility of the *colons* to his careful approach and to the lack of responsibility of his successors, particularly Theodore Steeg (1925–1929), Lucien Saint (1929–1933), Henri Ponsot (1933–1936), and Marcel Peyrouton (1936), who did absolutely nothing to prevent the best agricultural land from passing into the hands of the land-grabbing *colons*.

In urban areas the approach by Lyautey towards the question of land ownership was similar to the policy pursued by Lugard in Northern Nigeria. The ownership of *melk*, which includes houses and gardens, was not affected by the new land law of the protectorate. Land disputes and inheritance cases, unless settled amicably by the parties involved, were tried by Muslim judges (*quadi*) in local courts (*chrâa*) according to Maliki law.

In Marrakech, part of the land required for the construction of a new suburb to the west of the walled city was already in government hands (*makhzen* land), while the rest was acquired from local people who were given compensation.

Land tenure and transfer today

The investigation of land ownership and the transfer of land and houses described below is based on my survey of 75 houses in Marrakech in 1969.

Permanent transfer of land

In my survey, purchase of land and houses accounts for 45.3 per cent of the total sample, and is by far the most important mode of land transfer. (See Table A.14.1 on p. 418.) Compound heads* in need of more rooms normally sell their houses and buy larger ones, as the only way of increasing the floor area of a house in the tightly packed *medina* is to build an additional storey, which, for structural reasons, is not always possible. A total of 29 purchased houses in the survey were each owned by one individual who was usually the compound head; while another 5 purchased houses were owned by a group of related persons who had pooled their resources in order to buy the house.

Inheritance of houses accounted for 18.7 per cent of the total number of houses surveyed. Following the owner's death, a house or plot of land will pass to his children or, if there are none, to the care of the next senior agnatic relative. If the house is not required by the heirs, it may be rented or sold and the proceeds divided among them according to Maliki law.[10] Among the 14 inherited houses found in the sample, 9 were owned by a group of related persons while 5 were owned by one individual each.

Houses built on squatter land accounted for 8.0 per cent of the units sampled. All of these houses are located in the Douar Sidi Youssef b. Ali, an area situated south-west of the walled city. (See Plan 15.1 on p. 207.) The first inhabitants of this area arrived shortly after the Second World War. As the police were unwilling to evict the squatters, popular beliefs that they were permitted to settle there gradually strengthened. Hence the number of squatters and the area they occupied steadily increased until the town-planning authority put a stop to this development in the early 1960s. At that point, the sole owner of the land was compensated by the government, which is now reclaiming the money from the occupants at a rate of DH20 per square metre. According to my information only a few people had actually paid this amount to the government, a fact which caused us considerable difficulties when surveying this area.

The renting of houses

Unlike in Zaria and Ibadan, the renting of houses accounted for 20.0 per cent of the total sample in Marrakech. Of the 15 houses found in this category, 11 were let by absentee landlords, while 4 were *habous* property. The rent paid for these houses ranged from

* I retain the term 'compound head' to distinguish him from all other household heads who may be living in the same house.

DH60 per month for a small house with four rooms and one kitchen having a total floor area of 68 sq. m, to DH200 per month for a house with eight rooms, one kitchen, four stores, and a total floor area of 166 sq. m. Rent paid for an average sized room, on the other hand, was in the region of DH15 per month in 1969.

An additional arrangement which was found in three houses involved the payment of a deposit of between DH1,000 and 2,000 per room by a tenant to the owner of the house. Once such a contract has been signed the tenant pays no further rent, and there is usually no time limit on the right of occupancy which is heritable. However, the right of occupancy can be sold by the tenant subject to the house owner's approval. The owner can revoke the contract only after the refund of the deposit to the tenant. This type of arrangement, which plays an important role in the local economy, guarantees some security for the tenant, and provides the owner of the house with a substantial lump sum which he may use to pay for trading activities, marriage or funeral expenditures, building construction, and improvements.

Land use in the *medina* of Marrakech

The study of land use given below is based on an aerial survey of Marrakech carried out in 1960, and on a large-scale map, scale 1:2,000, published by the Sous-Secrétariat d'État à l'Agriculture, Service Topographique, Rabat, 1963. Excluding the Jardin de l'Aguedal to the south, the walled city of Marrakech covers a total area of 6,319,790 sq. m or 632.0 hectares (1,562 acres). The circumference of the wall is 13,000 m long. The diameter of the walled city varies between 2,930 m from east to west and 4,300 m from north to south. The area of the walled city has been divided into seven categories of land. These are:

1 Building sites, i.e. houses and courtyards which account for 64.1 per cent of the total area. (See Table A.14.2 on p. 418. This is by far the most important category and comprises all private and public buildings, as well as narrow alleyways and footpaths between houses unsuited to motor traffic. Land use within houses, i.e. courtyards, etc., will be discussed separately in Chapter 16.

2 Parks and public gardens account for 12.6 per cent of the total enclosed area and include *inter alia* the Jardin de la Koutoubia, and the Arset el Bahia.

3 Waste lands cover 7.2 per cent of the total walled city. These lands consist mainly of dilapidated buildings, uncultivated stony areas alongside the city wall, and land cleared for redevelopment.
4 Roads. If we define this category to include all roads and tracks wide enough to carry motor vehicles, then 7.1 per cent of the walled city area is appropriated to these ends.
5 Cultivated areas in the walled city account for 5.7 per cent of the total area and consist mainly of olive groves and irrigated gardens.
6 There are three Muslim, one small Christian, and one Jewish cemetery within the walled city, covering about 2.7 per cent of the total walled city area.
7 Other land accounts for 38,960 sq. m or 0.6 per cent of the total city area. This includes 31,200 sq. m used mainly for leather tanning and two reservoirs covering 7,760 sq. m.

Notes and references

1 R. Bidwell, *Morocco under Colonial Rule*, London, 1973, p. 207.
2 Bidwell, op. cit., p. 206. The amount of *habous* land seems to have been considerable, particularly in towns. Bidwell reports that according to an early French survey in Taza, no fewer than 349 shops in the city or about 60 per cent of the total were designated as *habous* land. Unfortunately there are no comparative figures available for Marrakech.
3 A. Scham, *Lyautey in Morocco*, Berkeley, Calif., 1970, pp. 191–205.
4 R. Besnard, *L'Oeuvre française au Maroc*, Paris, 1914, p. 194.
5 Bidwell, op. cit., p. 204.
6 H. Fazy, *Agriculture marocaine et protectorat*, Paris, 1948, p. 62.
7 E. Michaux-Bellaire, 'Les biens habous et biens du makhzen au point de vue de leur location et de leur aliénation', *Revue du monde musulman* (Paris), **V** (7) 1908, p. 439.
8 Scham, op. cit., pp. 118–126.
9 L. Barėty, *La France au Maroc*, Paris, 1932, p. 231. Barėty, who was a French minister and leader of the Moroccan lobby, wrote: 'Le peuplement! voilà la base fondamentale de la réussite et de la longévité de notre oeuvre au Maroc. Veillons à accroître là-bas notre population française'.
10 F. H. Ruxton, *Maliki Law*, London, 1916, Chapter LV, 'Succession (*fara'id*)', pp. 373–397.

Chapter 15

Demography

General characteristics

Morocco the demographic situation

In 1971, Morocco had a total population of about 15.4 million, that is, approximately 4.5 per cent of the total population in Africa.[1] It is the most populous of the Maghrib countries followed by Algeria with 14.5 million, Tunisia with 5.2 million, and Libya with about 1.9 million.[2] Earlier estimates indicate that the population of Morocco has trebled during the last 50 years from an estimated 5.0 million in 1921[3] to 15.4 million in 1971. During the 11 years from 1960 to 1971, the average annual growth rate of its population was in the region of 2.6 per cent. If present trends continue, the population of the country will reach an estimated 27.0 million by the mid-1980s.[4]

In the former French protectorate of Morocco, which covered about 90 per cent of the territory, crude population counts of limited statistical value were conducted in 1921, 1926, and 1931. All three estimates suffered from extremely poor enumerating techniques and from the crude guesses which they included for the populations in unpacified areas. According to these estimates, the population rose from approximately 4.3 million in 1921 to about 5.4 million in 1931.[5] An improved population estimate in 1936, which for the first time included the pacified areas of the former French protectorate, gave a population of about 6.2 million.[6] The first postwar census carried out in 1947 was less reliable because it consisted of a count of ration cards, a procedure which resulted in an overestimation of the population. The 1951/1952 census, the last that the French conducted in their zone, is undoubtedly the most reliable count taken during the period of the protectorate, and yielded a total population of approximately 8.1 million.[7]

For the former Spanish protectorate including the province of Tarfaya estimates were made in 1930, 1940, and 1950 and yielded populations of 0.75, 1.00 and 1.03 million respectively. The international zone of Tangier increased its population from an estimated 60,000 in 1927 to about 183,000 in 1954.[8]

Both the 1960 and 1971 censuses were national censuses which included the former French and Spanish protectorates as well as the international zone of Tangier and gave totals of 11.6 and 15.4 million respectively.

Population distribution and densities

During the period of the protectorate, 1912–1956, Morocco was divided into three political units: first, the French protectorate with a population of approximately 8.1 million or 87.0 per cent of the country's total population in 1952; second, the Spanish protectorate including the province of Tarfaya in the south, with about 1.06 million or 11.0 per cent; and finally, the international zone of Tanger with about 172,000 inhabitants in 1952 or about 2.0 per cent of the total. Following reunification in 1956, the province of Tarfaya was returned by Spain in April 1958, the country was then administratively divided into 16 provinces and 2 prefectures. By a reorganization in the mid-1960s, 19 provinces were formed, while the 2 prefectures of Casablanca and Rabat-Salé remained unaltered.

According to the *Annuaire statistique du Maroc 1971* the country's overall population density then was 34 per square kilometre,[9] but there were wide regional variations. Map A.15.1 on p. 419 shows the differing population densities per square kilometre of the 19 Provinces and two Prefectures in 1971. (For the names of these Provinces and Prefectures, see Map A.15.2 on page 420.) As can be seen, there are three broad areas with different population densities which roughly coincide with the country's social and economic geography. First, there are six coastal provinces stretching from Nador in the north to Safi in the south with densities that range between 60 and 100 persons per square kilometre. The only exception here is the province of Tangier with 590 persons per square kilometre, and the prefectures of Rabat-Salé and Casablanca with 1,210 and 1,430 persons per square kilometre respectively. The province of Settat on the other hand, with an overall density of only 55 persons per square kilometre, falls slightly below the lower limit of the coastal range. However, near the coast the population density rises to an estimated 80 persons per square kilometre. The concentration of population in these coastal provinces, and particularly in the highly urbanized and industrialized areas around Casablanca and Rabat-Salé, where most of the country's manufacturing industries are located, has been created by the French colonial administration which initially developed these coastal towns. This was followed by an increasing stream of Moroccan immigrants into Casablanca and Rabat which started in earnest in the mid-1920s.

The second area comprises a group of five provinces with densities of between 30 and 60 persons per square kilometre. These are located almost in the geographical centre of the country, and include the Meseta Plateau and the western slopes of the Middle and High Atlas. The population in this area secures a living from livestock raising, agriculture made possible by irrigation, and to some extent from phosphate mining. Three of the four old imperial cities, i.e. Fez, Meknès and Marrakech, with their traditional art and crafts industry as well as trading activities, are located in this belt.

The third group of six provinces, with densities of up to 30 persons per square kilometre, lie in the mountainous and cis-Saharan region of the country. This area is populated mainly by nomadic people of predominantly Berber stock. The only exception is the Taza Corridor where Arabic-speaking people dominate. Livestock raising and some cultivation on irrigated plots or alongside river beds are the main occupations of the people there.

Ethnic composition

The two major ethnic groups in Morocco – Berbers and Arabs – are distinguished mainly by language. As already mentioned in Chapter 13 on p. 187, an estimated 9 million people or approximately 60 per cent of the country's total population speak Arabic, while the rest speaks one of several Berber dialects. However, a steady flow of people from the Berber dominated mountainous regions into the Atlantic lowlands and the urban centres, where newcomers and their descendants are progressively integrated into the Arabic-speaking community, blurs the division between the two ethnic groups.[10]

Although significant in the economic life of colonial Morocco, the Jewish community was never large. In the 1951/1952 census the Jewish population numbered about 218,000 or 2.3 per cent of the country's total population. However, with independence in 1956 and the second Arab–Israeli war in 1967, the number of Jews in the country fell significantly to 162,400 or 1.4 per cent in 1960 and below 40,000 or 0.2 per cent of the total population in 1971.[11]

According to the 1951/1952 census, there were about 540,000 Europeans in the country or 5.8 per cent of the total population. They controlled over 80 per cent of all industrial and/or commercial enterprises, about 10 per cent of the arable land, and produced roughly one third of the country's entire tax revenue. However, following independence their number declined to 396,000 or 3.4 per cent in 1960 and to little more than 110,000 or 0.7 per cent of the total population in 1971.[12]

Level of urbanization

The urban population of Morocco* has increased progressively from an estimated 300,000 or about 8 per cent of the country's total population around the turn of the century to 544,000 or 12.5 per cent in 1921, 984,000 or 15.8 per cent in 1936, 1.8 million or 22.8 per cent in 1952, 3.4 million or 29.3 per cent in 1960, and 5.4 million or 35.2 per cent in 1971.

Between 1960 and 1971, the overall annual growth rate of the country's total population was in the region of 2.6 per cent, while at the same time the urban population grew by as much as 4.3 per cent per annum.[13] The most rapidly growing towns were, in order of importance, Rabat-Salé with an average annual growth rate of 5.1 per cent, followed by Casablanca with 4.2 per cent, Fez with 3.8 per cent, Meknès with 3.2 per cent, and Marrakech with only 2.9 per cent.

Marrakech

Population growth

Marrakech is Morocco's third largest town.[14] It is the regional capital of southern Morocco and a centre of administration, small-scale industry, and tourism. Early

* Cities with 20,000 or more inhabitants.

estimates of the city's population are extremely sketchy and range from 20,000 in the late seventeenth century to about 50,000–70,000 inhabitants in the early twentieth century.[15]

The first population count carried out by the French administration in 1921 gave the city a total of 102,000.[16] By 1971, the city's population had reached 332,700, a three-fold increase in only 50 years.[17]

Based on all available estimates and census results, Graph A.15.1 on p. 421 illustrates the pattern of population growth in Marrakech over the last 300 years. The population increase was very slight throughout the eighteenth and nineteenth centuries. However, with the beginning of the twentieth century and with the establishment of the French protectorate in 1912, this pattern changed drastically. From an estimated 50,000–70,000 inhabitants at the turn of the century, the population of the city increased sharply to reach a total of 332,700 in mid-1971. If this rate of increase continues, Marrakech is expected to reach the half-million mark well before the end of this century.

The growth of Marrakech

The growth of residential areas in Marrakech has been described by G. Deverdun[18] and more recently by A. Mandleur.[19] As a result of the population increases outlined above, the development of Marrakech can be broadly divided into three periods: first, the pre-protectorate period, which may be subdivided into the epochs of the five dynasties that ruled the city from the end of the eleventh century until the beginning of the twentieth century; second, the period of the protectorate from 1912 to 1956; and third, the period since independence.

The pre-protectorate period from 1070 to 1912

During the reign of 'Ali b. Yusuf, the second Almoravid sultan who ruled from 1107 to 1143, the built-up area within the city wall* concentrated around the Mosque of Ben Yusuf (Djema ben Youssef) and the central market (*souk*). According to local tradition, the built-up area extended from Bab Faz (the gate leading to Fez) (the modern Bab Khemis) in the north, to the Place Djemaa el

* The first city wall was built in 1126–1127.

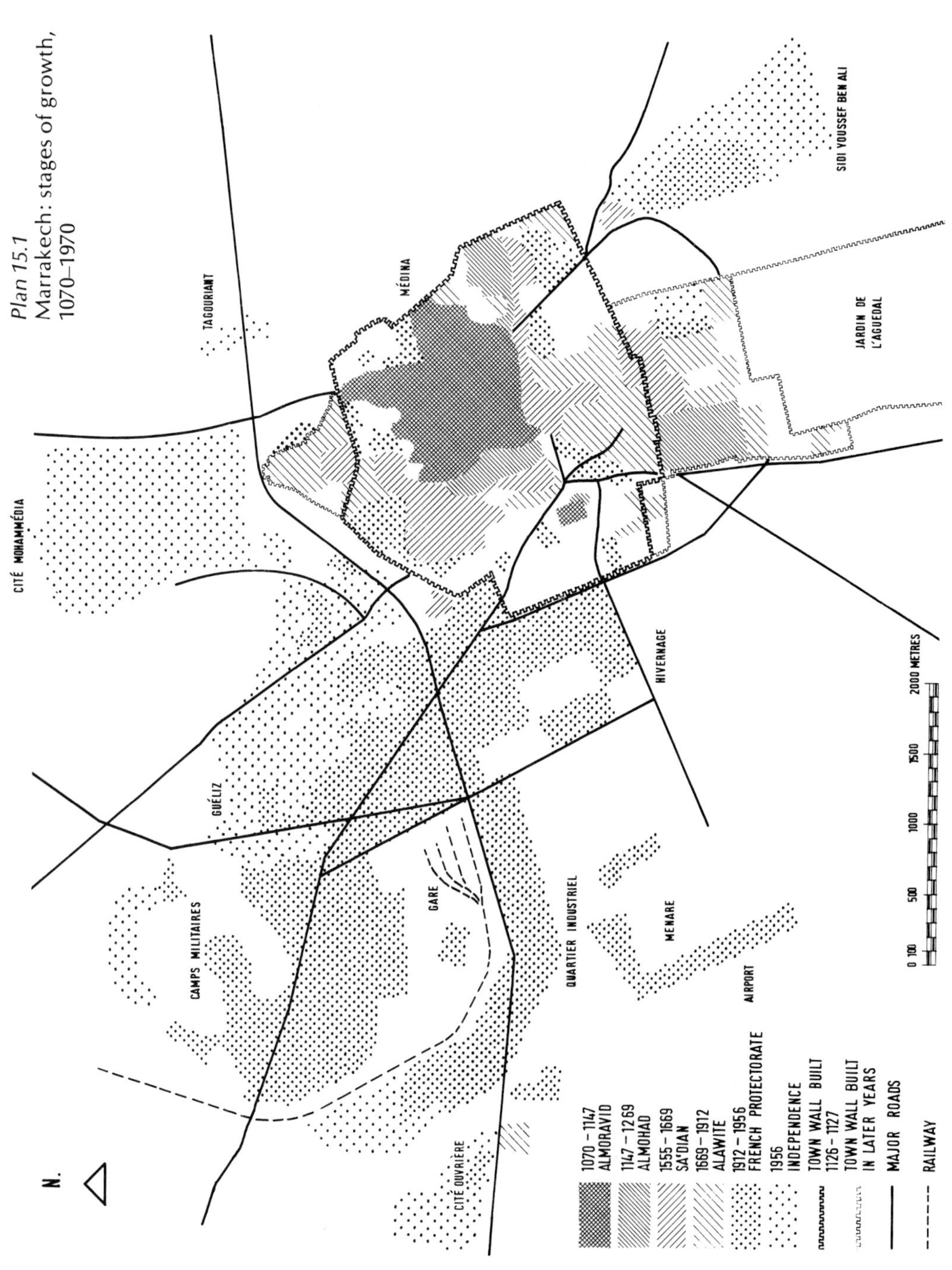

Plan 15.1
Marrakech: stages of growth, 1070–1970

Fna in the south, and from Bab ad Debagh in the east to a line west of the quarter of Riad el Arous.[20] (See Plan 15.1; also Plan A.15.3 on p. 423.)

The Almohad sultans and in particular Ya'kub al-Mansur (1184–1199) added the quarter (*derb*) known today as Mouassine, the area around Bab Haïlen and, most important of all, the Casba, an extension of the walled city to the south.

The Merinid sultans (1269–1470), who chose Fez as their capital, did not take much interest in the city, the population of which is believed to have decreased during the first century of their rule.

The decline of Marrakech was halted by the first Sa'dien sultan Ahmad al-A'radj (1517–1541) who again made the city the capital of the country. His successors, noticeably Abd Allah al-Ghalib (1557–1574) and Ahmad al-Mansur (1578–1603), also known as *al-dhahabi*, the golden, restored the city to its former splendour. The area known as Zaouia in the north, the quarters of Sidi ben Sliman and Arsat ben Chebli in the west, Dabachi and Kennaria in the south, and part of the Bab Haïlen in the east were developed by them. (For place names see Plan A.15.3.) In addition, a new quarter to rehouse the city's Jewish population (Mellah) was built alongside the eastern wall of the Casba.[21]

Although Mawlay Isma'il, the second Alawid sultan, chose Meknès as the capital of the new dynasty, and only Muhammad b. 'Abd Allah (1757–1790) lived in Marrakech for any length of time, the city grew slowly after assuming the status of the regional capital of southern Morocco. The new quarters built during the Alaouide dynasty include Kaa el Mechra in the north, most of the southern quarters between Sidi Mimoun in the west and Djenan bou Zekri in the east, as well as the area around Bab Ahmar in the south. On the eve of the French occupation nearly all open areas within the walled city, except the private gardens and parks, were occupied, leaving precious little space for further development.

The protectorate period, 1912–1956

No doubt, the period of the French protectorate has had the greatest impact on the city since its foundation in the eleventh century. After the French occupation of Marrakech in September 1912, the military administration under General Lyautey embarked on an ambitious plan to demarcate several areas for European township development outside the major cities of Morocco. The task of planning these new towns was given to H. Prost who came to Morocco in 1913.[22] In his capacity as head of the planning mission in Morocco, Prost designed new township areas at Fez, Marrakech, Rabat, Meknès, and Casablanca. The basic ideas which guided the design of these strictly segregated township areas were to establish an undisputed French presence, to limit the conflict between the French and Moroccan communities, and to preserve the character of the ancient walled cities.[23] A *dahir* of 16 April 1914 provided the legal base for the acquisition of *makhzen* and/or *habous* land for this purpose, while a *dahir* of 12 November 1917 created the Associations Syndicales Urbaines to organize and undertake part of the new construction.

At Marrakech, the initial construction work on the European township area started in 1913. By 1923, when Prost left Morocco, the core of the new township area, consisting of Camps Militaires and a residential area with shops, administrative buildings, hotels, cinemas, and sports facilities, was almost complete. In 1930, the Quartier Industriel and the Hivernage, a low-density living area, came into existence. Thus on the eve of independence the European township area, including Gueliz, Hivernage, and the Quartier Industriel, but excluding the Camps Militaires, had an estimated population of over 15,000 inhabitants or about 6 per cent of the total population at Marrakech.

The population of the walled city, on the other hand, almost doubled from an estimated 100,000 in 1921 to nearly 180,000 in 1951. This rapid population increase, which was mainly due to immigration, was not matched by an equally extensive building programme. Between 1921 and 1956, only about 35 hectares or about 10 per cent of the total built-up area within the walled city was redeveloped as residential areas,* while most newcomers had to settle in already overcrowded old quarters. Hence the overall population density in the walled city reached over 500 persons per hectare or 200 persons per acre in the early 1950s. (For more detailed information see Plan A.15.4 on p. 424.) With such increases of population inside the walled city, newcomers were forced to settle elsewhere. The new suburb of Sidi Youssef ben Ali proved to be the most popular area for immigrants. As a result, the settlement grew unplanned from a few hundred families in the mid-1940s to an estimated 15,000 people in 1956. Most of the inhabitants of this area live in self-built houses, which are often substandard and without basic sanitary facilities.[24]

* The districts built between 1921 and 1956 include *inter alia* Arsat Ihiri and Arsat ben Chebli in the west, Arsat el Maach in the south, and Arsat el Houta as well as Arsat Baraka in the south-west.

The period since independence

Between 1956 and July 1971, Marrakech increased its urban population from an estimated 230,000 to 332,700 inhabitants. There were two main areas outside the walled city where the bulk of the immigrants settled: in the already mentioned area of Sidi Youssef ben Ali which increased rapidly to 54,000 inhabitants in 1971; second, in the Cité Mohammédia, formerly the Extension Nord, a well-planned suburb, which was laid out in the early 1960s and housed about 25,000 inhabitants in 1971.

The area of Gueliz which, after the reduction of its French population that followed independence, increased to over 22,000 inhabitants in 1971, today houses the Moroccan elite, the remaining Europeans, and some Jews who have quit their traditional quarters in the walled city for better accommodation.

In spite of its already very densely populated quarters, the walled city or *medina* increased its population slightly from about 180,000 in 1951 to 208,000 in 1971, that is, by an average of 0.7 per cent per annum.

Administrative division

The walled city of Marrakech, where most of the houses surveyed were located, is governed by a *pasha* or mayor and is divided into four arrondissements, administered by *khalifas* or deputies. These are: the arrondissement Nord with 45,850 inhabitants, the Ouest or Bab Dukkala with 31,860, the Centre with 66,620, and the Sud with 63,960 inhabitants in 1971. These arrondissements are further subdivided into 32 quarters looked after by *mukaddimins*. (See Plan A.15.3 on p. 423.)

Migration

Although Arabic speaking, the indigenous population of Marrakech is almost entirely composed of Berber stock. According to the 1960 census (no data for the 1971 census being available at the time of writing), slightly under half of all household heads who took part in the census were born outside Marrakech.[25] This represents by far the lowest proportion of immigrant household heads for any Moroccan city of over 100,000 inhabitants. The age of these household heads when immigrating to Marrakech was given as between 15 and 29 years. This relatively restrained rate of immigration* is most likely due to the severely restricted employment opportunities in the city which has only a small-scale food-processing industry employing about 5 per cent of its total labour force.[26]

While the total population of Morocco increased by about 2.6 per cent per annum between 1960 and 1971, the population of Marrakech increased by 2.9 per cent per annum over the same period. Thus the theoretical influx of immigrants into the city may be estimated at 0.3 per cent per annum. This increase is relatively modest when compared with Rabat-Salé with an overall annual increase of 5.1 per cent and Casablanca with 4.2 per cent per annum between 1960 and 1971. The majority of immigrants who came to Marrakech were Berber, either from the surrounding countryside or from other southern and eastern provinces.

Of the sample population, 239 persons, namely 98 males and 141 females, or 26.7 per cent of the total, were born outside the city. Of 68 compound heads,† 27 or 39.7 per cent immigrated to Marrakech, while 62 or 50.8 per cent of the dependent and tenant household heads in the sample came to the city in their early manhood. The main reasons for coming to Marrakech were given by these household heads as economic, though some stressed the city's superior educational facilities for their children. In order of numerical importance, the birthplaces of all 89 immigrant household heads (including immigrant compound heads) were the province of Marrakech with 40 household heads or 45.0 per cent, followed by the provinces of Quarzazate with 20 or 22.5 per cent, Safi with 9 or 10.1 per cent, and Beni Mellal with 5 or 5.6 per cent. The remaining 15 household heads or 16.8 per cent came from further away including the provinces of Settat, Meknès, Agadir, El Jadida, Taza, and Fez. (For the location of these provinces see Map A.15.2 on p. 420.)

The majority of the 141 immigrant females came as wives to Marrakech. The birthplaces of these 83 wives were, in order of numerical importance, the province of Marrakech with 31 or 37.3 per cent, Quarzazate with 16 or 19.3 per cent, Safi with 11 or 13.2 per cent, and Beni Mellal with 5 or 6.0 per cent. Of the remaining 20 wives or 24.2 per cent, 17 came from various other Moroccan provinces, 2 came from Oran, and 1 from Austria.

* In Casablanca about 80 per cent of all household heads were born outside the city.

†There were seven tenement houses without compound heads included in the survey.

Sample survey

Age and sex distribution

The age composition of the sample population in Marrakech was collected with the help of the so-called Historical Calendar Method. The advantages and limitations of this method have already been discussed in some detail in Chapter 3.

Table 15.1 gives the age and sex ratios of the sample population for comparison with the census returns for Marrakech in 1960. No detailed data for the 1971 census return for Marrakech Town were available at the time of writing. In 1960 the proportion of the population under the age of 15 was high, namely 41.4 per cent; it was 44.0 per cent in 1971, and 44.6 per cent for the sample population studied in 1969. This large proportion of young people, which is a widely accepted feature in most African countries, is the result of high fertility and declining infant mortality. Diagram A.15.1 on p. 425 shows comparative percentage distribution for male and female at five-year intervals for the total population of Morocco in 1971, for the city of Marrakech in 1960, and for the sample population studied in 1969. As may be seen from the bar-chart for Marrakech, the population in the city was only slightly affected by age-selective immigration among the male population aged 25 to 44 and females aged 25 to 34. The sample population, on the other hand, shows a slight

Table 15.1 Population distribution by age and sex groups, in percentages

Age and sex groups	Marrakech, 1960[a] Pop. 243,134	Marrakech, 1971[b] Pop. 332,741	Sample survey, 1968–1969 Pop. 896
0–14	41.4	44.0	44.6
15–49	46.6	43.9	41.0
50+	12.0	12.1	14.4
Male	49.0	49.9	45.5
Female	51.0	50.1	54.5
Total	100.0	100.0	100.0

[a] *Résultats du recensement de 1960*, vol. 1, p. 108.
[b] Premier Ministre, Secrétariat d'État au Plan et au Développement Régional, Royaume du Maroc, Recueil de données par province, *d'aprés le recensement géneral de la population et de l'habitat 1971*, Direction de la Statistique. Figures represent the urban population of the Province of Marrakech.

excess of females between the ages of 30 and 39, while the male population aged 30–34 were underestimated, in all probability due to some mis-information and the smallness of the sample.

The sex ratio given in the lower part of Table 15.1 shows an excess of females over males in the 1960 and 1971 censuses, and even more so in the sample population. This may be partly due to the generally higher number of female immigrants (141 females against 98 males), and to the substantially larger number of divorced and widowed females (69) as against only 3 divorced and no widowed males observed in the sample (See Tables A.16.3 and A.16.4 on pp. 428, 430.)

Notes and references

1 Direction de la Statistique Royaume du Maroc, *Annuaire statistique du Maroc 1971*, Rabat, 1972, pp. 13–15. United Nations, *Demographic Yearbook 1971*, New York, 1972, pp. 111–112.
2 Ibid., pp. 112–113.
3 Comité de l'Afrique Française, *L'Afrique française*, bulletin mensuel du Comité de l'Afrique Française et du Comité du Maroc (Paris), no. 5, 1921, p. 156.
4 A. Imani, 'The family planning programme in Morocco', in *Population Growth and Economic Development in Africa*, ed. S.H. Ominde, and C.N. Ejiogu, London, 1972, pp. 365–368.
5 Service Central des Statistiques, Royaume du Maroc, *Résultats du recensement de 1960*, Rabat, 1964, vol. 1, p. 8.
6 Ibid., p. 8.
7 Servie Central des Statistiques, Royaume du Maroc, *Recensement général de la population de la zone française 1951/52*, Rabat, 1954, vols 1–4.
8 Service Central des Statistiques, Royaume du Maroc, *Résultats du recensement de 1960*, vol. 1, p. 8.
9 Direction de la Statistique, Royaume du Maroc, op. cit., p. 13.
10 A. Adam, 'Berber migrants in Casablanca', in *Arabs and Berbers*, ed. E. Gellner and C. Micand, London, 1972, pp. 325–343.
11 Africa Research Ltd, *African Research Bulletin* (London), 1971, p. 1902.
12 Direction de la Statistique, Royaume du Maroc, op. cit., pp. 13–14.
13 Kingsley Davis, *World Urbanization 1950–1970*, Population Monograph, Series No. 4, Berkeley, Calif., 1969, Vol. 1, p. 141. Davis Kingsley gives the annual growth rate for urban areas in Morocco as 5.0 per cent between 1950 and 1960 and 4.9 per cent between 1960 and 1970.
14 Casablanca had 1,506,400 and Rabat-Salé 523,200 inhabitants in 1971.
15 See Graph A.15.1 on p. 421.
16 Comité de l'Afrique Française, op. cit., p. 156.

17 Direction de la Statistique, Royaume du Maroc, *Population légale du Maroc 1971*, Rabat, 1971, p. 6.
18 G. Deverdun, *Marrakech des origines à 1912*, Rabat, 1959 and 1966, 2 vols.
19 A. Mandleur, 'Croissance et urbanisation de Marrakech', *Revue de géographie du Maroc* (Rabat), no. 22, 1972, pp. 31–60.
20 Deverdun op. cit., pp. 142–143.
21 J. Bénech, *Essai d'explication d'un mellah, un des aspects du Judaisme*, Paris, 1950, pp. 1–7.
22 J. Marrast, 'Maroc', in *L'Oeuvre de Henri Prost*, Paris, 1960, pp. 107–115.
23 H. G. Lyautey: '. . . le respect de l'intégrité artistique et morale des villes anciennes'. Quoted by Mandleur, op. cit., p. 42.
24 M. de Leenheer, 'L'Habitat précaire à Marrakech et dans sa zone périphérique', *Revue de géographie du Maroc* (Rabat), no. 17, 1970, pp. 43–51.
25 D. Noin *et al.*, *La Population rurale du Maroc*, Publication de l'Université de Rouen, Paris, 1970, vol. 2, pp. 256–279.
26 A. Mandleur, 'Les Industries alimentaires de Marrakech', in *Revue de géographie du Maroc* (Rabat), no. 17, 1970, pp. 53–69.

Chapter 16

Domestic groupings and the house

The courtyard house

Layout and organization

Historically, the courtyard house is probably one of the oldest known urban house types in the western hemisphere. Early examples excavated in present-day Turkey date from the seventh millennium BC.[1] It is interesting to observe that in the Muslim dominated countries of the Middle East and North Africa the basic pattern of the courtyard house has survived almost unchanged over the centuries. At least three factors have contributed to its apparently unchanged popularity: first, the relatively economical use of land, as this house type does not require large building sites; second, the courtyard house guarantees, even in crowded urban conditions, maximum security and privacy, which are of paramount importance where *purdah* is imposed by the household head; and third this house type, which frequently has a planted courtyard, is well adapted to the conditions of hot, dry climates.

Today, the Moroccan urban population distinguishes between two types of courtyard house: the *dar* which has a small paved courtyard (*oust-ad-dar*), and its larger counterpart, the *riad*, which always has an interior garden. As can be seen from Plans 16.1 and 16.2, in basic layout and organization these two house types are very similar. However, compared with the *dar*, the *riad* has on average

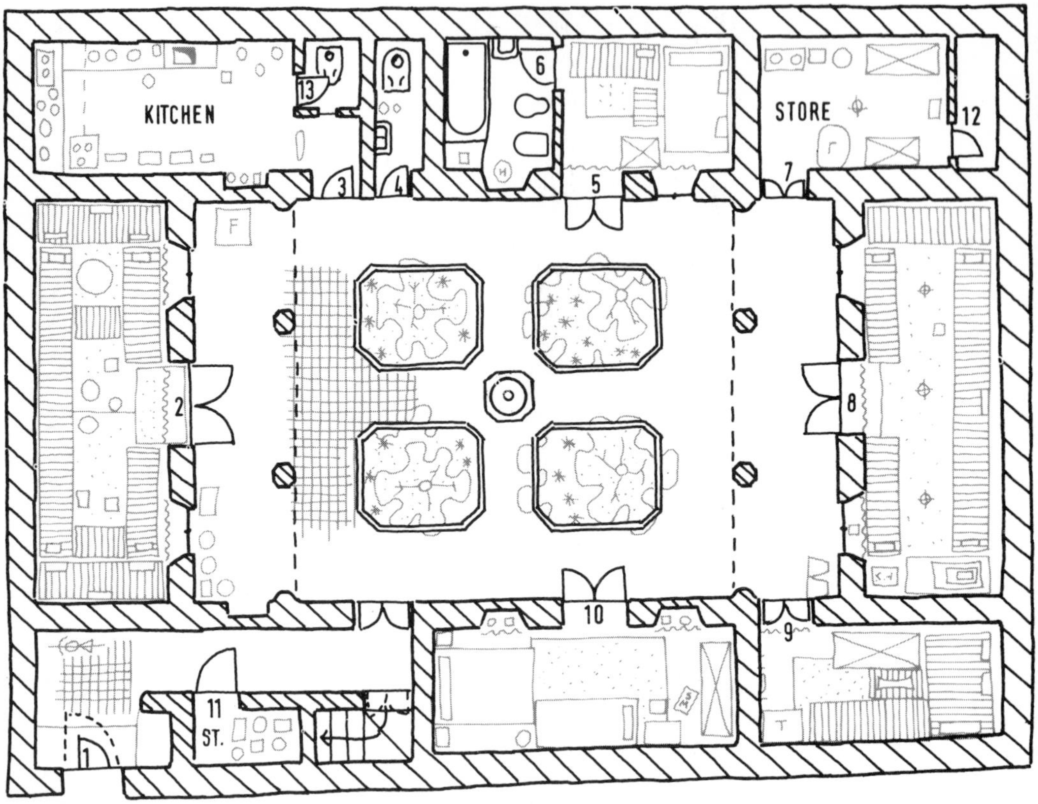

KITCHEN
STORE
ST.

RIAD

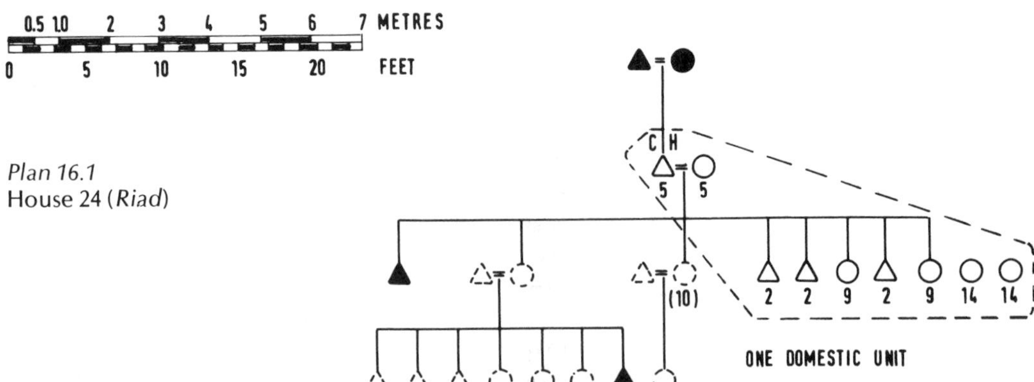

Plan 16.1
House 24 (*Riad*)

more rooms, better quality finish, and more expensive furniture. It goes without saying that the inhabitants of a *riad* usually belong to the upper income groups.

As shown in the two examples, all rooms open onto the central courtyard or garden. The rooms are usually long and narrow, their width being determined by the length of timber beams available on the local building material

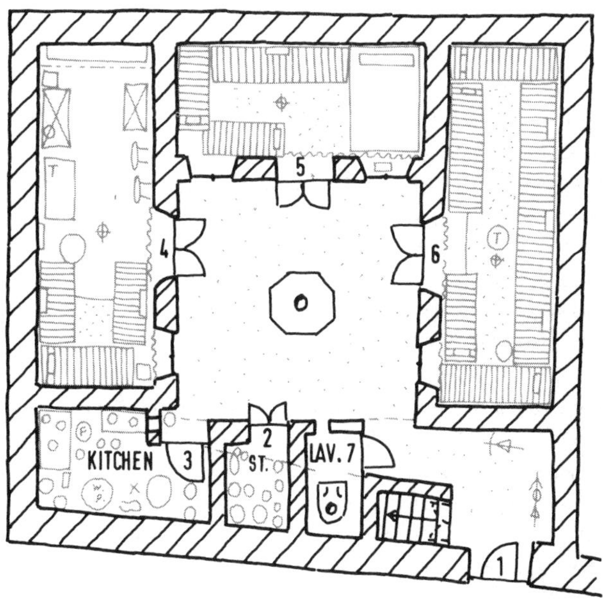

Plan 16.2
House 22 (*Dar*)

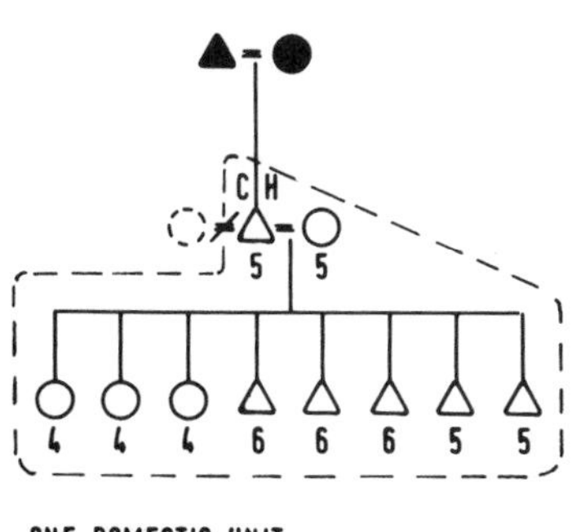

market for the construction of roofs and/or ceilings.* The position of the various types of rooms grouped around the courtyard are fairly uniform. The main living, sleeping, and reception rooms are always placed alongside the courtyard or interior garden, while the corners of the

* The length of wooden roof beams rarely exceeds 3 metres.

house are reserved for such rooms as kitchens, stores, toilets, bathrooms, entrance halls, and staircases.[2] The plain, nearly windowless elevations of most houses that face the narrow alleyways or streets contrast pleasantly with the enchanting atmosphere of their interiors. (See Pictures 16.1, 16.2, and 16.3.) In Marrakech, as in many other traditional Moroccan cities, courtyard houses vary greatly in size and appearance, but their basic characteristics are always the same.

In contrast to the above-mentioned two house types (*dar, riad*), *fondouks* are large courtyard houses which contain many rooms. Originally used as entrepôts or warehouses for the caravan trade to and from West Africa, these courtyard houses were adapted for permanent habitation soon after the trade across the Sahara came to an end at the turn of this century. Since then, the rooms have been let for a monthly rent to less well-off families and immigrants. Overcrowding, poor sanitary facilities, and lack of regular maintenance are the main features of the few remaining *fondouks*.[3] (See Plan 16.3.)

The modern houses situated in the western suburbs of the city, most of which were built or influenced by the French, were not investigated and are therefore excluded from this study.

Picture 16.1
Narrow street in Marrakech

Picture 16.2
Interior garden of courtyard house (*Riad*)

Picture 16.3
Room of courtyard house

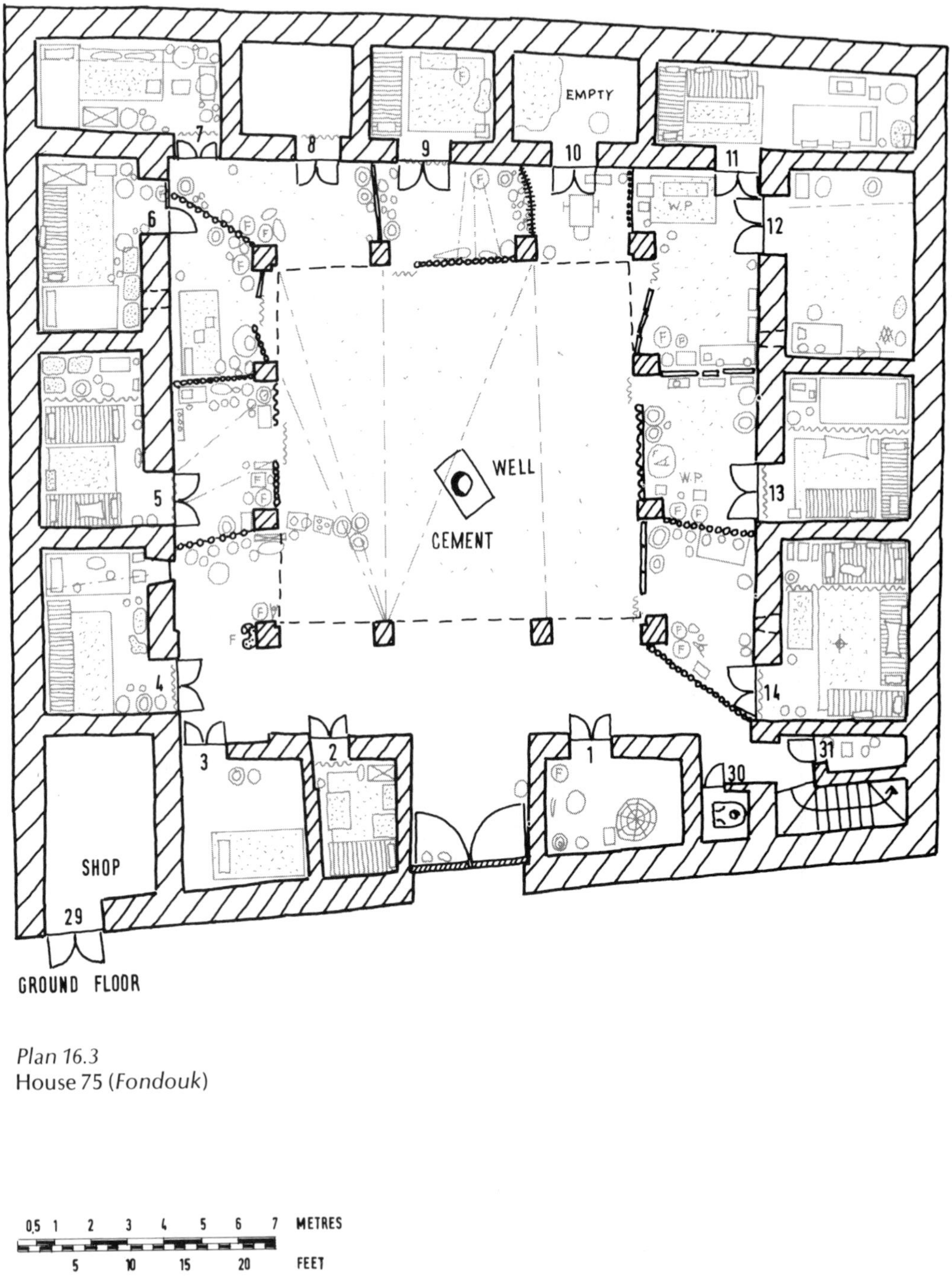

Plan 16.3
House 75 (*Fondouk*)

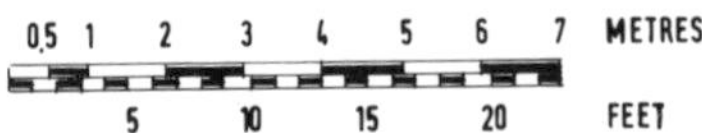

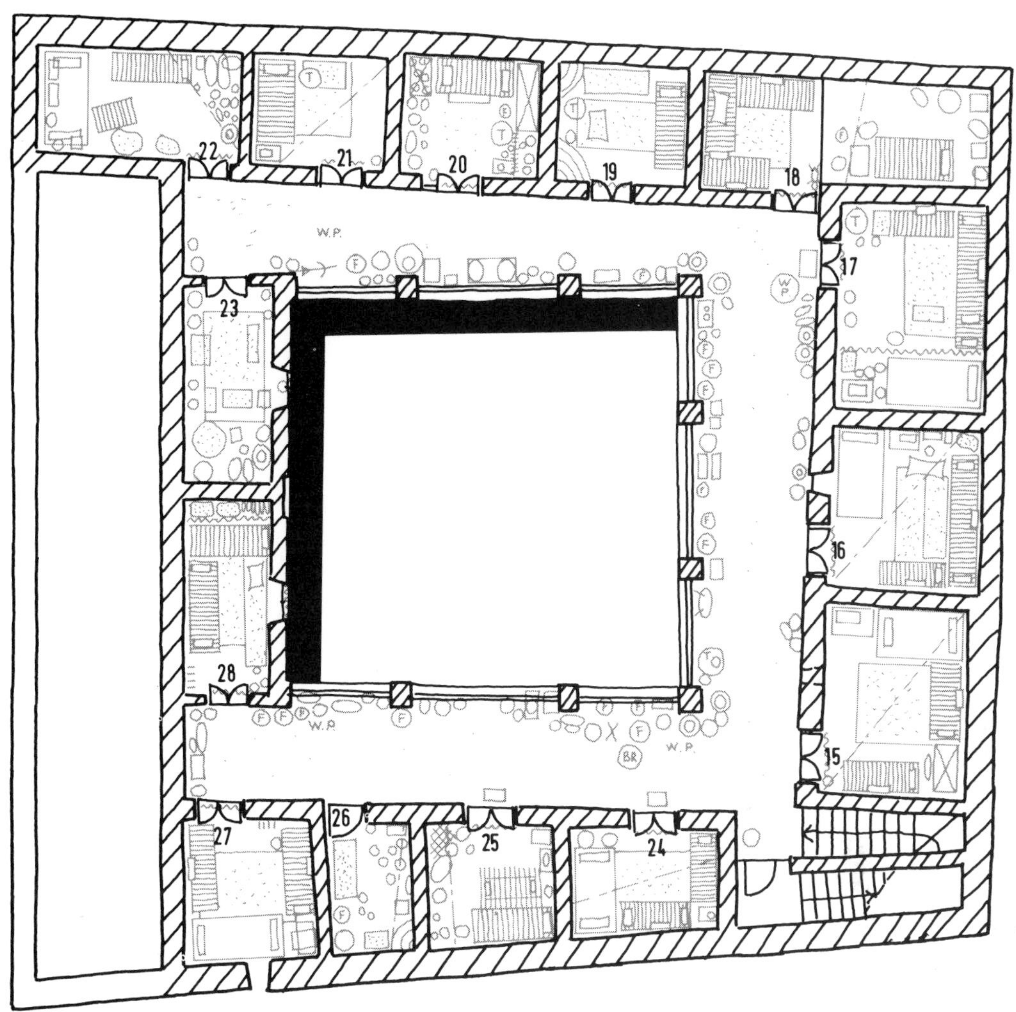

FIRST FLOOR

TENANT HOUSEHOLDS

PERSONS PER HOUSEH.	NUMBER OF HOUSEH.	NUMBER OF PERSONS	PERSONS PER HOUSEH.	NUMBER OF HOUSEH.	NUMBER OF PERSONS
1	8	8	5	1	5
2	5	10	6	2	12
3	2	6	8	1	8
4	5	20	TOTAL	24	69

Land use

The data on land use given below derive from measurements taken in 75 houses in the walled city of Marrakech.* The houses surveyed covered a total area of 11,089 sq. m† which may be divided into the built-up area of 8,809 sq. m or 79.4 per cent, and the open area of 2,280 sq. m or 20.6 per cent. The average size of the surveyed houses is 148.0 sq. m or 1,593 sq. ft. The open area of courtyards can be subdivided into two basic categories: first, the areas paved either with cement screed or ceramic tiles which accounted for 2,062 sq. m or 90.4 per cent of the total open area; and second, the planted areas with 218 sq. m or 9.6 per cent.

Type and size of rooms

The built-up area of the 75 houses surveyed contained a total of 776 rooms, averaging 10.3 per house. The total floor area of 8,326 sq. m is divided into four categories:

1 Living area accounted for 5,901 sq. m or 70.9 per cent of the total floor area. This includes 289 rooms with an average size of 12.0 sq. m used for sleeping, 35 sitting rooms or parlours with an average size of 14.6 sq. m, 36 storage rooms used for personal belongings with an average size of 6.7 sq. m, and 55 empty rooms, some of them under repair. A total of 11 verandahs were also included in the living area (see Plan 16.6). With a total of 415 rooms this is by far the most important group of rooms.
2 Common rooms accounted for 1,273 sq. m or 15.3 per cent of the total floor area. This category includes 78 entrance lobbies as well as all passages and staircases.
3 Basic ancillary facilities accounted for 1,030 sq. m or 12.3 per cent of the total floor area. This includes 86 kitchens having an average size of 6.1 sq. m, 80 general store rooms, and 104 toilets and/or bathrooms.
4 Commercially used rooms accounted for a mere 123 sq. m or 1.5 per cent of the total floor area in these houses, and comprises 13 shops and/or workshops. (See Table A.16.6 on p. 434.)

* There were 10 houses situated in Sidi Youssef ben Ali, a suburb just outside the walled city to the south-east.
† The total area includes only the house and the internal courtyard. Public or semi-public footpaths and other open areas alongside the house are excluded.

Social structure and kinship organization

As mentioned in Chapter 15 on p. 205, slightly over one third of Morocco's total population are now city-dwellers, while the rest live in rural areas where they are organized in various kinds of tribal groups, The following brief description of the social structure and kinship organization of these tribal groups is thus necessary in order to introduce the discussion of the mode of kinship organization in urban areas, and particularly among the people covered by the survey in Marrakech.

All Moroccan tribes, whether Arabic or Berber speaking, are agnatic and segmentary in character. Thus each tribe (*qabila* in Arabic; *taqbilt* in Berber) is divided into several clans though seldom more than five.[4] Each of these clans is again segmented into a number of subclans, which in turn are further divided into agnatic or patrilineal lineages. At this level of segmentation, the group usually refers to a widely known male ancestor, the lineage founder, who may be three to five generations removed from the oldest living member. All lineages are further divided into several patrilineal extended families (*adam* or *ighs* in Arabic; *tigmmi* or *adouar* in Berber) which, for example, may consist of a compound head's family, together with the families of his married son or sons, their descendants and/or collateral agnates, and their dependents. As each patrilineal extended family may occupy a common house, it is the basic kinship unit which will be analysed below. While in rural areas the patrilineal extended family is firmly embedded in the social structure of the larger kinship units, in the cities its affiliation to wider kinship groups is less important and is partly replaced by the ties of its members to occupational associations or guilds and other urban socio-economic institutions.

However, before analysing the various types of co-residential kinship groups found in my sample, we must once again turn our attention to the division of these groups into units of domestic economy or households. As already observed, the inhabitants of a house or compound are not necessarily divided into economic units along kinship lines. A household may contain, besides a nuclear or individual family (*kanoun* in Arabic; *taka* in Berber) consisting of a man, his wife, and their own unmarried children, several single, divorced, and/or widowed relatives and one or more unrelated persons. Some households may therefore contain several fragmented families, i.e. divorced or widowed persons and their children, while yet others may contain only a single person or persons.

The 75 houses surveyed in Marrakech contained a total of 190 households which fall into three categories: first, the compound head's household;* second, all other related dependent or semi-dependent households; and finally, tenant households who pay a monthly rent for their rooms.† In the following pages I will examine some aspects of these three different categories of households before discussing the various forms of kinship groupings and organizations found within them.

Population and household data

The population distribution of 75 houses surveyed is given below. As is shown in Diagram 16.1, 73.3 per cent of the sample houses have populations that range between 5 and 19 persons, the average being 11.9 per house. Of the three largest houses, two with 42 and 67 persons respectively were 'tenement houses' with absentee landlords, while the largest house, with a total 69 inhabitants, was a *fondouk*.

The sizes of the three types of households mentioned above are shown in Diagram 16.2. When compared, parts A, B, and C of Diagram 16.2 reveal some interesting patterns. The compound heads' households (first diagram) show the smallest number of 1–2 person households (6 or 8.8 per cent), while the majority of these households (72.1 per cent) have between 3 and 8 persons.

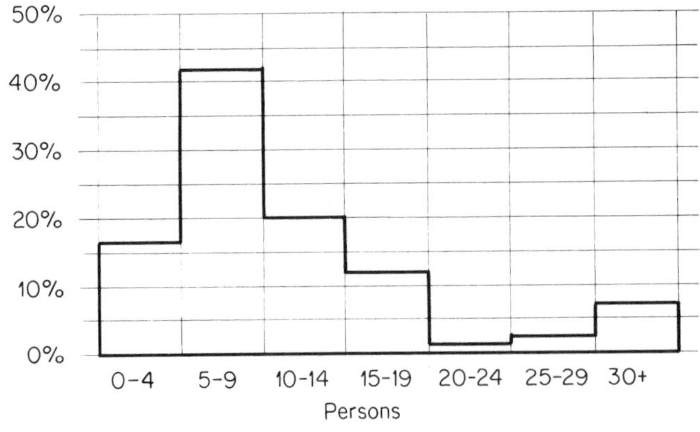

Diagram 16.1
Number of persons per house in percentages

* For a definition of this term see Chapter 4 on p. 34.
† Including households which lease their rooms. For discussion, see p. 200.

Over one third of the related dependent or semi-dependent households, on the other hand, have 3 or 4 persons. As expected, tenant households contain the largest number with one or two persons. The average size of household decreases from 6.0 persons in the compound head's household to 4.7 persons in dependent households and 3.8 persons in tenant households. It is interesting to observe that a very similar distribution of households by size and status has already been reported

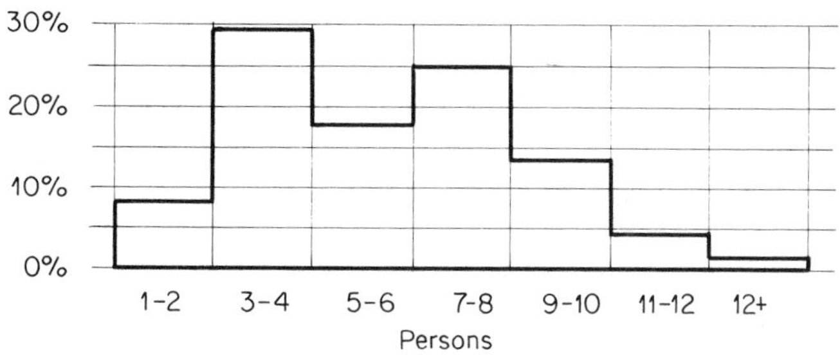

B. Related dependent or semi-dependent households (31)

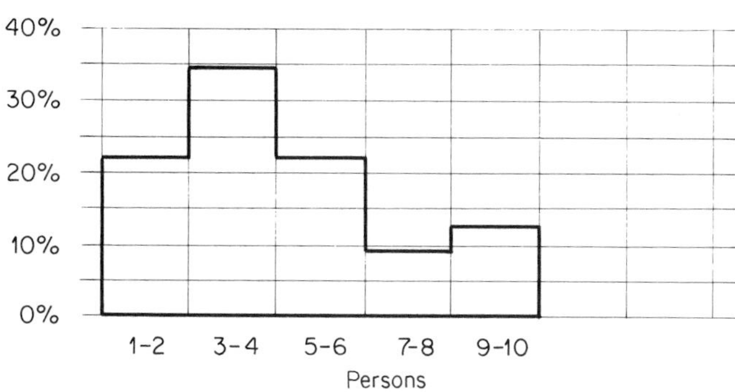

C.Tenant households (91)

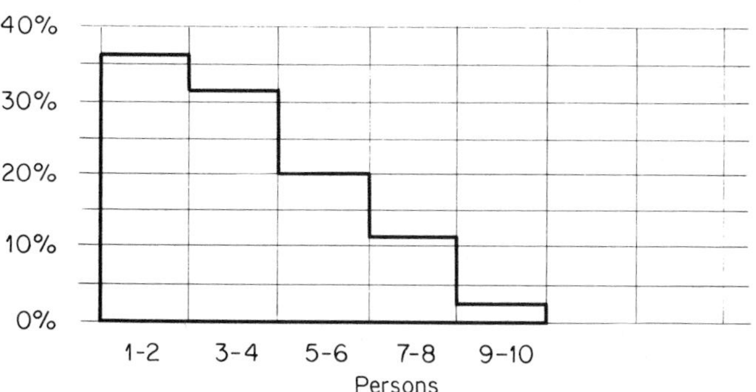

Diagram 16.2
Number of persons per household in percentages

for Ibadan, the only other sample which had a sizeable tenant population.* It seems that the relatively 'young households' among the dependent or semi-dependent households, the lack of cheap and suitable accommodation for tenant households, and generally lower incomes of both these categories may be partly responsible for the smaller size of these households.

Although permitted by Muslim law, polygamy is practised infrequently at Marrakech, and it did not play an important part in the sample population. Only two of 68 compound heads† and one of 91 tenant household heads had more than one wife. In all three cases the second wife did not live in the house surveyed. No case of polygamy was found among the related dependent or semi-dependent household heads.

The age and sex distribution as well as the marital status of the sample population is shown in Diagram 16.3 and Table 16.1. The bar-chart indicates quite clearly that young persons of both sexes, but particularly females, marry on average at the same age as their counterparts in Ibadan but generally later than in Zaria.‡ Among the 408 males included in the sample population, 254 or 62.2 per cent were single, 151 or 37.0 per cent were married, and 3 or 0.8 per cent were divorced. There were no widowed males among the sample population. On the other hand, the female population of 488 persons was divided into 263 or 54.0 per cent single persons, 156 or 32.0 per cent married, and 69 or 14.0 per cent were either divorced or widowed. (For more detailed information see Tables A.16.2, A.16.3, and A.16.4 on pp. 427, 428, 430.)

As can be seen in Table A.16.4, a total of 54 widowed females were found in the sample population. Ten of these women were compound heads; 14 were either mothers of compound heads or mothers of compound heads' wives. Another 13 widowed females were tenant household heads, while 7 females were mothers of unrelated household heads. The remaining 10 females belonged either to the compound heads' households or to tenant households. Eight out of 15 divorced females included in the table were tenant household heads. The remainder included 1 compound head and several other related kin. Some widows who were no longer able to work were supported by their next of kin, while younger widowed and/or divorced females will most likely leave the house on remarriage.

* See Chapter 10 on p. 134.
† As mentioned in Chapter 15 there were seven tenement houses without compound heads.
‡ See Table 4.1 on p. 38.

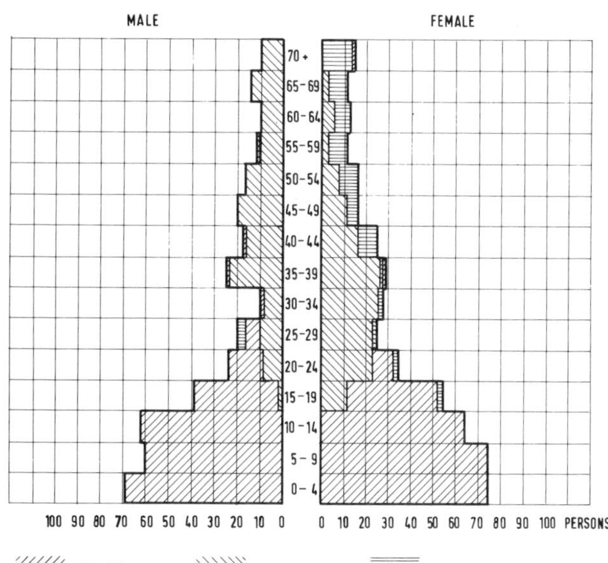

Diagram 16.3
Survey sample population by sex, age, and marital status

Table 16.1 Survey sample population by sex, age, and marital status

Age	Male					Female					Grand total
	Sing.	Mar.	Div.	Wid.	Total	Sing.	Mar.	Div.	Wid.	Total	
0–4	69				69	73				73	142
5–9	60				60	73				73	133
10–14	62				62	64				64	126
15–19	38	1			39	41	11	2		54	93
20–24	14	9			23	9	23	2		34	57
25–29	7	10	3		20	1	23	1		25	45
30–34	1	9			10		26	1	1	28	38
35–39	1	23			24	1	27	1		29	53
40–44	1	17			18		17	2	6	25	43
45–49		20			20		11	1	5	17	37
50–54		17			17		7	3	7	17	34
55–59	1	11			12		3		8	11	23
60–64		10			10		5		7	12	22
65–69		14			14		3		8	11	25
70+		10			10	1		2	12	15	25
Total	254	151	3	–	408	263	156	15	54	488	896

Family groupings

Before discussing the various modes of co-residential family groupings found in the 75 houses surveyed, I must briefly refer to some of the earlier findings regarding kinship patterns observed in the sample populations at Ibadan and Zaria. As already mentioned, household data alone are insufficient to explain satisfactorily the various changes which frequently occur in co-residential groups, and some additional kinship data, based on a common reference point – in our case, relations with the compound head – are essential. Most changes that affect the structure of co-residential kinship groups are due to either the marriage, migration, and/or death of one of its male members, and particularly of the compound head. How such changes may affect the co-residential kinship group and consequently modify the layout, size, and occupational pattern of courtyard houses will be the subject of the following analysis.

We may recall that in Zaria and Ibadan the survey data clearly showed that most co-residential kinship groups were based on agnatic descent. It could be established that the individual family consisting of a man, his wife or wives, and their own unmarried children was the first stage in a development cycle that gave rise to composite co-residential kinship groups. Altogether six such stages were identified, the last being that of a compound which housed paternal cousins and their descendants. However, it must be stressed again that at each stage of development co-residential kinship groups are liable to split into two or more independent units. The most important reasons for such splits are, in order of importance: the death of the compound head, marriage of male descendants, the differential economic success of some dependent or semi-dependent household heads, and family quarrels. A preliminary examination of the data collected in Marrakech revealed that the majority of co-residential kinship groups were based on agnatic descent. We may therefore apply a similar mode of analysis as for the kinship data collected in Zaria and Ibadan.

Let us begin with a few remarks about co-residential groups at Marrakech. Although the rule of patrilocal residence by which married daughters go to live with their husband's family is widely practised in Morocco, the survey revealed that no less than eight compounds contained the families of the compound heads' daughters, as against two in Zaria and none in Ibadan. Investigation of these families suggests that one reason for a daughter's residence in her father's house is economic. At 38.8 per cent, the proportion of tenants living in the 75 houses at Marrakech was considerably larger than in Ibadan where they reached only 23.0 per cent of the sample population. As these tenant families generally do not influence the development of the co-residential kinship groups of their compound heads, they are omitted from Table 16.2 and will be analysed separately later.

Table 16.2 shows the age distribution of the 68 compound heads, grouped according to the composition of

Table 16.2 Age of compound heads by stages of kinship development

Column	1	2	3	4	5	6	7
Stage	1	2	3	4 + 5	6	Joint hhs	Total
Age of CH							
25–29	1						1
30–34	1					2	3
35–39	7						7
40–44	8	1	1				10
45–49	9	2	1			1	13
50–54	5	1				2	8
55–59	5	1					6
60–64	6	3					9
65–69	4	2					6
70+	2	3					5
No. of CHs	48	13	2			5	68
No. of HHs	48	34	5			12	99
No. of persons	297	172	27			57	553
Av. households (hhs) per compound	1.0	2.6	2.5			2.4	1.5
Av. persons per compound	6.2	13.2	13.5			11.4	8.1
Av. persons per hh	6.2	5.1	5.4			4.8	5.6
Kinship diagrams	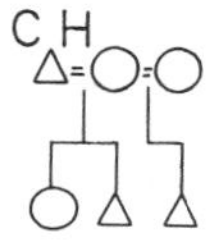	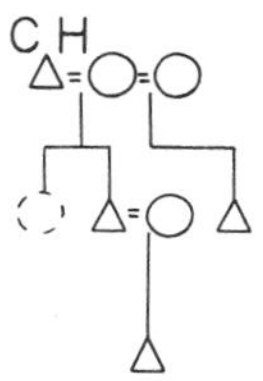	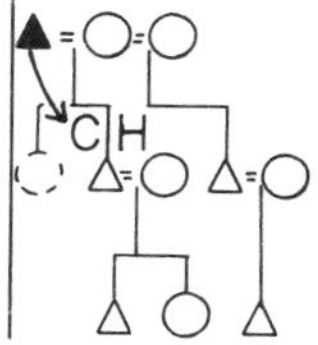			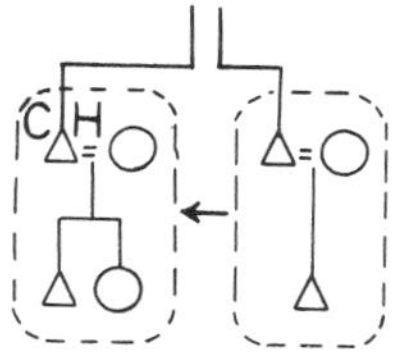	

their respective co-residential kinship groups. As indicated in the simplified kinship diagrams at the foot of the table, column 1 lists all compound heads responsible only for individual families; column 2 lists those compound heads whose co-residential kinship groups contained the compound head's family together with the families of his sons and/or daughters; while column 3 contains two paternal full brothers and their unmarried children; and column 6 lists five houses whose population had increased by the immigration of seven related families rather than by natural growth. (See also Table A.16.5 on p. 432.)

These three types of co-residential kinship groups (columns 1–3) represent the first three stages in the development of domestic groups based on agnatic kinship and virilocal residence that were discussed in some detail in Chapter 4 on pp. 39–42. It is interesting to note that none of the houses surveyed contains composite co-residential kinship groups beyond the third stage when a unit includes paternal full or half brothers and their married children. As expected, the modal age of compound heads in stage 2 is generally greater than that of their counterparts in stages 1 and 3, an observation already made for the sample populations in Ibadan and Zaria.

The centre of the table deserves special attention. It shows clearly that the average number of households per compound increases from 1 household with an average of 6.2 persons in stage 1 to 2.6 households having an average total of 13.2 persons in stage 2. The average number of persons per household, on the other hand, decreases from 6.2 persons in stage 1 to 5.1 persons in stage 2. The number of 'stage 3 households' is too small to yield any meaningful averages. Quantitatively speaking, the 68 compound heads interviewed had a total of 38 married sons, of whom only 10 or 26.3 per cent lived in their father's house. While the number of compound head's married brothers recorded is believed to be incomplete, the total indicates that less than 3 per cent lived together in the same house.

The data presented in Table 16.2 indicate that the division of composite co-residential kinship groups normally occurs during their second developmental phase when the compound head's family includes his married children and their descendants. This poses at least two important questions. First, is the process of division which occurs at this relatively early stage due to the lack of suitable space in the rather inflexible urban courtyard house; or, second, does the break-up occur because young dependent household heads regard their father's house as a valuable asset which can be readily turned into cash to provide them with the capital they need to lease, buy, or even build their own houses? If the latter suggestion is correct, it would partly explain why there are in Marrakech such a large number of divided courtyard houses owned by unrelated parties. However, in his study of the traditional rural society in Morocco, B. G. Hoffman has shown that patrilineal extended families are most likely to split up when reaching stage 3 in the development of composite co-residential kinship groups,[5] thus indicating that the pattern of division noted above is not entirely due to conditions which prevail in urban areas. We shall reconsider these questions further* after discussing the structure and size of the 91 tenant households which are not included in Table 16.2.

In Table 16. 3, the 91 tenant households have been divided into four main categories based on kinship organization in order to reveal their internal fabrics and their differences. The first category, columns 1–3, had heads who are either single, divorced, or widowed, while the second category, column 4, contains female heads whose husbands had been absent for more than one month preceding the date of interview. The third category, column 5, consists of couples without resident children, but includes some whose children were away, while the last category, column 6, contains individual families with married and/or unmarried children. As the table shows, 22 or 24.2 per cent of all tenant households consisted either of single, divorced, or widowed persons or of females whose husbands were away, while 69 or 75.8 per cent contained childless couples or couples without resident children, and individual families with married and/or unmarried children. Of 91 tenant household heads in these houses 38 or 41.8 per cent were born in Marrakech, while the remaining 53 or 58.2 per cent had immigrated to the city, mainly from villages situated in southern Morocco. Furthermore, it is interesting to observe that with a total of 343 members, these 91 tenant households financially supported 25 persons or 7.3 per cent who were either single, divorced, and/or widowed relatives of the household head or his wife's kinship group, and 3 unrelated persons. By comparison, the compound heads' households contained 64 such persons who represented 15.7 per cent of their total population. Table A.16.5 on p. 432, reveals yet another interesting feature of these tenant households. In four out of seven

* See discussion on p. 309.

Table 16.3 Structure of tenant households

Column	1	2	3	4	5	6	7	8	9
Type of HH	Sing.	Div.	Wid.	Female with temp. absent husband	Childless couple	Individual family	Fem. HH	Male HH	Grand total
Age of THH									
15–19					1	2		1	1
20–24		1	1	1	2	7	3	4	7
25–29	1	1				3	2	7	9
30–34					1	9		4	4
35–39					3	7		12	12
40–44		1	2	1	2	5	4	9	13
45–49		1	1		1	3	2	6	8
50–54		1			3	4	1	6	7
55–59			2		1		2	5	7
60–64					2	8		2	2
65–69			4		1	2	4	9	13
70+		1	3		2		4	4	8
M + F hh							22	69	
No. of households	1	6	13	2	19	50			91
No. of persons	1	7	24	4	46	261			343
Av. persons per hh	1.0	1.2	1.8	2.0	2.4	5.2			3.8
Kinship diagrams	H|H	HH	HH	H|H	H|H	H|H			

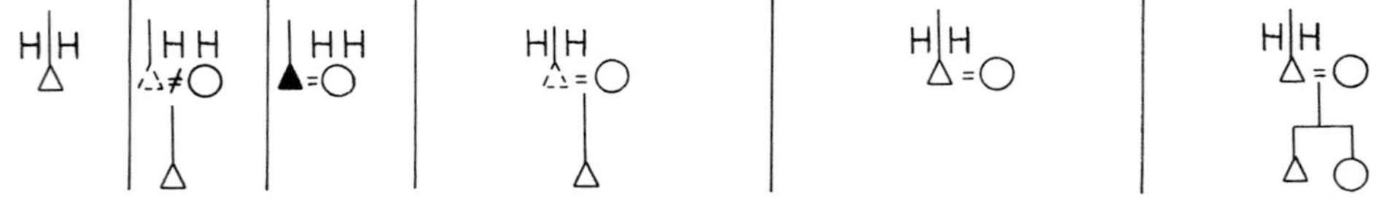

'tenement houses', some tenant families had formed composite co-residential kinship groups either through natural growth or by bringing related families to join them when a room became vacant in the house. This formation of extended kinship groups among tenant families, which was not found in the Ibadan sample, suggests a certain degree of stability, the length of residence of tenant households in rented accommodation as well as the need for mutual help among this group.

Finally, Table 16.4 compares the age distributions of tenant household heads and compound heads. It shows that, apart from a slightly larger proportion of younger tenant household heads, these age distributions do not differ markedly.

The age distribution of these tenant household heads and the substantial number of years that most of them have spent in rented accommodation indicate that the renting of rooms in Marrakech is a long-established practice which has helped immigrants and poorer local families to find suitable homes.

Courtyard house and kinship organization

Now I will apply some conclusions that emerged from the preceding discussion on household and kinship organization to a number of the houses surveyed. Altogether, four case studies have been chosen from the sample to illustrate the various stages in the development of co-residential kinship groups, their pattern of occupancy, and the modes of transferring real estate.

The first example is a house situated in the northern parts of the *medina*. (See Plan 16.4.) This house was bought for 850,000 Moroccan francs (DH8,500) in 1954 by the father of the present compound head. About three quarters of the money was raised by selling the old house, which, according to the compound head, had become too small, while the rest was given by the oldest son. Shortly after moving to the house the compound head built a new toilet (room no. 10) which has so far remained

Table 16.4 Age distribution of tenant household heads and compound heads, in percentages

Age group	15–24	25–39	40–54	55–69	70+	Total	No. of HHs
Tenant HHs	8.8	27.5	30.7	24.2	8.8	100.0	91
Compound heads	—	16.2	45.6	30.9	7.3	100.0	68

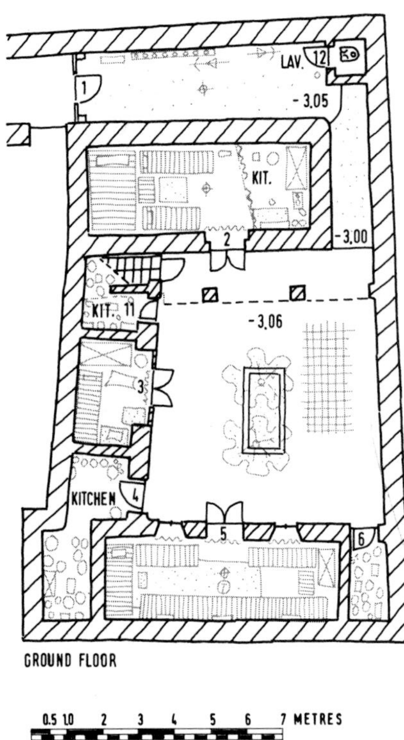

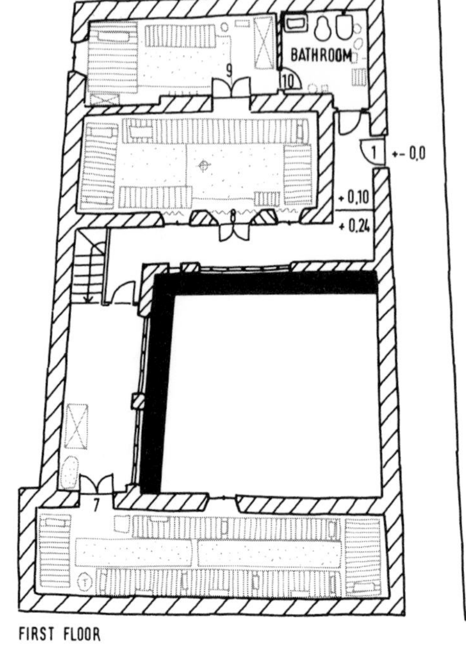

0.5 1.0 2 3 4 5 6 7 METRES
0 5 10 15 20 FEET

Plan 16.4
House 12

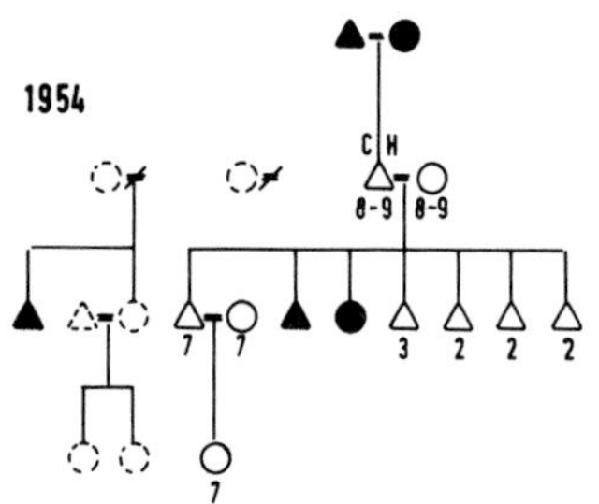

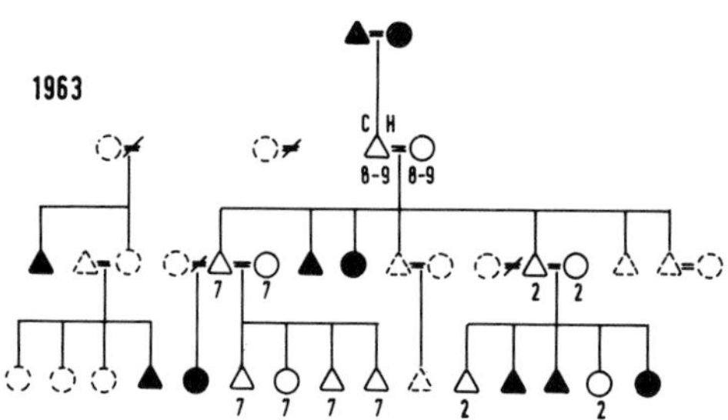

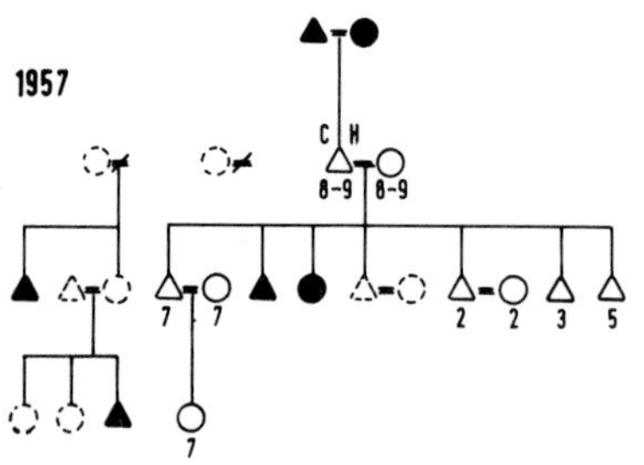

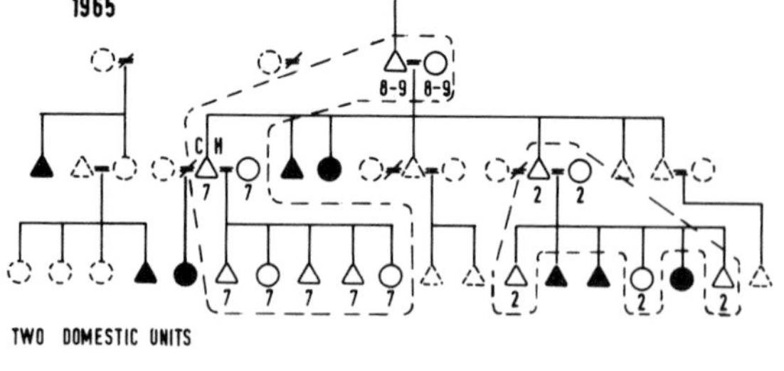

his only alteration to the house. During the mid-1950s the house contained a kinship group in the second stage of development and had the following pattern of occupancy. The compound head occupied two rooms numbered 8 and 9 on the plan, while his first-born son lived with his wife in room no. 7 on the same floor. The head's four unmarried sons shared two rooms on the ground floor until in 1957 two of them married. The elder of the two already had a bookshop in Gueliz and moved there with his wife, while the younger was given room no. 2 on the ground floor. The two remaining sons, one of whom is now married, moved out of the house in the early 1960s. In late 1965, when the compound head suffered a stroke, and was unable to carry out his responsibilities, he asked his first-born son to take over the headship. With this change of its headship the inhabitants of the house entered the third stage of its development as a co-residential kinship group. At the time of my interview in 1969, the young compound head was the only member of the group with a regular income and he supported his invalid father and, partly, his younger brother.

The second example, sketched in Plan 16.5, is of some interest because it illustrates a very common mode of dividing a courtyard house into two or more self-contained dwellings and the financial implications of this partition. This house is inhabited by the compound head's family and two of his married sons with their wives and children, as well as two individual tenant families. The present compound head and his younger full brother inherited the house from their father in 1938. After the Second World War, part of the upper floor was converted into two small self-contained dwellings. In 1952 a quarrel between the brothers resulted in the younger one moving out and demanding compensation for his share of the house. Obliged to pay, the compound head sold the two self-contained dwellings and, adding to this his own savings, paid his brother the sum of DH5,000. Unfortunately, I did not investigate the occupancy pattern of this house between 1938 and 1952, but since the younger brother and his family moved out there seem to have been few changes. In 1969 the compound head lived with his wife and two grandchildren in room no. 9 on the first floor, while his two sons and their families occupied all the rooms on the ground floor and room no. 8 on the first floor. The two self-contained dwellings which were sold in 1952 have been rented out to stranger families by their present owner.

The division of houses into two or more self-contained dwellings illustrated by this example represents but one of

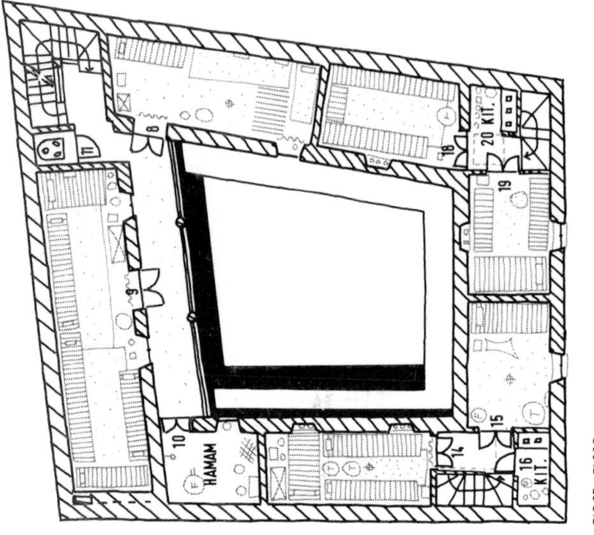

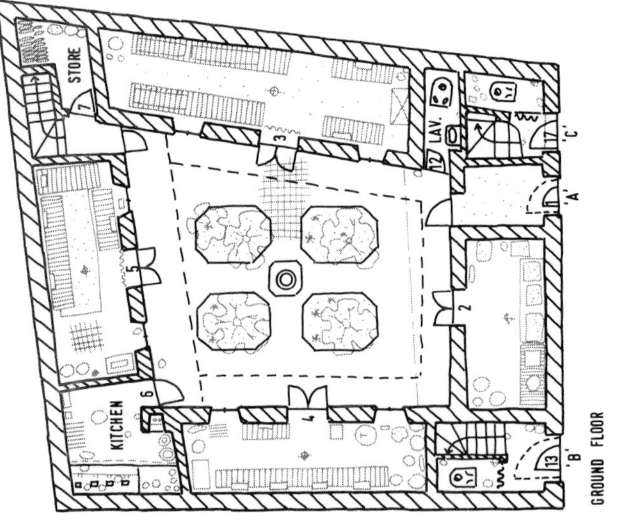

Plan 16.5
House 28

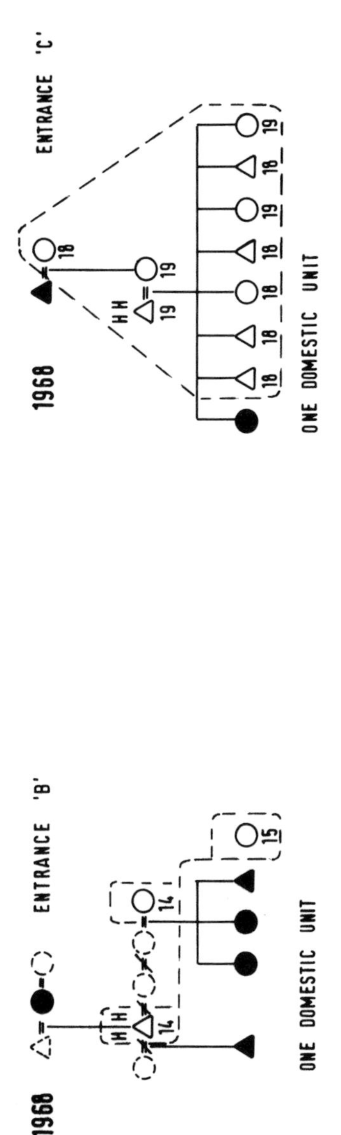
1968
ENTRANCE 'C'
ONE DOMESTIC UNIT
1968
ENTRANCE 'B'
ONE DOMESTIC UNIT

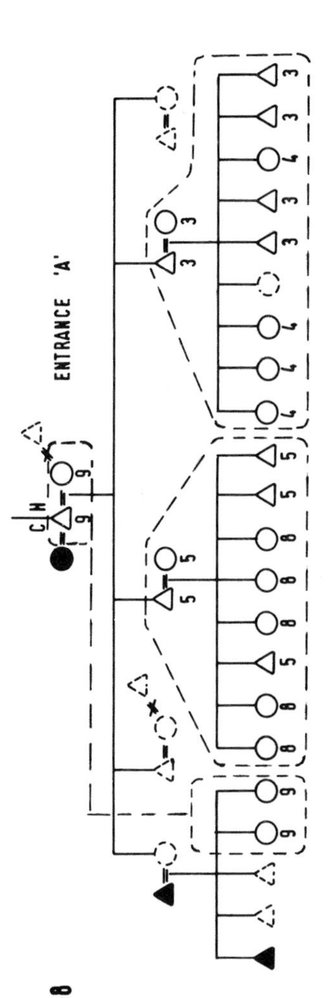
1968
ENTRANCE 'A'
THREE DOMESTIC UNITS

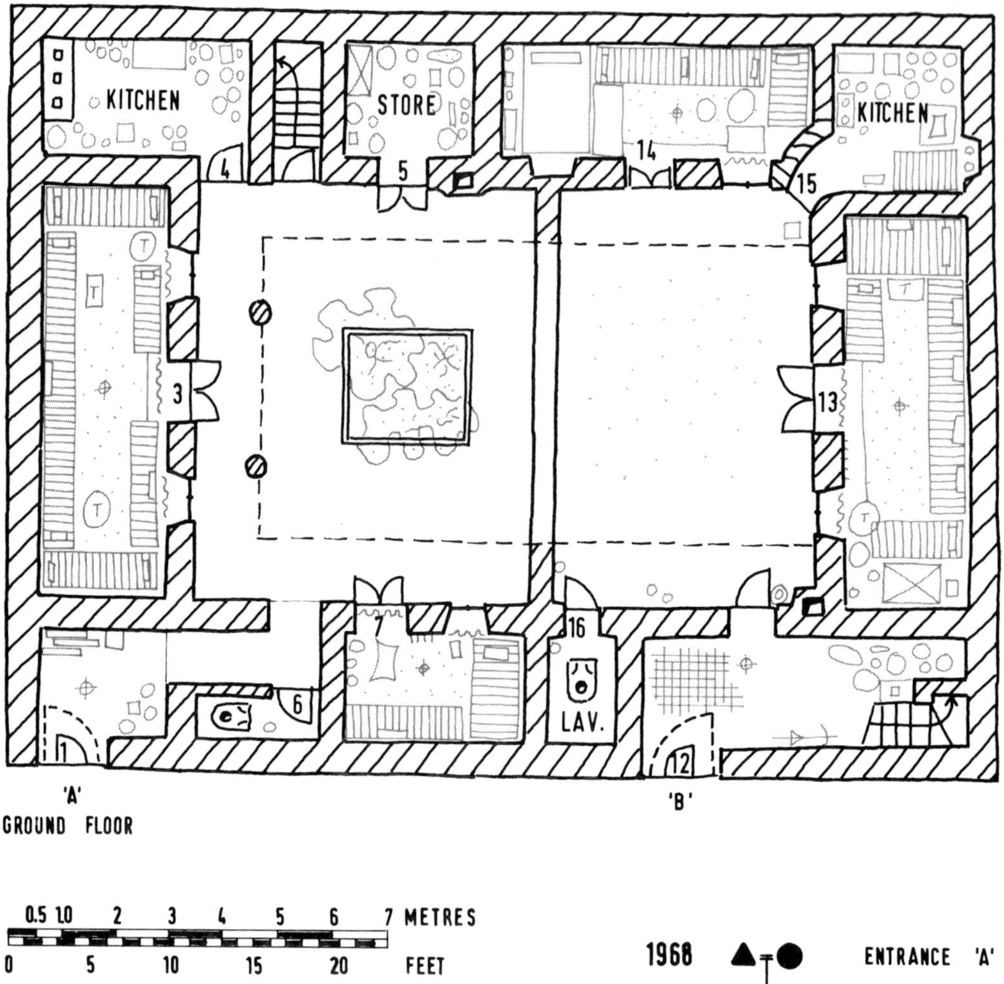

KITCHEN
STORE
KITCHEN
LAV.
'A'
'B'
GROUND FLOOR

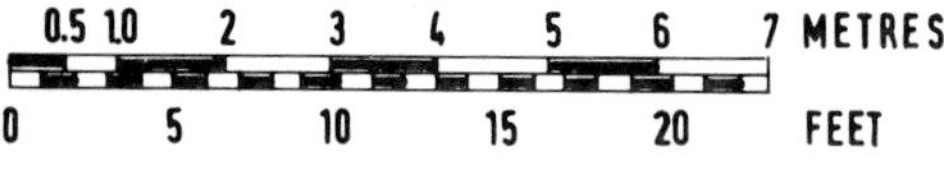

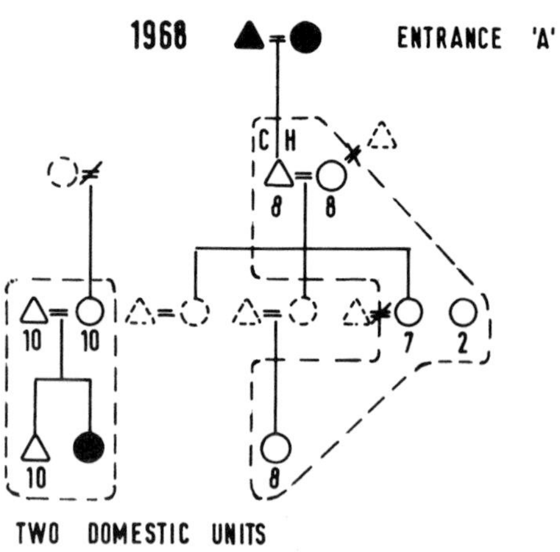

Plan 16.6
House 19

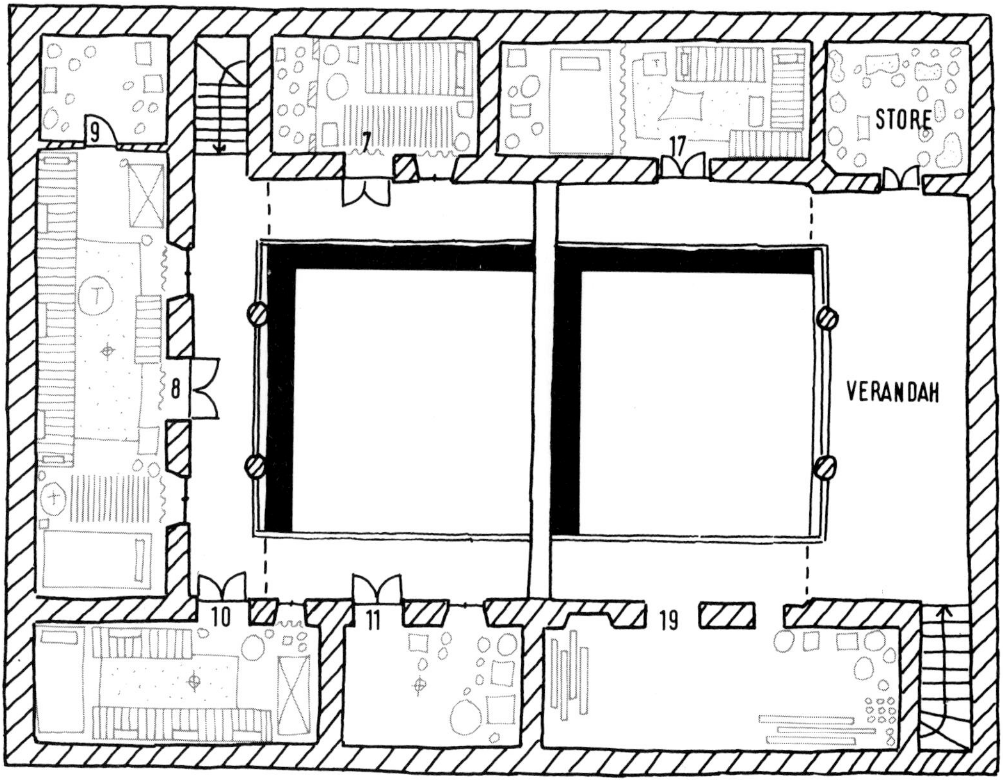

FIRST FLOOR

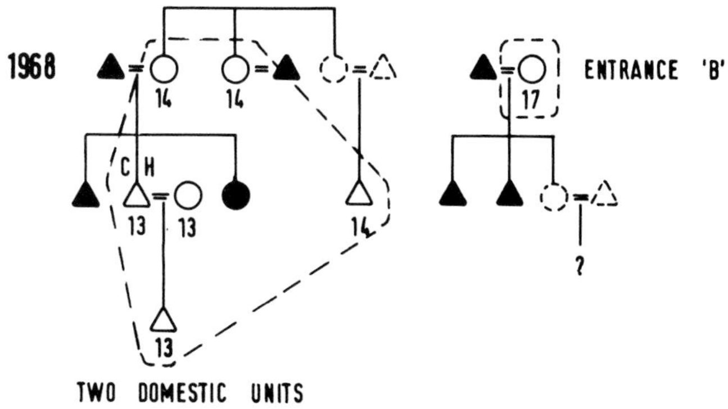

TWO DOMESTIC UNITS

two methods which are frequently found. The next example, Plan 16.6, illustrates the second mode of division, which is achieved by building a dividing wall through the courtyard of the house. The two individual families who now occupy this house are only casual acquaintances. According to the compound head who occupied section 'B', his grandfather bought the already divided house shortly after the First World War, and his neighbour bought the other section for DH4,300 in 1955. Neither of these two compound heads knew how old the house was or when the dividing wall was built. In both cases the family history and pattern of occupancy before the present compound heads' generation was not studied. The kinship diagrams beneath the house plans show the occupancy patterns of both families in 1969. Jean Gallotti in his book on *Le Jardin et la maison arabe au Maroc* gives an example of two small houses being joined together presumably to cater for the needs of an expanding family.[6] I did not find a similar example among the houses I surveyed.

The last example, shown in Plan 16.7, is situated in the suburb of Sidi Youssef ben Ali which stands just outside the walled city to the south-east. It is one of six houses included in the sample which were built by the present compound heads. In 1952, the compound head bought the land for 15,000 Moroccan francs (DH150) from a man who claimed to own it. However, this transaction, which was undertaken without exchanging a written contract, proved to be invalid as the whole area then belonged to a well-to-do merchant and had been taken over without his consent by squatters and self-styled property speculators. The compound head, himself a construction worker, built a wall around the plot and completed the first room in the second half of 1953. After moving into this room he built a second room for his wife and completed this a year later. Following a break of about one year in which he repaid at least some of the money he had borrowed, a third room was finished in 1956 and was immediately rented out to a tenant family. It took him over two years to build a kitchen, an entrance lobby, and a store room, and these were completed in 1959. In 1965 the compound head was able to let one room for a lump sum of DH500. This kind of transaction, which is based on a contract asking for no further payment from the tenant but which is repayable to him in full when he leaves the house, has been described in some detail in Chapter 14 on p. 200. This loan enabled the compound head to buy some building materials and to start the construction of a large upstairs room which was completed in 1967. On moving into the new room the

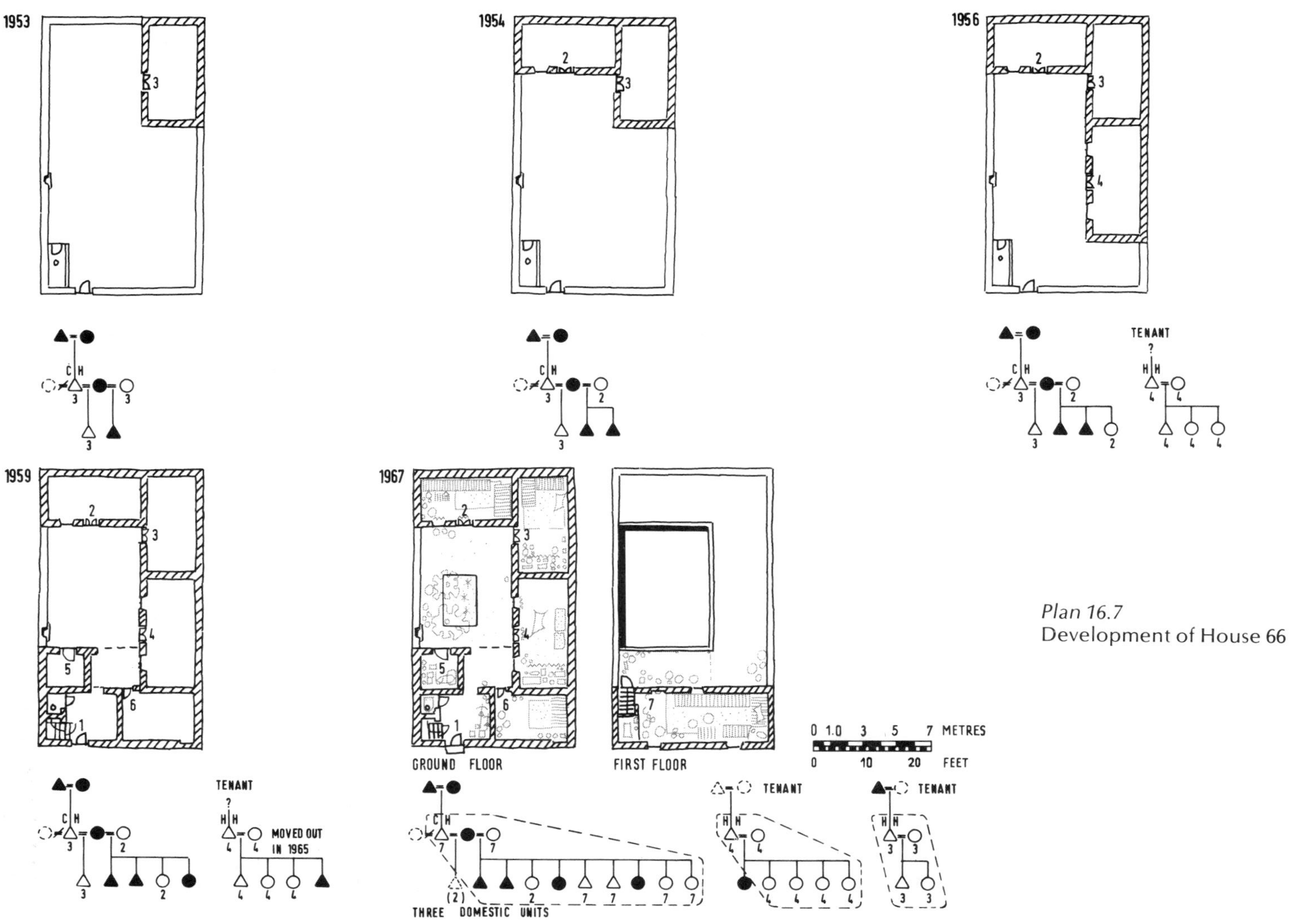

Plan 16.7
Development of House 66

compound head was able to let his old room (no. 3 on the plan) for DH15 per month.

These four examples indicate that most houses in Marrakech are regarded as a capital investment made by an individual or a group of individuals who may exchange them for something more suitable if the occasion arises. Hence, as shown in the last example, the construction of rooms need no longer reflect the requirements of a growing family but may illustrate the owner's ability to invest his money for a profitable return.

Distribution of floor area

As in the other two samples the distribution of the floor area among the sample population in Marrakech has been studied from two points of view: first, the average floor area per household and person classified by their relationship to the compound head; and second, the average floor area per household and person according to the number of persons per household. As already argued in Chapter 10 on p. 147, the first approach may tell us something about differential treatment of related and tenant households regarding the allocation of space, while the second approach will indicate the compound head's ability either to buy a bigger house or to adapt already available space for a growing family.

Type of floor area and household

The sample of houses surveyed in Marrakech included 190 households with a total of 896 persons. Columns 2 and 3 of Table 16.5 show the total average floor area and the average sleeping area available to each household for its members, these households being classified by the relationship of their heads to the compound head. As shown in the table, there is a substantial difference between the average floor area occupied by the households of compound heads (85.1 sq. m) and the average floor area of all other related dependent or semi-dependent households (22.1 sq. m) and tenant households (20.4 sq. m).

In part these differences are due to the larger average size of the compound head's households with 6.0 persons as against 4.7 and 3.8 persons for all dependent and tenant households respectively. As explained above, the area occupied by the compound head's own household includes all rooms such as entrance lobbies, passages,

Table 16.5 Average floor area per household and person in square metres

Column	1		2		3	
	No. of hhs	No. of persons	Total av. area per hh	per person	Av. sleeping area per hh	per person
CH's household	68	408	85.1	14.2	27.5	4.6
CH's sons' & daus' hhs	18	95	20.2	3.8	14.9	2.8
CH's brs' & sists' hhs	8	32	21.8	5.4	14.8	3.7
Other related hhs	5	18	29.0	8.1	13.4	3.7
Subtotal dep. hhs	31	145	22.1	4.7	14.6	3.1
Tenant hhs	91	343	20.4	5.4	12.6	3.4
Total hhs & persons	190	896				
Av. all hhs & persons			43.8	9.3	18.3	3.9

staircases, common kitchens, and stores for which he is directly responsible, even though these rooms are available for use by all other resident households. Hence the average floor area given above for the compound head's household illustrate the distribution of responsibility within the house, while the average floor area given for all other household heads represents a more precise allocation of space used almost exclusively by members of these households.

The average sleeping area per person, as shown in column 3, fluctuates between 4.6 sq. m for members of the compound head's household, 3.1 sq. m for all other related households, and 3.4 sq. m for tenant households, the average for the sample being 3.9 sq. m or 42.0 sq. ft. However, the average sleeping area per person in the compound head's household is slightly inflated by the fact that some compound heads have their own sleeping quarters, while most other household heads have to share their bedrooms with others in their family.

Graphs 16.1 and 16.2 derive from Table A.16.7 on p. 436. Graph 16.1 shows the average floor area (curve 1) and average sleeping area (curve 2) per household of differing sizes. As may be seen, the average floor area per household increases from 27.7 sq. m in households with 1 or 2 persons to 69.3 sq. m in households having 9 or 10 persons. At the same time the average sleeping area per household also increases from 10.1 sq. m for households with 1 or 2 persons to 30.6 sq. m for 9 or 10 person households.

Graph 16.2 shows the average floor area per person (curve 1) and the average sleeping area per person

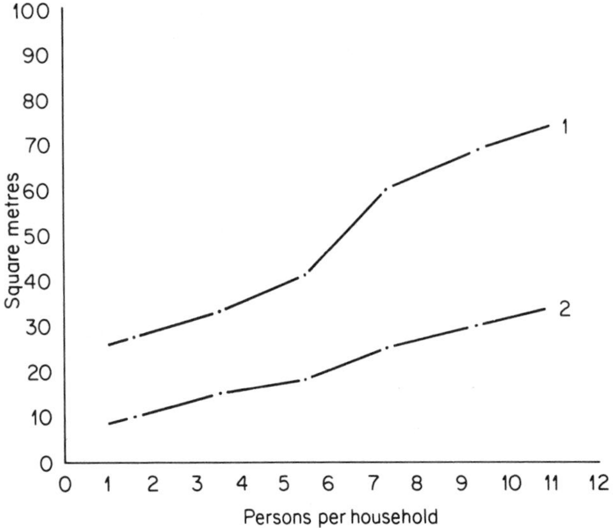

Graph 16.1
Average floor and sleeping area per household in square metres. (See Table A.16.7 on p. 436)

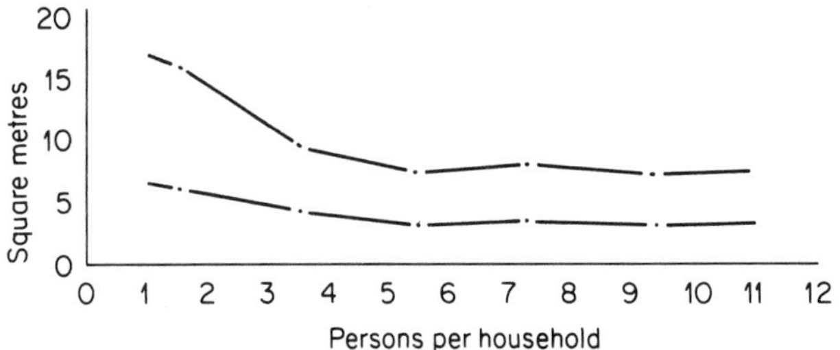

Graph 16.2
Average floor and sleeping area per person in square metres

(curve 2) in households of differing size. At 17.1 sq. m, the average floor area per person for households of 1 or 2 persons is relatively high when compared with 9.5 sq. m per person for households of 3 or 4 persons, and 7.4 sq. m per person for households having 9 or 10 persons. Average sleeping area, on the other hand, fluctuates between 6.2 sq. m per person in households with 1 or 2 persons and 3.3 sq. m per person in households having 9 or 10 persons, the sample average being 3.9 sq. m. It will be noted on Graph 16.2 that the average sleeping area per person decreases from about 6.0 sq. m in 1 or 2 person households to about 3.0 sq. m in households of 5 or 6 persons, but remains almost stable for all large households.

In conclusion, apart from a few very densely populated tenement houses including the *fondouk*, overcrowding is not worse in Marrakech than in Ibadan. For example, in Marrakech the total average floor area per person was 9.3 sq. m and the total average sleeping area 3.9 sq. m, while in Ibadan the comparable figures were 7.4 and 3.8 sq. m respectively. Thus the available floor and sleeping areas per person in Marrakech are very similar to the area found in Ibadan, and may not be a decisive factor in the early division of co-residential kinship groups as proposed earlier in this chapter. It is also interesting to observe that the high degree of residential mobility of the population is partly illustrated by the reluctance of many a compound head to undertake the major building operations required to enlarge a house, preferring instead to sell it and to buy a more suitable one elsewhere in the city. Furthermore, the economic value of urban houses and the possible opportunity open to compound heads to sell part of it and to give the money to their sons has no doubt enabled many of them to leave their fathers' homes and establish their own independent households elsewhere. However, as will be seen later, Islam and the influence of Islamic laws have also contributed to the decline of extended families in the urban areas of Morocco, (see pp. 307–309.)

Notes and references

1 P. Lampl, *Cities and Planning in the Ancient Near East*, New York, 1968, pp. 21–22 and 34.
2 J. Gallotti, *Le Jardin et la maison arabe au Maroc*, Paris, 1926, vol. 1, pp. 3–13.
3 M. de Leenheer, 'L'Habitat précaire à Marrakech et dans sa zone périphérique', *Revue de géographie du Maroc* (Rabat), no. 17, 1970, pp. 43–51.
4 D. M. Hart, 'Segmentary systems and the role of "five fifths" in tribal Morocco', *Revue de l'occident musulman et de la Méditerranée* (Aix-en-Provence), no. 3, 1967, pp. 65–95.
5 B. G. Hoffman, *The Structure of Traditional Moroccan Rural Society*, The Hague, 1967, p. 45. 'If this common ancestor [the lineage founder] is still living he heads the extended family and represents it on social and public occasions; if not his place is taken by his elder brother. If this brother dies the extended family splits up into units under each of the other brothers.'
6 Gallotti, op. cit., vol. 1, p. 11.

Chapter 17

Occupation and income

Morocco and Marrakech

Occupational pattern

According to the 1971 census report, about 4 million people or 26.3 per cent of the total Moroccan population were classified as belonging to the economically active population.[1] The division into sexes shows that 3.4 million or 44.5 per cent of the total male population were economically active, while only 0.6 million or 8.0 per cent of the total female population belonged to this group. It is thus obvious that the latter figure does not include an estimated 2.0 million females who are engaged in various kinds of unpaid agricultural and/or crafts activities, mainly in the rural areas of the country.

A broad division of the total working population into five major occupational groups revealed that in 1971 agriculture employed 51.4 per cent of the country's total labour force, followed by crafts and industry with 19.2 per cent, services including professional and administrative staff with 15.2 per cent, trade with 5.6 per cent, and finally miscellaneous occupations and the unemployed with 8.6 per cent.[2] The substantial differences between the occupational patterns in the rural and urban areas of the country* are noteworthy. As expected, 76.9 per cent of the economically active population in the rural areas work

* Urban areas include all towns with 20,000 or more inhabitants.

in agriculture, while only 4.7 per cent of the urban population do so. Crafts and industry employ 10.7 per cent of the rural but 34.7 per cent of the urban population. Services, including professional and administrative occupations, show a similar distribution with 6.0 per cent in the rural areas and 32.1 per cent in the towns, while trade accounted for 2.5 per cent in the rural and 11.3 per cent in the urban areas. Miscellaneous occupations including the unemployed account for 3.9 per cent of the rural and 17.2 per cent of the urban population. (See Table A.17.1 on p. 437.) The 1971 census report also showed that 37.2 per cent of the country's total labour force were wage and salary earners, 33.6 per cent were self-employed, 18.7 per cent were family workers, and 10.5 per cent were not classified.[3]

As no detailed data for the various occupational groups in the city of Marrakech are available, Table 17.1 shows the percentage distribution of the total economically active urban population of Marrakech Province in comparison with the country as a whole in 1971. Persons employed in crafts and industry together form 39.8 per cent of the total economically active population in the urban areas of Marrakech Province. They are followed by persons employed in services with 27.0 per cent, traders with 13.3 per cent, full-time farmers with 5.2 per cent, and finally miscellaneous occupations and the unemployed with 14.7 per cent.

Table 17.1 Percentage distribution of occupational groups in Morocco/Marrakech[a]

	Morocco total	Marrakech Prov. urban areas	Sample survey 1968/1969[b]
Crafts and industry	19.2	39.8	37.4
Services[c]	15.2	27.0	24.7
Trade	5.6	13.3	17.4
Agriculture	51.4	5.2	6.8
Miscellaneous occupations	8.6	14.7	13.7
Total	100.0	100.0	100.0

[a]Secrétariat d'État au Plan et au Développement Régional, Royaume du Maroc, *Recensement général de la population et de l'habitat 1971* vol. 2, Rabat, 1973, pp. 119, 120.

[b]See p. 249.

[c]Includes professional, administrative, and clerical staff.

Income

Minimum wage rates have been in operation in Morocco since 1936.[4] In 1971, the lowest established minimum wage per hour in industry and commerce was DH0.544 for females between 14 and 15 years of age, and DH0.956 for an adult man.[5] Since 1960, these minimum wages have been linked to a cost of living index, but wage increases have usually lagged behind the rise in prices. However, actual wages are often above the quoted minimum, and there are substantial variations between unskilled and highly skilled workers. Unfortunately, no reliable data for wage and income distribution among Moroccan workers are available except for the late 1950s and early 1960s.[6] Nevertheless, estimates for the early 1970s suggest that the average monthly income of unskilled and semi-skilled workers in manufacturing industry ranged from DH300 to DH500, while highly skilled workers, clerks, and teachers were earning between DH500 and DH800 per month.

Cost of living

The consumer price index for Casablanca is shown in Table A.17.2 on p. 438. Unfortunately no index is available for Marrakech. Column 1 in the table gives the general consumer price index, whereas columns 2–4 give separate figures for food including drinks, for clothing, and finally for rent which also contains fuel and lighting as well as the cost of kitchen utensils. As shown in the table, the increase of the general index was only 20.6 per cent over the previous 10 years (1963–1973) which represents a very modest average annual increase of 1.7 per cent.

Sample survey

Occupational pattern

The occupational pattern and income distribution of the 190 household heads interviewed will be analysed below. The main occupations of these household heads are given in Table 17.2. Among compound heads, the service category, which includes *inter alia* teachers as well as professional, administrative, and clerical staff, represents the most important group, followed by crafts, trade, and agriculture. Dependent and tenant household heads, on the other hand, worked more frequently in occupations related to crafts and industry, followed by services and

Table 17.2 Occupational pattern of 190 household heads

Column	1		2		3		4	
	Compound head		Dep. HH		Tenant HH		Total HHs	
	No.	%	No.	%	No.	%	No.	%
Crafts & industry	20	29.4	12	38.7	39	42.8	71	37.4
Services[a]	23	33.8	9	29.0	15	16.5	47	24.7
Trade	13	19.1	5	16.1	15	16.5	33	17.4
Agriculture	2	3.0	2	6.5	9	9.9	13	6.8
Miscellaneous	10	14.7	3	9.7	13	14.3	26	13.7
Total	68	100.0	31	100.0	91	100.0	190	100.0

[a] Includes professional, administrative, and clerical staff.

trade. The number of interviewed household heads who engaged in full-time agriculture was relatively small. (For comparison with Marrakech Province urban area see Table A.17.1 on p. 437.)

As shown in Table A.17.4 on p. 440, 27 or 14.2 per cent of the 190 household heads had some income from a secondary occupation. Twelve of these household heads worked in agriculture, 7 pursued some crafts, and 8 worked in several other occupations.

Table 17.3 shows how the household heads included in the survey were employed. Some 50.0 per cent of the compound heads were self-employed, 19.1 per cent were employed by private firms, and 16.2 per cent in the public sector. Slightly over one third of the dependent household heads were self-employed but, compared with the compound heads, a larger proportion was employed in the public sector. It is noteworthy that only 1 of 91

Table 17.3 How household heads are employed

Column	1		2		3		4	
	Compound head		Dep. HH		Tenant HH		Total HHs	
	No.	%	No.	%	No.	%	No.	%
Self-employed	34	50.0	11	35.5	31	34.1	76	40.0
Empl. priv. sector	13	19.1	6	19.4	45	49.4	64	33.7
Empl. publ. sector	11	16.2	8	25.8	1	1.1	20	10.5
Helps sen. fam. member	—	—	3	9.7	1	1.1	4	2.1
Retired	7	10.3	1	3.2	8	8.8	16	8.4
Miscellaneous	3	4.4	2	6.4	5	5.5	10	5.3
Total	68	100.0	31	100.0	91	100.0	190	100.0

tenant household heads was employed in the public sector, while 45 or 49.4 per cent worked for private firms, and 31 or 34.1 per cent were self-employed. It seems that tenant household heads, 58.2 per cent of whom were immigrants, had little chance of gaining employment from the local administration, and had to rely on private firms for employment or establish their own businesses.

Finally, the occupations of 240 women* (156 married, 15 divorced, 54 widowed, and 15 single) in the sample population must be briefly discussed. A total of 37 female household heads have already been included in the two previous tables.† Of the remaining 203 females, 119 or 58.6 per cent were housewives with no gainful occupation, 40 or 19.7 per cent practised handicrafts, 26 or 12.8 per cent were in services, 3 were engaged in part-time agriculture, and one was a beggar. A total of 14 women or 6.9 per cent had retired from active life and were supported by their next of kin. It is interesting to observe that none of the females interviewed was engaged in full-time trade, although 5 women – 3 who embroidered pillow-cases and 2 who baked bread – also sold their products in the local market.

Income groups and income distribution

The following division of households into low, middle, and high income categories is based on Table 5.3 on p. 69 which guided my classification of the sample households in Zaria and Ibadan. In 1971 the official conversion rate was about 14 dirhams to one Nigerian pound.[7] The converted income groups are given in Table 17.4.

The upper limit of the low income households (C) was found to be DH209.9 per month. As this is just above the minimum wage of DH198.85 per month fixed by the government for an adult unskilled labourer in industry or commerce, it may serve as a convenient boundary between the low and middle income households.[8] The minimum wage cited above is based on a 52-hour week, but with serious problems of underemployment some labourers may not reach even the minimum level and will thus receive a lower monthly income. Household heads in the middle income group are mainly skilled workers,

* This excludes single female children of compound heads and any other household heads, as well as other female children under the age of 15 living in the compound.

† Fourteen of these women practised crafts, 7 were in services, 5 each were in part-time agriculture and semi-retired, 4 were housewives, and 2 were beggars.

Table 17.4 Income groups

	Income per month in dirhams	Income per year in dirhams
Low-income households		
A.	Under 70.0	Under 840.0
B.	70.0–139.9	840.0–1,679.9
C.	140.0–209.9	1,680.0–2,519.9
Middle-income households		
D.	210.0–279.9	2,520.0–3,359.9
E.	280.0–419.9	3,360.0–5,049.9
F.	420.0–699.9	5,050.0–8,399.9
High-income households		
G.	700.0–1,399.9	8,400.0–16,799.9
H.	1,400.0–2,099.9	16,800.0–25,199.9
I.	2,100.0 and over	25,200.0 and over

teachers, and administrative and clerical staff, while those in the high-income groups are well-to-do traders, successful craftsmen, high-ranking government officials, and managers of private or public industries. (For a more detailed description of the occupational groups in these income categories, see Chapter 5 on p. 69.)

As explained above, the aim of my budgetary inquiries was to establish the annual cash income of compound heads and that of all other dependent and tenant household heads who lived in the houses surveyed. However, the cash income of women other than female household heads, and the cash value of non-monetary transactions such as barter, gifts of agricultural produce, or earnings in kind, are not included in this account. The incomes and expenditures of household heads were systematically investigated over a period of one year preceding the time of the interview. For purposes of inquiry, income was divided into six major categories: first, income from agriculture; second, from arts and crafts; third, from trade; fourth, from services and professional or clerical occupations; fifth, from rent and cash gifts; and finally, other financial receipts, including unearned incomes. However, before income was investigated, household heads were asked to give a detailed account of their cash expenditures, a subject on which most were far less reluctant to speak than about their income. In order of importance, the major items of expenditure investigated were: first, expenditure on food and drink; second, on accommodation; third, on clothing; fourth, on transport, firewood, and lighting; fifth, help given to relatives and friends; and finally, miscellaneous expenditures such as outlays for religious and public festivals, childbirth, marriages, or funerals. To the amount of regular daily, weekly, and monthly cash expenditure were added the reported irregular outlays, and only when this balanced within 10 per cent of the household head's reported cash income was the budget accepted as valid for inclusion in data analysed here. This method worked fairly well, particularly for the low and middle income households where small sums of money are in constant use and relatively few chances for saving and investment exist. However, in the high-income households I had to rely to a far greater extent on the household heads' willingness to cooperate. It must be stressed yet again that in spite of all precautions taken, it is unlikely that the budgetary data cited below are free from inaccuracies and omissions. Nevertheless they are sufficiently detailed to provide a valuable guide to the levels of cash incomes and expenditures among the household heads interviewed in Marrakech.

Table A.17.3 on p. 439 indicates the pattern of household consumption and expenditure in urban areas of Morocco.[9] It shows clearly that between 1957 and 1960 food and drinks, accommodation, clothing, fuel, and lighting accounted for 83.0 per cent of household expenditures in the traditional towns in Morocco. Hence, particular attention was paid to these four items, together with the financial help given to family members and friends. The table also shows that expenditure on food and drinks decreases from 68.0 per cent of the total in households with incomes of less than DH1,442 per year to 54.1 per cent in households with over DH5,977 per year. Clothing, on the other hand, increases from 4.1 per cent of the total in the lowest to 9.4 per cent in the highest income group.

Having given these preliminary explanations, I now examine the income distribution of the 190 household heads interviewed in Marrakech. A total of 6 household heads refused to cooperate in this inquiry, while another 11 gave such grossly misleading information regarding their incomes and expenditures that they had to be excluded from the analysis. Of the remaining 173 household heads, 95 or 54.9 per cent belonged to the low-income group with monthly incomes of DH209.9 or less; 66 or 38.2 per cent belonged to the middle-income group with incomes that ranged between DH210.0 and DH699.9 per month; and only 12 household heads or 6.9 per cent belonged to the high-income group with incomes exceeding DH700.0 per month. (For more detailed information see Tables A.17.5 and A.17.6 on pp. 442–443.)

Table A.17.7B–D on p. 444 gives the income distribution for compound heads dependent and tenant household heads separately. As expected, compound heads have the highest average monthly income, and only 25 per cent of them fell in the low-income group, while 57.8 per cent were in the middle, and 17.2 per cent in the high-income groups. This pattern is followed broadly by dependent or semi-dependent household heads, 36 per cent of whom fall in the low-income group, and 60 per cent and 4 per cent in the middle and high-income groups respectively. By contrast, tenant household heads have an astonishing 83.3 per cent in the low-income group, 16.7 per cent in the middle, and none in the high-income groups.

The income distribution by household size for all households is set out in Table A.17.7A on p. 444. This table shows the predominance of small households with 1–4 persons in the low-income group. However, as the number of persons per household increases, income tends to increase as well. This is clearly illustrated by the diagonal pattern of concentration which holds for households with up to 9–10 persons and with incomes of between DH210.0 and DH699.9 per month. From these points onwards, the few remaining households are scattered so widely that their distribution has uncertain statistical value.

The average per capita income of all households classified according to their size was for households with 1 or 2 persons DH102.5 per month; this decreased to DH64.6 for households with 3 or 4 persons, and DH45.5 per month for households consisting of 5 or 6 persons. Thereafter the per capita income for households with 7 or 8 persons increased slightly to DH53.5 per month and further to DH76.8 per month for households with 9 or 10 persons. A similar upward movement, which has already been observed in Ibadan, reflects to some extent the higher frequency of these larger households under compound heads who have generally higher incomes.

On Graph A.17.1 on p. 446 the cumulative income distribution of 173 households is plotted on logarithmic probability paper in order to show, first, the relationship of incomes between the three types of households cited above, and, second, their median income. The almost straight line of the cumulative income distribution curve for all households indicates a log-normal distribution. All three types of households are distinguished by separate curves which show approximately equal percentage changes but differing incomes. Hence the curves representing the income distributions of dependent and tenant household heads, who have generally lower incomes, shift leftwards. The median income for compound heads is DH380.0 per month and for dependent and tenant household heads DH245.0 and DH120.0 per month respectively. However, it must be remembered that part of the higher income of compound heads derives from rent and other financial benefits which are associated with compound headship. Some of this money is spent on improvement and repair of the house as well as on help given to other family members in need.

Finally, a Lorenz Curve was constructed from the collected data (Graph A.17.2 on p. 446) and illustrates clearly the considerable inequality in distribution of income among the 173 household heads included in this analysis. With a total of 46.1 per cent, the 'area of inequality' is by far the largest calculated so far, and shows that about 50 per cent of all households earn only about 20 per cent of the total recorded average monthly income of about DH51,000.

In conclusion, this analysis has shown that about 55 per cent of all household heads had cash incomes of less than DH209.9 per month. Despite the country's minimum wage legislation, a considerable number of small family enterprises are either unwilling or unable to pay their workers a minimum wage, and the high level of unemployment and underemployment, particularly in traditional cities such as Marrakech, keeps wage demands relatively low. In the following chapter I will show how household heads with such low incomes can manage to rent, buy, maintain, and even improve their houses.

Notes and references

1 Secrétariat d'État au Plan et au Développement Régional, Royaume du Maroc, *Recensement Général de la population et de l'habitat 1971*, vol. 2, 'Population Active', Rabat, 1973, p. 18.
2 Ibid., p. 119.
3 Ibid., p. 89.
4 Royaume du Maroc, *Dahir* of 18 June 1936.
5 Service Central des Statistiques, Royaume du Maroc, *Annuaire Statistique du Maroc 1972*, Rabat, 1973, p. 154.
6 International Labour Office, *Labour Survey of North Africa*, Geneva, 1960, Appendix II, p. 463. A. Lazraq, 'Les Salaires dans le revenu national de 1955 à 1966', *Bulletin economique et social du Maroc* (Rabat), **XXIX** (106–107), 1967, pp. 85–139.
7 International Labour Office, *Yearbook of Labour Statistics 1973*, Geneva, 1974, pp. 762–763.

8 Service Central des Statistiques, Royaume du Maroc, op. cit., p. 154.

9 International Labour Office, *Household, Income and Expenditure Statistics 1950–64*, Geneva, 1967, pp. 97, 130.

Chapter 18

Production, cost, and financing of houses in the *medina* of Marrakech

Building materials and the construction of houses

The local building industry needs only a few basic materials for the construction of houses in the *medina* of Marrakech. These include stones for foundations, earth, lime, and locally made bricks for the construction of walls. Forest timber is normally used for roof beams, while sawn wood is needed to make doors and window shutters. To finish the house, cement and/or lime is used for the laying of floor screed and to plaster the walls and ceilings which are usually painted white.

According to an industrial survey of 1970, building materials in Morocco were produced by 61 firms having a total of 6,300 employees. Together these firms produced a wide range of building materials, having a value of approximately DH233.3 million.[1] The index for the production of building materials rose from 100 in 1958 to 239 in 1971, which represents an average annual increase of about 8 per cent.[2] Morocco has adequate resources of all basic raw materials for the development of its building material industry, with the exception of timber and iron, most of which have to be imported. (See Tables A.18.1 and A.18.2 on pp. 447–448.)

Earth and clay

Locally burned bricks and rammed earth mixed with lime have been used since time immemorial for the construction of walls and ramparts in the walled cities of Morocco.

The production of burned bricks and roof tiles varied considerably during the decade beginning 1960. For example, in 1960 a total of 119,000 tonnes were produced by the country's brick and tile industry. This amount rose steadily to 138,000 tonnes in 1963. However, during the following three years the production fell to 90,000 tonnes in 1966, rising again to an all-time high of 180,000 tonnes in 1972. Production of fire-proof bricks was in the region of 9,000 tonnes in 1970.[3] In the same year, the ceramic industry, with 18 firms and about 960 workers, produced sanitary porcelain and glazed tiles having a total value of DH10.9 million and supplied about half the country's needs, the remainder being imported.[4]

Timber and wood products

According to the 1972 *Annuaire Statistique du Maroc*, the country's forest area was estimated at 5.2 million hectares or 11.3 per cent of the total land area.[5] This forest area includes 2.9 million hectares or 55.8 per cent under broad-leaved trees, 1.5 million hectares or 28.8 per cent under conifers, and 0.8 million hectares or 15.4 per cent of mixed secondary growth.[6] In 1970 Morocco produced about 97,000 cu. m of industrial timber* which represented between 15 and 20 per cent of the country's industrial timber consumption, the rest being imported.†

Cement and cement products

Between 1960 and 1972 the annual production of cement in Morocco increased nearly three-fold from 580,000 tonnes to 1,545,000 tonnes.[7] Imports of cement were restricted to special kinds of cement, and were estimated at 36,000 tons in 1970 or 2.3 per cent of the local production. In 1970 Morocco had five cement plants which employed a total of 1,190 persons. In the same year the gross output of the industry reached DH117.1 million. The price of cement on the home market was then in the region of DH90.0 per tonne.

Associated industries producing concrete blocks, asbestos-cement sheets, and pipes were served by 16 firms. These firms employed a total of 2,830 persons and produced goods valued at DH54.4 million in 1970.[8]

* This excludes 160,000 cu. m of pulp wood.

† In 1969, the country's imports of wood and wood-based products were valued at DH152.5 million, while its export, consisting mainly of cork and pulp wood, stood at DH64.0 million. BMCE, *Bulletin mensuel d'informations*, no. 118, p. 10.

Iron and steel consumption

The Moroccan iron and steel producing industry is in its infancy. In 1970 the industry produced about 8,000 tonnes of pig-iron and about 1,000 tonnes of crude steel for casting.[9] However, with the recent rapid expansion of the country's industry, an increasing amount of imported steel (some 325,000 tonnes in 1970) is being re-rolled and processed in Morocco. Of Morocco's total steel imports of approximately 325,000 tonnes in 1970, an estimated 110,000 tonnes or about 35 per cent was consumed by various branches of the construction industry.[10]

Marrakech type of construction

The type and method of construction prevalent in the walled city of Marrakech will be discussed briefly. The majority of extensions, improvements, and maintenance work on houses is still carried out by locally trained craftsmen who mainly use indigenous materials and building techniques, except for the increasing use of cement. Such kinds of building activities are normally not recorded in any government statistics, and their overall volume is unknown. However, as the more modern types of houses built in the former French township areas and, more recently, in the northern parts of the city were not investigated, they are not included in the following account.

Walls

Most houses within the walled city were built either with locally manufactured burned bricks laid in lime mortar, or with rammed earth. The latter method, which is still used today, requires description. Following a decision to build a house or room, a sufficient quantity of laterite earth is excavated and brought to the building site. Here the earth is mixed with lime and wetted slightly before being rammed into prepared shutters. (See Picture 18.1.) It is then left to dry sufficiently to carry the load of the next layer, each layer being on average 1 m high. This process is repeated until the wall has reached its required height. The thickness of both types of walls (brick and rammed earth) may reach half a metre for a one-storey dwelling and frequently exceeds one metre for a two-storey house. The internal walls of rooms are always rendered with lime, gypsum, or cement plaster and whitewashed. In more expensive houses courtyard walls are usually covered with

Picture 18.1
Construction of mud walls

brightly coloured glazed tiles to a height of about 1.5 m. Floors are finished with a lime or cement screed and are sometimes covered with tiles.

Roofs and ceilings

The traditional Moroccan town house has a flat roof. Rooms are usually long and narrow, their width seldom exceeding 2.5 m or about 8 ft. A ceiling or a roof is constructed from beams of forest timber which are laid across the top of the wall at intervals of about 0.3 m or 1 ft. These beams are covered first with bamboo and then with grass matting. (See Picture 18.2.) The wooden roof structure is then covered with about 0.2 m of mud and finished with several layers of specially prepared lime mortar which keeps the roof reasonably waterproof for at least one year. The undersides of roofs are normally plastered, whitewashed, and occasionally painted. A more elaborate and expensive roof made from sawn wood can be seen in Picture 18.3. However, it can only be found in the more expensive houses of the relatively prosperous.

The local building industry

As no detailed data for the 1971 census were available at the time of writing, the only information regarding the local building industry in Marrakech dates back to the

Picture 18.2
Underside of flat mud roof construction

Picture 18.3
Underside of ceiling constructed of sawn wood

1960 census report. According to this report, an estimated 2,700 persons or 3.6 per cent of the active labour force were engaged in the industry. Of these, 95.1 per cent were Moroccan Muslims, 1.9 per cent French, 1.5 per cent Moroccan Jews, and 1.5 per cent belonged to various other nationalities.[11] In the late 1960s it was estimated that the number of persons employed by the building industry had nearly doubled due to the construction of a new suburb in the northern parts of the city.

Sample survey

Data from the sample survey analysed below include the age distribution of rooms, the structural changes of houses over the five-year period from February 1964 to January 1969, and the distribution of such amenities as kitchens, lavatories, electricity, and piped water in the houses under investigation.

Age composition of rooms

The inquiry into the age distribution of rooms was only partly successful. Despite much effort, I could only establish the age of 79 rooms or 10.2 per cent of the total number of rooms in the 75 houses surveyed. To account for the apparent lack of knowledge among compound heads regarding the age of their houses, we have to look at Table A.14.1 on p. 418. That table shows that a total of 34 houses, or 45.3 per cent of the sample, were bought by their present inhabitants. Of the 14 inherited houses in the sample, 10 were purchased by their previous owners, and the history of the remaining 4 was uncertain. All 6 houses listed under 'others' were also bought by their present owners. The remaining 15 houses were rented by occupants who had no knowledge of their age.* On this information, it seems likely that most of the houses studied had changed hands several times over the previous years or so, thus making it virtually impossible to establish their age with reasonable accuracy. However, existing historic records indicate that about 65 per cent of all houses included in my survey were built before 1920, and that nearly 27 per cent were over 100 years old. A total of 6 houses (8 per cent of the sample), having 50 rooms, were constructed by their present compound heads, while another 7 houses were found to which their compound heads had added 29 rooms. The age of these 79 rooms ranged between 1 and 30 years.

Structural changes of houses

The 75 courtyard houses surveyed contained 776 rooms with a total area of 8,326 sq. m. Between February 1964 and January 1969, when my survey in Marrakech was con-

* I did not interview the owners of these houses.

cluded, only 19 rooms with a total area of 224.4 sq. m were built by 12 compound heads. Over the five-year period no rooms were destroyed or disintegrated, thus the increase was 19 rooms or 2.5 per cent, which yielded an average growth rate of about 0.6 per cent per annum. It is worth mentioning here that the population of the *medina* grew from 180,000 in 1951 to 208,000 in 1971. This represents an average annual increase of 0.7 per cent over the last 20 years. (See discussion on p. 83.) This very slow growth rate of both population and housing reflects the fact that the extension of houses in the tightly packed *medina* is partly restricted by the lack of space, partly by the structural limitations of existing mud walls, and also by lack of adequate financial help, a subject I shall discuss in some detail later in the chapter. Moreover, this minimal increase confirms that major housing developments during the two decades 1950–1970 have taken place in areas beyond the twelfth-century city wall, particularly in the suburbs of Sidi Youssef b. Ali and Cité Mohammédia. (For their location see Plan 15.1 on p. 207.) About three quarters of the 19 rooms built between 1964 and 1969 were constructed from locally manufactured burned bricks; the rest were built with cement blocks. (See Table A.18.3, p. 449.)

Amenities

The existence of basic amenities in the houses surveyed will be examined below. Kitchens were found in 73 houses that accommodated 150 households. Of these, 42 households, mostly those of the compound heads, had their own private kitchens, while the remaining 108 households shared 44 kitchens, yielding an average of one kitchen to 2.4 households. The remaining 40 households or 21 per cent who lived in the two biggest tenement houses surveyed had no kitchen at all and cooked their meals on verandas or other covered places in front of their rooms.

A total of only 11 bathrooms shared by 20 households was counted in 9 houses. Members of the remaining 170 households or 89.5 per cent in 66 houses used either the toilet, the courtyard, or their rooms for personal washing.

All houses surveyed had at least one toilet. A total of 52 households, mainly the households of compound heads, had their own private toilet, while 98 households had to share a toilet with other people. The worst situation was found in the two tenement houses where 16 households with 67 persons and 24 households with 69 persons respectively had to share two tiny toilets, one in each house. (See Plan 16.3 on p. 220.)

Electricity had been installed in 69 houses; but of the 175 households living in these houses, only 131 had at least one electric bulb in their rooms, while 59 households or 31 per cent of the total had no electricity supply at all.

Finally, 37 houses containing 72 households had piped water in their courtyards, kitchens, or toilets, whereas 118 households or 62.1 per cent in 38 houses used a public stand-pipe in one of the streets nearby.

In short, 21 per cent of all households surveyed had no kitchen at all, 31 per cent had no electric light, 62.1 per cent had to fetch water from public stand-pipes, and 89.5 per cent had no bathrooms of their own. (For official statistics see Table A.18.4 on p. 449.)

In spite of such a lack of basic amenities most compound heads had other problems to worry about. When asked 'What improvement do you think the house most needs?', a total of 18 compound heads or 24 per cent replied spontaneously that the repair of leaking roofs and damage done by rain water to ceilings and walls was most urgently needed. There were also constant complaints about rising damp in walls due to the lack of any damp course. Connected with this problem were the answers of 5 compound heads or 6.7 per cent who felt that a proper drainage system in the courtyard connecting their pit-latrines to the municipal sewerage system would help to get rid of the damp in the house. Thus nearly one third of the compound heads interviewed were seriously concerned about leaking roofs and damp conditions in their houses. This indicates a serious recurrent problem in winter, particularly common in traditional urban houses.

In reply to this question, another 15 compound heads or 20 per cent said they needed more living and sleeping rooms for their familes. Another 4 compound heads or 5.3 per cent wanted to sell their houses to buy larger ones, while 2 or 2.7 per cent thought it would be better to demolish the house and build a new and bigger one on the site. Thus 21 compound heads or 28 per cent needed more rooms, though their approaches to this objective varied greatly.

A third group of 12 compound heads or 16 per cent wanted to improve their houses either by decorating the courtyards and rooms with glazed tiles or by plastering and painting the whole or part of the house. The need for piped water in the house was felt by 7 compound heads or 9.3 per cent, while another 7 compound heads made various other suggestions, including 2 who said they needed a bathroom. Of the remaining 5 compound heads, 4 were satisfied, while one did not respond. (For more detailed information see Table A.18.5 on p. 450.)

Cost of building

The aim of the second part of this chapter is to analyse the cost of building and the financing of traditional private houses in Marrakech. The analysis is based on my survey of 75 houses. The period over which the costs of construction and improvements were studied extended over five years from the beginning of February 1964 to the end of January 1969; whereas my study on maintenance and repair costs was limited to the three years immediately preceding the date of the interview. However, before going into these matters, the cost of building materials and labour must be briefly discussed.

The cost of materials and labour

Over the five-year period from 1964 to 1969 the index of costs of building materials in Morocco rose from 143 to 186 (100 = 1958) or about 5 per cent per annum. A number of basic building materials such as cement and steel bars did not increase during the period under study, and the price of burned bricks actually fell from DH160.0 per thousand in 1964 to DH150.0 in 1968. On the other hand, the cost of plaster increased from DH65.0 per tonne to DH70.0, and the cost of cedar wood also rose from DH350.0 per cubic metre to DH361.0 per cubic metre.[12] In Marrakech the price of timber beams normally used for the construction of ceilings and roofs fluctuated between DH1.5 and DH2.0 per beam, depending on the quality and length.

In 1968, daily wages paid to building workers ranged from DH5.0 for unskilled labourers to DH10.0 and more for skilled builders. Usually, labourers and some builders were paid daily, while the client provided all necessary building materials.

The cost of construction

As shown in the following list, expenditure on building made by the compound heads and other household heads in my sample covers a wide range of activities and has been divided into five major groups:

1 cost of construction completed between 1964 and 1969,
2 cost of buildings still under construction on 31 January 1969,

3 cost of improvements,
4 cost of maintenance and repair, and
5 cost of such miscellaneous construction as wells and pit-latrines.

Table 18.1 shows that of about DH94,300, the adjusted total expenditure on buildings by these men, 41.7 per cent was spent on improvements to existing buildings, 24.8 per cent on maintenance and repair, 24.7 per cent on new construction, and 8.8 per cent on buildings still under construction at the time of interview.

During the five-year period from 1964 to 1969 only 19 rooms, having a total floor area of 224.4 sq. m, were built in 7 out of 75 houses surveyed. (See Table A.18.6 on p. 451.) The recorded cost of construction for these rooms was about DH23,300 or 24.7 per cent of the total expenditure on buildings. The average cost per square metre is DH104.7 for 17 comparable living, sleeping, and commercially used rooms having a total floor area of 217.3 sq. m. None of the 75 houses surveyed in Marrakech had been built entirely during the period under study (1964–1969), and only 2 had had major extensions added to them.* In the remaining 5 houses only a few rooms – not more than two at a time – were built between 1964 and 1969. Given this small number of new rooms, as well as the different mode of constructing these rooms,† no attempt was made to calculate the cost by element of building, or by element of cost. A tentative comparison of my data with those for houses built by the Ministère des Travaux Publics in the northern parts of the city indicate that the government built houses were on average about twice as expensive as those under investigation.

Only 6 rooms with a total area of 121.3 sq. m were under construction at the time of interview. The six compound heads who had undertaken these constructions paid DH8,250 which represents 8.8 per cent of the total expenditure on buildings.

Cost of improvements

The cost of improvements, which covers *inter alia* the installation of piped water and an electricity supply as well as the tiling and cementing of walls and floors, amounted

* By 'major', I mean extensions of more than 50 per cent of the original floor area.

† Two rooms were built by one compound head who was also a builder, 6 rooms by the brother of a compound head, and the rest were either constructed with the help of relatives or by local craftsmen.

Table 18.1 Cost of construction in 75 surveyed houses, 1964–1969

Column	1	2	3	4	5
	No. of rooms	Sq. m	Cost in DH	Cost per sq. m	%
New construction (completed)					
Living area, common and commercial rooms	17	217.3	22,755	104.7	
Basic ancillary facilities	2	7.1	567		
Subtotal	19	224.4	23,322		24.7
Improvements on existing buildings					
Wall and floor tiles (glazed)			13,005		
Cement plaster on walls			4,011		
Piped water installed			2,785		
Link with mun. sewerage system			2,755		
Cement screed on floors			2,459		
Electricity installed			1,443		
Other structural improvements			12,820		
Subtotal			39,278		41.7
Maintenance and repair					
Repair of roofs					
Painting					
Repair of walls					
Repair of cement plaster		For details see Table 18.2 on p. 268			
Repair of doors and windows					
Other repairs					
Subtotal (1964–1969, actual)			14,050		
Subtotal adjusted 1964–1969[a]			23,417		24.8
Buildings under construction					
Walls completed	2	34.2	800	23.4	
Roof completed	4	87.1	7,450	85.5	
Subtotal	6	121.3	8,250		8.8
Miscellaneous construction	—	—	—		—
Total			94,267		100.0

[a] $\frac{14{,}050}{3} \times 5 = 23{,}417$ dirhams.

to DH39,300 or 41.7 per cent and was the most important item of expenditure. Compared with expenditures on improvements in Zaria and Ibadan, only in the Marrakech sample does the cost of improvements surpass expenditures on new construction. This may be explained partly by the lack of space in Marrakech and partly by the mode of existing construction in the tightly packed *medina* which often makes it impossible to extend a house.* Hence, too, the frequent sale of old houses in order to buy more suitable ones. The newly bought houses are then improved according to the compound heads' financial ability.

More detailed data on these improvement expenditures reveal that DH13,000 or 33.1 per cent of the total was spent on glazed tiles, DH4,010 or 10.2 per cent on the rendering of walls with cement plaster, 7.1 and 7 per cent respectively for the installation of piped water and sewage channels, 6.3 per cent on new cement screeds in rooms and courtyards, 3.7 per cent on electricity supplies, and finally DH12,800 or 32.6 per cent on various other structural improvements.

Cost of maintenance and repair

At DH23,400 the cost of maintenance and repair was 24.8 per cent of the total building expenditure, and its second largest item. However, the cost of maintenance and repair was only collected for a three-year period preceding the date of the interview. This time limit was necessary as most compound heads could not remember accurately their expenditures on this beyond the three-year period. Nevertheless, the detailed annual data collected on this topic show clearly the recurrent tendency of this kind of expenditure, and enabled me to adjust the costs of maintenance and repair to cover the five-year period of study. None the less, it must be borne in mind that the costs for this item are rather difficult to check; and in doing so I accepted the compound head's statement on these counts after comparing his annual expenditure for each item with those of others. Any apparent discrepancy was discussed with the informant and corrected as necessary.

For more detailed analysis I have broken down the total actual maintenance cost of DH14,050 into six categories as shown in Table 18.2. Repairs on the roof absorbed nearly

* Old mud walls are often not designed to carry the load of another floor.

Table 18.2 Actual maintenance cost by element of building, 1966–1969

Element of building	DH	%
Repair to roof	4,434	31.5
Painting and whitewash	3,596	25.6
Repair to walls	3,075	21.9
Repair to cement plaster and screed	1,993	14.2
Repair to doors and windows	615	4.4
Miscellaneous repairs	337	2.4
Total	14,050	100.0

one third of the total maintenance cost, followed by painting and/or whitewash with 25.6 per cent, repairs to walls with 21.9 per cent, and cement plaster and screed with 14.2 per cent, while outlays for repairs to doors and windows and for miscellaneous items were 4.4 and 2.4 per cent respectively. It is of interest, that maintenance work on roofs was carried out most frequently and usually involved only relatively small sums of money. However, if neglected for any length of time, the roof structure tends to deteriorate quickly and its replacement is usually expensive. Damage to walls including the plaster was in the majority of cases caused by rising damp and leaking roofs which occur periodically during the winter months.

The financing of private houses

The financing of private houses is divided into two sections: first, finance for the purchase of old houses; and second, finance for the various building activities described above.

The purchase of houses

During the five years from 1964 to 1969, 13 houses or 17.3 per cent of the sample were bought by their present owners. In value, these houses ranged from DH3,150 for a one-storey house of 4 rooms to DH32,000 for a two-storey house with 14 rooms. How, one may ask, was the money raised to pay for these houses? Seven compound heads raised the money by selling an old house. However, 3 of these compound heads had to borrow additional money from close relatives to pay for the bigger and more expensive house. Another 3 compound heads sold some animals and received financial help from relatives; 6 compound heads saved some money before purchasing the house; and 1 compound head refused to reply to this question. It is of interest that all the compound heads who required additional funds to meet the cost of the new house turned for such help to their next of kin. The only compound head who received a government grant of DH2,500 towards building costs* put about half of it towards the purchase of a house for DH7,000, while spending the rest on various improvements. (See Table A.18.7 on p. 451.)

The financing of building activities

I have examined in some detail the type and cost of various building activities carried out in 75 houses surveyed. I now wish to show how these building activities were financed by the compound heads concerned. As indicated elsewhere the two main sources of funds for housing are personal and institutional.

Personal sources

Personal sources of funds to finance building activities include self-finance from personal savings and income, contributions from family members and friends, loans from private money-lenders, and such social security funds as pensions and/or gratuity. Contributions from family members and friends are further subdivided into gifts and loans.

During the five-year period from 1964 to 1969, loans totalling DH10,900 were made by private persons to 13 compound heads who used the money as follows: eight loans having a total of DH5,600 were spent on various improvements; four loans totalling DH4,100 paid for new construction; and one loan of DH1,200 was used to pay for urgent maintenance and repair work. The creditors of these loans were, in order of importance, as shown in Table 18.3.

There was only one recorded gift of DH2,000 by a father to his son who used the money to pay for various improvements to the house. It is noteworthy that of 13 loans, only two with a total value of DH1,600 or 14.7 per cent were advanced by relatives of the compound head,

* The compound head is a teacher in primary education with a monthly income of DH530.

Table 18.3 Types of creditors of private building loans

	No. of loans	DH	%
Personal friends of compound head	7	7,200	66.0
Close relatives of compound head	2	1,600	14.7
Contract with tenants[a]	2	1,000	9.2
Credit from craftsmen	1	750	6.9
Private money-lender	1	350	3.2
Total	13	10,900	100.0

[a]See Chapter 14 on p. 200.

while the rest came from unrelated persons. At the time of interview about half of these loans had been repaid. Information on the amount of interest charged for loans received from friends was difficult to obtain as most compound heads were rather evasive on this point. However, interest rates charged by private money-lenders are known to be high, between 30 and 50 per cent per annum; but the compound head who had received such a loan refused to comment.

The 13 loans listed above covered about 17.6 per cent of the total costs for new construction, 14.3 per cent of the expenditure on improvements, and 5.1 per cent of the outlays for maintenance and repair. The rest of these expenditures, amounting to DH83,370 or about 88 per cent, were met either from the compound heads' personal savings and income, by gifts from close relatives (some DH2,000), and from institutional sources.

Institutional sources

Institutional sources of funds for housing include all building loans and grants made directly by the government through its Ministère des Travaux Publics or indirectly through the various government sponsored agencies, the banks, and/or state-owned industries to their employees.

From 1964 to 1969 two compound heads received building loans from institutional sources totalling DH5,000. One loan of DH2,000 was for the construction of two additional rooms, another of DH3,000 was for the improvement of an existing building. The creditors of these loans are shown, in order of importance, in Table 18.4. As mentioned earlier, one government grant

Table 18.4 Types of creditors of institutional building loans

	No. of loans	DH	Years	Interest rate
Electricity Board to employee	1	3,000	5	3.0
Food prod. industry to employee	1	2,000	4	3.0
Total	2	5,000		

of DH2,500 was given to a primary school teacher who used about half of it to purchase a house and the other half for housing improvements. The two loans together with the grant covered about 8.6 per cent of the total expenditure on new construction and 10.8 per cent of the money was spent on improvements.

In short, between 1964 and 1969, a total of approximately DH94,300 was spent by 75 compound heads on new construction, improvements, and the maintenance of their houses. Slightly less than 80 per cent of this money came from the personal savings and income of the compound heads. Nearly 14 per cent came from loans and gifts made by family members, friends, and one moneylender, while the rest, or about 6 per cent, came from official loans and grants. (For more detailed information see Table A.18.8 on p. 452.) It is noteworthy that official loans and mortgages for the purchase of 'second-hand houses' were conspicuously absent in my survey.

Internal subsidy and investment

Thus far we have examined the financial help given by official agencies and private persons living outside the houses surveyed to assist compound heads either to build additional rooms or to improve and maintain their houses. In the following pages I will discuss internal subsidies and investment, by which I mean funds used to provide new or improved rooms either for close relatives who live inside the houses surveyed or for tenants. In internal subsidy, I include help given by the compound head to his newly-married son or daughter, or to any other married, divorced, or widowed family member in need of shelter, while expenditures on new or improved rooms for renting are listed as investment.

Under these terms, of the 19 rooms between 1964 and 1969 one was fully subsidized and given to his son

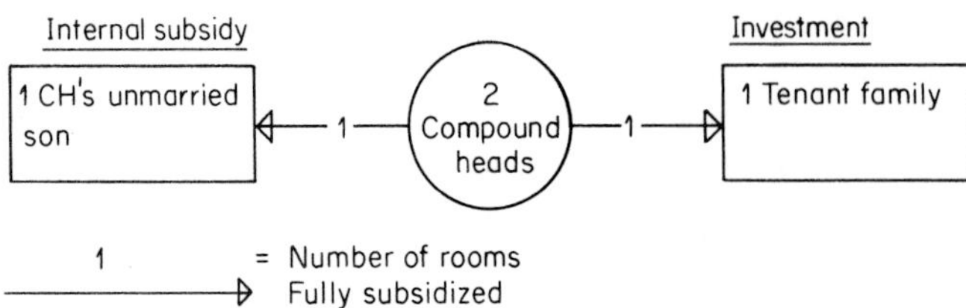

Diagram 18.1
Distribution of internal subsidy and investment

by a compound head, while another room was rented to a tenant family. Diagram 18.1 illustrates the main characteristics of internal subsidy and investment on new constructions made by these two compound heads during the five years from 1964 to 1969. One room, costing DH1,470, was fully financed by the compound head and given to his son who was expecting to marry, while a second room, costing about DH900, was rented to a tenant family after completion.

Improvements to four rooms costing about DH850 were carried out by two compound heads. Two of these rooms were given to a compound head's daughter and her family, while the other were rented to a stranger's family.

To conclude, my survey of 75 traditional houses in the walled city of Marrakech has revealed that of the total of DH94,300 spent on new construction, improvements, and maintenance during a period of five years, DH6,250 or 6.6 per cent was in the form of government loans and grants, DH12,900 or 13.7 per cent was in the form of private loans and gifts, while the rest, amounting to 79.7 per cent, derived from the private savings and incomes of the compound heads concerned. During the five-year period under study, only 19 rooms were built by seven compound heads in the sample. Preliminary data indicate that the cost of construction for these rooms was in the region of DH105 per square metre, which is about one half the cost per square metre of the modern 'low-cost houses' built by the Ministère des Travaux Publics in the northern parts of the city.

Notes and references

1 Banque Marocaine du Commerce Extérieur (BMCE), *Bulletin mensuel d'informations* (Casablanca), no. 123, 1972, pp. 16–17.
2 Service Central des Statistiques, Royaume du Maroc, *Annuaire statistique du Maroc 1960–1972*, Rabat, 1961–1973.
3 Service Central des Statistiques, Royaume du Maroc, op. cit., Tables: 'Ceramique-materiaux de construction'.
4 BMCE, op. cit., pp. 16–17.

5 Service Central des Statistiques, Royaume du Maroc, *Annuaire Statistique du Maroc 1972*, Rabat, 1973, p. 56.
6 BMCE, *Bulletin mensuel d'informations*, no. 118, 1971, 'Le Bois au Maroc', p. 3.
7 United Nations, *The Growth of World Industry 1971*, vol. 2, 'Commodity Production Data 1962–71', New York, 1973, p. 347.
8 BMCE, *Bulletin mensuel d'informations*, no. 123, pp. 16–17.
9 United Nations, *Statistical Yearbook 1972*, New York, 1973, pp. 304–305.
10 United Nations, *Yearbook of International Trade Statistics 1969*, New York, 1971, p. 579. This figure was estimated from the imports of various steel products mainly used by the construction industry. See also Table A.18.2 on p. 448.
11 Service Central des Statistiques, Royaume du Maroc, *Résultats du recensement de 1960*, vol. 2, Rabat, 1965, pp. 300, 344.
12 Service Central des Statistiques, Royaume du Maroc, *Annuaire statistique du Maroc 1964–1968*, Table: 'Indices de la production industrielle'.

Part IV

COMPARISON AND CONCLUSION

Chapter 19

Comparison

In preceding chapters I have analysed the survey data collected at Zaria, Ibadan, and Marrakech independently. In this chapter I intend to compare the most important data collected in these towns. As all three towns have a predominantly Muslim population, an attempt must also be made to evaluate the influence of Islam on their traditional houses and co-residential kinship groups. We may recall that the aim of this study was to investigate traditional urban housing in three different pre-industrial Muslim African cultures, and to determine the relationship between the size and composition of co-residential kinship groups and the type and layout of houses. It was also intended to learn how these houses were built, maintained, and financed.

The towns

The towns of Zaria, Ibadan, and Marrakech were founded in the fifteenth, nineteenth, and eleventh centuries respectively. Zaria, a Hausa city, is located in the savannah belt of Northern Nigeria; Ibadan, the modern Yoruba metropolis, lies within the high rain forest of Southern Nigeria; while Marrakech, the ancient capital of Morocco, is situated on the western slopes of the High Atlas Mountains in North Africa. At the time of my field studies, all three towns had a predominantly Muslim population. In each, the people were mainly engaged in farming for subsistence and/or sale, in handicrafts, trade, and local administration. Building activities initiated by or linked with colonial interests have mostly taken place outside the old established towns, thus leaving them virtually untouched by modern development until quite recently.

Growth of population

By the early 1970s the Zaria Urban Area had an estimated population of about 170,000, while Ibadan had over 1 million inhabitants, and Marrakech 333,000. Over the decades 1950–1970, the population of the Zaria Urban area increased by about 6 per cent per annum, Ibadan by over 7 per cent, and Marrakech by 2.9 per cent. On the other hand, the populations of the walled cities at Zaria and Marrakech had a much lower growth rate and increased by only 1.5 per cent and 0.7 per cent per annum respectively during this period.

Type of buildings

In Chapters 4, 10, and 16 I briefly described the traditional types of urban houses most frequently found in the three cities under investigation. In the following pages I will summarize some of the most salient features of these houses.

In Zaria the layout and organization of compounds with several courtyards surrounded by high mud walls were designed to provide a high degree of security and privacy for the compound head and his wife or wives, many of whom were living in complete or partial seclusion. Normally, each adult member of the compound has his own room or rooms which are usually abandoned after his or her death and in many cases are allowed to collapse. Each new generation of compound heads usually rebuild part of their compounds according to the needs of their families and dependents. This entails that the construction of compounds is a continuous process which reflects the size and changes of the co-residential kinship group that occupies it.

In Ibadan most houses consist of a double row of rooms which open onto a central hall or passageway. Doors and windows are usually open during daytime to allow for some cross-ventilation essential for the comfort of the inhabitants in this warm and humid climate. Women are not restricted by purdah and play active parts in the economic life of the city.

At Marrakech the most common house type is the two-storey central courtyard house. All rooms in these houses open onto the central courtyard or garden. This house type is well adapted to the hot and dry summer months, needs comparatively little space, and provides a high degree of privacy and seclusion even in such a densely populated place as the *medina* of Marrakech.

All houses included in my survey were constructed with locally manufactured building materials except for corrugated iron sheets used as roofing material in Ibadan, and all building was carried out by locally trained labourers with the help of family members or small indigenous building contractors.

Age and sex distribution

The age and sex distribution of my sample populations at Zaria, Ibadan, and Marrakech are given in Table 19.1. A comparison between the three towns shows a roughly similar pattern of inner-city populations covered by the survey, but there are regional differences. As expected, young people up to the age of 15 contribute over 40 per cent of the total sample population. This relatively high proportion of young people is a typical feature of rapidly growing towns in Third World countries. A comparison of the latest census data for each whole town with the findings of the sample survey shows very similar age distributions. Hence, we can dismiss the possibility that we have depicted ageing populations which have congregated in these inner-city areas, as opposed to younger populations in the peripheral areas of these cities.

With 41.3 per cent of the sample population, Ibadan, of the three samples, had the lowest proportion of young people in the age group 0–14. This is mainly due to the high rate of immigration of people in the age group 15–50 who came to Ibadan in search of work. This was not found

Table 19.1 Age and sex distribution of sample populations, in percentages

Age and sex	Zaria	Ibadan	Marrakech
0–14	46.7	41.3	44.6
15–50	44.3	49.6	41.0
50+	9.0	9.1	14.4
Male	45.2	48.1	45.5
Female	54.8	51.9	54.5
Total	100.0	100.0	100.0

in the walled cities of Zaria and Marrakech. Of the sample populations in Zaria and Ibadan, about 9 per cent were over the age of 50, while in Marrakech this age group accounted for 14.4 per cent. According to the last census data for Marrakech, this ratio held also for the whole city. We can thus assume that differing customs, more favourable climatic conditions, and the improved health service in Marrakech may together have been largely responsible for the higher proportion of old people in the city.

In all three sample populations, females exceeded males, but various factors contributed to this imbalance. First, polygamy as practised in Zaria and Ibadan has certainly brought some women from elsewhere as wives into these cities. Second, prostitution normally flourishes in towns, bringing or keeping there an excessive number of females. Third, many able-bodied men have left Zaria and particularly Marrakech – which has the lowest male sample population – in search of better employment opportunities elsewhere.

Composition of domestic groups

Throughout this study the units of analysis are the occupants of a house or compound divided into households. As units of domestic economy households consist of all related or unrelated persons who occupy a common domicile, eat together for most of the year, and contribute in kind, labour, and/or money to the household budget. However, as data on household composition alone are insufficient to explain the growth and decline of co-residential kinship groups, all persons living within a house or compound were classified for analysis by their relationship to the compound head. This procedure enabled me to discern and trace the cyclical tendency which regulated the development of co-residential agnatic groups. As we have seen, the individual family consisting of a man, his wife or wives, and their unmarried children is the first and simplest stage in a development cycle which often gives rise to composite co-residential kinship groups. Altogether six stages in the developmental cycle of such domestic groups were identified, the last being that of a compound which housed paternal first cousins and their descendants. However, it must be remembered that at any stage these groups are liable to constant changes due either to the marriage or death of one of their male members, particularly the compound head, or to the emigration of dependent households caused by differential economic success, the lack of space, or tension, or disagreements among these households.

Table 19.2 compares differences in the percentage distributions of households related to the compound heads that illustrated each of the developmental stages in the samples at Zaria, Ibadan, and Marrakech. It is of interest that domestic groups at the first two stages of development – i.e. the compound head with his wife or wives and their own unmarried children, and/or married children accounted for only 18.1 per cent of all households surveyed in Ibadan, while in Marrakech the corresponding figure was 82.8 per cent. It is obvious that in Marrakech kinship groups split at an early stage, with only 5.1 per cent of all households found in houses with kinship groups at stage 3, whereas at Ibadan large co-residential kinship groups are the norm and account for about 69.0 per cent of all households interviewed. The population surveyed at Zaria lies somewhat between these two extremes, with 32.2 per cent of all related households in the first two stages of the developmental cycle, and 58.9 per cent of the sample households in stages 3 to 6.

Households related to the compound head which had joined their compounds of residence in recent years accounted for 8.9 per cent in Zaria, 12.9 per cent in Ibadan, and 12.1 per cent in Marrakech. These households were listed separately because their immigration into their host compounds neither influences nor contributes to the natural development of co-residential kinship groups.

We may now ask why domestic families divide at a relatively early stage in Marrakech and much later, if at all, in Zaria and Ibadan. To what extent do the layout and structure of the house or compound, the mode of land tenure, differing incomes of dependent household heads, and the influence of Islam, to cite only some important factors, impede or promote the division of co-residential kinship groups in the three samples? I will examine these questions in the light of my survey data and with the additional historic, religious, social, and economic background information given earlier on.

Table 19.2 Related households by stages of development, in percentages

	No. of hhs	Stage 1	Stage 2	Stage 3	Stages 4 + 5	Stage 6	Joint hhs	Total
Zaria	180	17.2	15.0	22.8	34.4	1.7	8.9	100.0
Ibadan	171	11.1	7.0	25.7	22.2	21.1	12.9	100.0
Marrakech	99	48.5	34.3	5.1	–	–	12.1	100.0

However, before pursuing these questions, we should briefly discuss the 226 unrelated households included in the three surveys. Of these, 215 or 95.1 per cent paid a weekly or monthly rent for their room or rooms. Together these households accounted for one third of the total sample of households. As they do not belong to the kinship group of the compound head, they were listed and analysed separately. The differing incidence of these unrelated households in the three samples is noteworthy. At Zaria, only 5.8 per cent of all households surveyed were unrelated, while at Ibadan and Marrakech these figures rose to 42 per cent and 47.9 per cent respectively. Most of these stranger households are small and consisted of single, divorced, and widowed persons, childless couples, or individual families. The ratio of immigrants among the heads of stranger households was 100 per cent in Zaria, 95.2 per cent in Ibadan, and 58.2 per cent in Marrakech. While the varying distribution of tenant households within these three samples suggests different rates and volumes of immigration in these towns, the proportion of first-generation immigrants among these household heads indicates that these cities have recently experienced different patterns of growth.

The building of houses

The volume of new construction in the three samples of compounds differs widely. Table 19.3 shows the total area and the area which was constructed during the five-year period that preceded the date of each survey. In Zaria construction in this period accounted for 1,773 sq. m or 16.9 per cent of the total floor area of the sample compounds, whereas in Ibadan and Marrakech these figures dropped to 575 sq. m or 6 per cent, and 224 sq. m or 2.7 per cent respectively. As we have seen in Zaria, most new rooms were built as a direct response to the housing needs of expanding families, while at Ibadan and Marrakech increasing demand for rented accommodation motivated some compound heads to build more rooms. However, it should be stressed that the layout and organization of compounds at Zaria are relatively flexible by comparison with those of Ibadan and Marrakech, while construction costs are also much lower. These conditions enable compound heads to add more rooms as the need arises. By comparison with Zaria, the cities of Ibadan and Marrakech have much higher population densities, and as building plots become increasingly scarce, building activities are naturally more restricted and costs tend to rise.

Table 19.3 Total floor area and area of new construction built between 1963 and 1969

	Zaria			Ibadan			Marrakech		
	Total m² in 1968	Built 1963–1968	% of total area	Total m² in 1968	Built 1963–1968	% of total area	Total m² in 1969	Built 1964–1969	% of total area
Floor area	10,473.4	1,772.5	16.9	9,522.3	575.1	6.0	8,326.0	224.4	2.7

Directly connected with these different volumes of new construction in the three samples are differences in the median age of sample rooms. At Zaria, for example, the median age of rooms is around 12 years, which indicates that nearly all living and sleeping rooms are replaced at each new generation of compound heads. In other words, a room lasts as long as its occupants are alive. Such periodic rebuilding of rooms at short intervals requires low construction costs and the recycling of building materials such as mud, used for the construction of walls, and roof beams. In Ibadan the median age of rooms was found to be about 26 years. The increased 'life expectancy' of these Yoruba houses may be primarily due to their corrugated iron roofs which protect the mud walls much better than traditional thatched roofs. The survey at Ibadan also revealed that a large number of inherited houses were used almost unaltered by the second and even third generation of their compound heads. Unfortunately, the median age of rooms in Marrakech could not be calculated as most compound heads did not know the age of their houses. However, historic data suggest that the median age of houses surveyed exceeded 50 years. During the five-year period from 1964 to 1969 only 2.7 per cent of the total floor area was built by 13 out of 68 interviewed compound heads. This was partly due to the lack of building plots, the mode of existing construction, and the relatively high building costs in the *medina* of Marrakech.

Expenditure on housing

Expenditure on housing in the three cities follows closely the pattern of building activities discussed above. Table 19.4 compares the percentage distribution of the various types of expenditure on house building. In Zaria and Ibadan the cost of new construction was the most important item of housing expenditure, while in Marrakech expenditure on improvements rank first. This indicates that in Zaria and to a lesser extent in Ibadan land

Table 19.4 Types of building expenditure, in percentages

	Zaria	Ibadan	Marrakech
Cost of new construction	44.4	48.5	24.7
Cost of improvements	27.7	22.1	41.7
Cost of repair	23.6	26.3	24.8
Cost of build. under constr.	2.4	–	8.8
Cost of misc. constructions	1.9	3.1	–
Total percentage	100.0	100.0	100.0

for new construction is still available, whereas in Marrakech the lack of suitable building land forces many compound heads to sell their houses and to buy bigger ones which are then improved according to the compound heads' financial abilities.

Distribution of floor area

The distribution of floor area among the populations of the sample houses was studied in two ways. First, I calculated the average floor area per person classified by their relationship to the compound head; and second I calculated the average floor area per person according to the number of persons per household. However, as these calculations of average floor area per person cover all rooms including entrance halls, store rooms, kitchens, bathrooms, and workshops, it seems that the area of rooms used for sleeping provides a more useful measure of space standards among the populations in the houses surveyed. Table 19.5 sets out the average sleeping areas for members of compound heads' households, of dependent households, and of tenant households separately. As can be seen, the average sleeping area of members of the compound heads' households was very similar in all three samples, namely, 4.8 sq. m in Zaria, 4.7 sq. m in Ibadan, and 4.6 sq. m in Marrakech. This convergence is especially significant, given the wide differences in the house types and in the composition of co-residential kinship groups in the three samples. The average sleeping area per person belonging to dependent or semi-dependent households was 3.9 sq. m in Zaria, 3.0 sq. m in Ibadan, and 3.1 sq. m in Marrakech, all of which are lower than comparable figures for compound heads' households. The average sleeping area per person belonging to tenants' households was 3.6 sq. m in Ibadan and 3.4 sq. m in Marrakech.

Table 19.5 Average area per person, in square metres

Type of Household	Zaria		Ibadan			Marrakech		
	CH	DHH	CH	DHH	THH	CH	DHH	THH
Average sleeping area	4.8	3.9	4.7	3.0	3.6	4.6	3.1	3.4
Total av. floor area	12.8	6.0	12.7	4.2	4.8	14.2	4.7	5.4

CH = compound head. DHH = dependent household head. THH = tenant household head.

It is interesting to recall that in all three samples the average sleeping area per person fell slightly as the number of persons per household increased, but levelled off in households containing 3 or 4 persons and remained almost stable for all larger households. This suggests that in Zaria and to some extent in Ibadan, new rooms were constructed as the need arose, whereas at Marrakech dependent households had to emigrate when the compound head was unable to provide the extra accommodation required. This procedure enabled resident households to maintain a minimum space standard in spite of an increasing household population. The inquiry into the sleeping area per person revealed that in spite of differences in these cultures, in the type of houses surveyed and in the composition of co-residential kinship groups, a striking convergence of the space standards obtains in all three samples. This may indicate that a common minimum space standard is unconsciously observed by the urban populations from which these samples were drawn.

The use of space

For analysis, the floor area of all houses surveyed was divided into four main categories: first, living area, which includes all sitting and sleeping rooms; second, such common rooms as entrance lobbies and corridors; third, such basic ancillary facilities as kitchens, bathrooms, and store rooms; and fourth, rooms used commercially. Table 19.6 shows that at Zaria and Marrakech the percentage distribution of the first three categories, namely, living area, common rooms, and basic ancillary facilities, represented about 70 per cent, 15 per cent, and 12 per cent of total floor area respectively. Commercially used rooms accounted for 3.8 per cent of the total floor area surveyed in Zaria, and 1.5 per cent of that in Marrakech. By contrast, in Ibadan nearly 84 per cent of the total floor space was living area, commonly used rooms accounted for 5.7 per cent, basic ancillary facilities for 7.6 per cent, and commercially used rooms for 3.1 per cent. It is

Table 19.6 The use of floor area, in percentages

	Zaria	Ibadan	Marrakech
Living area	67.6	83.6	70.9
Commonly used rooms	16.1	5.7	15.3
Basic ancillary facilities	12.5	7.6	12.3
Commercially used rooms	3.8	3.1	1.5
Total	100.0	100.0	100.0

interesting to note that 8.2 per cent of the total floor area in Zaria consisted of empty rooms, 3.6 per cent in Ibadan, and 9.2 per cent in Marrakech. These empty rooms are frequently used by the compound head to accommodate newly married wives or relatives in need of shelter. Hence houses were most economically used in Ibadan where 84 per cent of the floor area represented the living area, as compared with about 70 per cent in Zaria and Marrakech.

Land tenure

Besides housing itself, two other factors also influence the size and composition of domestic groups in these samples. One is the mode of land tenure which plays an important part in structuring the composition of co-residential kinship groups. For example, as we have seen in the walled city of Zaria and in the centre of Ibadan, most land is held by agnatic descent groups. Normally, these groups distribute their lands among their members who all enjoy usufructuary rights but cannot alienate the plots they occupy without the consent of all adult male members of the descent group. In spite of such restrictions, some land is none the less sold, but the bulk of it, including 'family compounds', still passes down within the lineage or lineage segment, unaffected by modern developments. If anything the increasing cash value of urban land and its growing scarcity, as well as the urban population increases, have probably strengthened the role of the descent group as a corporate landholder. In consequence, descent groups tend to congregate in ancestral family compounds and on their corporately owned lands, thus ensuring the development of those large and complex co-residential kinship groups I found in Zaria and Ibadan. At Marrakech, on the other hand, most houses included in my sample were owned by individuals. With few exceptions, these individuals are free to sell the house in whole or part. This situation has enabled many a compound head to sell part of the house in order to provide his son or sons with the necessary funds to buy, lease, or even build their own houses elsewhere, often outside the old city walls.

Income distribution

The level and distribution of income among the various categories of household heads is the second factor which influences the size and composition of domestic groups. As shown in Table 19.7, while compound heads had on average the highest incomes in all three samples, most heads of dependent and tenant households were in the low-income category. The major exception to this pattern is found among the heads of dependent households in Marrakech, 60 per cent of whom belonged to the middle income group, and were thus financially in a better position to leave their father's or brothers' house and establish their own independent household elsewhere should the need arise. However, it seems likely that the very low overall incomes of most heads of dependent and tenant households included in the sample severely restrict their mobility and above all their choice of residence.

The financing of houses

As mentioned above, the financial resources used for housing construction and other building activities derive from three main sources. First, there are the personal savings and incomes of the compound heads; second, gifts or loans from family members and friends; and third, loans or grants from government sponsored housing

Table 19.7 Distribution of income, in percentages

	Zaria		Ibadan			Marrakech		
	CH	DHH	CH	DHH	THH	CH	DHH	THH
Low-income group[a]	53.2	85.8	32.8	63.6	58.7	25.0	36.0	83.3
Middle-income group[b]	41.6	14.2	50.0	36.4	39.1	57.8	60.0	16.7
High-income group[c]	5.2	–	17.2	–	2.2	17.2	4.0	–
Total	100.0	100.0	100.0	100.0	100.0	100.0	100.0	100.0

[a]Under 300s. or DH210 per month.
[b]Under 1,000s. or DH700 per month.
[c]Over 1,000s. or DH700 per month.

agencies, from building societies, or from banks. Table 19.8 compares the percentage distribution of funds drawn from these alternative sources for the three samples. The table shows that in Zaria, Ibadan, and Marrakech between 80 and 94 per cent of the total cash expenditure on buildings over a five-year period preceding my surveys came from the personal incomes and savings of compound heads and any other dependent household heads engaged in building activities. Gifts and loans from family members and friends accounted for about 14 per cent of these expenditures in Zaria and Marrakech, but only for 6.2 per cent in Ibadan. Financial help received from institutional sources accounted for 6.6 per cent of the total cash expenditure on housing in Marrakech, as against 1.7 per cent in Zaria and zero in Ibadan. Thus, in these three surveys, institutional aid for house building is absent or marginal.

This lack of official support, particularly in Zaria and Ibadan, may be due to three reasons. First, the mode of land tenure may discourage financial institutions modelled on Western prototypes from investment, as these agencies insist on clear titles to land and regard corporately owned land as a security risk in case of litigation and mortgage default. Second, most institutions that lend for housing require borrowers to use only permanent building materials for the construction of houses that they finance. Third, the low average cash income of most compound heads frustrates provision of credit. My sample at Marrakech has shown that most houses were owned by individuals who had a clear title to the land which is also registered in the municipality's land registrar's office. If required, these titles could be used as security to obtain housing loans either from the government or from the compound heads' employers.

Cost of traditional buildings

The cost per 'unit area' in the traditional housing sector was found to be roughly one third of that of modern houses constructed by building societies, housing corporations, and government agencies in Zaria and Ibadan, and about half the cost of modern buildings in Marrakech. This is mainly due to the use of relatively inexpensive building materials and cheap labour, as well as to the lack of such services as piped water, sewerage, and an electricity supply which are normally provided in modern houses.

Table 19.8 Sources of housing funds, in percentages

	Zaria	Ibadan	Marrakech
CH's personal income	83.9	93.8	79.7
Loans & gifts from family	14.4	6.2	13.7
Loans & grants from Institutions	1.7	–	6.6
Total	100.0	100.0	100.0

The influence of Islam on houses

The religious background

As shown in Chapters 1, 7, and 13, the older parts of the three towns investigated have a predominantly Muslim population. We may recall that about 60 per cent of the inhabitants of Ibadan and over 90 per cent in the walled cities of Zaria and Marrakech call themselves Muslims. What effect, one may ask, has this had or does it still have on the traditional types of housing to be found in these three African cities? The impact of Islam on traditional houses and their inhabitants varied according to the cultural and historic development of the town, its ethnic base, the length of time the society had been exposed to Islam, the mode of its Islam, and the way in which Islam was initially adopted. However, before discussing their differences, we have to look at the religious and civil laws of Islam common to all these towns.

The Shari'a, or sacred law based on the Koran, formally governs the entire lives of Muslims. Its most important aspects are the religious laws that regulate purification, ritual prayer, fasting, pilgrimage, and alms giving, and the civil law which regulates the conduct of the individual *vis-à-vis* the community and its members.

The outward signs of a Muslim community are the mosque, the Koranic school, a system of qadi's courts, the Islamic rites of naming, marriage, and burial, as well as the law of succession and, last but not least, markets and distinctive trading classes.

The seclusion of women practised today with various degrees of rigidity in most Muslim countries has influenced the design of houses probably more than any other single factor. Its justification derives from the Koran, chapter 33, Al-Ahzab, verse 33 'And stay in your houses and display not your beauty . . .'[1] Originally applied only to the wives of the Prophet, that verse was later interpreted to mean the wives of Muslims, and thus their seclusion or purdah was accordingly practised. It should be pointed out that the Koran never forbids women to go out of the house for their needs, nor was any occupation forbidden to them. However, the seclusion of women is an ancient custom, and it was practised in one form or another among people of the Middle East long before the appearance of Islam.

The Koran is explicit on the privacy it grants to the inhabitants of houses, making homes practically inaccessible to all strangers unless permission is given.[2] In addition, the Prophet disapproved strongly of idol-worship, and this has eliminated most pre-Islamic altars or religious symbols in houses, particularly in societies where Islam was introduced early.[3]

Maliki law, as outlined in the *Mukhtasar* of Sidi Khalil, forms the basis of the religious and civil law practised in North and West Africa except in Egypt.[4] Maliki law gives no recommendations or rules about how to design or build a house, thus leaving these matters to popular choice. Instead, the law considers certain areas of conflict such as disputed rights of way between a house owner and the community, and between individuals, especially neighbours over the use of a common wall.[5] Furthermore, the law stresses the need for friendly cooperation as far as the construction of buildings is concerned.

We must now consider briefly the main historical events which have characterized the expansion of Islam in North and West Africa.[6] As already remarked, the spread of Islam along the Mediterranean coast of Africa from the seventh to the eleventh centuries was carried out by nomad Arabs. The Arabization of towns by conquest was completed throughout this region by the twelfth century, but in the mountainous regions of Morocco the indigenous Berber tribes retained their social structure and language (see pp. 187 and 223).

The spread of Islam across the Sahara into the Sudan belt of West Africa started in the eleventh century and was mainly the work of traders and clerics. Although adopted then as the imperial cult by the ruling classes in states such as Mali and Kanem, and somewhat later by most Habe dynasties of Hausaland, its effect on the mass of people was rather limited.

The second half of the eighteenth and the beginning of the nineteenth century saw the appearance of several militant Islamic movements led by such outstanding reformers as Uthman dan Fodio, Shehu Hamadu, and Al-hajj Umar who, after proclaiming their respective holy wars, brought large areas of the Sudan belt under their control.

The result was the emergence of several theocratic states, which represented the first serious attempt to bring Islam to the majority of people in these states. Islamic religious and civil laws were enforced and a large number of people were converted, particularly in urban centres.

The occupation of West Africa by France and Britain in the late nineteenth century and early twentieth centuries brought peace and stability to the whole area, a condition under which Islam could expand again rapidly.[7] Stability and the expansion of trading activities were accompanied by other changes which flowed from the colonial occupation, such as the introduction of Western culture, languages, government, education, and technology, which together wrought in a relatively short time more drastic changes in the design and construction of houses than Islam had achieved despite its long history in North and West Africa.

The influence of Christianity which spread during the colonial era should also be briefly considered, since this was accompanied by the diffusion of secular outlook on religion hitherto unknown to Africans whether Muslim or not, all of whom regarded religion and life as a completely integrated entity. In areas where Islam and Christianity penetrated simultaneously, such as Yorubaland, these secular conceptions had their effect on newly converted Muslims who, in order to avoid conflicts either with traditional customs and beliefs or with Christianity, frequently adopted rather secular attitudes towards Islam, similar to those adopted by their brethren who became Christians. Such orientations encouraged religious tolerance so that religion was redefined as a matter of personal belief, and has come to be regarded merely as one of the many important dimensions of life. It is thus not surprising that such attitudes had a strong influence on the development of the traditional house in Ibadan.

The introduction of Islam into Africa over the last millennium, then, depended on several factors which included *inter alia* tribal movements, trading relations, conquests, political domination, as well as linguistic and cultural assimilation. J. S. Trimingham has identified three successive stages which he has called 'germination, crisis and gradual reorientation'.[8] The first stage is characterized by the adoption of some aspects of Islamic material culture, while during the second and third stages Islamic socio-religious culture becomes an integral part of life in the community. Except perhaps in the theocratic states of the nineteenth century and in the Christian south, the process of conversion may have taken three or more generations. Thus the houses and compounds of commoners were probably only affected by Islamic models, whether social or architectural, during the latter part of the conversion process, if at all.

The house

As already mentioned, Islam has no explicit religious or civil laws regulating the design of private houses. However, there is little doubt that Islam has influenced domestic architecture.

As shown on p. 215, the courtyard house, which is regarded today as almost synonymous with the 'Muslim house', was in existence long before Islam made its appearance on the Arabian Peninsula in the seventh century AD. Archaeological evidence suggests that the courtyard house was in existence in the seventh millennium BC in Mesopotamia and what is now known as Turkey, from where it probably spread throughout the mediterranean countries. Climatic and socio-economic factors rather than religious considerations are most likely the predominant factors which governed its development. Other non-religious factors such as building materials, techniques and skills available to communities, their need for security, and the scarcity of land, particularly in urban centres, must also have contributed to the final shape of these pre-Islamic courtyard houses. Hence, Islam has at best modified a much older house type that prevailed in Arabia, although Arabic culture as well as socio-political organizations and kinship forms has certainly influenced its form.[9] In order to isolate those features of design[10] which may have had their roots in Islamic religious and civil laws, we need to look again at the various urban house types found in the three cities under study.

Marrakech

Long before the Arab invasion of North Africa, the Graeco-Roman courtyard house was the predominant type of homestead in all coastal towns. One of its design characteristics was the direct access through a narrow corridor or room into the courtyard, allowing passers-by occasional glimpses into the courtyard or atrium.[11]

The principal characteristics of the Marrakech courtyard house have been described on pp. 214–222. However, some further comments are necessary here. As mentioned earlier, the entrance to a house is usually in one of its corners and a visitor has to pass through a succession of small rooms and/or corridors in order to reach the courtyard. No direct view from the street or alleyway into the courtyard is possible. A visitor is normally entertained in a large reception room situated either on the ground floor or the first floor but always near the main entrance. No special area of the house is reserved for women. Purdah is not strictly enforced and women are allowed to go out, some partly veiled. To what extent the entrance to the house has been influenced by Islamic laws, which lay great emphasis on domestic privacy, and to what extent it was determined by pre-Islamic cultures of Berber and other earlier civilizations, is difficult to say. However, at least two non-religious factors – the protection of the inhabitants and the traditional secrecy of the Arab life-style – are also partly responsible for this arrangement.

The house shown in Plan 19.1 has two courtyards. The main courtyard has a marble fountain surrounded by four large flower-beds, while the smaller courtyard was originally reserved for women and servants. Although the present owner no longer observes purdah, and the second courtyard is little used by the family, it is an excellent example of a traditional Muslim house. Visitors are normally received in a well-furnished room facing the main courtyard, while the female occupants of the house can go about their daily work without being seen. The layout of the house is ideally suited for the segregation of women if required.

The dotted line in the plan indicates the route visitors have to take in order to reach the reception room, as well as the way to the women's quarters.

In the house shown in Plan 19.2 the reception room is located on the first floor. A staircase in the entrance lobby leads directly to the reception room. The window-sill in this room is placed about 0.8 m above floor level preventing visitors, who normally sit on the narrow mattress alongside the wall, from looking into the courtyard below where the women work.

As in the previous example, the reception room in Plan 19.3 is located on the first floor, while the ground floor of the house, including the courtyard, is reserved for the inhabitants of the house. However, it must be pointed out here that among the urban poor in Marrakech who live in very crowded conditions, the segregation of women or purdah has never been practised nor can it be enforced. (For more information see Plan 16.3 on p. 222.)

Zaria

Islam may have arrived at Zaria in the fifteenth century. However, it was not until the successful Fulani holy war

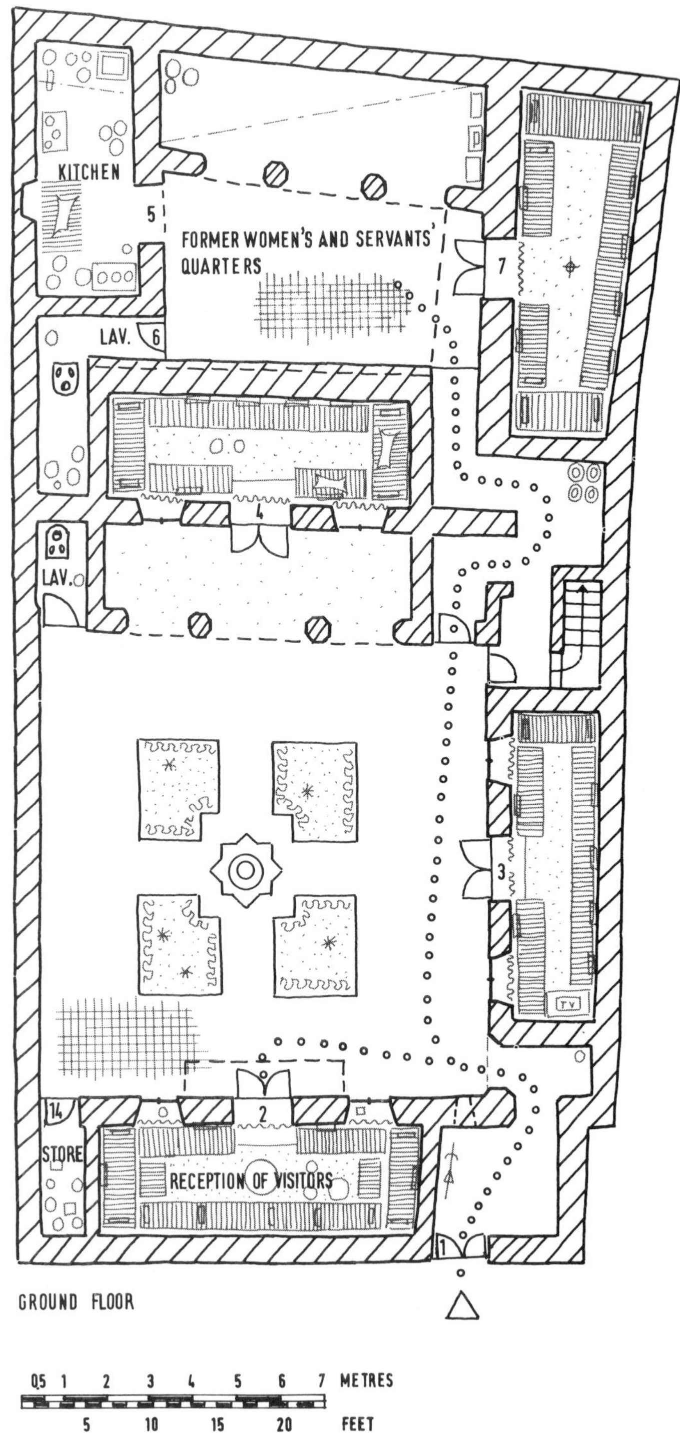

Plan 19.1
House 45 (Marrakech)

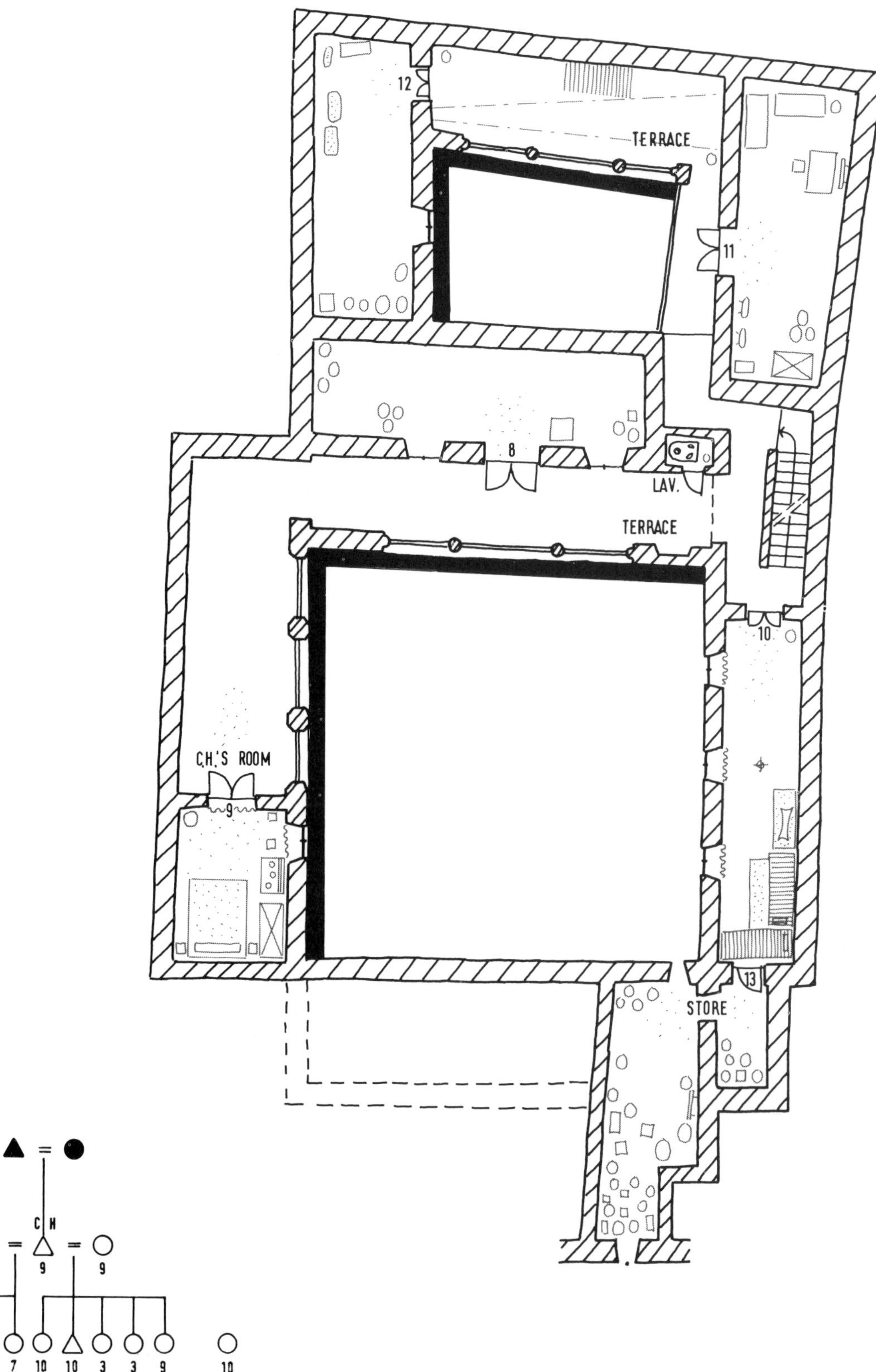
12
TERRACE
11
8
LAV.
TERRACE
10
C.H.'S ROOM
9
13
STORE
C H
9
9
9
7
10
10
3
3
9
10

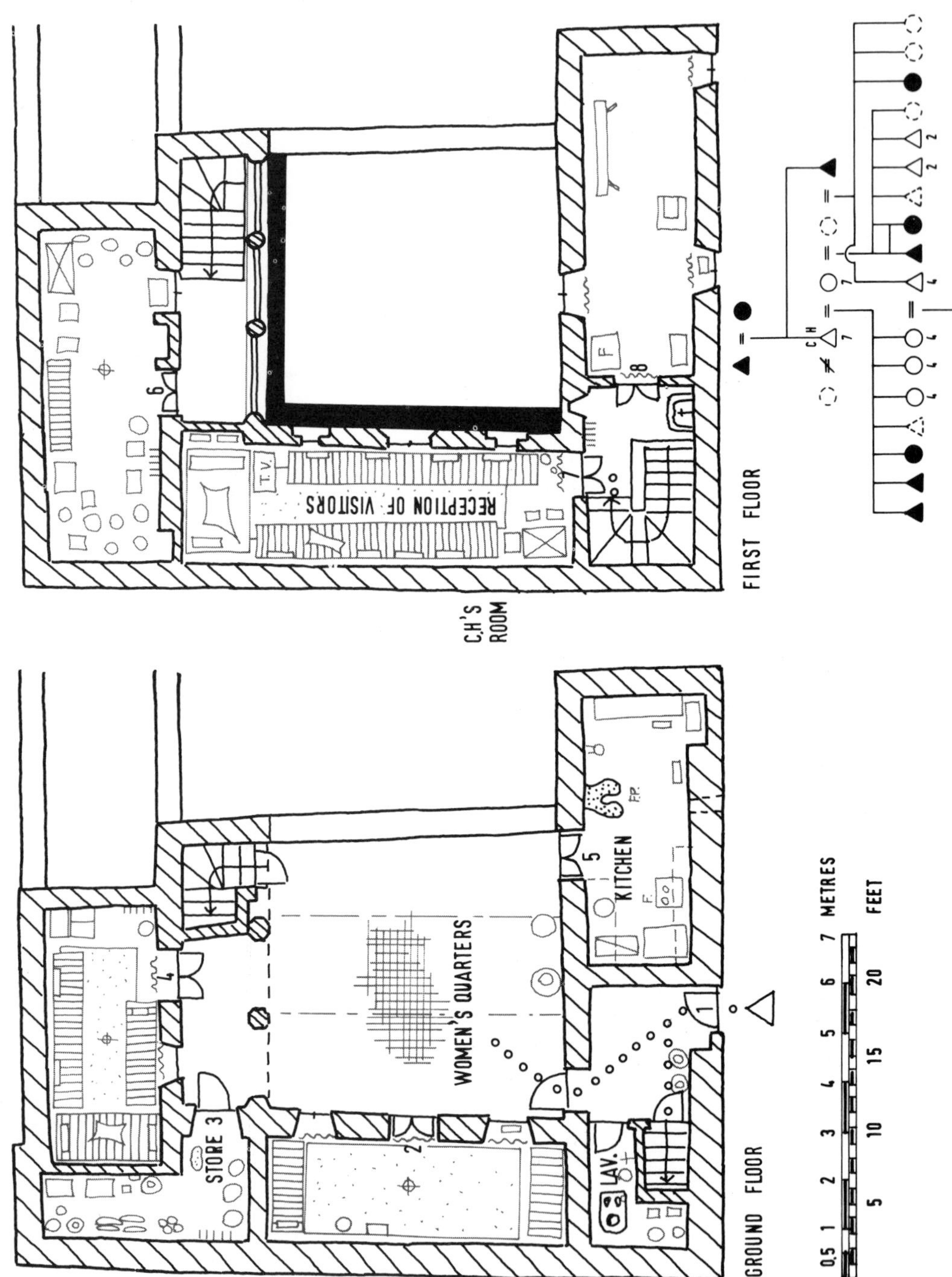
GROUND FLOOR
FIRST FLOOR
WOMEN'S QUARTERS
KITCHEN
STORE 3
LAV.
F.P.
RECEPTION OF VISITORS
T.V.
C.H'S ROOM
C H
METRES
FEET
0.5 1 2 3 4 5 6 7
5 10 15 20

Plan 19.2

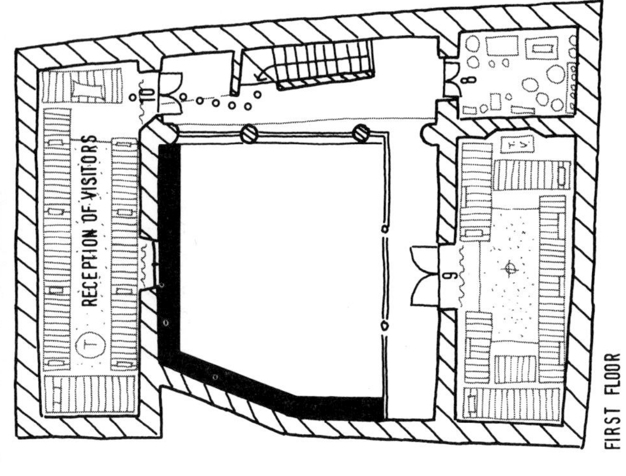

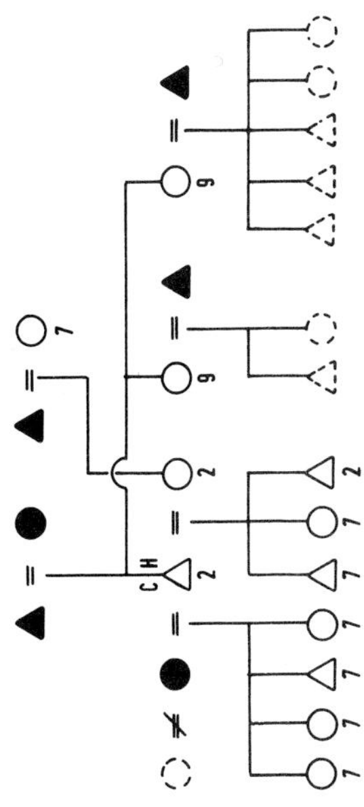

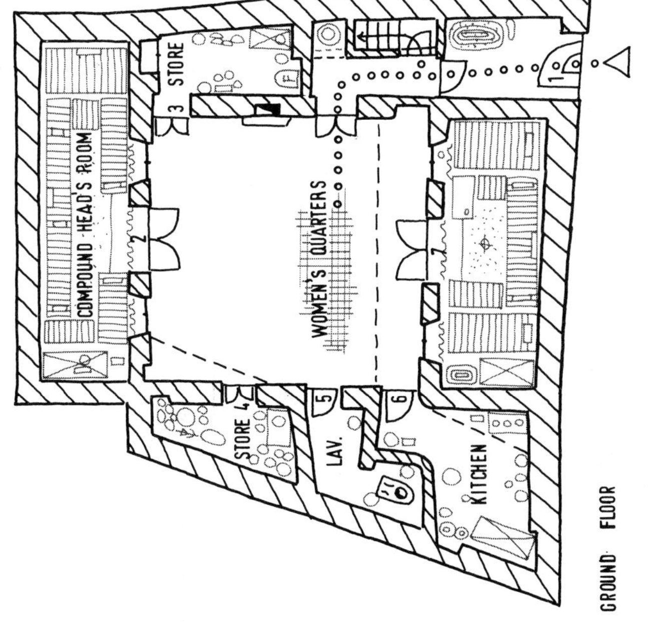

Plan 19.3
House 26 (Marrakech)

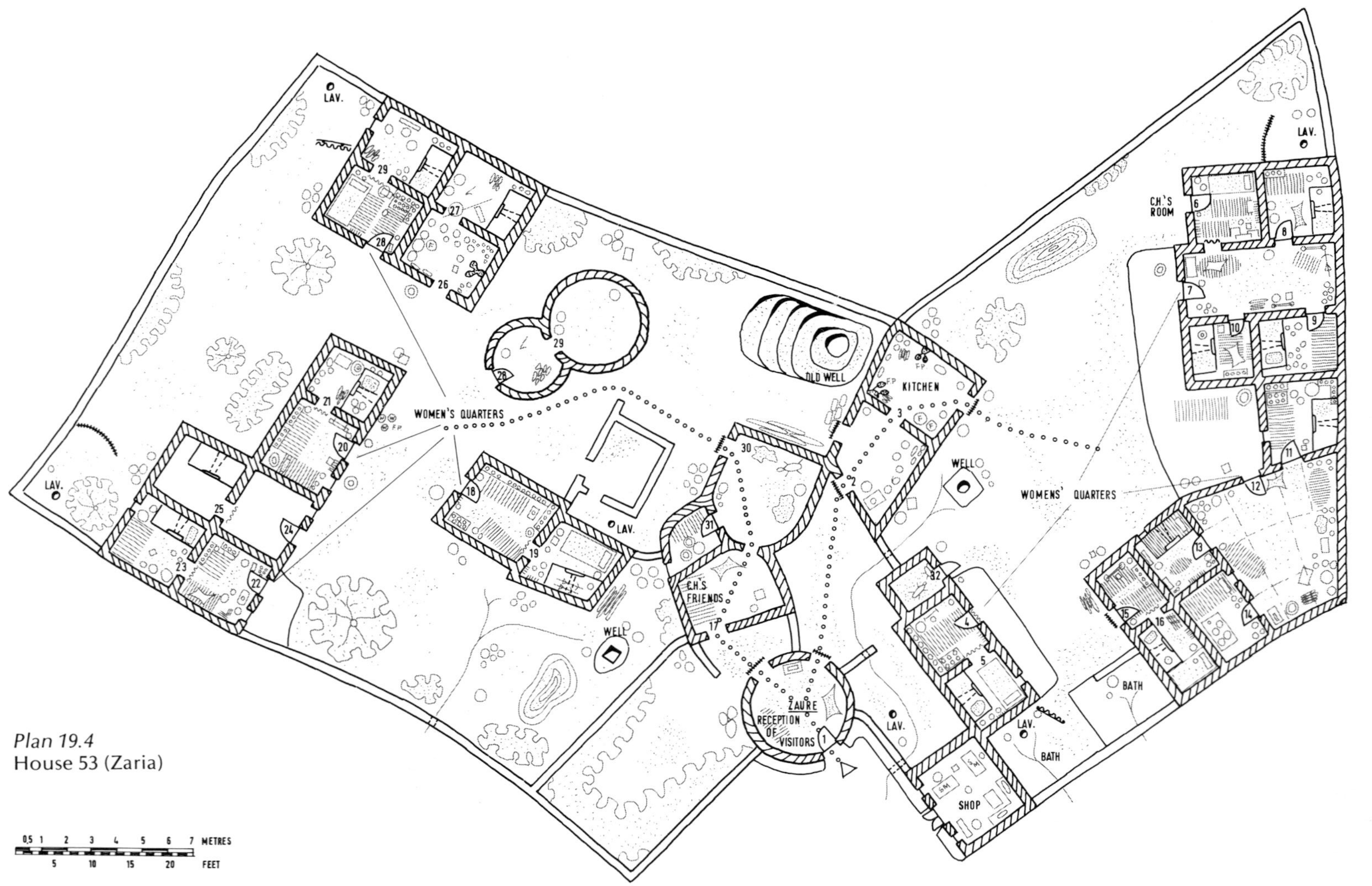

Plan 19.4
House 53 (Zaria)

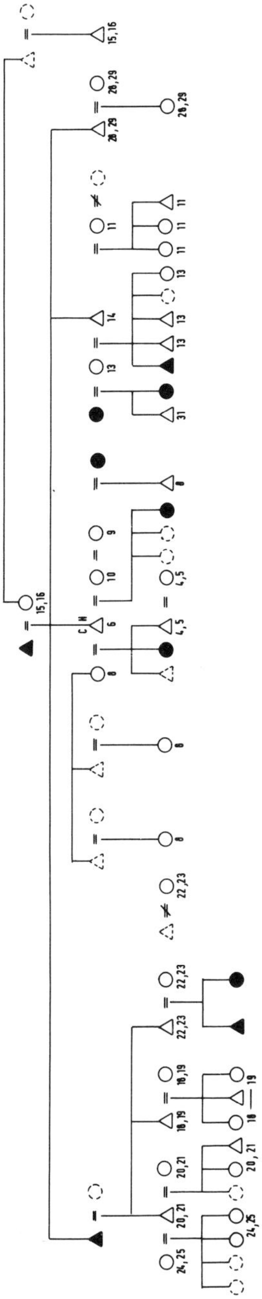

or *jihad* against the Habe dynasties of Hausaland at the start of the nineteenth century that the population of Zaria was obliged to observe Islam.

The major physical characteristics of the traditional Hausa compound in the walled city of Zaria have already been described on pp. 28–33. While very little is known about their origin and early development, these general patterns are believed to be very old and have probably little changed over the centuries.

The compound entrance is again of interest. To reach the interior of the compound one has to pass through an entrance hut, and then either through a forecourt and a second entrance room, or through a succession of rooms and/or corridors before reaching the central courtyard where the women's quarters are located. Strangers are normally not allowed into the interior, and will meet the compound head in the entrance hut. Heinrich Barth, who travelled through Bornu and Hausaland in the early 1850s, found very similar compound layouts.[12] The often very elaborate entrance arrangements clearly date from pre-Muslim times and reflect the need for the safety of the inhabitants rather than a domestic privacy motivated by religion, although it may now be interpreted in this way. It must also be remembered that Islam had only about 200 years in which to consolidate its influence on the community in Zaria. It is likely that the religious demand for domestic privacy and the seclusion of women, which is widely practised among the ruling class and the rich traders, fitted perfectly into the prevailing design patterns of urban compounds, which needed little or no alteration.

The compound shown in Plan 19.4 was originally built and occupied by two brothers who were mainly engaged in farming. Beyond a common entrance hut the compound is divided into two clearly distinguishable sections. To reach the centre of each house, the occupants have to pass through a small courtyard and two rooms. This arrangement indicates the importance Hausa urban society attaches to domestic privacy. The public and private areas of the house are clearly defined and are respected by the public. Men visiting the compound head are normally not allowed beyond the entrance room.

The compound shown in Plan 19.5 belongs to a wealthy trader who has some of his merchandise stored in the front part of the house. The private rooms of the compound head are situated almost in the centre of the house, close to the women's quarters. Friends of the compound head are usually not allowed beyond his rest room off the first courtyard.

The last example from Zaria, Plan 19.6, belongs to a

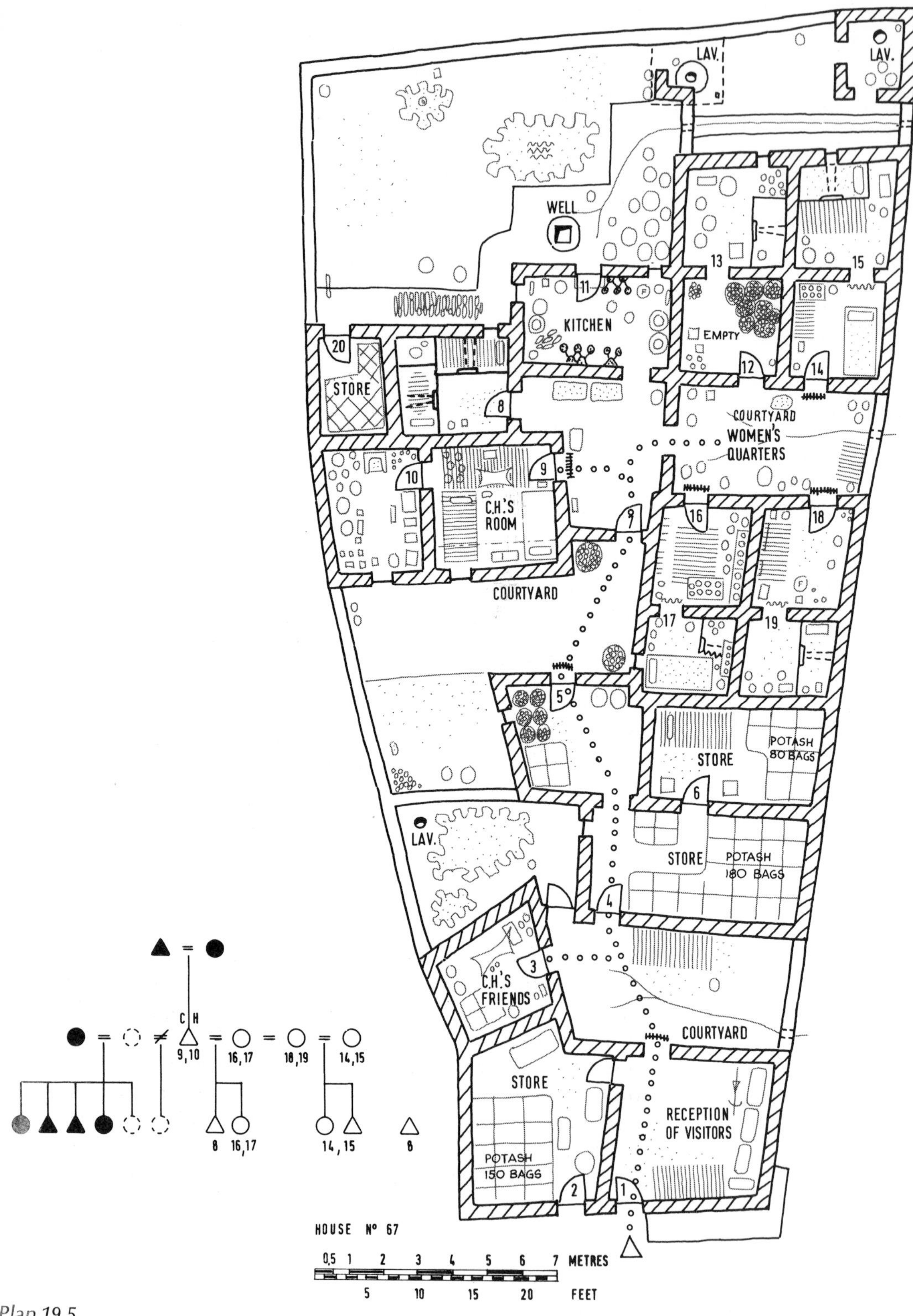

Plan 19.5
House 67 (Zaria)

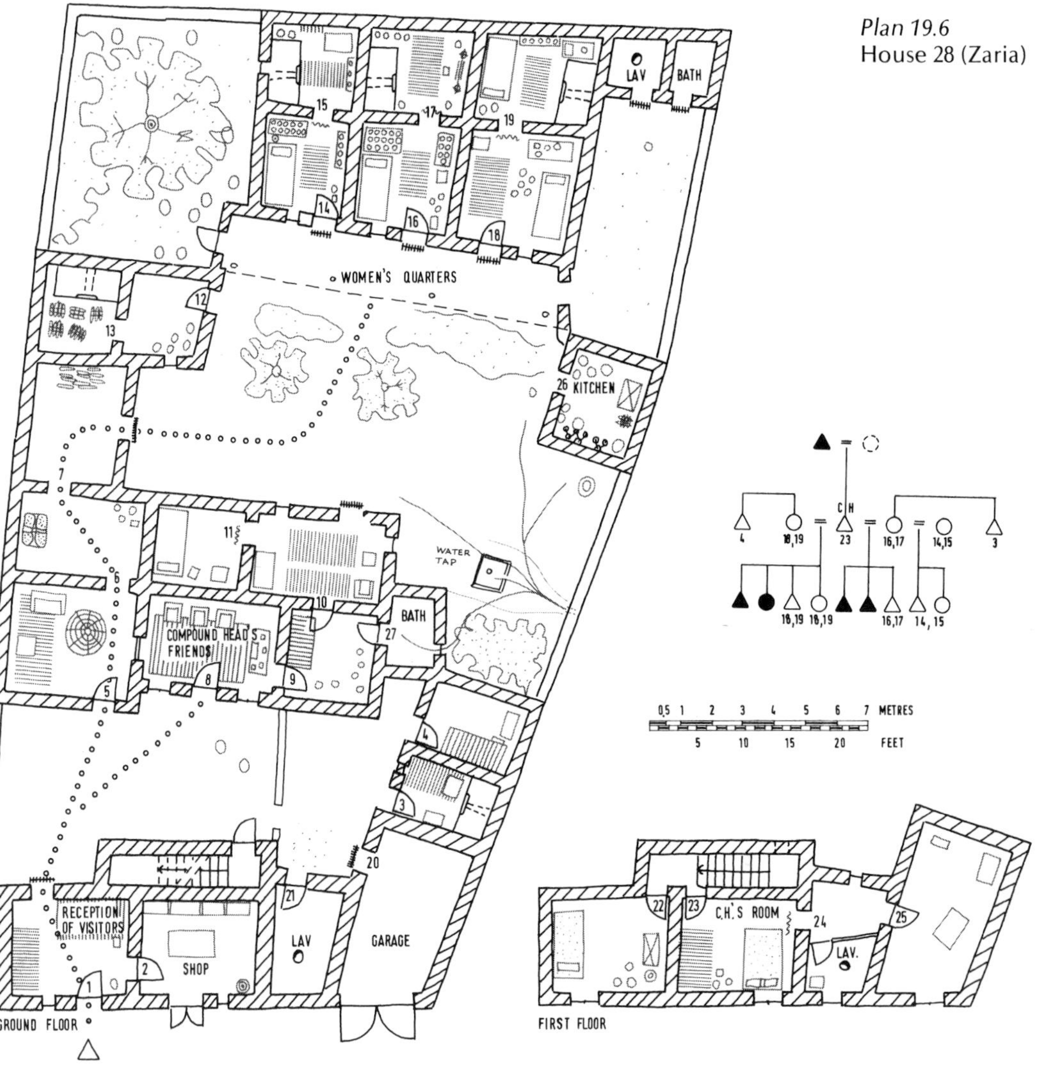

Plan 19.6
House 28 (Zaria)

compound head employed by local government. Friends and important male visitors will be received in a well-furnished room just beyond the first courtyard. The occupants of the house have to pass through another three rooms to reach the interior of the compound where the women's quarters are located. The two adolescent boys, who are related to the compound head's wives, are housed in rooms in the forecourt, while the compound head's sleeping room is on the first floor of the house.

Ibadan

Ibadan was founded at the beginning of the nineteenth century by refugees fleeing from the Fulani army. The two basic house types built by these refugees were a courtyard house and a normally smaller house with a central hall flanked by rooms on two sides. (See pp. 124–131.)

As already mentioned, among the founders of Ibadan was a small group of Muslims. The Muslim community in the city grew slowly, reaching an estimated 30 per cent of the city's population at the beginning of the twentieth century. Christianity was introduced into Ibadan in the 1850s but it had hardly any following. At the start of this century only about 1 per cent of the city's population professed Christianity, while the traditional Yoruba religion accounted for between 60 and 70 per cent. Following the establishment of colonial rule, the percentage distribution of the various religious groups changed. According to the 1952/1953 census report, the Muslim population of the city had grown to nearly 60 per cent, Christians accounted for 32 per cent, and only 8 per cent still followed the traditional Yoruba religion.

Of the 63 houses surveyed in Ibadan, 39 or 61.9 per cent had Muslim populations, 14 or 22.2 per cent had mixed Muslim–Christian populations, and 10 or 15.9 per cent were inhabited by Christians. Among the 295 household heads living in these houses, 187 or 63.4 per cent were Muslims, while 108 or 36.6 per cent professed Christianity.

In spite of the rapid growth of the Muslim community, the layout of their houses has not changed except for the more recent addition of the central corridor house which has developed from the older central hall type. All these houses have little privacy, no surrounding walls or entrance room(s), and are sometimes inhabited by several unrelated families. In contrast to the situation in Marrakech and Zaria, women play a very important part in the economic life of the city and a sizeable proportion of the retail trade passes through their hands. Yoruba society has always granted its women a high degree of unrestricted movement within towns, and Islam has not changed this in any way.

During my survey of Ibadan, the traditional Yoruba religion, Islam, and Christianity were often practised by people living in the same co-residential kinship group. The peaceful coexistence of two or more religions in a family is only possible if secular attitudes towards religion are shared by all its members. Then, religious differences are not regarded as undermining family unity. On the contrary, family members cooperate in building houses, help each other financially, share all family celebrations, and participate in all the festivals of these differing religions. Thus religion has largely become a matter of personal choice and observance, open to individuals who usually respect the religious beliefs and customs of other family members. Given these conditions, it is understandable that building arrangements to assure domestic privacy in a Yoruba house are restricted to a minimum, and that high walls and complicated entrance ways which block access and views into the compound interior will serve no useful purpose and become, indeed, nonsensical.

While there is no doubt that Islam will continue to influence the Yoruba deeply, it no longer has a dominant effect on the design of houses. In Ibadan and other Yoruba cities, non-religious orientations have taken over a decisive role, fuelled by Western education, technology, and attitudes.

The core of the house shown in Plan 19.7 was built in the early 1920s with rooms added in 1931 and 1943. According to the compound head, the family was converted to Islam at the end of the last century. The women's quarters, situated around the central courtyard, are well protected from the public gaze. However, in the part of the house built in 1931, one enters directly into a long room with little domestic privacy for the women who are normally cooking there. The reception room in the main house is spacious and reflects the important position of the compound head and his family in Ibadan's local affairs.

Little or no domestic privacy can be found in the house shown in Plan 19.8, although its inhabitants are Muslims. The central hall serves as a multi-purpose room where male strangers, friends, and family members meet freely. The cooking is done on the open veranda which faces the main road, while the women keep a watchful eye on their merchandise displayed under the big tree in front of the house.

Plan 19.9 shows a house built in the early 1960s, a typical central corridor house. All members of the family are Muslims. Women work mainly in the kitchen yard, and occasionally in the central corridor to which male acquaintances and friends of the family have free access. The household head's sitting and reception room is located in the front of the house.

Apart from religious considerations, all houses in these three urban surveys – i.e. the courtyard house in Marrakech, the typical compound in Zaria, and the central corridor house in Ibadan – are divided clearly into three major zones, namely a public zone, a semi-public zone, and a private zone.

The public zone includes all footpaths and alleyways leading to the house as well as the area immediately in front of the main entrance.

Plan 19.7
House 4 (Ibadan)

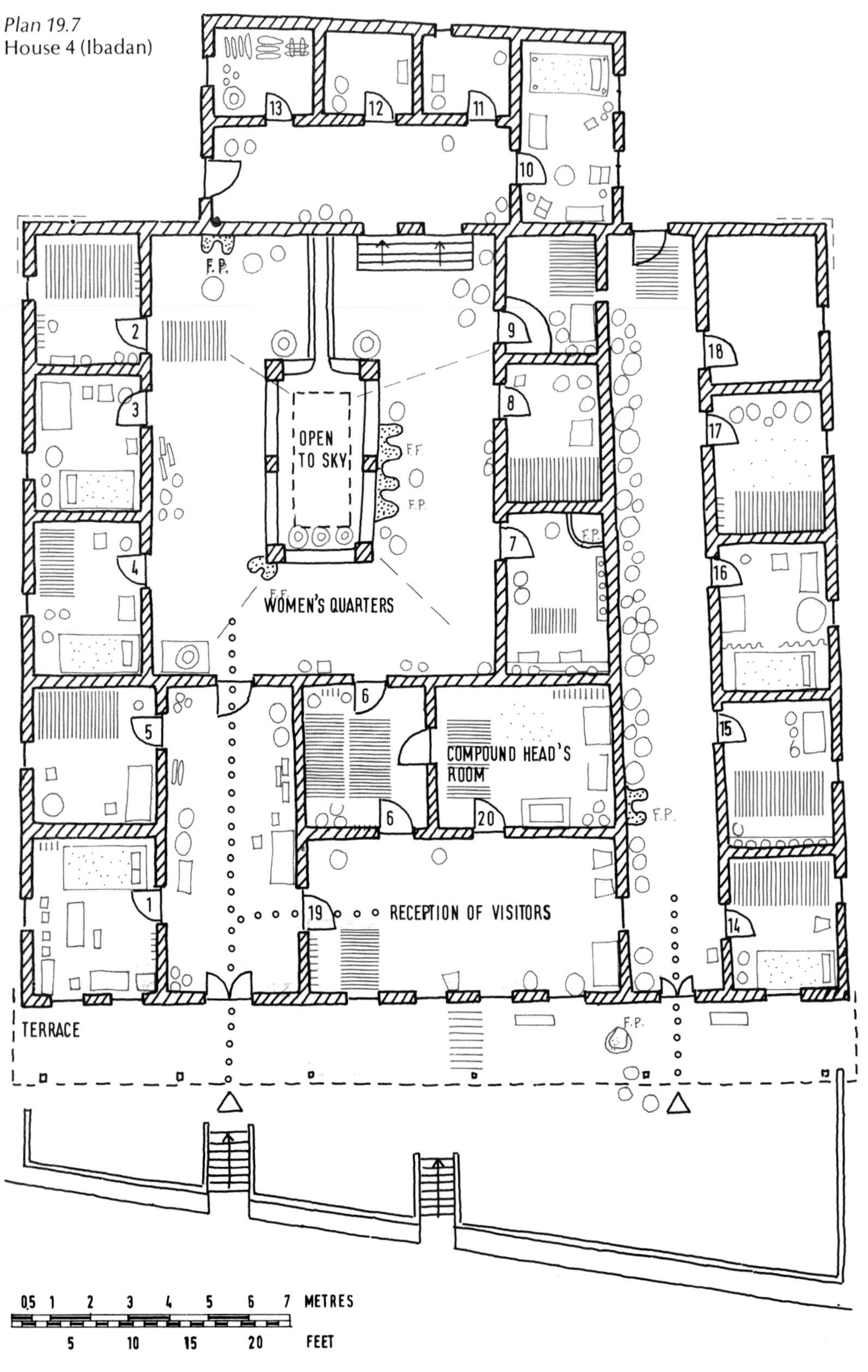

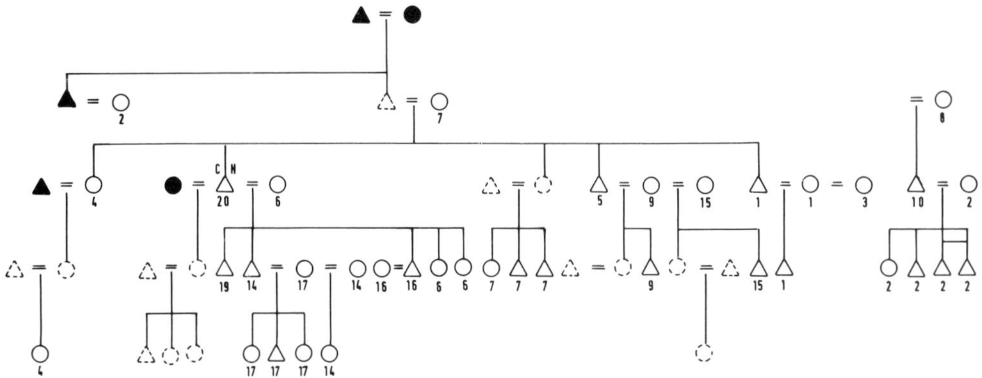

The semi-public zone can be defined as consisting of the entrance lobby or room and the forecourts if there are any. This zone may extend to include the reception room of a courtyard house in Marrakech, the second entrance room of a traditional compound in Zaria, and the central corridor or hall as well as the kitchen yard in a typical Yoruba house in Ibadan.

The private zone comprises all sleeping and living rooms belonging to the compound head and any other married male kinsmen, tenants, or clients and their wives, including the courtyard which is usually not accessible to strangers.

However, these zones may change according to personal and/or religious interpretation. In Marrakech and particularly in Zaria, where purdah is practised with various degrees of severity, these zones are clearly defined and respected by the public, whereas in Ibadan their definition and boundaries are subject to individual judgement and are generally regarded as more flexible. Notwithstanding this, these zones fulfil the important function of reserving various areas in the homestead for the common or exclusive use of particular individuals or sets of individuals; and such demarcation is surely essential for peace and stability within extended co-residential kinship groups.

The influence of Islam on the design and layout of traditional urban houses covered by the survey thus seems marginal; perhaps this is partly due to the lack of Islamic laws on the subject. The segregation of women, which has no doubt influenced the layout of these urban houses and their ancient prototypes, is not necessarily religious in origin,[13] and was practised in the Middle East long before the advent of Islam. The same point holds for the origin and development of the basic courtyard house type that underlies the compound structures found in Marrakech, Zaria, and Ibadan. Such courtyard houses are certainly

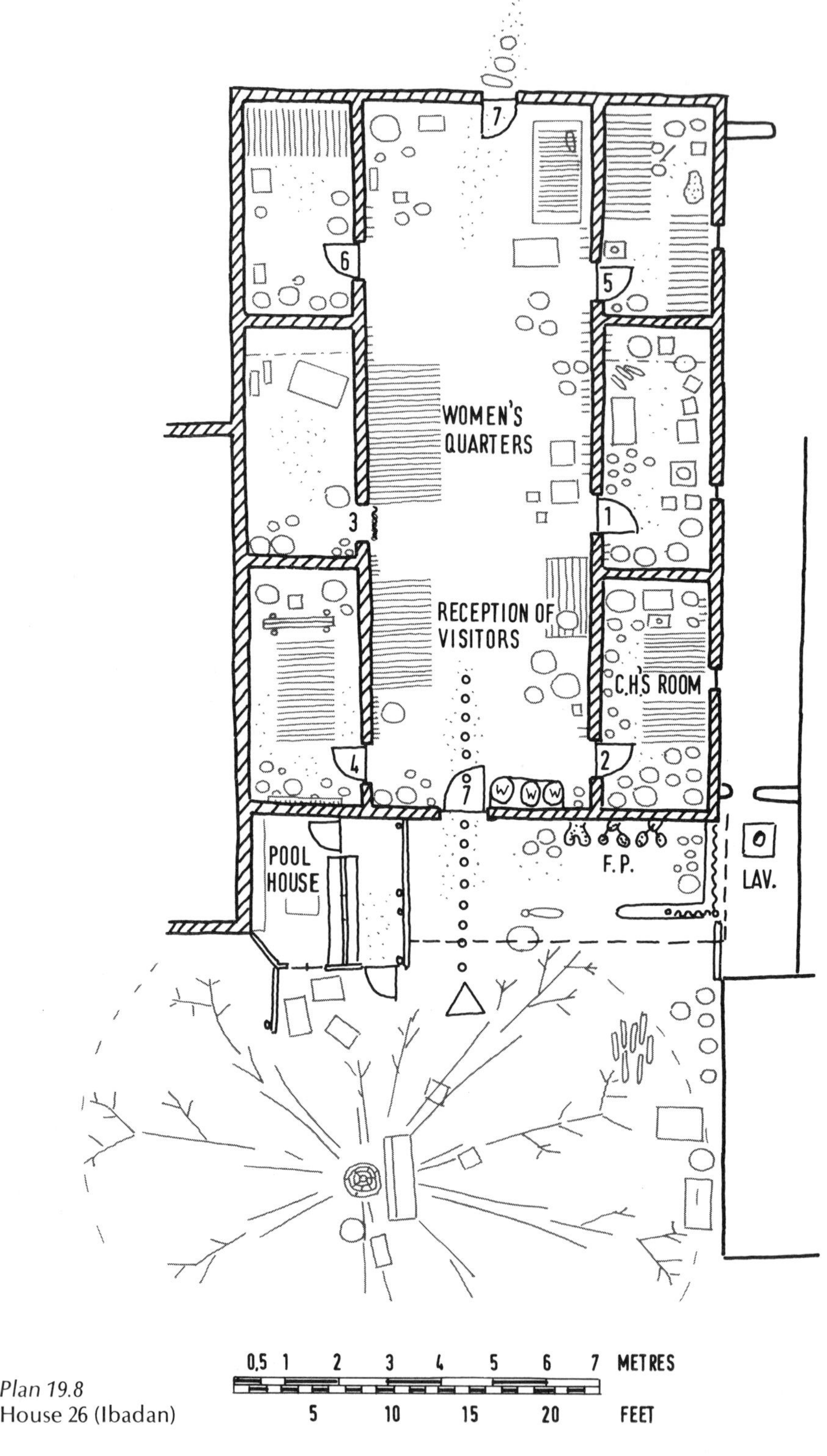

Plan 19.8
House 26 (Ibadan)

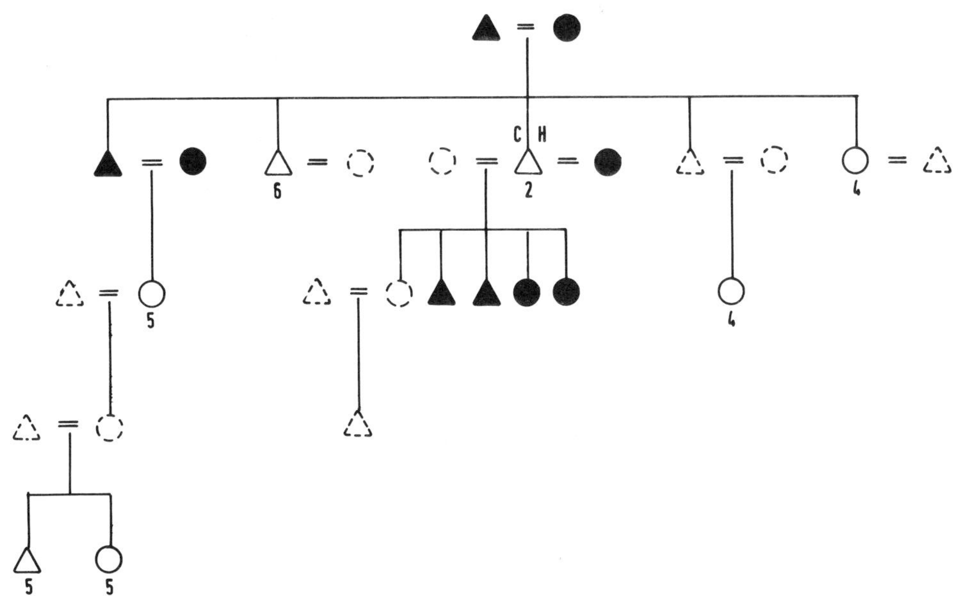

much older than Islam in Arabia and preceded the introduction of Islam in all three towns. Security and safety considerations in pre-Islamic times have probably contributed more to the development of restricted entrances and high surrounding walls, as found in houses in Marrakech and Zaria, than any factors motivated by religion, although religion may well have been used later to justify these features.

However, though the influence of Islam on the traditional urban house styles at Zaria, Marrakech, and Ibadan was marginal, its influence on people and society in Africa has been, and remains, considerable. The social structure and family patterns changed substantially as Islam made its impact on African societies. In the Sudan belt of West Africa the extended family unit is still the norm, while among the urban Berber of North Africa the individual family as a residential unit predominates. Islamic laws of succession *'fara'id* recognize only the individual family, hence fraternal succession is giving way to succession in the direct line of descent.[14] This law has challenged the African system of the extended family by weakening the position of its traditional head. However, in areas where Islam has been introduced effectively only during the last 200 years, the extended family as an institution has so far resisted any major changes. The Islamic law of succession as applied at Zaria, and sometimes at Ibadan, has been modified to allow all persons in the direct line of descent a share in the personal, but not necessarily in the inherited, property of a deceased person. Inherited property, i.e. land, houses, fruit-bearing trees, and certain

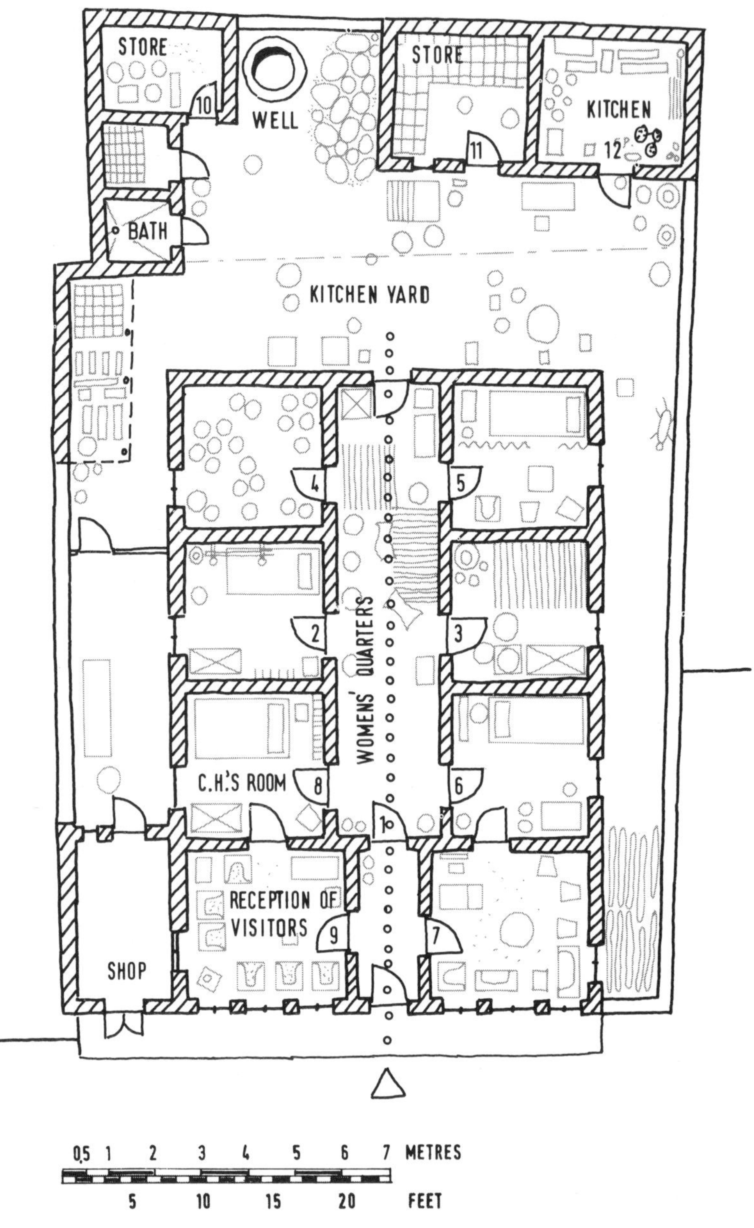

Plan 19.9
House 42 (Ibadan)

3
C H
8
2
5
3 3 3 3 2
6

other capital assets, will revert to the extended family group and be re-allocated according to traditional custom and law.[15]

As indicated, the extended family in Zaria and Ibadan is still the dominant residential unit, and most of its powers and responsibilities are concentrated in the hands of its head, but there are subtle changes. As shown in Table 19.2 on p. 281, co-residential kinship groups at stages 1 and 2 – i.e. consisting of the compound head with his wife or wives and their married and unmarried children – together accounted in Ibadan for only 18.1 per cent of the survey population, in Zaria for 32.2 per cent, and in Marrakech for 82.8 per cent. These figures suggest that a gradual breakdown of the extended family groupings characteristic of Zaria and Ibadan is leading to smaller, self-contained domestic units or individual families. This development is closely related to the length of time the populations of the three towns were exposed to the influence of Islam. While Marrakech has been Islamized for nearly 1,000 years, the Islamization of Zaria and Ibadan is still in progress, and at least from the beginning of the twentieth century this has been further complicated by the influence of Western culture and technology. To what extent Western culture and contacts have promoted the decline of the extended family unit is difficult to say, though both will certainly play increasing roles in future.

There is little doubt that Islam and Western culture have both contributed to the decline of extended family compounds. Islam has made its greatest impact on these communities in the past, while Western culture and technology will influence living patterns and, above all, the design of houses in the future. Together they may well effect the gradual disappearance of large compounds and the increase of smaller, self-contained houses occupied by individual families.

Notes and references

1 Maulana Muhammad Ali, trans., *The Holy Qur'an*, Lahore, 1963, p. 808. Other restrictions on women are included in chapter 24, Al-Nur, verses 30–31, pp. 684–685.
2 Maulana Muhammad Ali, op. cit., chapter 24, Al-Nur, verses 27–28, p. 684.
3 Ancestor worship and family altars were still in use in some houses in Ibadan.
4 The Hanafi school is followed in Egypt.
5 F. H. Ruxton, trans., *Maliki Law*, London, 1916, pp. 197–198 §650–662.
6 For an excellent account of these events see S. J. Trimingham, *The Influence of Islam upon Africa*, London, 1980, *Islam in West Africa*, London, 1959.

7 According to Nigerian census reports, the Muslim population of Ibadan increased from about 35 per cent in 1913 to almost 60 per cent in 1952/1953, while Christianity increased from about 1 per cent to 32 per cent over the same time span.

8 Trimingham, *The Influence of Islam upon Africa*, p. 43.

9 Referring to the Prophet's house in Medina, G. Marcais continued: 'Tradition brings us an interesting detail on the subject of these rooms. Their entrance on to the courtyard was fronted by a porch of palm branches which could be shut off, if required, by curtains of camel-hair. This front annexe of the room, which recalls the *riwak*, the movable screen of the nomadic tent, which keeps the dwelling in touch with the outside world, and plays the part of a vestibule, was to be perpetuated in the Muslim house'. *Encyclopaedia of Islam*, Vol. 2, C–G (Dar), London, Leiden, 1965, p. 113.

10 These do not include any decorative features.

11 A. W. Lawrence, *Greek Architecture*, London, 1975, p. 332. D. Yarwood, *The Architecture of Europe*, London, 1974, p. 64.

12 H. Barth, *Travel and Discoveries in North and Central Africa,* vol. I, London, 1890, p. 377.

13 Trimingham, *The Influence of Islam upon Africa*, p. 95. 'We have referred to the ritual segregation of women, but their physical segregation is based on class, town life or prestige – non-Islamic factors, though justified by clergy on Islamic grounds.'

14 Ruxton, op. cit., pp. 373–397.

15 For more information see J. D. M. Derret, ed., *Studies in the Laws of Succession in Nigeria*, Oxford, 1965.

Chapter 20

Conclusion

The main object of this book has been to provide detailed information on a limited number of traditional houses and their inhabitants in three African cities. My basic interest centred on the relationship between co-residential kinship groups and the layout of their houses. To achieve these objectives I had to develop a systematic method of study to investigate this relationship. From the outset it was clear that only a cross-disciplinary approach – including *inter alia* aspects of history, social and cultural anthropology, economics, and architecture – could expose the complex cultural relationships which hold between traditional houses and their inhabitants.

A second important feature of this inquiry is its comparative character. Data for each town were collected independently according to set criteria. Comparative analysis of houses and their inhabitants within and between each of our three urban samples has contributed substantially to our understanding of the cyclic tendency which underlies the growth and decline of agnatic co-residential kinship groups, and revealed its effect on their houses. The comparative study has also revealed the striking similarities in the composition and use of space by these people of widely different ethnic origin and historic cultural backgrounds.

A third feature of my study is its emphasis on the process of cultural change. Cultural change through the assimilation of new ideas is a continuous process which involves indigenous African culture, Islam, and Western influence, all of which have contributed to the reduction in the size of co-residential families, the change in attitudes of people, and consequently the modification of traditional house styles or the outright adoption of foreign patterns of housing.

The relationship between domestic groups and the layout of houses, which is basic for our understanding of these survey data, needs further attention. We may recall that in Zaria and Ibadan the majority of households surveyed lived in compounds having large and complex co-residential kinship groups, whereas at Marrakech small domestic groups predominated.

In Zaria the construction of new rooms and the abandonment of old ones correspond closely with events that mark stages in the growth and decline of these co-residential kinship groups. Hence, when the development of the co-residential kinship group was known, the physical development of compounds at Zaria could be explained in detail. Moreover, the adaptability of the layout of most compounds in Zaria walled city with their spacious arrangement of detached huts, and the relatively low cost of construction, which are partly assured by the recycling of such building materials as roof beams and mud for wall construction, enables compound heads to provide adequate accommodation for the changing requirements of their families at the *right time*. Up to 1970, changes affecting the design and construction of compounds in the walled city of Zaria were rare and limited, and the few modern building materials, such as cement and corrugated iron roofing sheets, available in the local market, were used to supplement and protect existing buildings, rather than to construct new, different, and more durable houses, but this is now changing.

In spite of many shortcomings, the major advantage of the traditional building practice in Zaria is undoubtedly the flexibility of compounds which enables each new generation of compound heads to provide exactly the accommodation needed for their families. It is difficult to estimate what impact the increased use of modern building materials for the construction of new houses within compounds will have on the future development of co-residential kinship groups in Hausaland. However, it must be stressed that the higher capital outlay, the substantially increased life expectancy, and the undoubted comfort of well-built modern houses constructed on Western models with permanent building materials, will make it unlikely that the compound heads who inherit such houses will abandon them and build their own, though accelerating changes in the traditional patterns of compound occupancy and subsequently in the structure and size of co-residential kinship groups.

At Ibadan and Marrakech the relationship between domestic groupings and the layout of houses is more complex. This is partly due to the shortage of suitable building sites which tends to restrict the construction of new rooms, and partly due to the larger number of tenant households who occupy rented accommodation in both cities. Once tenant households are accepted and established, some compound heads find it increasingly difficult to house their own growing families within their compounds. Hence, in Ibadan compound heads, faced with the problem of housing their rapidly expanding families, try to build new rooms where space is available, to distribute existing accommodation more economically, and to re-allocate rooms of deceased family members. Failing this, family members have to look for alternative accommodation elsewhere. In the *medina* of Marrakech, where space for new construction is even more restricted, houses which had become too small for their owners' families were sold to facilitate the purchase of larger ones. Unlike Zaria where the construction of new rooms is a direct response to an increase of co-residential kinship groups, mainly through marriages, building activities in the compounds at Ibadan and Marrakech are not necessarily undertaken for such a reason, but new rooms are built as a capital investment, to be rented out to stranger households on completion. Hence, large proportions of the houses studied at Ibadan and Marrakech have become sources of additional income for their owners. The inhabitants of these latter houses are also the ones most likely to suffer from overcrowding.

The different systems of land tenure in Zaria and Ibadan on the one hand and in Marrakech on the other have no doubt influenced the size and composition of domestic groups. Particularly at Zaria and Ibadan, traditional modes of land tenure, by which most land is owned corporately by agnatic descent groups, have promoted the development of large and complex co-residential groups based on kinship, whereas at Marrakech, the regime of individual holdings and freehold properties which can be sold if necessary tends to facilitate the continuous division of co-residential kinship groups into small, economically independent family units.

Although the direct influence of Islam on the houses investigated appears to be marginal, Islam has contributed substantially to the decline of large domestic kinship groups, particularly through its law of succession. As shown in Marrakech, Zaria, and Ibadan, the incidence of large, co-residential extended families seems to be directly linked to the length of time Islam has influenced these societies. However, the trend towards the individual family as a residential unit is now accelerated by Western influences as well.

As we have seen, the generally lower income of most dependent or semi-dependent household heads found in Zaria and Ibadan has no doubt restricted their mobility and their ability to establish their own independent households. At Marrakech the slightly higher income of such household heads has made this move less difficult for them. The restriction of our surveys to compounds in the older parts of the three selected towns has concentrated the study on populations which are economically disadvantaged when compared with the immigrant communities in the rapidly growing new urban districts that surround these towns. Even without detailed comparison, it is evident that the immigrant communities living on the outskirts have seized the economic initiative and established new centres of commerce that have attracted a fair amount of old trade and younger people from the old walled cities. Family composition, life-style, housing, occupations, and incomes of these immigrant communities thus differ markedly from those of the indigenous population which live in the older parts of the three cities under investigation.[1] Interest in modern building materials and new construction techniques is now increasing among the urban populations included in these surveys. However, the capital investment needed to employ these new materials and techniques effectively is still beyond the reach of most compound heads. Furthermore, the rapidly increasing populations of the new towns, and the inability of governments, building societies, and other financial institutions to provide at least some of the building funds required by the poorer section of the community in the centre of old towns, have led to the deteriorating housing conditions which can be found in traditional sections of many African towns. Only sustained economic growth and changes of government attitudes towards the traditional housing sector can create an environment in which the state could improve the urban housing situation of their citizens who dwell in the traditional sections of their most historic and distinctive towns.

Reference

1 F. W. Schwerdtfeger, 'Urban settlement patterns in Northern Nigeria', in *Man, Settlement and Urbanism*, ed. P. Ucko *et al.*, London, 1972, pp. 547–556.

Appendixes – Part I

ZARIA

Appendix 1

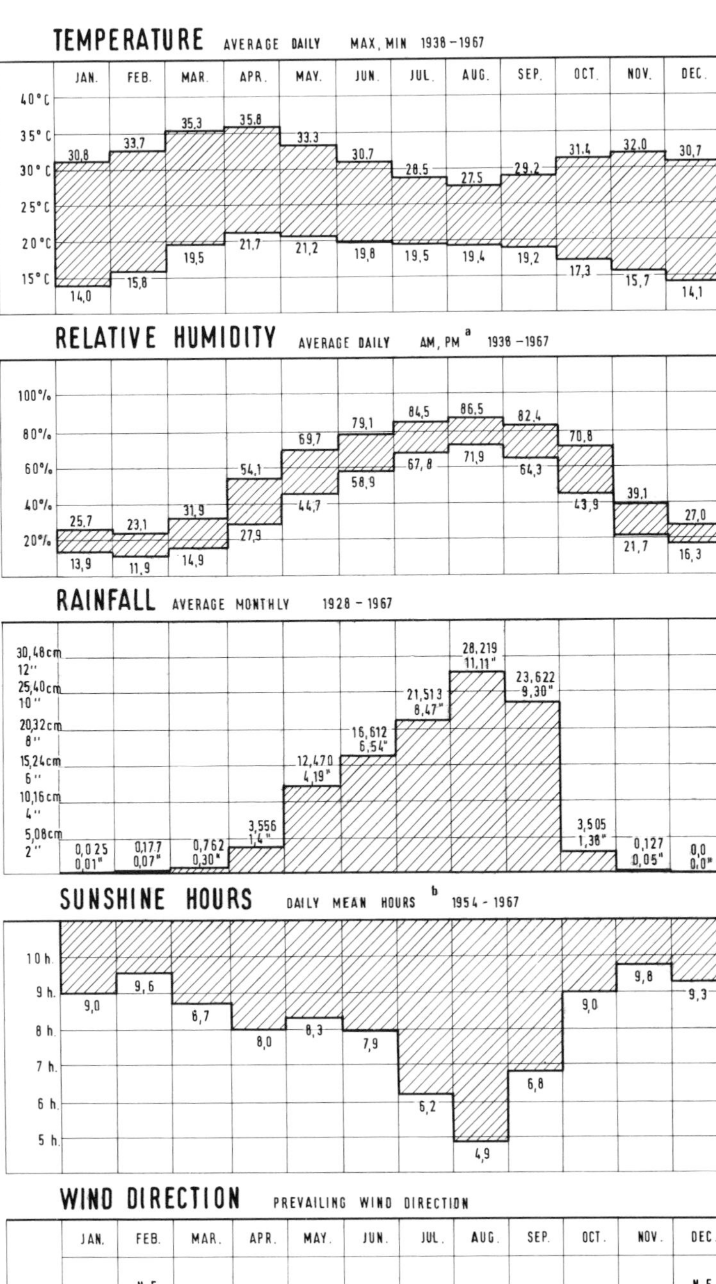

Diagram A.1.1
Climatic data, Zaria.
[a] Before 1953, observation taken at 08.00 and 13.00 GMT; after 1953, at 09.00 and 15.00 hours GMT.
[b] Sunshine records from Campbell and Stokes's recorder

Table A.1.1 List of Fulani rulers of Zaria

1804–1821	Mallam Musa	Founder of the Mallawa dynasty.
1821–1834	Yamusa	Founder of the Bornuawa dynasty.
1834–1846	Abdulkarim	Founder of the Katsinawa dynasty.
1846	Hamada	Son of Yamusa. (Reigned 52 days)
1846–1860	Mommon Sani	Son of Yamusa.
1860	Sidi Abdulkadiri	Son of M. Musa, deposed by Sultan of Sokoto.
1860–1863	Audusallami	Member of the Suleibawa clan.
1863–1873	Abdullahi	Son of Hamada. Deposed by Sultan of Sokoto.
1873–1876	Abubakar	Son of M. Musa.
1876–1881	Abdullahi	Restored by Sultan of Sokoto and again deposed.
1881–1890	Sambo	Son of Abdulkarim. Deposed by Sultan of Sokoto.
1890–1897	Yero	Son of Abdullahi.
1897–1902	Kwassau	Son of Yero. Deposed by British.
1902–1903	Galadima Suleimanu	Acting regent for six months.
1903–1920	Aliyu	Son of Sidi Abdulkadiri. Deposed by British.
1920–1924	Dalhatu	Son of Yero.
1924–1936	Ibrahim	Son of Kwassau.
1936–1959	Ja'afaru	Grandson of Yero.
1959–1975	Muhammadu Aminu	Great-grandson of Abdulkarim.
1975–	Shehu Idris	Grandson of Sambo.

Source: M. G. Smith, *Government in Zazzau 1800–1950*, London, 1960, pp. 141–238.

Table A.1.2 Gross Domestic Product at 1962 factor cost; 1960–69 in £N million; 1970 and 1971 in Naira million

	1960	1961	1962	1963	1964	1965	1966	1967	1968	1969	1970	1971
Agriculture	798.9	774.9	802.9	868.9	865.7	871.1	790.9	679.0	669.0	763.9	1,887.7	1,985.2
Distribution	158.8	153.9	156.5	180.9	199.1	209.2	194.9	166.5	166.1	205.8	512.9	544.5
Manufacturing and crafts	59.8	65.1	73.2	85.0	90.5	110.5	110.8	95.0	100.2	131.7	317.6	307.7
Transport and communication	56.9	64.1	62.7	65.5	74.6	73.1	71.0	56.7	62.8	63.8	137.9	168.0
Building construction	50.0	52.7	56.4	59.2	64.0	81.1	80.1	67.9	58.5	70.0	221.0	312.0
Crude oil and mining	14.9	21.7	27.0	29.4	39.8	74.9	105.2	81.9	42.5	127.0	501.5	704.3
General government	39.9	38.6	38.8	38.9	44.8	48.4	49.6	42.3	69.5	119.9	327.6	338.8
Education	32.0	35.1	38.9	41.4	46.7	48.5	55.4	44.9	45.9	52.1	133.1	153.1
Health	6.2	7.1	8.4	8.9	10.1	11.3	13.1	10.0	9.5	13.6	39.5	40.8
Electricity and water supply	4.0	4.8	5.8	6.8	7.8	9.1	10.0	7.5	8.7	10.4	24.0	28.9
Other services	25.3	28.1	28.2	27.9	30.7	36.2	41.4	34.4	39.2	44.7	116.2	132.2
Total	1,246.7	1,246.1	1,298.8	1,412.8	1,473.8	1,573.4	1,522.4	1,286.1	1,271.9	1,602.9	4,219.0	4,715.5
GDP at current factor cost	1,123.7	1,179.8	1,298.8	1,372.9	1,447.2	1,555.0	1,687.4	1,376.3	1,328.1	1,752.0	5,281.1	6,650.9

Source: Federal Office of Statistics, Nigeria, *Annual Abstract of Statistics 1971*, Lagos, 1972, pp. 140–141; *Annual Abstract of Statistics 1973*, Lagos, 1974, pp. 148–149.

Note: Although the Naira as the new Nigerian currency was not introduced until 1 January 1973, figures for 1970 and 1971 are not available in Nigerian pounds. The exchange rate was two Naira for one Nigerian Pound.

Table A.1.3 Gross Domestic Product at 1962 factor cost, in percentages

	1960	1961	1962	1963	1964	1965	1966	1967	1968	1969	1970	1971
Agriculture	64.1	62.2	61.8	61.5	58.7	55.3	51.9	52.8	52.6	47.7	44.7	42.1
Distribution	12.7	12.4	12.0	12.8	13.5	13.3	12.8	12.9	13.1	12.8	12.2	11.6
Manufacturing and crafts	4.8	5.2	5.6	6.0	6.1	7.0	7.3	7.4	7.9	8.2	7.5	6.5
Transport and communication	4.6	5.1	4.8	4.6	5.1	4.6	4.7	4.4	4.9	4.0	3.3	3.5
Building construction	4.0	4.2	4.4	4.2	4.4	5.2	5.3	5.3	4.6	4.4	5.2	6.6
Crude oil and mining	1.2	1.7	2.1	2.1	2.7	4.8	6.9	6.3	3.3	7.9	11.9	14.9
General government	3.2	3.1	3.0	2.8	3.0	3.1	3.2	3.3	5.5	7.5	7.8	7.2
Education	2.6	2.8	3.0	2.9	3.2	3.1	3.6	3.5	3.6	3.3	3.1	3.3
Health	0.5	0.6	0.7	0.6	0.7	0.7	0.9	0.8	0.7	0.8	0.9	0.9
Electricity and water supply	0.3	0.4	0.4	0.5	0.5	0.6	0.7	0.6	0.7	0.6	0.6	0.6
Other services	2.0	2.3	2.2	2.0	2.1	2.3	2.7	2.7	3.1	2.8	2.8	2.8
Total	100.0	100.0	100.0	100.0	100.0	100.0	100.0	100.0	100.0	100.0	100.0	100.0

Table A.1.4 Export of principal products, in £N million

	1960	1961	1962	1963	1964	1965	1966	1967	1968	1969	1970	1971
Agriculture	133.2	133.6	123.2	135.1	143.1	156.2	139.7	128.0	127.6	134.8	136.3	120.6
Crude petroleum	4.4	11.5	16.7	20.2	32.1	68.1	92.0	72.1	37.0	131.0	254.9	476.5
Metal ore	8.3	8.1	9.3	11.2	14.1	16.1	16.6	14.1	14.3	10.2	9.6	8.5
Timber	8.1	7.9	7.0	7.8	8.9	7.5	6.7	4.2	4.1	5.1	3.9	3.4
Miscellaneous	11.6	9.0	7.9	10.6	12.3	15.3	23.7	19.7	23.5	33.5	33.8	31.4
Total domestic export	165.6	170.1	164.1	184.9	210.5	263.2	278.7	238.1	206.5	314.6	438.5	640.4

Source: Federal Office of Statistics, Nigeria, *Annual Abstract of Statistics 1971*, Lagos, 1972, pp. 84–86.

Table A.1.5 Export of principal products, in percentages

	1960	1961	1962	1963	1964	1965	1966	1967	1968	1969	1970	1971
Agriculture	80.4	78.5	75.0	73.1	68.0	59.3	50.1	53.7	61.8	42.9	31.1	18.9
Crude petroleum	2.7	6.8	10.2	10.9	15.3	25.9	33.0	30.3	17.9	41.6	58.1	74.4
Metal ore	5.0	4.8	5.7	6.1	6.7	6.1	6.0	5.9	6.9	3.2	2.2	1.3
Timber	4.9	4.6	4.3	4.2	4.2	2.9	2.4	1.8	2.0	1.6	0.9	0.5
Miscellaneous	7.0	5.3	4.8	5.7	5.8	5.8	8.5	8.3	11.4	10.7	7.7	4.9
Total domestic export	100.0	100.0	100.0	100.0	100.0	100.0	100.0	100.0	100.0	100.0	100.0	100.0

Table A.1.6 Value of external trade and visible balance, in £N million

	1960	1961	1962	1963	1964	1965	1966	1967	1968	1969	1970	1971
Merchandise import	215.9	222.5	203.2	207.6	253.9	275.4	257.0	223.5	192.6	248.7	378.2	539.5
Domestic export	165.6	170.1	164.0	184.9	210.5	263.2	278.7	238.1	206.5	314.6	438.5	640.4
Re-export	4.1	3.6	4.5	4.8	4.2	5.0	5.4	3.7	4.6	3.5	4.2	6.2
Total export	169.7	173.7	168.5	189.7	214.7	268.2	284.1	241.8	211.1	318.1	442.7	646.6
Visible balance	–46.2	–48.8	–34.7	–17.9	–39.2	–7.1	+27.1	+18.3	+18.5	+69.5	+64.5	+107.2

Source: Federal Office of Statistics, Nigeria, *Annual Abstract of Statistics 1971*, Lagos, 1972, p. 68.

Table A.1.7 Gross Fixed Capital Formation at 1962–1963 constant prices; 1960–69 in £N million; 1970 and 1971 in Naira million

	1960	1961	1962	1963	1964	1965	1966	1967	1968	1969	1970	1971
Buildings	64.9	67.1	70.8	71.1	76.4	94.3	89.2	65.0	61.1	65.3	152.5	238.6
Civil engineering works	27.2	30.1	34.3	39.3	42.5	55.7	58.9	61.1	47.5	64.3	213.4	305.0
Land improvements	11.5	31.0	25.6	33.1	32.1	34.1	32.4	29.7	21.4	17.4	25.0	24.5
Transport equipment	24.0	20.9	12.0	16.6	26.1	28.1	26.1	24.9	21.4	30.3	122.9	151.9
Machinery and equipment	32.9	36.0	33.3	34.2	73.5	80.3	68.4	55.3	49.4	44.3	176.1	234.4
Total	160.5	185.1	176.0	194.3	250.6	292.5	275.0	236.0	200.8	221.6	689.9	954.4
GFCF at current fact or cost	159.4	178.3	176.0	196.5	251.5	307.6	300.8	241.8	217.0	263.8	844.9	1,234.9

Source: Federal Office of Statistics, Nigeria, *Annual Abstract of Statistics 1971*, Lagos, 1972, p. 142; *Annual Abstract of Statistics 1973*, Lagos, 1974, p. 150.
Note: Although the Naira as the new Nigerian Currency was not introduced until 1 January 1973, figures for 1970 and 1971 are not available in Nigerian Pounds. The exchange rate was two Naira for one Nigerian Pound.

Table A.1.8 Gross Fixed Capital Formation at 1962–1963 constant prices, in percentages

	1960	1961	1962	1963	1964	1965	1966	1967	1968	1969	1970	1971
Buildings	40.4	36.3	40.2	36.6	30.5	32.2	32.4	28.1	30.4	29.5	22.1	25.0
Civil engineering works	16.9	16.3	19.5	20.2	17.0	19.0	21.4	26.5	23.6	29.0	30.9	32.0
Land improvements	7.2	16.7	14.6	17.0	12.8	11.7	11.8	10.7	10.7	7.8	3.6	2.6
Transport equipment	15.0	11.3	6.8	8.6	10.4	9.6	9.5	10.8	10.7	13.7	17.8	15.9
Machinery and equipment	20.5	19.4	18.9	17.6	29.3	27.5	24.9	23.9	24.6	20.0	25.6	24.5
Total	100.0	100.0	100.0	100.0	100.0	100.0	100.0	100.0	100.0	100.0	100.0	100.0

Appendix 2

Table A.2.1 Type of tenure of 77 compounds in Zaria walled city, 1968

	Compounds	% of total
1 Inherited compounds	50	65.0
2 Purchased compounds	19	24.6
3 Allotted compounds/land	5	6.5
4 Gift of compounds	2	2.6
5 Compound built on reclaimed land	1	1.3
Total	77	100.0

Table A.2.2 Use of land within the walled city of Zaria, 1963

	Sq. m	% of total
1 Cultivated land	10,982,660	66.2
2 Building sites	3,077,640	18.6
3 Waste land	1,502,620	9.1
4 Roads	353,400	2.1
5 Rock surfaces	347,740	2.1
6 Borrow-pits and brooks	313,610	1.9
Total area	16,577,670	100.0

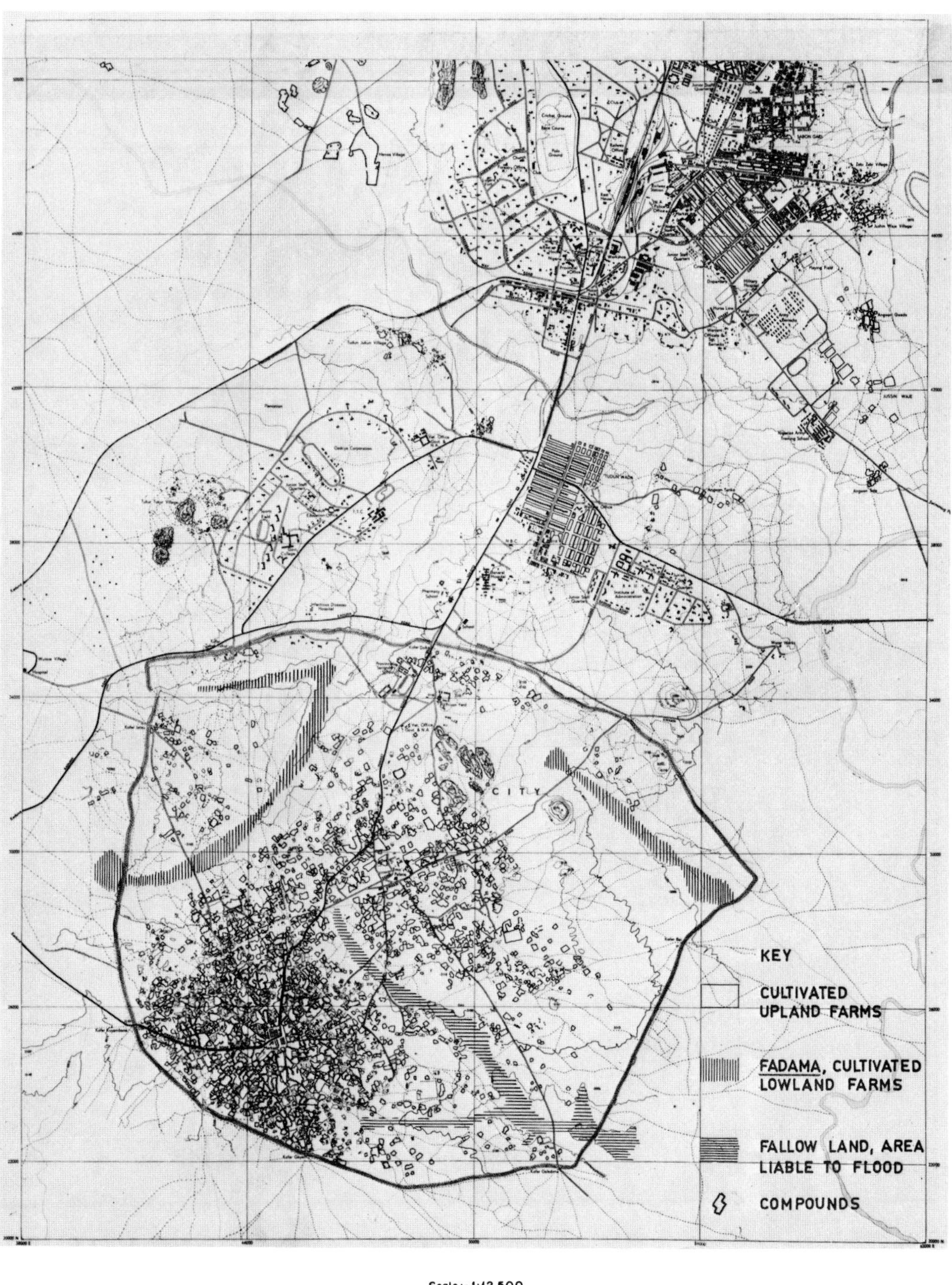

Map A.2.1
Use of land in the walled city of Zaria

Appendix 3

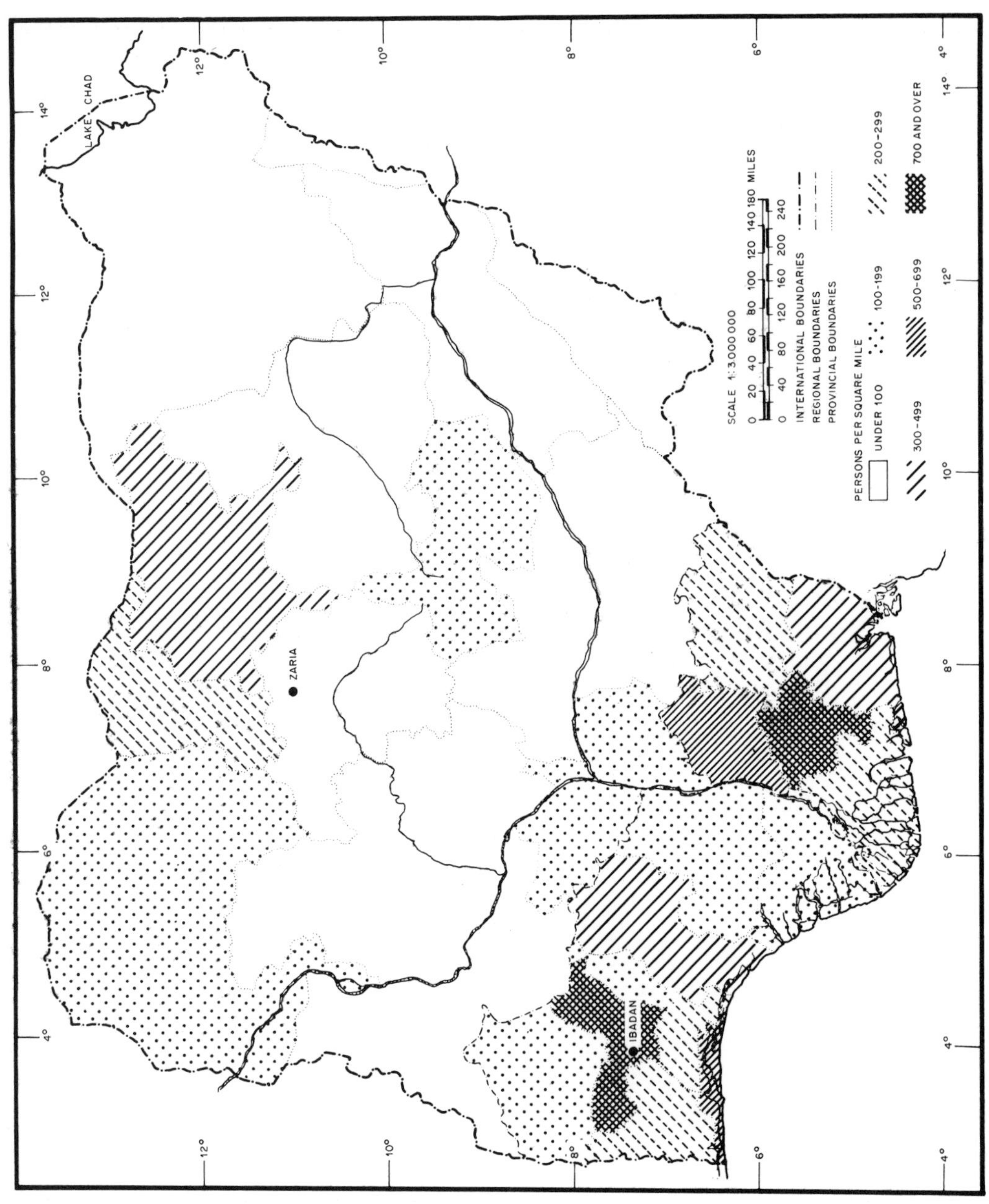

Map A.3.1
Nigeria: population density by provinces, 1963

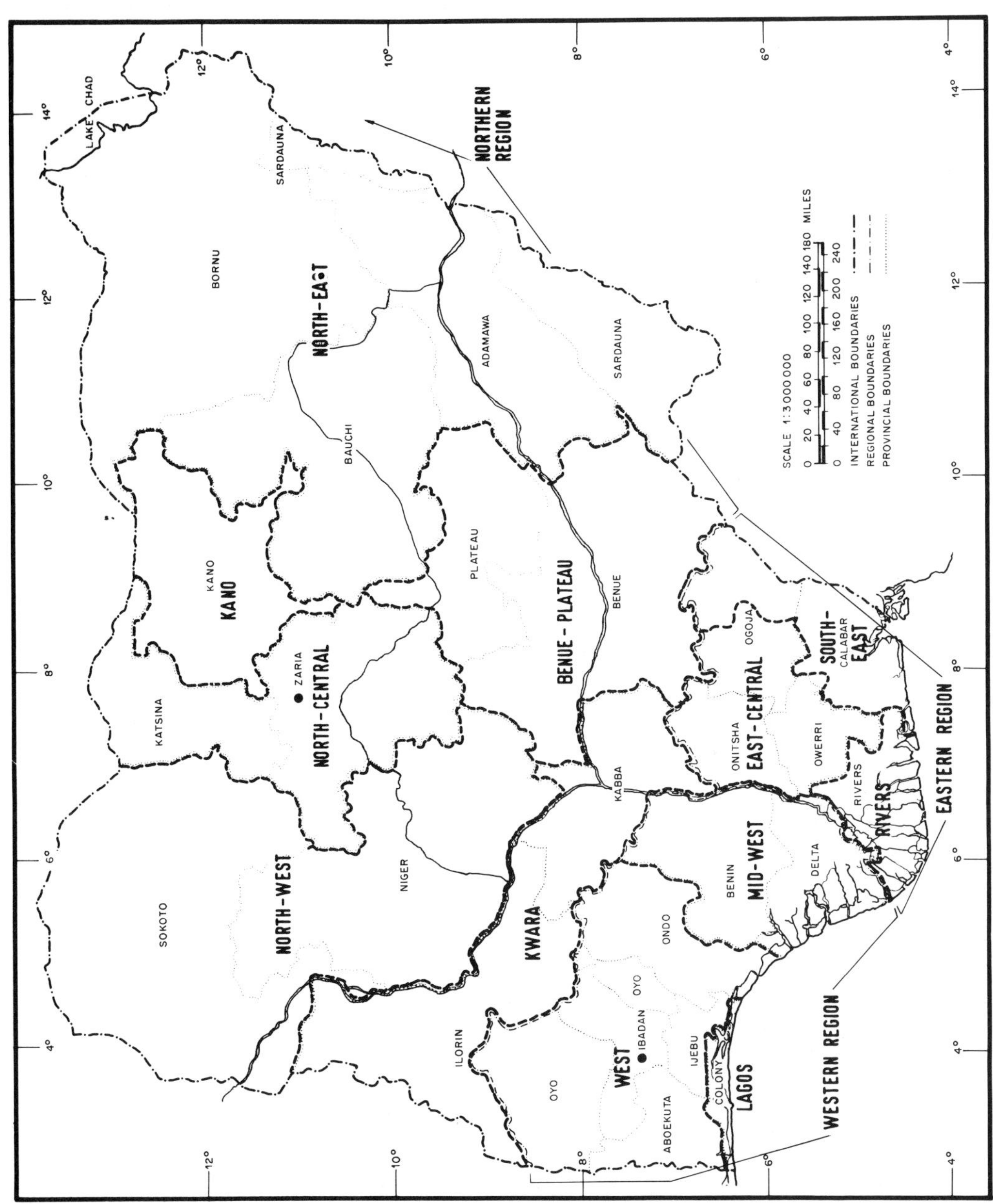

Map A.3.2
Administrative division of Nigeria in 1972

Table A.3.1 Reported age distribution, 1963 census and sample population in percentages

Age	Total national		Total urban		Total rural		Zaria, total division		Zaria div., urban		Zaria div., rural		Survey sample 1968	
	M	F	M	F	M	F	M	F	M	F	M	F	M	F
0–4	8.5	8.7	7.1	7.2	8.7	9.0	9.7	10.0	7.6	7.8	10.0	10.0	9.2	11.4
5–9	7.9	7.3	6.4	6.3	8.1	7.5	8.5	7.8	6.5	6.4	8.9	8.4	8.8	8.5
10–14	5.8	4.8	5.6	4.7	5.9	4.8	5.7	4.2	5.8	3.9	5.6	4.5	5.2	3.6
0–14	43.0		37.3		44.0		45.9		38.0		47.4		46.7	
15–19	4.5	4.9	5.4	4.5	4.3	5.0	3.9	6.6	4.4	5.8	3.8	6.7	3.1	4.6
20–24	5.7	6.8	8.0	6.8	5.2	6.8	4.9	6.9	7.1	6.0	4.6	7.0	2.4	6.4
25–29	4.7	5.3	6.6	5.6	4.3	5.3	4.2	4.7	6.5	4.9	3.9	4.6	3.8	6.3
30–34	3.8	4.0	4.5	3.9	3.7	4.0	3.6	3.7	4.8	3.8	3.4	3.7	2.3	3.4
35–39	2.4	2.0	3.0	2.1	2.3	2.0	2.2	1.6	3.3	1.9	2.1	1.5	2.3	2.6
40–44	2.4	2.0	2.4	1.9	2.3	2.0	2.1	1.7	2.6	2.0	2.0	1.6	2.4	1.7
45–49	1.2	0.9	1.4	0.9	1.2	0.9	1.0	0.6	1.3	0.8	0.9	0.6	1.5	1.5
15–49	50.6		57.0		49.3		47.7		55.2		46.4		44.3	
50–54	1.2	1.0	1.2	0.9	1.2	1.0	1.2	0.9	1.3	1.2	1.2	0.9	1.7	1.6
55–59	0.5	0.3	0.5	0.3	0.5	0.3	0.5	0.3	0.6	0.4	0.4	0.3	0.7	1.3
60–64	0.8	0.6	0.7	0.5	0.9	0.6	0.8	0.5	0.8	0.7	0.8	0.5	0.6	1.3
65–69	0.3	0.2	0.2	0.2	0.3	0.2	0.3	0.2	0.3	0.1	0.3	0.1	0.5	0.1
70+	0.9	0.6	0.6	0.6	1.0	0.7	1.0	0.7	0.8	0.6	1.1	0.6	0.7	0.5
50+	6.4		5.7		6.7		6.4		6.8		6.2		9.0	
Total M/F	50.6	49.4	53.6	46.4	49.9	50.1	49.6	50.4	53.7	46.3	49.0	51.0	45.2	54.8
Total	100.0		100.0		100.0		100.0		100.0		100.0		100.0	

Source: Federal Office of Statistics, Nigeria, 'Population census of Nigeria, 1963' (mimeo), Lagos, 1968, vol. 3.

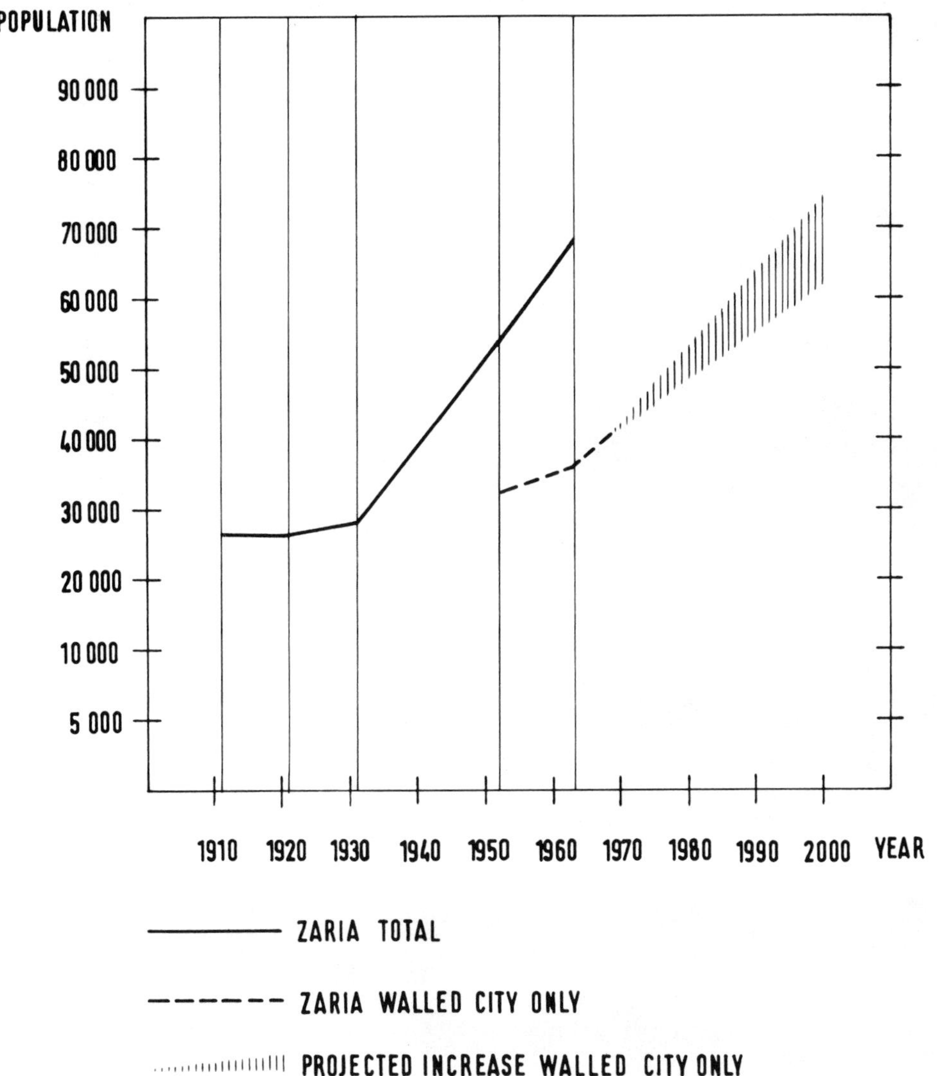

Graph A.3.1
Population trends and projections in Zaria

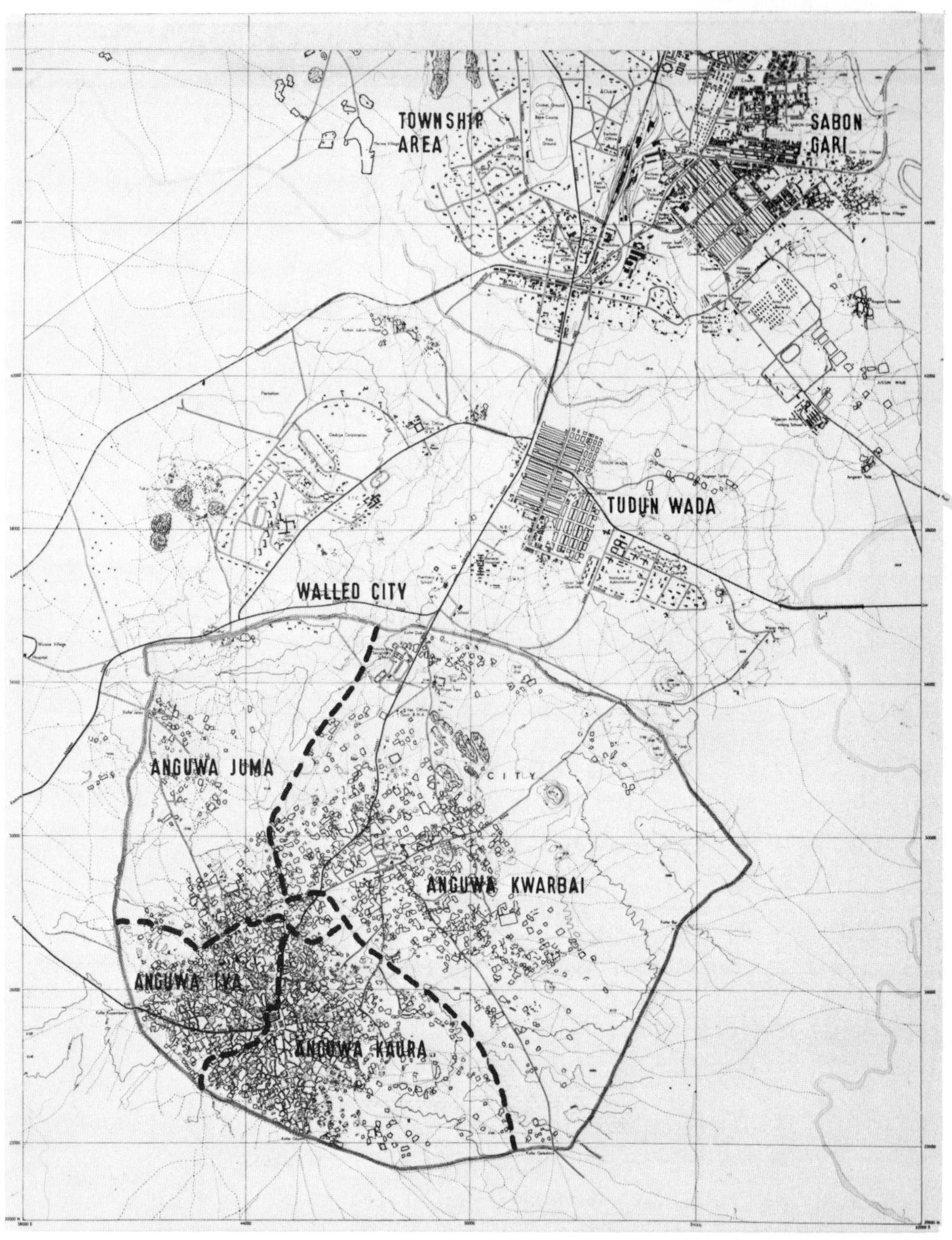

Map A.3.3
Administrative division of Zaria

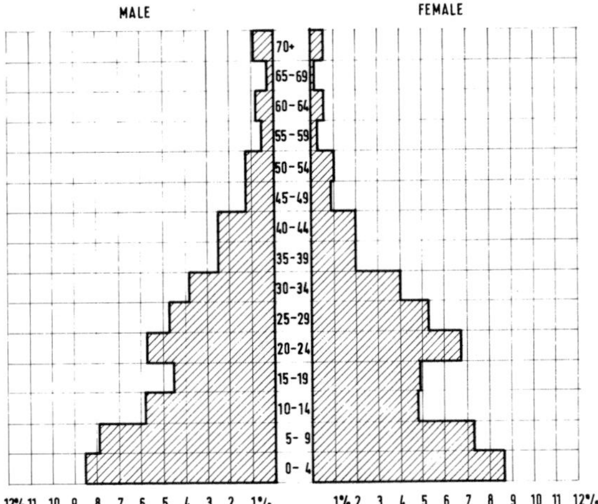

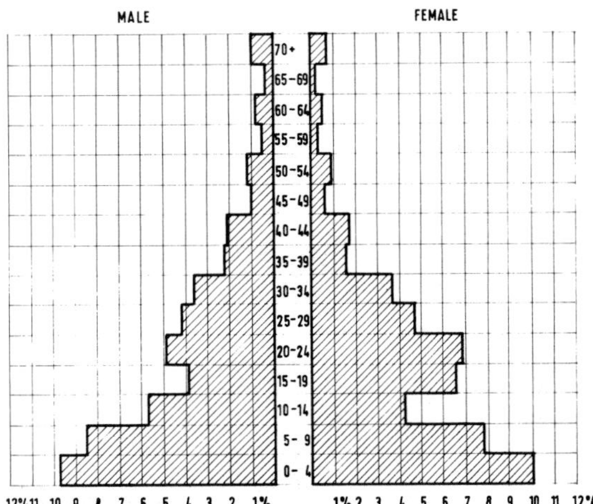

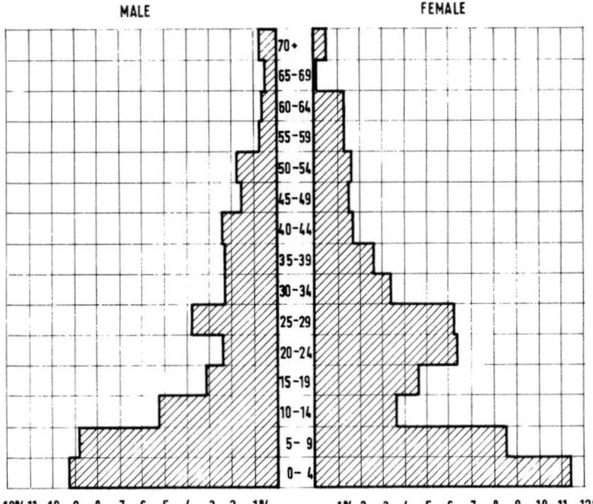

Diagram A.3.1
Age and sex distribution

Appendix 4

Stage		
1	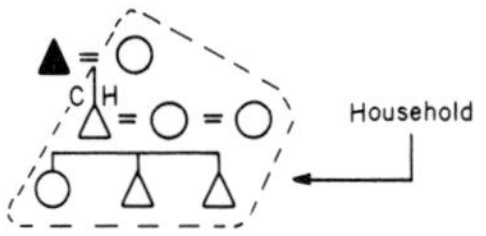 C H Household	Nucleus or elementary family Parents and children
2	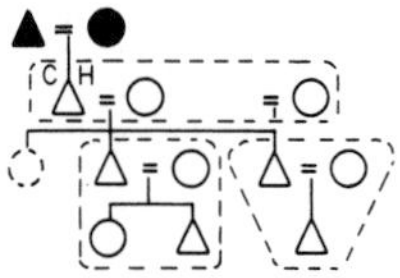 C H	Lineal extended family CH's family & CH's sons' families Change: Marriage
3	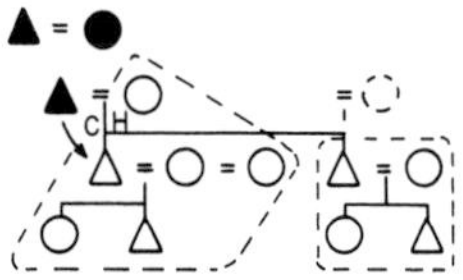 C H	Collateral agnates and families Change: Death of compound head
4	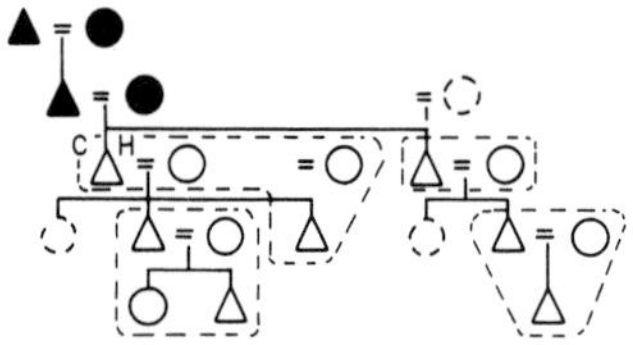 C H	Ditto Stage 3 Change: Marriage
5	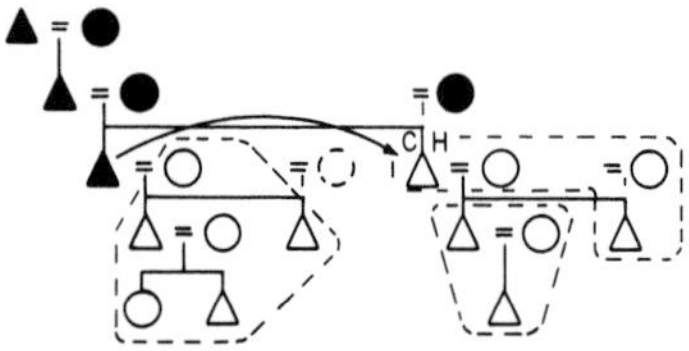 C H	Ditto Stage 3 Change: Death of compound head
6	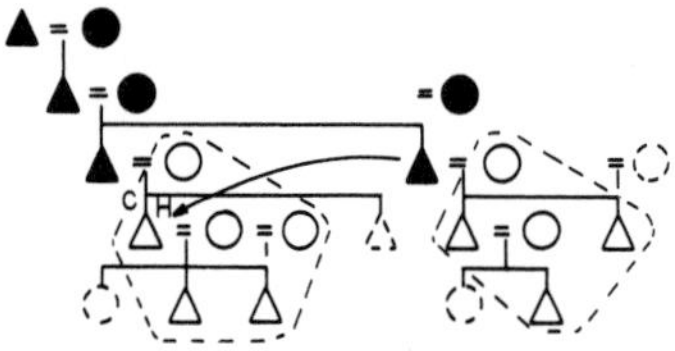 C H	Combination of parallel agnatic cousins and with families Change: Death of compound head

Diagram A.4.1
Stages of kinship groups
(development model)

Table A.4.1 Land use inside compounds (open area)

Category of land	No. of comp.	Sq. m	%	Av. area in sq. m
1 Courtyard area, unpaved	77	23,902	76.4	310.4
2 Cultivated land	44	4,088	13.1	92.9
3 Cement platforms	63	2,122	6.8	33.7
4 Washing places	73	1,012	3.2	13.9
5 Storage space	37	160	0.5	4.3
Total open area	77	31,284	100.0	406.3

Table A.4.2 Rooms and

	Compound head's hhs 77 hhs, 603 pers.			CH's f & h brs' hhs 39 hhs, 172 pers.			CH's sons' hhs 29 hhs, 106 pers.		
	Rms	Sq. m	%	Rms	Sq. m	%	Rms	Sq. m	%
1. Living area									
Rooms used for sleeping	359	2,896.3	27.65	93	706.8	6.75	55	415.5	3.97
Sitting rooms & central halls	88	815.8	7.79	20	219.9	2.10	7	55.2	0.53
Stores for personal articles	29	215.4	2.06	10	61.6	0.59	3	20.2	0.19
Empty living & sleeping rooms	96	754.6	7.20	5	42.6	0.41	3	23.7	0.23
Total	572	4,682.1	44.70	128	1,030.9	9.85	68	514.6	4.92
2. Common rooms									
Entrance hut	70	811.2	7.74				1	7.5	0.07
Second entrance hut	85	745.9	7.13	2	20.9	0.20	4	24.8	0.24
Passages and staircases		72.3	0.69		3.3	0.03			
Total	155	1,629.4	15.56	2	24.2	0.23	5	32.3	0.31
3. Basic ancillary facilities									
Kitchens	70	508.5	4.85	15	79.8	0.76	4	26.2	0.25
Kitchen stores	17	101.3	0.97	2	11.5	0.11			
Other stores	40	337.7	3.22	3	25.8	0.25			
Toilets and bathrooms	27	143.3	1.37	1	4.2	0.04			
Total	154	1,090.8	10.41	21	121.3	1.16	4	26.2	0.25
4. Commercial rooms									
Shops and workshops	12	111.1	1.06						
Stores for trading articles	9	131.0	1.25						
Stables	19	98.4	0.94	4	32.0	0.30	2	10.2	0.10
Total	40	340.5	3.25	4	32.0	0.30	2	10.2	0.10
Grand total	921	7,742.8	73.9	155	1,208.4	11.5	79	583.3	5.6

floor area per household

CH.s f & h brs' sons' hhs 25 hhs, 118 pers.			Other related hhs 10 hhs, 29 pers.			Clients' & strangers' hhs 11 hhs, 39 pers.			Total no. of hhs 191 hhs, 1,067 pers.		
Rms	Sq. m	%	Rms	Sq. m	%	Rms	Sq. m	%	Rms	Sq. m	%
58	400.0	3.82	15	121.1	1.16	18	148.1	1.41	598	4,687.8	44.7
10	84.6	0.81	6	39.2	0.37	1	7.0	0.07	132	1,221.7	11.7
			2	17.2	0.16				44	314.4	3.0
2	10.5	0.10	3	26.2	0.25				109	857.6	8.2
70	495.1	4.73	26	203.7	1.94	19	155.1	1.48	883	7,081.5	67.6
									71	818.7	7.8
									91	791.6	7.6
										75.6	0.7
									162	1,685.9	16.1
4	26.8	0.26	2	14.8	0.14	2	11.1	0.11	97	667.2	6.4
			1	6.6	0.06				20	119.4	1.1
1	4.4	0.04							44	367.9	3.5
			1	4.8	0.04				29	152.3	1.5
5	31.2	0.30	4	26.2	0.24	2	11.1	0.11	190	1,306.8	12.5
									12	111.1	1.0
									9	131.0	1.3
2	8.5	0.08	1	8.0	0.07				28	157.1	1.5
2	8.5	0.08	1	8.0	0.07				49	399.2	3.8
77	534.8	5.1	31	237.9	2.3	21	166.2	1.6	1,284	10,473.4	100.0

Table A.4.3 Male members of 77 compounds by relationship to the compound head

	Marital status						Age group							
	Adopted sing.	Sing.	Mar.	Div.	Wid.	Temp. absent[a]	0–4	5–14	15–24	25–39	40–54	55–69	70+	Total
1 Compound head			76						1	20	34	15	6	76
2 CH's sons		126	27			2	55	53	26	15	4			153
3 CH's sons' sons	2	24					12	12	2					26
4 CH's daughters' sons	3						1	2						3
Total	5	150	103			2	68	67	29	35	38	15	6	258
5 CH's father			1										1	1
Total			1										1	1
6 CH's full brothers		2	24			1			3	11	9	2	1	26
7 CH's full brothers' sons	20	32	18			2	9	34	10	14	3			70
8 CH's full brothers' sons' sons		16				2	6	10						16
9 CH's full sisters' sons	5	1	1			1		5	1	1				7
10 CH's full sisters' sons' sons		1					1							1
Total	25	52	43			6	16	49	14	26	12	2	1	120
11 CH's half brothers		4	14					1	5	9	2	1		18
12 CH's half brothers' sons		9	5				3	5	1	4	1			14
13 CH's half brothers' sons' sons		8					1	7						8
14 CH's half sisters' sons	1							1						1
Total	1	21	19				4	14	6	13	3	1		41
15 CH's father's brother		1						1						1
16 CH's father's brothers' sons	1		2					1		2				3
17 CH's father's brs' sons' sons	1	2					2		1					3
Total	2	3	2				2	2	1	2				7

18 CH's mother's brother			1						1				1
19 CH's mother's brothers' sons	2		1			1			2				3
Total	2		2			1			3				4
20 CH's daughters' husbands					2								
21 CH's full sister's husband			1		1				1				1
Total			1		3				1				1
22 CH's wives' brothers	3	1					3	1					4
23 CH's wives' brothers' sons	2						2						2
24 CH's wives' other kin	2						2						2
25 CH's full brs' wives' other kin	1	1					1	1					2
26 CH's half brs' wives' other kin	1						1						1
Total	9	2					9	2					11
27 CH's client		13	4				7	7	2	1			17
28 CH's clients' sons		2				1	1						2
Total		15	4			1	8	7	2	1			19
29 Unrelated males		3	9	2	1				8	6			14
30 Unrelated males' sons		6				6							6
Total		9	9	2	1	6			8	6			20
Grand total male	44	252	184	2	12	98	149	59	90	60	18	8	482

[a] Not counted in total population.

Table A.4.4 Female members of 77 compounds by relationship to the compound head

	Marital status						Age group							
	Adopted sing.	Sing.	Mar.	Div.	Wid.	Temp. absent[a]	0–4	5–14	15–24	25–39	40–54	55–69	70+	Total
1 Compound head					1							1		1
2 CH.s daughters		85	2				42	43		2				87
3 CH's sons' daughters	5	23					16	12						28
4 CH's daughters' daughters		5					4	1						5
Total	5	113	2		1		62	56		2		1		121
5 CH's full sisters		1	2	2	2			1		3	1	2		7
6 CH's full sisters' daughters		2					1	1						2
7 CH's full sist's daus' daughters	2						1	1						2
8 CH's full brothers' daughters	5	29			2		19	15		2				36
9 CH's full brs' sons' daughters		26					17	9						26
Total	7	58	2	2	4		38	27		5	1	2		73
10 CH's half sisters		1		1				1			1			2
11 CH's half sisters' daughters	3						2	1						3
12 CH's half brothers' daughters		9					4	5						9
13 CH's half brs' sons' daughters		3					2	1						3
Total	3	13		1			8	8			1			17
14 CH's widowed mother					19						4	12	3	19
15 CH's half brs' wid. mother					4					1	3			4
16 CH's dead father's wives					5						2	2	1	5
Total					28					1	9	14	4	28
17 CH's father's mother					1								1	1
18 CH's father's sister				1							1			1
19 CH's mother's sisters					2							2		2
20 CH's mo's sist's br's daughter	1							1						1
Total	1			1	3			1			1	2	1	5

21 CH's wives' brs' daughters	15						7	8						15
22 CH's wives' sisters	4	1					1	4						5
23 CH's wives' other kin	3		2	1			1	2	1	1	1			6
24 CH's full brs' wives' other kin	1	1	1					2			1			3
25 CH's half brs' wives' other kin	3						1	2						3
26 CH's sons' wives' other kin	2							2						2
Total	28	2	3	1			10	20	1	1	2			34
27 CH's wives			152			4		5	46	64	30	7		152
28 CH's sons' wives			34			1		5	19	10				34
29 CH's full brothers' wives			36	1	1	2			11	22	4	1		38
30 CH's full brs' sons' wives			25					1	14	10				25
31 CH's full sists' sons' wives			2						2					2
32 CH's half brothers' wives			15		1	1		2	8	5	1			16
33 CH's half brs' sons' wives			7						4	3				7
34 CH's father's brs' sons' wives			2						1	1				2
35 CH's father's wife			1								1			1
36 CH's mother's brs' wife			1					1						1
37 CH's mother's brs' sons' wife			1						1					1
38 CH's clients' wives			3						2	1				3
39 Unrelated males' wives			9						5	4				9
Total			288	1	2	8		14	113	120	36	8		291
40 CH's clients' daughters		2					1	1						2
41 Unrelated males' daughters		5					2	3						5
42 Other unrelated females		1	1	5	2		1		3	2	1	2		9
Total		8	1	5	2		4	4	3	2	1	2		16
Grand total female	44	194	296	11	40	8	122	130	117	131	51	29	5	585

[a] Not counted in total population.

Table A.4.5 Distribution of household sizes

No. of persons	Hh group	CH's household			Dependent households			Total households		
		No. of hhs	%	No. of persons	No. of hhs	%	No. of persons	No. of hhs	%	No. of persons
1	1–2	1	3.9	1	2	27.2	2	3	17.8	3
2		2		4	29		58	31		62
3	3–4	5	14.3	15	25	36.7	75	30	27.8	90
4		6		24	17		68	23		92
5	5–6	10	24.6	50	17	23.7	85	27	24.0	135
6		9		54	10		60	19		114
7	7–8	6	16.9	42	6	6.2	42	12	10.5	84
8		7		56	1		8	8		64
9	9–10	6	15.6	54	5	5.3	45	11	9.4	99
10		6		60	1		10	7		70
11	11–12	7	15.6	77	1	0.9	11	8	6.8	88
12		5		60				5		60
Over 12	Over 12	7	9.1	106				7	3.7	106
Total		77	100.0	603	114	100.0	464	191	100.0	1,067
Average				7.8			4.1			5.6

Table A.4.6 Age of household heads

Age	Compound heads	Dependent household heads
15–19	–	3
20–24	1	14
25–29	6	33
30–34	9	17
35–39	5	18
40–44	13	12
45–49	12	4
50–54	9	7
55–59	7	–
60–64	6	2
65–69	3	2
70+	6	2
Total HHs	77	114

Table A.4.7 Household composition

	No. of com-pounds	No. of house-holds	A	B	C	D	E	F	G	H	I	J	K	L	M	N	O	Total no. of hhs	Total no. of persons
1. A	26	1	26															26	217
A + O	2	2	2														2	4	12
A + O2	2	3	2														4	6	26
A + O + N	1	3	1													1	1	3	9
Total stage 1	31		31													1	7	39	264
2. A + B	3	2	3	3														6	38
A + B2	4	3	4	8														12	63
A + B4	1	5	1	4														5	17
A + B + F2	1	4	1	1				2										4	23
Total stage 2	9		9	16				2										27	141
3. A + E	6	2	6				6											12	77
A + E2	4	3	4				8											12	77
A + I	4	2	4								4							8	41
A + I2	2	3	2								4							6	34
A + I + L	1	3	1								1			1				3	15
Total stage 3	17		17				14				9			1				41	244
4. A + E2 + B + F	1	5	1	1			2	1										5	20
A + E2 + B + F3	1	7	1	1			2	3										7	39
A + E + B3 + F3	1	8	1	3			1	3										8	38
A + E + B + F2	1	5	1	1			1	2										5	18
A + E + F	1	3	1				1	1										3	13
A + E + F2	2	4	2				2	4										8	37
A + E + I + B + F	1	5	1	1			1	1			1							5	26
A + I + B3 + F + J2	1	8	1	3				1			1	2						8	34
A + I2 + J2 + N	1	6	1								2	2				1		6	28
A + I + J	1	3	1								1	1						3	18
Total stage 4	11		11	10			10	16			5	5				1		58	271

5. A + B3 + F + N	1	6	1	3				1								1		6	27
Total stage 5	1	6	1	3				1								1		6	27
6. A + E + K	1	3	1				1						1					3	28
Total stage 6	1		1				1						1					3	28
Joint households																			
A + F + D	1	3	1			1		1										3	12
A + C	1	2	1		1													2	9
A + C + O	1	3	1		1												1	3	17
A + G	1	2	1						1									2	10
A + G + H	1	3	1						1	1								3	16
A + H	1	2	1							1								2	6
A + M	1	2	1												1			2	22
Total	7		7		2	1		1	2	2					1		1	17	92
Grand total	77		77	29	2	1	25	20	2	2	14	5	1	1	1	3	8	191	1067

Key: Symbols

A Compound head's family
B CH's sons' families
C CH's daughters' families
D CH's father's family
E CH's full brothers' families
F CH's full brothers' sons' families
G CH's full sisters' families
H CH's full sisters' sons' families
I CH's half brothers' families
J CH's half brothers' sons' families
K CH's father's brothers' sons' families
L CH's mother's brothers' families
M CH's mother's brothers' sons' families
N CH's clients' families
O Strangers' families

Example: A + B2 (Compound head's family plus two CH's sons' families)

Table A.4.8 Average floor area per household and person according to household size

No. of persons per household	No. of households	No. of persons	Average persons per household	Total floor area			Sleeping area		
				Total floor area, m^2	Average area in m^2 per household	Average area in m^2 per person	Sleeping area, m^2	Average sleeping area in m^2 per household	Average sleeping area in m^2 per person
1–2	34	65	1.91	586.7	17.2	9.0	312.8	9.2	4.8
3–4	53	182	3.43	1,614.5	30.5	8.9	836.3	15.8	4.6
5–6	46	249	5.41	2,369.6	51.5	9.5	1,098.6	23.9	4.4
7–8	20	148	7.40	1,354.2	67.7	9.2	598.3	29.9	4.0
9–10	18	169	9.39	1,745.5	97.0	10.3	682.0	37.9	4.0
11–12	13	148	11.38	1,538.8	118.4	10.4	661.5	50.9	4.5
13+	7	106	15.14	1,264.1	180.6	11.9	498.3	71.2	4.7
Total	191	1,067		10,473.4			4,687.8		
Average			5.59		54.8	9.8		24.5	4.4

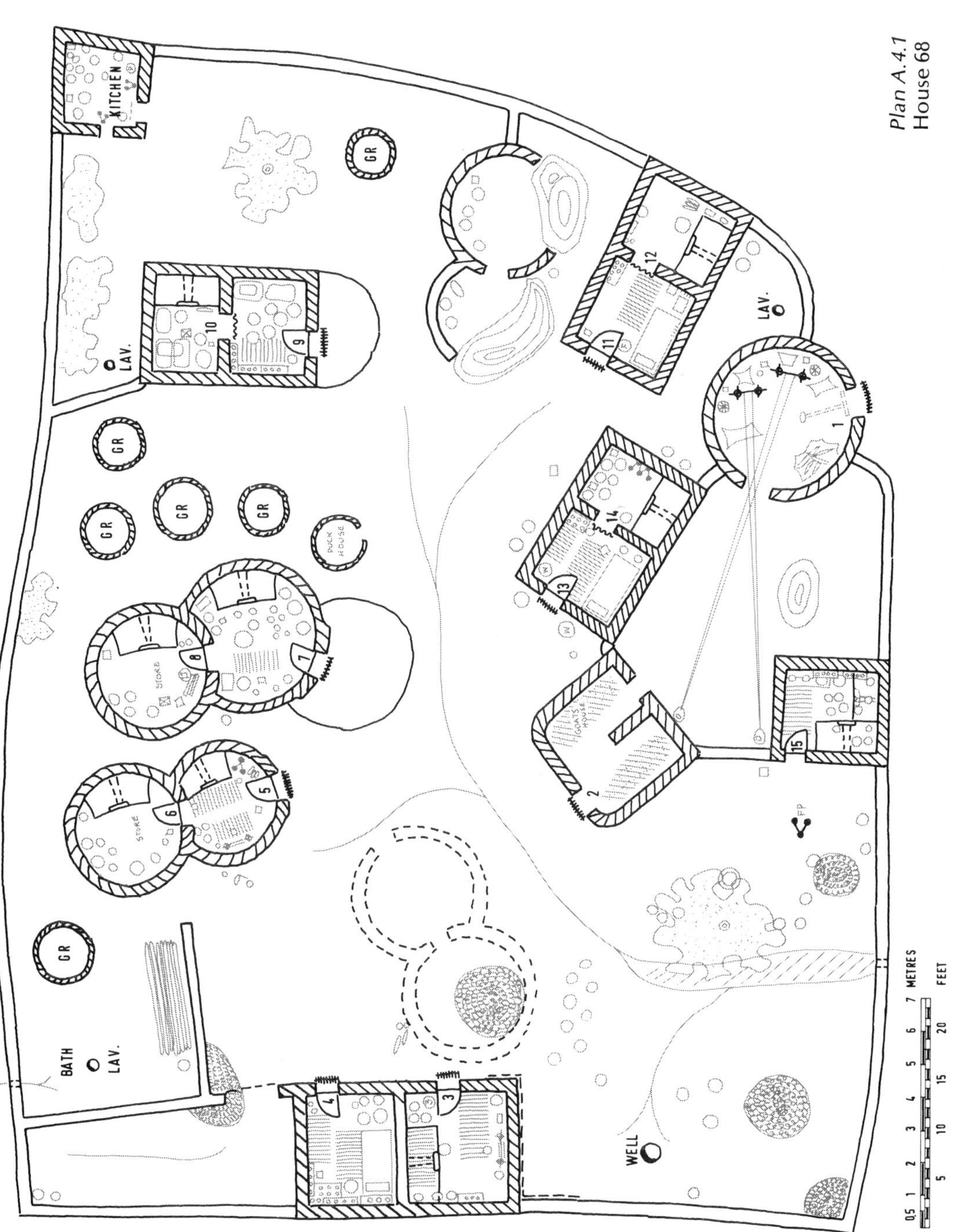

Plan A.4.1
House 68

Plan A.4.2
House 71

Appendix 5

Table A.5.1 Ibadan consumer price index

Base: average 1953 = 100

	All items	Accommodation fuel and light	Food and drink	Tobacco and kola	Clothing	Transport	Other goods and services
Weights	100	10	56	5	11	6	12
1961	127	121	131	145	107	101	131
1962	137	122	143	147	130	106	137
1963	128	119	125	146	143	107	135
1964	127	118	123	141	143	113	138
1965	131	120	131	127	145	118	135
1966	146	120	158	130	146	119	135
1967	141	121	145	130	159	120	137
1968	136	120	135	133	154	126	145
1969	148	128	142	129	167	131	161
1970	166	137	174	129	178	146	170
1971	173	147	235	128	175	143	187

Source: Federal Office of Statistics, Nigeria, *Annual Abstract of Statistics 1971*, Lagos, 1972, p. 106.

Table A.5.2 Kaduna consumer price index

Base: average 1957 = 100

	All items	Accommodation	Food	Drinks	Tobacco and kola	Fuel and light	Clothing	Other goods	Transport and other services
Weights	100	8	50	6	5	5	13	6	7
1961	115								
1962	122	112	120	128	132	146	128	110	118
1963	119	112	111	130	134	160	127	110	130
1964	118	112	107	135	132	148	136	108	135
1965	122	112	113	147	114	152	139	111	138
1966	131	112	133	136	111	152	138	112	140
1967	128	112	122	142	111	191	140	117	131
1968	130	112	111	159	118	199	170	149	128
1969	147	112	135	163	129	197	200	150	131
1970	157	112	159	154	114	154	190	177	143
1971	168	112	200	144	123	212	196	187	146

Source: Federal Office of Statistics, Nigeria, *Annual Abstract of Statistics, 1971*, Lagos 1972, p. 107.

Table A.5.4 Number of valid and omitted households

	CH's hhs		Dep. hhs		Tenant hhs		Total hhs	
	No.	%	No.	%	No.	%	No.	%
Valid	77	100.0	70	61.4	–	–	147	77.0
Omitted	–	–	44	38.6	–	–	44	23.0
Total hhs	77	100.0	114	100.0	–	–	191	100.0

Table A.5.5 Income distribution of valid households

	CH's hhs		Dep. hhs		Tenant hhs		Total hhs	
Income group	No.	%	No.	%	No.	%	No.	%
Low	41	53.2	60	85.8	–	–	101	68.7
Middle	32	41.6	10	14.2	–	–	42	28.6
High	4	5.2	–	–	–	–	4	2.7
Total hhs	77	100.0	70	100.0	–	–	147	100.0

Table A.5.3 Occupational pattern, survey sample

	Main occupation			Sec. occ., CH						Sec. occ., DHH						
	CH	DHH	Total hhs	1[a]	2	3	4	5	Total	1	2	3	4	5	Total	Total sec. occ.
1. Agriculture																
Farmer or farm lab.	2	8	10			1		1	2			5		3	8	10
Subtotal	2	8	10			1		1	2			5		3	8	10
2. Art and crafts																
Tailor	6	18	24	4	1				5	10					10	15
Embroiderer	3	11	14	1	1				2	10					10	12
Malam	4	7	11		2				2	1		1			2	4
Builder	2	4	6	1	1				2	4					4	6
Weaver, dyer	1	2	3	1					1	2					2	3
Butcher	1		1	1					1							1
Barber, baker	2		2	1					1							1
Other crafts	2	7	9		1		1		2	4		2	1		7	9
Subtotal	21	49	70	9	6		1		16	31		3	1		35	51
3. Trade																
Textiles	10	11	21	2	4	2			8	5		1			6	14
Prov. & cooked food	9	12	21	4	3				7	7					7	14
Potash (natron)	3	1	4	1	2				3	1					1	4
Kola nuts	2	4	6		2				2	1	1				2	4
Miscellaneous	2	4	6	1					1	1					1	2
Subtotal	26	32	58	8	11	2			21	15	1	1			17	38

4. Services																
NA police	4	6	10	1	2				3							3
Army		4	4													
NA clerk	5		5	1	2				3							3
Gen. labourers, watchmen	4	2	6	3			1		4	2					2	6
NA messenger	2	3	5	1					1	2				1	3	4
Car driver	3	1	4		1				1							1
NA vet. assistant	3		3		2				2							2
Gov. produce exam.	1	1	2	1					1		1				1	2
Station master, NR		1	1													
Subtotal	22	18	40	7	7		1		15	4	1			1	6	21
5. Miscellaneous																
Retired	6	1	7	2	1	1			4							4
Invalid		1	1													
Student, ABU, Kano		1	1							1					1	1
No response		4	4													
Subtotal	6	7	13	2	1	1			4	1					1	5
Total	77	114	191	26	25	4	2	1	58	51	2	9	1	4	67	125

CH = Compound head
DHH = Dependent household head

[a] 1 = Agriculture (paid labour)
2 = Agriculture (self)
3 = Art and crafts
4 = Trade
5 = Miscellaneous

Table A.5.6 Distribution of income for different size households

A. TOTAL HOUSEHOLDS

Av. month. inc. / Persons in hh	1–2	3–4	5–6	7–8	9–10	11–12	13+	Total	%	Cum. %
Sh. 0–99.9	6	7	6	2				21	14.3	14.3
100–199.9 low	10	19	10	2	2	2		45	30.6	44.9
200–299.9	6	5	10	7	3	2	2	35	23.8	68.7
300–399.9	1	5	5	2	5	4	4	26	17.7	86.4
400–599.9 middle		1	1	2	3	4		11	7.5	93.0
600–999.9			2		3			5	3.4	97.3
1,000–1,999.9			1		1	1		3	2.0	99.3
2,000–2,999.9 high							1	1	0.7	100.0
3,000+										
Total households	23	37	35	15	17	13	7	147	100.0	
Percentage	15.6	25.2	23.8	10.2	11.6	8.8	4.8	100.0		

B. COMPOUND HEADS' HOUSEHOLDS

Av. month. inc. / Persons in hh	1–2	3–4	5–6	7–8	9–10	11–12	13+	Total	%	Cum. %
Sh. 0–99.9	2	1		1				4	5.2	5.2
100–199.9 low	1	4	6	1	2	1		15	19.5	24.7
200–299.9		1	7	7	3	2	2	22	28.5	53.2
300–399.9		4	2	2	1	4	4	17	22.1	75.3
400–599.9 middle		1	1	2	3	4		11	14.3	89.6
600–999.9			2		2			4	5.2	94.8
1,000–1,999.9			1		1	1		3	3.9	98.7
2,000–2,999.9 high							1	1	1.3	100.0
3,000+										
Total households	3	11	19	13	12	12	7	77	100.0	
Percentage	3.9	14.3	24.6	16.9	15.6	15.6	9.1	100.0		

C. DEPENDENT OR SEMI-DEPENDENT HOUSEHOLDS

Av. month. inc. / Persons in hh	1–2	3–4	5–6	7–8	9–10	11–12	13+	Total	%	Cum. %
Sh. 0–99.9	4	6	6	1				17	24.3	24.3
100–199.9 low	9	15	4	1		1		30	42.9	67.2
200–299.9	6	4	3					13	18.6	85.8
300–399.9	1	1	3		4			9	12.8	98.6
400–599.9 middle										
600–999.9					1			1	1.4	100.0
1,000–1,999.9										
2,000–2,999.9 high										
3,000+										
Total households	20	26	16	2	5	1		70	100.0	
Percentage	28.6	37.1	22.9	2.9	7.1	1.4		100.0		

Table A.5.7 Budget no. 10

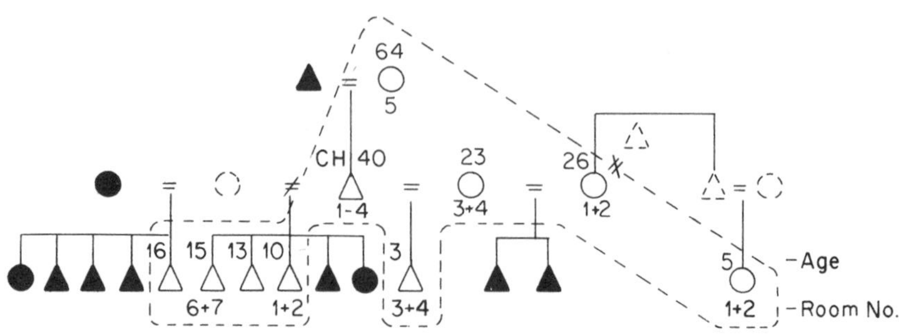

Total population: 6 males, 4 females
Occupation of household head: farmer and farm labourer

Household income and expenditure, 1967/1968

Cash income	£N	Cash expenditure	£N
Rainy season		Food	
Household head works in the morning as a farm labourer gets 5s. per day; total income in season about	18. 0.0	The harvest of guinea corn and millet lasted about 5 to 6 months. During this time he bought only stew ingredients at 7d. per day and meat at 6d., 3 or 4 times per week.	
In the afternoon he works on his own farm; sons help him	–		
Sells groundnut harvest	7.10.0	Expenditure about	7. 5.0
and two goats	3.12.0	Buys extra staple food for about 6 months at 2s. per day plus stew ingredients and meat. Expenditure about	28.10.0
Dry season		Stimulants and drinks	
Household head helps builder for about 7 weeks gets 6s. per day. Total income about	12. 0.0	Spends 3–4d. on kola nuts per day, total	5.10.0
Household head goes to village to cut and sell firewood and grass. Profit made after two months	9. 5.0	Firewood and lighting	
During the time of absence his mother helped with about 5s. per week to buy food; she spins and receives some money from her brother who she says is a rich man	2. 0.0	Spends 6d. per day (but sometimes collects firewood on farm or in village) plus 1d. kerosene per day	8. 0.0
Household head borrowed not paid back yet.	5. 0.0	Clothing	
Received some gifts from ward head and friends, about	3. 0.0	Bought some clothing with money given by father's brother.	?
Father's brother gave him some money to buy clothes but he can't remember how much	?	Accommodation	
		Maintenance: roof repair	1.10.0
		Other expenditure	
		Muslim festivals	3.15.0
		Tax paid last year according to ward head's tax file; but household head insists he paid £N 1.10.0.	1. 8.0
Total known cash income per annum	60. 7.0	Total known expenditure per annum	55.18.0
Average monthly income 100.6 shillings			

Table A.5.8 Budget no. 63

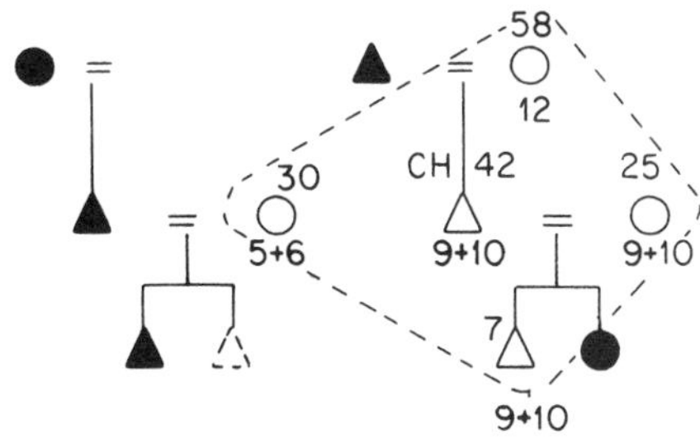

Total population: 2 males 3 females
Occupation of household head: barber–doctor (*wanzami*)
Household head has small farm

Household income and expenditure, 1967/1968

Cash income	£N	Cash expenditure	£N
All seasons		Food	
Household head has on average 8 to 10 customers a day, shave 2s.3d., haircut 3d. Income per month about £N 3.10.0: per annum about	42. 0.0	The harvest of guinea corn and millet lasted about 3 months. During this time he buys only stew ingredients at 5–6d. per day and meat at 6d. 4 times per week.	3.10.0
He spends about 7 days on his farm during the farming season, brother's son helps him. He says this does not affect his craft income much; he has more business before the Muslim festivals, can't say how much.		Buys extra staple food for about 9 months at 1s. per day plus stew ingredients and meat. Expenditure about	23.10.0
		Stimulants and drinks	
		Spends no money on kola nuts as he gets them free from customers.	
Household head performs approximately 3–4 circumcisions per month. Average earning over the last 2 months was 9s. per circumcision, but gives his helper 1s. each time;		Firewood and lighting	
		Firewood 4d. and kerosene 1d. per day	7.11.0
Annual income about	20. 0.0	Clothing	
One customer paid about £N 1 10s., he says; also gets food, clothing and some extra money as gifts, but does not know how much.		Bought clothing for himself, his wife and child at Lesser Beiram, total about	9.10.0
Attends 2–3 naming ceremonies per month, shaves the child's head and makes any tattoos the father requests, gets on average 5s. per		Accommodation	
		Improvement: new cement floor	2.15.0
		Maintenance: roof repair, whitewash on walls, total	2. 5.0
ceremony.	9. 0.0	Other expenditure	
Gets also some food and cash gifts, does not know how much.		Expenses at Muslim festivals, does not know precisely but thinks about	17. 0.0
		Tax paid last year	2. 0.0
Total known cash income per annum	71. 0.0	Total known expenditure per annum	68. 1.0
Average monthly income 118.3 shillings			

Table A.5.9 Budget no. 67

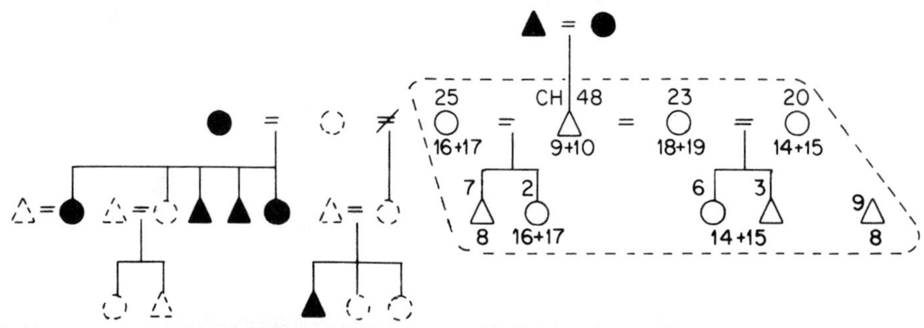

Total population: 4 males, 5 females
Occupation of household head: trader in potash (natron), old paper, and clothes
Household head has farm

Household income and expenditure, 1967/1968

Cash income	£N	Cash expenditure	£N
All seasons		Food	
Household head bought up to 500 bags of potash from Guru in Kano. Price at Zaria railway station 23s. per bag. Sold 300 bags in bulk for 5s. profit each. Total profit	75. 0.0	The harvest of guinea corn lasts about 7 months. At this time he buys each day meat at 1s., stew ingredients at 1s.6d. and yam or rice at 6d. Expenditure about	31.10.0
In the dry season sold about 150 bags at his market stall at 6d. per *mudu*, average profit per bag is 7s. Total income	52.10.0	For about 5 months he buys additional staple food for 3s. per day plus meat and stew ingredients. Gives some food to students.	46.10.0
Sold about 80 bags in wet season. Total income.	28. 0.0	Stimulants and drinks	
At the time of interview he stored 450–500 bags of potash in his house.		6d. for kola nuts per day	9. 3.0
Bought 200 gowns for £N 120 in wet season, sold in dry season at £N 30 profit.	30. 0.0	Firewood and lighting	
		Firewood 9d. per day, electricity about 15s. per month, total	23. 0.0
Buys on average 4 bundles of old newspapers or cement bags per month, sells one bundle at £N 2 profit, pays helper £N 1, profit about £N 7 per month	84. 0.0	Clothing	
		Bought clothing for himself, his wives and children at Lesser Beiram, about	38. 0.0
Household head farms with paid labour (*kodago*).		Accommodation	
Sold millet harvest for £N 15 and groundnuts at £N 8, but keeps guinea corn which lasted about 7 months.	23. 0.0	Improvement: new cement floor	4. 3.0
		Maintenance: roof repair	1. 2.0
		Other expenditure	
		Festival expenses about	28. 0.0
		Tax paid	8.10.0
		Pays helper in shop 10s. per week, rent for market stall 8s. per month, total	30.15.0
		£N 2 to relatives per month	24. 0.0
Average monthly income 487.5 shillings		Koranic teacher 2s. per week	5. 4.0
		Bought watch for himself	4. 0.0
		Paid farm labourers about	18. 0.0
Total known cash income per year	292.10.0	Total known expenditure per year	271.17.0

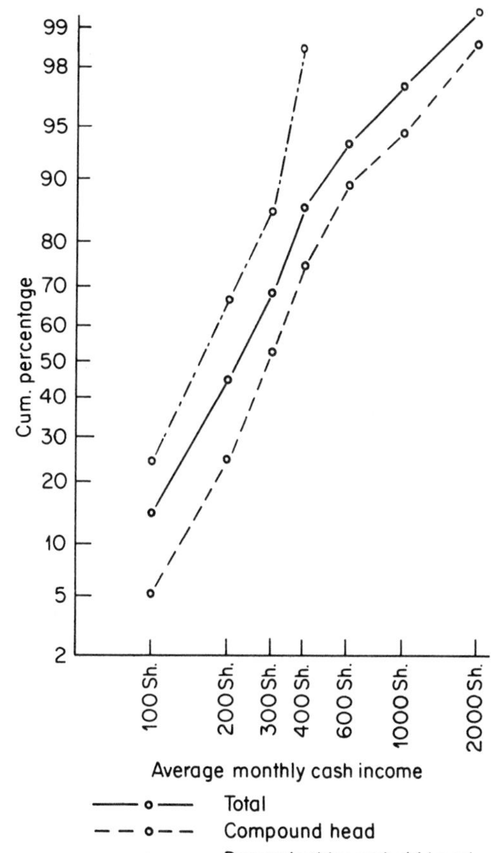

Graph A.5.1
Distribution of household income in Zaria. (See Table A.5.6 on p. 350)

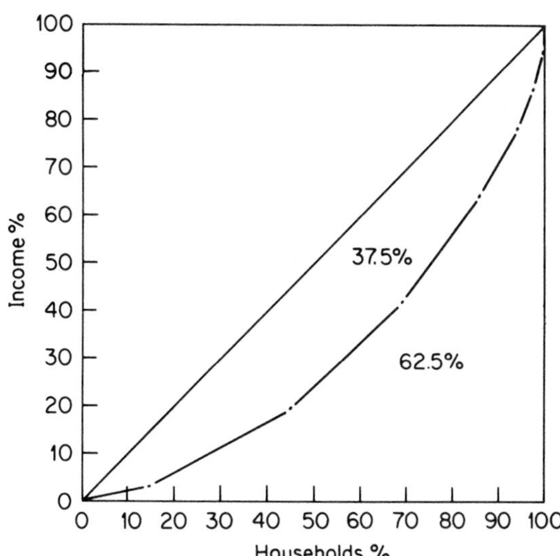

Graph A.5.2
Income distribution (Lorenz Curve) in Zaria

Appendix 6

Table A.6.1 Production, export, and consumption of sawn wood in Nigeria

	Production cu. m	Export cu. m	Home consumption cu. m
1960	–	62,302	–
1961	–	–	–
1962	–	–	–
1963	198,240	77,228	121,012
1964	209,568	76,314	133,254
1965	288,864	81,751	207,113
1966	320,000	74,000	246,000
1967	226,560	52,521	174,039

Source: Organization for Economic Co-operation and Development (OECD), *Tropical Timber*, Paris, 1969.

Table A.6.2 Consumption of sawn wood by end uses in percentages

Column	1	2	3
	West Africa 1959/1961	Nigeria 1962/1963	Nigeria 1964
Construction industry	73	82	80
Furniture industry	15	10	12
Packing and other uses	12	8	6
Engineering (bridges)	–	–	2
Total	100	100	100

Sources: Columns 1 and 2 United Nations FAO, *Timber Trends and Prospects in Africa*, Rome, 1967, pp. 000.
Column 3 National income estimates by the Federal Department of Statistics, 1964 (unpublished).

Table A.6.3 Production and import of cement in tons

	Production	%	Import	%	Total supply	%
1960	164,000	20.8	626,000	79.2	790,000	100.0
1961	358,000	44.5	446,000	55.5	804,000	"
1962	476,000	58.7	335,000	41.3	811,000	"
1963	518,000	63.3	300,000	36.7	818,000	"
1964	653,000	78.6	178,000	21.4	831,000	"
1965	967,000	85.0	171,000	15.0	1,138,000	"
1966	986,000	86.7	151,000	13.3	1,137,000	"
1967	722,000	84.3	134,000	15.7	856,000	"
1968	565,000	86.3	90,000	13.7	655,000	"
1969	557,000	84.4	103,000	15.6	660,000	"
1970	587,000	56.1	459,000	43.9	1,046,000	"

Source: Federal Office of Statistics, Nigeria, *Digest of Statistics* Lagos, 20 (2) April 1971, Table 5.4, p. 20.

Table A.6.4 Steel import and consumption, 1965 and 1970 (*'000 tons*)

		1965	1970
1	Tubes	99.3	223.9
2	Wire rod and bars	51.3	75.0
3	Sections	24.1	51.9
4	Sheets (uncoated)	36.9	44.6
5	Sheets galv. and corrugated in Nigeria		40.0
6	Sheets galvanized flat	7.0	3.9
7	Plates	7.2	19.4
8	Tinplates	9.3	12.2
9	Wire	2.1	6.4
10	Metal strips	1.9	6.0
11	Other steel	7.2	6.3
	Total	246.3	489.6

Source: British Steel Corporation, 'Nigeria: economic prospects and steel import potentials in 1975', compiled by Ifor A. Ffowcs Williams, London, 1970, (Unpublished report), p. 16.

Table A.6.5 Steel processing from imported material in 1970 (*'000 tons*)

		1970
1	Galvanizing and corrugating sheets	40.0
2	Tubes from metal strips	6.0
3	Re-rolling bars or sections	75.0
4	Enamelware industry	35.0
	Total	156.0

Source: British Steel Corporation, 'Nigeria', p. 17.

Table A.6.6 Structural development of 77 surveyed compounds from 17 December 1963 to 1 November 1968

	Total no. of rooms 1 Nov. 1968		No. of rooms built 1963–1968		No. of rooms dis-appeared 1963–1968		No. of rooms with roof structure converted 1963–1968		Total no. of rooms 17 Dec. 1963		No. of rooms decreased 1963–1968	No. of rooms increased 1963–1968	Total growth rate % 1963–1968	Annual growth rate %
	No.	m²	No.	m²	No.	m²	No.	m²	No.	m²	–	+		
A. Palace area														
35 compounds														
Thatched roof	181	1,419.6	43	311.8	60	[a]			223	[a]	42		–18.8	–3.9
Mud roof	322	2,746.4	82	609.0	6		25	197.6	256			66	25.8	5.3
C. iron roof	61	567.7	19	194.1			32	272.3	10			51	510.0	104.5
Ceil. gd flr rm	6	60.8					3	36.3	3			3	100.0	
Total	570	4,794.5	144	1,114.9	66		60	506.2	492		–42	+120	15.9	
Increase												78		+3.25
B. Market area														
42 compounds														
Thatched roof	180	1,444.4	17	114.2	71				249		69		–27.7	–5.7
Mud roof	376	2,985.8	51	381.0	7		15	112.2	364			12	3.3	0.7
C. iron roof	87	815.9	15	162.4			43	391.6	29			58	200.0	41.0
Ceil gd flr rm	14	123.4					4	31.0	10			4	40.0	
Total	657	5,369.5	83	657.6	78		62	534.8	652		–69	+74	0.8	
Increase												5		+0.16
C. Combined area														
77 compounds														
Thatched roof	361	2,864.0	60	426.0	131				472		111		–23.5	–4.8
Mud roof	698	5,732.2	133	990.0	13		40	309.8	620			78	12.6	2.6
C. iron roof	148	1,383.6	34	356.5			75	663.9	39			109	279.5	57.3
Ceil gd flr rm	20	184.2					7	67.3	13			7	53.8	
Total	1,227	10,164.0	227	1,772.5	144		122	1,041.0	1,144		–111	+194	7.3	
Increase												83		+1.47

[a]Not known.

Table A.6.7 'What improvement do you think the compound most needs?'

	Answers by compound head	Number of compound heads	%
1	Corrugated iron roof	31	40.2
2	More sleeping rooms	15	19.5
3	Cement plaster on walls	9	11.7
4	Change thatch to mud roof	7	9.1
5	If new rooms, walls in concrete blocks	6	7.8
6	Cement floors	1	1.3
7	Outdoor cement working platform	1	1.3
8	Electricity	1	1.3
9	Bathroom	1	1.3
10	Other improvement	2	2.6
11	No response	2	2.6
12	Satisfied	1	1.3
	Total compound heads	77	100.0

Table A.6.8 Age distribution of rooms

Column	1	2	3	4
Year	Age of rooms	No. of rooms built	No. of rooms survived	Cum. %
1968/1969	<1	48[a]	967	100.0
1966/1967	1–2	119	919	95.0
1964/1965	3–4	99	800	82.7
1962/1963	5–6	70	701	72.5
1960/1961	7–8	80	631	62.6
1958/1959	9–10	73	551	57.0
1956/1957	11–12	79	478	49.4
1954/1955	13–14	54	399	41.3
1952/1953	15–16	40	345	35.7
1950/1951	17–18	37	305	31.5
1948/1949	19–20	34	268	27.7
1946/1947	21–22	16	234	24.2
1944/1945	23–24	7	218	22.5
1942/1943	25–26	17	211	21.8
1940/1941	27–28	14	194	20.1
Before 1940	29+	180	180	18.6
No. of rooms		967		
Age unknown		299		
Total rooms		1,266		

[a]Includes 39 rooms under construction.

Table A.6.9 Costs of construction in Zaria walled city, October 1968 (*in Shillings*)

PLAN

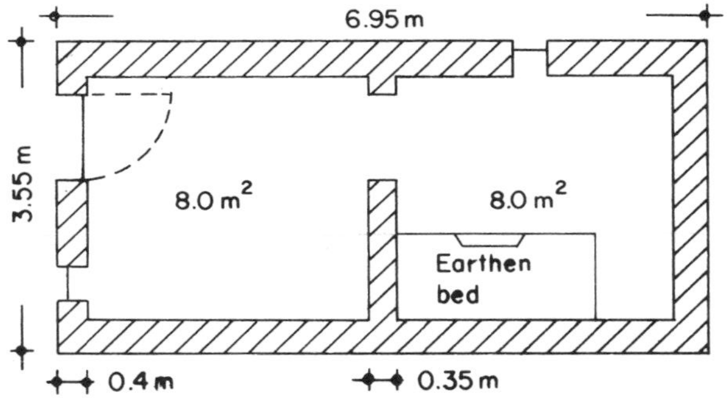

6.95 m
3.55 m
8.0 m²
8.0 m²
Earthen bed
0.4 m
0.35 m

Two-roomed building with three different roof types. Height of mud walls 2.80 m

Total floor area 16 sq. m

Type of roof	Thatched roof			Mud roof			C. iron roof		
Element of building	Min.[a]	Max.[b]	% max.	Min.	Max.	% max.	Min.	Max.	% max.
Walls (26.3 m^3 mud)[d]									
Lintels	14	192[c]	31.3						
Lintels & shear reinforcement				38	220	25.5	38	220	15.3
Roof									
Beams, thatch & rope	163	235	38.5						
Azara beams				338[e]	459	53.1			
Azara & C. iron sheets							762	1,030	71.8
Door and windows 1 door 0.85 x 2.00 m 2 windows 0.4 x 0.4 m	45	45	7.3	45	45	5.2	45	45	3.1
Finishes Floor, cement screed Int. walls, whitewash Out. waterproof plaster	62	140	22.9	62	140	16.2	62	140	9.8
Total	284	612	100.0	483	864	100.0	907	1,435	100.0

Cost per sq. m in s.	17.7	38.2		30.2	54.0		56.7	89.7	
% of material cost			46.4			55.9			63.2
% of labour cost			53.6			44.1			36.8
Improvements									
Flat mud roof[f]				256	398				
C. iron roof[g]							420	571	
Total in s.				256	398		420	571	
Cost per sq. m in s.				16.0	24.9		26.5	35.7	

[a]Material cost only.
[b]Material and labour cost.
[c]Labour cost, experienced builder about 10 shillings per day, assistant builder 6 shillings per day, and unskilled labourer about 3 shillings per day.
[d]Material for mud walls is taken from a dilapidated hut inside the compound, extras will have to be allowed if mud is carried from borrow-pit to the compound.
[e]See p. 363.
[f]Change thatch into mud roof.
[g]Corrugated iron sheets on top of mud roof.

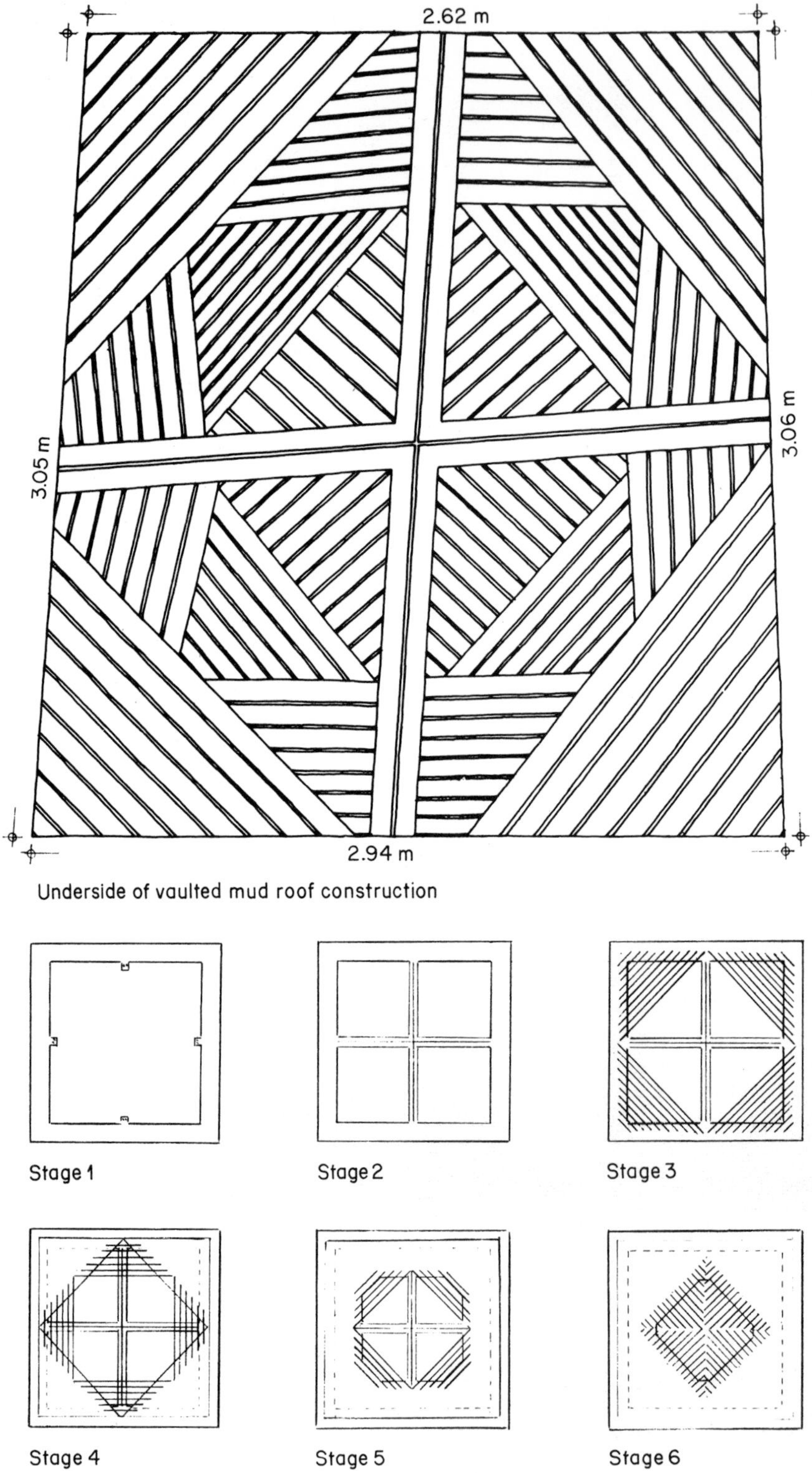

2.62 m

3.05 m

3.06 m

2.94 m

Underside of vaulted mud roof construction

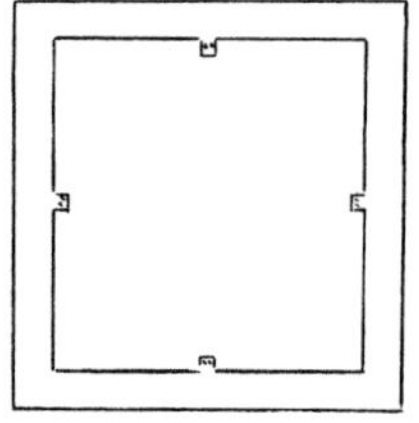

Stage 1

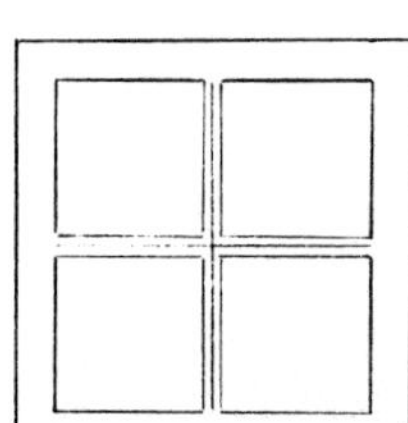

Stage 2

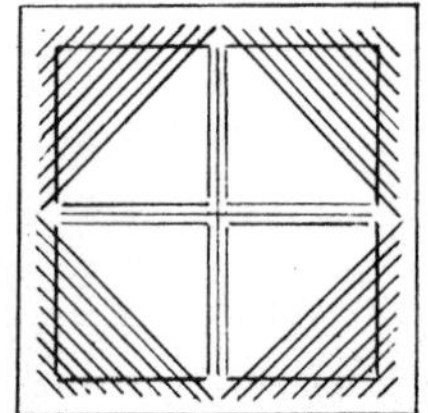

Stage 3

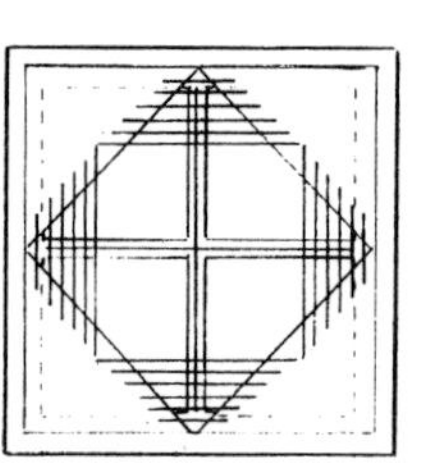

Stage 4

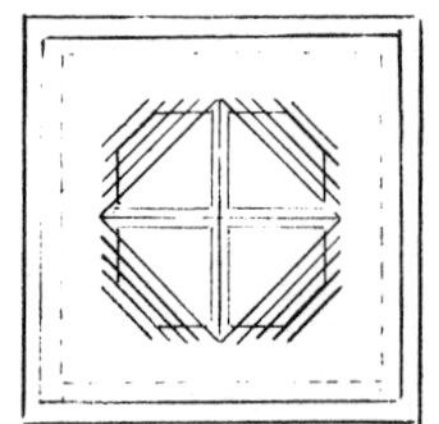

Stage 5

Stage 6

Diagram A.6.1
Construction of vaulted mud roof

Table A.6.10 Number of azara beams needed for mud roof construction

Stage	No. of beams		Metres	No. of beams @ 2.3 m long
1	8 10	In lower part of double arch and as additional shear reinforcement in walls. Total length	41.4	18
2	16	In double arch (*daurin gaga*)	36.8	16
3	36	Varying between 2.3 m and 0.6 m Total length	56.8	25
4	60	Varying between 1.1 m and 0.6 m Total length	46.6	20
5	30	Varying between 1.6 m and 0.6 m Total length	33.5	15
6	50	Varying between 1.0 m and 0.6 m Total length	37.7	16
		Total number of *azara* beams, average length 2.3 m		110

Table A.6.11 The financing of houses

	No. of loans	Gifts and grants	Shillings	%
New construction				
CH's personal income and savings			59,684	74.7
Personal sources, loans, and gifts	10	12	17,230	21.6
Institutional sources	2	1	3,000	3.7
Total expenditure			79,914	100.0
Improvements				
CH's personal income and savings			45,004	90.1
Personal sources, loans, and gifts		5	4,940	9.9
Institutional sources			—	
Total expenditure			49,944	100.0
Maintenance and repair				
CH's personal income and savings			39,088	92.0
Personal sources, loans, and gifts		8	3,400	8.0
Institutional sources			—	
Total expenditure			42,488	100.0
Buildings under construction				
CH's personal income and savings			3,913	90.3
Personal sources, loans, and gifts		1	420	9.7
Institutional sources			—	
Total expenditure			4,333	100.0
Miscellaneous construction				
CH's personal income and savings			3,392	100.0
Personal sources, loans, and gifts			—	
Institutional sources			—	
Total expenditure			3,392	100.0
Total building activities				
CH's personal income and savings			151,081	83.9
Personal sources, loans, and gifts	11	25	25,990	14.4
Institutional sources	2	1	3,000	1.7
Total expenditure			180,071	100.0

Table A.6.12 Direction and distribution of internal subsidy

No.			No.		No. of rooms	Floor area, sq. m	Shillings
	Fully subsidized						
4	Compound heads	to	5	CH's sons' fam.	12	92.0	3,920
2	CHs	,,	2	CH's full brs' sons' fam.	3	20.1	623
1	CH	,,	1	CH's full sist's son's fam.	1	7.2	222
1	CH	,,	1	CH's full sister's fam.	1	8.3	230
1	CH	,,	1	CH's father's fam.	1	6.6	173
1	CH	,,	1	CH's client's fam.	1	10.7	286
1	CH's sons' fam.	,,	1	CH's fam.	1	7.9	318
1	CH's full brs' sons' fam.	,,	1	CH's full brother's fam.	1	9.4	246
	Total				21	162.2	6,018
	Partly subsidized[a]						
5	Compound heads	to	6	CH's full & half brs' fam.	17	119.4	2,124
1	CH	,,	1	CH's full sist's sons' fam.	3	22.7	210
1	CH	,,	1	CH's mother's brs' fam.	3	14.4	425
2	CH's sons' fam.	,,	2	CHs' fam.	3	17.5	380
1	CH's full br's fam.	,,	1	CH's full br's son's fam.	1	8.1	148
	Total				27	182.1	3,287
	Not subsidized by compound head						
9	CH's full and half brothers' fam.				15	122.2	6,222
7	CH's sons' fam.				23	165.9	7,253
5	CH's full brothers' sons' fam.				6	37.4	1,201
1	CH's full brother's fam.						
1	CH's full brother's son's fam.				1	8.1	258
	Total				45	333.6	14,934

[a]At least one quarter of the total cost.

Appendixes – Part II

IBADAN

Appendix 7

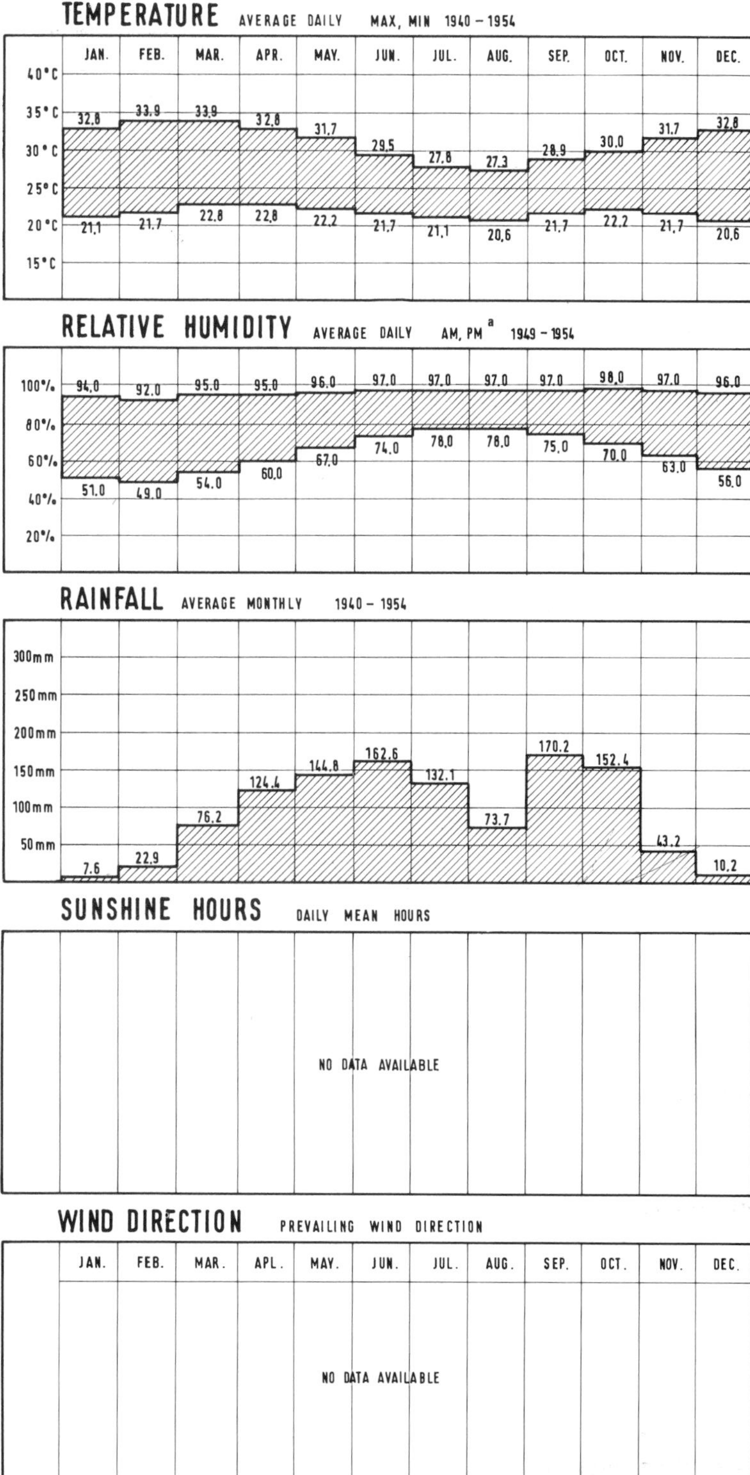

Diagram A.7.1
Climatic data, Ibadan.
[a]Observation taken at 06.30 and 12.30 GMT

Picture A.7.1
Church and Mission House at Ibadan, c. 1858. Source: Anna Hinderer, *Seventeen Years in Yoruba Country*, London, 1873

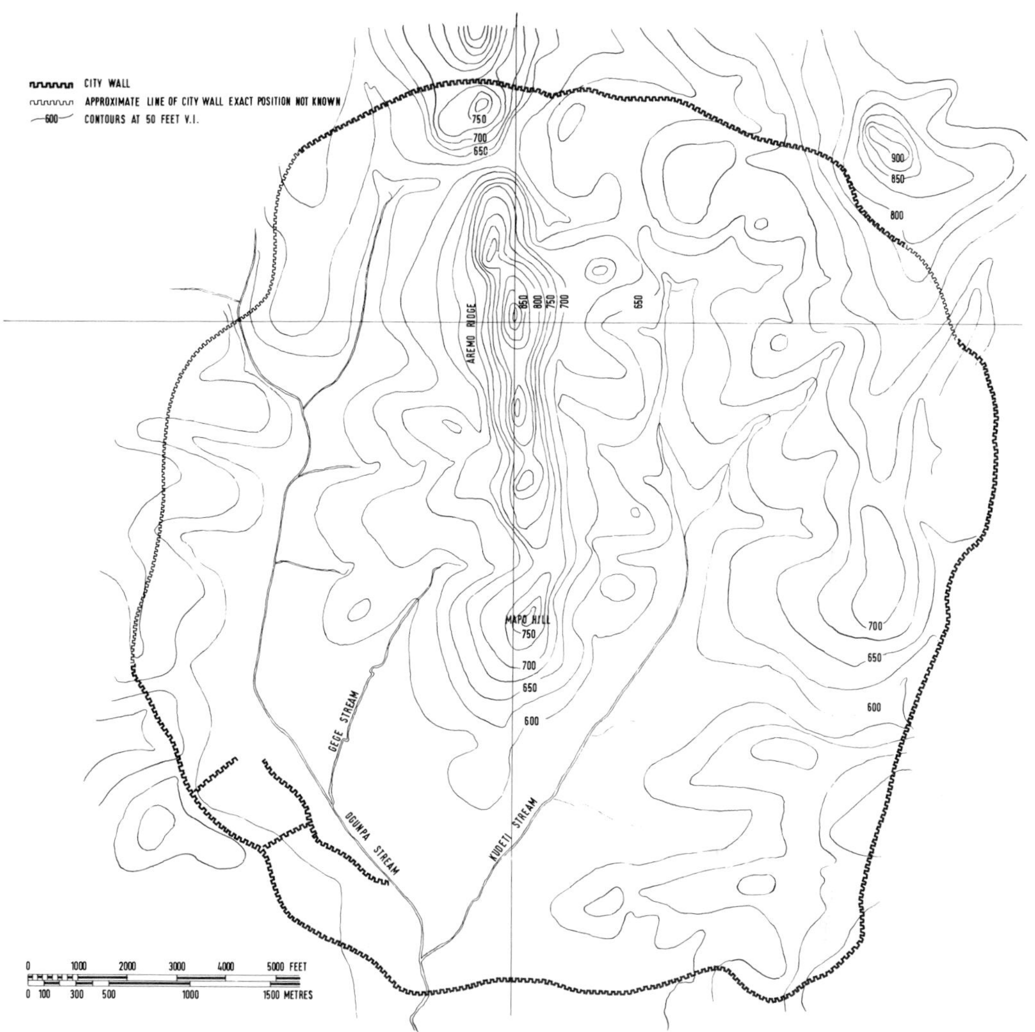

Map A.7.1
Ibadan: relief and drainage

Table A.7.1 Important rulers of Ibadan

Bashorun[a] Oluyole	Early	1830s–1847
Balogun Ibikunle	Early	1850s–1864
Otun Balogun/Bashorun Ogunmola	Early	1850s–1867
Are Onakakanfo[a] Latosa		1872–1885
Balogun Osungbekun		1885–1893

[a]*Bashorun* and *Are Onakakanfo* are titles which combine the military and civil leadership of the town. These are imperial titles which can only be taken with the consent of the Alafin of Oyo.

Source: B. A. Awe, 'The Rise of Ibadan as a Yoruba Power in the 19th Century' Ph.D. Thesis, Oxford University, 1964, p. 361.

Map A.7.2
Ibadan: principal localities

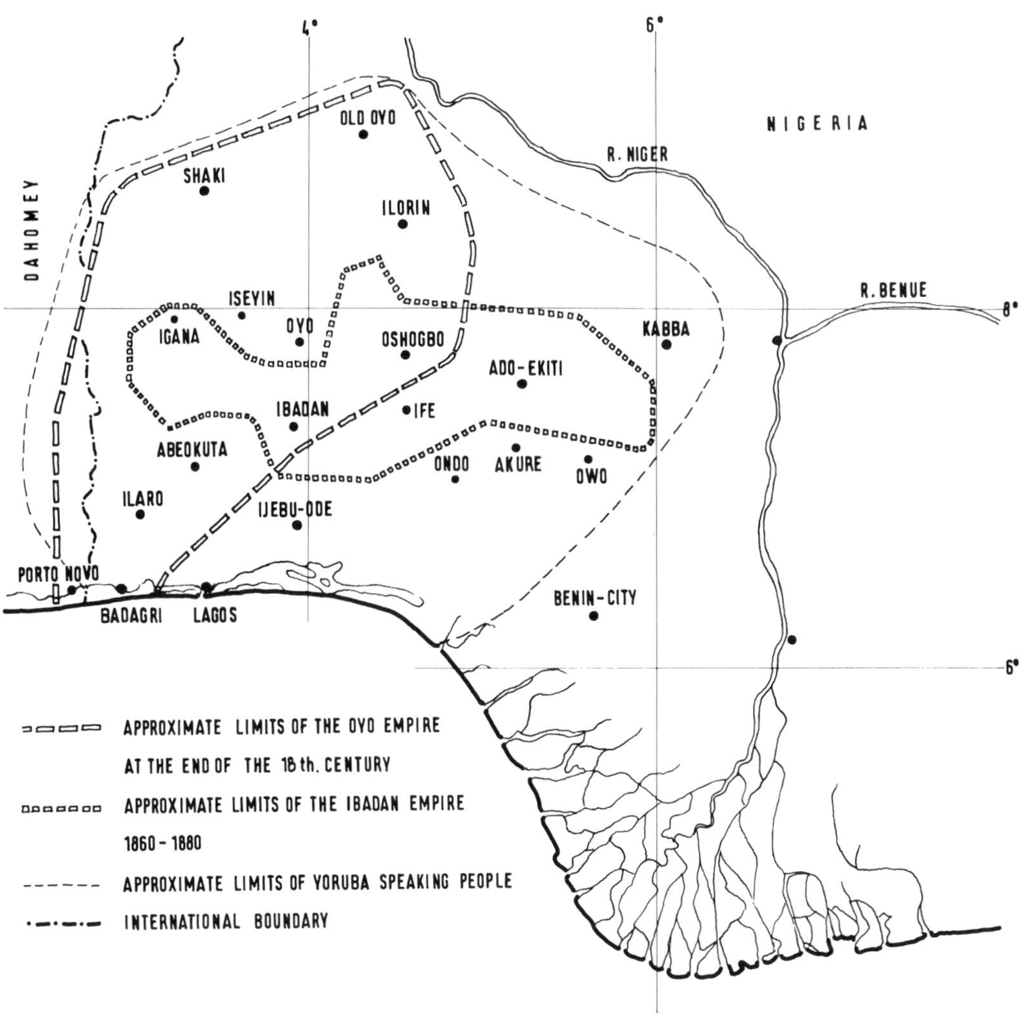

Map A.7.3
The Oyo and Ibadan empires in the eighteenth and nineteenth centuries.
Source: B. Awe, 'Ibadan, its early beginnings' in *The City of Ibadan*, P. C. Lloyd (ed.), Cambridge, 1967, p. 12.

Appendix 8

Table A.8.1 Type of land tenure of 63 compounds in Ibadan, 1968

	No.	% of total
1. *Inheritance*		
Houses	32	
Land	4	
Total	36	57.1
2. *Purchase*		
Houses	1	
Land	13	
Total	14	22.2
3. *Allotted*		
Houses	–	
Land	11	
Total	11	17.5
4. *Long lease* (rent)		
Houses	2	
Land	–	
Total	2	3.2
Grand total	63	100.0

Table A.8.2 Land use in Ibadan city, 1965

	Hectares	% of total
1 Cultivated land	4,049	39.0
2 Built-up area	3,471	33.4
3 Fallow and woodland	1,954	18.8
4 Forest reserves	780	7.5
5 Lakes and reservoirs	125	1.2
Total	10,379	99.9

Source: J. O. Oyelese, 'The growth of Ibadan city and its impact on land-use patterns, 1961–65', *Journal of Tropical Geography* (Singapore), **32**, 1971. This table represents an extract of Tables 1 and 3 on pp. 51 and 54.

Appendix 9

Table A.9.1 Population growth of Ibadan city

Sources	Population	Average annual rate of growth %
1. *Missionaries' estimates*		
Hinderer, 1851[a]	60,000	–
Tucker, 1853[b]	60,000	–
Bowen, 1856[b]	70,000	
2. *British Government officials' estimates*		
Moloney, 1890[c]	150,000	–
Millson, 1891[c]	120,000	–
Carter, 1893[c]	150,000	–
3. *Colonial administration official estimates*		
1911[d]	175,000	–
1921[d]	238,000	3.1
1931[d]	387,000	5.0
4. *Census results*		
1952[e]	459,000	0.8
1963[f]	627,000	2.9

[a]See Chapter 9, note 1.
[b]See Chapter 9, note 2.
[c]See Chapter 9, note 3.
[d]See Chapter 9, note 4.
[e]See Chapter 9, note 5.
[f]See Chapter 9, note 6.

Table A.9.2 Area, population, and number of houses in Ibadan city

Column	1	2	3	4	5	6	7
	Ward	Area in hectares	Population	Persons per hectare	No. of houses	Houses per hectare	Persons per house
Group I	C.1	15.4	11,557	750	307	20	38
	C.2	17.8	16,437	923	598	34	27
	N.1	33.2	16,307	491	985	30	17
	N.2	29.9	9,446	316	539	18	18
	N.W.1	16.2	6,820	421	378	23	18
	E.1	35.2	12,856	365	754	21	17
	E.2	20.2	7,595	376	300	15	25
	S.1	32.8	11,391	347	725	22	16
	S.2	21.4	7,897	369	634	30	12
	S.W.1	44.5	15,200	342	793	18	19
	S.W.2	25.9	8,132	314	584	22	14
	Total	292.5	123,638	423	6,597	23	19
Group II	E.3	39.7	9,122	230	639	16	14
	E.4	76.9	7,028	91	470	6	15
	E.5	40.1	9,850	246	740	18	13
	E.6	111.7	9,825	88	430	4	23
	E.7	67.6	12,045	178	750	11	16
	E.8	19.4	8,646	446	422	22	20
	S.3	35.6	7,963	224	521	15	15
	S.4	121.0	15,120	125	585	5	26
	S.6	131.9	11,365	86	964	7	12
	S.W.3	48.6	20,913	430	1,175	24	18
	S.W.4	52.6	13,743	261	759	14	18
	S.W.5	26.3	12,179	463	532	20	23
	N.W.2	21.4	13,658	638	617	29	22
	N.W.3	47.3	26,859	568	1,160	24	23
	Total	840.1	178,316	212	9,764	12	18
Group III	N.3	133.5	20,503	154	800	6	26
	N.4	135.6	15,964	118	850	6	19
	N.5	617.1	20,420	33	692	1	30
	E.9	129.5	9,206	71	454	3	20
	S.5	75.3	7,808	104	377	5	21
	S.7	125.4	11,654	93	359	3	32
	S.W.6*	21.4	55,214	2,580	554	26	100
	S.W.7*	229.4	70,687	308	650	3	109
	N.W.4	52.6	6,913	131	418	8	17
	N.W.5	65.1	3,980	61	476	7	8
	N.W.6	118.2	5,602	47	300	3	19
	Total	1,703.1	227,951	134	5,930	4	38
Group IV	N.6	784.3	45,964	59	1,061	1	43
	S.W.8	346.4	33,687	97	792	2	43
	S.W.9	1,942.5	15,362	8	545	–	28
	Abadina	3,854.2	7,632	2	–	–	–
	Total	6,927.4	102,645	15	2,398	–	–
Grand total		9,763.1	632,550	65	24,689	–	–

*Figures given are incorrect.

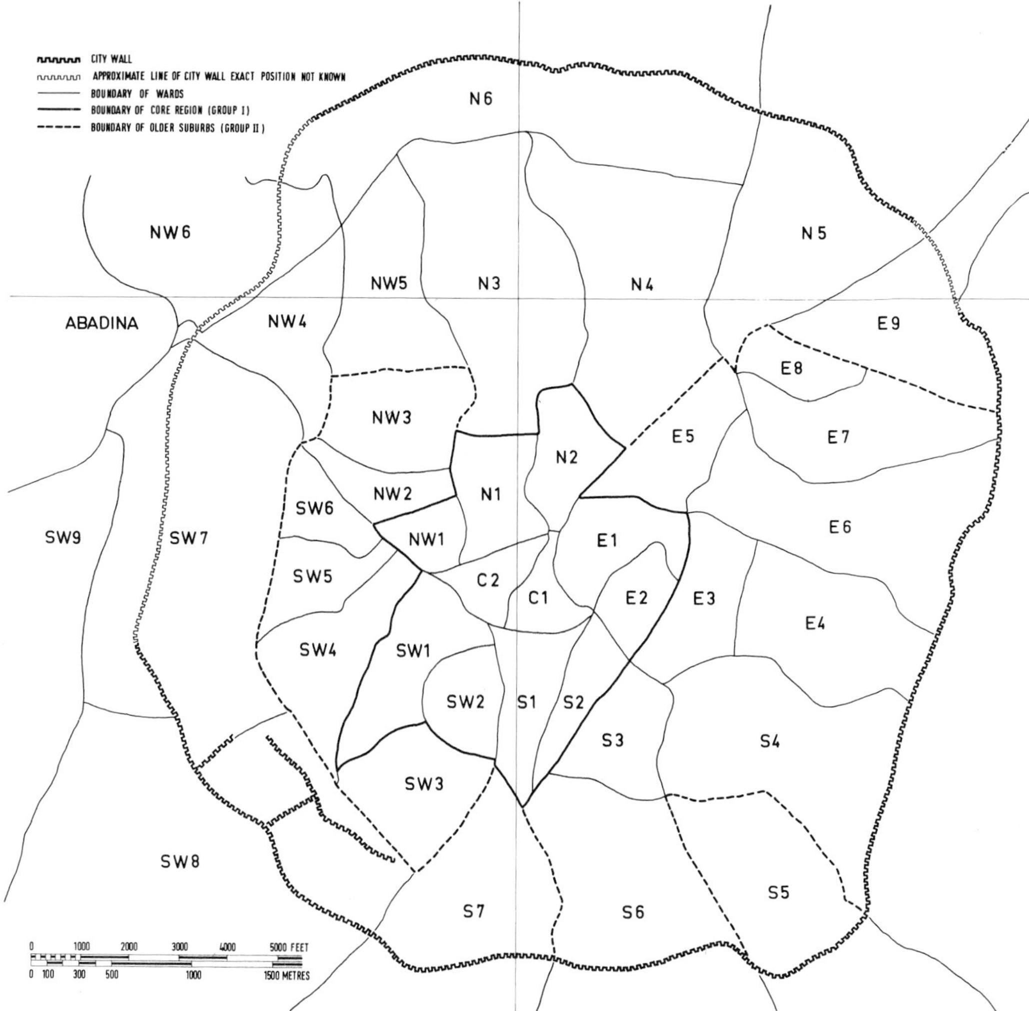

Map A.9.1
Ibadan: division into wards

Sources and Reliability of Data. Table A.9.2, p. 374

Areas per ward given in column 2 were obtained from the Ibadan Townplanning Authority and checked against the map 'Ibadan and environs', 1:12,500, Sheet 2, second edition, 1967. The populations per ward in column 3 are taken from a mimeographed edition of the 'Population Census of Nigeria 1963', vol. 1, p. 56, published by the Federal Office of Statistics, Lagos, 1968. The numbers of houses per ward in column 5 were supplied by the Ibadan District Council, and allegedly represent the number of houses in the city in 1962.

The population figures and numbers of houses per ward, which cannot be checked, are likely to be inaccurate, particularly for wards S.W.6 and S.W.7, and to a lesser extent for wards N.6, S.W.8, S.W.9, and Abadina, the latter certainly being highly erroneous and incomplete both for population and for houses. Apart from these wards the consistency in the number of persons per hectare (column 4), number of houses per hectare (column 6), and number of persons per house (column 7) cannot be dismissed as entirely improbable, although these ratios only give a very rough approximation of the situation in the city in the early 1960s. Group IV is incomplete and cannot be taken into account.

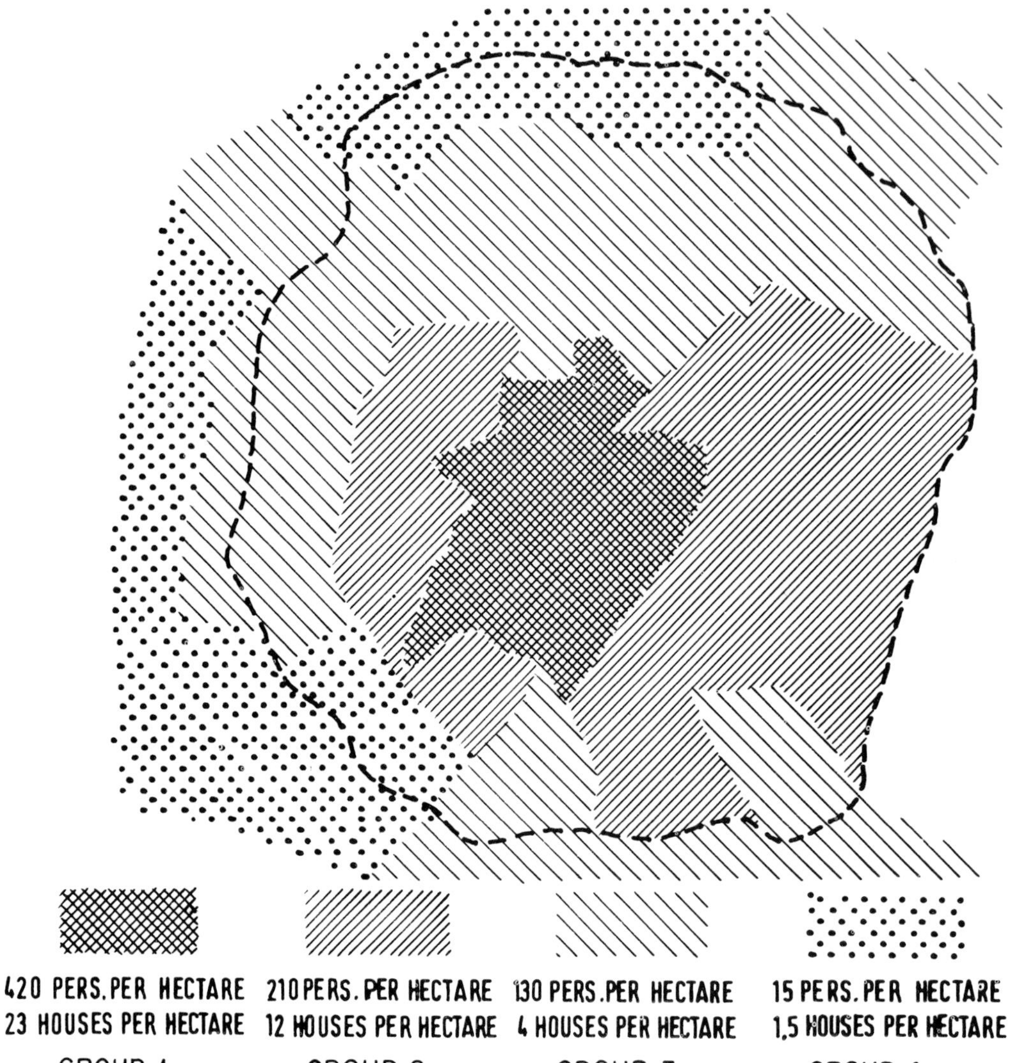

Map A.9.2
Population density in Ibadan

Grouping of Wards. Map A.9.1, p. 375

The grouping of 40 city wards into four major divisions corresponds roughly with the three periods of development in Ibadan distinguished on pp. 117 and 374. The first group of 11 wards covers approximately the area on which Ibadan was built in the first half of the nineteenth century. The second group of 14 wards represents the area which developed in the second half of the nineteenth century prior to the British occupation in 1893. The third group of 11 wards is roughly identical with the area that developed during the colonial period up to the Second World War, while the fourth group of 4 wards covers the areas which have been occupied since the late 1940s, except for the European reservations.

The average population density per house of 18 to 22 persons seems to be fairly stable throughout the city (excluding wards S.W.6 and S.W.7 in Group III). However, the average number of persons per house in predominantly immigrant areas to the west of the old city is most likely to be above 20 persons, while the average number in the older parts of the city, with generally smaller houses, is below 20 persons per house.

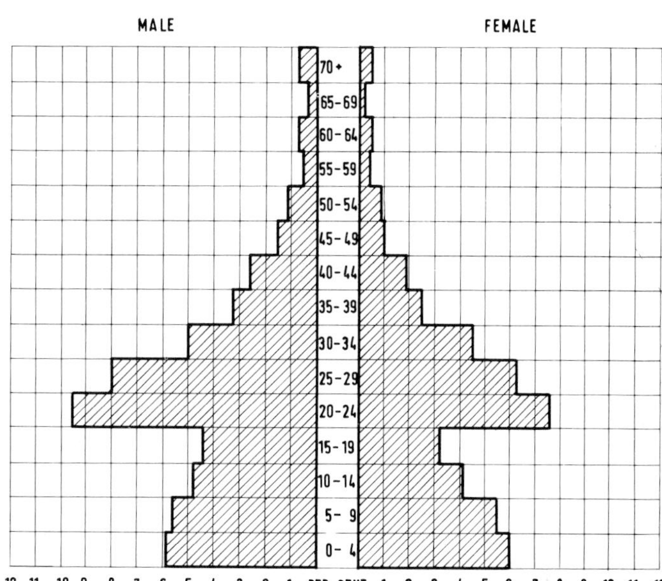

Diagram A.9.1
Age and sex distribution
Ibadan Division, 1963

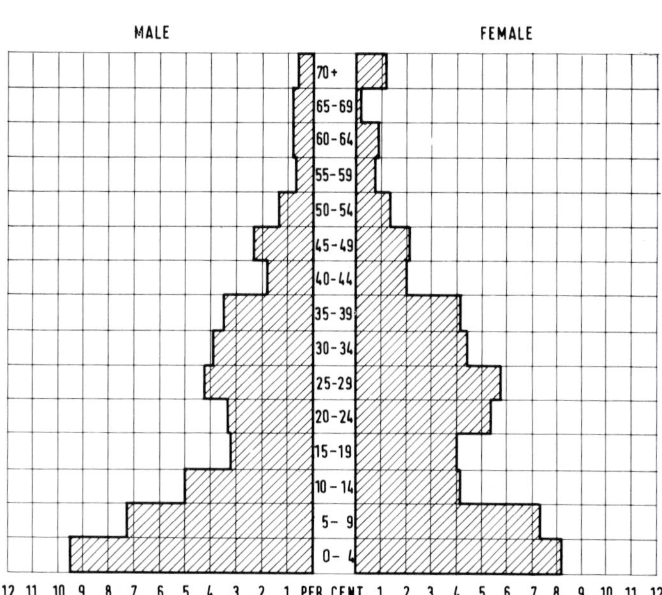

Diagram A.9.2
Age and sex distribution,
Survey Sample, 1968

Table A.9.3 Ethnic composition and birthplace of household heads

	No.	%
Household head Yoruba born in Ibadan	160	54.2
Household head Yoruba born outside Ibadan		
Abeokuta	29	9.8
Ijebu	15	5.1
Oyo	11	3.7
Lagos	10	3.4
Ilesha	9	3.1
Ilorin	6	2.0
Ekiti	6	2.0
Ede	4	1.4
Ondo	4	1.4
Owo	3	1.0
Oshogbo	3	1.0
Other Yoruba towns and villages	14	4.8
Unknown	1	0.3
Total Yoruba household heads born outside Ibadan	115	39.0
Total Yoruba household heads	275	93.2
Household heads from other Southern Nigerian tribes	14	4.8
Household heads from Northern Nigeria	6	2.0
Total household heads	295	100.0

Appendix 10

Table A.10.1 Land use: open area

Category of land	No. of comp.	Sq. m	%	Av. area in sq. m
1 Unpaved area	63	3,878	67.2	61.5
2 Cement platforms	54	1,549	26.8	28.7
3 Pit-lat. & washplaces	35	162	2.8	4.6
4 Storage space	38	184	3.2	4.8
Total open area	63	5,773	100.0	91.6

Table A.10.2 Distribution of household size

No. of persons	Hh group	CH's households			Dependent households			Tenant households			Total households		
		No. of hhs	%	No. of persons	No. of hhs	%	No. of persons	No. of hhs	%	No. of persons	No. of hhs	%	No. of persons
1	1–2		9.5		1	16.7	1	40	53.2	40	41	30.5	41
2		6		12	17		34	26		52	49		98
3	3–4	4	20.6	12	25	44.4	75	12	25.8	36	41	31.6	123
4		9		36	23		92	20		80	52		208
5	5–6	5	17.5	25	23	27.8	115	9	11.3	45	37	18.6	185
6		6		36	7		42	5		30	18		108
7	7–8	6	20.6	42	3	10.2	21	8	6.5	56	17	10.9	119
8		7		56	8		64				15		120
9	9–10	5	15.9	45	1	0.9	9	2	2.4	18	8	4.7	72
10		5		50				1		10	6		60
11	11–12	2	6.4	22				1	0.8	11	3	1.7	33
12		2		24							2		24
Over 12	Over 12	6	9.5	94							6	2.0	94
Total		63	100.0	454	108	100.0	453	124	100.0	378	295	100.0	1,285
Average				7.2			4.2			3.0			4.4

Table A.10.3 Marital status of household population

Age	Male Sing.	Male Mar.	Male Div.	Male Wid.	Male Total	Female Sing.	Female Mar.	Female Div.	Female Wid.	Female Total	Grand total
A. Compound heads' households											
0–4	35				35	31				31	66
5–9	37				37	32				32	69
10–14	27				27	22	1			23	50
15–19	23				23	12	5			17	40
20–24	15				15	3	13			16	31
25–29	6	2	1		9	1	17			18	27
30–34	4	6			10		15			15	25
35–39		8			8		13	1		14	22
40–44	1	3	1		5		12	1	2	15	20
45–49	1	11			12		16		1	17	29
50–54		5	1		6		6		2	8	14
55–59		7			7		6		3	9	16
60–64		7		1	8		2		3	5	13
65–69		8		1	9		1		1	2	11
70+		5		1	6		3		12	15	21
Total	149	62	3	3	217	101	110	2	24	237	454
B. Dependent households											
0–4	40				40	42				42	82
5–9	27				27	38				38	65
10–14	22				22	21				21	43
15–19	8				8	9	11			20	28
20–24	8	9			17	1	32			33	50
25–29	4	19	1		24		23			23	47
30–34		18			18		20		1	21	39
35–39	1	17			18		17		4	21	39
40–44		8			8		6		4	10	18
45–49		8			8		3		5	8	16
50–54		5			5		7		2	9	14
55–59		1			1		1			1	2
60–64		2			2		1		4	5	7
65–69		1			1						1
70+				1	1				1	1	2
Total	110	88	1	1	200	111	121		21	253	453
C. Tenant households											
0–4	48				48	32				32	80
5–9	27				27	23				23	50
10–14	16				16	9				9	25
15–19	9				9	9	4			13	22
20–24	9	1			10	2	16	1		19	29
25–29	9	13			22		30	3		33	55
30–34	1	19	1		21		20	1		21	42
35–39	1	18			19		18			18	37
40–44		10			10						10
45–49		10			10		1		1	2	12
50–54		6			6		2			2	8
55–59		1			1			1		1	2
60–64		1			1		1		1	2	3
65–69				1	1				1	1	2
70+									1	1	1
Total	120	79	1	1	201	75	92	6	4	177	378

Table A.10.4 Male members of 63 compounds by relationship to compound head

	Marital status				Temp absent[a]	Age group							Total
	Sing.	Mar.	Div.	Wid.		0–4	5–14	15–24	25–39	40–54	55–69	70+	
1 Compound head		58	1		1				15	19	20	5	59
2 CH's sons[b]	93	12				26	46	20	11	2			105
3 CH's sons' sons	14					5	8	1					14
4 CH's daughters' sons	7	1				4	2	1	1				8
5 CH's daughters' sons' sons	2					1	1						2
Total	116	71	1		1	36	57	22	27	21	20	5	188
6 CH's full brothers	5	30		2	3			4	16	11	5	1	37
7 CH's full brothers' sons	34	10			1	17	10	6	11				44
8 CH's full brothers' sons' sons	12					6	6						12
9 CH's full brother's dau's dau's son	1						1						1
10 CH's full sisters' sons	6	1				2	2	1	2				7
Total	58	41		2	4	25	19	11	29	11	5	1	101
11 CH's half brothers	9	8	1	1			1	6	7	3	2		19
12 CH's half brothers' sons	22	5				4	12	5	6				27
13 CH's half brothers' sons' son	1						1						1
14 CH's half sisters' son	1					1							1
Total	33	13	1	1		5	14	11	13	3	2		48
15 CH's father's brother			1						1				1
16 CH's father's brothers' sons	5	14	1		3		4	2	9	5			20
17 CH's father's brs' sons' sons	11					2	8	1					11
18 CH's father's brs' dau's son		1							1				1
19 CH's father's brs' daus' sons' sons	3					2	1						3
20 CH's father's sister's son		2						1		1			2
21 CH's father's sisters' daus' sons	2						1	1					2
22 CH's father's wives' relatives	3				1	1	1	1					3
Total	24	17	2		4	5	15	6	11	6			43

23 CH's mother's brother				1								1	1
24 CH's mother's brothers' sons	5	2			1	1		4	2				7
25 CH's mother's brs' sons' sons	3					2	1						3
26 CH's mother's sisters' sons	1	1						1	1				2
27 CH's mother's sists' relatives	2					1	1						2
Total	11	3		1	1	4	2	5	3			1	15
28 CH's half sister's husband		1			3				1				1
29 CH's full sist's husb's wife's son	1							1					1
Total	1	1			3			1	1				2
30 CH's wives' brothers	1	1					1		1				2
31 CH's son's wife's brother	1							1					1
Total	2	1					1	1	1				3
32 CH's concubines' sons	4						2	2					4
33 CH's father's concubine's son	1									1			1
Total	5						2	2		1			5
34 Other CH's relatives		1							1				1
Total		1							1				1
35 Unrelated males	28	81	1	1	19		3	14	62	28	4		111
36 Unrelated males' sons	94					48	41	5					94
Total	122	81	1	1	19	48	44	19	62	28	4		205
37 Unrelated males' full brs.	4						1	2	1				4
38 Unrelated males' full br's son	1						1						1
39 Unrelated male's half brother	1							1					1
Total	6						2	3	1				6
40 Unrelated males' wife's brs	1							1					1
Total	1							1					1
Grand total male	379	229	5	5	32	123	156	82	149	70	31	7	618

[a]Not counted in total population. [b]1 CH's son is acting compound head.

Table A.10.5 Female members of 63 compounds by relationship to compound head

	Marital status				Temp. absent[a]	Age group							Total
	Sing.	Mar.	Div.	Wid.		1–4	5–14	15–24	25–39	40–54	55–69	70+	
1 Compound head		1		2						1	1	1	3
2 CH's daughters	76	7				27	39	13	3	1			83
3 CH's sons' daughters	21					6	13	2					21
4 CH's daughters' daughters	6					1	5						6
5 CH's daughter's son's dau	1					1							1
Total	104	8		2		35	57	15	3	2	1	1	114
6 CH's full sisters	1	5	1	1					1	6	1		8
7 CH's full sisters' daughters	2					1	1						2
8 CH's full sister's dau's dau	1						1						1
9 CH's full brothers' daughters	32	2				13	17	2	1	1			34
10 CH's full br's daughter's dau	1						1						1
11 CH's full br's dau's dau's dau	1						1						1
12 CH's full brs' sons' daughters	6					4	2						6
Total	44	7	1	1		18	23	2	2	7	1		53
13 CH's half sisters	7	5				1	5	3	3				12
14 CH's half sisters' daughters	4					1	1	2					4
15 CH's half brothers' daughters	12	1				4	8		1				13
16 CH's half brs' daus' daughters	2					1	1						2
17 CH's half br's son's daughter	1					1							1
Total	26	6				8	15	5	4				32
18 CH's mother		2		12						1	5	8	14
19 CH's father's wives		1		11					2	7	2	1	12
Total		3		23					2	8	7	9	26

20 CH's mother's sisters		1		3								4	4
21 CH's mother's sists' relatives	1	1					1		1				2
22 CH's mother's brs' daughters	3						2	1					3
23 CH's mother's br's dau's dau	1					1							1
Total	5	2		3		1	3	1	1			4	10
24 CH's father's sister				1						1			1
25 CH's father's sist's dau's dau	1					1							1
26 CH's father's sis' son's dau	1						1						1
27 CH's father's brs' daughters	3			1			3					1	4
28 CH's father's brs' sons' daus	17					9	5	3					17
29 CH's father's brs' daus' sons' daus	2						2						2
Total	24			2		10	11	3		1		1	26
30 CH's wives		91			15		1	14	38	29	8	1	91
31 CH's wive's br's wife		1							1				1
32 CH's sons' wives		16			4			8	7	1			16
33 CH's daughter's son's wife		1						1					1
34 CH's full brothers' wives		46		2	2			12	25	9	2		48
35 CH's full brs' sons' wives		9			1			5	4				9
36 CH's half brothers' wives		10		3	2			2	10	1			13
37 CH's half brs' sons' wives		5			2			4	1				5
38 CH's father's wive's br's wife				1					1				1
39 CH's father's wives' brs' sons' wives		2						1	1				2
40 CH's father's brothers' wives				4					1	1	2		4
41 CH's father's brs' sons' wives		15		1	4			7	7	2			16
42 CH's father's sists' sons' wives		2							1	1			2
43 CH's father's brs' daus' sons' wives		2							2				2
44 CH's mother's brothers' wives		1	1	2						3	1		4
45 CH's mother's brs' sons' wives		2						1	1				2
46 CH's mother's sist's son's wife		1						1					1
Total		204	1	13	30		1	56	100	47	13	1	218

[a] Not counted in total population.

continued

Table A.10.5 (*continued*)

	Marital status				Temp. absent[a]	Age group							Total
	Sing.	Mar.	Div.	Wid.		1–4	5–14	15–24	25–39	40–54	55–60	70+	
47 CH's wives' sis' relatives	4						1	3					4
48 CH's wives' br's relatives	2					1	1						2
49 CH's father's brs' sons' wives relatives	1						1						1
50 CH's mother's brs' wives' relatives		1								1			1
Total	7	1				1	3	3		1			8
51 CH's father's brs' son's concubine	1							1					1
52 CH's concubine's daughter	1						1						1
Total	2						1	1					2
53 Unrelated males' wives		91	5	1	16			20	71	3	2	1	97
54 Unrelated male's full br's wife		1						1					1
Total		92	5	1	16			21	71	3	2	1	98
55 Unrelated males' daughters	63					31	30	2					63
Total	63					31	30	2					63
56 Unrelated male's full br's dau	1						1						1
57 Unrelated male's full sister	1							1					1
Total	2						1	1					2
58 Unrelated male's mother				1							1		1
Total				1							1		1
59 Unrelated males' wives' relatives	6		1	2		1	1	4	1	1	1		9
Total	6		1	2		1	1	4	1	1	1		9
60 Other unrelated females	4			1				4		1			5
Total	4			1				4		1			5
Grand total	287	323	8	49	46	105	146	118	184	71	26	17	667

[a] Not counted in total population.

Symbols

A	Compound head's family
B	CH's sons' families
D	CH's father's family
E	CH's full brothers' families
F	CH's full brothers' sons' families
I	CH's half brothers' families
J	CH's half brothers' sons' families
K	CH's father's brothers' sons' families
L	CH's mother's brothers' families
M	CH's mother's brothers' sons' families
N	CH's full brothers' daughters' families
P	CH's half brothers' daughters' families
Q	CH's father's brothers' families
R	CH's father's brothers' daughters' sons' families
S	CH's father's sisters' sons' families
T	CH's daughters' sons' families
U	CH's half sisters' families
V	CH's mother's sisters' sons' families
W	CH's mother's sisters' husbands' sisters' daughters' families
X	Relationship to CH uncertain
Y	CH's wives' brothers' families
Z	CH's father's wives' brothers' sons' families
O	Strangers' families

On Table A.10.6 there is one household containing parallel cousins and their families (symbol K) which is not included in stage 6 because this household joined its host compound, increasing the population by immigration rather than by natural growth.

Table A.10.6 Household composition

	No. of com- pounds	No. of house- holds	A	B	D	E	F	I	J	K	L	M	N	P	Q	R	S	T	U	V	W	X	Y	Z	O	Total no. of hhs	Total no. of persons
1. A	10	1	10																							10	77
A + O	2	2	2																						2	4	19
A + O2	1	3	1																						2	3	15
A + O3	2	4	2																						6	8	39
A + O5	1	6	1																						5	6	23
A + O7	1	8	1																						7	8	21
A + O10	1	11	1																						10	11	23
A + O16	1	17	1																						16	17	76
Total, stage 1	19		19																						48	67	293
2. A + B	1	2	1	1																						2	10
A + B2 + T	1	4	1	2														1								4	16
A + B + O	2	3	2	2																					2	6	27
A + B + O7	1	9	1	1																					7	9	40
Total, stage 2	5		5	6														1							9	21	93
3. A + E	5	2	5			5																				10	54
A + E2	1	3	1			2																				3	17
A + E + X	1	3	1			1																1				3	8
A + E + O	1	3	1			1																			1	3	15
A + E + O2	1	4	1			1																			2	4	12
A + E2 + O	1	4	1			2																			1	4	9
A + E2 + O4	1	7	1			2																			4	7	33
A + E + O10	1	12	1			1																			10	12	52
A + E3 + V + O3	1	8	1			3														1					3	8	35
A + E + I + Y + O7	1	11	1			1		1															1		7	11	31
A + I2 + R + O2	1	5	1					2								1									2	6	38
A + I + K + O	1	4	1					1		1															1	4	23
Total, stage 3	16		16			19		4		1						1				1		1	1		31	75	327
4. A + E + F + O3	1	6	1			1	1																		3	6	24
A + E3 + B + F	1	6	1	1		3	1																			6	47
A + E2 + I + B2	1	6	1	2		2		1																		6	37
A + E + I + J + Z2	1	6	1			1		1	1															2		6	26
A + E + I + B2 + F + J2	1	8	1	2		1	1	1	2																	8	24
A + I + J + O3	1	6	1					1	1																3	6	20
Total, stage 4	6		6	5		8	3	4	4															2	6	38	178

5. A + F2	1	3	1				2																			3	22
A + F2 + O	1	4	1				2																		1	4	17
Total, stage 5	2		2				4																		1	7	39
6. A + K	1	2	1							1																2	12
A + E + K	1	3	1			1				1																3	18
A + E2 + K3	1	6	1			2				3																6	27
A + U + K + O4	1	7	1							1										1						4	7	34
A + E2 + P2 + K6 + P	1	12	1			2	2			6				1													12	45
A + E2 + F2 + K6 + P	1	10	1		3	1		1		3					1												10	48
A + E + I + D3 + K3 + Q																												
Total, stage 6	6		6		3	6	2	1		15				1	1				1							4	40	184
Joint households																												
A + N	1	2	1										1														2	7
A + Q + O5	1	7	1												1											5	7	17
A + K + O3	1	5	1							1																3	5	16
A + J + U + O	1	4	1						1										1							1	4	13
A + S + U + O	1	4	1														1		1							1	4	19
A + M2 + L	1	4	1								1	2															4	21
A + W + O2	1	4	1																		1					2	4	18
A + S + O6	1	8	1														1									6	8	24
A + U + O7	1	9	1																1							7	9	36
Total	9		9						1	1	1	2	1		1		2		3		1					25	47	171
Grand total	63		63	11	3	33	9	9	5	17	1	2	1	1	2	1	2	1	4	1	1	1	1	2	124	295	1285

Table A.10.7 Number of rooms

	Compound head's hhs 63 hhs, 454 pers.			CH's f & h brs' hhs 42 hhs, 195 pers.			CH's sons' hhs 11 hhs, 54 pers.			CH's brs' sons' hhs 14 hhs, 48 pers.		
	Rms	Sq. m	%	Rms	Sq. m	%	Rms	Sq. m	%	Rms	Sq. m	%
1. Living area												
Sleeping rooms	240	1,992.6	20.9	82	619.3	6.5	17	127.6	1.3	23	164.1	1.7
Sitting rooms	25	305.9	3.2	3	39.0	0.4	4	35.9	0.4	1	9.0	0.1
Central halls	66	1,696.2	17.8	6	99.4	1.1	3	75.6	0.8	1	12.4	0.2
Stores for personal articles	39	248.2	2.6	1	4.0	0.1				1	3.7	
Empty rooms	45	301.3	3.2	91	5.5					3	22.1	0.3
Total	415	4,544.2	47.7	93	767.2	8.1	26	250.1	2.6	29	211.3	2.3
2. Common rooms												
Entrance lobbies	52	303.0	3.2	2	10.0	0.1				1	6.8	
Passages and staircases	14	128.0	1.3							2	10.0	0.1
Total	66	431.0	4.5	2	10.0	0.1	1	1.5		3	16.8	0.1
3. Basic ancillary facilities												
Kitchens	45	334.3	3.5	2	11.8	0.1	1	9.3	0.1	1	5.2	
Kitchen stores	4	23.3	0.2									
Other stores	23	109.1	1.2	2	5.0	0.1						
Toilets and bathrooms	47	112.2	1.2	3	4.7		3	4.3		1	1.3	
Total	119	578.9	6.1	7	21.5	0.2	4	13.6	0.1	2	6.5	0.1
4. Commercial rooms												
Shops and workshops	28	199.1	2.1				1	9.3	0.1			
Stores for trading articles	4	32.4	0.3									
Total	32	231.5	2.4				1	9.3	0.1			
Grand total	632	5,785.6	60.7	102	798.7	8.4	32	274.5	2.8	34	234.6	2.5

and floor area per household

CH's f brs' sists' hhs 17 hhs, 69 pers.			Other related hhs 24 hhs, 87 pers.			Tenant hhs 124 hhs, 378 pers.			Total hhs 295 hhs, 1285 pers.		
Rms	Sq. m	%	Rms	Sq. m	%	Rms	Sq. m	%	Rms	Sq. m	%
25	193.0	2.1	30	211.2	2.2	161	1,328.9	13.9	578	4,636.7	48.7
1	9.0	0.1	3	34.5	0.4	13	111.4	1.2	50	544.7	5.7
2	48.6	0.5	1	61.9	0.7	7	130.8	1.4	86	2,124.9	22.3
1	11.5	0.1				5	32.4	0.3	49	310.8	3.3
			1	7.8	0.1	1	4.8	0.1	51	341.5	3.6
29	262.1	2.8	35	315.4	3.3	187	1,608.3	16.9	814	7,958.6	83.6
3	14.8	0.1	1	5.6	0.1	7	40.0	0.4	66	380.2	4.0
						2	25.2	0.3	19	164.7	1.7
3	14.8	0.1	1	5.6	0.1	9	65.2	0.7	85	544.9	5.7
						8	44.2	0.5	57	404.8	4.3
									4	23.3	0.2
						6	30.1	0.3	31	144.2	1.5
						15	33.5	0.3	69	156.0	1.6
						29	107.8	1.1	161	728.3	7.6
			1	15.4	0.2	5	34.3	0.4	35	258.1	2.8
									4	32.4	0.3
			1	15.4	0.2	5	34.3	0.4	39	290.5	3.1
32	276.9	2.9	37	336.4	3.6	230	1,815.6	19.1	1,099	9,522.3	100.0

Table A.10.8 Average floor area per household and person according to household size

No. of persons per household	No. of households	No. of persons	Average persons per household	Total floor area			Sleeping area		
				Total floor area, m^2	Average area in m^2 per household	Average area in m^2 per person	Sleeping area, m^2	Average sleeping area in m^2 per household	Average sleeping area in m^2 per person
1–2	90	139	1.54	1,228.4	13.6	8.8	756.3	8.4	5.4
3–4	93	331	3.56	2,010.1	21.6	6.1	1,109.5	11.9	3.4
5–6	55	293	5.33	1,938.2	35.2	6.6	1,092.3	19.9	3.7
7–8	32	239	7.47	1,792.1	56.0	7.5	846.3	26.4	3.5
9–10	14	132	9.43	1,307.0	93.4	9.9	527.1	37.6	4.0
11–12	5	57	11.40	532.1	106.4	9.3	233.8	46.8	4.1
13+	6	94	15.67	714.4	119.1	7.6	356.4	59.4	3.8
Total	295	1,285		9,522.3			4,921.7		
Average			4.35		32.3	7.4		16.7	3.8

Appendix 11

Table A.11.2 Number of valid and omitted households

	CHs' hhs		Dep. hhs		Tenant hhs		Total hhs	
	No.	%	No.	%	No.	%	No.	%
Valid	58	92.1	77	71.3	92	74.2	227	76.9
Omitted	5	7.9	31	28.7	32	25.8	68	23.1
Total hhs	63	100.0	108	100.0	124	100.0	295	100.0

Table A.11.3 Income distribution of valid households

	CHs' hhs		Dep. hhs		Tenant hhs		Total hhs	
Income group	No.	%	No.	%	No.	%	No.	%
Low	19	32.8	49	63.6	54	58.7	122	53.8
Middle	29	50.0	28	36.4	36	39.1	93	40.9
High	10	17.2			2	2.2	12	5.3
Total hhs	58	100.0	77	100.0	92	100.0	227	100.0

Table A.11.1 Occupational pattern survey sample

Column	1	2	3	4	5						6						7						8
	Main occupation				Sec. occ., CH						Sec. occ., DHH						Sec. occ., THH						
	CH	DHH	THH	Total hhs	1[a]	2	3	4	5	Total	1	2	3	4	5	Total	1	2	3	4	5	Total	Total sec. occ.
1. Agriculture																							
Farmer	9	4	2	15			2	2		4		1	1			2							6
Subtotal	9	4	2	15			2	2		4		1	1			2							6
2. Art and crafts																							
Tailor	4	7	8	19	1		1			2									1	1		2	4
Mechanic	1	7	4	12	1					1				1		1							2
Carpenter	1	5	5	11															1			1	1
Skilled worker	2	1	6	9	1					1													1
Bricklayer	2	5	2	9		1				1	1					1							2
Building contr.	5	2		7							1					1							1
Printer	1	2	3	6																			
Barber	1	1	2	4				1		1													1
Goldsmith		1	2	3															1			1	1
Painter	1		1	2																			
Butcher	1		1	2	1					1													1
Other crafts	1	2	2	5			1			1													1
Subtotal	20	33	36	89	4	1	2	1		8	2			1		3			3	1		4	15
3. Trade																							
Food, provisions	6	16	18	40	2			1		3		1				1		2				2	6
Textiles	1	4	4	9																			
Cooked food		2	3	5																			
Motor spare parts		5		5										1		1							1
Shoes			4	4															1			1	1
Livestock	1	1	1	3																			
Timber, firewood	1	2		3				1		1													
Mats			2	2																			1
Other trade	3	3	1	7																			
Subtotal	12	33	33	78	2			2		4		1		1		2		2	1			3	9

	CH	DHH	THH	Total																
4. Services																				
Clerk	7	9	15	31													1		1	1
Transport	1	15	10	26																
Unskilled labour			13	13											1		1		2	2
Police, army		5	3	8							1			1						1
Teacher	1	3	2	6																
Church minister	3		1	4		1			1											1
Washerman/dry cl.		3	1	4												1			1	1
Mallam	1	1	1	3	1				1											1
Nightwatchman	2	1		3	1				1											1
Musician			2	2													1		1	1
Other services	2		2	4																
Subtotal	17	37	50	104	2	1			3		1			1	1	1	3		5	9
5. Miscellaneous																				
Retired	5			5																
Temp. out of work			1	1																
DK		1	2	3																
Subtotal	5	1	3	9																
Grand total	63	108	124	295	8	2	4	5	19	2	3	1	2	8	1	3	7	1	12	39

CH = Compound head
DHH = Dependent household head
THH = Tenant household head

[a]1 = Agriculture
2 = Art and crafts
3 = Trade
4 = Services
5 = Miscellaneous

Table A.11.4 Distribution of incomes for different size households

A. TOTAL 227 HOUSEHOLDS

Av. month. inc. \ Persons in hh	1–2	3–4	5–6	7–8	9–10	11–12	13+	Total	%	Cum. %
Sh. 0–99.9	7	6	1					14	6.2	6.2
100–199.9 low	26	20	8	2				56	24.7	30.9
200–299.9	12	18	12	8	2			52	22.9	53.8
300–399.9	7	13	11	9	2		1	43	18.9	72.7
400–599.9 middle	4	8	9	4	2		1	28	12.3	85.0
600–999.9	1	4	5	5	3	3	1	22	9.7	94.7
1,000–1,999.9				1	4	2	2	9	4.0	98.7
2,000–2,999.9 high		1						1	0.4	99.1
3,000+			1				1	2	0.9	100.0
Total households	57	70	47	29	13	5	6	227	100.0	
Percentages	25.1	30.8	20.7	12.8	5.7	2.2	2.7	100.0		

B. COMPOUND HEADS' HOUSEHOLDS

Av. month. inc. \ Persons in hh	1–2	3–4	5–6	7–8	9–10	11–12	13+	Total	%	Cum. %
Sh. 0–99.9		2						2	3.5	3.5
100–199.9 low	3	3	1	1				8	13.8	17.3
200–299.9	1	3	1	2	2			9	15.5	32.8
300–399.9	1		2	2	1		1	7	12.1	44.9
400–599.9 middle		2	2	2	2		1	9	15.5	60.4
600–999.9	1	2	2	3	2	2	1	13	22.4	82.8
1,000–1,999.9				1	2	2	2	7	12.1	94.9
2,000–2,999.9 high		1						1	1.7	96.6
3,000+			1				1	2	3.4	100.0
Total households	6	13	9	11	9	4	6	58	100.0	
Percentages	10.3	22.4	15.5	19.1	15.5	6.9	10.3	100.0		

C. DEPENDENT OR SEMI-DEPENDENT HOUSEHOLDS

Av. month. inc. / Persons in hh	1–2	3–4	5–6	7–8	9–10	11–12	13+	Total	%	Cum. %
Sh. 0–99.9	2	3	1					6	7.8	7.8
100–199.9 low	5	12	7	1				25	32.4	40.2
200–299.9	1	9	7	1				18	23.4	63.6
300–399.9		4	4	5	1			14	18.2	81.8
400–599.9 middle	2	3	3	2				10	13.0	94.8
600–999.9		1	2	1				4	5.2	100.0
1,000–1,999.9										
2,000–2,999.9 high										
3,000+										
Total households	10	32	24	10	1			77	100.0	
Percentages	13.0	41.5	31.2	13.0	1.3			100.0		

D. TENANT HOUSEHOLDS

Av month. inc. / Persons in hh	1–2	3–4	5–6	7–8	9–10	11–12	13+	Total	%	Cum. %
Sh. 0–99.9	5	1						6	6.5	6.5
100–199.9 low	18	5						23	25.0	31.5
200–299.9	10	6	4	5				25	27.2	58.7
300–399.9	6	9	5	2				22	23.9	82.6
400–599.9 middle	2	3	4					9	9.8	92.4
600–999.9		1	1	1	1	1		5	5.4	97.8
1,000–1,999.9					2			2	2.2	100.0
2,000–2,999.9 high										
3,000+										
Total households	41	25	14	8	3	1		92	100.0	
Percentages	44.5	27.2	15.2	8.7	3.3	1.1		100.0		

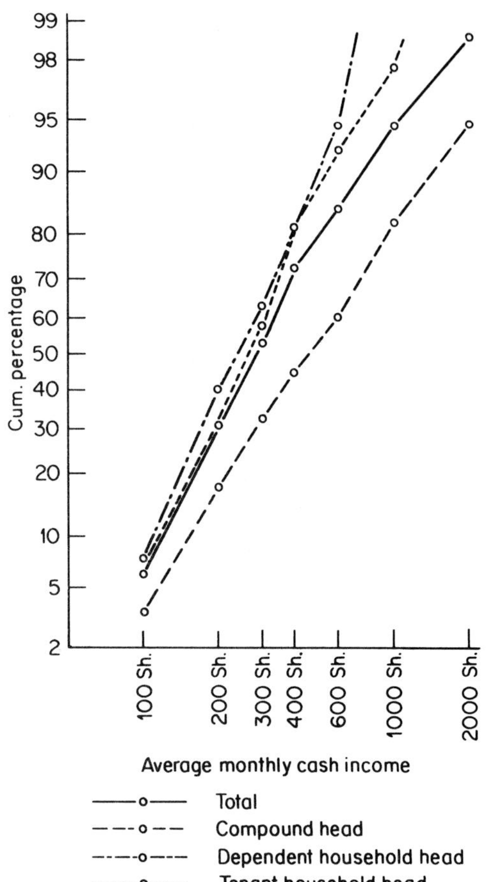

Graph A.11.1
Distribution of household income in Ibadan. (See Table A.11.4 on pp. 396–397)

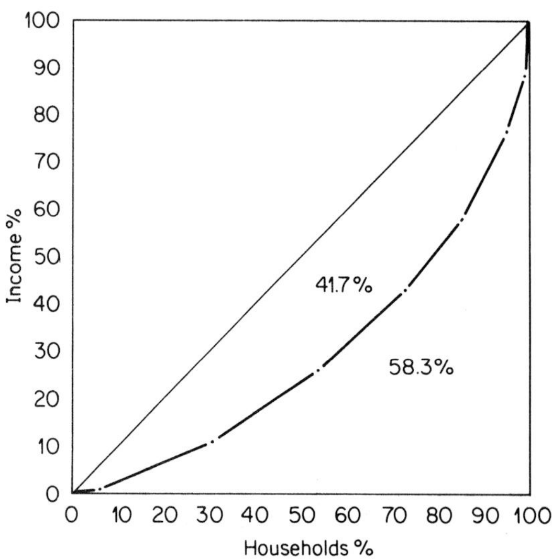

Graph A.11.2
Income distribution (Lorenz Curve), Ibadan

Appendix 12

Table A.12.1 Classification and structure of the Western State building industry, 1971

	Building contractors				Civil engineering contractors				Electrical contractors				All contractors			
	Western State		Based in Ibadan		Western State		Based in Ibadan		Western State		Based in Ibadan		Western State		Based in Ibadan	
	No.	%	No.	%	No.	%	No.	%	No.	%	No.	%	No.	%	No.	%
Small contractors																
Categories A–C	200	73.8	61	58.1	14	28.6	6	22.2	30	81.1	16	72.7	244	68.3	83	53.9
Medium contractors																
Categories D–F	62	22.9	37	35.2	23	46.9	14	51.9	5	13.5	4	18.2	90	25.2	55	35.7
Large contractors																
Categories G+	9	3.3	7	6.7	12	24.5	7	25.9	2	5.4	2	9.1	23	6.5	16	10.4
Total	271	100.0	105	100.0	49	100.0	27	100.0	37	100.0	22	100.0	357	100.0	154	100.0
% firms based in Ibadan				38.7				55.1				59.5				43.1

Source: *Western State of Nigeria Gazette* (Ibadan), **20** (44), August 1971.

Table A.12.2 Age distribution of rooms

Column	1	2	3	4
Year	Age of rooms	No. of rooms built	No. of rooms survived	Cum. %
1968/1969	0–1	3	1,093	100.0
1966/1967	1–2	14	1,090	99.7
1964/1965	3–4	28	1,076	98.4
1962/1963	5–6	25	1,048	95.9
1960/1961	7–8	19	1,023	93.6
1958/1959	9–10	52	1,004	91.9
1956/1957	11–12	91	952	87.1
1954/1955	13–14	62	861	78.8
1952/1953	15–16	36	799	73.1
1950/1951	17–18	70	763	69.8
1948/1949	19–20	66	693	63.4
1946/1947	21–22	50	627	57.4
1944/1945	23–24	35	577	52.8
1942/1943	25–26	59	542	49.6
1940/1941	27–28	37	483	44.2
1930–1939	29–38	123	446	40.8
1920–1929	39–48	111	323	29.6
1910–1919	49–58	84	212	19.4
1900–1909	59–68	82	128	11.7
Before 1900	69+	46	46	4.2
No. of rooms		1,093		
Age unknown		6		
Total rooms		1,099		

Table A.12.3 Structural development of 63 surveyed compounds in Ibadan from 1 May 1963 to 30 April 1968

	Total no. of rms on 30 April 1968		No. of rms built 1963–1968			No. of rms disappeared 1963–1968		Rms converted from earth to cement floor		Total no. of rms on 1 May 1963	
	No.	Sq. m	No.	Sq. m	% 1968	No.	Sq. m	No.	Sq. m	No.	Sq. m
Living areas	814	7,958.6	44	445.2	5.6	10	86.0			780	7,599.4
Communally used rooms	85	544.9	4	23.6	4.3					81	521.3
Basic ancillary facilities	161	728.3	18	86.2	11.8	2	11.7			145	653.8
Commercially used rooms	39	290.5	3	20.1	6.9					36	270.4
Total	1,099	9,522.3	69	575.1	6.0	12	97.7			1,042	9,044.9
Cement floor	761	6,255.6	39	300.1	4.8			46	342.9	676	5,612.6
Rammed earth floor	242	2,343.6	22	173.3	7.4	12	97.7			278	2,610.9
Wooden floor, upstairs rooms	96	923.1	8	101.7	11.0					88	821.4
Total	1,099	9,522.3	69	575.1	6.0	12	97.7	46	342.9	1,042	9,044.9

Table A.12.4 'What improvement do you think the house most needs?'

Answers by compound head	No. of compound heads	%
1. Building a second floor	19	30.2
2. Painting the house	11	17.5
3. Ceilings in rooms	5	7.9
4. Lavatory and bathroom	4	6.3
5. Rebuild the whole house	4	6.3
6. Piped water	3	4.8
7. More bedrooms	3	4.8
8. Electricity	3	4.8
9. Repair roof	3	4.8
10. Other needs	5	7.9
11. No response	2	3.1
12. Undecided	1	1.6
Total compound heads	63	100.0

Table A.12.5 Construction of new buildings, 1963–1968

	No.	Sq. m
1. Living area		
Sleeping rooms	29	266.7
Sitting rooms	4	44.9
Central halls	5	87.8
Store rooms (personal)	2	13.2
Empty rooms	4	32.6
Subtotal	44	445.2
2. Common rooms		
Entrance lobbies	4	23.6
Passages	–	–
Subtotal	4	23.6
3. Basic ancillary facilities		
Kitchens	5	34.4
Kitchen stores	1	3.4
Other stores	5	30.4
Toilets and bathrooms	7	18.0
Subtotal	18	86.2
4. Commercially used rooms		
Shops	1	4.3
Stores and stables	2[a]	15.8
Subtotal	3	20.1
Total	69	575.1

[a]Grouped in Table 12.1 on p. 173 under 'Miscellaneous construction'.

Table A.12.6 Cost of construction, House 6

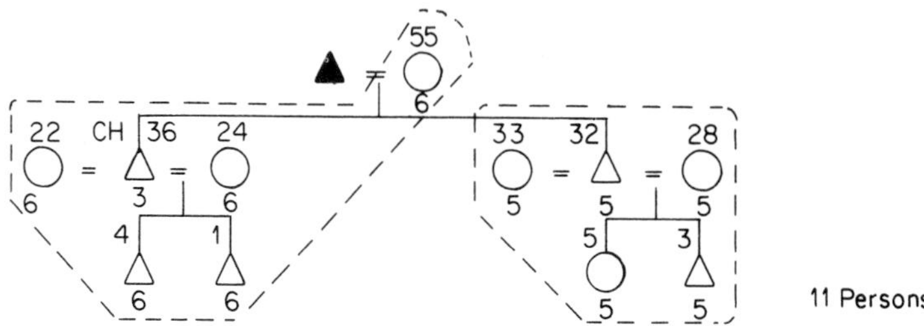

Compound head	Bookshop manager	Salary 1967/1968 £N 325 p.a.
CH's full brother	Washerman	Known cash income 1967/1968 £N 89 p.a.

CH built house in 1963–1965 with some financial help from his family and full brother

Size of house:		
	6 rooms	59.8 sq. m
	1 cent. hall	14.0 sq. m
	1 ent. lobby	5.1 sq. m
	1 cov. verandah	8.8 sq. m
	Total area	87.7 sq. m

House contained very little furniture: 1 table, 3 chairs, 4 mats, 3 wooden boxes, various baskets, and cooking pots. There was no electricity or water supply.

Breakdown of cost by element of building and element of cost

Material	s.	Labour	s.	Subtotal s.	%
SUPERSTRUCTURE					
Foundation and walls					
Stones for foundation	820				
Cement, 65 bags @ 15 s.	975	Foundation	300		
Sand	100	Walls £N 10 per room	1,200		
Subtotal	1,895		1,500	3,395	34.2
Roof					
Timber	800				
CIR sheets, 10.5 bundles	1,050				
Nails, etc.	160	Roof construction	675		
Subtotal	2,010		675	2,685	27.0
FINISHES					
Ceilings					
45 asbestos-cement sheets	270				
Timber	135				
Nails, etc.	80	Fixing of ceilings	360		
Subtotal	485		360	845	8.5
Doors and windows					
Internal doors 9 @ £N 3.75					
External doors 2 @ £N 5.25	800[a]				
Small windows 5 @ £N 1.25					
Big windows 4 @ £N 4.00					
Glass	135	Building doors and windows	530		
Subtotal	935		530	1,465	14.8

Table A.12.6 (*continued*)

Material	s.	Labour	s.	Subtotal s.	%
Cementing rooms					
Cement, 55 bags @ 15 s.	825				
Sand	80	Contractor	390		13.0
Subtotal	905		390	1,295	13.1
Paint and whitewash					
Paint	155				
Subtotal	155	Painter	90	245	2.5
Total	6,385		3,545	9,930	
Percentages	64.3		35.7		100.0

[a]Estimated proportion of material and labour cost.

Table A.12.7 Cost of construction, House 12

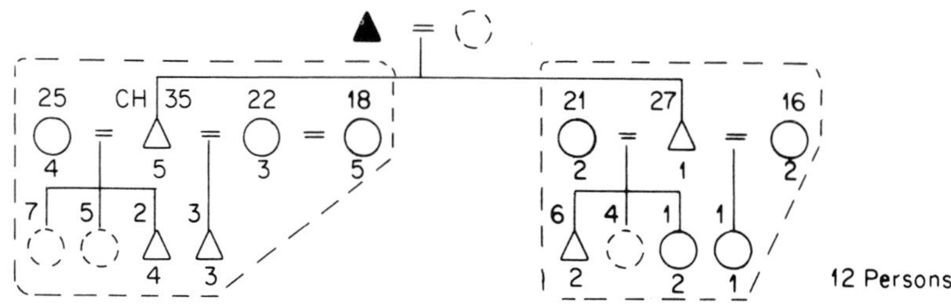

Compound head Bricklayer, Min. of Works & Trans. Salary 1967/1968 £N 230 p.a.
CH's full brother Police since 1964, carpenter Salary 1967/1968 £N 210 p.a.
CH and brother built house together in 1964–1965. Some help from family

Size of house:

6 rooms	66.1 sq. m
1 cent. hall	16.1 sq. m
1 ent. lobby	5.4 sq. m
1 cov. verandah	10.5 sq. m
Total area	98.1 sq. m

House contained 4 beds, 4 cupboards, 3 boxes, 7 chairs, 16 mats, 3 tables, 1 sewing machine, 1 mirror, several baskets, cooking pots. No electricity or water supply.

Breakdown of cost by element of building and element of cost

Material	s.	Labour	s.	Subtotal s.	%
SUPERSTRUCTURE					
Foundation and walls					
Stones for foundation	260				
Cement, 60 bags @ 14.2 s.	852				
Sand	110				
Reinforcement bars	158	Helpers	250		
Subtotal	1,380		250	1,630	25.8
Roof					
Timber	700				
CIR sheets, 12 bundles	1,200				
Nails, etc.	90	Helpers	160		
Subtotal	1,990		160	2,150	34.1
FINISHES					
Ceilings					
Fibreboard sheets	390				
Nails, etc.	40				
Subtotal	430	Self	–	430	6.8
Doors and windows					
Timber	580				
Hinges	175				
Glass	210				
Subtotal	965	Self	–	965	15.3

Table A.12.7 (*continued*)

Material	s.	Labour	s.	Subtotal s.	%
Cementing rooms					
Cement, 60 bags @ 14.2 s.	852				
Sand	100				
Subtotal	952	Self	–	952	15.1
Paint and whitewash					
Paint	180				
Subtotal	180	Self	–	180	2.9
Total	5,897		410	6,307	
Percentages	93.5		6.5		100.0

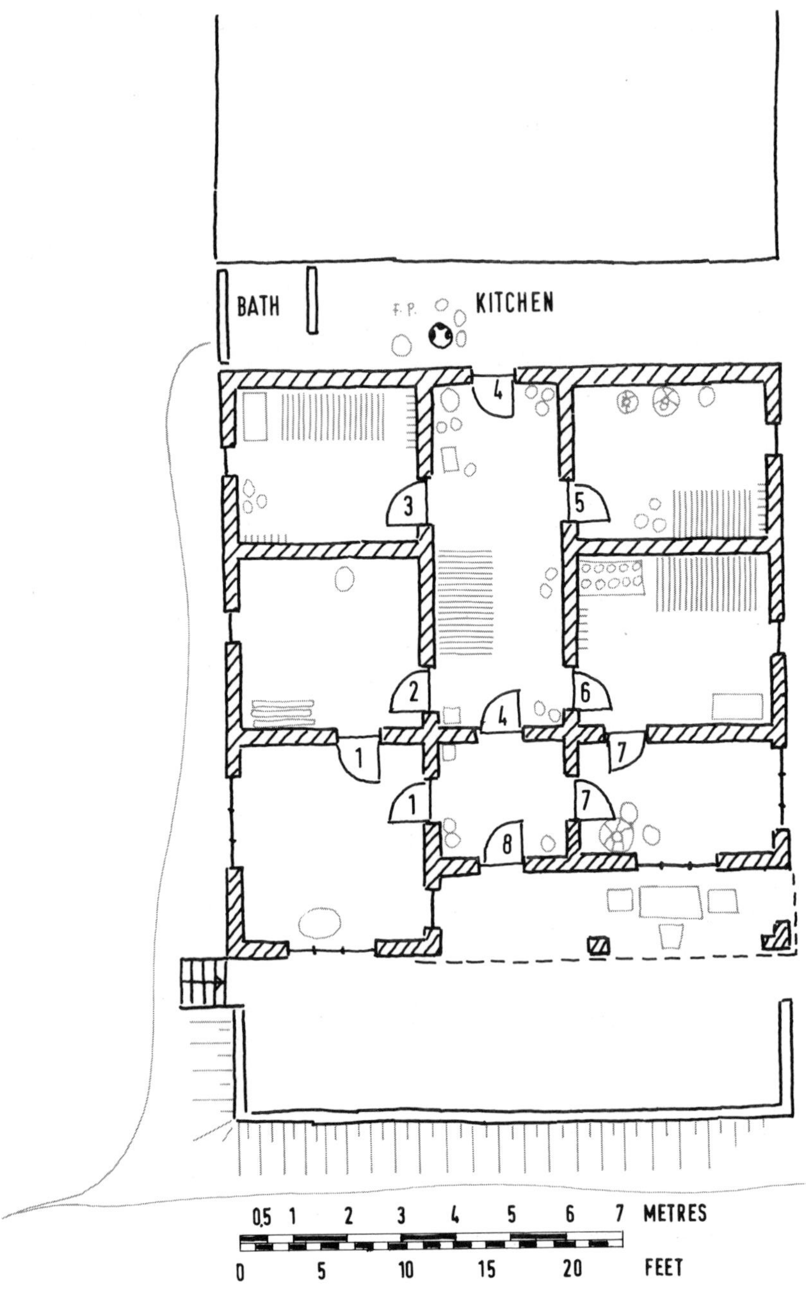

Plan A.12.1
House 6

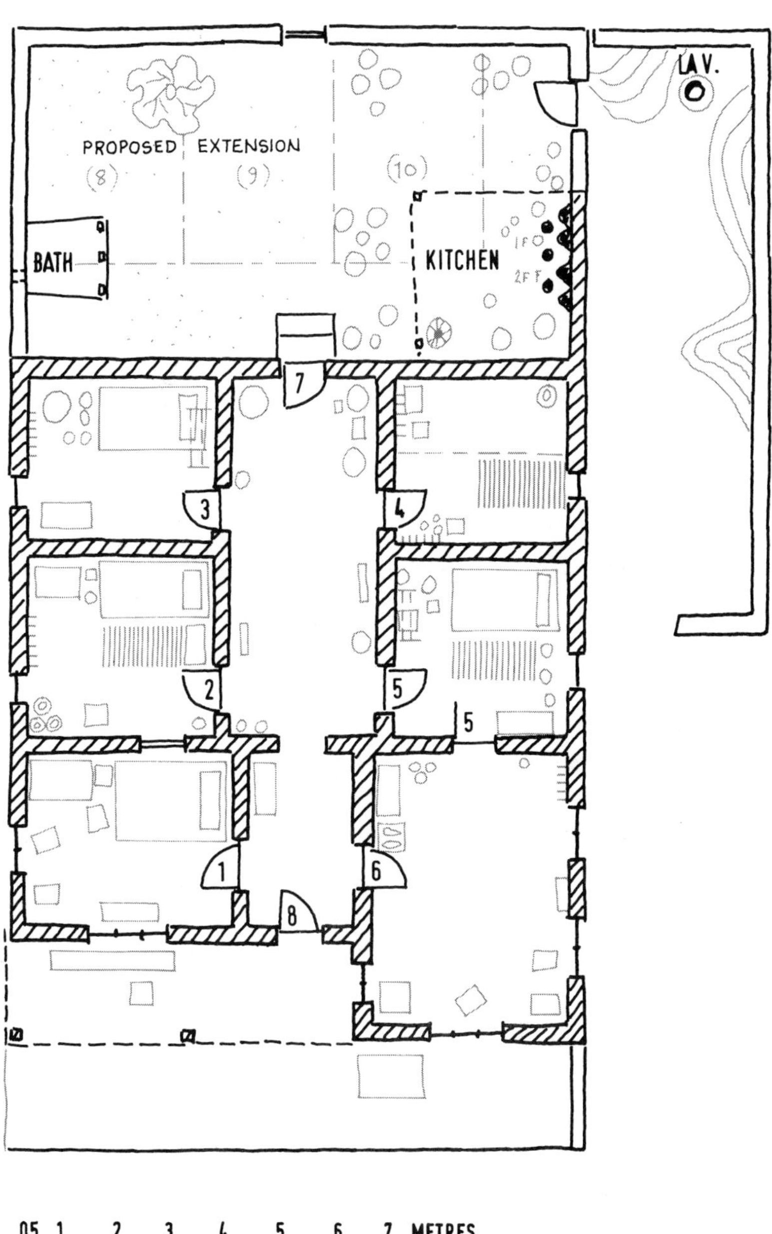

Plan A.12.2
House 12

Table A.12.8 The cost of construction of rural buildings in Western Nigeria

Houses built	No. of houses surveyed at each age group[a]	Average no. of rooms per house[b]	Total average cost per house in £N[c]	Total average cost per room in £N[d]	% total cost					
					Walls	Roof	Woodwork	Metalwork	Others[e]	Total
Before 1920	7	—	40.8	—	14.0	20.4	43.8	6.2	15.6	100.0
1920–1924	22	6.7	81.7	12.2	28.0	27.8	25.3	5.3	13.6	100.0
1925–1929	50	7.7	132.2	17.2	22.1	28.5	29.8	7.2	12.4	100.0
1930–1934	87	6.7	101.7	15.2	28.2	22.6	29.1	6.5	13.6	100.0
1935–1939	164	6.5	118.2	18.2	31.1	25.3	28.0	5.6	10.0	100.0
1940–1944	106	5.5	89.0	16.2	35.6	23.1	28.1	5.2	8.0	100.0
1945–1949	161	6.1	158.7	26.0	27.3	29.8	29.7	5.0	8.2	100.0
1950–1951	90	7.5	244.0	32.5	30.6	31.9	27.0	4.8	5.7	100.0
Total	687	6.5	136.7	21.0	29.5	27.6	28.5	5.3	9.1	100.0
1965[f]	1	6.0	224.0	37.3	33.4	42.8	———	23.8	———	100.0

[a]R. Galletti, *Nigerian Cocoa Farmers*, Oxford, 1956, Table 118, p. 255.
[b]Ibid., Table 119, p. 257.
[c]Ibid., Table 116, p. 254.
[d]Ibid., Table 117, p. 255.
[e]Including entertainment and sacrifices.
[f]P. Crooke, 'Sample survey of Yoruba rural building', *Odu, University of Ife Journal of African Studies* (Ibadan), **2** (2), 1966, p. 60.

Table A.12.9 'Who built the core or main part of the house?'

		No.	%
1	The present compound head	25	39.7
2	The present CH's father	24	38.1
3	The present CH's father's or mother's father	7	11.1
4	The present CH's deceased husband	2	3.2
5	Absentee landlord	2	3.2
6	Others include CH's father's brother and CH's mother. One compound head who bought the house	3	4.7
	Total compound heads	63	100.0

Table A.12.10 The financing of houses in Ibadan

	No. of loans	Gifts and grants	s.	%
New construction				
CH's personal income and savings			45,060	89.4
Personal sources, loans, and gifts	2	2	5,350	10.6
Institutional sources				
Total expenditure			50,410	100.0
Improvements				
CH's personal income and savings			21,890	95.2
Personal sources, loans, and gifts	2	1	1,105	4.8
Institutional sources				
Total expenditure			22,995	100.0
Maintenance and repair				
CH's personal income and savings			27,315	100.0
Personal sources, loans, and gifts				
Institutional sources				
Total expenditure			27,315[a]	100.0
Under construction				
CH's personal income and savings				
Personal sources, loans, and gifts	–			
Institutional sources				
Total expenditure			–	–
Miscellaneous construction				
CH's personal income and savings			3,260	100.0
Personal sources, loans, and gifts				
Institutional sources				
Total expenditure			3,260	100.0
Total building activities				
CH's personal income and savings			97,525	93.8
Personal sources, loans, and gifts	4	3	6,455	6.2
Institutional sources				
Total expenditure			103,980	100.0

[a]Adjusted expenditure, actual expenditure 16,389 shillings.

Appendixes – Part III

MARRAKECH

Appendix 13

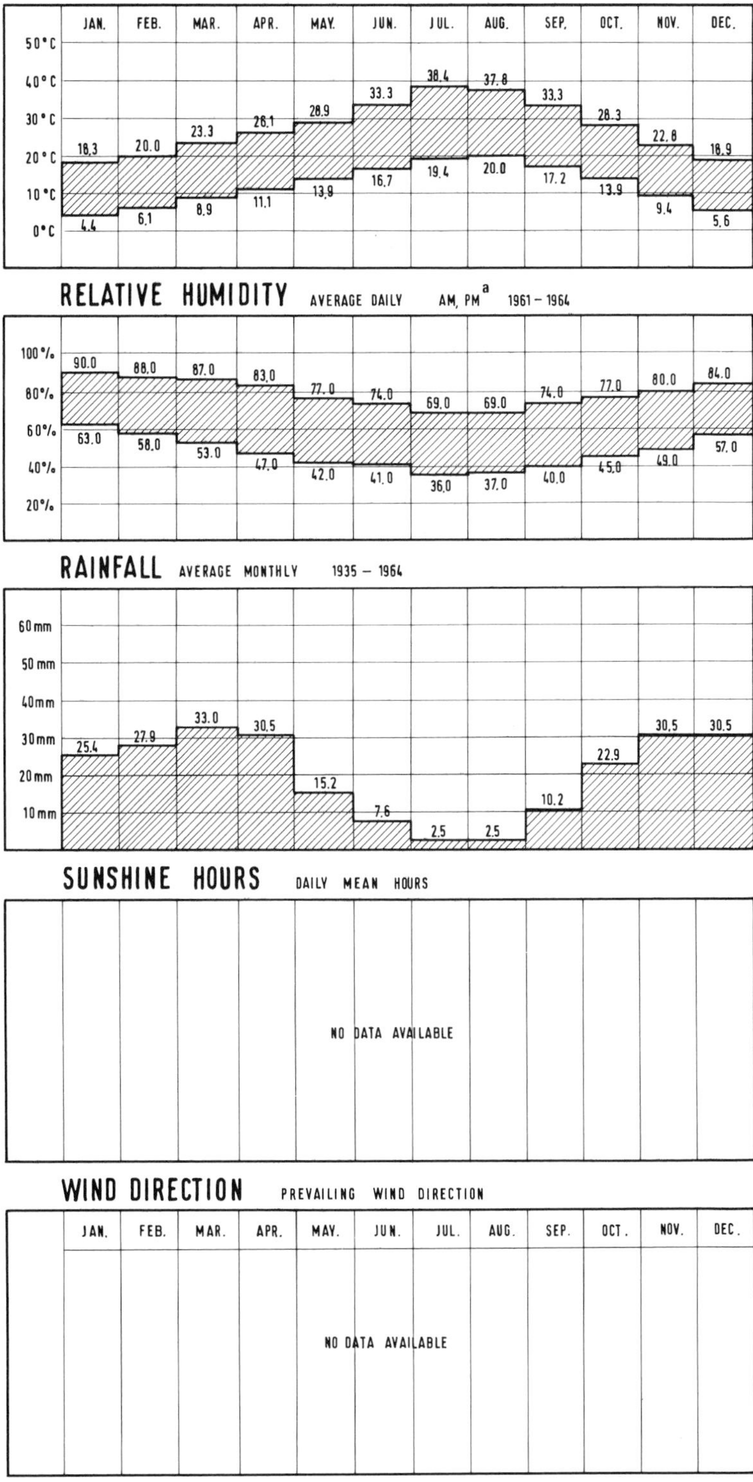

Diagram A.13.1
Climatic data, Marrakech
[a]Observation taken at 05.30 and 11.30 GMT

Table A.13.1 Gross Domestic Product at 1960 factor cost, in DH million

	1960	1961	1962	1963	1964	1965	1966	1967	1968	1969	1970	1971[a]
Agriculture	2,650	2,260	2,870	3,060	2,990	3,150	2,780	3,070	3,980	3,650	3,720	3,940
Commerce	1,910	1,880	2,060	2,180	2,150	2,130	2,140	2,280	2,440	2,550	2,730	2,840
Transp. and non-gov. services	1,500	1,530	1,600	1,660	1,720	1,780	1,820	1,890	2,010	2,090	2,190	2,300
Manufacturing and crafts	1,100	1,150	1,210	1,290	1,330	1,320	1,370	1,420	1,490	1,580	1,700	1,780
Government services	890	940	1,010	1,020	1,090	1,100	1,140	1,230	1,380	1,430	1,530	1,630
Mining	540	570	540	530	590	590	580	580	580	620	620	630
Construction	320	370	420	460	450	470	500	580	570	610	700	730
Energy	180	180	220	230	250	260	280	280	310	330	350	370
Total	9,090	8,880	9,930	10,430	10,570	10,800	10,610	11,330	12,760	12,860	13,540	14,220
GDP at current factor cost	9,090	9,040	10,620	11,860	12,490	13,160	12,840	13,600	15,310	15,920	16,960	18,530

Source: Ministère du Développement, Royaume du Maroc, *Annuaire statistique du Maroc,* 1965 and 1972.
[a]Provisional figures.

Table A.13.2 Gross Domestic Product at 1960 factor cost, in percentages

	1960	1961	1962	1963	1964	1965	1966	1967	1968	1969	1970	1971[a]
Agriculture	29.2	25.5	28.9	29.3	28.3	29.2	26.2	27.1	31.2	28.4	27.5	27.7
Commerce	21.0	21.2	20.7	20.9	20.3	19.7	20.2	20.1	19.1	19.8	20.1	20.0
Transp. and non-gov. services	16.5	17.2	16.1	15.9	16.3	16.5	17.2	16.7	15.8	16.3	16.2	16.2
Manufacturing and crafts	12.1	12.9	12.2	12.4	12.6	12.2	12.9	12.5	11.7	12.3	12.5	12.5
Government services	9.8	10.6	10.2	9.8	10.3	10.2	10.7	10.9	10.8	11.1	11.3	11.5
Mining	5.9	6.4	5.4	5.1	5.6	5.5	5.5	5.1	4.5	4.8	4.6	4.4
Construction	3.5	4.2	4.3	4.4	4.3	4.3	4.7	5.1	4.5	4.7	5.2	5.1
Energy	2.0	2.0	2.2	2.2	2.3	2.4	2.6	2.5	2.4	2.6	2.6	2.6
Total	100.0	100.0	100.0	100.0	100.0	100.0	100.0	100.0	100.0	100.0	100.0	100.0

Source: Ministère du Développement, Royaume du Maroc, *Annuaire Statistique du Maroc*, 1965 and 1972.
[a]Provisional figures.

Table A.13.3 Export of principal products, in DH million

	1960	1961	1962	1963	1964	1965	1966	1967	1968	1969	1970	1971
Food, drink, tobacco	822	749	817	943	1,074	1,049	1,052	1,062	1,169	1,185	1,250	1,206
Fuel and energy	15	16	14	15	16	13	7	11	16	8	10	9
Raw materials–minerals	777	808	772	847	937	982	777	754	738	768	784	762
Other raw materials	—	—	—	—	—	—	174	141	134	238	167	153
Manufactured products	160	159	159	138	159	132	158	179	221	256	261	395
Total export	1,774	1,732	1,762	1,943	2,186	2,176	2,168	2,147	2,278	2,455	2,472	2,525

Source: Ministère du Developpement, Royaume du Maroc, *Annuaire Statistique du Maroc*, 1965 and 1972.

Table A.13.4 Export of principal products, in percentages

	1960	1961	1962	1963	1964	1965	1966	1967	1968	1969	1970	1971
Food, drink, tobacco	46.3	43.2	46.4	48.5	49.1	48.2	48.5	49.5	51.3	48.3	50.6	47.8
Fuel and energy	0.9	0.9	0.8	0.8	0.7	0.6	0.3	0.5	0.7	0.3	0.4	0.3
Raw materials–minerals	43.8	46.7	43.8	43.6	42.9	45.1	35.9	35.1	32.4	31.3	31.7	30.2
Other raw materials	—	—	—	—	—	—	8.0	6.6	5.9	9.7	6.7	6.1
Manufactured products	9.0	9.2	9.0	7.1	7.3	6.1	7.3	8.3	9.7	10.4	10.6	15.6
Total export	100.0	100.0	100.0	100.0	100.0	100.0	100.0	100.0	100.0	100.0	100.0	100.0

Table A.13.5 Gross Fixed Capital Formation at current prices, in DH million

	1960	1961	1962	1963	1964	1965	1966	1967	1968	1969	1970	1971
Plant, machinery, equipment	360	400	410	570	550	580	600	780	860	980	1,210	1,130
Public works	310	370	470	510	480	540	590	750	730	790	890	900
Buildings	250	280	270	330	340	320	340	360	380	310	510	590
Total	920	1,050	1,150	1,410	1,370	1,440	1,530	1,890	1,970	2,080	2,610	2,620

Source: Ministère du Développement, Royaume du Maroc, *Annuaire statistique du Maroc*, 1965 and 1972.

Table A.13.6 Gross Fixed Capital Formation at current prices, in percentages

	1960	1961	1962	1963	1964	1965	1966	1967	1968	1969	1970	1971
Plant, machinery, equipment	39.1	38.1	35.6	40.4	40.2	40.3	39.2	41.3	43.6	47.1	46.4	43.1
Public works	33.7	35.2	40.9	36.2	35.0	37.5	38.6	39.7	37.1	38.0	34.1	34.4
Buildings	27.2	26.7	23.5	23.4	24.8	22.2	22.2	19.0	19.3	14.9	19.5	22.5
Total	100.0	100.0	100.0	100.0	100.0	100.0	100.0	100.0	100.0	100.0	100.0	100.0

Appendix 14

Table A.14.1 Type of land tenure of 75 houses in Marrakech, 1969

	No.	% of total
1 Purchased houses	34	45.3
2 Rented accommodation	15	20.0
3 Inherited houses	14	18.7
4 Houses built on squatter land	6	8.0
5 Others	6	8.0
Total	75	100.0

Table A.14.2 Land use inside the walled city of Marrakech, 1969

	Sq. m	% of total
1 Built-up area	4,053,396	64.1
2 Parks and public gardens	798,166	12.6
3 Waste land	452,319	7.2
4 Roads	450,755	7.1
5 Cultivated land	356,940	5.7
6 Cemeteries	169,250	2.7
7 Other land	38,960	0.6
Total	6,319,786	100.0

Appendix 15

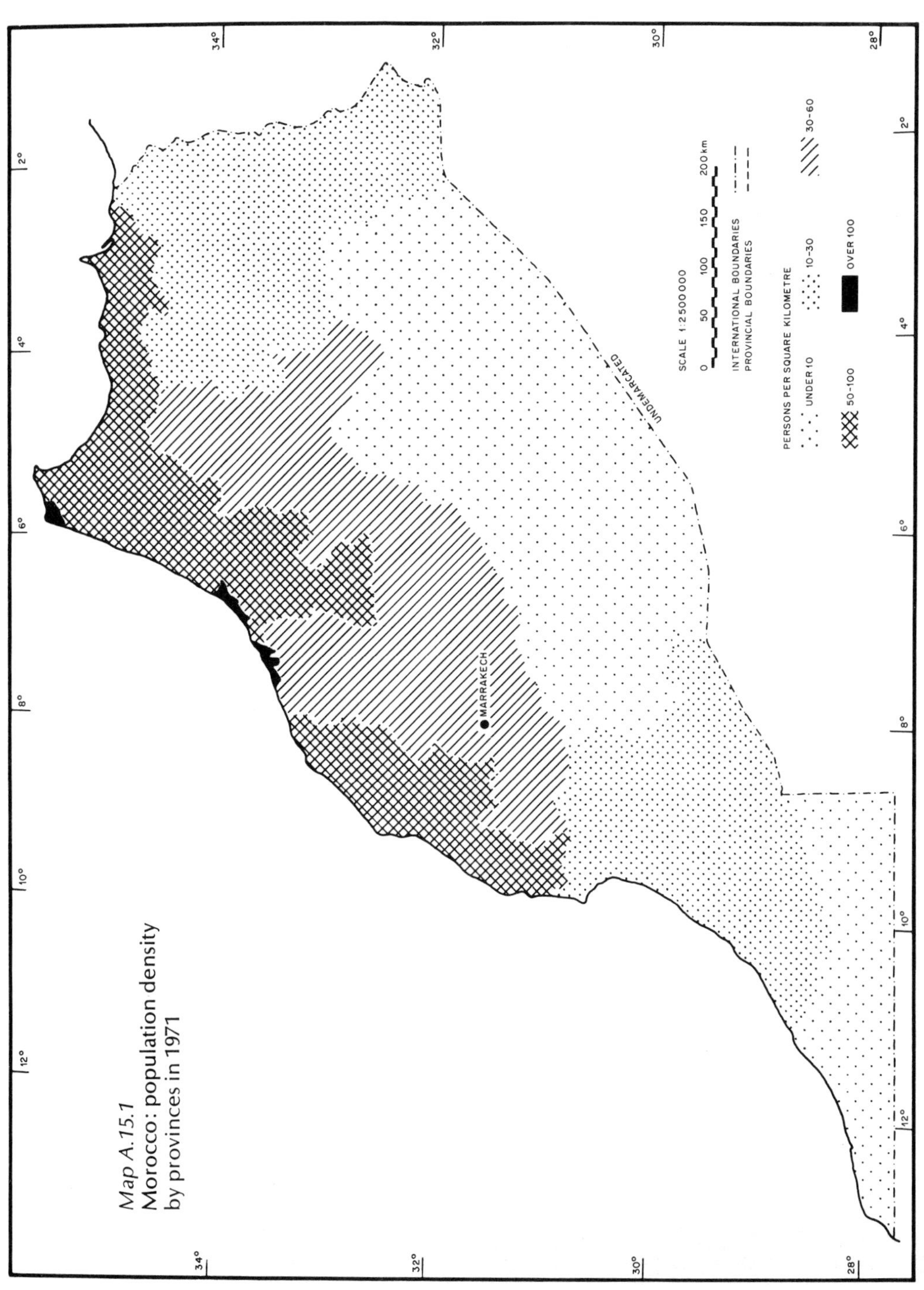

Map A.15.1
Morocco: population density by provinces in 1971

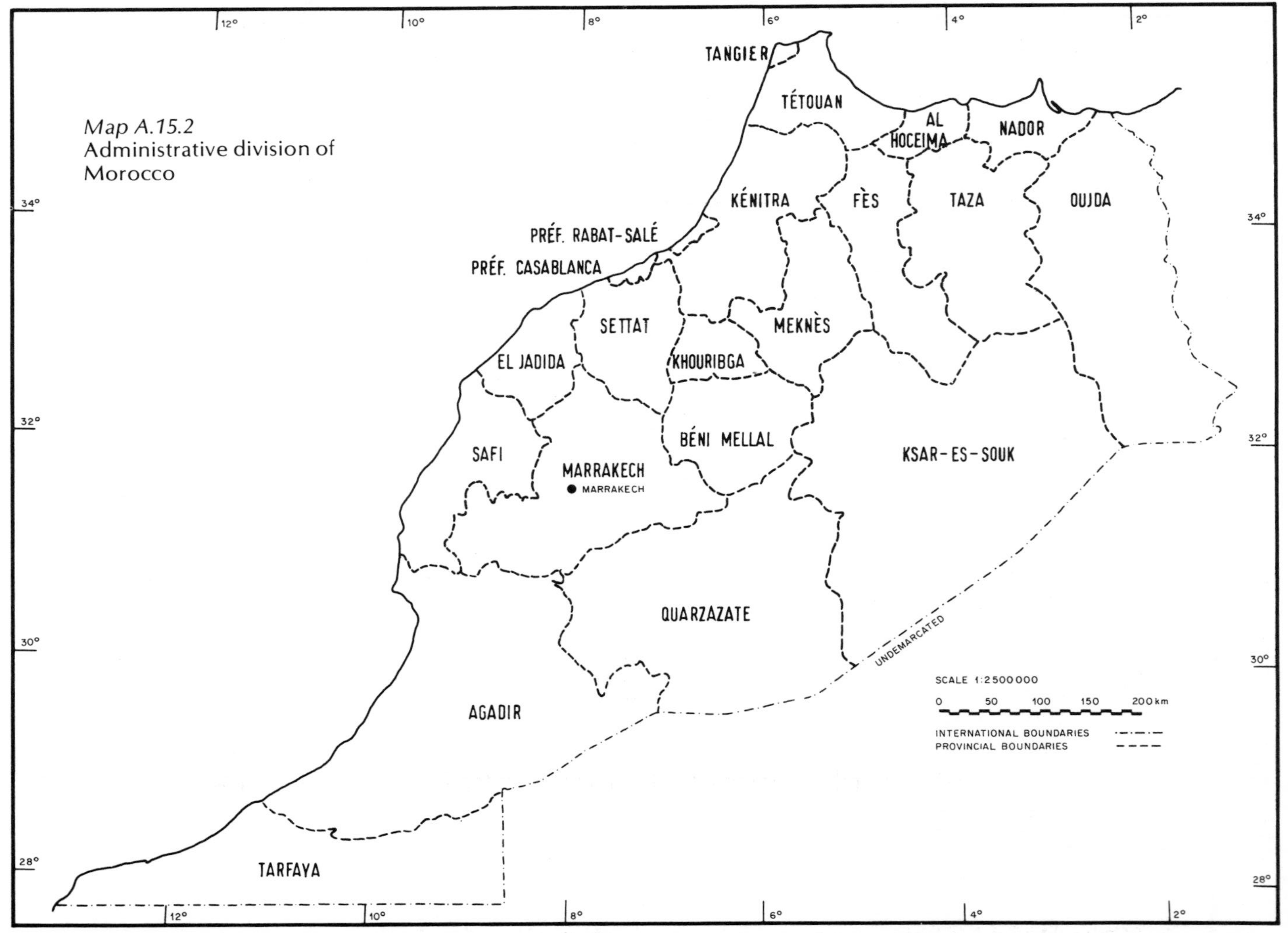

Map A.15.2
Administrative division of Morocco

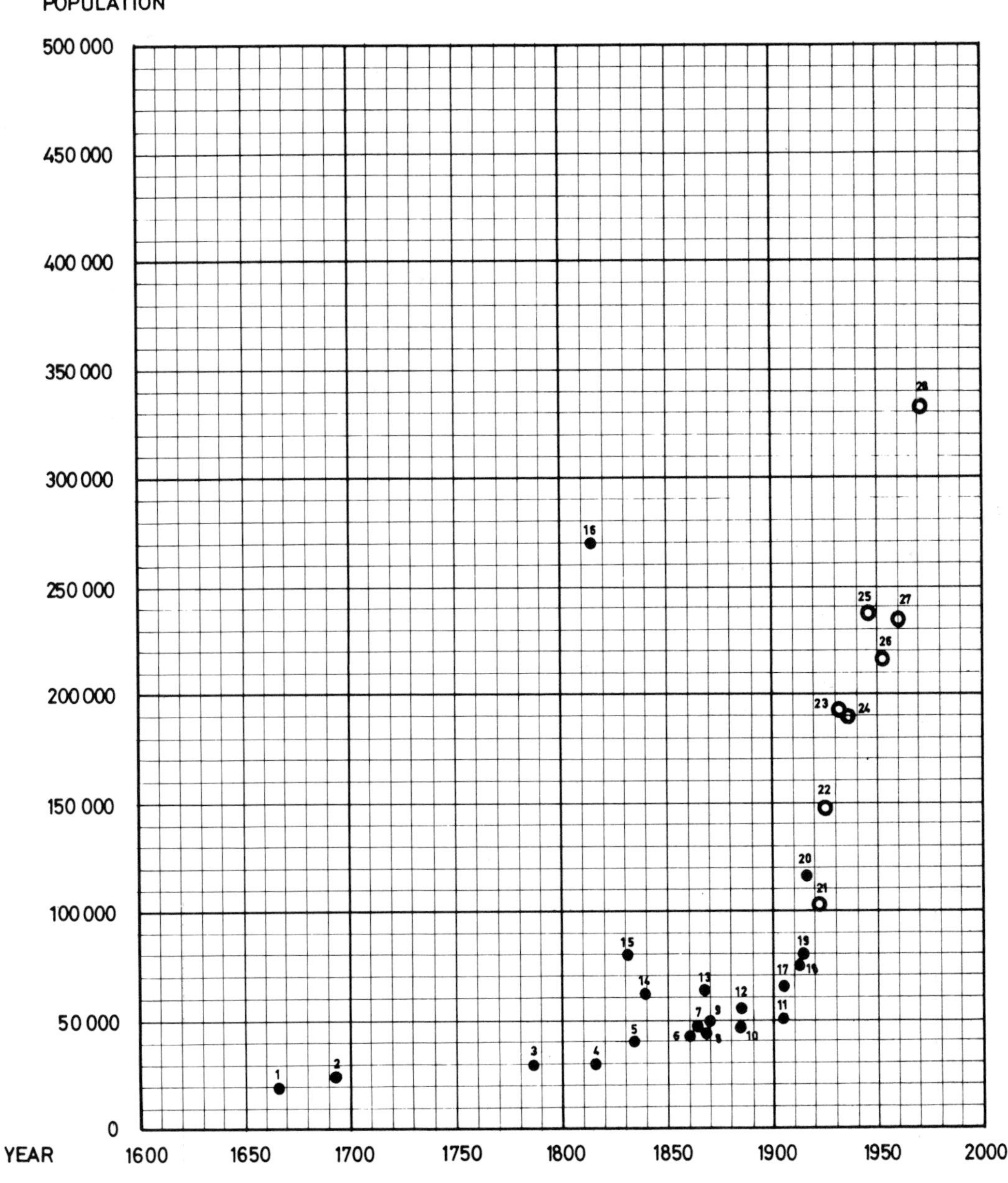

Graph A.15.1
Population trends and projections for Marrakech

Numbers referring to Graph A.15.1 on p. 421

1 D. de Torrés, *Relation de l'origine et succez des chérifs, et de l'estat des royaumes de Marroc, Fez et Tarudant, et autres provinces*, Paris, 1667, p. 81.
2 P. de Saint-Olon, 'Estat présent de l'empire de Maroc', *Relation de l'empire de Maroc*, Paris, 1693, p. 16.
3 L. de Chénier, *Recherches historiques sur les maures et histoire de l'empire de Maroc*, Paris, 1787, vol. 3, p. 50.
4 Ali Bey el Abbassi, *Travels of Ali Bey in Morocco ... between 1803 and 1807*, London, 1816, vol. 1, p. 149.
5 J. Craberg di Hamso, *Specchio geografico e statistico dell' imperio di Marocco*, Genoa, 1834, p. 68.
6 J. Richardson, *Travels in Morocco*, London, 1860, vol. 2, p. 150.
7 J. Gavira, *El viajero español por Marruecos, Don Joaquin Gatell*, Madrid, 1949, p. 114.
8 P. Lambert, 'Notice sur la ville de Maroc', *Bulletin de la Société Géographie* (Paris), no. 107, 1868, p. 441.
9 J. L. Miège, 'Note sur l'artisanat marocain en 1870', *Bulletin économique et social du Maroc* (Rabat), no. 2, 1953, p. 91.
10 O. Lenz, *Reise durch Marokko die Sahara und den Sudan*, vol. 1, Leipzig, 1884, p. 258.
11 E. Aubin, *Le Maroc d'aujourd'hui*, Paris, 1904, p. 37.
12 J. Erckmann, *Le Maroc moderne*, Paris, 1885, p. 38.
13 A. Beaumier, *Description sommaire du Maroc*, Paris, 1868, p. 23.
14 A. Balbi, *Abrégé de géographie*, Paris, 1934, pp. 885–886.
15 R. N. Washington, 'Geographical notice of the empire of Morocco', *Journal of the Royal Geographical Society* (London), vol. 4, p. 138.
16 J. G. Jackson, *An account of the empire of Morocco and the district of Suse and Tafilet*, London, 1814, p. 25.
17 A. Cousin and D. Saurin, *Le Maroc*, Paris, 1905, p. 374.
18 H. Bardon, 'Les deux capitales du Maroc: Fèz et Marrakech', *Bulletin de la Société de géographie de Marseille*, **XXXVI** (2), 1912, p. 134.
19 Capt. Cornet, *À la conquête du Maroc-Sud avec la Colonne Mangin 1912–13*, Paris, 1914, p. 192.
20 V. Piquet, *Le Maroc*, 3rd edition, Paris, 1920, p. 215.
21 Comité de l'Afrique française, *L'Afrique française* (Bulletin Mensuel du Comité de l'Afrique Française et du Comité du Maroc; Paris), no. 5, 1921, p. 156.
22 Ibid., no. 2, 1927, p. 59.
23 Author not given, *Bulletin de la société de géographie d'Alger et de l'Afrique du Nord* (Paris), vol. 34 (133), p. 30. Comité de l'Afrique française, op. cit., no. 5, 1931, p. 362.
24 Ibid., no. 7, 1937, p. 386.
25 Secrétariat Générale du Protectorat, Service des Statistiques, Royaume du Maroc, *De nombrement générale de la population de la zone française de l'Empire Chérifien 1947*, Paris, 1948, vol. 1, p. 6, and vol. 2, pp. 4–5.
26 Service Central des Statistiques, Royaume du Maroc, *Recensement général de la population de la zone française de l'Empire Chérifien 1951/52*, Rabat, 1954, vol. 1, p. 17, vol. 2, p. 15, and vol. 3, p. 22.
27 Service Central des Statistiques, Royaume du Maroc, *Résultats du recensement de 1960*, Rabat, 1964, vol. 1, pp. 81–82 and 22.
28 Service Central des Statistiques, Royaume du Maroc, *Population légale du Maroc 1971*, Rabat, 1971, p. 6.

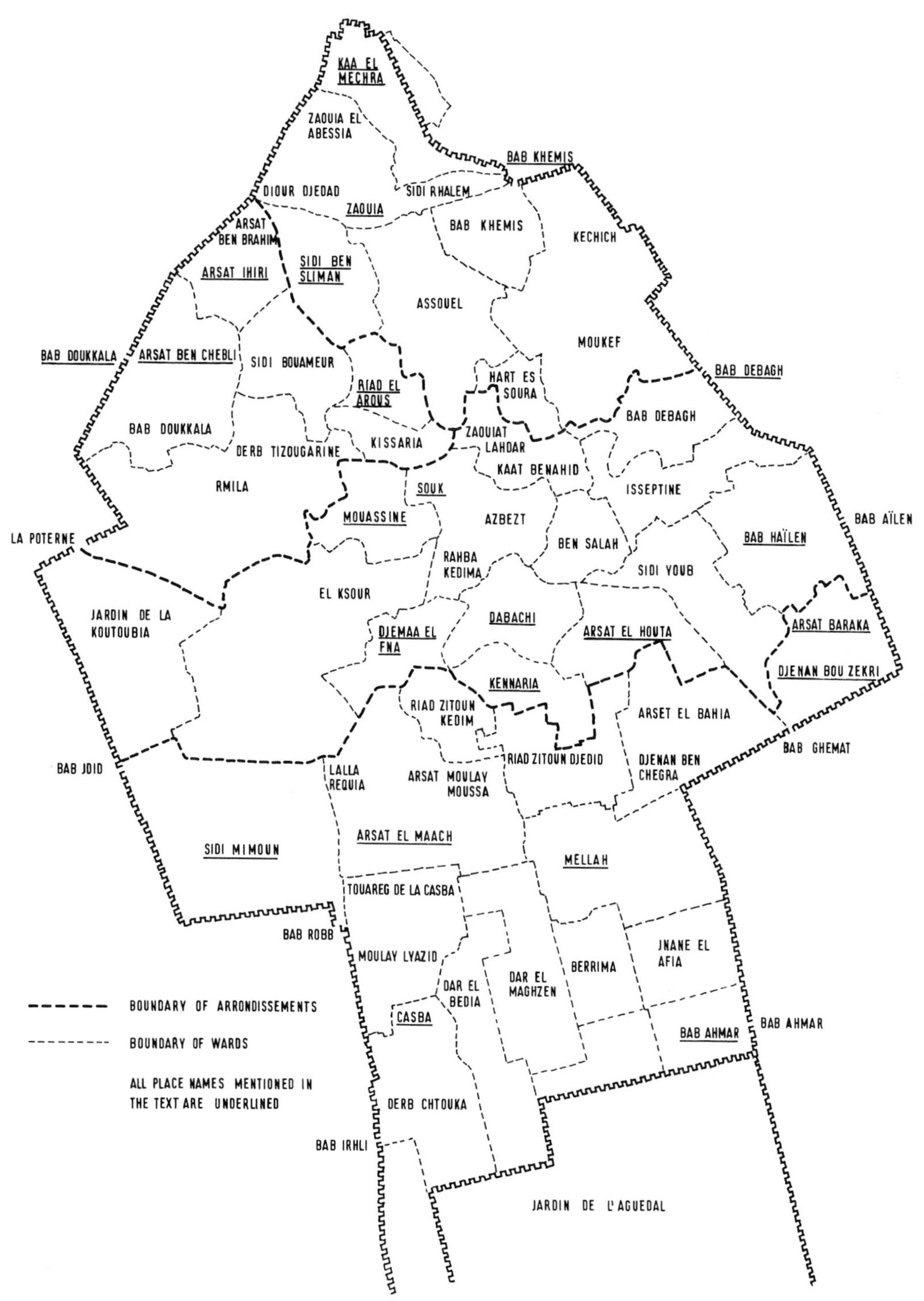

Plan A.15.3
Marrakech: principal localities and administrative divisions

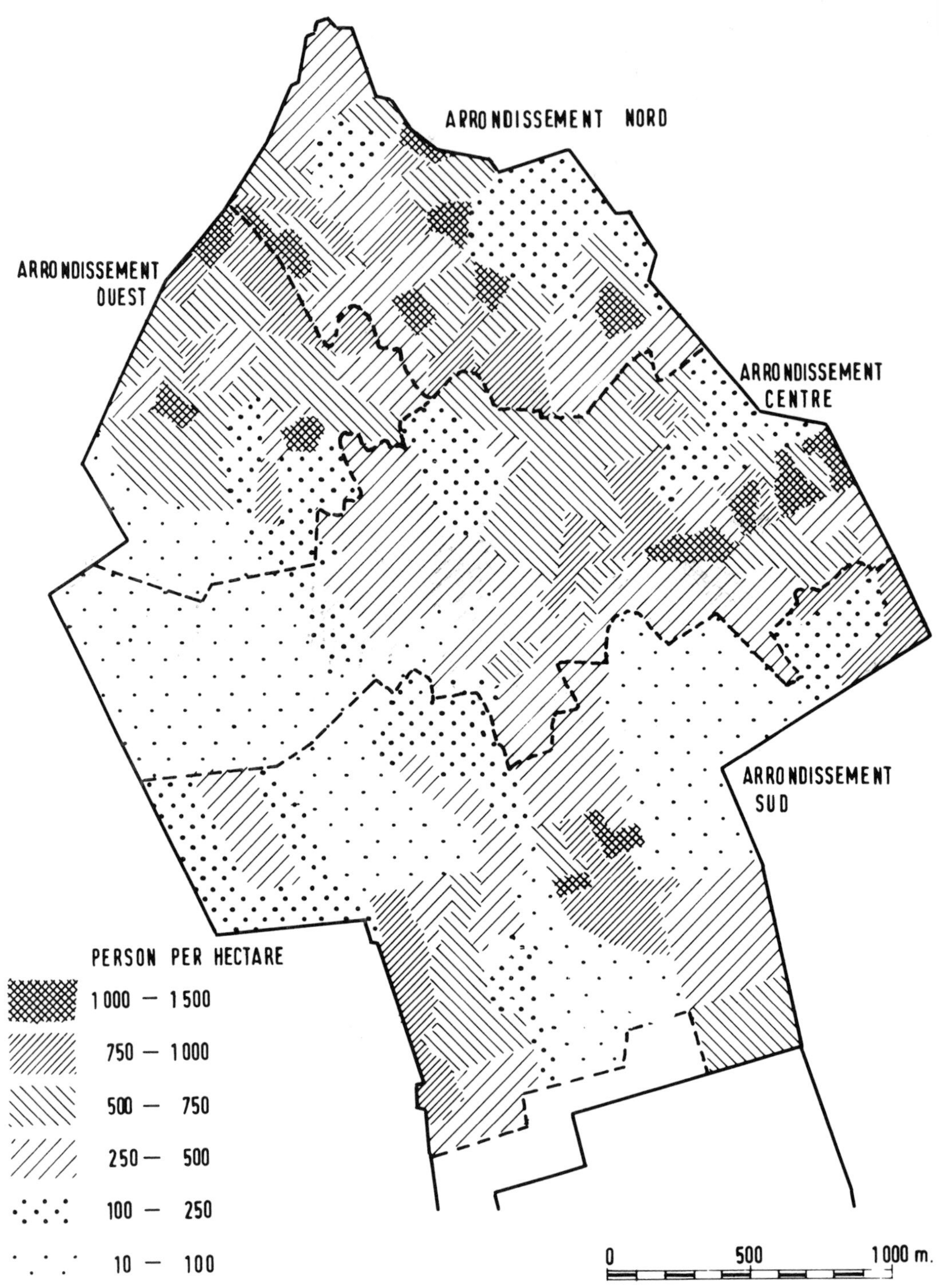

Plan A.15.4
Population density in the walled city of Marrakech in 1971. Source: A. Mandleur, 'Croissance et urbanisation de Marrakech, *Revue de géographie du Maroc* (Rabat), no. 22, 1972

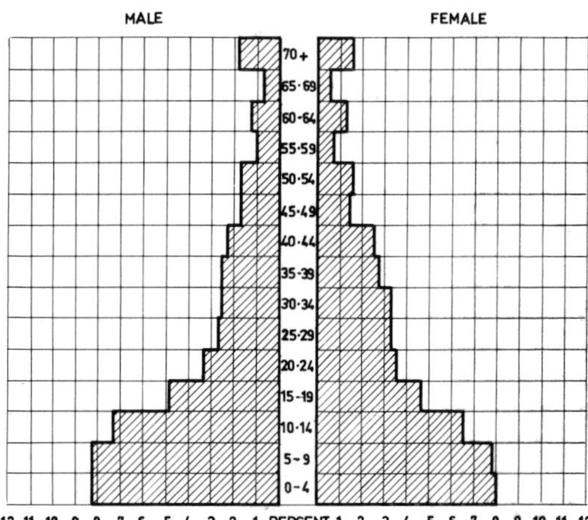

MARRAKECH TOTAL POPULATION 1960

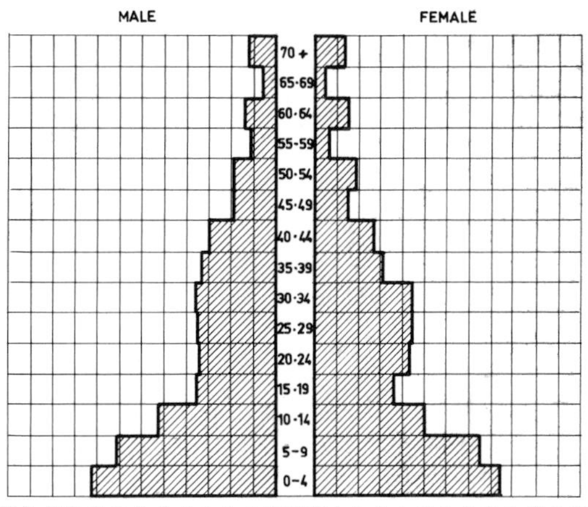

SURVEY SAMPLE POPULATION 1969

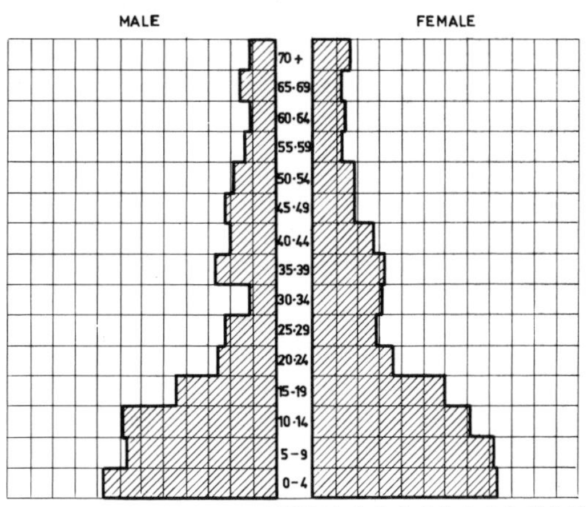

Diagram A.15.1
Age and sex distribution

Appendix 16

Table A.16.1 Distribution of household size

No. of persons	Hh group	CH's households			Dependent households			Tenant households			Total households		
		No. of hhs	%	No. of persons	No. of hhs	%	No. of persons	No. of hhs	%	No. of persons	No. of hhs	%	No. of persons
1	1–2	1	8.8	1	1	22.6	1	15	35.1	15	17	23.7	17
2		5		10	6		12	17		34	28		56
3	3–4	6	29.4	18	6	35.5	18	14	30.8	42	26	31.0	78
4		14		56	5		20	14		56	33		132
5	5–6	5	17.7	25	2	19.3	10	11	20.9	55	18	19.5	90
6		7		42	4		24	8		48	19		114
7	7–8	12	25.0	84	2	9.7	14	6	11.0	42	20	15.8	140
8		5		40	1		8	4		32	10		80
9	9–10	6	13.2	54	2	12.9	18	1	2.2	9	9	7.9	81
10		3		30	2		20	1		10	6		60
11	11–12	1	4.4	11							1	1.6	11
12		2		24							2		24
Over 12	Over 12	1	1.5	13							1	0.5	13
Total		68	100.0	408	31	100.0	145	91	100.0	343	190	100.0	896
Average				6.0			4.7			3.8			4.7

Table A.16.2 Marital status of household population

A. Compound head's households

Age	Male Sing.	Male Mar.	Male Div.	Male Wid.	Male Total	Female Sing.	Female Mar.	Female Div.	Female Wid.	Female Total	Grand total
0–4	22				22	29				29	51
5–9	28				28	37				37	65
10–14	33				33	35				35	68
15–19	24				24	24		2		26	50
20–24	11				11	7	6			13	24
25–29	4	1	3		8		5			5	13
30–34	1	2			3		14	1	1	16	19
35–39		5			5	1	12	1		14	19
40–44	1	6			7		6	1	3	10	17
45–49		11			11		3		3	6	17
50–54		8			8		5	1	5	11	19
55–59	1	3			4		1		5	6	10
60–64		8			8		2		5	7	15
65–69		5			5		1		2	3	8
70+		5			5	1		1	6	8	13
Total	125	54	3	–	182	134	55	7	30	226	408

B. Dependent households

Age	Male Sing.	Male Mar.	Male Div.	Male Wid.	Male Total	Female Sing.	Female Mar.	Female Div.	Female Wid.	Female Total	Grand total
0–4	14				14	17				17	31
5–9	9				9	13				13	22
10–14	10				10	11				11	21
15–19	2				2	7	5			12	14
20–24		5			5	1	7			8	13
25–29	2	2			4		3			3	7
30–34		3			3		3			3	6
35–39		6			6		7			7	13
40–44		2			2		3			3	5
45–49		3			3						3
50–54		3			3			1		1	4
55–59		3			3						3
60–64							2			2	2
65–69											
70+		1			1						1
Total	37	28	–	–	65	49	30	1	–	80	145

C. Tenant households

Age	Male Sing.	Male Mar.	Male Div.	Male Wid.	Male Total	Female Sing.	Female Mar.	Female Div.	Female Wid.	Female Total	Grand total
0–4	33				33	27				27	60
5–9	23				23	23				23	46
10–14	19				19	18				18	37
15–19	12	1			13	10	6			16	29
20–24	3	4			7	1	10	2		13	20
25–29	1	7			8	1	15	1		17	25
30–34		4			4		9			9	13
35–39	1	12			13		8			8	21
40–44		9			9		8	1	3	12	21
45–49		6			6		8	1	2	11	17
50–54		6			6		2	1	2	5	11
55–59		5			5		2		3	5	10
60–64		2			2		1		2	3	5
65–69		9			9		2		6	8	17
70+		4			4			1	6	7	11
Total	92	69	–	–	161	80	71	7	24	182	343

Table A.16.3 Male members of 75 houses by relationship to compound head

	Marital status				Temp. absent[a]	Age group							Total
	Sing.	Mar.	Div.	Wid.		0–4	5–14	15–24	25–39	40–54	55–69	70+	
1 Compound head	2	54			1				8	26	17	5	56
2 CH's sons	110	10	3			21	56	29	15	2			123
3 CH's sons' sons	16					9	7						16
4 CH's daughters' sons	15					3	10	2					15
Total	143	64	3			33	73	31	23	28	17	5	210
5 CH's full brothers	4	2						4	1	1			6
6 CH's full brothers' sons	3						2	1					3
7 CH's full sisters' sons	5					2	3						5
Total	12	2				2	5	5	1	1			14
8 CH's father		1										1	1
Total		1										1	1
9 CH's sisters' husbands		5			1				1	2	2		5
10 CH's sist's husb's father's son	1						1						1
11 CH's daughters' husbands		8			1			3	1	3	1		8
12 CH's daus' daus' husband		1							1				1
Total	1	14					1	3	3	5	3		15
13 CH's wife's brother	1				1			1					1
14 CH's wife's brother's son		1						1					1
15 CH's wife's sister's son	1						1						1
Total	2	1					1	2					3

16 Unrelated male HHs	7	60			2	1	3	4	19	20	16	4	67
17 Unrelated HHs' sons	75	3				28	33	14	3				78
18 Unrelated HHs' sons' sons	4						4						4
19 Unrelated HHs' daus' sons	4					3	1						4
Total	90	63				32	41	18	22	20	16	4	153
20 Unrelated HH's full brother		1								1			1
21 Unrelated HH's sist's dau's son	1						1						1
Total	1	1					1			1			2
22 Unrelated HH's father's br's son		1							1				1
23 Unrelated HH's fa's br's son's son	1					1							1
24 Unrelated HH's mo's br's son		1						1					1
25 Unrelated HH's mo's br's son's br	1							1					1
Total	2	2				1		2	1				4
26 Unrelated HHs' daus' husbands		2							2				2
Total		2							2				2
27 Unrelated HHs' wives' brothers	2								2				2
28 Unrelated HHs' wife's sist's son		1						1					1
29 Unrelated HHs' wife's sist's son's son	1					1							1
Total	3	1				1		1	2				4
Grand total, male	254	151	3	–	6	69	122	62	54	55	36	10	408

[a]Not counted in total population.

Table A.16.4 Female members of 75 houses by relationship to compound head

	Marital status				Temp. absent[a]	Age group							Total
	Sing.	Mar.	Div.	Wid.		0–4	5–14	15–24	25–39	40–54	55–69	70+	
1 Compound head		1	1	10					3	5	4		12
2 CH's daughters	111	8	2			27	57	33	3	1			121
3 CH's daughters' daughters	19	1				7	11	2					20
4 CH's daughter's dau's dau	1					1							1
5 CH's sons' daughters	17					4	9	4					17
Total	148	10	3	10		39	77	39	6	6	4		171
6 CH's full sisters	1	6	2	3				1	4	6		1	12
7 CH's full sisters' daughters	10					4	5	1					10
8 CH's full brothers' daughters	3		1				2	2					4
9 CH's full br's daughter's dau	1					1							1
Total	15	6	3	3		5	7	4	4	6		1	27
10 CH's mother		1		9							6	4	10
11 CH's mother's sister				1								1	1
12 CH's mo's sist's son's daughter	1						1						1
Total	1	1		10			1				6	5	12
13 CH's wives		54	1		3			6	30	15	4		55
14 CH's father's wife				1							1		1
15 CH's sons' wives		10						5	5				10
16 CH's brothers' wives		2							2				2
Total		66	1	1	2			11	37	15	5		68
17 CH's wives' mothers				5						3	1	1	5
18 CH's wife's mo's sister's dau	1						1						1
19 CH's ws' mo's br's dau's dau	1						1						1
20 CH's wife's sister	1							1					1
21 CH's wife's br's daughter	1						1						1
22 CH's wives' brs' sons' daughters	3					2	1						3
23 CH's wife's br's son's wife		1						1					1
24 CH's sister's husband's mother		1									1		1
Total	7	2		5		2	4	2		3	2	1	14

25 Unrelated females	13	2	8	13			7	6	3	8	7	5	36
26 Unrelated HHs' wives		60			2			9	29	17	5		60
27 Unrelated HHs' sons' wives		3						2	1				3
28 Unrelated HH's brother's wife		1							1				1
29 Unrelated HH's mo's br's wife				1						1			1
30 Unrelated HH's mo's br's son's wife		1						1					1
31 Unrelated HH's fa's br's son's wife		1						1					1
32 Unrelated HHs' brs' sons' wives' relatives	3			1			1	2		1			4
Total	16	68	8	15	2		8	21	34	27	12	5	107
33 Unrelated HHs' daughters	69	2				23	37	11					71
34 Unrelated HH's dau's dau	1					1							1
35 Unrelated HHs' sons' daus	3					2	1						3
Total	73	2				26	38	11					75
36 Unrelated HHs' sisters				2						1	1		2
37 Unrelated HH's sist's dau's dau	1					1							1
Total	1			2		1				1	1		3
38 Unrelated HHs' mothers				7						1	3	3	7
Total				7						1	3	3	7
39 Unrelated HH's wife's sister	1						1						1
40 Unrelated HH's wife's sist's son's wife		1							1				1
41 Unrelated HH's wife's br's dau	1						1						1
42 Unrelated HH's wife's mother				1							1		1
Total	2	1		1			2		1		1		4
Grand total	263	156	15	54	5	73	137	88	82	59	34	15	488

[a]Not counted in total population.

Table A.16.5 Household composition

	No. of comps	No. of hhs	A	B	C	D	E	G	K	M	T	V	W	Y	Z	O	Total no. hhs	Total persons
1. A	38	1	38														38	245
A + O	6	2	6													6	12	47
A + O2	1	3	1													2	3	14
A + O3	3	4	3													9	12	45
Stage 1	48		48													17	65	351
2. A + B	3	2	3	3													6	24
A + B3	1	4	1	3													4	18
A + B2 + O2	1	5	1	2												2	5	37
A + B + C + Z	1	4	1	1	1										1		4	29
A + B + C + O	1	4	1	1	1											1	4	19
A + C	4	2	4		4												8	41
A + C ÷ G	1	3	1		1			1									3	6
A + C + T + O	1	4	1		1						1					1	4	16
Stage 2	13		13	10	8			1			1				1	4	38	190
3. A + E	1	2	1				1										2	11
A + E + D	1	3	1			1	1										3	16
Stage 3	2		2			1	2										5	27
Joint households																		
A + G	2	2	2					2									4	23
A + G + O	1	3	1					1								1	3	11
A + G2 + W	1	4	1					2					1				4	18
A + V	1	2	1									1					2	9
Joint hhs	5		5					5				1	1			1	13	61

Tenant hhs																		
O2	1	2														2	2	15
O3 + Y	1	4												1		3	4	15
O6	1	6														6	6	31
O7	1	7														7	7	28
O7 + B + K + M	1	10		1					1	1						7	10	42
O15 + E	1	16					1									15	16	67
O20 + B2 + C2	1	24		2	2											20	24	69
Tenant hhs	7			3	2		1		1	1				1		60	69	267
Grand total	75		68	13	10	1	3	6	1	1	1	1	1	1	1	82	190	896

Symbols

A Compound head's family
B CH's sons' families
C CH's daughters' families
D CH's father's family
E CH's full brothers' families
G CH's full sisters' families
K CH's father's sons' families
M CH's mother's brothers' sons' families
T CH's daughters' daughters' families
V CH's wife's brothers' sons' families
W CH's sisters' husbands father's family
Y CH's wife's sisters' sons' families
Z CH's divorced wife's family
O Strangers' families

Table A.16.6 Number of rooms and

	CH's hh 68 hhs 408 pers.			CH's sons' & daus' hhs 18 hhs 95 pers.			CH's brs' & sists' hhs 8 hhs 32 pers.		
	Rms	Sq. m	%	Rms	Sq. m	%	Rms	Sq. m	%
1. Living area									
Sleeping rooms	148	1,867.8	22.4	20	267.4	3.2	8	118.1	1.4
Sitting rooms	27	400.4	4.8	3	50.4	0.6			
Stores for personal articles	24	180.2	2.2	2	13.1	0.2	3	16.7	0.2
Empty rooms	51	719.0	8.6						
Verandas	–	678.0	8.2	–	33.2	0.4	–	7.4	0.1
Total	250	3,845.4	46.2	25	364.1	4.4	11	142.2	1.7
2. Common rooms									
Ent. lobbies	66	437.8	5.2						
Passages and staircases	–	497.2	6.0				–	22.8	0.3
Total	66	935.0	11.2				–	22.8	0.3
3. Basic ancillary facilities									
Kitchens	67	433.4	5.2				2	6.9	0.1
Kitchen stores	17	64.5	0.8						
Other stores	57	223.5	2.7				1	2.4	–
Toil. & bathrms	89	174.8	2.1						
Total	230	896.2	10.8				3	9.3	0.1
4. Commercial rooms									
Shops and workshops	11	110.0	1.3						
Stores for trading articles									
Total	11	110.0	1.3						
Grand total	557	5,786.6	69.5	25	364.1	4.4	14	174.3	2.1

floor area per household

Other related hhs 5 hhs 18 pers.			Tenant hhs 91 hhs 343 pers.			Total hhs 190 hhs 896 pers.		
Rms	Sq. m	%	Rms	Sq. m	%	Rms	Sq. m	%
6	66.8	0.8	107	1,149.4	13.8	289	3,469.5	41.7
1	17.0	0.2	4	42.9	0.5	35	510.7	6.1
			7	31.0	0.4	36	241.0	2.9
1	12.2	0.1	3	36.6	0.4	55	767.8	9.2
–	16.5	0.2	–	176.5	2.2	–	911.6	11.0
8	112.5	1.3	121	1,436.4	17.3	415	5,900.6	70.9
1	5.1	0.1	11	55.2	0.7	78	498.1	6.0
–	13.5	0.1	–	241.5	2.9	–	775.0	9.3
1	18.6	0.2	11	296.7	3.6	78	1,273.1	15.3
1	6.6	0.1	16	76.7	0.9	86	523.6	6.3
						17	64.5	0.8
			5	14.1	0.1	63	240.0	2.8
2	7.4	0.1	13	19.3	0.2	104	201.5	2.4
3	14.0	0.2	34	110.1	1.2	270	1,029.6	12.3
			2	12.7	0.2	13	122.7	1.5
			2	12.7	0.2	13	122.7	1.5
12	145.1	1.7	168	1,855.9	22.3	776	8,326.0	100.0

Table A.16.7 Average floor area per household and person according to household size

No. of persons per household	No. of households	No. of persons	Average persons per household	Total floor area			Sleeping area		
				Total floor area, m^2	Average area in m^2 per household	Average area in m^2 per person	Sleeping area, m^2	Average sleeping area in m^2 per household	Average sleeping area in m^2 per person
1–2	45	73	1.62	1,247.3	27.7	17.1	455.5	10.1	6.2
3–4	59	210	3.56	1,989.7	33.7	9.5	901.2	15.3	4.3
5–6	37	204	5.51	1,525.5	41.2	7.5	675.0	18.2	3.3
7–8	30	220	7.33	1,807.1	60.2	8.2	768.6	25.6	3.5
9–10	15	141	9.40	1,040.1	69.3	7.4	458.9	30.6	3.3
11–12	3	35	11.67	644.6	214.9	18.4	173.8	57.9	5.0
13+	1	13	13.00	71.7	71.7	5.5	36.5	36.5	2.8
Total	190	896		8,326.0			3,469.5		
Average			4.72		43.8	9.3		18.3	3.9

Appendix 17

Table A.17.1 Structure of economically active population, distribution by occupational groups in 1971

	Morocco, total		Morocco urban areas		Morocco rural areas		Marrakech Prov., urban	
	No.	%	No.	%	No.	%	No.	%
Agriculture	2,047,210	51.4	65,370	4.7	1,981,840	76.9	5,580	5.2
Crafts and industry	762,440	19.2	487,780	34.7	274,660	10.7	42,590	39.8
Services/army	327,200	8.2	248,350	17.7	78,850	3.1	17,040	15.9
Trade	222,980	5.6	157,970	11.3	65,010	2.5	14,180	13.3
Prof. tech. scient. staff	158,010	4.0	98,030	7.0	59,980	2.3	6,990	6.6
Administration	119,170	3.0	104,310	7.4	14,860	0.6	4,850	4.5
Miscellaneous	343,510	8.6	241,560	17.2	101,950	3.9	15,740	14.7
Total	3,980,520	100.0	1,403,370	100.0	2,577,150	100.0	106,970	100.0

Source: Secrétariat d'État au Plan et au Developpement Regional, Royaume du Maroc *Recensement général de la population et de l'habitat 1971*, Rabat, 1973, vol. II, Serie 'S'.

Table A.17.2 Consumer price indices for Casablanca

Column	1	2	3	4
Year	General index	Food index	Clothing index	Rent index
1963	100.0	100.0	100.0	100.0
1964	104.1	105.8	103.0	99.2
1965	107.6	109.5	106.1	101.2
1966	106.5	106.4	111.2	102.0
1967	105.7	105.2	110.9	101.0
1968	106.2	105.5	110.3	103.6
1969	109.3	108.9	111.4	105.5
1970	110.7	110.1	112.3	106.8
1971	115.3	117.0	114.2	108.0
1972	119.6	123.0	114.6	113.1
1973	120.6	123.7	—	—

Source: International Labour Office, *Yearbook of Labour Statistics 1973*, Geneva, 1974, pp. 700, 705, 714, 719.

Table A.17.3 Distribution of consumption and expenditure among urban households in Morocco, 1957–1960

All urban areas				% of consumption expenditure						
Average income per year	month	Average persons per household	No. of households surveyed	Food and drinks	Rent and housing expenditure	Clothing	Fuel and lighting	Household equipment and operations	Others	Income group
DH 1,442.0	120.0	6.1	392	68.0	12.7	4.1	6.8	1.9	6.5	B[a]
2,242.0	187.0	5.9	346	65.8	12.4	5.0	6.9	1.9	8.0	C
2,705.0	225.0	5.4	324	64.1	11.3	6.4	6.8	2.2	9.2	D
3,235.0	270.0	5.0	340	64.9	11.3	6.9	5.9	2.3	8.7	D
5,977.0	498.0	5.1	553	54.1	11.1	9.4	5.1	2.8	17.5	F
Traditional towns only										
3,414.0	285.0	5.7	583	57.6	11.9	8.0	5.5	2.6	14.4	E

[a]These letters refer to income groups shown in Table 17.4 on p. 251.
Source: International Labour Office, *Household, Income and Expenditure Statistics 1950–1964*, Geneva, 1967.

Table A.17.4 Occupational pattern survey sample

Column	1	2	3	4	5						6						7						8
	Main occupation			Total hhs	Sec. occ., CH						Sec. occ., DHH						Sec. occ., THH						Total sec. occ.
	CH	DHH	THH		1[a]	2	3	4	5	Total	1	2	3	4	5	Total	1	2	3	4	5	Total	
1. Agriculture																							
Farmer	2	2	4	8															1			1	1
Olive picker			5	5														2		1	1	4	4
Subtotal	2	2	9	13														2	1	1	1	5	5
2. Art and crafts (ind.)																							
Builder	5	1	15	21	1			1		2	1					1	2					2	5
Spinn., weav., embroy.	7	3	8	18																			
Tailor	2	1	4	7	1					1													1
Baker	1	1	2	4			1			1													1
Mechanic, etc.		2		2																			
Electrician	2			2																			
Leatherworker		1	2	3																			
Carpenter			2	2																			
Gen. labourer			4	4													1					1	1
Photographer		1		1																			
Store keeper, foreman	2			2	1					1													1
Other crafts	1	2	2	5			1			1				1		1							2
Subtotal	20	12	39	71	3		2	1		6	1			1		2	3					3	11
3. Trade																							
Food, provisions	9	2	7	18	2	1				3	1					1	1					1	5
Textiles, carpets	3		3	6	1					1													1
Livestock			4	4														1				1	1
Books		2		2																			
Shoes	1	1		2																			
Perfumes			1	1																			
Subtotal	13	5	15	33	3	1				4	1					1	1	1				2	7

4. Services																						
Teacher	3	3		6																		
Transport	4		1	5																		
Watchman	1	1	3	5																		
Waiter, Cook	3		2	5																		
Barber	1	1		2								1				1						1
Admin. officer	1	2		3																		
Washer woman (and man)	1		1	2																		
Gen. labourer (and servant)	3	1	5	9		1				1									1			1	2
Petrol stat. attendant	2			2																		
Entertainer		1	1	2																		
Prostitute	1		2	3														1				1	1
Money-lender	1			1																		
Lawyer	1			1																		
Policeman	1			1																		
Subtotal	23	9	15	47		1				1		1				1		1	1			2	4
5. Miscellaneous																						
Retired	7	1	8	16																		
Beggar	1		5	6																		
Housework (women)	2	2		4																		
Subtotal	10	3	13	26																		
Total	68	31	91	190	6	2	2	1		11	2	1		1		4	4	4	2	1	1	12	27

CH = Compound head
DHH = Dependent household head
THH = Tenant household head

[a]1 = Agriculture
2 = Art and crafts
3 = Trade
4 = Services
5 = Miscellaneous

Table A.17.5 Number of valid and omitted households

	CHs' hhs		Dep. hhs		Tenant hhs		Total hhs	
	No.	%	No.	%	No.	%	No.	%
Valid	64	94.1	25	80.6	84	92.3	173	91.1
Omitted	4	5.9	6	19.4	7	7.7	17	8.9
Total hhs	68	100.0	31	100.0	91	100.0	190	100.0

Table A.17.6 Income distribution of valid households

Income group	CHs' hhs No.	%	Dep. hhs No.	%	Tenant hhs No.	%	Total hhs No.	%
Low	16	25.0	9	36.0	70	83.3	95	54.9
Middle	37	57.8	15	60.0	14	16.7	66	38.2
High	11	17.2	1	4.0	—	—	12	6.9
Total hhs	64	100.0	25	100.0	84	100.0	173	100.0

Table A.17.7 Distribution of incomes for different size households

A. TOTAL HOUSEHOLDS

Av. month. inc. / Persons in hh	1–2	3–4	5–6	7–8	9–10	11–12	13+	Total	%	Cum. %
DH 0–69.9	15	2						17	9.8	9.8
70–139.9 low	11	23	8	3				45	26.0	35.8
140–209.9	9	8	12	3	1			33	19.1	54.9
210–279.9	4	7	6	4	2			23	13.3	68.2
280–419.9 middle	2	5	3	9	1			20	11.6	79.8
420–699.9		3	5	7	7		1	23	13.3	93.1
700–1,399.9		1	1	1	2	3		8	4.6	97.7
1,400–2,099.9 high	1	1		1				3	1.7	99.4
2,100+					1			1	0.6	100.0
Total households	42	50	35	28	14	3	1	173	100.0	
Percentages	24.3	28.9	20.2	16.2	8.1	1.7	0.6	100.0		

B. COMPOUND HEADS' HOUSEHOLDS

Av. month. inc. / Persons in hh	1–2	3–4	5–6	7–8	9–10	11–12	13+	Total	%	Cum. %
DH 0–69.9		2						2	3.1	3.1
70–139.9 low	2	3	1					6	9.4	12.5
140–209.9	2	4	1	1				8	12.5	25.0
210–279.9	1	2	2	2				7	10.9	35.9
280–419.9 middle		3	2	7				12	18.8	54.7
420–699.9		2	4	5	6		1	18	28.1	82.8
700–1,399.9		1	1	1	1	3		7	10.9	93.7
1,400–2,099.9 high	1	1		1				3	4.7	98.4
2,100+					1			1	1.6	100.0
Total households	6	18	11	17	8	3	1	64	100.0	
Percentages	9.4	28.1	17.2	26.5	12.5	4.7	1.6	100.0		

C. DEPENDENT OR SEMI-DEPENDENT HOUSEHOLDS

Av. month. inc. / Persons in hh	1–2	3–4	5–6	7–8	9–10	11–12	13+	Total	%	Cum. %
DH 0–69.9	1							1	4.0	4.0
70–139.9 low	1	1						2	8.0	12.0
140–209.9	3	2	1					6	24.0	36.0
210–279.9	1	2	2		2			7	28.0	64.0
280–419.9 middle		2	1	2				5	20.0	84.0
420–699.9		1	1		1			3	12.0	96.0
700–1,399.9					1			1	4.0	100.0
1,400–2,099.9 high										
2,100+										
Total households	6	8	5	2	4			25	100.0	
Percentages	24.0	32.0	20.0	8.0	16.0			100.0		

D. TENANT HOUSEHOLDS

Av. month. inc. / Persons in hh	1–2	3–4	5–6	7–8	9–10	11–12	13+	Total	%	Cum. %
DH 0–69.9	14							14	16.7	16.7
70–139.9 low	8	19	7	3				37	44.0	60.7
140–209.9	4	2	10	2	1			19	22.6	83.3
210–279.9	2	3	2	2				9	10.7	94.0
280–419.9 middle	2				1			3	3.6	97.6
420–699.9				2				2	2.4	100.0
700–1,399.9										
1,400–2,099.9 high										
2,100+										
Total households	30	24	19	9	2			84	100.0	
Percentages	35.7	28.6	22.6	10.7	2.4			100.0		

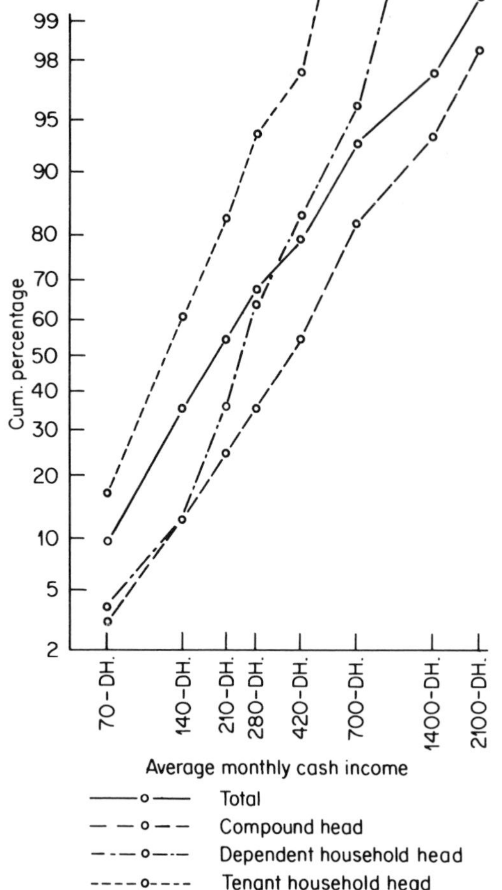

Graph A.17.1
Distribution of household income in Marrakech. (See Table A.17.7 on p. 444)

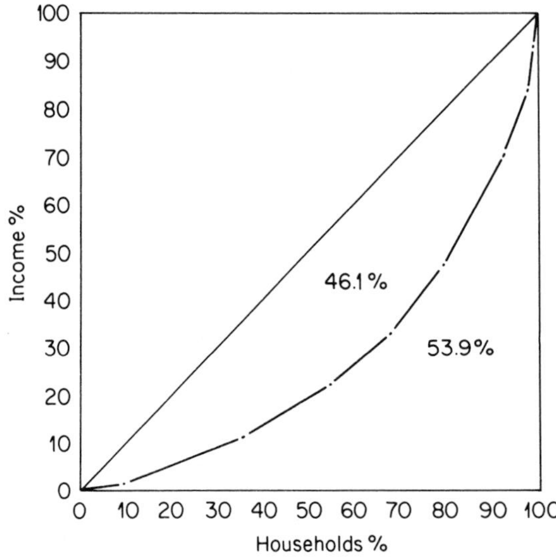

Graph A.17.2
Income distribution (Lorenz Curve), Marrakech

Appendix 18

Table A.18.1 The production of building materials

	Units	1960	1961	1962	1963	1964	1965	1966	1967	1968	1969	1970	1971
Bricks and tiles[a]	1,000 t	119	124	134	138	115	96	90	101	120	126	151	167
Pulp wood	1,000 cu. m								125	130	150	160	180
Sawn wood, veneer, sleepers	,,	72	60	79	84	54	48	89	68	70	67	70	56
Mine wood (pitprops)	,,	4	5	6	5	2		9	9	12	15	16	5
Other industrial wood	,,								15	10	10	11	30
Total industrial wood product.[b]	,,	181	—	—	—	—	165	227	217	222	242	257	271
Cement production[a]	1,000 t.	579	638	701	769	832	788	856	875	1011	1165	1421	1481
Cement pipes	,,	42	35	14	24	18	21	30	35	41	42	46	
Asbestos-cement sheets	,,	20	23	19	25	21	25	18	18	24	25	30	26
Pig-iron production[c]	,,			6	7	7	7	6	7	7	8	8	
Crude steel production[c]	,,					1	1	1	1	1	1	1	1
Building material index	100 = 1958	110	118	123	137	143	139	145	145	168	186	224	239

Sources:

[a]Ministère du Développement, Royaume du Maroc, *Annuaire statistique du Maroc.*
[b]United Nations, *FAO Yearbook of Forest Products*, 1960–1971.
[c]United Nations, *Statistical Yearbook 1972*, New York, 1973.

Table A.18.2 Wood and steel import

Year	1966		1967		1968		1969		1970		1971	
Weight and value	1000 t	DH million	1000 t	DH million	1000 t	DH million	1000 t	DH million	1000 t	DH million	1000 t	DH million
Wood and wood products												
Wood rough or roughly squ.	106.4	27.9	103.7	27.0	95.8	26.3	118.3	32.8	143.3	42.7	155.8	47.9
Sawn wood, veneer, logs	54.5	16.7	51.4	15.9	55.6	17.4	71.7	23.1				
Wood shaped or simply worked	130.1	48.9	106.6	42.9	140.3	54.7	124.9	52.7	134.6	62.4	113.7	59.6
Lumber	111.1	46.2	101.1	40.8	137.0	39.6	118.7	49.8				
Total wood	402.1	139.7	362.8	126.6	428.7	138.0	433.6	158.4	–	–	–	–
Iron and steel products												
Iron & steel bars, rods	87.6	48.7	98.9	52.1	111.8	61.8	132.5	76.6	170.7	135.4	156.2	104.0
Other bars and rods, etc.	54.3	28.2	55.7	29.1			69.4	39.8				
Angles, sections, 804 mm +	7.4	4.4	12.3	7.4								
Plates and sheets	43.0	43.0	57.7	59.7	58.8	57.1	83.7	85.6	74.4	84.0	69.0	76.4
Sheets coated – 3 mm	23.0	28.1	34.1	44.7								
Steel wire excl. wire rods	6.3	6.4	7.7	7.7	8.3	8.8	8.4	9.0	8.6	11.2	6.2	8.1
Tubes, pipes, and fittings	10.9	14.0	15.8	21.1	17.7	20.0	18.3	20.9	22.7	32.0	17.0	23.9
Building fixtures & fittings	2.8	8.9	3.4	9.7	3.3	10.7	4.1	14.0	5.3	18.3	5.0	17.1
Total iron and steel	235.3	181.7	285.6	231.5	–	–	–	–	–	–	–	–

Source: United Nations, *Yearbook of International Trade Statistics 1969*, New York, 1971, p. 579; Yearbook of International Trade Statistics 1972–3, New York, pp. 585–586.

Table A.18.3 Structural changes in 75 surveyed houses

	No. of rms 31.1.1969		No. of rms built 1.2.1964–31.1.1969		No. of rms 1.2.1964	
	No.	Sq. m	No.	Sq. m	No.	Sq. m
Living area	415	5,900.6	14	183.9	401	5,716.7
Common rooms	78	1,273.1	2	14.8	76	1,258.3
Basic ancillary facilities	270	1,029.6	2	7.1	268	1,022.5
Commercially used rooms	13	122.7	1	18.6	12	104.1
Total	776	8,326.0	19	224.4	757	8,101.6

Table A.18.4 Basic ancillary facilities in urban dwellings in Morocco

	% of facilities in dwellings		
	Private	Shared	Total
Kitchen	60.8	4.2	65.0
Bathroom	17.9	0.8	18.7
Piped water	39.1	12.6	51.7
W.C.	62.3	19.9	82.2
Electricity	68.4	–	68.4

Source: Secrétariat d'État au Plan, au Développement Regional et a la Formation des Cadres, *Recensement général de la population et de l'habitat 1971*, Rabat, 1972, vol. 1, Serie 'S', p. 20.

Table A.18.5 'What improvement do you think the house most needs?'

Answers by compound head	No. of compound heads	%
1 Repair roof (leaks)	11	
2 New ceilings (collapsed)	4	
3 Stop damp in wall	3	
4 Sewage and rainwater channels	5	
Subtotal	23	30.8
5 Build more living & sleeping rooms	15	
6 Sell house; buy bigger one	4	
7 Demolish house; build bigger one	2	
Subtotal	21	28.0
8 Glazed tiles in rooms & courtyard	7	
9 Plaster and paint rooms	5	
Subtotal	12	16.0
10 Piped water	7	
Subtotal	7	9.3
11 Better furniture	2	
12 Bathrooms	2	
13 Repair screed in rooms & courtyard	1	
14 Cement courtyard	1	
15 Prefer to live on ground floor	1	
Subtotal	7	9.3
16 Satisfied	4	
Subtotal	4	5.3
17 No response	1	
Subtotal	1	1.3
Total	75[a]	100.0

[a] A total of seven tenement houses had no compound head; instead I asked the oldest resident household head.

Table A.18.6 Construction of new rooms, 1964–1969

	No. of rooms	Sq. m	%
1. Living area			
Sleeping rooms	7	90.6	
Sitting rooms	2	27.1	
Personal store rooms	1	6.2	
Empty rooms	4	60.0	
Subtotal	14	183.9	81.9
2. Common rooms			
Entrance lobbies	2	11.7	
Passages		3.1	
Subtotal	2	14.8	6.6
3. Basic ancillary facilities			
Kitchens	1	5.8	
Kitchen stores	–	–	
Other stores	–	–	
Toilets and bathrooms	1	1.3	
Subtotal	2	7.1	3.2
4. Commercially used rooms			
Shops	–	–	
Workshops	1	18.6	
Subtotal	1	18.6	8.3
Total	19	224.4	100.0

Table A.18.7 The financing of 'second-hand' houses

Column	1	2	3	4	5	6
House no.	Sold old house	Loans from relatives	Own savings	Sold animals	Gov. grant & gift	Total cost of house
74			150	3,000		3,150
72		300	2,000	1,100		3,400
1	4,000					4,000
5			5,750		1,250	7,000
15		2,000		5,000		7,000
20	5,200	1,800				7,000
39	8,000					8,000
57		3,000	12,000			15,000
7	17,000					17,000
28	10,000	7,000				17,000
45	13,000		7,000			20,000
43	7,000	23,000	2,000			32,000
62*	–	–	–	–	–	–
Total	64,200	37,100	28,900	9,100	1,250	140,550
Percentage	45.7	26.4	20.6	6.5	0.8	100.0

*Refused to answer.

Table A.18.8 The financing of houses

	No. of loans	Gifts & grants	DH	%
New construction				
CH's personal income and savings			17,222	73.8
Personal sources, loans, and gifts	4		4,100	17.6
Institutional sources	1		2,000	8.6
Total expenditure			23,322	100.0
Improvements				
CH's personal income and savings			27,428	69.8
Personal sources, loans, and gifts	8	1	7,600	19.4
Institutional sources[a]	1	1	4,250	10.8
Total expenditure			39,278	100.0
Maintenance and repair				
CH's personal income and savings			22,217	94.9
Personal sources, loans, and gifts	1		1,200	5.1
Institutional sources			—	—
Total expenditure			23,417[b]	100.0
Under construction				
CH's personal income and savings			8,250	100.0
Personal sources, loans, and gifts			—	—
Institutional sources			—	—
Total expenditure			8,250	100.0
Total building activities				
CH's personal income and savings			75,117	79.7
Personal sources, loans, and gifts	13	1	12,900	13.7
Institutional sources	2	1	6,250	6.6
Total expenditure			94,267	100.0

[a]Excluding DH 1,250 government grant used for buying a second-hand house.
[b]Adjusted expenditure, actual expenditure DH 14,050.

Questionnaire

GENERAL INFORMATION SHEET

URBAN HOUSING SURVEY

Town

Address
House No.

1. CONTACT

When

Dimensions	
General Family Data	
Questionnaire completed	
Climatic Data taken	
Finished	

2. OBSERVATION

House

Family

3. CLIMATIC INVESTIGATION

4. MISCELLANEOUS

F1 GENERAL FAMILY DATA

Date
Time

Town
House No.

No.	House member	Rm no.	Relationship to compound head	Household (same pot)	Birthplace and age	Rural/ Urban	Eth. gr.	Rel.	Mat. status	Years in town	Years in house
1											
2											
3											
4											
5											
6											
7											
8											
9											
10											
11											
12											
13											
14											
15											
16											
17											
18											
19											
20											
21											
22											
23											
24											
25											
26											
27											
28											
29											
30											

Education standard reached	Occupation: Primary	Secondary	Other information
1			
2			
3			
4			
5			
6			
7			
8			
9			
10			
11			
12			
13			
14			
15			
16			
17			
18			
19			
20			
21			
22			
23			
24			
25			
26			
27			
28			
29			
30			

F2 FAMILY HISTORY

F2.2 What was the occupation of your father? Birthpl.

F2.3 What was the occupation of your grandfather? Birthpl.

F2.4 Are your parents still alive?

F2.5 Where did you live before coming to this town? When?

F2.6 When did you become compound head?

HOUSEHOLD DATA

F3 AGRICULTURE

F3.1 Do you farm?

F3.2 How many acres do you have?

F3.3 Where are they located? Give nearest town and distance.

F3.4 Do you have a farmhouse there?

F3.5 How much time do you spend on farm?

F3.6 List house member helping you.

Person					
Time spent farm/animal	1	2	3	4	5

F3.7 How many labourers do you employ?

F3.8 How much do you pay them? Year/season/week/day.

F3.9 List crops you mainly grow.

This year's figures.

Cash-crop	Amount sold (turnover)	Food crop	Amount sold (turnover)	Amount kept, profit
1				
2				
3				
4				
5				

F3.10 What was your total profit from farm products last year?

F3.11 List animals belonging to your household.

Kind	Within the compound	On farm	Sold last year (turnover)	Other information
1				
2				
3				
4				
5				

F3.11a How many labourers do you employ for your animals?

F3.12 What was your total profit from animals or animal products last year?

F4 ART AND CRAFT

F4.1 Are you or your family members engaged in crafts?

Person	Article produced	How many per hr/day/wk	Price per article	Profit per article
1				
2				
3				
4				
5				

F4.2 How much did you spend on raw materials last day/week/month?

How long will they last?

F4.3 Where did you practise your craft?

F4.4 How much rent do you pay for your site?

F4.4a How many labourers do you employ?

How much do you pay them?

F4.5 What is your total profit from crafts per day/week/month?

F5 INTERMEDIATE TRADE

F5.1 Do you or your family members trade?

Person	Kind of trade (items)	Hours per day	Good day inc.	Good day prof.	Normal day inc.	Normal day prof.	Bad day inc.	Bad day prof.
1								
2								
3								
4								
5								

F5.2 How much capital have you invested in your stock?

1	2	3	4	5	6

F5.3 How much do you spend on new stock and how long will it last?

F5.5 How much rent do you pay for your trading site?

F5.6 What is your average profit from trade in a day/week/month?

F6 OTHER PROFESSION OR SERVICE

F6.1 Describe your occupation.

F6.2 How long employed in that job?

F6.3 Where do you work?

F6.4 How many hours do you work?

F6.5 What is your income per week/month?

F7 FOOD

F7.1 List food you normally eat daily.

Morning	Noon	Evening

F7.2 How much do you spend on food per day/week?
Give details. (See separate sheet.)

F7.2a How much do you spend on fuel per week? (Light/cooking.)

F7.3 How much do you spend on (per day/week/month):

Kola	Cigar	Wine/beer	Soft drinks	Cinema	Others

F8 HYGIENE

F8.1 Where do you obtain water for drinking? Own tap/public tap/well.

F8.1a How much do you pay for water?

F8.2 Where do family members wash themselves?

F8.3 If no latrine in the house where do you go?

F8.4 General cleanliness in the compound

+3	+2	+1	fair	−1	−2	−3

F9 CHILDREN

F9.1 Are your children born in hospital or at home?

F9.2 If you have children in school, how much do you pay in fees?

Where	1	2	3	4	5	6
How much						

F9.3 Account for children of school age not attending school.

F10 WIDER KIN RELATIONSHIPS

F10.1 Do you have close relatives in town not living here?

		1	2	3	4
F10.2	Where?				
F10.3	How often do you meet your relatives?				

F10.4 List relatives to whom help was given during the last year.

	1	2	3	4	5	6
State kind of help.						
How much?						
When?						
How often?						

F10.5 List relatives from whom help was received during the last year.

State kind of help.						
How much?						
When?						
How often?						

F11 MISCELLANEOUS

F11.1 How much did you spend on technical goods last year?
(e.g. radio, record player, fan, etc.)

F11.2 How much did you spend on clothes for yourself last year?

For your wife/wives?

For your children?

F11.3 How much do you spend on electricity?

F11.4 How much did you spend on furniture last year?

F11.5 Other expenditures, religious, state, personal festivities?

H1 HOUSE

H1.1 Do you own the house? Built/bought/inherited. When?

H1.2 If not, how much rent do you pay?

H1.3 When was the house built? (Core.) Total cost up to now?

H1.3a What was the cost of the land?

H1.4 When were the extensions added?

No. of rooms										
Year										
Cost										

H1.5 Do you own other property in town?

H1.6 How many rooms do you rent out?
Income from rent per month?

H1.7 Did somebody break in, or attempt to break in to your house?
Give details.

H2 CONSTRUCTION (last five years)

H2.1 If you built the house, or part of it, did your relatives or friends help you?

	1	2	3	4	5
Who?					
When?					
State kind of help.					
How much?					
Terms of repayment.					

H2.2 Did you employ paid labour? Or a contractor?

H2.3 Cost of house by items. (See separate sheet [p. 460])

H2.4 When did you start to build the house?
And when did you move into the house?

H2.5 What was your occupation and income when you built the house?

H2.6 How long did you save for the house How much?

H2.8 Is any part of the house still under construction?
If yes, how much has it cost you up till now?

H2.9 When do you hope to complete it?
How much more do you think it will cost you?

H2.11 Did you receive a mortgage or loan from government, a society, bank, or private sources? How much? When?
Terms of repayment?

H3 IMPROVEMENT

H3.1 Have you carried out any improvement on the house (in the last five years)?

	Walls House/ courtyard	Roof Ceiling	Floor	Window Doors	Outside
Describe					
When?					
Cost?					

H3.3 What improvement do you think the house most needs?

H4 MAINTENANCE

H4.1 Have you carried out any repair work on the house (in the last three years)?

	Walls House/ courtyard	Roof Ceiling	Floor	Window Doors	Outside
Describe					
When?					
Cost?					
Misc.					

H5 EQUIPMENT

Room no.	1	2	3	4	5	6	7	8	9	10	11	12	13	14	15	16	17	18	19	20	21	22	23	24	25	26	27	28
Walls mud																												
Burnt bricks																												
Concrete blocks																												
Plastered																												
Painted																												
Roof mud																												
Roof cement																												
Roof tiles																												
Corr. iron																												
Ceiling mats																												
Hardboard																												
Floor cement																												
Rammed earth																												
Lino																												

(continued)

Room no.	1	2	3	4	5	6	7	8	9	10	11	12	13	14	15	16	17	18	19	20	21	22	23	24	25	26	27	28
Carpet																												
Bed Iron/Wood																												
Mosquito net																												
Cupboards																												
Tables																												
Stools																												
Bench																												
Chairs																												
Easy chairs																												
Couch, sofa																												
Boxes																												
Curtain																												
Car																												

H5 EQUIPMENT *(continued)*

Room no.	1	2	3	4	5	6	7	8	9	10	11	12	13	14	15	16	17	18	19	20	21	22	23	24	25	26	27	28
Motorbike																												
TV																												
Radio																												
Radiogram																												
Record player																												
Sewing machine																												
Refrigerator																												
Fan																												
Iron																												
Electric bulb																												
Clock																												
Bicycles																												
Shelf/rack																												
Mirrors																												

H23 COST OF HOUSE BY ITEMS

Town House Date NEW CONSTRUCTION
IMPROVEMENT
REPAIR

	Comp. wall	Room 1	2	3	4	5	6	7	8	9
WALLS										
Builder										
Labour										
Materials										
ROOF										
Builder										
Labour										
Grass										
Sticks										
Rope/nails										
Wood/sawn wood										
Corr. iron										
FINISHING FLOOR/WALLS										
Builder										
Labour										
Cement										
Windows/doors										
Paint										
Outside										
TECH. INSTALLATION										
Piped water										
Electricity										
MISCELLANEOUS										
TOTAL										

Bibliography

Abou-Obeid-El-Bekri, *Kitab al-Masalik* Trans. by Mac Guckin de Slane as *Description de L'Afrique septentrionale*, Paris, 1965.

Abun-Nasr, J. M., *A History of the Maghrib*, Cambridge, 1971.

Adam, A., 'Berber migrants in Casablanca', in *Arabs and Berbers*, ed. E. Gellner and C. Micand, London, 1972.

Africa Research Ltd, *Africa Research Bulletin*, 1971 (Exeter), (7), 1974.

Ahmadu Bello University, Zaria, Institute of Administration, *Northern States of Nigeria Local Government Year Book 1968*, Zaria, 1968.

Akinola, R. A., 'Ibadan: A study in urban geography', London, 1963. Unpublished Ph.D. thesis.

Akinyele, I. B., *The Outlines of Ibadan History*, Lagos, 1946.

Ali Bey el Abbassi, *Travels of Ali Bey in Morocco . . . Between 1803 and 1807*, London, 1816.

Aluko, S. A., 'How many Nigerians? An analysis of Nigeria's census problems, 1901–63', *Journal of Modern African Studies* (Cambridge), **III** (3), 1965.

Anonymous, *Bulletin de la Société de Géographie d'Alger et de l'Afrique du Nord*, Paris, **34** (133), 1933.

——— 'Yoruba brickmaking', *Nigeria Journal* (Ibadan), no. 25, 1946.

Ardener, S., 'The comparative study of rotating credit associations', *Journal of the Royal Anthropological Institute* (London), **XCIV** (2), 1964.

Arnett, E. J., 'A Hausa chronicle', *Journal of the Royal African Society* (London), **IX**, 1909–1910.

Aubin, E., *Le Maroc d'aujourd'hui*, Paris, 1904.

Awe, B. A., 'The rise of Ibadan as a Yoruba power in the 19th century', Oxford, 1964. Unpublished Ph.D. thesis.

——— 'Ibadan, its early beginnings', in *The City of Ibadan*, ed. P. C. Lloyd, A. L. Mabogunje, and B. Awe, Cambridge, 1967.

Balbi, A., *Abrégé de géographie*, Paris, 1934.
Banque Marocaine du Commerce Extérieur (BMCE), *Bulletin bimestriel d'informations*, Casablanca, 1973.
——— *Bulletin mensuel d'informations* (Casablanca), no. 123, 1972.
Barber, J., *Journals*, Church Missionary Society, London, 1857.
Bardon, H., 'Les Deux Capitales du Maroc: Fèz et Marrakech', *Bulletin de la Société de Géographie de Marseille*, **XXXVI**, 1912.
Barêty, L., *La France au Maroc*, Paris, 1932.
Barth, H., *Travel and Discoveries in North and Central Africa*, 2 vols., London, 1890.
Bascom, W. R., 'The Esusu: A credit institution among the Yoruba', *Journal of the Royal Anthropological Institute of Great Britain and Ireland* (London), **LXXII**, 1952.
——— 'Urbanization among the Yoruba', *American Journal of Sociology*, **LX** (5), 1955.
Baumann, H., and Westermann, D., *Les Peuples et les civilisations de l'Afrique*, Paris, 1948.
Beaumier, A., *Description sommaire du Maroc*, Paris, 1868.
Bedawi, H. Y., 'Variation in residential space standards in Zaria', *Savanna: A Journal of the Environmental and Social Sciences* (Zaria), **5** (1), June 1976, pp. 75–78.
——— 'Housing in Zaria, present conditions and future needs', Department of Urban and Regional Planning, ABU, Zaria, 1977.
Bénech, J., *Essai d'explication d'un mellah, un des aspects du Judaisme*, Paris, 1950.
Besnard, R., *L'Oeuvre française au Maroc*, Paris, 1914.
Bidwell, R., *Morocco under Colonial Rule*, London, 1973.
Bourdieu, P., 'The Berber house', in *Rules and Meanings*, ed. Douglas, M., Penguin, Harmondsworth, 1973.
Boutillier, J. L., et *al.*, *La Moyenne Vallée du Sénégal*, Paris, 1962.
Bovill, E. W., 'The Moorish invasion of the Sudan', *Journal de la Société des Africanistes* (Paris), **XXVI** and **XXVII**, 1927.
Bowen, T. J., *Central Africa: Adventures and Missionary Labors in Several Countries in the Interior of Africa, from 1849–1856*, Charleston, South Carolina, 1857.
Brass, W., *et al.*, *The Demography of Tropical Africa*, Princeton, NJ, 1968.
British Steel Corporation, 'Nigeria: economic prospects and steel import potentials in 1975', London, 1970. Unpublished report.
British West African Meteorological Services, Nigeria, *Preliminary Notes on Rainfall of Nigeria*, Lagos, 1955.
Buchanan, K. M., and Pugh, J. C., *Land and People in Nigeria*, London, 1955 and 1966.

Callaway, A., 'From traditional crafts to modern industry', in *The City of Ibadan*, ed. P. C. Lloyd, A. L. Mabogunje, and B. Awe, Cambridge, 1967.
Carter, Sir G., *Report of the Lagos Interior Expedition 1893*, Lagos, 1893.
Castries, Ho de, 'La Conquête du Soudan', *Hesperis*, **3**, 1923.
Chénier, L. de, *Recherches historiques sur les maures et histoire de l'empire de Maroc*, Paris, 1787.
Church Missionary Society (CMS), *Review*, London, 1908.
Cohen, A., *Custom and Politics in Ibadan*, London, 1969.
——— 'The Hausa', in *The City of Ibadan*, ed. P. C. Lloyd, *et al.*, Cambridge, 1967.

Coker, J. O., *Family Property among the Yoruba*, London, 1958.

Cole, C. W., *Report on Land Tenure, Zaria Province*, Kaduna, 1952.

Colonial Office, *Annual Report Northern Nigeria*, London, 1902–1903.

——— *Blue Book*, Lagos.

——— *Land and Native Rights Ordinance No. 1 of 1916.*

——— *Official Report on the Southern Nigeria Census 1911*, Lagos, 1912.

——— C.D. 5102, *Report of the Northern Nigeria Land Committee*, London, 1910.

Comité de l'Afrique Française, *L'Afrique française* (Paris), 1921.

Cornet, Capt. *À la conquête du Maroc-Sud avec la Colonne Mangin 1912–13*, Paris, 1914.

Cousin, A., and Saurin, D., *Le Maroc*, Paris, 1905.

Cox, H. B., *Census of the Southern Provinces*, London, 1932.

Crooke, P., 'Rural settlement and housing trends in a developing country: An example in Nigeria', *International Labour Review* (Geneva), **96** (3), 1967.

——— 'Sample survey of Yoruba rural building', *Odu, University of Ife Journal of African Studies* (Ibadan), **2** (2), 1966.

Daily Times, Nigeria Year Book 1971, Lagos, 1971.

Daldy, F. A., 'Temporary buildings in Northern Nigeria', Technical Paper No. 10, Public Works Department, Lagos, 1945.

Davis, Kingsley, *World Urbanization 1950–1970*, Berkeley Calif., 1969.

Department of Economic and Social Affairs, United Nations, *Soil-Cement, its Use in Building*, New York, 1964.

Department of Statistics, Nigeria, *Population Census of Nigeria 1952/53*, Lagos, 1956.

——— *Population Census of Northern Nigeria 1952*, Zaria Province, Kaduna, 1956.

——— *Population Census of the Western Region of Nigeria 1952*, Lagos, 1956.

Department of Statistics, Northern Nigeria, *Statistical Yearbook 1966*, Kaduna, 1967.

Derret, J. D. M., ed., *Studies in the Laws of Succession in Nigeria*, Oxford, 1965.

Deverdun, G., *Marrakech des origines à 1912*, Rabat, 1959 and 1966.

Direction de la Statistique, Royaume du Maroc, *Annuaire statistique du Maroc 1971*, Rabat, 1972.

Douglas, M., 'Symbolic orders in the use of domestic space', in *Man, Settlement and Urbanism*, Ucko, P. J. *et al.*, eds., London, 1972.

Elias, T. O., *Nigerian Land Law and Custom*, London, 1951.

El-Masri, F. H., 'Religion in Ibadan', B. 'Islam', in Lloyd, P. C. *et al.*, eds., *The City of Ibadan*, Cambridge, 1967.

Encyclopaedia of Islam, London, Leiden, 1965.

Encyclopédie Mensuelle d'Outre-mer, Morocco 1954, Paris, 1954.

Erckmann, J., *Le Maroc moderne*, Paris, 1885.

Fazy, H., *Agriculture marocaine et protectorat*, Paris, 1948.

Federal Census Office, *Population Census of Nigeria, Northern Region*, Lagos, 1968.

Federal Department of Statistics, Nigeria, *Urban Consumer Surveys in Nigeria*, Lagos, 1959.
Federal Ministry of Information, Nigeria, *Conclusion of the Federal Government on the Report of the Morgan Commission on the Review of Wages, Salaries and Conditions of Service of the Junior Employees of the Government in the Federation and Private Establishment 1963–64*, Lagos, 1964.
——— *Report of the Commission on the Review of Wages, Salaries and Conditions of Service of the Junior Employees of the Government of the Federation and in Private Establishments 1963 to 1964*, Lagos, 1964.
——— *Second National Development Plan 1970–4*, Lagos, 1970.
Federal Office of Statistics, Nigeria, *Annual Abstract of Statistics*, Lagos.
——— *Digest of Statistics* (Lagos), **20** (2), April 1971.
——— 'Ibadan housing enquiry', Lagos, 1963. Unpublished MS.
——— *Industrial Survey of Nigeria 1967*, Lagos, 1968.
——— 'Population census of Nigeria 1963' (mimeo), Lagos, 1968.
Fletcher, B., *A History of Architecture*, London, 1975.

Galletti, R., *Nigerian Cocoa Farmers*, Oxford, 1956.
Gallotti, J., *Le Jardin et la maison arabe au Maroc*, Paris, 1926.
Gavira, J., *El viajero espanol por Marruecos, Don Joaquin Gatell*, Madrid, 1949.
Goldziher, I., *Mohammed Ibn Toumert et la théologie de l'Islam dans le Nord de l'Afrique au XIe siècle*, Algiers, 1903.
Graberg di Hamso, J., *Specchio geografico e statistico dell' imperio di Marocco*, Genoa, 1834.
Greenberg, J. A., *Languages in Africa*, The Hague, 1966.
Greenberg, V. J., 'Islam and clan organization among the Hausa', in *Southwestern Journal of Anthropology*, **3**.

Habitat International, 'Iuccio Turin Memorial Issue' (ed. O. Koenigsberger), **3**, Nos. 1 and 2 (London), 1978.
Hance, W., *The Geography of Modern Africa*, New York, 1964.
Hart, D. M., 'Segmentary systems and the role of "five fifths' in tribal Morocco', *Revue de l'occident musulman et de la Méditerranée* (Aix en Provence), no. 3, 1967.
——— 'The tribe in modern Morocco: Two case studies', in *Arabs and Berbers*, ed. E. Gellner and C. Micand, London, 1973.
Hinderer, A., *Seventeen Years in the Yoruba Country*, London, 1872.
Hinderer, D., *Journals*, Church Missionary Society, London, 1851.
——— The reports and letters of David Hinderer can be found in the Church Missionary Archives at 4 Salisbury Square, London EC4, under the serial number CA2/0.
Hodder, B. W., 'The markets of Ibadan', in *The City of Ibadan*, P. C. Lloyd, A. L. Mabogunje, B. Awe, Cambridge 1967.
Hoffman, B. G., *The Structure of Traditional Moroccan Rural Society*, The Hague, 1967.

Idowu, E. B., 'Religion in Ibadan', A. 'Traditional religion and Christianity', in Lloyd, P. C. *et al.*, eds., *The City of Ibadan*, Cambridge, 1967.
Imani, A., 'The family planning programme in Morocco', in *Population Growth and Economic Development in Africa*, ed. S. H. Ominde and C. N. Ejiogu, London, 1972.

International Labour Office, *Household, Income and Expenditure Statistics 1950–64*, Geneva, 1967.

——— *Labour Survey of North Africa*, Geneva, 1960.

——— *Yearbook of Labour Statistics 1973*, Geneva, 1974.

Jackson, J. G., *An Account of the Empire of Morocco and the District of Suse and Tafilet*, London, 1814.

Jacob, S. M., *Census of Nigeria 1931*, London, 1933.

Johnson, S., *The History of the Yorubas*, Lagos, 1960.

Julien, C.-A., *Histoire de l'Afrique du Nord*, Paris, 1956.

Keay, R. W. J., *An Outline of Nigerian Vegetation*, Lagos, 1949.

Koll, M., *Crafts and Cooperation in Western Nigeria*, Freiburg i.B., 1969.

Kuper, A. 'Symbolic dimensions of the southern Bantu homestead', in *Africa*, **50**, No. 1.

Lambert, P., 'Notice sur la ville de Maroc', *Bulletin de la Société de Géographie* (Paris), no. 107, 1868.

Lample, P., *Cities and Planning in the Ancient Near East*, New York, 1968.

Lawrence, A. W., *Greek Architecture*, Harmondsworth, Middx, 1973.

Lazraq, A., 'Les Salaires dans le revenu national de 1955 à 1966', in *Bulletin économique et social du Maroc* (Rabat), **XXIX** (106–107), 1967.

Leenheer, M. de, 'L'Habitat précaire à Marrakech et dans sa zone périphérique', *Revue de géographie du Maroc* (Rabat), no. 17, **1970**.

Lenz, O., *Reise durch Marokko die Sahara und den Sudan*, vol. I, Leipzig, 1884.

Le Tourneau, R., 'La Décadence sa'dienne et l'anarchie marocaine au XIIe siècle', *Annales de la Faculté des Lettres d'Aix*, **XXXII**, 1960.

Littlejohn, J., 'The Temne house', in *Sierra Leone Studies*, no. 14.

Lloyd, B., 'Indigenous Ibadan', in *The City of Ibadan*, ed. P. C. Lloyd et *al.*, Cambridge, 1967.

Lloyd, P. C., 'Agnatic and cognatic descent among the Yoruba', *Man. The Journal of the Royal Anthropological Institute*, **I** (4), 1966.

——— 'The Yoruba lineage', *Africa*, **XXV** (3), 1955.

——— *Yoruba Land Law*, Oxford, 1962.

——— et *al.*, eds., *The City of Ibadan*, Cambridge, 1967.

Lubega, A., 'Financing and production of private houses in urban districts of Kampala (Uganda)', London, 1970. Unpublished Ph.D. thesis.

Mabogunje, A. L.,

——— 'The growth of residential districts in Ibadan', *Geographical Review*, **52**, 56–57, 1962.

——— 'The morphology of Ibadan', in *The City of Ibadan*, ed. P. C. Lloyd, Cambridge, 1967.

——— *Urbanization in Nigeria*, London, 1968.

Mabogunje, A. L., and Omer-Cooper, J. D., *Owu in Yoruba History*, Ibadan, 1971.

Mandleur, A., 'Les industries alimentaires de Marrakech', in *Revue de Géographie du Maroc*, Rabat, 1970.

——— 'Croissance et urbanisation de Marrakech', *Revue de géographie du Maroc* (Rabat), 1972.

Marrast, J., 'Maroc', in *L'Oeuvre de Henri Prost*, Paris, 1960.

Marris, P., *Family and Social Change in an African City*, London, 1961.

Marshall, J. R. N., *Traditional Land Tenure Survey 1963*, 'Report in parts of Zaria province' by I. A. Bijimi. Institute of Administration, ABU, Zaria, 1965, mimeo.

Maulana Muhammad Ali, trans., *The Holy Qur'an*, Lahore, 1963.

Meek, C. K., *Land Tenure and Land Administration in Nigeria and the Cameroons*, London, 1957.

Meteorological Office, *Tables of Temperature, Relative Humidity and Precipitation for the World*, London, 1964.

Michaux-Bellaire, E., 'Les biens habous et biens du makhzen au point de vue de leur location et de leur aliénation', in *Revue du monde musulman*, Paris, 1908.

Michie, C. W., 'Notes on land tenure in the northern districts of Zaria emirate', in *Report on Land Tenure, Zaria Province*, by C. W. Cole, Kaduna, 1952.

Miége, J. L., 'Note sur l'artisanat marocain en 1870', *Bulletin économique et social du Maroc* (Rabat), no. 2, 1953.

Millson, A., 'The Yoruba Country, West Africa', *Proceedings of the Royal Geographical Society*, **13** (10), October 1891.

Ministère du Développement, Royaume du Maroc, *Annuaire statistique du Maroc 1964–1965* and *1971*, Rabat, 1966 and 1972.

Ministry of Economic Planning and Reconstruction, Western State of Nigeria, *Statistical Abstract*, Ibadan, 1971.

Mitchell, N. C., 'Some comments on the growth and character of Ibadan's population', Research Notes No. 4, Department of Geography, University College, Ibadan, 1953.

Moloney, A., 'Notes of Yoruba land and the colony and protectorate of Lagos', *Proceedings of the Royal Geographical Society* (London), New series, **12** (10), 1890.

Montagne, R., *La vie sociale et la vie politique des Berbères*, Paris, 1931.

Morgan, Lewis H., 'Houses and house-life of the American aborigines', contribution to *North American Ethnology*, Vol. IV, Government Printing Office, Washington, DC (reprinted 1965, University of Chicago Press).

Morgan, W. B., 'The change from shifting to fixed settlements in Southern Nigeria', University College, Ibadan, 1955.

Mortimore, M. J., 'Zaria and its region' Ahmadu Bello University, Department of Geography, Occasional Paper no. 4, Zaria, 1970.

Moughtin, J. C., 'The Friday Mosque, Zaria City', in *Savanna, A Journal of Environmental and Social Sciences*, ABU, Zaria, **1** (2), 1972.

Mouline, M. R., *The Era of al-Mansur the Almohad, or the Political, Intellectual and Religious Life of the Maghrib from the Year 580 to the Year 595 (1185–1199)*, Rabat, 1946.

Native Authority Housing Corporation, Northern Region of Nigeria *First Annual Report and Accounts for the Period 18th May 1961 to 31st March 1962*, Kaduna, 1962.

Noin, D., *La Population rurale du Maroc*, Paris, 1970.

Northern States of Nigeria, *Local Government Year Book 1968*, Kaduna, 1968.

Nyrop, R. F., et al., *Area Handbook for Morocco*, Washington, DC, 1972.

Ogunpola, G. A., 'The pattern of organization in the building industry – A Western Nigerian case study', *Nigerian Journal of Economic and Social Studies* (Ibadan), **10** (3), 1968.

Okigbo, L., *Sawmill Industry in Nigeria*, Ibadan, 1964.

Oliver, P., ed., *Shelter and Society*, New York, 1969.

——— *Shelter in Africa*, London, 1971.

——— *Shelter, Sign and Symbol*, London, 1975.

Organization for Economic Co-operation and Development (OECD), *Tropical Timber*, Paris, 1969.

Oyelese, J. O., 'The growth of Ibadan city and its impact on land-use patterns, 1961–1965', *Journal of Tropical Geography* (Singapore), **32**, June 1971.

Parrinder, G., *Religion in an African City*, London, 1953, pp. 63–85.

——— *The Story of Ketu, an Ancient Yoruba Kingdom*, Lagos, 1956.

Peel, J. D. Y., *Aladura: A Religious Movement among the Yoruba*, London, 1968.

Piquet, V., *Le Maroc*, Paris, 1920.

Rapoport, A., *House Form and Culture*, Englewood Cliffs, NJ, 1969.

Richardson, J., *Travels in Morocco*, London, 1860.

Rowling, C. W., *Land Tenure in Ijebu Province*, Ibadan, 1956.

——— *Report on Land Tenure, Kano Province*, Kaduna, 1949.

Royaume du Maroc, *Dahir* of 18 June 1936.

Ruxton, F. H., trans., *Maliki Law*, London, 1916.

Saint-Olon, P. de, 'Estat présent de l'empire de Maroc', *Relation de l'empire de Maroc*, Paris, 1893.

Scham, A., *Lyautey in Morocco*, Berkeley, Calif., 1970.

Schwab, W. B., 'Kinship and lineage among the Yoruba', *Africa*, **XXV** (4), 1955.

Schwerdtfeger, F. W., 'Housing in Zaria', in *Shelter in Africa*, ed. Oliver, Paul, London, 1971.

——— 'Urban settlement patterns in Northern Nigeria', in *Man, Settlement and Urbanism*, ed. P. Ucko, R. Tringham, and G. W. Dimbleby, London, 1972.

Secrétariat d'État au Plan au Développement Régional et a la Formation des Cadres, Royaume du Maroc, *Recensement général de la population et de l'habitat 1971*, Rabat, 1972.

Secrétariat d'État au Plan et au Développement Régional, Royaume du Maroc, *Bulletin mensuel d'informations*, Casablanca, 1971.

——— *Recensement général de la population et de l'habitat 1971*, Rabat, 1973.

Secrétariat Générale du Protectorat, Service des Statistiques, Royaume du Maroc, *De nombrement générale de la population de la zone française de l'Empire Chérifien 1947*, Paris, 1948.

Service Central des Statistiques, Royaume du Maroc, *Annuaire statistique du Maroc*.

——— *Recensement général de la population de la zone française de l'Empire Chérifien 1951/52*, Rabat, 1954.

——— *Résultats du recensement de 1960*, Rabat, 1964 and 1965.

——— 'Population légale du Maroc 1971', Royaume du Maroc, Rabat, 1972.

Service de Statistique Haute-Volta, *La Situation démographique en Haute-Volta*, Paris, 1962.
Skinner, E. P., 'Strangers in West African societies', *Africa*, **XXXIII**, 1963.
Smith, A., 'Some notes on the history of Zazzau under the Hausa kings', in *Zaria and its Region*, ABU, Department of Geography, Occasional Paper No. 4, Zaria, 1980.
Smith, M. G., *Government in Zazzau*, Oxford, 1960.
——— 'Hausa inheritance and succession', in *Studies in the Laws of Succession in Nigeria*, by J. D. M. Derrett, J. Duncan and M. Derrett, Oxford, 1965.
——— 'The beginning of Hausa society AD 1000 to 1500', in *The Historian in Tropical Africa*, by J. Vansina, R. Mauny, and L. V. Thomas, London, 1964.
——— *The Economy of Hausa Communities of Zaria*, London, 1955.
Smith, R. S., *Kingdoms of the Yoruba*, London, 1969.

Térrasse, H., *Histoire du Maroc des origines à l'establissement du protectorat français*, Casablanca, 1949–50.
Torrés, D. de, *Relation de l'origine et succez des chérifs, et de l'estat des royaumes de Marroc, Fez et Tarudant, et autres provinces*, Paris, 1667.
Trimingham, S. J.,
——— *Islam in West Africa*, London, 1959.
——— *The Influence of Islam upon Africa*, London, 1968.
——— *A History of Islam in West Africa*, Oxford, 1978.
Tucker, A. W., *Abeokuta or Sunrise within the Tropics*, London, 1853.

Ugoh, S. U., 'The Nigerian cement industry', *Journal of Economic and Social Studies* (Ibadan), **8** (1), 1966.
United Nations, *Demographic Yearbook 1971*, New York, 1972.
——— *Housing in Africa*, New York, 1965.
——— *Statistical Yearbook 1972*, New York, 1973.
——— *The Growth of World Industry 1971*, New York, 1973.
——— *World Population Prospects as Assessed in 1963*, New York, 1965.
——— *Yearbook of International Trade Statistics 1969*, New York, 1971.
——— *Yearbook of National Accounts Statistics 1971*, New York, 1973.
United Nations, Economic Commission for Africa, *Summaries of Economic Data, Morocco 1971*, Addis Ababa, 1972.
United Nations, FAO, *Timber Trends and Prospects in Africa*, Rome, 1967.
——— *Yearbook of Forest Products*, Rome.
Urquhart, A. W., *Planned Urban Landscapes of Northern Nigeria*, Zaria, 1977.

Wallé, E. van de, 'Fertility in Nigeria', in *The Demography of Tropical Africa*, by W. Brass *et al.*, Princeton, NJ, 1968.
Walter, M. W., 'Observation on rainfall at the Institute for Agricultural Research', Samaru Miscellaneous Paper no. 15, Ahmadu Bello University, Zaria, 1967.
Ward Price, H. L., *Land Tenure in the Yoruba Provinces*, Lagos, 1939.
Washington, R. N., 'Geographical notice of the empire of Morocco', *Journal of the Royal Geographical Society* (London), **1**, 1931.

Western State of Nigeria (Government), *Gazette 1971*, Ibadan, 1971.

Western State of Nigeria, Ministry of Economic Planning and Reconstruction, *Statistical Abstract*, Ibadan, 1970.

Yarwood, D., *The Architecture of Europe*, London, 1974.

Zanzibar Protectorate, 'Report of the (1958) census of the population of Zanzibar Protectorate', Zanzibar, 1960.

Index